Oran's Dictionary of the Law

Daniel Oran, J.D.

WEST PUBLISHING COMPANY

St. Paul   New York   Los Angeles   San Francisco

Cover: Colored ink triptych *Beyond a Reasonable Doubt* by Joyce E.
Murphy, from the art collection of West Publishing Company.

Library of Congress Cataloging in Publication Data

Oran, Daniel.
    Oran's Dictionary of the law.

    1. Law—United States—Dictionaries. I. Title.
II. Title: Dictionary of the law.
KF156.069 1983   349.73'03'21   82-8504
ISBN 0-314-68800-5   347.300321

3rd Reprint—1986

for Christina Alexandra Oran
and Stuart Robert Surick

Contents

Introduction

This is a guidebook to a foreign language. The language of Law uses mostly English words, but they rarely mean what they seem. Many look like everyday English, but have technical definitions totally different from their ordinary uses. Some mean several different things, depending on the area of law or business they come from. The language of Law also contains more "leftovers" than most languages. Hundreds of Latin, Old French, Old English and obsolete words are still used in their original forms.

The dictionary has two main purposes. Like any specialized dictionary, it helps the reader to understand and use a technical vocabulary. It also tries to do one more thing: help the reader to recognize and discard the vague, fuzzy words that sound precise and that lawyers often use as if they were precise.

The book was written with the needs of many different readers in mind: lawyers, law and pre-law students, paralegals, legal secretaries, consumers, businesspersons, and persons in law-related fields such as criminal justice, social work, and government. Because the dictionary covers so many different fields, I need suggestions for additional words and definitions. If you have any ideas for the next edition, please send them to me care of West Publishing Company.

I have tried to make this guidebook as complete, clear and easy to use as possible. Using it, you will be able to understand a contract, a law, a court decision, and even a lawyer under full sail. But always remember: *omnis definitio in lege periculosa*. Look it up.

Acknowledgments

The more books I write, the more personal and professional debts I owe (and inexcusably forget). An alphabetical listing of names cannot begin to thank all those people who have helped me. Some, like Thomas Emerson, taught me how to "think like a lawyer." Others, like Fred Rodell, taught me how to stop writing like one. The list includes people like Bill Statsky, who gave me several excellent ideas for this book; Judith Fifer and Lenore Johns, who shepherded it through publication; Sara Ann Determan and Mark Tosti, who corrected large portions, and my wife Elaine, who read the whole thing. Finally, the list includes those who, like Jonah Brown, "merely" gave me the encouragement I needed to see the project through. I hope that everyone has been properly listed, but no one has been properly thanked: Sylvia Arrom, Sandy Augliere, Edwin Barrett, Max Baucus, Henry Black, David Boris, Elizabeth Boris, Jay Boris, Paul Boris, Fred Brandow, Margery Braunstein, David Brodsky, Jonah Brown, Steve Browning, Edgar Cahn, Jean Cahn, Karen Clark, Dean Determan, Sara Ann Determan, Charles Docter, Marcie Docter, Ashley Doherty, Thomas Emerson, Larry Evans, Marcie Evans, Stanley Field, Judith Fifer, Joseph Fortenberry, Leslie Foster, Robert Foster, Robert Fracasso, William Fry, Ronald Greene, Sunny Greene, John Hodges, Jeanne Hoene, Lonn Hoklin, Carolyn Hunter, David Hunter, Richard Jackson, Lenore Johns, Barbara Lampe, Martin Lampe, Judith Lhamon, William Lindberg, Sam Mansfield, Susan Marsnik, Barbara Martin, Rick Martin, Edward Mattison, Steve Merlin, Kirsten Mueller, Edward Oberhofer, David Oran, Elaine Oran, Max Oran, Minerva Oran, Victoria Powell, Charles Reich, David Robinson, Ruth Robinson, Sandra Robinson, Fred Rodell, Martin Seligman, Jay Shafritz, William Statsky, John Stein, Diane Surick, Herman Surick, Stuart Surick, Charles Todd, Mark Tosti, Thomas Weck, Dorothy Weitzman, Thomas Willging, and Kenneth Zeigler. Not on this list are the many people who wrote to suggest additions and corrections to my prior books. This dictionary would not have been the same without their help.

Reading the Definitions

FINDING THE WORD
Skim the area near where the word should be. The word you want may be printed in the definition of a nearby word. Also, look up both halves of a compound word.

BOLDFACE
If a word in a definition is in **Boldface**, it is defined in the dictionary. You can look it up if you need it.

BOLDFACE PLUS "SEE THAT WORD"
If you are told to "see that word," you *must* know what that word means to understand the definition you are reading. *Look it up.*

ITALICS
Italics are used to emphasize a word or to illustrate its use.

ORDINARY ENGLISH
Everyday English definitions of legal words are omitted unless they are necessary to avoid confusion.

"PERSON"
"Person" is used in this dictionary to mean "person," "man or woman," "human being," and "corporation." Also, the old feminine suffix "ix" (executor/executrix) is omitted.

Pronunciation

MOST WORDS

Most words in this dictionary are easy to pronounce. No pronunciations are given for these words.

ACCENT MARKS

Some words need only accent marks for the strong syllable. This is done by underlining the emphasized part of the word. For example, "Testimony" means that the "Tes" is spoken more strongly than the rest of the word.

PROBLEM WORDS

Legal words with pronunciation problems have the pronunciations in square brackets after the definitions. For example, after the definition for "Indictment" you will see: [in-dite-ment]. This dictionary uses English sounds, not technical pronunciation marks.

LATIN WORDS

Most Latin words may be pronounced almost any way they are read. This is because there are at least three acceptable pronunciations: "Classical" Latin, "Church" Latin and "English" Latin. Pronunciations are given for Latin words only when one way is heard most often.

The Basic 50

These fifty words are used frequently in definitions. They are among the most basic words in the law. If you are using this dictionary as a learning tool, rather than as an occasional reference, look up those words you do not know and those for which you know only an ordinary English meaning:

Action	Duty	Opinion
Agency	Estate	Party
Appeal	Evidence	Plaintiff
Bill	Executive	Pleading
Case	Federal	Property
Civil	Grounds	Regulate
Complaint	Judgment	Right
Constitutional	Judicial	Security
Contract	Jury	Sentence
Conviction	Law	Statute
Corporation	Liability	Testimony
Court	Legislate	Title
Creditor	Mortgage	Tort
Criminal	Motion	Trust
Debtor	Negligence	Verdict
Deed	Negotiable	Will
Defendant	Instrument	Witness

A **1.** (Latin) From, for, with (and when translated into smooth English can also mean in, of, by, etc.). **2.** Atlantic Reporter (see **National Reporter System**).

A.A. **Affirmative action** (see that word).

A.A.A. **1.** Agriculture Adjustment Act. **2.** American Accounting Association. **3. American Arbitration Association** (see that word).

A.A.L.S. Association of American Law Schools.

A.A.P. Affirmative action plan (or program).

A.B.A. **American Bar Association** (see that word).

A.B.A.J. American Bar Association Journal.

ABC **1.** The *ABC Test* states that an employee need not be covered by **unemployment** insurance if the employee is an independent worker who performs jobs free of the employer's control and away from the employer's place of business. **2.** An *ABC Transfer* was a complicated exchange of mining or oil rights meant to lower taxes. Current tax law eliminates the advantage of these transfers.

ACLU American Civil Liberties Union. A group that supports basic **constitutional** freedoms by going to court, by supporting and fighting **legislation,** and by public education.

A.C.R.S. **Accelerated cost recovery system** (see that word).

A.D.R. **Asset depreciation range** (see that word).

AFDC Aid to Families with Dependent Children. The largest federally funded welfare program.

AFL–CIO American Federation of Labor–Congress of Industrial Organizations. The largest organization of **labor unions** in the United States.

A.G. **Attorney general** (see that word).

A.I.C.P.A. American Institute of Certified Public Accountants.

A.k.a. Also known as.

A.L.I. **American Law Institute** (see that word).

ALJ **Administrative law judge.**

A.L.R. **American Law Reports**.

A.L.T.A. American Land Title Association.

A.P.A. **Administrative Procedure Act.**

A.P.R. **Annual percentage rate** (see that word).

A.R. Anno Regni (Latin) "In the year of the reign of." An abbre-

A.R.M.

viation used to date famous cases and laws by year within the rule of a particular English king or queen.

A.R.M. An "adjustable rate **mortgage**" with payments and other terms that can be easily changed during the course of the mortgage.

A.S.P.R. Armed Services Procurement Regulations.

A.T.L.A. American Trial Lawyers Association.

A.W.O.L. "Absent without leave"; a military offense similar to but less serious than **desertion.**

A coelo usque ad centrum (Latin) "From the heavens to the center of the earth" (a landowner's supposed property right). This may be limited by other conflicting rights, such as the right of planes to pass (**air rights**) or the right of others to drill for oil (**mineral rights**).

A contrario sensu (Latin) On the other hand; in a contrary sense.

A force (Latin) Of necessity.

A fortiori (Latin) With stronger reason. For example, if it is true that a twenty-one-year-old person is an adult, then, *a fortiori*, a twenty-five-year-old person is an adult. [pronounce: ah-for-she-o-ri]

A gratia (Latin) By **grace** (see that word).

A large (Latin) Free or **at large.**

A latere (Latin) **Collateral;** from the side.

A mensa et thoro (Latin) "From bed and board" (literally, "from bed and table"). A type of legal **separation** or limited **divorce** (see that word).

A posteriori (Latin) From the effect to the cause. A method of reasoning that starts with experiments or observations and attempts to discover general principles from them.

A prendre (French) See **profits a prendre.** [pronounce: ah-pran]

A priori From the cause to the effect. A method of reasoning that starts with general principles and attempts to discover what specific facts or real-life observations will follow from them. [pronounce: ah pri-o-ri]

A quo (Latin) From which. For example, a *court a quo* is a court from which a case has been removed, and a *court ad quem* is the court to which it is taken.

A rendre (French) See **profits a rendre.**

2

Abatement

A rubro ad nigrum (Latin) "From red to black." Interpreting a **statute** by its title.

A vinculo matrimonii (Latin) "From the marriage bonds." **1.** A complete **divorce**. **2.** An **annulment**.

Ab (Latin) **1.** See **A**. **2.** Abridgment.

Ab actis (Latin) A court **clerk** or a **registrar**.

Ab ante (Latin) In advance; before.

Ab antiquo (Latin) Since ancient times.

Ab inconvenienti (Latin) "From inconvenience." A weak argument, offered only because you are forced to put up some sort of argument in a difficult case.

Ab initio (Latin) From the very beginning; entirely and completely since the start. [pronounce: ab in-ish-i-o]

Abaction Forcibly carrying something away.

Abandon Give up something completely and finally (see **abandonment**).

Abandonment **1.** Complete and final giving up of property or rights with no intention of reclaiming them and to no particular person. For example, throwing away a book is *abandonment,* but selling or giving it away is not. **2.** A lawsuit may be thrown out of court if it is *abandoned* by failure to take any action on it for too long a time. **3.** Children are *abandoned* if they are either deserted or no longer cared for or looked after. **4.** A husband or wife is abandoned if the other leaves without consent and with the intent to stay away permanently. **5.** Abandonment of a **patent** (see that word) right might occur if the inventor fails to apply for a patent or if too many other people are allowed to see the invention. **6.** Abandonment of service occurs if a public utility permanently cuts off a customer.

Abatable nuisance A **nuisance** (see that word) that is easily or practically stopped or made harmless.

Abate **1.** Destroy or completely end. **2.** Greatly lessen or reduce.

Abatement **1.** Reduction or decrease. **2.** Proportional reduction. For example, if a pot of money does not have enough to pay everyone it owes, each person may have to be satisfied with an *abatement* of his or her share. **3.** Complete elimination. For example, see **abatable nuisance**. **4.** An ending or delaying of a lawsuit for technical reasons such as failure to include all necessary persons. This ending is now usually called a **dismissal** (see that word).   **5.** The order of reduction or elimination. For example, if a person leaves "five hundred dollars to John and five hundred dollars to my heirs," John gets five hundred dollars and the heirs' share may *abate* to zero if there is only five hundred dollars.

Abbroachment   Buying up goods at wholesale to control the supply and then resell at much higher resale prices.

Abdication   **1.** The act of giving up the throne (by a king or other monarch).   **2.** Giving up a public office by ceasing to perform its functions rather than by formally resigning.

Abduction   **1.** The criminal offense of taking away a person who is in the care of another.   **2. Kidnapping** (see that word).   **3.** Tricking or persuading a wife or husband to leave the other.

Abet   Encourage, request, order, or help another person to commit a crime.

Abettor   A person who **abets** (see that word) a crime.

Abeyance   In suspension, waiting, or held off for a while.

Abide   **1.** Accept the consequences (usually of a court's **judgment**).   **2.** Be satisfied with.   **3.** Wait for.   **4.** Obey; for example, most persons *abide* by the law.

Ability to pay   A standard that juries are rarely permitted to use in deciding how much money a **defendant** must pay a **plaintiff** (one exception is some types of **punitive damage** awards). An **arbitrator,** however, may consider *ability to pay* in deciding a wage or benefit increase dispute between an employer and a union.

Abjudication   A judge's decision that takes something away from a person. (*Not* **adjudication.**)

Abjuration   Taking an oath to give up property, rights, or personal convictions and opinions. For example, when you become a citizen, you *abjure* allegiance to all foreign governments.

Abnegation   Denial or renunciation.

Abode   Home or dwelling place.

Abolish   Completely do away with something previously thought to be permanent, such as the longstanding legality of slavery.

Aboriginal   Belonging to the first natives or residents since ancient times.

Abortion   The intentional destruction of a fetus.

About   Near in time, distance, quantity, or quality. *About* is an imprecise word, but not so imprecise as to legally undo a deal based on a phrase like "about a million widgets" or "about May first."

Above   **1.** Higher. Usually refers to a higher or **appellate** court. **2.** Before. *Above cited* or *above mentioned* may mean "appears earlier on this page," "earlier in this chapter," "earlier in this book," etc., without telling the reader which one is meant.

Abr.   Abridgment.

Abridge   **1.** Shorten. An *abridgment* of a book is a condensation of its ideas into a shorter work.   **2.** Infringe upon. To *abridge* a right is to make the right less useful or complete.

Abrogation   The destruction, ending, or **annulling** of a former law.

Abscond   Hide or sneak away to avoid arrest, a lawsuit, or creditors.

Absentee landlord   An owner or other **lessor** who does not live on the premises. Usually one who cannot be reached by the tenants.

Absentee voting   Voting by mail or other means if the voter has an approved reason to miss going to the polls on election day.

Absolute   Complete, final, and without restrictions. For example, an absolute **deed** is a transfer of land without a **mortgage** or other restrictions; absolute law is natural, as opposed to human-made; and absolute **liability** is responsibility for harm to another whether or not you are at fault.

Absolute nuisance   A **nuisance** (see that word) that involves no **negligent** conduct.

Absolution   Freedom or release from an obligation or a debt.

Absolutism   Government power unchecked by legal restraints or safeguards. A king, dictator, or ruling group with nearly complete power over the people.

Absorption   The continued life of a thing (a right, a company, etc.) by its becoming a part of another thing. For example, when one business **merges** with another, the continued right of **seniority** for employees is called *absorption*.

Absque   (Latin) Without; but for. For example, *absque hoc*, "but for this," was a technical phrase used by a **defendant** to introduce new facts that hurt the **plaintiff's** case even if the plaintiff's facts were correct. [pronounce: ab-skway]

Abstain

Abstain   Refrain, hold off, keep hands off.

Abstention doctrine   The principle that a federal court should refuse to decide some cases even though it has the power to do so. For example, when a case can be taken care of purely by applying state law, and the case involves only persons from the same state, the court should **abstain.**

Abstract   **1.** A summary. For example, an abstract of **title** is a condensed history of the ownership of a piece of land that includes transfers of ownership and any rights (such as **liens**) that persons other than the owner might have in the land; and an **abstract of record** is a summary of a **trial** record for an **appeals** court.   **2.** See **abstraction.**

Abstraction   Taking something (usually money) with the intent to commit **fraud.**

Abuse   **1.** Misuse.   **2.** Sexually molesting a child.   **3.** Regularly injuring a child.   **4.** Insult forcefully.   **5.** *Abuse of discretion* is the failure to use sound, reasonable judgment as a judge or as an administrator.   **6.** *Abuse of process* is using the legal process unfairly; for example, prosecuting a person for writing a bad check simply to put on pressure to pay.

Abut   **1.** Touch or border on with nothing in between. Closer than **adjacent.**   **2.** For *"abutter's right,"* see **ancient lights.**

Academic freedom   The right of teachers and students to teach and learn without being harassed for their political, religious, or other beliefs. This is *not* a **constitutional** right, like many other freedoms, but it is protected primarily by those freedoms (freedom of speech, religion, etc.), plus longstanding traditions and institutions such as **tenure.**

Accede   **1.** Come into a job or public office.   **2.** Agree, consent, or give in.

Accelerated cost recovery system   An **accounting** method that uses a range of time, usually shorter than an **asset's** useful life, over which a business may take **depreciation** on the asset.

Accelerated depreciation   See **depreciation.**

Acceleration   **1.** Shortening of the time before a future event will happen.   **2.** An *acceleration clause* is a section of a contract that makes an entire debt come immediately due because of a failure to pay on time or because of some other failure.

Accept   Receive with approval, satisfaction, or the intention to keep (see **acceptance**).

Acceptance **1.** Agreeing to an **offer** and becoming bound to the terms of a **contract.** **2.** Taking something offered by another person with the intention of keeping it. For example, the **Uniform Commercial Code** explains several ways a buyer can *accept* goods from a seller: by telling the seller that the goods received are right; by saying that the goods will be taken despite problems; by failing to reject the goods in reasonable time; or by doing something that makes it seem like the buyer now owns the goods. **3.** In **negotiable instruments** law, a person's *acceptance* of a check may be by signing and depositing it, and a bank can *accept* the check by cashing it. There are technical rules of acceptance for more complicated negotiable instruments. **4.** A *banker's acceptance* is a trade device in which a bank promises to pay a certain amount at a future date (a negotiable time **draft** or a guaranteed **bill of exchange**). A *trade acceptance* is the same thing promised by a company instead of a bank. These are both called "acceptance credit" and are often used to finance international trade and are bought and sold as investments.

Access **1.** Opportunity to approach. For example, most city lots have *access* to the street. **2.** Right to approach. For example, *access* to public records includes both their practical availability and the right to see them. **3.** In **paternity suits,** claiming that the mother had several lovers is called a **defense** of *multiple access.*

Accession **1.** The right to own things that become a part of something already owned. For example, if land builds up on a riverbank, the bank's owner will also own the new land by *accession.* **2.** The right to things, such as crops, produced on owned property. **3.** See **accede.**

Accessory **1.** A person who helps commit a crime without being present. **2.** An *accessory before the fact* is a person who encourages, orders or helps another to commit a crime without being present. **3.** An *accessory after the fact* is a person who knows that a crime has been committed and helps to conceal the crime or the criminal. **4.** Anything connected to something more important.

Accident A general word for an unexpected event (usually with harmful effects). The word has no precise legal meaning. It can include events that are predictable or unpredictable, somebody's fault or nobody's fault.

Accommodation

Accommodation   A favor done for another person, usually involving **co-signing** to help another person get a loan or credit.

Accommodation line   Business that is accepted not on its own merits but to get other business or as part of a "package."

Accommodation paper   A **bill** or **note** that is signed on by one person as a favor to help another person get a loan. The person signing promises to pay if the person getting the loan fails to pay.

Accommodation party   A person who signs an **accommodation paper** (see that word) as a favor to another person.

Accommodation personnel **Dummy** incorporators (see that word).

Accomplice   A person who knowingly and voluntarily helps another person to commit a crime. This includes persons who **aid, abet,** or act as **accessory.**

Accord   **1.** An agreement to pay (on one side) and to accept (on the other side) less than all a debt or obligation is worth as full payment for that obligation. For example, there is an *accord* if a person agrees to take one hundred dollars as payment in full for one hundred and fifty dollars worth of damages to an auto, and the person who did the damage agrees to pay the one hundred dollars.   **2.** An *accord and satisfaction* is an accord that has been completed by payment and a full **release. 3.** Any agreement.

Account   **1.** A list of money paid and owed by one person or business to another.   **2.** An *account payable* is a regular business debt not yet paid.   **3.** An *account receivable* is a regular business debt not yet collected; for example, a store's charge accounts.

Account stated   An exact figure for money owed, calculated by the person to whom the money is owed, and accepted as accurate by the person who owes the money.

Accountable   Responsible or **liable** for something.

Accountant   A person who specializes in the accuracy of financial records. This includes setting up financial record keeping systems, filling them in, and checking up on them. These duties include **auditing, bookkeeping,** and preparing financial **statements.** Normally, persons who do just bookkeeping do not have accounting skills. The next level of skill is accountant. Some accountants are specially trained and certified as *certified public accountants* by satisfying state professional requirements.

Accounting   1. A system of setting up financial record books, especially for tax purposes. Two of the most common methods are the *accrual method* (recording debts owed to and by a company when the debt becomes a legal obligation, which may be before the money is actually paid) and the *cash method* (recording debts when paid).   **2.** Giving a full financial explanation of a transaction or of an entire business.   **3.** Making good on money owed. For example, a court may order one partner to pay another. This is called an *accounting for profits*.

Accounting changes   See **statement.**

Accounting identity   A statement that two numerical things are equal by accepted definition; for example, "**assets** equal **liabilities** plus stockholder's **equity.**"

Accounting period   See **fiscal.**

Accounts payable   Money owed to suppliers.

Accounts receivable   Money owed by customers.

Accredit   Give official status or recognition. For example, an *accredited* law school has been approved by a state, by the Association of American Law Schools (see **A.A.L.S.**), or by the **American Bar Association.**

Accretion   1. The gradual adding on of land by natural causes such as the deposit of dirt by a river on its bank.   **2.** Any gradual accumulation.

Accroachment   Taking over or exercising power with no authority to do so.

Accrual basis   A method of **accounting** that shows expenses **incurred** and income earned in a given time period, whether or not cash payments have actually changed hands during that period.

Accruals   Regular, short-term business obligations, such as employees' wages.

Accrue   1. Become due and payable. For example, in tax law, income *accrues* to a taxpayer when the taxpayer has an unconditional right to it and a likelihood of being able to receive it.   **2.** An accrued **dividend** is a share of a company's earnings that has been formally declared as payable to the stockholders, but not yet paid.

Accumulated earnings tax   A federal tax on **corporations** that pile up profits without either distributing them to stockholders in the form of **dividends** or plowing the money back into the business.

Accumulated retained earnings See **retained earnings.**

Accumulation trust A **trust** that keeps its income during the trust period rather than paying it out regularly to a **beneficiary.**

Accumulative sentence (or judgment) A **cumulative sentence** (see that word).

Accusation A formal charge, made to a court, that a person is guilty of a crime.

Accusatory instruments Papers that charge a person with a crime; for example, an **indictment,** an **information,** etc. (see these words).

Accused The person against whom an **accusation** is made; the **defendant** in a criminal case.

Acid test See *quick ratio* under **quick assets.**

Acknowledgment **1.** An admission or declaration that something is genuine. For example, a father's statements that a child is his may be an *acknowledgment.* **2.** Signing a formal paper and swearing to it as your act before a court official such as a **notary public.**

Acquest Something bought.

Acquiescence Silent agreement; knowing about an action or occurrence and remaining quietly satisfied about it or, by silence, appearing to be satisfied.

Acquisition charge A charge for paying off a loan before it comes due. Also called a *"prepayment penalty."*

Acquit Set free from an obligation or an accusation; see **acquittal.**

Acquittal **1.** A formal legal determination that a person who has been charged with a crime is innocent. **2.** A **release** from an obligation.

Acquittance A written **discharge** of an obligation. For example, a **receipt** is an *acquittance* of an obligation to pay money owed.

Act **1.** A law passed by one or both **houses** of a **legislature,** such as Congress. **2.** Something done voluntarily that triggers legal consequences.

Act in pais Something done out of court and without being a part of the court's official proceedings.

Act of bankruptcy Any one of several actions (such as hiding property from creditors) that *used to* make a person **liable** to be proceeded against as a **bankrupt** by **creditors. Bankruptcy** law now provides for this sort of *involuntary bankruptcy* only when a person cannot pay debts as they come due.

Act of God   An event caused entirely by nature alone.

Act of State doctrine   The rule that a court in the United States should not question the legality of acts done by a foreign government in its own country.

Acting   Holding a temporary rank or position. Filling in for someone else.

Actio   (Latin) A **right** and also the legal proceedings taken to enforce the right; an "**action**" or lawsuit; for example, in Roman law, an "*actio damni injuria*" was a lawsuit for **damages.**

Action   **1.** Conduct or behavior.   **2.** The formal legal demand of your rights from another person made in court. Types of lawsuits are often grouped under various types of "actions" such as "**civil action**," "**common law action**," "**real** action," etc. (see these words). Actions may overlap. For example, one lawsuit may be both a common law action and a real action.

Action on the case   See **trespass** (on the case) or see **case.**

Actionable   An act or occurrence is *actionable* if it provides legal reasons for a lawsuit. For example, "*actionable words*" are statements by one person that are serious enough to support a lawsuit (or "action") for **libel** or **slander** by another person.

Active trust   A **trust** for which the **trustee** must actually perform some service.

Acts and Resolves   See **Statutes at Large.**

Actual   Real, substantial, and presently existing as opposed to possible or theoretical.

Actual authority   In the law of **agency** (see that word), the right and power to act that a **principal** (often an employer) intentionally gives to an **agent** (often an employee) or at least allows the agent to believe has been given. This includes both **express** and **implied** authority (see these words).

Actual cash value   The fair, usual, or reasonable cash price that something will bring on the open market; the same as "**fair market value.**"

Actuarial method   The way of accounting for finances in a record book. For example, the *actuarial method* mentioned in the Uniform Consumer Credit Code is a company's method of applying payments made by a consumer first to **interest** and finance charges, then to paying off **principal** (the basic debt).

Actuary   A person who specializes in the mathematics of **insurance**; for example, the possibility of a person dying by a certain age, the money that should be paid for a certain type of insurance, etc.

Actus   (Latin) An **act** (see that word). For example, an "*actus reus*" is a "wrongful deed" (such as killing a person) which, when combined with **mens rea**, a "guilty mind" (such as "*malice aforethought*"), equals a crime (such as **murder**).

Ad   (Latin) To; for (when translated into smooth English, it can also mean by, because, until, near, etc.).

Ad damnum   (Latin) "To the **damages**." That part of a **plaintiff's** original court papers that sets out the money loss or "damages."

Ad hoc   (Latin) "For this"; for this special purpose; for this one time; for example, an *ad hoc* committee is a temporary one set up to do a specific job.

Ad hominem   (Latin) "To the person." Arguments or statements made against an opponent personally, rather than against the opponent's argument or position.

Ad idem   (Latin) To the same point; proving the same thing.

Ad infinitum   (Latin) Forever; limitless.

Ad interim   (Latin) Meanwhile; for now.

Ad litem   (Latin) "For the suit"; for the purposes of this lawsuit. For example, a *guardian ad litem* is a person who is appointed to represent a child (or other person lacking legal **capacity**) in a lawsuit.

Ad quem   (Latin) To which (see **a quo** for its use).

Ad sectam   (Latin) At the suit of. "Ad sectam Jones" means that Jones is the **plaintiff.**

Ad valorem   (Latin) According to value. For example, an *ad valorem* tax is a tax on the value of an item, rather than a fixed tax on the type of item. An *ad valorem* tax might tax a ten-dollar hat fifty cents and a twenty-dollar hat one dollar, while a specific hat tax might tax all hats seventy-five cents regardless of price or value.

Ad vitam   (Latin) For life.

Addict   A person who regularly uses something (such as a drug) to the extent that he or she no longer has control over the use.

Additur   **1.** The power of a trial court to increase the amount of money awarded by a **jury** to a **plaintiff.**   **2.** The power of an **appeals** court to deny a new trial to the **plaintiff** if the **defendant**

agrees to pay the plaintiff a certain amount of extra money. **3.** See also **remittitur.**

Add-on More goods bought before old goods are paid for; often, the contract for the original goods is rewritten to include the new things. An *add-on clause* is a provision in an **installment** contract that combines payment obligations for previously bought and newly bought things so that nothing is owned "free and clear" until everything has been paid for.

Adduce Present or bring forward **evidence** in a **trial.**

Adeem "Take away" (see **ademption**).

Ademption **1.** Disposing of something left in a **will** before death, with the effect that the person it was left to does not get it. **2.** The gift, before death, of something left in a will to a person who was left it. For example, Ed leaves a chair to Joan in his will, but gives her the chair before he dies. **3.** See also **advancement.**

Adequate A general word for "enough." It has no precise legal meaning.

Adhesion "Stick to." For example, a *"contract of adhesion"* is one in which all the bargaining power (and all the contract terms) are unfairly on one side. This often occurs when buyers have no choice among sellers of a particular item, and when the seller uses a pre-printed form contract.

Adjacent Near or close by. Perhaps touching, but not necessarily so.

Adjective law Procedural law. The rules by which courts and agencies operate as opposed to what is usually thought of as "the law" or **substantive law** (see that word).

Adjoining owners Persons whose land touches a particular piece of land and who may have special rights against it under local **zoning** laws and under general laws of property.

Adjourn Postpone or suspend business (see **adjournment**).

Adjournment Putting off business or a session to another time or place. The decision of a court, legislature, or other meeting to stop meeting either temporarily or permanently. See also **recess.**

Adjudge Old word for performing a judge's duties (pass **judgment,** make a decision, etc.).

Adjudicate To judge (see **adjudication**).

Adjudicated form

Adjudicated form A **form** may be called *"adjudicated"* if a court has called it legally binding or has interpreted it in a way that makes it useful for later users.

Adjudication The formal giving, pronouncing, or recording of a **judgment** (see that word) for one side or the other in a lawsuit.

Adjudicative facts Facts about the persons who have a dispute before an **administrative agency.** These are the "who, what, where, etc." facts that are similar to the facts that would go to a jury in a court trial. They are different from **legislative facts** (see that word).

Adjunction Permanent attachment; for example, a patch sewn onto a coat.

Adjuration Swearing to something under **oath.**

Adjust Settle or arrange; bring persons to agreement, especially as to amount of money owed. The process is called *"adjustment."*

Adjusted basis The worth of property for tax purposes after subtracting for **depreciation** (see that word) and adding in **capital** improvements.

Adjusted gross income A technical federal income tax word that means, in general, the money a person makes minus deductions such as certain travel, work, business, or moving expenses, etc. For most persons, it is the same as "gross" or total income. The word is used for personal taxes, not for business taxes.

Adjuster A person who either determines or settles the amount of a claim or debt. For example, an *insurance adjuster* acts for an insurance company to determine and settle claims.

Adjustment securities Stocks, etc. that are issued during a **corporate reorganization**. The "adjustments" are usually changes that make the new stock worth less than the stock it replaced.

Admeasure Divide and give out by shares.

Administer **1.** Manage; take charge of business. **2.** Settle and distribute the **estate** (property, money, etc.) of a dead person. **3.** Give; for example, *administer* an **oath.**

Administration **1.** Managing or running a business, organization, or part of a government. **2.** Supervision of the estate of a dead person. This usually includes collecting the property, paying debts and taxes, and giving out what remains to the **heirs.** **3.** The persons and political party currently running the government.

Administrative agency A sub-branch of the government set up to carry out the laws. For example, the police department is a local *administrative agency* and the **I.R.S.** is a national one.

Administrative board A broad term which sometimes means "**administrative agency**" (see that word) and sometimes means a courtlike body set up by an agency to hold **hearings.**

Administrative Conference of the U.S. A federal organization set up to improve the legal procedures by which federal **agencies** operate.

Administrative discretion A public official's right to perform acts and duties that are not precisely "covered" by a law or rules and that require the use of professional judgment and common sense within the bounds set by the law.

Administrative law **1.** Laws about the duties and proper running of an **administrative agency** (see that word) that are handed to agencies by **legislatures** and courts. **2.** **Rules** and **regulations** set out by administrative agencies.

Administrative law judge An official who conducts **hearings** for an **administrative agency.** Also called "hearing officer" or "examiner."

Administrative Procedure Act A law that describes how U.S. agencies must do business (hearings, procedures, etc.) and how disputes go from these federal agencies into court. Some states also have an Administrative Procedure Act.

Administrative remedy A means of enforcing a right by going to an **administrative agency** (see that word) either for help or for a decision. Persons are often required to "exhaust administrative remedies," which means to fully submit their problems to the proper agency before taking them to court.

Administrator A person appointed by the court to supervise handing out the **estate** (property) of a dead person. If the administrator is named in the dead person's **will**, the proper name is **executor.** For administrators **cum testamento annexo (CTA)** and **de bonis non (DBN),** see those words.

Admiralty **1.** A court that handles most maritime (seagoing) matters, such as collisions between ships and shipping claims. This is usually a federal **district court.** **2.** Maritime law.

Admissible Proper to be used in reaching a decision; **evidence** that should be "let in" or introduced in court; evidence that the **jury** may use.

Admission **1.** An "*admission*" is a voluntary statement that a fact or a state of events is true (see **Admissions**). **2.** "*Admis-*

Admissions

sion to the bar" is the formal procedure in which a lawyer is permitted to practice law.   **3.** *"Admission to bail"* is the court's decision to allow a person accused of a crime to be released if **bail** money is put up.   **4.** *"Admission of evidence"* is a decision by a judge to allow **evidence** to be used by the jury (or, if no jury, by the judge).

Admissions   Confessions, concessions, or voluntary acknowledgments. Statements made by a **party** to a lawsuit (or the party's representative) that a fact exists which helps the other side or that a point the other side is making is correct. An *admission against interest* is a prior statement, usually made out of court, by a person involved in a lawsuit that contradicts something that person's side needs to prove.

Admit   See **admission.**

Admonition   **1.**   Oral advice by a judge to a jury.   **2.** A reprimand given by a judge to a lawyer.   **3.** A reprimand given by a judge in place of a jail **sentence** or other serious punishment.

Admonitory tort   An intentional **tort** of the type in which punishing the wrongdoer is more important than compensating the person hurt.

Adopt   **1.**   Accept, choose, or take as your own property, acts, or ideas.   **2.** Pass a law and put it into effect.   **3.** Take a child of another as your own, with all of the rights and duties there would have been if it had been your own originally. (In some states, it is possible to adopt an adult in order to make that person your **heir.**)

Adoption   The legal process by which an adult gives to a child, who is not the adult's own, all the rights of a natural child and gains parental control over the child. See **adopt.**

Adoptive admission   Approval of another's statements by approval, by silence, by actions, or by failure to deny them.

Ads.   Abbreviation for **ad sectam** (see that word).

Adult   A person over the legal age a state has set for full rights (such as voting) to begin.

Adulteration   Mixing inferior, cheaper, or harmful things in with better ones (to increase volume, lower costs, etc.).

Adultery   Voluntary sexual intercourse between a married person and a person who is not the husband or wife.

Advance   **1.** Pay money before it is due; loan money; supply something before it is paid for.   **2.** An increase in price.   **3.** A *motion to advance* is a request for an immediate trial.

Advance sheets   "Hot off the press" unbound copies of case **decisions** that will later be printed with other cases in bound form.

Advancement   Money or property given by a parent to a child (or to another **heir**) that the parent intends to be deducted from the child's eventual share in the parent's **estate** when the parent dies. See also **ademption.**

Adventure   **1.** A risky commercial venture; any commercial venture.   **2.** A shipment of goods by sea; any shipment of goods.

Adversary proceeding   A **hearing** (see that word) with both sides represented.

Adversary system   The system of law in America. The judge acts as the decision maker between opposite sides (between two individuals, between the state and an individual, etc.) rather than acting as the person who also makes the state's case or independently seeks out **evidence.** This latter method is called the "**inquisitorial system.**"

Adverse   Opposed; having opposing interests; against. For example, "*adverse actions*" by employers towards employees include firing, demoting, etc., and an "*adverse land use*" is a use, such as a factory in a neighborhood of single-family homes, that harms the local properties.

Adverse inference rule   An **administrative agency's** inference that, when relevant information is withheld from the agency with no good excuse, the information is **adverse** to the person or organization keeping it back.

Adverse interest   Having opposing needs and desires from those of a person with whom you are associated.

Adverse party   A **party** (see that word) who, when a case is **appealed,** might be hurt by a successful appeal. **Notice** of the appeal must be given to all *adverse parties* even if they were originally on the side that is now appealing.

Adverse possession   A method of gaining legal **title** to land by occupying the land openly and continuously for a number of years set by state law and openly and aggressively claiming the right to both own and occupy the land.

Advice   **1.** View or opinion.   **2.** The **counsel** given to clients by their lawyers.   **3.** This is *not* "*advise*" (give advice).

Advice and consent   The **constitutional** right of the U.S. **Senate** to advise the president on **treaties** and major presidential appointments and to give its consent to these actions (by a two-thirds vote for treaties and a majority vote for appointments).

Advisement

Advisement　Consideration. A case "under advisement" means that the judge has heard the **evidence** or **arguments** and will delay a **decision** in the case until it has been thought over for a while.

Advisory jury　A jury that a federal judge can call to help decide **questions** of fact even though the judge has the right to decide them alone.

Advisory opinion　A formal opinion by a judge or judges about a question of law submitted by the **legislature** or by an **executive** (administrative) officer, but not actually presented to the court in a concrete lawsuit.

Advocacy　Forceful persuasion; arguing a cause, right, or position.

Advocate　**1.** A person who speaks for another person, for a "cause," or for an organization in order to persuade others. **2.** A lawyer. **3.** To speak in favor of something.

Aequitas　(Latin) **Equity** (see that word).

Affair　A **lawsuit**, or an action or event that could turn into a lawsuit.

Affect　To change; to act upon or influence. *Affect* and *effect* are often confused in legal writing. Proper use of the words is illustrated by these sentences: When you effect (cause) a change, you affect (change) something. When you affect (change) something, you produce an effect (the change itself).

Affected class　**1.** Persons who suffer the present effects of past job discrimination. **2.** Persons who make up a "class" for a **class action.**

Affecting commerce　**1.** An activity that generally concerns business or commerce. **2.** An activity that is likely to lead to a **labor dispute** that could obstruct the free flow of commerce.

Affiant　A person who swears to a written statement; a person who makes an **affidavit** (see that word). [pronounce: a-fi-ant]

Affidavit　A written statement sworn to before a person officially permitted by law to administer an **oath.** For example, an *affidavit of service* is a sworn statement that a legal paper has been "served" (mailed, handed to, etc.) upon another person in a lawsuit.

Affiliate　A person or company with an inside business connection to another company. Under **bankruptcy, securities,** and other laws, if one company owns more than a certain amount of another company's voting **stock,** or if the companies are under common control, they are *affiliates.*

Affiliation proceedings   Same as **paternity suit** (see that word).

Affinity   Relationship by marriage. For example, a wife is related by *affinity* to her husband's brother.

Affirm   **1.** Make firm; repeat agreement; confirm. **2.** When a higher court declares that a lower court's action was valid and right, it *"affirms"* the decision. **3.** Reaccept and make solid a **contract** that is breakable. **4.** State positively. **5.** Make a formal declaration in place of an **oath** (if oath taking is against your principles).

Affirmance   See **affirm.**

Affirmation   A solemn and formal declaration in place of an **oath** for those persons whose religious beliefs forbid oath taking.

Affirmative action   **1.** The requirement that an organization take steps to remedy past **discrimination** in hiring, promotion, etc.; for example, by recruiting more minorities and women. **2.** Any administrative action taken to right a wrong, rather than to punish anyone for causing it.

Affirmative defense   That part of a **defendant's answer** to a **complaint** (see these words) that goes beyond denying the facts and arguments of the complaint. It sets out new facts and arguments that might win for the defendant even if everything in the complaint is true. For example, an *affirmative defense* to a lawsuit for injuries caused by an auto accident might be the **contributory negligence** of the person who was hurt. Some other affirmative defenses in **civil** cases are **accord** and satisfaction, **assumption of risk,** and **estoppel.** Affirmative defenses in **criminal** cases include **alibi, insanity,** and **self-defense.**

Affirmative order   A judge's or **administrative agency's** order that a person (or organization) not only stop doing something but that the person take positive steps to undo the damage.

Affirmative relief   **1.** A court's **judgment** or other help given to a **defendant** that goes beyond merely denying the **plaintiff's** claim and gives the defendant something. **2.** A request for more than money **damages;** for example, for **specific performance.**

Affix   Attach physically (as a tree to the ground or a gutter to a house) or place upon (as a signature on a document). To affix something usually means to put it in place permanently. See **fixture.**

Afforce

Afforce   Make something larger or stronger.

Affreightment   A shipping contract.

Aforesaid   A vague legal word meaning "preceding" or "already mentioned."

Aforethought   Planned in advance; **premeditated.**

After-acquired property   Property received after a certain event, such as the date a person **mortgages** other property. Some mortgages have an *"after-acquired property clause"* which means that anything added to the mortgaged property is subject to the mortgage just as if it were mortgaged directly.

After-acquired title   The legal principle that if a person transfers ownership to land for which he or she has no good **title** (right of ownership) and then gets good title to it, the title automatically goes to the person to whom the property was transferred.

After-born child   A legal principle that if a child is born after a **will** is made, the child should still inherit whatever children inherit (under the will or by state law) unless the will specifically excludes later-born children.

After-market   Secondary market.

Against interest   A statement made against interest is one which hurts a person's claims in a lawsuit. It may be used by the other side even though most out-of-court statements may not be used in court. See **hearsay** and **admissions.**

Against the evidence   A **trial** judge may order a new trial if the **jury** has clearly given its **verdict** by mistake or bias "against the evidence." This is different from a **directed verdict** and a **judgment** non obstante veredicto (see these words).

Age of consent   The age at which persons may marry without parents' approval or the age at which a person is legally capable of agreeing to sexual intercourse. If a man engages in sex with a woman below that age (usually sixteen), most states call the crime **statutory** rape.

Age of majority   Age at which a child gains full right to enter into binding **contracts,** make a **will,** vote, etc. This age varies from state to state (though often eighteen) and from purpose to purpose.

Age of reason   Age at which a child may be capable of acting responsibly. This is often the age of seven. Below that age, a child's actions are never a crime, and the child's **testimony** may rarely be used.

Agency 1. A relationship in which one person acts for or represents another by the latter's authority. 2. Short for "**administrative agency**" (see that word).

Agency shop An arrangement between an employer and a **union** that requires all nonmembers of the union to pay the union as much money as if they were dues-paying members.

Agent A person authorized (requested or permitted) by another person to act for him or her; a person entrusted with another's business. Some of the many types of agent include: **bargaining agent** (see that word); *independent agent* (a **contractor.** Someone who is responsible for results only, who is not under the direct control of the employer, and not on the regular payroll); *managing agent* (A company employee who runs a part of the company's business and acts with independent judgment much of the time). A person need not be called an agent to be one for legal purposes. Many employees are agents.

Aggravated assault A general term (defined more specifically by some state laws) that means an **assault** that is more serious or dangerous than normal. *Aggravated assault* often means with a deadly weapon or with the intent to kill, rob, or rape. It does *not* mean "because aggravated by the person you harmed."

Aggravation Actions or occurrences that increase the seriousness of a crime, but are not part of the legal definition of that crime.

Aggregate method Projecting costs for a whole pension or insurance plan rather than for each individual in it.

Aggregation doctrine A rule that forbids combining separate money claims in order to reach a total equal to the minimum **jurisdictional** amount required to bring a lawsuit in federal court.

Aggressive collection Various means of collecting a debt, such as **attachment, execution, garnishment,** etc. (see these words).

Aggrieved party A person whose personal or property rights have been violated by another person or whose interests are directly harmed by a court's **judgment.**

Agio Extra money paid to convert from one currency to another. The *interest agio* is the difference between the interest rates of two countries.

Aging schedule A list showing how long **accounts receivable** (short term money owed to a company) have been owed and which ones are overdue. See also **collection ratio.**

Agrarian reform   Laws that break up large landholdings and give the land to small farmer–owners.

Agreed case   A lawsuit in which all the important facts are stipulated (agreed upon) between the sides, so that the judge needs to answer only the legal questions in dispute.

Agreement   **1.** A "meeting of minds."   **2.** An intention of two or more persons to enter into a **contract** with one another combined with an attempt to form a valid contract. An *agreement* may include the language used plus background facts and circumstances.   **3.** A contract.

Agricultural Marketing Agreement Act   A federal law that regulates the sale of farm products and gives price protection to farmers. See **parity.**

Aid and abet   Intentionally help another person to commit a crime. The term often includes encouraging or inciting another person to commit a crime.

Aid and comfort   **1.** Help or encourage.   **2.** To *"aid and comfort the enemy"* is committing **treason** according to the U.S. Constitution.

Aider   The legal conclusion that once a jury gives a **verdict,** those facts that the jury logically needed to reach the verdict are assumed to be properly **alleged** and proved.

Air rights   **1.** The right to build above a piece of land; for example, the right to put a building over a sunken road.   **2.** The right to reasonable use of all airspace above a property. For example, while airplanes may fly over a property, if they regularly fly so low as to reduce the property's value, they may have to pay for this reduction.

Airbill   A **bill of lading** (see that word) for shipment by air.

Alcometer   See **breathalyzer.**

Alderman   **1.** A person elected to a city council or other local governing body.   **2.** A low-level local judge.

Aleatory contract   A **contract** with effects and results that depend on an uncertain event; for example, **insurance** agreements are *aleatory.* [pronounce: a-le-a-to-ri]

Alia   (Latin)   **1.** Other things.   **2.** Other persons.

Alias   (Latin)   **1.** Short for "alias dictus" or "otherwise called"; a fictitious name used in place of a person's real name.   **2.** An *alias* **writ** or **summons** (see those words) is a second (or third, etc.) one put out through the court if the first one did not work.

Alibi (Latin) "Elsewhere"; the excuse that at the time a crime was committed a person was somewhere else.

Alien **1.** Any person who is not a U.S. **citizen**, whether or not that person lives here permanently. **2.** A foreigner generally.

Alien Registration Act A federal law that requires the finger-printing and annual registration of all noncitizens over the age of thirteen.

Alienable Subject to removal, taking away, transfer, or denial.

Alienate Transfer, convey, or otherwise dispose of property to another person. The process is called *"alienation"* when land is transferred.

Alienation clause A part of an **insurance** policy that **voids** (ends) the policy if the property being insured is sold or otherwise transferred.

Alienation of affection Taking away the love, companionship, or help of another person's husband or wife. (This can no longer be the basis for a lawsuit in most states.)

Alienee A person to whom property is transferred.

Alieni juris (Latin) Under another person's legal control.

Alienor A person who transfers property to another person.

Alimony Court-ordered payments by a divorced husband to his ex-wife (or occasionally by wife to ex-husband) for ongoing personal support. Unlike child **support**, periodic alimony is considered to be income of the recipient, who must pay taxes on it, and not of the person who pays the alimony and who may deduct it. Also see **lump-sum settlement.**

Aliquot (Latin) A part; a fractional or proportional part. [pronounce: al-i-quo]

Aliunde **1.** (Latin) From another place; from outside this document. Sometimes a document may be explained by information *aliunde* (other papers, **testimony** by the person who drew up the document, etc.), and sometimes not. **2.** The *aliunde rule* is that a **jury's** verdict may not be called into question by a **juror** unless new **evidence** (from some separate, independent source) is first used to set up the juror's statements. [pronounce: al-i-und]

Alive A word with no definite legal meaning. A child may be alive for purposes of **inheritance** once the child is conceived; alive for other purposes once it is capable of independent life if artificially removed from the mother's body; alive if actually breathing or giving other more technical signs of life, no matter how briefly; etc. For the similar problem of when life legally ends, see **death**.

All events test   When taxes are paid on an **accrual basis,** income is considered to belong to the taxpayer once all events have occurred that give the taxpayer a legal right to the income and once the amount can be closely figured.

All faults   See **as is**.

All fours   Two cases or decisions are *on all fours* if they are generally similar and are exactly alike in all legally important ways.

Allegation   A statement in a **pleading** that sets out a fact that one side expects to prove.

Allege   State; assert; charge; make an **allegation;** for example, *"alleged"* often means *"merely* stated" or *"only* charged."

Allegiance   Loyalty and obedience to the government of which a person is a citizen. *Local allegiance* is the temporary obedience (but not personal loyalty) that a person owes to the country he or she is living in temporarily.

Allen charge   A judge's instruction to a **jury** sometimes used when the jury has difficulty reaching a decision. The judge tells the **jurors** to listen more favorably to each other's opinions. This charge has also been called the *dynamite instruction, shotgun charge*, etc., and is prohibited in some states.

Allocation   Putting something in one place rather than in another. For example, crediting all of a payment to one **account** when it is not specifically marked and the customer has two accounts at the store is called *allocation. Allocation of income* refers to the process in **trust** accounting by which income is put into one pot to continue the trust or into another pot to be paid out. *Allocation of income* also refers to the **I.R.S.'s determination** (see those words) that income belongs to one of two companies controlled by the same persons, rather than to the other company.

Allocution   The procedure in which a judge asks a prisoner whether he or she has any way to show that **judgment** should not be **pronounced** against him or her or has any last words to say before a sentence is given out. This is sometimes called "calling the prisoner."

Allodial   An old word describing land that was owned freely and completely.

Allograph   A document written or signed by one person for another person.

Allonge   A piece of paper attached to a **negotiable instrument** (see that word) to provide space for **endorsements** (signatures).

Allotment   A share or portion; sometimes, the dividing-up process itself. For example, an *"allotment certificate"* is a document that tells prospective buyers of **shares** in a company how many shares they may buy and the **schedule** of payments for the shares; and a *"land allotment"* is a dividing-up of a piece of land for sale as building lots.

Allowance   1. A **deduction**. **2.** A regular payment. For example, a *temporary allowance* in a divorce may be **alimony** plus child **support** (see these words).

Alluvion (or alluvium)   See **accretion**.

Alter ego   Second self. The rule that if persons use a **corporation** as a mere front for doing their own private business, a court may disallow some of the protections that the law gives to the corporation's owners. Under the "alter ego rule" the court may hold the persons individually **liable** for their actions taken through the corporation. See also **corporate veil** and ınstrumentality.

Alteration   1. Making a thing different from what it was before without destroying its identity; a change or modification. **2.** Writing or erasing on a document that changes its language or meaning.

Alternate valuation date   Under federal tax rules, the **administrator** of a dead person's property may set a value for the property based on the date of death or on the "alternate valuation" day, the date the property is sold or given out. If six months go by before the property is disposed of, the choice is between the value as of the day of death and six months thereafter.

Alternative contract   A **contract** that gives one or both of the persons making the agreement the choice of more than one way to fulfill the contract's terms.

Alternative pleading   Asserting facts that are mutually exclusive (that cannot logically, physically, etc., exist at the same time) in the same **pleading** (see that word). This is now permitted in federal court and most state courts as long as each alternative fact or statement could stand on its own without the others.

Alternative relief   Asking the court, in a **pleading**, for help in ways that might contradict one another; for example, asking for either the return of a borrowed book or for payment of its value. Most courts allow this type of request.

Alternative writ   See **show cause** order.

Am.Jur.   *American Jurisprudence*, a legal encyclopedia.

Amalgamation   A complete joining or blending together of two or more things into one. For example, the amalgamation of two **corporations** usually creates a single **board** of directors, a single company name, new company stock, etc.

Ambassador   The top representative of one country to another.

Ambiguity   Uncertainness; the possibility that something (usually a document) can be interpreted in more than one way.

Ambit   Boundary line; limit; border.

Ambulance chaser   **1.** A lawyer or a person working for a lawyer who follows up on street accidents to try to get the legal business involved.   **2.** A lawyer who improperly solicits business or tries to get others to bring lawsuits.

Ambulatory   Movable; capable of being changed or revoked.

Amend   Improve; correct; change or review.

Amendment   **1.** A change in a **bill** during its passage through a **legislature** or in a law already passed.   **2.** One of the provisions of the U.S. Constitution enacted since the original Constitution became law.   **3.** The correction of a **pleading** that is already before a court.

Amercement   A fine imposed on an official for misconduct.

American Arbitration Association   An organization that supplies **arbitrators** who help settle labor and other disputes.

American Bar Association   The largest voluntary organization of lawyers in the country. Its branches and committees are involved in almost every area of legal practice and government activity.

American clause   A provision in some marine **insurance** policies that makes the insurance company **liable** for the full amount of certain claims even if other insurance covers the same claims.

American Digest System   A giant collection of summaries of every **reported** case (written **opinion**) in America since the sixteen hundreds. The years up to 1896 are in a *Century Digest*, each ten year period after that is in a *Decennial Digest* and the latest few years are in a *General Digest*. Each Digest has many volumes. The cases are organized by subjects according to the Key Number System (see **key numbers**).

American Jurisprudence   A legal encyclopedia that is cross-referenced with **American Law Reports** (see that word).

American Law Institute   An organization that writes model laws and carries out an educational program for lawyers and others. Among its projects are the **Restatement of Law** and the **Uniform Laws,** which are often adopted by many states.

American Law Reports   A large series of books that selects important cases, prints them in full, and gives an **annotation** (a commentary) that is often long and that discusses a whole area of the law.

American rule   The rule that the winner of a lawsuit may not collect attorney fees from the loser. This "rule" has many exceptions. For example, if the opponent has brought the lawsuit in **bad faith,** a court may award attorney fees to the winner.

Amicable action   A lawsuit (involving a real, not a made-up problem) that is started by agreement of the two sides.

Amicus curiae   (Latin) "Friend of the court." A person who is allowed to appear in a lawsuit (usually to file arguments in the form of a **brief**, but sometimes to take an active part) even though the person has no right to appear otherwise. [pronounce: a-me-kus cure-e-eye]

Amnesty   A wiping out, by the government, of guilt for persons guilty of a crime; a general governmental forgiving.

Amortization   **1.** Paying off a debt in regular and equal payments. To *amortize* an ordinary loan, figure out the total interest for the whole time until the loan is paid off, add that total to the amount of the loan, and divide the total by the number of payments.   **2.** Breaking down the value and costs of an intangible asset (such as money owed, a **copyright**, or a **patent**) year-by-year over the estimated useful life of the asset.   **3.** Any dividing up of benefits or costs by time periods, primarily for tax purposes. It is called *amortization* for **intangibles** such as money owed, **depreciation** (see that word) for physical objects used in a business, and **depletion** (see that word) for natural resources such as oil.

Amotion   Putting or taking out; for example, evicting a tenant from a house, removing a person from a public or corporate office, taking someone's personal property, etc.

Analogy   Reasoning or arguing by similarities. For example, when there is no previous case exactly deciding an issue (a "**pre-**

cedent"), lawyers will argue from cases that are similar or are decided by the same general principles.

Analytical jurisprudence   A method of studying legal systems by analyzing and comparing legal principles in the abstract without considering their ethical backgrounds or practical applications.

Anarchist   **1.** A person who advocates the violent overthrow of all governments.   **2.** A person who believes that no government is the best government.

Anarchy   Absence of government; absence of law. *"Anarchism"* is the belief that no government is the best government and that people will cooperate voluntarily if left alone.

Anathema   A religious punishment in which all members of a church are forbidden to have anything to do with the person being punished.

Ancient   A word meaning "old," without having a precise legal definition. For example, an *ancient watercourse* is a stream that has existed "beyond memory"; an *ancient deed* is thirty (in some states twenty) years old and kept in proper custody; and *ancient streets* having nothing to do with time, but with the fact that a landowner is presumed to have given a street to the surrounding lot owners and to the public use if the lots were sold by the landowner.

Ancient lights   Windows that have had outside light for over a certain length of time (usually twenty years) cannot be blocked off by an adjoining landowner in some states. Both the windows themselves and the rule about blocking them are called *ancient lights*.

Ancient writings   Documents over a certain age (usually thirty years) that are presumed to be genuine if they have been in continuously proper **custody** (keeping).

Ancillary   Aiding; a proceeding "on the side" that helps a main proceeding.

Ancillary administration   A proceeding in a state where a dead person had property, but which is different from the state where that person lived and has his or her main **estate administered** (see those words).

Ancillary jurisdiction   The power of a court to handle matters that are a "side" part of a case even if it could not handle them without their being tacked on to the main subject of the case.

And/or A vague term, best replaced by words that say exactly what you mean. For example, "I like ham and/or eggs" could be "I like ham; I like eggs; and I like them served together."

Animo (Latin) With intention; for example, *animo furandi* (with intention to steal), *animo testandi* (with intention to make a will), or *revertandi* (return); *donadi* (make a gift); *manendi* (remain, make the place a **domicile** or permanent **residence**); or *revocandi* (revoke).

Animus (Latin) Mind or intention (see **animo**).

Animus et factum (Latin) "Intention plus fact"; the intention to do something plus the act itself.

Ann. (or An.) Annual; annotated.

Annex Attach (usually something small to something large); for example, attaching a small piece of land to a large one or a small school district to large one. *Annex* can also refer to attaching a side document to the main one or putting a permanent light fixture on a wall.

Annotated statutes A set of books containing the laws plus commentary (history, explanations, cases discussing each law, etc.); for example, Connecticut General Statutes Annotated.

Annotation **1.** A note or commentary intended to explain the meaning of a passage in a book or document. **2.** A legal *annotation* is usually an explanation of a **case** and a description of other similar cases. It usually follows the text of the **decision** in a collection of cases.

Annual exclusion The amount of money a person can give away each year without paying a **gift tax** and without using up any of the **unified credit** each person has.

Annual percentage rate The true cost of borrowing money, expressed in a standardized, yearly way to make it easier to understand **credit** terms and to "shop" for credit.

Annual report (or statement) **1.** A report most **corporations** are legally required to provide each year to stockholders and to the government. Most companies also make it freely available to the public. The report usually contains a **balance sheet, statements** (see that word) of income, spending, **retained earnings**, and other financial data, plus a breakdown of the company's **stocks** and **bonds**, an explanation of **accounting** principles used, an **auditor's** report, comments about the year's business and future prospects, etc. Parts of the report may have different names from those given here. **2.** Any yearly report of an organization.

Annuity **1.** A fixed sum of money, usually paid to a person at fixed times for a fixed time period or for life. If for life, or for some other uncertain period of time, it is called **contingent**. **2.** A *retirement annuity* is a right to receive payments starting at some future date, usually retirement, but sometimes a fixed date. There are many ways a retirement annuity can be paid. For example, *life* (equal monthly payments for the retiree's life); *lump sum* (one payment); *certain and continuous* (like *life*, but if the person dies within a set time period, benefits continue for the rest of that period); and *joint and survivor* (a slightly lower level of benefits, but it will continue for the life of either the retiree or the spouse.)

Annul Make void; wipe out; see **annulment**.

Annulment **1.** The act of making something **void** or wiping it out completely. **2.** The *annulment* of a marriage wipes the entire past and past validity of the marriage off the books, as opposed to a **divorce**, which only ends the marriage. A marriage will not usually be *annulled* by a court unless it was **invalid** in some way from the beginning.

Anomalous Unusual; an exception to a rule; abnormal.

Anon Anonymous (author unknown).

Answer **1.** The first **pleading** by the **defendant** in a lawsuit. This pleading responds to the charges and demands of the **plaintiff's complaint.** The defendant may deny the plaintiff's charges, may present new facts to defeat them, or may show why the plaintiff's facts are legally invalid. **2.** Take on the **liability** of another person, as in to "answer" for someone's debt.

Ante (Latin) Before.

Ante litem motam (Latin) Before the lawsuit was started; before anyone would have a reason to lie.

Ante natus (Latin) Born before. A person born before another person or before a major political event such as a revolution.

Antecedent debt A debt that is prior in time to another transaction. In **contract** law, the prior debt may sometimes make a fresh promise to pay enforceable even if the debt itself is too old to collect. And in **bankruptcy** law, an *antecedent debt* is one owed for a long enough time before the **filing** of bankruptcy that it is considered a valid debt rather than an attempt to give money to one person in preference to other **creditors**.

Antedate   Predate. Date a document earlier than the date it was actually signed. This may be a crime.

Antenuptial   Before a marriage. An *antenuptial agreement* is a contract between persons about to marry. It usually concerns the way property will be handled during the marriage, the way it will be divided in case of **divorce**, and the way it will be passed on in case of death.

Anticipation   **1.** The act of doing a thing before its proper time or simply doing it "before" something else.   **2.** The right to pay off a **mortgage** before it comes due without paying a "prepayment penalty."   **3.** The right under some **contracts** to deduct some money (usually equal to the current interest rate) when paying early.   **4.** In **patent** law, a person is *anticipated* if someone else has already patented substantially the same thing.

Anticipatory breach   Breaking a contract by refusing to go through with it once it is entered into, but before it is time actually to perform (do your side or share).

Antidumping act (or duty)   See **dump.**

Antilapse statute   Laws passed in most states to allow the **heirs** of someone who will inherit under a will to inherit themselves if the person who was supposed to inherit dies before the person making the will dies. Otherwise, that part of the property in the will would **lapse** (go to others).

Antinomy   An inconsistency between ideas, authorities, laws, or provisions in a law.

Anti-Racketeering Act   A federal law prohibiting **extortion** and other interference with interstate commerce. Also called the Hobbs Act.

Antitrust acts   Federal and state laws to protect trade from **monopoly** control and from **price-fixing** and other **restraints of trade** (see those words). The main federal antitrust laws are the Sherman, Clayton, Federal Trade Commission, and Robinson-Patman Acts.

Apex Rule   In mining law, a miner may follow and exploit a mineral vein on public land from the top (usually the discovery point) to any underground point on public land to which the vein leads, even if it goes outside the surface boundary of the miner's claim or passes under another claim. Also called "extralateral right."

App. Ct. Appellate court (see **appellate**).

Apparent Easily seen; superficially true. For example, *"apparent authority"* is the **authority** an agent (such as an employee) seems to have, judged by the words and actions of the person who gave the authority and by the **agent's** own words and actions.

Appeal **1.** Ask a higher court to review the actions of a lower court in order to correct mistakes or injustice. **2.** The process in no. 1 is called *"an appeal."* An appeal may also be taken from a lower level of an **administrative agency** to a higher level or from an agency to a court.

Appeal bond Money put up by someone appealing a court's decision. This money is to pay the other side's costs in case the person appealing fails to go forward with an honest appeal.

Appealable order An action by a judge that is sufficiently final so that an appeal from the order will not disrupt the way the judge is handling the case. See **interlocutory** for examples of when an order is "final enough" to be *appealable.*

Appeals council The place to **appeal** when dissatisfied with the ruling of an **administrative law judge** in a Social Security case.

Appearance **1.** The coming into court as a **party** (**plaintiff** or **defendant**) to a lawsuit. A person who does this *"appears."* **2.** The formal coming into court as a lawyer in a specific lawsuit; often also called "entering" the case.

Appellant The person who **appeals** a case to a higher court.

Appellate A higher court that can hear **appeals** from a lower court.

Appellate jurisdiction The power and authority of a higher court to take up cases that have already been in a lower court for trial and the power to make decisions about these cases without holding a trial. This is called appellate review. Also, a trial court may have *appellate jurisdiction* over cases from an **administrative agency.**

Appellee The **party** in a case against whom an **appeal** is taken (usually, but not always, the winner in the lower court).

Append Add or attach. Something *appendant* is added or attached to another thing.

Appoint **1.** Give a person a job or duty; for example, to *appoint* a person to serve on a committee. Nonelected government jobs, especially high-level ones, are called *appointments.* **2.** Give a **power of appointment** (see that word).

Apportionment   Dividing something up by shares. For example, "one person—one vote" is now the rule for the *apportionment* of voters to each Congressional District in a state so that each person is fairly represented.

Appose   Examine the keeper of written records about those records.

Appraisal (or appraisement)   1. Estimating the value of something by an impartial expert. This is not the same as an **assessment** (see that word).   **2.** Fixing the fair value of **stock** by a court when stockholders in a **corporation** quarrel and some must be bought out. *Appraisal remedy* (*or rights*) is the provision of law in most states giving **minority stockholders** the right to be bought out at the price the stock was before the corporation took an unusual action, such as a **merger** or sale of major **assets.**

Appraiser   An impartial expert chosen to set a value on a piece of property.

Appreciable   1. Can be estimated, weighed, or perceived by the senses.   **2.** Existing, but *not* necessarily substantial or great in size, quantity, or value.   **3.** Capable of increasing in value. See **appreciate**.

Appreciate   1. Increase in value.   **2.** Estimate the value of something.   **3.** Understand or realize.

Appreciation   1. The increase in value of a piece of property excluding increases due to improvements.   **2.** Any increase in value.

Apprehension   1. The capture or arrest of a person on a criminal charge.   **2.** Fear.   **3.** Understanding; knowledge of something.

Appropriation   1. A legislature's setting aside for a specific purpose a portion of the money raised by the government; for example, a *"highway appropriation."*   **2.** A governmental taking of land or property for public use.   **3.** Taking something wrongfully; for example, using a person's picture and name in an advertisement without permission.   **4.** In private business, an appropriation is setting aside money for a major purchase or long-term project.   **5.** Any setting aside or application of money or property for a particular purpose.   **6.** *"Appropriations"* is the name of the committee of Congress that makes the spending decisions in no. 1.

Approval   A sale *"on approval"* means that the buyer may return the goods if they are unsatisfactory even if they are all the seller claims they are.

Approximation   When a **charitable trust** cannot be carried out, a court may, in order to save the trust from failing, under the **doctrine** of *approximation*, carry out the general purposes of the trust even though the particular method set up in the trust will no longer work. See also **cy pres**.

Appurtenance   Something that belongs to or is attached to something else. For example, both a **right of way** and a barn may be an *appurtenance* to land.

Appurtenant   Belonging to or added onto (see **appurtenance**).

Arbiter   A person who is chosen to decide a disagreement.

Arbitrage   Buying **stocks** or other financial papers in one market and selling them in another for the profit from price differences.

Arbitrary   **1.** Action taken according to a person's own desires; without supervision, general principles or rules to decide by.   **2.** Action taken capriciously, in bad faith, or without good reason.

Arbitration   Formally submitting a dispute to a person (other than a judge) whose decision is binding. This person is called an *arbitrator*. If arbitration is required by law, it is called "compulsory."

Arbitration acts   Laws that help (and sometimes require) the submission of certain types of problems (often **labor** disputes) to an **arbitrator**.

Arbitration of exchange   The **arbitrage** of **bills** of exchange (see those words) in order to take advantage of the different values of national currencies in different international money markets.

Arbitrator   A person who conducts an **arbitration** (see that word). This person is usually not a public official, is often chosen by the persons having the dispute, and is usually an impartial expert in the field.

Architect's lien   See **lien**.

Area-wide agreement   One **union** making the same **labor contract** with many companies in one geographical area. This is called "area bargaining."

Arguendo (Latin) Assume something as true (whether true or false) for the sake of argument.

Argument **1.** Persuasion by laying out facts, law, and the reasoning that connects them. **2.** The oral, in-court presentation of no. 1.

Argumentative Stating not only facts, but conclusions.

Arise Originate or come into being. For example, a lawsuit *arises* when a person first has the *right* to take it to court. This is before the lawsuit *commences*, or when it actually begins. Also, a case *arises* under the **Constitution** when a constitutional right is claimed or when the case cannot be decided without referring to the Constitution.

Aristocracy Government by a nobility based on birth, wealth, social position, etc.

Armed robbery Taking property from a person by using or threatening violence and while carrying a dangerous weapon.

Armistice A complete suspension of fighting between nations with the hope that the suspension will become permanent. An armistice is more than a truce (which can be for a limited time or place) and less than a peace treaty (which is permanent or long-lasting).

Arms length Not on close terms; not an "inside deal"; not done by a lawyer, **trustee**, or other person especially responsible to a person for faithfulness. Whether a deal is *arms length* is often tested by its result: was the price paid a fair one; was it a price that would have been reached on the open market?

Arms, right to The right given by the **Second Amendment** to the U.S. **Constitution** for the people to "keep and bear arms" in order to guarantee "a well regulated militia." This right does not allow a person to carry a gun in violation of state or federal laws.

Arraign To bring a **defendant** before a judge to hear the charges and to enter a **plea** (guilty, not guilty, etc.).

Arraignment See **arraign**.

Arrangement with creditors A plan under the federal **Bankruptcy** Act that allows a financially weak person or company to settle debts for less than full value, to gain additional time to pay, or to otherwise keep from going under completely. See **Chapter Eleven** for **corporations** and **Chapter Thirteen** for persons and small businesses.

Array The entire **jury panel** (see those words). A "challenge to the array" is an objection to the procedures by which the panel was chosen.

Arrears (or arrearages) Money owed that is overdue and unpaid.

Arrest The official taking of a person to answer criminal charges. This involves at least temporarily depriving the person of liberty and may involve the use of force.

Arrest of judgment A judge's temporary stopping of the enforcement of the court's **judgment** because of some apparent defect in the proceedings.

Arrest record 1. The official form filled out by the police when a person is arrested. 2. A list of times a person has been arrested, with convictions also noted.

Arrogation 1. Claiming something or taking something without having any right to it. 2. The **adoption** of an adult.

Arson The **malicious** and unlawful burning of a building.

Art 1. Special knowledge or skill. 2. A process or method. 3. *Words of art* are technical or scientific words, or ordinary words used in a special way in a particular area of business or science. 4. "Art." is **article**.

Article A separate and distinct part of a document.

Articled clerk A lawyer's apprentice in England. Few states in America still allow entry into the legal profession by apprenticeship and examination rather than by graduation from law school and examination.

Articles 1. The separate parts of a document, book, set of rules, etc. 2. A law with several parts. 3. A system of rules; for example, "*articles of the navy.*" 4. Certain types of contracts; for example, "*articles of partnership,*" which set up a partnership, or "*articles of association,*" which set up non **stock** (often non-profit) organizations.

Articles of Confederation The document that held together the thirteen original American colonies before the adoption of the **Constitution**.

Articles of incorporation The document that sets up a **corporation**. This document must be filed with the right state agency (usually the secretary of state).

Articulated pleading Using separate paragraphs, separately numbered, for each important fact in a court paper such as a **complaint** or **answer**.

Articulo mortis (Latin) Death throes; at the point of death.

Artificial person An **entity** or "thing" that the law gives some of the legal rights and duties of a person; for example, a **corporation**.

Artisan's lien See **mechanic's lien**.

As is A thing sold "*as is*" is sold in a possibly defective condition, and the buyer must take it with no promises other than it is as seen and described.

As per A general phrase used for "in accordance with" or "with reference to."

Ascendants Parents, grandparents, etc. Ascendants can **inherit** property in the same way descendants (children, etc.) can, and "ascent" is the word that describes this type of inheritance.

Ascent See **ascendants**.

Asportation Taking things and carrying them away illegally.

Assault An intentional show of force or a movement that could reasonably make the person approached feel in danger of physical attack or harmful physical contact.

Assay **1.** Examine something to discover its size, weight, number, or quality. **2.** The chemical testing of a metal's purity.

Assemblage **1.** See **assembly**. **2.** Combining many things (such as small lots of land) into one.

Assembly **1.** A large meeting. **2.** The lower **house** of many state **legislatures**. **3.** The *right of assembly* in the **First Amendment** to the U.S. **Constitution** guarantees the right of the people to meet for political purposes, especially to protest government actions. **4.** *Unlawful assembly* is the gathering of people in a disruptive way, such as obstructing traffic on a busy street.

Assent Approval; demonstrated agreement.

Asservation See **asseveration**.

Assess **1.** Set the value of something. **2.** Set the value of property for the purpose of taxing it. **3.** Charge part of the cost of a public improvement (such as a sidewalk) to each person or property directly benefiting from it.

Assessable **1.** Liable to pay extra. For example, *assessable stock* is **stock** that may require the owner to pay more than the original investment to keep a share in the company; and *assessable insurance* may require the person **insured** to start paying higher **premiums** if a loss is too expensive. **2.** Liable to be put on the tax rolls and taxed.

37

Assessed valuation

Assessed valuation   The value placed on real estate for tax purposes by the government. It is usually less than "**market value**."

Assessment   **1.** Deciding on the amount to be paid by each of several persons into a common fund. **2.** The process of listing and evaluating the worth of property for taxing it. This is not "**appraisal**" (see that word). **3.** A payment beyond what is normally required of members of a group. **4.** Periodic payments by persons who have **subscribed** to buy **stock** from a **corporation**. **5.** Deciding the amount of **damages** that the loser of a lawsuit must pay. **6.** An extra payment. For example, when the **I.R.S.** decides that you owe more taxes than you paid.

Assessment ratio   The percentage of the **market value** of a property at which the government values it for tax purposes.

Assessment work   Mining or improvements on a mining **claim** on public land in order to avoid losing your right to the claim.

Assessor   **1.** A person who evaluates the worth of things; usually a government official who evaluates land and building for tax purposes. **2.** A person who advises a judge on scientific or technical matters during a lawsuit.

Asset depreciation range   The choice of "lifetimes" the **I.R.S.** will let you use when you claim **depreciation** on a particular **asset** (property). See **accelerated cost recovery system** for new rules.

Assets   All money, property, and money-related rights (such as money owed) owned by a person or an organization. In a business, "*capital assets*" or "*fixed assets*" are those things that cannot be turned into cash easily (such as buildings); "*current assets*" or "*liquid assets*" are those things that can be turned into cash easily (such as cash or goods for sale); and "*frozen assets*" are those things that are tied up because of a lawsuit. For other types of assets, such as **quick assets**, see those words.

Asseveration   A solemn **oath** or **declaration**.

Assign   **1.** To appoint or select for a particular purpose or duty. **2.** To transfer or make over formally; for example, to **deed** over land to another person. **3.** To point out, set forth, or specify. For example, to "*assign errors*" is to specify them in a legal document, and an "*assignable error*" is an error that can be used as the basis for an **appeal**.

Assigned account   A debt owed to a company that the company uses as **security** for its own debt to a bank. Also called *pledged accounts receivable*.

Assigned counsel   A lawyer appointed by the court to represent someone, usually in a criminal case, who is too poor to hire a lawyer.

Assigned risk   A type of **insurance** (such as automobile insurance for a person who has had many accidents) that insurance companies handle only because state law requires it. These persons pay extra for insurance and are often assigned to each insurance company by a list.

Assignee   Person to whom something is given or transferred. The *assignee clause* in federal law prohibits lawsuits in federal courts that got there only because one person transferred rights to another person in another state in order to get the necessary diversity **jurisdiction** to bring the lawsuit (see **diversity of citizenship**).

Assignment   **1.** See **assign**.   **2.** The transfer of property, rights in property, or money to another person. For example, an *assignment of wages* is an employer paying part of an employee's salary directly to someone to whom the employee owes money. Most states limit this. An *assignment of income* is an attempt to have income taxed to someone else by turning over either the income or the income-producing property to that person. Tax laws make this hard to do.

Assignor   Person who assigns (see **assign**) something to another person.

Assigns   Old word for persons to whom property is or will be transferred.

Assise (or Assize)   Old word with various meanings including: certain English courts, laws, and **writs**.

Assistance of counsel   The Sixth Amendment to the Constitution gives every person the right to a lawyer in a criminal prosecution. See **assigned counsel**.

Assistance, writ of   A *writ of assistance* is a judge's command that the **sheriff** help a person take possession of land once the court has decided that the person has a right to the land.

Associate company   A company owned or controlled by a **holding company**.

Associate justice   The title of each judge (other than the chief justice) on an **appeals** court.

Association   **1.** A general word meaning a group of persons joined together for a particular purpose.   **2.** A type of **limited**

partnership, trust, or other financial entity that the **I.R.S.** will tax as a **corporation** because it acts like a corporation.

Assume **1.** To take up or take responsibility for. See **assumption.** **2.** To pretend; to take deceitfully on the appearance of something.

Assumpsit "He promised"; an old word meaning a promise to do or pay something. Certain types of lawsuits had this name. For example, *"indebitatis assumpsit"* was "he promised to pay the debt," but it was based not on an actual promise but on the fact that money was owed, whether or not there was an actual promise to pay.

Assumption The assumption of a **mortgage** is the taking over of a mortgage debt (for example, on a house) when buying the property.

Assumption of risk If you expose yourself or your property to certain kinds of known dangers, you cannot collect **damages** if harmed. This is a legal rule in some states.

Assurance **1. Insurance** (see that word); and *assured* means insured. **2.** A **pledge** or **guarantee.** **3.** An old word for the document that transfers real property and for the transfer itself.

Assured **Insured** person.

Asylum The right of one country to protect a fugitive from criminal **prosecution** by another country. This right is greatly limited by **extradition treaties.**

At bar Currently being handled in court; "before this court."

At issue A legal point is "at issue" in a lawsuit when one side clearly asserts it and the other side clearly denies it. The lawsuit itself is "at issue" when all major legal points are clearly asserted and denied.

At large **1.** Unlimited, fully, in detail, everywhere. **2.** Free, unrestrained, uncontrolled. **3.** See **statutes at large. 4.** An *at large* election is one where each person chooses from among all the candidates, rather than just candidates from one geographic subarea.

At risk The amount of money a person could actually lose if an investment goes bad.

Ats. Abbreviation for **Ad sectam** (see that word) or, now, "At The Suit of."

Attaché An official attached to an embassy, an ambassador's staff, or some other diplomatic mission, especially for a particular reason, such as a naval attaché. [pronounce: at-ah-<u>shay</u>]

Attachment   1. The act of taking or seizing property or persons in order to bring them under the control of the court. For example, a bank account may sometimes be *"attached"* in order to make sure that a person pays a debt that might result from a successful lawsuit.   2. A document added onto another document.   3. A **security** interest, such as a **mortgage**, *attaches* if it is valid and can be enforced by the person who has it against the person who holds the attached property.

Attachment bond   Money put up to free property that has been attached. The bond substitutes for the property and guarantees that if the person who attached it wins in court, there will be money to pay the claim.

Attainder   The wiping out of **civil rights** that occurs when a person receives a death **sentence.** It usually includes the government's taking of all the person's property. This is no longer done in America. A *bill of attainder* was a **legislative** act pronouncing a person guilty (usually of **treason**) without a trial and sentencing the person to death and *attainder.* This is now prohibited by the Constitution.

Attaint   1. An old English process, no longer done, of conducting an investigation into whether a **jury** had given a deliberately false **verdict.** If so, the person wronged was given back everything lost and the jurors were sent to prison and stripped of all they owned.   2. What happens in **attainder** (see that word).

Attempt   1. An act that goes beyond preparation, but which is not completed.   2. An effort to commit a crime that goes beyond preparation, and which would have succeeded if it had not been prevented.

Attenuation   The breaking of a connection. For example, if many things happen between two events, the connection between these two events becomes *"attenuated"* or broken.

Attest   Swear to; act as a witness to; certify formally, usually in writing.

Attestation   The act of witnessing the signing of a document and signing that you have witnessed it.

Attorn   An old word that means to agree to pay rent and be a tenant to a new landlord who buys the land. The process is called *attornment.*

Attorney   1. Lawyer (*"attorney at law"*).   2. Any person who acts formally for another person (*"attorney in fact"*).

Attorney general   The chief law officer of each state and also of the United States. The U.S. attorney general is also the head of the Department of Justice and a **cabinet** member.

Attorney of record   The lawyer listed in court papers as representing a person and who is responsible to the person and the court for all work done (and not done) in the lawsuit. The *attorney of record* is the person who receives all legal papers from the court and from the other side in the case.

Attorney–client privilege   See **privilege.**

Attorney's lien   The right of lawyers, in some circumstances, to hold a client's money (or property, such as legal papers) already in the lawyer's hands or to get at a client's money in the court's hands, to pay for attorney's fees.

Attractive nuisance   A legal principle, used in some states, that says if a person keeps dangerous property in a way that children might be attracted to it and be able to get at it, then that person is responsible even if the children are at fault when they get hurt.

Attribution   Saying (or deciding) that something that looks like it belongs to one person really belongs to another.

Att'y   Attorney.

Audit   An official examination of an **account** or of a person's or an organizations' financial situation. The two most common audits are the annual outside examination of a company's total financial picture by "auditors" and the inspection by the **I.R.S.** of a person's tax records. This I.R.S. examination can be a *field audit* (at home or place of business), a *correspondence audit,* or an *office audit* (at the I.R.S. office).

Audit trail   A cross-reference from a bookkeeping record to its source to properly explain it, document it, or check its accuracy.

Auditor   An official who examines **accounts** and decides whether they are accurate.

Augmented estate   The property left by a dead person after subtracting for various claims and expenses and adding in the value of property held by the husband or wife and of certain other property disposed of to "insiders."

Authentication   1. A formal act certifying that a public document (a law, a record of **deeds,** etc.) is official and correct, so that it may be admitted as **evidence.**   2. Any **evidence** that proves that a document actually is what it seems to be. **3.** An *"authentic act"* may be something sworn to before a **notary public.**

Authoritarianism **Absolutism** (see that word), whether or not there is a formal legal system in place that makes it look like government power is *not* **absolute.**

Authorities **Citations** or references taken from laws, decisions, texts, etc., in support of a legal position argued by an advocate, a decision maker, or a scholar.

Authority **1.** Permission to act. **2.** Power to act. **3.** Legal right to act. **4.** See **authorities.** **5.** For **apparent, express,** and **implied** authority, see those words.

Authorization card A form signed by a worker giving a **union** the right to represent him or her. If a union gets a majority of employees to sign cards, the company must deal with that union in **collective bargaining.** Another way a union can get these rights is through an authorization election.

Authorize Give the right to act. *"Authorized"* means officially permitted.

Autocracy One person with total power over a country.

Autopsy Examination of a dead body to find out the cause of death. Evidence from an autopsy is called "autoptic evidence."

Autre (or Auter) (French) Another. For example, *"autre vie"* means "during another person's life-time," and *autre droit* means "in another's right" or for another person. [pronounce: oh-tr vee; oh-tr dwa]

Autrefois acquit (or convict) (French) Formerly **acquitted** (or **convicted**). A person cannot be tried for a crime for which he or she has already been acquitted or convicted, or for a crime based upon the same facts and law.

Auxiliary Aiding, **subsidiary, ancillary.**

Avails Profits or **proceeds.**

Aver Declare, assert, **allege,** set out clearly and formally.

Average **1.** A general mathematical term that can mean the *mean,* the *median,* or the *mode* (see these words in a good general dictionary). When used in a contract without further definition, *average* may be obvious from the context of the contract or from the general use of the word in the trade, or it may be so vague as to make the contract fail. **2.** For **general** and **particular average loss,** terms in marine **insurance,** see those words.

Averment Statement of facts.

Aviation Act   Federal law that governs the Federal Aviation Administration (**F.A.A.**) and the Civil Aeronautics Board (**C.A.B.**).

Avoidance   **1.** Escaping or evading.   **2.** In **pleading,** avoidance is a statement admitting the facts in a pleading by the other side, but showing why these facts should not have their ordinary legal effect.   **3. Annulling** or cancelling.

Avowal   An offer of **proof** (made out of the **jury's** hearing) in order to have it just in case an **appeals** court says that the witness should have been allowed to **testify** before the jury.

Avulsion   The sudden loss or gain of land, such as when a storm tears away part of a riverbank and deposits land on the other side.

Award   **1.** To give or grant by formal process. For example, a jury *awards* **damages** and a company awards a **contract** to a bidder.   **2.** The decision of an **arbitrator** or other nonjudge in a dispute submitted to him or her.

Axiom   A basic truth or principle from which others are deduced.

Bb

B.B.B.   **Better Business Bureau.**

B.F.   Old abbreviation for the Latin "bona fides" (good faith); also for "bonum factum" (a good act). This meant "approved."

B.F.O.Q. (or B.F.Q.)   "Bona fide occupational qualification." An employer's legitimate need to discriminate in hiring based on race, sex, age, etc. There are very few BFOQs permitted.

B.F.P.   **Bona fide** purchaser.

B.I.A.   Bureau of Indian Affairs. The branch of the U.S. **Interior** Department that acts as **trustee** for Indian lands and handles Indian problems.

B.J.   Bar Journal.

B.N.A.   Bureau of National Affairs. A publisher of **loose-leaf services** in specialty areas of the law.

Baby act *"Pleading the baby act"* means using a person's **minority** (underage) as a **defense** against a lawsuit based on a contract made by the minor.

Back **1.** To **indorse,** sign, or assume financial responsibility for something; for example, co-signing a loan **note. 2.** To supply money for a business venture.

Backbond A bond given by a person to the **surety** who backs the person's debt. For example, when John promises to pay Mary's debt to Sue if Mary fails to pay it, Mary may give a *backbond* to John, promising to repay any losses.

Backdoor spending Government spending, such as the authority to enter into debts and to make payments on them, that is not a direct part of an **appropriation bill** and, thus, is not directly controllable each year by the **legislature.**

Bad debt A debt that has become completely uncollectable. A *bad debt* can be a tax **deduction.** There are different rules for loans due to business, investment, and personal bad debts. A typical business bad debt might be an unsecured bank loan with no monthly payments made for several months despite collection efforts.

Bad faith Dishonesty in dealing with another person, whether or not actual **fraud** is involved.

Bad tendency A test for whether free speech should be limited because it might lead to action that is illegal and dangerous. This test has been replaced by the **clear and present danger** test.

Badge of fraud A strong suspicion of fraud. The phrase is usually used when examining a transfer of property to see if it is a fake used to keep the property away from **creditors.** In this case a *badge of fraud* might be a sale totally different from one made in the ordinary course of business or a sale made to relatives.

Bail **1.** Persons who put up money or property to allow the release of a person in jail until time of trial. **2.** The money or property put up by the person in no. 1. This money, often in the form of a **bail bond,** may be lost if the person released does not appear in court. **3.** The process of releasing the person for whom a bail bond was supplied.

Bail bond A written statement of debt that is put up by an arrested person and others who back it up. It promises that the arrested person will show up in court or risk losing the amount of the bond.

Bailee

Bail<u>ee</u> A person to whom property is loaned or otherwise entrusted.

Bailiff **1.** A **sheriff's** deputy or a low-level court official who keeps the peace in court. **2.** A low-level official; a superintendent or steward.

Bailment A temporary delivery of property by the owner to another person. Examples of *bailments* include: the loan of a book to a friend, the storage of property in a commercial warehouse, the repair of an automobile in a repair shop, etc. A *bailment for term* is a delivery of property for a set length of time.

Bail<u>or</u> A person who entrusts property to another.

Bail-out **1.** Any situation in which one person saves another from financial loss. **2.** A conversion of **ordinary income** to **capital gains,** or any other attempt by the owner of a business to get better tax treatment of profits.

Bait and switch Advertising one item to get people to come into a store and then persuading them to buy a different item. This may be illegal if the original item was never really available or if it was not really as advertised.

Baker v. Carr A 1962 Supreme Court case that started a series of cases requiring "one person, one vote" standards for the **reapportionment** of all state and federal election **districts.**

Balance **1.** An amount left over. For example, the difference between a debt and the payments already made on the debt is called a *balance due.* In bookkeeping a *balance* is the difference between the amounts in the **debit** and **credit** columns. If the debit total is larger, the account has a *debit balance.* **2.** Nothing left over. For example, if the debit and credit columns in no. 1 add up to the same amount, the account is called *"in balance"* or *"balanced."*

Balance of payments **Balance of trade** plus certain other financial transactions such as international loans.

Balance of trade The figure that shows the value of exports to a country compared with imports from it.

Balance sheet A complete summary of the financial worth of a company, broken down by **assets** and **liabilities** (see these words). A corporation's annual balance sheet will show what it owns and owes as of a given day and will include **stockholder's equity** as a separate item.

Balancing test A **doctrine** in **constitutional law** that says a court should balance constitutional rights such as *free speech* against the right of the government to control conduct it calls harmful. The court should decide for the side with more important needs in each individual situation. The doctrine says that no rights are **absolute.**

Balloon payment (or Balloon loan) A loan in which the last payment is much larger than any of the other regular payments. This gives the customer a feeling that low payments will pay off a debt, but the *balloon payment* at the end is rarely noticed and must often be **refinanced.** The federal Truth-in-Lending law requires the clear disclosure of a balloon payment, and many state laws prohibit them entirely.

Ballot **1.** Pieces of paper or levers on a machine used to cast a (usually secret) vote in an election **2.** The total vote in an election. **3.** A list of candidates running for office.

Ban **1.** An old word for a public notice or proclamation of an intended marriage, a law, a public command, a fine, etc. **2.** Now a prohibition.

Banc (French) Bench; place where the court normally does business. A court "sitting in banc" (or "en banc") is a session of all the judges together.

Banishment See **deportation.**

Bank **1.** A commercial business that the laws allow to receive deposits, make loans, and perform other money-related functions. **2.** See **banc.** **3.** For *bank book,* see **passbook.** A *bank bill* or *bank note* is a document that promises to pay a certain sum of money to the **bearer** on **demand** and is intended to serve as money. *Bank credit* is a written promise by a bank (based on a **credit** rating or on **security**) that a person may borrow up to a certain amount from the bank. A *bank draft* is a check or similar document made out by a bank officer to take out funds from the bank or from another bank where the bank has funds. *Bank paper* is a commercial document (such as a banknote or bill of **exchange**) good enough to be **discounted** (bought by a bank or used as **collateral** for a bank loan).

Bank Holding Company Act A federal law that places restrictions on companies that have partial control of more than one bank.

Bank Secrecy Act A federal law that requires banks to report all large cash transfers, requires persons to report all carrying or sending of large amounts of money in or out of the country, and to report on any foreign bank accounts.

Banker's lien

Banker's lien   A bank's right to take for its own the money or property left in its care by a customer if the customer owes an overdue debt to the bank and if the money, to the bank's knowledge, belongs fully to the customer.

Bankrupt   A person going through a **bankruptcy** proceeding.

Bankruptcy   The procedure, under the Federal Bankrupty Act, by which a person is relieved of all debts once the person has placed all property and money under the court's supervision or by which an organization in financial trouble is either restructured by the court or ended and turned into cash to pay **creditors** and owners. *Bankruptcy* is a legal word and, while triggered by **insolvency** (see that word), does not mean the same thing. A bankruptcy can be *voluntary* (chosen by the person in financial trouble) or *involuntary* (caused by the person's creditors). Bankruptcies are handled by the **federal district courts.** A typical bankruptcy involves a **trustee** appointed by the court who takes charge of the **bankrupt's** property, gets a list from the bankrupt of all debts owed, and distributes the property proportionally among those **creditors** who **file** and prove their claims. When this is done, the court allows the bankrupt to keep some personal property and grants a **discharge** which frees the bankrupt from all listed debts. This is done under **Chapter Seven** of the Bankruptcy Act. See also **Chapter Eleven** for business reorganizations short of full bankruptcy and **Chapter Thirteen** for personal and small business "partial" bankruptcies with special plans.

Bar   **1.**   The entire group of lawyers permitted to practice law before a particular court.   **2.** The part of some courtrooms where prisoners stand.   **3.** A barrier or prohibition.   **4.** The court itself or the judge at work in court. See **at bar.**

Bar act   A state law that sets up what a lawyer may and may not do.

Bar association   A voluntary group of lawyers, as opposed to a group of lawyers who are required to be members of a court's **"integrated bar"** (see that word). There are bar associations on the national, state, and local levels, and bar associations of specialists in legal areas.

Bar examination   The written test that a new lawyer must pass in order to practice law. Some states use the "multi-state" exam and some rely on their own tests or a combination of the two.

Bare   With very limited legal rights, duties, or effect.

Bargain   A mutual understanding, **contract,** or agreement.

Bargain and sale   **1.** An old two-step method of transferring land ownership, which is now an ordinary sale with full transfer of **title.**   **2.** A sale **deed** with no title **warranties.**

Bargaining agent   A **union** that has the exclusive right to represent all the employees of a certain type at a company.

Bargaining unit   Those employees in a company who are best suited to be treated as one group for purposes of being represented by a union. The workers must have a "mutuality of interest."

Barometer   A business index (such as the unemployment rate) that shows general economic trends; or a stock that tends to go up (or down) in price when the general stock market goes up (or down).

Barratry   **1.** The offense of stirring up quarrels or lawsuits (usually applied to a lawyer's trying to stir up a lawsuit from which the lawyer can profit).   **2.** A **fraudulent** or illegal act done by a captain or crew of a ship that harms the ship's owner.

Barrister   **1.** An English lawyer who argues in actual court trials. See also **solicitor.**   **2.** A lawyer.

Barter   An exchange of things for things, as opposed to a sale of things for money.

Base   **1.** Inferior or subordinate; mixed or impure.   **2.** Basic or underlying; that upon which something is added or calculated. For example, a *base period* is a minimum time something must happen before something else can legally happen, or it is a time period used for financial comparison and calculations based on a fixed standard.

Basic form (or policy)   A standard **homeowners' policy** that covers the most common insurable **risks** to a home.

Basic patent   An entirely new and unpredicted process or product. A **patent** that may open up a whole new field of discovery. A pioneer patent.

Basis   The assumed cost of property used in calculating gain or loss for tax purposes when property is sold or exchanged. This is usually, but not always, purchase price. Sometimes it is original cost plus **improvements** minus **depreciation**, sometimes the cost to the person who gave the current owner the property, and sometimes another cost.

Basis point   One percent of one percent.

Basket buy

Basket buy   A purchase of several different things for one price.

Bastardy action   Same as **paternity suit** (see that word).

Bath   **1.** A big loss, *"Taking a bath"* is losing big in a **stock** or business deal, and a *"big bath"* is a company's abandoning of an unprofitable line of business and taking a **write-off** for taxes. **2.** See **immunity bath.**

Battery   Any intentional, unwanted, unprovoked, harmful physical contact by one person (or an object controlled by that person) with another person.

Bear arms   See **arms, right to.**

Bear market   A general drop in stock or other security prices. A "bear" is someone who thinks the market will fall.

Bear raiding   An illegal attempt by a group of investors to drive down the price of a stock by a rapid series of sales.

Bearer   A person in possession of a **negotiable instrument** (for example, a check) that is made out "payable to bearer," that is indorsed in **blank** (signed, but no name filled in on the "payable to" line), or that is made out to "cash" or other indication that no one specific person is meant to cash it.

Bearer instrument (or paper)   A check or other financial document as described in **bearer** (see that word).

Behoof   Old word for use or benefit.

Belief   A sense of firmness about the truth of an idea that lies somewhere between "suspicion" and "knowledge."

Belief–action rule   The principle that a person may believe anything without restriction, but when belief turns into action, that action is only sometimes protected by the **Constitution.** See **symbolic speech.**

Belligerent   **1.** A country at war with another country, as opposed to a neutral country that takes absolutely no part and chooses no "side" to support.   **2.** Rebels who have organized a government while they fight, so that their war is considered lawful by international standards.

Below   A lower court.

Bench   **1.** The place where judges sit in court.   **2.** Judges collectively are "the bench."

Bench conference   A private meeting at the judge's bench of lawyers for both sides of a lawsuit. It is often called to discuss something out of the jury's hearing, and it may or may not be made part of the **record** of the case.

Bench warrant   A paper issued directly by a judge to the police or other **peace officers** to permit the arrest of a person.

Beneficial   Giving a profit or advantage.

Beneficial association   See **benefit society.**

Beneficial interest   The right to profits resulting from a contract, **estate,** or property rather than the legal ownership of these things.

Beneficiary   **1.** A person (or organization, etc.) for whose benefit a **trust** is created.   **2.** A person to whom an **insurance** policy is payable.   **3.** A person who inherits under a **will.**   **4.** Anyone who benefits from something or who is treated as the real owner of something for tax purposes.

Benefit   **1.** Any advantage, profit, or privilege.   **2.** Money paid by an insurance company, a retirement plan, an employer (other than wages), etc.

Benefit of bargain rule   In normal lawsuits based on **fraud** in the sale of something for more than it is worth, the buyer can get only the difference between what was paid and what the item is really worth. In some lawsuits where the value of an item was *promised* to be a certain amount, the buyer can get the difference between the promised value and the real value under the *benefit of bargain rule.*

Benefit of cession   The right that some **debtors** had in old England to avoid imprisonment for debts if the debtor turned over all property to the **creditors.**

Benefit of clergy   **1.** The right that clergymen had in old England to avoid trial by all nonchurch courts.   **2.** Married; not merely living together.

Benefit–security ratio   The money a pension plan must pay out compared to what it has set aside to make the payments.

Benefit society   A general name for an organization that uses its members' payments to give or lend money to other members who need it.

Benevolent corporation (or Benevolent association)   A nonprofit charitable organization that may receive certain tax advantages.

Bequeath   **1.** Give **personal** property or money (as opposed to real estate) by **will.**   **2.** Give anything by will.

Bequest   **1.** A gift by will of personal property.   **2.** Any gift by will.

Best evidence

Best evidence   A rule of **evidence** that requires that the most reliable available proof of a fact must be produced. For example, if a painting is available as evidence, a photograph of the painting will not do.

Bestiality   Sexual intercourse between a human and an animal, a crime in most states.

Best use   The value a piece of property would have if it were used in the most lucrative way. See **highest and best use.**

Bestow   Give or **grant** something.

Beta   A measure of how closely the value of a **stock** (and the money it pays its owners) parallels that of the stock market generally. *Beta* figures are often used to describe the variability of an entire **portfolio** of stocks.

Better Business Bureau   A local business-supported organization that handles complaints about business practices, provides consumer information, and generally promotes ethical business dealings. National standards and support for these local bureaus are provided by the Council of Better Business Bureaus.

Betterment   **1.** An improvement rather than a repair.   **2.** A "betterment act" (or "betterment theory") is a law (or a legal rule) that allows a tenant to recover the cost of necessary permanent improvements to property from the landlord.

Beyond a reasonable doubt   The level of proof required to **convict** a person of a crime. For a **jury** to be convinced "beyond a reasonable doubt," it must be fully satisfied that the person is guilty. This is the highest level of proof required in any type of trial. It does not mean "convinced 100 percent," but it comes close to that meaning.

Biannual   Twice a year. See also **biennial.**

Bias   **1.** A preconceived opinion that makes it difficult to be impartial.   **2.** A preconceived opinion by the judge about one or more of the persons involved in a lawsuit, as opposed to an opinion about the subject matter.

Bicameral   Two chambers. A legislature with two "houses," such as the U.S. Senate and House of Representatives, is bicameral.

Bid   **1.** An offer to pay an asking price at an auction. *Bidding up* or *by-bidding* is artificially raising the price at an auction by an insider who has no real intention of actually buying.   **2.** An offer to perform work or supply goods at a given price. An *open* *bid* reserves the right to reduce the price to meet the competition.   **3.** An application for a new job with the same employer.

Bid and asked   The range of prices quoted in an **over-the-counter** exchange of **stock.** *Bid* is the selling price and *asked* is the purchase price. The difference is dealer profit. Another way of looking at it is that *asked* is the average price asked by those persons recently willing to sell and *bid* is the average price bid by those persons recently willing to buy.

Bid shopping   Disclosing low bids on **contract** work in order to get lower ones from other persons.

Biennial   Once every two years. See also **biannual**.

Biennium   A two-year period. A spending period for a state with a **legislature** that meets only once every two years.

Bifurcated trial   Separate hearings for different issues in the same case; for example, for guilt and sanity or guilt and punishment in a criminal trial, or for **liability** and **damages** in a complicated auto injury trial.

Big board   A popular term for the listing of **stock** prices at the New York Stock Exchange.

Big eight   The eight largest accounting firms.

Bigamy   The crime of having two husbands or wives at the same time.

Bilateral contract   A deal that involves promises, **rights,** and **duties** on both sides. For example, a **contract** to sell a car is *bilateral* because one person promises to turn over the car and the other person promises to pay for it.

Bill   **1.** A formal written statement sent to a higher court, either to inform it of certain facts or to request certain actions. For example, a *bill of exceptions* is a list of objections to the rulings and actions of the trial judge by one side.   **2.** A **draft** of a law proposed to a **legislature** or working its way through the legislature.   **3.** A law passed by a legislature when it proceeds like a court; for example, a *bill of impeachment.*   **4.** An unusually important declaration; for example, the **Bill of Rights** (see that word).   **5.** A list of debts, contract terms, or items; for example, a *bill of lading* (list of goods shipped).   **6.** A type of **negotiable instrument** (see that word), promising the payment of money; for example, a *bill of exchange* (a written **order** from A. to B., telling B. to pay C. a certain sum of money).   **7.** A statement of details in court; for example, a *bill of particulars* (a breakdown

Bill of attainder

of one side's demands against the other in a lawsuit) or a *bill of indictment* (the formal accusation of a crime presented to a grand jury. **8.** The old word for the first court paper in an **equity** trial. The modern word for all first **pleadings** is a **complaint.**

Bill of attainder See **attainder.**

Bill of lading A document given by a railroad, shipping company, or other **carrier** that lists the goods accepted for transport and sometimes lists the terms of the shipping agreement. Some of the laws concerning bills of lading are Article 7 of the **Uniform Commercial Code,** the Federal Bills of Lading Acts, and the **Interstate Commerce Act.**

Bill of pains and penalties Similar to a **bill of attainder** (see that word), but with lesser punishment. It is prohibited by the Constitution.

Bill of particulars A detailed statement of charges or claims by a **plaintiff** or the **prosecutor** (given upon the **defendant's** request).

Bill of review A request that a court **set aside** a prior **decree.** It is a new **suit,** not a reopening of the old one.

Bill of Rights The first Ten Amendments (changes or additions) to the U.S. Constitution that provide for: **1. Freedom of speech,** religion, press, assembly, and to petition the government. **2.** The right to keep weapons. **3.** Freedom from being forced to give room or board to soldiers. **4.** Freedom from unreasonable searches and seizures and the requirement that **warrants** be supported by **probable cause. 5.** The requirement that crimes be **indicted,** the prohibition against **double jeopardy,** the freedom from being a witness against yourself in a criminal trial, and the requirement that no rights or property be taken away without **due process of law** and just compensation. **6.** The rights to a speedy criminal trial, an impartial jury, knowledge of the charges, **confrontation** of adverse witnesses, **compulsory process** of witnesses, and the help of a lawyer. **7.** The right to a jury trial in most civil cases. **8.** The prohibition against excessive **bail,** excessive fines, and cruel and unusual punishment. **9.** The fact that some rights are spelled out in the Constitution does not mean that these are all the rights the people have. **10.** Any powers not kept solely for the U.S. belong to the states and to the people.

Billing cycle The regular time interval (often one month) between dates when bills are sent out to customers.

Bind 1. Hold by legal obligation. **2.** See **binding over.**

Binder **1.** A temporary, preliminary **insurance** contract. **2.** The agreement made when a deposit is paid on a home purchase.

Binding authority Sources of law that *must* be taken into account by a judge in deciding a case; for example, **statutes** from the same state or decisions by a higher court of the same state.

Binding instructions A judge telling a jury that it must decide the case a certain way if it decides that certain facts are true.

Binding over **1.** An act by which the court requires a **bond** or **bail** money. **2.** An act by which a court transfers a criminal defendant to another court in the same system.

Black Acre A made-up name for a piece of real estate for use in teaching law; often used together with *"White Acre."*

Black code The pre-Civil War laws of southern states that controlled the conduct of slaves and regulated slavery.

Black letter law Important legal principles that are accepted by most judges in most states.

Black Lung Act A federal law providing for payments and treatment for coal miners with black lung disease.

Black market Selling goods that are stolen, prohibited, or under government control and taxation without submitting to that control.

Blacklist A list of persons to be avoided, such as a list circulated by merchants of persons who cannot be counted on to pay their bills.

Blackmail Illegal pressure or **extortion** of money by threatening to expose a person's illegal act or threatening to destroy a person's reputation. Some states require this to be in writing for it to be the crime of blackmail and not just **extortion.**

Blackstone *Blackstone's Commentaries on the Common Law,* an influential treatise on the law of England, written in the eighteenth century.

Blank **1.** A space left in a written or printed document. **2.** A printed document (a "form") with spaces to be filled in; a model document.

Blank indorsement Signing a **negotiable instrument,** such as a check, without specifying to whom it is being signed over (leaving a blank in that space) and thus not limiting who can cash it.

Blanket Covering most (or many) things.

Blasphemy Cursing or ridiculing God or the majority religion.

Block positioning

Antiblasphemy laws violate the *establishment of religion clause* of the U.S. **Constitution.**

Block positioning   A **broker's** buying a part of a large block of **stock** from a client because it cannot be sold immediately and then selling it off piece by piece.

Blockage rule   The value of large blocks of **stock** for tax purposes may be lower than the sum of the values of each **share** because it is often hard to sell large blocks all at once without driving down the value of the stock.

Blockbusting   Convincing owners to sell their homes because another ethnic group is rumored to be moving into the area. This may be illegal if done by real estate agents.

Blocked   **1.** Money is *"blocked"* when there are government restrictions on taking it out of the country or exchanging it for foreign currency.   **2.** *"Blocked"* also refers to bank accounts, checks, and other financial things that are temporarily kept from payment for any reason.

Blotter   **1.** The police record form for **booking** (see that word) a **defendant.** Also, the cumulative record of arrests and other events kept by the police.   **2.** See **waste-book.**

Blue book   **1.** A book showing the proper form of case **citations.**   **2.** A book that gives the organization of and lists the persons in a state government.   **3.** The National Blue Book of parallel **citations** of court **opinions.**   **4.** The A.L.R. Blue Book of Supplemental Decisions to update A.L.R. **annotations.**   **5.** A book of estimated prices, such as for used cars.

Blue chip   A large company with a history of stability and profits.

Blue flu   Police officers calling in sick because they are not allowed to strike. Other city employees have similar names for similar **job actions.**

Blue law   A state law that forbids selling or other activities on Sunday; originally, any law based on religious restrictions.

Blue list   Daily listing of **municipal** bond offerings.

Blue ribbon jury   A **jury** specially chosen to try important or complex cases. This practice is rarely permitted.

Blue sky bargaining   Making obviously unreasonable demands at the start of a negotiating session, often to impress those you represent, to delay real "nuts and bolts" discussions, or to set a far-out basis for later compromise.

Blue sky law   A law **regulating** and supervising sales of **stock** and other activities of investment companies to protect the public from fly-by-night or **fraudulent** stock deals.

Board   **1.** A publically appointed or elected group of persons chosen to oversee a public function. For example, a *board of aldermen* is the governing body of some local governments; a *board of supervisors* runs some county governments; a *board of elections* runs many elections; the *Board of Patent Appeals* reviews decisions in patent application cases; and a state professional licensing board examines the qualifications of various specialists.   **2.** A private governing body or looser-knit organization. For example, a *board of directors* is the group that runs a corporation, and a *board of trade* is an association of merchants with common interests.

Board lot   **Round lot.**

Boarder   A person who pays for regular meals (or meals plus a room) in a house.

Body   **1.** A person or an organization, such as a *"body corporate"* (a **corporation**).   **2.** The main or most important part of a document.   **3.** A collection of laws.

Body execution   Legal authority to deprive a person of freedom and to take that person to jail.

Body of the crime   See **corpus delicti.**

Body politic (or corporate)   The government; the citizens of a government as a group; a city, state, county, or even a school district.

Bogus   False and intended to deceive. For example, a *"bogus check"* is a check given by a person who has no active account at the bank named on the check.

Boiler plate   A form for a document, such as those sold by a stationery store. The word implies standardization or lack of tailoring to the individual legal problem.

Boiler-room sales   High-pressure sales of **stock,** usually by telephone, and often of doubtful value.

Bona   (Latin) **1.** Goods, property, or possessions.   **2.** Good. As in **bona fide** (see that word), "good faith," or honesty.

Bona fide   (Latin) Honest; in good faith; real. For example, a *bona fide purchaser* in commercial law is a person who buys something honestly, pays good value, and knows of no other person's claim to the thing bought.

Bona immobilia

Bona immobilia   (Latin) Immovable property or land.

Bond   **1.** A document that shows a debt owed by a company or a government. The company or government agency promises to pay the owner of the bond a specific amount of interest for a set period of time and to repay the debt on a certain date. A bond, unlike a **stock**, gives the holder no ownership rights in the company. Examples of this type of bond include: *adjustment bond* (**issued** when a corporation is reorganized); *convertible bond* (can be turned into stock); *coupon bond* (with coupons that are clipped and presented for interest); *debenture bond* (backed by the general credit of a company or government, rather than by specific property); *guaranteed bond* (backed by a company other than the one that put it out); *industrial development bond* (put out by a local government to build business facilities that are then leased to pay off the bond); *municipal bond* (put out by state and local governments to finance government projects; the interest paid on these is usually exempt from taxes); *registered bond* (the bond owner's name is kept by the company); *serial bond* (several bonds issued at the same time with different payback times); *series bond* (of the same exact type, but put out at intervals); *term bond* (all come due at the same time); and *U.S. savings bond.*   **2.** A document that promises to pay money if a particular future event happens, or a sum of money that is put up and will be lost if that event happens. Examples of this type of bond include: *appeal bond* (to cover the costs of the other side if the judge orders it when an **appeal** is taken); *attachment bond* (to get back property that has been attached [see **attachment**] and guarantee that the person who attached it will be paid if you lose the lawsuit concerning the property); *completion bond* (to make sure that a builder finishes a job properly and within a time limit); *fidelity bond* (to protect a business against an employee's stealing); and a **peace bond** (see that word).   **3.** Other words frequently used when discussing bonds are: *bond conversion* (exchanging bonds for stock); *bond discount* (the amount a bond sells for if it is cheaper than its face price); *bond issue* (all the bonds put out at one time); *bond premium* (the amount a bond sells for if it is more expensive than its face price); and *bond rating* (the appraisal of soundness and value given to bonds by one of several rating companies such as Standard and Poor's and Moody's. Rating systems differ, but the highest rating given is often AAA and the lowest rating of an "investment quality" bond is often Baa).

Bonded warehouse A special storage place for goods that are held until a federal tax is paid for the right to sell the goods. This system is used for alcoholic beverages and imported goods stored for possible exportation.

Bondsman Person who puts up a bond such as a **bail bond** (see that word).

Bonification A **waiving** of taxes, especially on export goods.

Book value 1. Net worth (see **net worth method**); clearly proven **assets** minus **liabilities.** 2. The worth of something as recorded on a company's **financial statement.**

Booking 1. The writing down, by the police, of facts about a person's arrest and charges along with identification and background information. This is recorded on the police **blotter** in the police station. 2. The process in no. 1 plus questioning the person, setting bail, etc. "Booking," if this extensive, may take place in a courthouse, jail, etc.

Bookkeeping Writing down the financial transactions of a business in a systematic way.

Boot Something extra thrown into a bargain.

Bootstrap sale Using the **assets** of a newly bought company to pay part of the cost of buying the company.

Borough A division of land within a state ranging from very big to very small, depending on the state. It may be equivalent to a **county,** a **town,** or other things. [pronounce: <u>burr</u>-oh]

Bottomry A loan to repair or equip a ship.

Bought and sold notes A **broker's** notifications to a buyer and a seller that a transaction has taken place.

Boycott The refusal to do business with and the attempt to stop others from doing business with a company. In labor law, a *primary boycott* involves a union and an employer while a *secondary boycott* involves companies that do business with (usually by buying from) the union's employer.

Bracket See **tax rate.**

Brain death rule According to this rule a person is dead if the brain has totally and irreversibly stopped functioning, even if other bodily processes still go on without outside help. For a person to be brain dead there must be no response to external stimuli; no spontaneous movements, breathing, or reflexes; and a flat reading for a full day on a machine that measures the brain's electrical activity.

Brandeis brief   A **brief** (see that word) in a lawsuit, usually on **appeal,** that includes economic and sociological studies in addition to the usual legal material.

Breach   Breaking a law or failing to perform a duty.

Breach of contract   Failure, without legal excuse, to perform any promise or to carry out any of the terms of a **contract.** Breach also includes refusing to perform your part of the bargain or making it hard for the other person to perform his or her part of the bargain.

Breach of peace   A vague term for a disturbance of public order. It is defined and enforced differently in different states.

Breach of promise   Short for "breach of promise to marry." See **heart-balm act** for its legal effect.

Breach of trust   The failure of a **trustee** to do something that is required. This includes doing things illegally, **negligently,** or even forgetfully.

Breaking   Using force or some kind of destruction of property (including things that do not permanently destroy, such as picking a lock), usually to illegally get into a building.

Breaking a case   **1.** Solving a crime.   **2.** An informal agreement among appeals court judges that is enough to form sides for written **opinions.**

Breaking bulk (or bail)   The crime of opening a container entrusted to your care and stealing part of the contents.

Breathalyzer   A test to discover the percentage of alcohol in the blood of a person arrested for drunk driving.

Breve   (Latin; plural is *brevia*) Old word for a **writ** (see that word). *Brevia de cursu* are writs issued automatically or "as a matter of course."

Bribery   The offering, giving, receiving, or soliciting of anything of value in order to influence the actions of a public official.

Bridge loan   Temporary, short-term financing; for example, to buy a new house before the old one can be sold.

Brief   **1.** A written summary or condensed statement of a series of ideas or of a document.   **2.** A written statement prepared by one side in a lawsuit to explain its case to the judge. It usually contains a fact summary, law summary, and an argument about how the law applies to the facts.   **3.** A summary of a published **opinion** in a case prepared for studying the case.   **4.** A document prepared by a lawyer to use at a trial. It usually contains lists of **witnesses, evidence,** and **citations** as well as arguments to be presented.

Bring suit (or bring an action)   Start a lawsuit, usually by filing the first papers.

Broad form (or policy)   A type of **homeowners' insurance** that covers more **risks** than the **basic form.**

Broad interpretation   Giving a law or **constitutional** provision a meaning that aims to bring about the law's "real intent," as opposed to a "narrow" or literal reading of the law.

Brocage   Brokerage.

Broker   An **agent** who is employed by different persons to buy, sell, make bargains, or enter into **contracts.** For example, an *insurance broker* sells insurance for more than one company; a *real estate broker* acts for the seller or buyer of land and buildings; and a *securities broker* buys and sells stocks, bonds, etc., for others.

Brother   Old expression for "fellow lawyer."

Brown decision   A **Supreme Court** case declaring racial segregation in public schools to be in violation of the equal protection clause of the **Fourteenth Amendment** to the **Constitution.**

Brutum fulmen   (Latin) An empty threat; a **judgment** that is unenforceable due to an obvious imperfection.

Bubble   A gigantic business project based on exaggerated hopes and unsound claims.

Bucket shop   An illegal business where persons accept orders to buy and sell stock, commodities, and other securities without actually placing the orders.

Budget   **1.** Money allowed for a particular purpose.   **2.** An estimate of money that will be taken in and spent in a particular time period.

Budget authority   An **appropriation** or other law permitting the government to spend money.

Budget Reform Act   A 1974 U.S. **congressional act** that set up budget committees, required annual budget **resolutions** with spending targets, moved the **fiscal** year to begin October 1, and made other changes designed to gain greater congressional control of the federal budget.

Buggery   **Sodomy** or **bestiality** (see those words).

Building code   Rules and standards for the construction or use of buildings. Some codes are part of local law and others are statewide or national, such as the requirements of **FHA** financed housing.

Building line   A certain distance inside the border of a lot, outside of which no building may extend.

Bulk transfer   According to the **Uniform Commercial Code,** a *"bulk transfer"* is "not in the ordinary course of business" and of "a major part of materials, supplies, or other inventories." Rules against "bulk sales," "bulk mortgages," or "bulk transfers" are to protect a merchant's **creditors** from being cheated.

Bull market   A general rise in **stock** or other **security** prices. A *"bull"* is someone who thinks the **market** will rise.

Bulletin   Name for many different types of legal publications, such as pamphlets with **agency** rules or **law journals.**

Bumping   **1.** An employee taking the job of another employee with weaker job rights (fewer years of service, lower rank, etc.). This usually happens during layoffs.   **2.** An airline's refusing a place to a ticketed customer because more airplane seats were sold than are available. The bumped customer may have special financial and other rights.

Burden of going forward (or burden of proceeding)   The requirement to come forward with evidence on a particular question in a lawsuit, rather than wait for the other side to do it.

Burden of proof   The requirement that to win a point or have an issue decided in your favor in a lawsuit you must show that the weight of evidence is on your side, rather than "in the balance" on that question.

Bureaucracy   An organization, such as an administrative agency or the army, with the following general traits: a chain of command with fewer people at the top than at the bottom; well-defined positions and responsibilities; fairly inflexible rules and procedures; "red tape" (many forms to be filled out and difficult procedures to go through); and **delegation** of authority downward from level to level.

Burford doctrine   The principle that federal courts will generally refuse to meddle with cases that involve complex state **regulations.**

Burglary   Breaking and entering the house of another person at night with the intention of committing a **felony** (usually theft). Some states do not require a "**breaking,**" or that the building be a house, or that it be at night for the entry to be called a **burglary.**

Bursar **Treasurer** or person who dispenses money.

Business agent **1.** A nonemployee that represents a company commercially; sometimes, any sales **agent.** **2.** A **labor union** employee who handles worker complaints and other union business, usually by traveling from one union workplace to another.

Business expense In tax law a business expense includes any expense necessary for producing income, not only those expenses that are a part of a trade or business. The I.R.S. has complex rules for deciding whether or not these expenses may be deducted from taxable income. Two areas of particular confusion are entertainment expenses and whether or not a collection (stamps, coins, etc.) is an investment or a hobby.

Business judgment rule The principle that if persons running a **corporation** make honest, careful decisions within their corporate powers, no court will interfere with these decisions even if the results are bad.

Business record exception An exception to the *"hearsay exclusion rule"* that allows original, routine records (whether or not part of a "business") to be used as **evidence** in a trial even though they are **hearsay** (see that word).

Business trust A company set up in the form of a **trust** (see that word) that is similar to a **corporation** (see that word) in most ways. One difference is that the **trustees** are permanent, but a corporation's **directors** are usually elected for a year or a few years.

"But for" rule **Negligence** alone will not make a person responsible for damage unless *"but for"* that negligence the damage would not have happened. For example, a failure to signal a turn may be negligent, but if the other driver was looking the other way, the failure to give a turn signal was not the cause of the accident.

Buy American acts Various state and national laws that require government agencies to give a preference to American-made goods when making purchases.

Buy and sell agreement An agreement among partners or owners of a company that if one dies or withdraws from the business, his or her share will be bought by the others or disposed of according to a prearranged plan.

Buyer 60 contract A purchase of **stock** at higher than the going price with the right to pay for the stock sixty days later.

By-bidding

By-bidding See **bid**.

Bylaws **Rules** or **regulations** adopted by an organization such as a **corporation,** club, or town.

Byrnes Act A federal law that prohibits bringing in strikebreakers from out of state.

C. **1.** An old abbreviation for the Latin "cum" (with). **2.** *"Circa"* (Lat'n) About. Approximately a certain date, as in c.1917. **3.** © means **copyright.**

C.A. **Court of appeals.**

C.A.B. Civil Aeronautics Board. The power of the *C.A.B.* is being gradually scaled down as airline routes and rates are deregulated. It may be eliminated.

C.A.F. Cost and freight.

C.A.T.V. Community Antenna Television System.

C.B.O.E. Chicago Board of **Options** Exchange.

C.C. **Circuit,** city or county court; **civil, criminal, crown,** or **chancery** case; civil or criminal code; chief **commissioner;** etc.

C.C.A. Circuit court of appeals.

C.C.C. Commodity Credit Corporation.

C.C.H. Commerce Clearing House. A publisher of **loose-leaf services.**

C.D. **Certificate** of deposit.

C.E.A. *Council of Economic Advisors* (to the U.S. president).

C.E.O. Chief Executive Officer.'

C.F. & I. (or C.I.F.) The price includes cost, freight, and insurance (all paid by seller).

C.F.R. **Code of Federal Regulations.**

C.F.T.C. **Commodity Futures Trading Commission.**

C.I.A. Central Intelligence Agency. The U.S. international spying department.

CIO See **AFL-CIO.**

C.J.   1. Chief judge; chief justice; circuit judge.   **2. Corpus Juris.**

CJS   Corpus Juris Secundum.

C.L.   Civil law.

C.L.A.   A Certified Legal Assistant who has passed the **N.A.L.A.** exams.

C.O.D.   Collect on delivery. The price of goods or the delivery charges are paid to the person who delivers them.

C.O.G.S.A.   Carriage of Goods by Sea Act.

C.O.L.A.   1. Cost of living adjustment (see that word).   **2. Cost of living allowance** (see that word).

C.P.   Common pleas (see that word).

C.P.A.   Certified public accountant (see **accountant).**

C.P.I.   Consumer Price Index.

C.P.S.C.   Consumer Products Safety Commission.

C.R.S.   Congressional Research Service.

C.S.C.   Civil Service Commission. It used to **regulate** federal employment (job classification, merit-system examinations, etc.), but now that this task has been split among other federal agencies, the name is used by only a few *state* employment regulatory boards.

C.T.A.   Cum testamento annexo (see that word).

Ca. sa.   Abbreviation for **Capias** ad satisfaciendum.

Cabinet   The advisory board of the head of a government. For example, the *cabinet* of the U.S. president is composed of the heads of the government departments such as State, Defense, Treasury, etc., plus a few other high government officials such as the vice-president; about fifteen persons in all.

Cachet   See **lettres de cachet.**

Caducary   Forfeit.

Caeterorum   (Latin) "As to the rest." When an **administrator** has not been given enough authority by a court to handle all of a dead person's property, the court may give power *caeterorum.*

Cafeteria plan   A **benefit** plan that allows employees to choose benefits from a list up to a certain dollar value. Also called *smorgasbord plan.*

Calendar   The trial list or **docket** of lawsuits ready for the court. A *calendar call* is the announcing in court of a list of active cases to find out the status of each, primarily whether or not they are ready for trial, and sometimes to assign trial times or dates.

Call **1.** Public announcement (usually of a list). **2.** A formal demand for payment according to the terms of a contract. For example, a **contract** or **option** that allows its owner to buy a certain number of **shares** of **stock** at a certain price on or by a certain day is a *call*. Also, the demand by a company that persons who promised to buy stock now actually come up with the money is a *call*. **3.** See **calling**.

Call numbers A way of identifying authors and books by a combination of letters and numbers. In most systems, the first letter is the first letter of the author's last name. No two authors or books share the same numbers. See **Dewey Decimal System** and **Library of Congress** for *subject* identification systems.

Call premium The amount over the **par** or **face** value of a **bond** or other **security** that a company must pay when the company calls it in for repurchase.

Callable Subject to being gathered in and paid for. *Callable bonds* may be paid off before **maturity** (coming due) by the company that put them out. This is often done when interest rates go down.

Call-in pay Pay that is guaranteed whether or not work is available.

Calling **1.** *"Calling the docket"* is a **calendar call.** **2.** *"Calling the jury"* is the selection of a **jury list** (see that word for the different meanings). **3.** *"Calling the plaintiff"* is the final in-court call for an absent **plaintiff** before awarding **judgment** to the **defendant. 4.** *"Calling a prisoner"* is **allocution. 5.** See **call.**

Calumny Defamation, **slander,** and false accusations.

Calvo doctrine The idea that a country should not normally be held responsible to outsiders for harm done by disturbances or fighting within the country, and that no other country has a right to intervene in a disturbance to protect its citizens' property or claims.

Cambism Foreign exchange.

Camera Chamber; see **in camera.**

Campbell's act See **Lord Campbell's Act.**

Cancel **1.** Wipe out, cross out, or destroy the effect of a document by defacing it (by drawing lines across it, stamping it "canceled," etc.). **2.** Destroy, **annul,** set aside, or end. The process is called *"cancellation."*

Cancellation   Under the **Uniform Commercial Code,** *"cancellation"* means ending a **contract** because the other side has **breached** (broken) the agreement.

Candidate for office   A person may be a candidate for office under various laws if he or she takes formal steps to run for office, raises or spends money on it, etc. A person may even be a candidate if he or she is put forward as a **nominee** of a group or receives any votes, whether or not that person agrees to run.

Canon   A law, rule, or principle.

Canon law   Christian religious law.

Canonical disability   Impotence that can permit the **annulment** of a marriage.

Canons of construction   Principles to guide the **interpretation** or **construction** of written documents to decide their legal effect.

Canons of Ethics   Old form (until 1969) for the **Code of Professional Responsibility** (see that word), the rules governing the legal profession.

Canons of Judicial Ethics   Old rules for judges' conduct, still used by some states, but gradually being replaced by the **Code of Judicial Conduct.**

Canvass   1.   Examine and count votes in an election to determine the authenticity of each vote and the accuracy of the totals. **2.** Solicit sales orders, votes, opinions, etc., by going door-to-door or phoning.

Capacity   1.   Ability to do something.   **2.** Legal right to do something.   **3.** Legal ability to do something. For example, a child of four lacks the *capacity* to commit a crime or make a contract.

Capacity costs   Fixed costs (see **fixed charges**) that give a business the ability to produce or sell goods and services. The opposite of **programmed costs.**

Capias   (Latin) "That you take." A **writ** from a judge to the **sheriff** or the police commanding them to take a **defendant** into **custody.** A *capias ad respondendum* is a writ to bring a person to court to answer a claim or defend a charge, and a *capias ad satisfaciendum* is a writ to bring a person to court to pay a **judgment.**

Capital   1.   Head, chief, or major. For example, *capital crimes* are those punishable by death, and *capital punishment* is the death penalty.   **2. Assets** or worth.   **3.** This is *not "capitol"* (a building).   **4.** Relating to wealth, especially to wealth or assets held

Capitalism

for a long time. For example, *capital assets* (almost all property owned other than things held for sale; *personal capital assets* include personally owned **stocks,** land, trademarks, jewelry, etc., and *business capital assets* are described under **assets**); *capital budget* (a list of planned spending on large, long-term projects); *capital charges* (money needed to pay off an investment's **interest** plus **amortization**); *capital cost* (an improvement to property that can be depreciated by taking tax **deductions** little by little during the life of the improvement); *capital gains tax* (a tax on the profit made on the increase in value of a *capital asset* when it is sold; to qualify for a low capital gains rate, property must be held for a certain length of time); *capital goods* (things used to produce other things, rather than for final sale); *capital market* (the way long-term **securities** such as **bonds** are bought and sold); *capital rationing* (a company's choice among long-term projects because of a shortage of funds or the inability to borrow at good interest rates); *capital return* (payments received that are not taxed as income because they are merely the return of money paid out); *capital stock* (all stock put out by a corporation in exchange for money invested in the company; a *capital stock tax* is a tax on the **face** or **par** value of the stock); *capital surplus* (money paid into a corporation by shareholders over the par value of the stock); and *capital structure* (the amount of a company's assets compared to its long-term debt and to its short-term debt).

Capitalism   Private ownership of most means of production and trade combined with a generally unrestricted marketplace of goods and services.

Capitalization rate   See **discounting.**

Capitalization ratio   The proportion of **bonds** and of each type of **stock** put out by a company compared to its total financing. A *bond ratio*, for example, might show that twenty percent of the company's finances comes from (and is tied up in) bonds.

Capitalize   1. Treat the cost of something (a purchase, an improvement, etc.) as a **capital** asset.   **2.** Issue **stocks** or **bonds** to cover an investment.   **3.** Figure out the **net worth** or **principal** on which an investment is based. For example, figure out what the sale price should be for a **mortgage** that brings in a hundred dollars a month for ten years. (This figure will be *much* less than one hundred dollars times twelve months times ten years.)

Capitation tax   A tax on a person at a fixed rate, regardless of income, assets, etc.; a "head tax."

Capitulary   A collection of laws. A **code** (see that word).

Capricious   Not based on fact, law, or reason.

Caption   **1.** The heading or introductory section of a legal paper that has, for example, the names of the **parties,** the court, the case number, etc.   **2.** An illegal taking.

Care   **1.** Safekeeping or **custody.**   **2.** Attention, heed or caution. There are various types of *care,* each defined in many ways, that apply to different situations. For example, in a normal driving situation, a person must act with *"reasonable care."* One definition of reasonable care is "ordinary or due care; what may be expected from a normal person under the circumstances."

Carnal knowledge   Sexual intercourse.

Carrier   A person or organization that transports persons or property. A *common carrier* does this for the general public.

Carrier's lien   The right of a shipping company or other mover of property to hold the things shipped until the shipping costs have been paid.

Carrol doctrine   The rule in **F.C.C.** cases that a broadcast **license** holder can challenge the grant of a competitive license.

Carry back (and Carry over)   A tax rule that allows a person or company to use losses to reduce taxes in the years prior to (or the years following) the loss.

Carrying charges   **1.** The costs of owning property, such as land taxes, mortgage payments, etc.   **2. Interest.**

Cartel   A close (often formal) association of companies carrying on the same or similar businesses. The companies limit competition among themselves and drive out competition by others.

Case   **1.** Lawsuit; a dispute that goes to court.   **2.** The judge's **opinion** deciding the dispute in no. 1.   **3.** Short for *trespass on the case,* an old form of lawsuit that preceded modern **contract** and **tort** law.

Case in point   A prior decision of the same court, or of a higher court, that decides a similar legal question.

Case method (or Case system)   The way most law schools teach law: by studying **cases** (judicial opinions) in each subject of the law historically, and by drawing general legal principles from them.

Casebook   A collection of written court opinions, usually by **appeals** judges. It is used for law school teaching.

Case-in-chief

Case-in-chief   The main **evidence** offered by one side in a lawsuit. This does not include evidence offered to oppose the other side's case.

Caselaw   All reported judicial decisions; the law that comes from reading judges' **opinions** in lawsuits.

Cases and controversies   The U.S. Constitution gives to the courts the power to decide *"cases or controversies."* These are real (not hypothetical or faked) disputes that turn into lawsuits.

Cash basis   A system of **bookkeeping** that shows a profit or loss when the money actually comes in or goes out.

Cash cycle   The time between a company's payment for raw materials (or wholesale goods) and its collection of payment for the finished product (or for the goods' resale).

Cash dividend   An ordinary **dividend** as opposed to a **stock dividend**, but it is paid by check, not in cash.

Cash flow   **1.** What is taken in minus what is paid out in a given time period.   **2.** A company's **net** profits plus **depreciation**.

Cash out   Sell.

Cash price   The price at which a merchant sells (or would sell) goods or services to consumers when no **credit** is given. If the merchant charges a higher price than his or her normal *cash price*, federal law may call the difference **interest** for credit.

Cash surrender value   The amount of money an insurance policy will bring if cashed in with the company.

Cash value   **1.** The same as **market value**; the price something would bring if it sold for cash on the open market.   **2.** See **cash surrender value**.

Cashier's check   A **certified check** (see that word) made out in the bank's own name and signed by a bank official.

Castle doctrine   The principle (now greatly restricted) that a person can use any force necessary to protect a home or its inhabitants from attack. Also called, "dwelling defense."

Casual   Accidental, by chance, unexpected, unintentional.

Casual ejector   See **ejectment**.

Casualty   **1.** Any accident; an unexpected accident; an inevitable accident.   **2.** An injured or killed person.

Casualty loss   A loss of property due to fire, storm, accident, or similar occurrence. It is **deductible** for tax purposes if certain tax rules are followed.

Casus (Latin) An occurrence, chance event, or accident that causes something. For example, *casus belli* is an event that causes (or is used to justify) a war; and *casus fortuitus* is a chance event or unavoidable accident.

Catch 22 An unwritten rule, or an unreasonable combination of otherwise reasonable rules, that keeps you from getting what you want.

Catch time charter A boat rental with payment for the time it is in actual use.

Catching **Unconscionable** (see that word). A *catching bargain* was originally a high interest loan to someone who would eventually inherit money or property.

Categorical assistance Financial help programs that have requirements in addition to financial need; for example, "Aid to the Blind."

Caucus **1.** A meeting of voters to choose **delegates** to a convention or **candidates** for public office. **2.** An informal subgroup of a large group such as a **legislature** or a convention.

Causa (Latin) Cause, reason, or motive. [pronounce: cow-sa]

Causa causans (Latin) See **proximate cause.**

Causa mortis (Latin) "In thinking about approaching death." For example, a gift *causa mortis* may be treated by the law as an attempt to avoid a tax on property given by **will** if the gift comes too close to death.

Causa proxima (Latin) See **proximate cause.**

Cause **1.** That which produces an effect. **2.** Motive or reason. **3.** Lawsuit or legal action. **4.** Short for *"just cause"* in the removal of a person from office or dismissal of a person from a job.

Cause of action **1.** Facts sufficient to support a valid lawsuit. For example, a *cause of action* for **battery** (see that word) must include facts to prove an intentional, unwanted physical contact. **2.** The legal theory upon which a lawsuit is based.

Caution A formal warning.

Cautionary instructions **1.** Part of a judge's **charge** to a **jury** that tells the jury it may use a particular piece of evidence only to answer certain specific questions and not to form any more general impressions from it. **2.** Part of a judge's charge that cautions the jury against talking with outsiders about the case and against being influenced by anything outside the trial itself.

Cautionary lien (or judgment) **1.** A **lien** put on a **defendant's** property to make sure that if the defendant loses there will be something available to pay the lien. **2.** A lien put on a property primarily to warn others that **title** to the property is not **clear**. This may be **recorded** in the land records or in a **judgment book**.

Caveat **1.** (Latin) "Let him or her beware." For example, *caveat emptor* (let the buyer beware) is a rule of law that has been greatly weakened by recent laws and judicial decisions. **2.** Warning. [pronounce: kav-e-at]

Caveator A person who makes a formal **objection**.

Cease and desist order A command from an **administrative agency** that is similar to a court's **injunction**.

Cede **1.** **Assign**, **grant**, or give up. **2.** To transfer land from one government to another. [pronounce: seed]

Cedent A person who **cedes** something. (*Not* the person who gets it.)

Celebration Formal ceremony.

Censorship **1.** The denial of **freedom of speech** or freedom of the press. **2.** The review of books, movies, etc., to prohibit publication and distribution, usually for reasons of morality or state security.

Censure A formal reprimand.

Census Bureau The federal agency that counts the population every ten years and maintains records of its characteristics.

Center of gravity doctrine The rule that a court should use the law of the state which has the most important contact with the events, persons, and issues involved in the lawsuit.

Century Digest (Abbreviated Cent. Dig.) See **American Digest System**.

Ceremonial marriage A marriage performed by a legally approved person, based on a legally valid license, and complying with all state laws as to blood tests, etc.

Certificate A written assurance that something has been done or some formal requirement has been met. For example, a *certificate of acknowledgment* is a confirmation made out by a public official such as a notary; a *certificate of convenience and necessity* is an operating license for a public utility such as a bus or gas company; a *certificate of deposit* is either a written receipt for a bank deposit or a bank deposit for a certain number of months or years that is permitted to pay a higher rate of interest than an ordinary **demand** savings account; and a *certificate of occupancy* permits a building or apartment to be used because it meets building, **zoning**, or health requirements.

Certification 1. See **certificate** and **certified**. 2. The process by which a federal court refers a question concerning state law to the state's highest court and holds off from deciding a case until that question is decided.

Certification mark A mark or label placed on goods by an organization (other than the manufacturer or seller of the goods) to show that the goods meet the organization's quality standards, come from a particular region, or were made by certain unions, etc. The mark is the property of the organization and its use is protected by law.

Certification proceeding A procedure taken by the National Labor Relations Board (see **N.L.R.B.**) to find out if the employees of a company want a particular **union** to represent them.

Certified Officially passed, "checked out," or approved.

Certified check A check that a bank has marked as "guaranteed cashable" for its customer.

Certiorari (Latin) "To make sure." A request for *certiorari* (or "cert." for short) is like an **appeal**, but one which the higher court is not required to take for decision. It is literally a **writ** from the higher court asking the lower court for the **record** of the case. [pronounce: sir-sho-rare-ee]

Cession A giving up of something; see **cede**.

Cessionary bankrupt A person who gives up everything he or she owns to be divided among **creditors**.

Cestui que (French) "He or she who." For example, a "cestui que trust" is a person who has a right to the property, money, and **proceeds** being managed by another. The modern phrase is "**beneficiary** of a **trust**." [pronounce: set-i kuh]

Cf. (Latin abbreviation) "Compare." For example, "*cf. Hamlet*" means "look at Hamlet for a comparison with or explanation of what is being discussed."

Ch. Chapter; **chancellor**; **chancery**; chief; etc.

Chain discount A discount on an already discounted price, so that the total discount is not as much as the sum of the discount percentages.

Chain of custody   The person who presents physical **evidence** (such as a gun) at a trial must account for its possession from time of receipt to time of trial. This proof of continuous possession is the *chain of custody.*

Chain of title   A list of the consecutive passing of the legal right to a piece of land.

Chain picketing   1. A tightly grouped, moving picket line to prevent anyone from crossing.   2. Picketing several retail outlets of one company.

Chain referral   See **pyramid sales scheme**.

Challenge   An objection; for example, an objection to the right of a **juror** or a judge to hear a case.

Chamber of commerce   A local association of businesses that promotes the area's trade. Also called *board of trade*.

Chambers   A judge's private office. Business that takes place there is *"in chambers."*

Champerty   Taking over a lawsuit being brought by another person, either by buying the other person's claim or by sharing any "winnings" of the suit. This practice is illegal.

Chancellor   1. Once the king or queen's **minister** who handed out royal justice, now the judge of a court of **equity** or **chancery**.   2. The head of a state university system.

Chance-medly   An old word for a sudden (usually free-for-all) fight during which a person kills in self-defense.

Chancery   An old court that handled **equitable** actions. The **equity** power is now part of regular courts in most states.

Change in financial position   See **statement**.

Chapter Eleven   A reorganization of an **insolvent** (broke) **corporation** under the federal **bankruptcy** laws, supervised by a federal bankruptcy court, in which ownership is transferred to a new corporation made up of old owners and **creditors**. In some cases the business can continue to operate during the process.

Chapter Seven   See **bankruptcy.**

Chapter Thirteen   A procedure under the federal **bankruptcy** laws for an individual or small business in financial trouble to pay off only a proportion of its debts (called a *"composition"*), get extra time to pay them (called an *"extension"*), or both. This process used to be called a *"wage earner's plan,"* but is now called a *"rehabilitation"* because the person's **credit** and finances are made good again. Payments may be made from a regular source of income or from a combination of income and the sale of property. Once the court approves the plan, all unsecured creditors must accept it, and even **secured** creditors may have to take less **interest** on their debts.

Character evidence   **Testimony** about a person's personal traits and habits that is drawn from the opinions of close associates, from the person's reputation in the community, or from the person's past actions.

Characteristic line   See **beta**.

Charge   **1.** A **claim, obligation,** burden, or **liability. 2.** The judge's final summary of a case and instructions to the jury. **3.** A formal accusation of a crime.   **4.** Paying for something "on time."

Charge d'affairs   A diplomatic representative of high, but not highest rank who often takes care of a country's business in another country when there is no **ambassador.**

Charge-off   Lowering the value of something in a company's records. For example, when a debt becomes too difficult to collect, it may be charged off (also called *write-off*).

Charitable   A gift or organization is *charitable* for tax purposes if it meets several tests. A gift must be made to a government-qualified nonprofit organization to benefit humankind in general, the community in general, or some specific type of people (so long as the individuals are not specified). Also, the organization's and the gift's purpose must be for the relief of poverty; protection of health or safety; prevention of cruelty; government; or advancement of education, religion, literature, science, etc. A qualified organization must use its money and staff to advance these purposes, rather than to benefit specific individuals. With few exceptions, it may not lobby or otherwise try to influence **legislation.** If the gift and the organization meet these standards, the giver may **deduct** the gift from income and the organization is exempt from paying taxes.

Charitable remainder trust   A **trust** that gets money (or property) for **charitable** purposes after others get use of the money first.

Charitable trust   A **trust** set up for a public purpose such as a school, church, charity, etc.

Charta   An old English word for **charter, deed,** or other formal document. More loosely, any written document.

Charter   **1.** An organization's basic starting document (for example, a corporation's **articles of incorporation**) combined with the law that gives the right to **incorporate** or otherwise exist. **2.** Renting a ship or other large means of transportation.

Chartered accountant   An English Certified Public **accountant.**

Chattel   Personal property or animals. Any property other than land.

Chattel mortgage   A **mortgage** on personal property.

Chattel paper   A document that shows both a debt and the fact that the debt is **secured** (see that word) by specific goods.

Check   **1.** A document in which a person tells his or her bank to pay a certain amount of money to another person. It is a type of **negotiable instrument** (see that word).   **2.** A restraint. For example, each branch of the U.S. federal government *"checks and balances"* the others so that no one branch can take over running the country.

Check-off   A system in which **union** dues are collected directly from a worker's pay for the union by the company.

Chicanery   **Fraud**.

Chilling   **1.** Holding down the sales price of an item to get it cheaply (usually at an auction and usually by telling lies about the property's value).   **2.** A law or practice has a *"chilling effect"* if it discourages a person from taking advantage of a **constitutional right.**

Chirograph   An old word for a document protected against fraud by different means (handwritten, signed by **witnesses**, written twice and torn in half with half given to each person, etc.).

Choate   Complete; valid against all later claims; opposite of **inchoate** (see that word). For example, a choate **lien** is one that needs nothing more to be done to make it enforceable.

Chose   (French) A thing; a piece of personal property. [pronounce: shows]

Chose in action   A right to recover a debt or to get **damages** that can be enforced in court. These words also apply to the thing itself that is being sued on; for example, an accident, a contract, stocks, etc.

Churning   The act of a **broker** who makes more trades (for example, of stock) than are beneficial to a customer's **account** in order to increase the broker's own **commissions.**

Cir. Ct.   **Circuit court.**

Circuit   An area of the United States or of a state which certain judges serve.

Circuit court The name given to different types and levels of courts in different states, originally because judges "rode circuit" (held court for a while in each place) to serve outlying areas.

Circuit court of appeals See **United States Court of Appeals**.

Circular note See **letter of credit**.

Circumstantial evidence Facts that *indirectly* prove a main fact in question. For example, **testimony** that a person was seen walking in the rain is **direct evidence** that the person walked in the rain, but testimony that the person was seen indoors with wet clothing is *circumstantial evidence* that the person walked in the rain. Another example of circumstantial, or indirect evidence: a live dodo-louse offered to prove that dodos are not extinct.

Citation **1.** A notice to appear in court or risk losing a right; for example, to inherit money. **2.** A reference to a legal authority and where it is found. For example, 17 U.Dl.L.R. 247 is a citation to an article that begins on page 247 of volume 17 of the University of Dull Law Review. **3.** A notice of a violation of law; for example, a *traffic citation*.

Citator A set of books that tells what happened to a **case** or **statute** after it came out. It will tell, for example, if a case has been **overruled, distinguished,** or **followed** (see these words). This is done by looking up the case by its **citation** (see that word) and checking whether there are citations to other cases listed under it. If there are, it means that the case was mentioned in these later cases. Some of these citations will be preceded by explanatory letters (such as "d," which means that the later case shows why the earlier one was different). The most used citator is called *Shepard's Citations*. It lists almost every case and law printed in the U.S. "Shepardizing" now means the same thing as "using a citator" because most citators are printed by that company. Shepardizing can now be done by computer.

Cite **1.** Summon a person to court. **2.** Refer to specific legal references or **authorities**. **3.** Short for "**citation**."

Citizen **1.** A person born in or naturalized in the U.S. **2.** A person is a citizen of the state where he or she has permanent residence, and a corporation is a citizen of the state where it was legally created.

Citizen's arrest An arrest by a private person, rather than by a police or other law enforcement officer. A person may arrest

Civil

another for any crime committed in his or her presence or for a **felony** (serious crime) committed elsewhere.

Civil 1. Not **criminal**. (See **civil action, civil commitment, civil procedure,** etc.) 2. Having to do with the government. See **civil law, civil rights, civil service,** etc.

Civil action Every lawsuit other than a **criminal** proceeding. A lawsuit that is brought to enforce a right or gain payment for a wrong, rather than a court action involving the government trying to punish a crime; in general, a lawsuit brought by one person against another.

Civil commitment Confinement by a non**criminal** process in a mental hospital or other treatment facility for insanity or for alcohol or drug addiction. The usual justification for confining a person who has not committed a crime is that he or she "is a danger to self or others." See **insanity**.

Civil death The loss of all rights, such as the right to make contracts or to sue, that occurs in some states to persons who are **convicted** of serious crimes (usually those persons **sentenced** to life imprisonment).

Civil disabilities The loss of some rights that occurs when a person has once been **convicted** of a crime. These may include the right to vote, to hold public office, to hold certain state-**licensed** jobs, etc.

Civil disobedience Breaking a law to demonstrate its unfairness or to focus attention on a problem. It may imply a willingness to pay a penalty, serve a **sentence**, etc., as part of the demonstration.

Civil law 1. Law handed down from the Romans. 2. Law that is based on one elaborate document or "**code,**" rather than a combination of many laws and judicial **opinions**. 3. Government by civilians as opposed to government by the military. 4. See **civil action**. 5. The law of an organized government as opposed to **natural law** or **anarchy**.

Civil liberties See **civil rights**.

Civil procedure The laws and rules that govern how non**criminal** lawsuits are handled by the individuals involved and by the court.

Civil rights 1. The rights of all citizens that are guaranteed by the Constitution; for example, **freedom of speech**. 2. The *Civil Rights Amendments* are the 13th, 14th, and 15th **Amendments**

to the **U.S. Constitution** that deal with slavery, **discrimination**, and the right to vote.   **3.** The Civil Rights Acts are federal laws passed after the Civil War and during the last four decades that prohibit discrimination based on race, color, age, sex, religion, or national origin.

Civil service   The largest category of government employment. Government employees who are chosen by a standardized, supervised method rather than by political appointment or election are "civil servants."

Civil suit   See **civil action**.

Civilian   **1.** Not a member of the armed forces.   **2.** Not a member of the police department.

Cl.   **Clause**.

Clafin trust   A **trust** in which the termination is precisely set, so that the **beneficiary** cannot end it.

Claim   **1.** Demand as your own; assert; urge; insist.   **2.** One side's case in a lawsuit.

Claim and delivery   An old form of lawsuit to get back property wrongfully withheld plus **damages**.

Claim for relief   The core of a modern **complaint** (first **pleading** in a lawsuit). It may be a short, clear statement of the claim being made that shows that if the facts **alleged** can be proved, the **plaintiff** should get help from the court in enforcing the claim against the **defendant**.

Claim jumping   Staking out or filing a mining claim on land that has been claimed by another.

Claim of right doctrine   A rule in tax law that if a person receives money under a *claim of right* (the assertion or honest impression that it belongs to or was owed to the person), he or she must pay taxes on the money that year even if there is a good chance that it must be returned later.

Claimant   **1.** A person who claims property or a right.   **2.** A **plaintiff**.

Claims Collection Act   The law that each federal **agency** must try to collect all overpayments it makes and all other claims it has.

Class action   A lawsuit brought for yourself and all other persons in the same situation. To bring a class action you must convince the court that there are too many persons in the class (group) to make them all individually a part of the lawsuit and that your interests are the same as theirs, so that you can adequately represent their needs.

Class directors

Class directors Corporate **directors** whose terms of office are staggered. This assures continuity of leadership and makes takeover attempts more difficult.

Class gift A gift, usually in a **will**, to a group of persons (such as "my grandchildren") whose shares will depend on the number of people in the "class" at the time the gift takes place.

Classified **1.** Secret. **2.** Put into a special category or "class."

Clause A single paragraph, sentence, or phrase.

Clayton Act A federal law, passed in 1914, that extended the **Sherman Act's** prohibition against **monopolies** and price discrimination.

Clean bill **1.** A **bill** (see that word) that has been substantially rewritten by a legislative committee. **2.** Any bill (such as a **bill of lading**) that is clear and in final form with no marginal notation or other qualifying words.

Clean hands Acting fairly and honestly in all matters connected with a lawsuit you are bringing, especially in a request for **equitable relief** (see these words).

Clean-up clause A part of an ongoing loan agreement that requires all loans to be paid off by a certain time, after which no new loans will be given for a short time, the "clean-up period."

Clear **1.** Final payment on a check by the bank on which it was drawn *clears* the check. The process of sending it to that bank and making payment is called *clearing*, and it takes place in an association or at a place called a *clearinghouse*. **2.** Free from doubt or restrictions. **3.** Free of taxes; free of **liens** or other **encumbrances**; free of any claims at all.

Clear and convincing proof Stronger **evidence** than simply better than fifty-fifty (what is required in normal **civil** cases), but not necessarily as strong as "**beyond a reasonable doubt**" (what is required in criminal cases).

Clear and present danger A test of whether or not speech may be restricted or punished. According to this standard, it may be punished if it will probably lead to violence soon or if it threatens a serious, immediate weakening of national safety and security.

Clear title Legal ownership that is free from all restrictions and doubt.

Clear view doctrine See **plain view doctrine**.

Clearance card 1. A document given to a ship by **customs** authorities allowing it to leave port. 2. A document given to a worker leaving a job that states the worker was a good worker (or at least in good standing) when employment ended.

Clearing 1. See **clear**. 2. The departure of a boat from a port after receiving a **certificate** that it has complied with all local **customs** and health laws. 3. The actions or legal proceedings needed to get a **clear title** to something.

Clemency 1. Lenient treatment of a criminal. 2. Reducing the punishment of a criminal.

Clerical error A mistake made while copying something or writing it down, as opposed to a mistake in judgment or decision-making.

Clerk A court official who keeps court records, official files, etc.

Clerkship 1. The employment of a law student or lawyer in a temporary position by a judge or a lawyer. 2. The employment of a law student by a lawyer in order to qualify that student for legal practice.

Client A person who employs a lawyer. For some purposes, a person who merely discusses a possible attorney–client relationship with a lawyer is a *client*.

Clifford trust A **trust** that is set up to give the income to someone else, eventually return the **principal** (original money put in) to yourself, and get tax benefits while the trust exists.

Close 1. Old word for an enclosed or well-marked piece of land. 2. See **closing**.

Closed corporation (or Close corporation) A **corporation** with total ownership in a few hands.

Closed mortgage A mortgage that cannot be paid off in advance (before **maturity**) without the mortgage-holder's agreement. See also **open-end mortgage** and **closed-end mortgage**.

Closed shop A company where only members of a particular **union** may work in certain jobs. This is now prohibited in most cases.

Closed-end mortgage A **mortgage** that allows no additional borrowing under the same agreement. See also **closed mortgage** and **open-end mortgage**.

Closely held Stock, or a company, that is owned by a family or by another company.

Closing The final meeting for the sale of land at which all payments are made, the property is formally transferred, and the

mortgage is fully set up by filling out all necessary papers for the mortgage lender. "Closing costs" are all charges for finishing the deal, such as transfer taxes, mortgage fees, credit reports, etc. These costs are all set down on a "closing statement" also known as a "**settlement sheet.**"

Cloture   A formal process of ending debate in a meeting.

Cloud on title   A **claim** or **encumbrance** against property which, if valid, would lower the value or add difficulties to its legal ownership.

Co   **1.** A prefix meaning with, together, or unitedly. For example, a *co-defendant* is a person who is a full defendant along with another person in a trial. **2.** An abbreviation for **county** or company.

Coaching   A lawyer telling a **witness** how to **testify**. This may be improper, or even illegal, if the lawyer tells the witness to lie or "coaches" while the witness is actually testifying.

Cobuyer   A vague term that includes both persons with and without an ownership right in the thing purchased.

Coconspirators rule   The rule that statements by a member of a proven **conspiracy** may be used as **evidence** against any of the members of the conspiracy.

Code   **1.** A collection of laws.   **2.** A complete, interrelated, and exclusive set of laws.

Code Civil   The law of France as first established in 1804 and used with revisions ever since.

Code of Federal Regulations   The compilation of all the **rules** and **regulations** put out by federal **agencies**. It is updated each year and divided into subject areas.

Code of Hammurabi   The first full-scale set of laws, written four thousand years ago in Babylon. It was "modern" in many of its provisions.

Code of Judicial Conduct   New rules for judges' conduct adopted by the **American Bar Association** and in use in many states.

Code of Military Justice   The laws and rules governing all of **military law**. The Code sets up a system of military courts, judges, and lawyers; a system of punishments for crimes; and all the rules for trial and appeal.

Code of Professional Responsibility   The rules that govern the legal profession. It contains both general ethical guidelines and specific rules prohibiting things that may be punished. It was written by the **American Bar Association** and adopted (with modifications) by the states.

Code pleading   The system of **pleading** that replaced **common law** and **equity** pleading with a standardized system. See **pleading** for descriptions.

Codex   (Latin) A **code** or collection of laws; any book.

Codicil   A supplement or addition to a **will** that adds to it or changes it. [pronounce: cod-i-sill]

Codification   The process of collecting and arranging the laws of an area into one complete system, approved in one piece by the **legislature**. To *codify* in this way includes arranging the laws by subject.

Coemption   Buying up all of a particular thing.

Coercion   Compulsion or force; making a person act against free will.

Cognation   **1.** Relationship by blood, rather than by marriage. **2.** A **lineal**, rather than **collateral** relationship. **3.** Any family ties.

Cognizance   **Judicial** power to decide a matter; the judicial decision to "take notice" of a matter and accept it for decision.

Cognovit note   A written statement that a **debtor** owes money and *"confesses judgment,"* or allows the **creditor** to get a **judgment** in court for the money whenever the creditor wants to or whenever a particular event takes place (such as a failure to make a payment).

Cohabitation   **1.** Living together. **2.** Living together as husband and wife. **3.** Living together and having sexual intercourse. **4.** Having sexual intercourse.

Cohan rule   The rule of tax law that, while a taxpayer must keep adequate records of **deductions**, if a deduction is proved but the amount is uncertain, a reasonable amount should be allowed (often fifty percent of that claimed).

Coif   A headpiece once worn by judges and lawyers to cover a wig.

Coinsurance   **1.** A division of **risk** between an insurance company and its customer on all losses less than 100 percent if the amount of insurance is less than the value of the property. For example, if a watch worth 100 dollars is insured for 50 dollars and suffers 50 dollars worth of damage, the company will pay only 25 dollars. **2.** Any sharing of an insurance risk between insurance company and customer.

Collapsible corporation   A company set up to earn money by building up its **assets**, then going out of business and distributing its profits back to the owners. The **I.R.S.** has rules that limit this sort of deal by preventing the owners from converting what would otherwise be **ordinary** income (taxed at a high rate) into **capital** gains (taxed at a low rate).

Collateral   **1.** "On the side." For example, *"collateral ancestors"* include uncles, aunts, and all persons similarly related, but not direct ancestors such as grandparents.   **2.** Money or property put up to back a person's word when taking out a loan.

Collateral attack   An attempt to avoid the *effect* of a court's action or decision by taking action in a different court proceeding. The opposite of a **direct attack** (see that word).

Collateral estoppel   Being stopped from making a claim in one court proceeding that has already been disproved by the facts raised in a prior, different proceeding. (In most states, *collateral estoppel* occurs only if the facts were important for the judge's decision in the prior case. And in some states, the lawsuit must be between the same persons.)

Collateral inheritance tax   A tax on money and property inherited by *collateral relatives* (relatives other than spouses, parents, grandparents, children, etc.).

Collateral order rule   The principle that a court's **order** may be **appealed**, even if it is not a final order in a case, if it is final as to important rights or claims that are totally separate from the main issues in the case.

Collateral source rule   The principle that if a person gets payments for an injury from a source other than the person who caused it (such as the injured person's own insurance company), the person who caused the injury must still pay for it.

Collateral warranty   **1.** A guarantee about land or buildings that was made by an ancestor.   **2.** A **warranty** of **title** to land made by someone other than the person selling it. Such a promise can be enforced only by the buyer, not by others who later buy the land.

Collation   **1.** Comparing a copy to the original to assure correctness.   **2.** **Hotchpot** (see that word).

Collection ratio   A comparison of **accounts receivable** and sales that shows a business's debt-collecting efficiency. See also **aging schedule.**

Collective bargaining **1.** The requirement that under certain circumstances employers must bargain with official **union** representatives about wages, hours, and other employment conditions. **2.** The process of negotiating described in no. 1.

Collective bargaining agreement The contract between a **union** and its employer that results from negotiation between the employer and union representatives.

Collective bargaining unit All the employees of one type or all the employees of one department in a company.

Collective mark A distinctive design used to indicate membership in an organization, such as a union.

Collective work Under **copyright** law, a *collective work* is a collection of individual works by different persons, such as an issue of a magazine or an encyclopedia.

Collectivism See **Communism** and **Socialism.**

Collector A temporary **executor** or **administrator** of an **estate.**

Colloquium A **plaintiff's** explanation of a **defendant's** possibly harmless words in such a way that they become offensive and so connected to the plaintiff that they are **defamation (libel** or **slander).**

Colloquy A conference, often in private, among lawyers and the judge during a trial.

Collusion **1.** Secret action taken by two or more persons together to cheat another or to commit **fraud.** For example, it is *collusion* if two persons agree that one should sue the other because the second person is **covered** by insurance. **2.** An agreement between husband and wife that one of them will commit (or appear to commit) an act that will allow the other one to get a **divorce.**

Color Appearance or semblance; looking real or true on the surface, but actually false. For example, acting *"under color of law"* is taking an action that looks official or backed by law, but which is not. In most cases ("color of authority," "color of office," etc.) "color" implies deliberate falseness, but in other cases ("color of right," "color of title," etc.) "color" implies no attempt to deceive.

Color of title Apparent **title,** based on a document such as a **deed,** a court **decree,** etc. Probably not a real or valid title.

Colorable

Colorable False; counterfeit; having the appearance, but not the reality.

Comaker A second (or third or more) person who signs a **negotiable instrument,** such as a check, and by doing so promises to pay on it in full.

Combination **1.** A group of persons working together, often for an unlawful purpose. **2.** A putting together of inventions, each of which might be already **patented**, but which by working together produce a new, useful result. This *combination* might get a patent.

Comfort letter A letter from an **accounting** firm saying that, upon informal review, a company's financial records seem to be in order although full, official approval requires an **audit**.

Comity Courtesy and respect. A willingness to do something official, not as a matter of right, but out of goodwill and tradition. For example, nations often give effect to the laws of other nations out of *comity*, and state and federal courts depend on comity to keep many of their results in line with one another.

Comment upon evidence A rule that a **trial** judge may not give the jury his or her opinion about whether **evidence** offered is true or false.

Commerce Department of Commerce. The **cabinet** department that promotes U.S. trade, economic development, and technology. It includes the **patent** office and many scientific and business-development branches.

Commerce clause The part of the U.S. **Constitution** that allows Congress to control trade with foreign countries and from state to state. This is called the *"commerce power"* (Article One, Section Eight of the Constitution). If anything "affects interstate commerce" (such as labor unions, product safety, etc.), it is fair game for the federal government to **regulate** what goes on or even to take over all regulation. See **pre-emption.**

Commercial code See **Uniform Commercial Code.**

Commercial insurance **1.** Insurance against a business loss due to another company's failure to perform a **contract**. **2.** Insurance against general business losses beyond the company's control.

Commercial paper All **negotiable instruments** (see that word) related to business; for example, **bills** of exchange. Sometimes, the word is restricted to a company's short-term **notes**.

Commercial unit   An item or group of goods which, if separated, would lose value. For example, a two-part machine or a suite of furniture.

Commingling   Mixing together; for example, putting two different persons' money into one bank account.

Commission   **1.** A written grant of authority to do a particular thing, given by the government to one of its branches or to an individual or organization.   **2.** An organization like one mentioned in no. 1.   **3.** Payment (to a salesperson or other **agent**) based on the amount of sales or on a percentage of the profit.   **4.** Doing a criminal act.

Commission merchant   A **factor** (see that word).

Commissioner   **1.** The name for the heads of many government **boards** or **agencies**.   **2.** A person appointed by a court to handle special matters, such as to conduct a court-ordered sale or to take **testimony** in complicated, specialized cases.

Commitment   The formal process of putting a person into the official care of another person, such as the warden of a prison or the head of a psychiatric hospital. See **civil commitment**.

Commitment fee   A payment to a lender for making a loan or opening an ongoing **line of credit**.

Committee   **1.** A subgroup that a larger group appoints to do specialized work; for example, the Agriculture Committee of the House of Representatives.   **2.** A person or group of persons appointed by a court to take care of the money and property of a person who is legally **incompetent**. A type of **trustee**.

Committee of the whole   A procedure in which a **legislature** works as if it were a **committee** in order to get business done more quickly and informally. Decisions of the *"committee of the whole"* are then voted on by the legislature acting as a "real" legislature.

Commodity   **1.** Anything produced, bought, or sold.   **2.** A raw or partially processed material.   **3.** A farm product such as corn.

Commodity Credit Corporation   A federal agency that stabilizes the price and supply of crops by making loans and **price support** payments, controlling acreage under production, etc.

Commodity Futures Trading Commission   The federal agency that regulates contracts to buy and sell future supplies of raw products such as corn, silver, etc. See **futures**.

Common

Common **1.** A piece of land used by many persons. **2.** Usual; ordinary; regular; applying to many persons or things.

Common carrier See **carrier**.

Common council A local (town or city) **legislature**.

Common count See **count**.

Common disaster When two people die in the same accident with no way to tell who died first (for **insurance** or **inheritance** purposes). A *common disaster clause* in a **will** spells out what the person making the will wants to happen to his or her property if the person to whom the property is left dies at the same time.

Common enemy doctrine The right of a landowner to keep out river or other surface water even if the water is diverted to another person's property.

Common fund rule If a person goes to court to get a particular fund of money and if others benefit from the lawsuit, the person receives all lawsuit costs and lawyers' fees from the fund before the others take their shares.

Common law **1.** Judge-made law (as opposed to **legislature**-made law). **2.** Law that has its origins in England and grows from ever-changing custom and tradition. **3.** Religious law compiled in writing; originally ancient Catholic law.

Common law action **1.** A **civil** lawsuit (as opposed to **criminal**) that is between private individuals or organizations and contains a request for money **damages**. **2.** A lawsuit, such as those in no. 1, that is not based on a written law or **statute**.

Common law marriage A marriage created by a couple publicly holding themselves out as married and living together as married in a way and for a time period sufficient to create a legal marriage in some states.

Common law trust **Business trust** (see that word).

Common pleas The name for several different types of **civil** trial courts.

Common scheme (or plan or design) **1.** Two or more different crimes planned together. **2.** Two or more persons planning the same crime. **3.** Dividing a piece of land into lots with identical restrictions on land use.

Common situs picketing **Picketing** an entire construction site by a union having a dispute with one of the **contractors** doing work. This is generally illegal.

Common stock **Shares** in a **corporation** that depend for their value on the value of the company. These shares usually have voting rights (which other types of company stock lack). However, they earn a **dividend** (profit) only after all other types of the company's obligations and stocks have been paid.

Commonwealth **1.** A state or country, especially a democratic one. **2.** The **people** (see that word) of a state or country. Also, the people as a group are called "*the commonalty*," and the public good or welfare is called "*the commonweal*."

Communication intelligence Intercepting others' messages by wiretapping, radio surveillance, and other means.

Communism A system in which most property is owned by the state and most economic and social decisions are made by the government in a theoretically classless society run by "the masses."

Community **1.** Neighborhood, locality, etc. A vague term that can include very large or very small areas. **2.** A group with common interests. **3.** Shared. See **community property**.

Community property Property owned in *common* (both persons owning it all) by a husband and wife. "*Community property states*" are those states that call most property acquired during the marriage the property of both partners no matter whose name it is in.

Community trust An organization set up to administer a **charitable** or public **trust**.

Commutation Changing a criminal punishment to one less severe.

Commutative contract A **contract** with **mutual** rights and duties.

Comp. **1.** Compiled. **2.** Compensation.

Compact An agreement or contract (usually between governments).

Compact clause The **constitutional** provision that prohibits states from entering into agreements with other states or foreign countries without congressional approval.

Company Any organization set up to do business.

Comparative negligence A legal rule, used in most states, by which the amount of "fault" on each side of an accident is measured and the side with less fault is given money **damages** depending on the difference between the seriousness of each side's fault. (Another rule is that any **negligence** at all stops that side from getting any damages in most situations.)

Comparative rectitude   A legal rule by which a divorce is given to the person in a marriage who the judge decides has behaved better. It is also called a "least fault" divorce.

Compelling state interest   A reason for a state law, **rule**, **policy**, or action that is strong enough to justify limiting a person's **constitutional rights.**

Compensating balance   A minimum amount of money that a person or company must keep in a no-interest checking account to compensate a bank for loans or other services.

Compensation   **1.** Payment for loss, injury, or damages.   **2.** Payment of any sort for work or services performed.

Compensatory damages   Payment for the actual loss suffered by a **plaintiff**, as opposed to **punitive damages** (see that word).

Competency proceeding   A **hearing** to determine a person's mental capacity. It may be for a **civil commitment** (see that word) or to determine whether a person is **competent** to stand trial in a **criminal** case. Competency to stand trial depends on the ability to understand what is happening and why and to assist in the **defense** of the case. *Competency* may be different from *sanity* (see **insanity**).

Competent   Properly qualified, adequate, having the right natural or legal qualifications. For example, a person may be *competent* to make a **will** if he or she understands what making a will is, knows that he or she is making a will, and knows generally how making the will affects persons named in the will and affects relatives.

Competent evidence   **Evidence** that is both relevant to the point in question and the proper type of evidence to prove the point; evidence that is not kept out by any **exclusionary rule** (see that word).

Compiled statutes   See **code.**

Complainant   **1.** A person who makes an official complaint.   **2.** A person who starts a lawsuit (see **plaintiff**).

Complaint   **1.** The first main paper filed in a **civil** lawsuit. It includes, among other things, a statement of the wrong or harm done to the **plaintiff** by the **defendant**, a request for specific help from the court, and an explanation why the court has the power to do what the plaintiff wants.   **2.** Any official "complaint" in the ordinary sense; for example, a complaint to the police about a noisy party.

Complete voluntary trust   A trust that has been set up in all its details (**trustee**, **beneficiary**, limits, methods, etc.).

Complex trust   Any **trust** other than a **simple** trust, especially one in which **trustees** have wide **discretion** to pay out or accumulate income.

Compliance   Acting in a way that does not violate a law. For example, when a state gets federal money for a state project, the project must be in *compliance* with the federal law that allows the money and, sometimes, with the **regulations** of the federal agency that gives it out.

Compos mentis   (Latin) Of sound mind; sane and **competent**.

Composition   A formal agreement, involving a **debtor** and several creditors, that each **creditor** will take less than the whole amount owed as full payment. For a *"composition in bankruptcy,"* see **Chapter Thirteen**.

Compound   **1.** Combine parts or ingredients into a whole. **2.** Compromise. Rid yourself of a debt by convincing the **creditors** to accept a smaller amount.   **3.** See **compound interest**. **4.** See **compounding a felony**.

Compound interest   Interest on interest. Adding interest to the **principal** (the main debt) at regular intervals and then computing the interest on the last principal plus interest.

Compounding a felony   Accepting money or other gain in exchange for not prosecuting a major crime committed against you.

Comprises   Made up of; includes.

Compromise verdict   A jury's agreement reached by **jurors** giving up strongly held opinions in exchange for other jurors giving up different strongly held opinions, rather than by jurors changing opinions due to reasoned persuasion. This type of **verdict** is not permitted in many circumstances.

Comptroller   The financial officer of a company or a government agency. For example, the comptroller general of the U.S. heads the Government Accounting Office, which **audits** government agencies and investigates their problems. [pronounce: con-troll-er]

Compulsory process   Official action to force a person to appear in court or to appear before a **legislature** as a witness. This is usually by **subpoena**, but sometimes by **arrest**.

Compurgator   See **wager of law**.

Con

Con **1.** Short for "contra"; against; on the other hand. **2.** A prefix meaning "with" or "together." **3.** Short for *"constitutional."*

Concentration banking See **lockbox system**.

Conception In **patent** law, *conception* is an inventor's completed idea for an invention. The *date of conception* is the day this idea, and not merely its general principles, is put down on paper. See also **reduction to practice.**

Concert of action rule The rule that it is not also a **conspiracy** (see that word) for two persons to agree to commit a crime if the definition of the crime itself includes two or more persons committing it. Also called *Wharton Rule*.

Conciliation The process of bringing together two sides to agree to a voluntary compromise.

Conclusion of law An argument or answer arrived at by not only drawing a conclusion from facts, but also by applying law to the facts. For example, it is only a conclusion of fact to say that a person hit another person with a car, but it is a *conclusion of law* to say that the accident was the driver's fault.

Conclusive Beyond dispute; ending inquiry or debate; clear. For example, a *"conclusive presumption"* is a legal conclusion that cannot be overturned by any facts.

Concordat A formal agreement between two countries; a **compact**.

Concur Agree. For example, a *"concurring opinion"* is one in which a judge agrees with the result reached in an **opinion** by another judge, but not necessarily with the reasoning that the other judge used to reach the conclusion.

Concurrent "Running together"; having the same authority; at the same time. For example, courts have *concurrent jurisdiction* when each one has the power to deal with the same subjects and cases; *concurrent sentences* are prison terms that run at the same time; and federal and state governments have *concurrent power* to govern in many areas.

Condemn (or Condemnation) **1.** Find guilty of a criminal charge. **2.** A governmental taking of private property with payment, but not necessarily with consent. **3.** A court's decision that the government may seize a ship owned privately or by a foreign government. **4.** An official ruling that a building is unfit for use.

Confidential relation

Condition   **1.** A future, uncertain event that creates or destroys rights and obligations. For example, a **contract** may have a *condition* in it that if one person should die, the contract is ended. **2.** Conditions may be **express** or **implied** (see these words). Also, they may be **precedent** (if a certain future event happens, a right or obligation is created) or *subsequent* (if a certain future event happens, a right or obligation ends).

Conditional   Depending on a **condition** (see that word); unsure; depending on a future event. For example, a *conditional sale* is a sale in which the buyer must wait for full ownership of the thing bought until it is fully paid for.

Condominium   Several persons owning individual pieces of a building (usually an apartment house) and managing it together.

Condonation   Willing forgiveness by a wife or husband of the other's actions that is enough to stop those actions from being **grounds** for a **divorce**.

Conduit   A company, **trust**, **estate**, etc., is considered a *conduit* for tax purposes if certain tax benefits or consequences (such as long-term capital losses) merely *pass through* on their way to the actual owners of the company, trust, etc.

Confederacy   **1.** A general word for persons who band together to do an illegal act. A more usual word for this is "**conspiracy**" (see that word).   **2.** A loose union of independent governments. A more usual word for this is *"confederation."*

Conference committee   A meeting of both **houses** of a **legislature** to work out differences between versions of a **bill** passed by each house. Agreements are then usually voted on by each house.

Confession   **1.** A voluntary statement by a person that he or she is guilty of a crime.   **2.** Any admission of wrongdoing.

Confession and avoidance   Same as **affirmative defense** (see that word).

Confession of judgment   A process in which a person who borrows money or buys on credit signs in advance to allow the lawyer for the lender to get a court judgment without even telling the borrower. See **judgment** and **cognovit**.

Confidential relation   Any relationship where one person has a right to expect a higher than usual level of care and faithfulness from another person; for example, client and attorney, child

Confidentiality

and parent, employee and employer. Another name for these relationships, if a strong duty exists, is a **fiduciary** relationship.

Confidentiality   **1.** The requirement that a lawyer, or anyone working for a lawyer, not disclose information received from a client. There are exceptions to this requirement; for example, if the lawyer is told that the client is about to commit a crime. **2.** The requirement that certain other persons (such as clergy, physicians, husbands, wives, etc.) not disclose information received under certain circumstances. This is called "privileged communication."

Confirmation   **1.** Formal approval, especially formal written approval.   **2.** A notice that something has been received, sent, ordered, etc.   **3.** Agreeing that something is correct. For example, a document in which a company's supplier or customer verifies financial figures or item counts for a review of the company's **books** by an **auditor**.   **4.** The transfer of legal **title** to land to a person who has possession of the land.   **5.** A **contract** that reaffirms a prior agreement that might have been otherwise difficult to prove or enforce.   **6.** The approval of a presidential appointment by Congress.

Confiscation   The government's taking of private property without payment. Government action may be called *confiscation* if it has nearly the effect of confiscation; for example, when an electric company is not permitted to charge enough ever to make a profit.

Conflict of interest   Being in a position where your own needs and desires could possibly lead you to violate your duty to a person who has a right to depend on you. A conflict need not even be intentional. For example, a judge who holds XYZ stock may be unconsciously influenced in a case concerning the XYZ Company.

Conflict of laws   The situation that exists when the laws of more than one state or country may apply to a **case** and a judge must choose among them. *Conflict of laws* is also the name for the legal subject of the rules to use in making this choice.

Conformed copy   An exact copy of a document with written explanations of things that could not be copied. For example, the handwritten signature and date might be replaced on the copy by the notation "signed by Jonah Brown on July 27, 1977."

Conformity hearing   After a judge decides in favor of one side in a lawsuit, the judge may tell the lawyer for the winner to draw up a **judgment** or **decree** to carry out the judge's decision. A *conformity hearing* may then be held to decide whether the judgment or decree is correct.

Confrontation The **constitutional** right of a criminal **defendant** to see and cross-examine all **witnesses** against him or her.

Confusion **1.** Mixing or blending together. For example, *confusion of goods* is a mixing together of the property of two or more persons with the effect that it is not possible to tell which goods belong to which person. **2. Merger**. When a **creditor** and a **debtor**, a landlord and a tenant, etc., become the same person, usually because of an **inheritance**, and separate legal rights and duties become one, often ending the duty.

Conglomerate A company that owns, or is made up of, companies in many different industries.

Congress **1.** The **legislature** of the United States (the House of Representatives plus the Senate); often abbreviated "Cong." **2.** A meeting of officials (often of different countries).

Congressional Record A daily printed record of proceedings in **Congress**. It tells how each **bill** was voted upon, which bills were sent to and from each **committee**, etc.

Conjoint **Joint**. Together as one.

Conjugal Having to do with marriage. For example, *conjugal rights* are a husband and wife's rights to companionship, love, and sex from the other.

Conjunctive Containing several interconnected parts, rights, duties, etc.

Connecting up A thing may be put into **evidence** subject to "connecting up" with later evidence that will show its **relevance**, etc.

Connivance The consent or help of a husband or wife to the other's acts in order to obtain a **divorce** based on those acts.

Consanguinity Blood relationship; kinship.

Conscientious objector A person who has religious objections to participating in a war. To avoid serving in the armed forces, a person need not necessarily belong to an organized religion.

Consecutive sentence See **cumulative sentence.**

Consensus ad item (Latin) **Meeting of minds** (see that word).

Consent Voluntary and active agreement.

Consent decree **1.** A **divorce** that is granted against a person who is in court or represented by a lawyer in court and who does not oppose the divorce. **2.** A settlement of a lawsuit or prosecution in which a person or company agrees to take certain actions without admitting fault or guilt for the situation causing the lawsuit.

Consequential damages Indirect losses or injuries; results of a wrongful act that do not show up immediately or upon superficial examination; for example, the loss of business a taxi-driver suffers from an accident that damages the taxi.

Conservator A guardian or preserver of property appointed for a person who cannot legally manage it.

Consideration The reason or main cause for a person to make a **contract**; something of value received or promised to induce (convince) a person to make a deal. Without *consideration* a contract is not valid. For example, if Ann and Sue make a deal for Ann to buy a car from Sue, Ann's promise to pay a thousand dollars is *consideration* for Sue's promise to hand over the car and vice versa.

Consignment Handing over things for transportation or for sale, but keeping ownership.

Consol **1.** A **bond** that keeps on paying interest forever and never gets paid off. **2.** An abbreviation for *consolidated*. **3.** This is *not* a **consul, counsel,** or **council.**

Consolidated statements **1.** Financial statements of legally separate companies combined as if they were one company. **2.** See **statement** of income.

Consolidation **1.** The combined trials of different lawsuits that are on the same general subject and between the same persons. They are treated as only one lawsuit. **2.** Generally, bringing together separate things and making them into one thing; often abbreviated "consol." **3.** Two **corporations** joining together to form a third, new one.

Consonant statement rule If a witness's believability has been damaged, the witness's prior out-of-court statements that back up his or her current **testimony** may be used to prove that the witness is believable. These "consonant statements" may be used even though out-of-court statements are **hearsay** and are not normally permitted as **evidence**, but because they are hearsay, they may *not* be used to directly prove what the witness claims.

Consortium The right of a husband or wife to the other's love and services. *"Loss of consortium"* might be sued for by, for example, the husband of a woman who was badly injured in an accident. [pronounce: con-<u>sore</u>-shum]

Conspiracy   Two or more persons joining together to do an unlawful act. The joining together itself is sometimes unlawful even if the act planned is not.

Constable   A low-level peace officer who does court-related work.

Constant dollars   Current costs or prices as measured in preinflated dollars of a set prior year.

Constant payment mortgage   The usual type of homeowner's **mortgage**, in which equal monthly payments are made, with the proportion of each payment going to **principal** increasing and **interest** decreasing until the mortgage is paid off. (Contrast this with a **direct reduction mortgage**.)

Constitute   Make up. For example, "duly *constituted*" means properly put together and formally valid and correct.

Constitution   **1.** The basic first document of a country, state, or organization that sets out its basic principles and most general laws.   **2.** The U.S. Constitution is the basic law of the country, from which most other laws are drawn, and to which all other laws must yield. Often abbreviated "Const." or "Con."

Constitutional   **1.** Consistent with the constitution; not in conflict with the fundamental law of the state or country.   **2.** Depending on the **Constitution**. For example, a *constitutional court* is one set up by the Constitution.

Constitutional convention   Representatives of the people of a country who meet to write or change a **constitution**. Article V of the U.S. Constitution allows a convention if two-thirds of the state **legislatures** call for one.

Constitutional law   The study of the law that applies to the organization, structure, and functions of the government, the basic principles of government, and the validity (or *constitutionality*) of laws and actions when tested against the requirements of the **Constitution**.

Constitutional right   A right guaranteed to the people by the **Constitution** (and, thus, safe from **legislative** or other attempts to limit or end the right).

Construction   A decision (usually by a judge) about the meaning and legal effect of ambiguous or doubtful words that considers

Construction draw

not only the words themselves but also surrounding circumstances, relevant laws and writings, etc. (Looking at just the words is called "**interpretation**.")

Construction draw   A type of **mortgage** or other agreement in which a builder gets money as it is needed for building.

Constructive   True legally even if not factually; "just as if"; established by legal interpretation; inferred; implied. For example, a *constructive eviction* might occur when a landlord fails to provide heat in winter. This means that the tenant might be able to treat the legal relationship between landlord and tenant *as if* the landlord had tried to throw the tenant out without good reason. This might give the tenant the right to stop paying the rent.

Constructive contract   See **quasi-contract**.

Constructive desertion   Forcing a husband or wife to leave. For example, when Mary is forced to leave because conditions at home are so bad that it amounts to John's forcing her out of the house, John has "constructively deserted" Mary, and Mary may get a divorce based on this in some states.

Constructive knowledge (or notice)   Knowledge that a person in a particular situation should have; that the person would have if he or she used reasonable care to keep informed; that is open for all to see; for example, knowledge of a properly recorded mortgage on a house you plan to buy.

Constructive receipt of income   A person who gains actual control of income will be taxed on it whether he or she actually takes the cash. For example, taxes must be paid in the year that savings account interest is earned, not in the later year it might actually be collected.

Constructive trust   A situation in which a person holds legal **title** to property, but the property should, in fairness, actually belong to another person (because the title was gained by **fraud**, by a clerical error, etc.). In this case, the property may be treated by a court *as if* the legal owner holds it in **trust** for the real owner.

Consuetudo   (Latin) A custom or common practice. For example, consuetudo mercatorum is the **law merchant** (see that word).

Consul   A country's foreign representative, below the rank of **ambassador**, who usually can handle the country's and its citizens' business and private matters, but not usually political matters. *Consuls* usually work in *consulates* in foreign cities where there are no embassies. (This is *not* a **council, counsel,** or **consol.**)

Consular court   A court held by the **consuls** (representatives) of one country inside another country.

Consumer   A person who buys (or rents, travels on, etc.) something for personal, rather than business use.

Consumer credit   Money, property, or services offered to a person for personal, family, or household purposes "on time." It is *"consumer credit"* if there is a finance charge or if there are more than four **installment** payments.

Consumer Credit Protection Act   A federal law adopted with changes by many states, requiring the clear **disclosure** of **consumer credit** (see that word) information by companies making loans or selling on credit. The act requires that **finance charges** (see that word) be given as a standard **annual percentage rate (APR)**, gives consumers the right to back out of certain deals, **regulates** credit cards, restricts wage **garnishments,** etc. It is also called the *Truth-in-Lending Act.*

Consumer Price Index   A federal Labor Department statistic that traces prices for goods and services bought by an "average consumer."

Consumer Product Safety Commission   A federal agency that sets product safety standards, bans hazardous consumer products, etc.

Consummate   Finish; complete what was intended.

Consummation   **1.** Completion of a thing; carrying out an agreement.   **2.** "Completing" a marriage by having sexual intercourse.

Contemner   A person who commits **contempt** of court.

Contemplation of death   An act taken *in contemplation of death* is one caused by or influenced strongly by thinking about your own probable imminent death. It may have tax consequences. See **causa mortis.**

Contempt   **1.** An act designed to obstruct a court's work or lessen the dignity of the court.   **2.** A willful disobeying of a judge's command or official court order. Contempt can be *direct* (within the judge's notice) and *indirect* (outside the court and punishable only after proved to the judge).   **3.** It is also possible to be in *contempt* of a **legislature** or an **administrative agency.**

Content validation   Making sure a test used to select people for

public jobs actually tests for the skills and characteristics needed to perform the job.

Contest **1.** Oppose or defend against a lawsuit or other action.
2. Oppose the validity of a **will.**

Context Surrounding words.

Contingent Possible, but not assured; depending on some future
events or actions (contingencies) that may or may not happen.
For example, a *contingent estate* is a right to own or use property that depends on an uncertain future event for the right to
take effect; and a *contingency reserve* is a fund of money set
aside by a business to cover possible unknown future expenses
such as a **liability** from a lost lawsuit.

Contingent fee Payment to a lawyer of a percentage of the possible "winnings" from a lawsuit rather than a flat amount of
money.

Continuance The postponement of a lawsuit to a later day or session of court.

Continuing appropriation **1.** An **appropriation** of money by a
government that continues automatically until it is revoked,
used up, or the authorization is revoked. **2.** An appropriation
passed by a **continuing resolution** (see that word).

Continuing jurisdiction The power of a court to keep its hands
on a case if changes in its orders are needed. This happens most
often in child **custody** or **support** cases.

Continuing offense A single crime, such as a **conspiracy**, that
can contain many individual acts over time. Even if the earlier
acts might be too old to prosecute individually (because of a
statute of **limitations**), the continuing nature of the crime allows these acts to be included in the crime prosecuted.

Continuing resolution An act of a **legislature** that allows a government agency to continue spending at past levels when its **appropriation** has run out. Compare with **continuing appropriation.**

Contra (Latin) **1.** Against; on the other hand; opposing. For example, *contra bonos mores* is "against good morals" or offending the public conscience, and *contra pacem* is "against the
peace" or offending public order. **2.** In **accounting**, *contra accounts* are set up to show subtractions from other **accounts,**
and *contra balances* are account **balances** that are the opposite
(positive or negative) of what usually appears.

Contraband   Things that are illegal to import or export or that are illegal to possess.

Contract   An agreement that affects the legal relationships between two or more persons. To be a *contract*, an agreement must involve: at least one promise, **consideration** (something of value promised or given), persons legally capable of making binding agreements, and a reasonable amount of agreement between the persons as to what the contract means. A contract is called **bilateral** if both sides **expressly** make promises (such as the promise to deliver a book on one side and a promise to pay for it on the other) or **unilateral** if the promises are on one side only (usually because the other side has already done its part). According to the **Uniform Commercial Code,** a contract is the "total legal obligation which results from the parties' agreement," and according to the Restatement of the Law of Contracts, it is "a promise or set of promises for the breach of which the law in some way recognizes a duty." For different types of contracts, such as **output, quasi,** etc., see those words.

Contract clause   The provision in Article I of the U.S. **Constitution** that no state may pass a law abolishing contracts or denying them legal effect.

Contract for deed   See **land sales contract.**

Contract sale   See **conditional** sale.

Contract under seal   An old form of **contract** that required a **seal** (see that word), but no **consideration** (see that word).

Contractor   A person who takes on work (usually building or related work) and has control over his or her own work, methods, details, etc. A *"prime contractor"* or *"general contractor"* is in charge of the whole project and makes *"subcontracts"* with others for parts of the job.

Contravention   Something done in breaking a legal obligation. For example, speeding in a downtown area is usually in *contravention* of the traffic laws.

Contribution   **1.** The sharing of payment for a debt (or **judgment**) among persons who are all **liable** for the debt.   **2.** The right of a person who has paid an entire debt (or judgment) to get back a fair share of the payment from another person who is also responsible for the debt. For example, most **insurance** policies require that if another insurance company also **covers** a loss, each must share payment for the loss in proportion to the maximum amount each covers.

Contributory

Contributory   A person who must pay up in full the price of **stock** owned in a company because the company is going out of business and owes money.

Contributory negligence   **Negligent** (see that word) conduct by a person who was harmed by another person's negligence; a **plaintiff's** failure to be careful that is a part of the cause of his or her injury.

Controlled substances acts   Federal and state laws to control the manufacture, sale, and use of dangerous drugs.

Controller   Top financial officer. (See **comptroller**).

Controversy   Any **civil** lawsuit that involves real legal rights at stake, rather than an assumed or potential invasion of rights.

Controvert   Dispute, deny, or oppose.

Contumacy   **1.** The refusal to appear in court when required to by the law.   **2.** The refusal to obey a court. See **contempt**.

Contumely   Rudeness; scornful treatment.

Convenience and necessity   See **certificate**.

Convention   **1.** A meeting of representatives for a special purpose, such as to draw up a **constitution** or to nominate a **candidate** for an election.   **2.** An agreement between countries on nonpolitical and nonfinancial matters; for example, fishing rights.

Conventional   **1.** Usual or ordinary.   **2.** Caused by an agreement between persons rather than by the effect of a law. For example, a *conventional mortgage* is one that involves just a person lending and a person borrowing money on a house as opposed to a mortgage involving a government subsidy or guarantee, and a *conventional lien* is one created by an agreement, rather than by a law or a lawsuit.

Conversion   **1.** Any act that deprives an owner of property without that owner's permission and without just cause. For example, it is *conversion* to refuse to return a borrowed book.   **2.** The exchange of one type of property for another; for example, turning in one type of **stock** to a company and getting another in return. The *conversion ratio* would be the number of shares you get for each share turned in and the *conversion price* the value of each new share.

Convertible   A **bond** or preferred **stock** that can be exchanged for **common stock** (see these words).

Conveyance   **1.** A transfer of **title** to land.   **2.** Any transfer of title.

Convict 1. Find a person guilty of a **criminal** charge. 2. A person in prison.

Conviction The result of a criminal trial in which a person is found **guilty**.

Cooley *Constitutional Limitations*, a **treatise** by Cooley. Also, the *Cooley doctrine* is the rule that a state may not **regulate** matters that are purely national and that require national regulation. See also **pre-emption**.

Cooling off period 1. A period of time in which no action of a particular sort may be taken by either side in a dispute; for example, a period of a month after a union or a company files a **grievance** against the other. During this period the union may not strike and the company may not **lock out** the employees. 2. A period of time in which a buyer may cancel a purchase. Many states require a three-day cancellation period for door-to-door sales. 3. An automatic delay in some states, in addition to ordinary court delays, between the filing of **divorce** papers and the divorce **hearing**.

Cooperative An organization set up to help the persons who form it and who use it. The word covers many different types of organizations set up for many different purposes. Cooperatives include: *apartment co-ops* (an apartment building owned by residents who **lease** the individual apartments; see also **condominium**); *consumer co-ops* (stores, utilities, health facilities, etc.); *marketing co-ops* (for example, one set up by milk producers in a certain area); *financial co-ops* (like **credit unions**); etc. Organizations like **labor unions** and **trade** associations may also be called *cooperatives*.

Coordinate jurisdiction **Concurrent** jurisdiction (see that word).

Cop a plea Agree as a **defendant** to a **plea bargain** that exchanges a charge of a lesser offense for a **guilty** plea.

Coparcenary An old word for a situation where several persons **inherit** property to share as if they were one person. These persons were called *parceners*.

Copartnership **Partnership** (see that word).

Copeland Act A federal law prohibiting wage **kickbacks** on federal building contracts.

Copyhold An old form of holding land at the **will** of the lord of an area, but recorded in the record books in keeping with local custom.

Copyright

Copyright The author's (or other originator's) right to control the copying and distributing of books, articles, movies, etc. This right is created, **regulated**, and limited by federal statute. The symbol for copyright is ©. The legal life of a copyright is the author's life plus fifty years or a flat seventy-five years for one held by a company.

Coram (Latin) Before; in the presence of. For example "*coram nobis*" (before us) is the name for a request that a court change its **judgment** due to the excusable failure of a **defendant** to raise facts that would have won the case. "*Coram vobis*" is a request for a higher court to order a lower one to correct the same sort of problem as *coram nobis*. These writs are no longer used in most places. And "*coram non judice*" means "before a non-judge." It is a judgment of a court with no **jurisdiction** to hear the case, so **void**.

Corbin *Corbin on Contracts*. A **treatise.**

Co-respondent The "other man" or "other woman" in a divorce suit based on **adultery**. Sometimes spelled "corespondent." See also **correspondent**.

Corner **1.** Owning enough of some **stock** or **commodity** to have control over the selling price in the general marketplace. **2.** Owning **contracts** for more future delivery of a commodity than is produced of that commodity. When the persons who have promised to deliver cannot do it, the price shoots sky high and the person with the "corner" greatly profits.

Corollary A secondary or "side" deduction or inference in logic or argument.

Coroner A doctor or other public official who conducts inquiries into the cause of any violent or suspicious death. If the case is serious, there is a *coroner's inquest* or hearing. Many places have replaced coroners with **medical examiners** (see that word).

Corporal punishment Physical punishment (beating, etc.).

Corporate Belonging to a **corporation.**

Corporate veil The legal assumption that actions taken by a **corporation** are not the actions of its owners, and that these owners cannot usually be held responsible for corporate actions.

Corporation An organization that is formed under state or federal law and exists, for legal purposes, as a separate being or an "**artificial person.**" It may be public (set up by the government) or private (set up by individuals), and it may be set up to carry on a business or to perform almost any function. It may be owned by the government, by a few persons, or by the general public through purchases of stock. Abbreviated "corp."

Corporation counsel The lawyer who represents a city or town in **civil** matters.

Corporeal Having body or substance; visible and tangible.

Corpus (Latin) "Body"; main body of a thing as opposed to attachments. For example, *"corpus juris"* means "a body of law" or a major collection of laws.

Corpus delicti (Latin) "The body of the crime." **1.** The material substance upon which a crime has been committed; for example, a dead body or a house burned down. **2.** The fact that proves that a crime has been committed.

Corpus Juris A legal encyclopedia that also ties in with the **American Digest System**. *Corpus Juris Secundum* is its most recent update.

Corpus juris civilis "The body of the civil law"; the main writings of Roman law.

Correlative Ideas that have a mutual relationship and depend on one another to exist. For example, "parent" and "child" are *correlative* terms, as are "right" and "duty."

Correspondent **1.** A person who collects **mortgage** loan payments for the lender. **2.** One bank or other financial institution that performs regular services for another. **3.** See **co-respondent**.

Corroborate Add to the likely truth or importance of a fact; give additional facts or evidence to strengthen a fact, an assertion, etc.; back up what someone else says.

Corrupt practices act **1.** A state law that **regulates** political campaign methods and spending. **2.** A federal law that regulates international corporate financial activities.

Corruption of blood An old punishment for a crime by which a person was deprived of the right to take property, hold it, or pass it on to **heirs** at death.

Cosigner A general term for a person who signs a document along with another person. Depending on the situation and on the state, a cosigner may have *primary* responsibility (for example, to pay a debt if the person who made the cosigned loan comes first to the cosigner for the money) or only a *secondary* responsibility (to pay a debt only after the person who took out the loan doesn't pay).

Cost and freight

Cost and freight   The price quoted includes cost and freight, but not insurance or any other charge.

Cost effective   **1.** Benefits exceed (or will exceed) costs; profits exceed (or will exceed) losses.   **2.** The alternative course of action with the highest benefits-divided-by-costs ratio is called *"cost effective."*

Cost of living adjustment   A wage increase automatically tied to the inflation rate.

Cost of living allowance   Extra pay or expenses for working in a high-cost living area.

Cost of living clause   A provision in a **contract**, such as a **labor agreement** or a retirement plan, that gives an automatic wage or benefit increase tied to inflation as measured by a standard indicator, such as the consumer price index.

Cost-plus contract   A **contract** that pays a **contractor** for the cost of labor and materials plus a fixed percentage of cost as profit.

Costs   Expenses of one side in a lawsuit that the judge orders the other side to pay or reimburse. *"Costs to abide the event"* are given by an **appeals** court and include the cost of the appeal and sometimes the cost of a retrial.

Council   A local or city **legislature**, sometimes called *"common council."* (This is *not* a **consul, counsel,** or **consol.**)

Counsel   **1.** A lawyer for a client.   **2.** Advice (usually professional advice).   **3.** *"Of counsel"* usually means not the primary lawyer in court, but an assistant lawyer on the case.   **4.** This is *not* a **consul, council,** or **consol.**

Counsel, right to   The **constitutional** right of a poor **defendant** to have a free court-appointed lawyer at every important stage of a **criminal** proceeding from formal **charge** through all **hearings, sentencing,** and **appeal.** This **Sixth Amendment** right applies in all crimes that might be punished by a jail term and applies also to juvenile delinquency proceedings.

Counsellor   Lawyer.

Count   **1.** Each separate part of a **civil complaint** or a **criminal indictment** (see these words). Each *count* must be able to stand alone as a separate and independent **claim** or **charge.**   **2.** The *"common counts"* were once the various **forms of action** (see that word) for money owed (for example, **assumpsit**).

Counter   Opposing or contradicting. For example, a counter-**affidavit** disputes the claims of another person's affidavit.

Counterclaim   A claim made by a **defendant** in a **civil** lawsuit that, in effect, sues the **plaintiff.** It can be based on entirely different things from the plaintiff's **complaint**, and may even be for more money than the plaintiff is asking. A counterclaim often must be made if it is based on the same subject or transaction as the original claim. Otherwise, the person with the counterclaim may not be permitted to sue for it later.

Counterfeit   **1.** Forge, copy, or imitate without authority or right, with the purpose of passing off the copy as the original.   **2.** The copy in no. 1.

Countermand   Take back or greatly change orders or instructions.

Counteroffer   **1.** A **rejection** of an **offer** and a new offer made back. A *counteroffer* sometimes looks like an **acceptance** with new terms or conditions attached, but if these terms or conditions have any substance at all, it is really a rejection, and no contract is made until the counteroffer is accepted. *But see no. 2.*   **2.** Under the **Uniform Commercial Code**, a *counteroffer* for the sale of goods may be an acceptance with new terms proposed for the **contract.**

Counterpart   **1.** A copy or duplicate of a document.   **2.** An unsigned copy of a signed original document.   **3.** A copy of a document that is signed by one person in a deal and given to the other person, who has signed the original in exchange.   **4.** A *counterpart* **writ** is a copy that is issued to **defendants** in a county other than the one in which a lawsuit is tried, but one in which the court does have **jurisdiction.**

Countersign   Sign a document in addition to the primary or original signature in order to approve the validity of the document. A bank may ask a person to countersign his or her own check made out to "cash," and a company may require a supervisor to countersign all orders written by lower-ranking employees.

Countervailing   Opposing; equal to; balancing out.

County   Division of a state.

County commissioner   Elected county officials who have different duties in different counties. These include running the county government; managing its financial affairs, its police, its low-level judicial work, etc.

Coupon   A **certificate** of interest or a **dividend** due on a certain date. The coupons are detached one by one from the primary document (**bond,** loan agreement, etc.) and presented for payment when due.

Course of business   What is normally done by a company. This is different from *"custom"* or *"usage,"* which is what is normally done in a particular *type* of company.

Course of dealing   The prior history of business between two persons.

Course of employment   Directly related to employment, during work hours, or in the place of work.

Court   **1.** The place where judges work.   **2.** A judge at work. For example, a judge might say "the court (meaning 'I') will consider this matter."   **3.** All the judges in a particular area.   **4.** A few different types of courts are defined here under "court of _____," but most are listed by their individual names or subject matters.

Court hand   An old system of Latin shorthand once used in England for legal documents.

Court martial   A *court martial* is a military court for trying members of the armed services according to the **Code of Military Justice**. There are three types of *courts martial*. A *"summary court martial"* is for the least serious military crimes, allows only sentences under two months or lesser penalties, and gives very few procedural protections to the person accused. For example, there need be no lawyer present, and the officer who acts as a judge is the fact-finder as well as decider. A *"special court martial"* is an intermediate military trial. It has most of the protections of a regular criminal trial and may hand out punishments ranging from a "bad conduct" discharge to several months in prison. A *"general court martial"* can try the most serious military cases and can hand out sentences up to the death penalty. It has all the procedural protections of a regular criminal trial and usually includes a panel of officers, a trained judge, and trained military lawyers.

Court of appeals   A court that decides appeals from a trial court. In most states it is a middle level court (like the U.S. Courts of Appeals), but in some states it is the name for the highest court.

Court of claims   A specialized federal court that handles money claims against the U.S.

Court of inquiry   A military court.

Court of probate   A court that handles **wills** and **estates** and sometimes handles the problems of **minors** or other legally **incompetent** persons.

Court packing An attempt to restructure a court so that persons who agree with the appointing executive's views can be chosen.

Covenant A written promise, agreement, or restriction usually in a **deed**. For example, a *covenant for quiet enjoyment* is a promise that the seller of land will protect the buyer against a defective **title** to the land and against anyone who claims the land; and a *"covenant running with the land"* is any agreement in a deed that is binding for or against all future buyers of the land.

Cover **1.** Make good. **2.** Protect (for example, insurance **coverage**). **3.** Protect yourself from the effects of a business deal that falls through or isn't made good on; for example, buy what you need from a new company when the original one can't make good on a sale.

Coverage **1.** The amount and type of **insurance** on a person, an object, a business venture, etc. **2.** The *ratio* of a company's income that is available to pay **interest** on its **bonds** (or to pay **dividends** on its preferred **stock**) to the interest itself (or to the dividends).

Coverture The status that married women used to have; the special rights and legal limitations of a married woman.

Craft union A **labor union** whose members all do the same kind of work (plumbing, carpentry, etc.) for different types of industries and employers.

Created See **fixed work**.

Creative financing Any financing (usually home-purchase) outside the normal pattern. It is used to complete a deal that would have failed otherwise. It may be risky.

Credentials The right to represent a country, a group of voters, or a branch of an organization (or the document that proves that right). A *"credentials committee"* is a group that sorts out who has the right to represent subgroups at a political convention.

Credibility The believability of a **witness** and of the **testimony** that the witness gives.

Credit **1.** The right to delay payment for things bought or used. **2.** Money loaned. **3.** See **credits**. **4.** A deduction from what is owed. For example, a *tax credit* is a direct subtraction from

Credit bureau

tax owed (for other taxes paid, for certain special purposes such as a part of child care expenses, etc.). See also **deduction, exemption,** and **exclusion.**

Credit bureau   A place that keeps records on the **credit** used by persons and on their financial reliability.

Credit line   See **line of credit.**

Credit rating   An evaluation of the ability of a person or business to pay debts. Usually, a **credit bureau** makes an evaluation based on past payments and current finances, then uses the information in credit reports to businesses that are considering making a loan or offering other **credit.**

Credit union   A financial setup that uses money deposited by a closed group of persons and lends it out again to persons in the same group.

Creditor   A person to whom a debt is owed.

Creditor beneficiary   When Alan and Betty have a contract in which Alan promises to do something that financially benefits Charles, Charles is a *creditor beneficiary.*

Creditors' meeting   The first meeting of persons to whom a **bankrupt** person owes money or who hold **security** interests in a bankrupt's property.

Creditor's position   The part of a property's sale price that is put up by the **mortgage** lender.

Credits   Records in an account book of money owed to you or money you have paid out. (The opposite of **debits.**)

Crim. Con.   **Criminal conversation** (see that word).

Crime   Any violation of the government's **penal** laws. An illegal act or failure to act.

Crime against nature   See **sodomy.**

Crimen   (Latin) Crime. For example, a *crimen falsi* is a "crime of fraud or falsehood" and includes **fraud, perjury, embezzlement,** and any other crime that involves lying or **deceit** and that might affect a person's believability as a **witness.**

Criminal   **1.** Having to do with the law of crimes and illegal conduct.   **2.** Illegal.   **3.** A person who has committed a crime.

Criminal action   The procedure by which a person accused of a crime is brought to trial and given punishment.

Criminal conversation   Causing a married man or woman to commit **adultery.** Most states now prohibit lawsuits against the seducer.

Criminal forfeiture   The loss of property to the government because it was involved in a crime; for example, an automobile used to smuggle narcotics.

Criminology   The study of the causes, prevention, and punishment of crime.

Critical stage   That point in a **criminal** proceeding at which a person's rights might be damaged. The **Constitution** requires that a person must have the opportunity to get a lawyer (or, if poor, have one provided) at this point. It may be as early as the first questioning by the police, but never later than the first **hearing.**

Cross-action   **1.** A **counterclaim** or a **cross-claim. 2.** A separate lawsuit against someone suing you.

Cross-claim   A claim brought by a **defendant** against a **plaintiff** or a codefendant. It must be based on the same subject matter as the plaintiff's lawsuit.

Cross-complaint (or Cross-action or Cross-demand)   Other words for either a **counterclaim** or a **cross-claim** (see these words).

Cross-examination   The questioning of an opposing **witness** during a trial or **hearing.** See **examination.**

Cross-picketing   **Picketing** by two or more **unions** that claim to represent the same workers.

Cross-remainder   Property that is inherited by several persons as a group. As each person dies, the others share that person's interest.

Cross-rules   An old word for **show cause** (see that word) orders that are given to both sides in a lawsuit.

Crossing   A **broker's** buying a **stock** or other **security** from one client and selling it to another without going through an **exchange.**

Crown cases   In English law, **criminal** cases brought by the crown (government).

Cruel and unusual punishment   Punishment, by the government, that is prohibited by the Constitution. Recently, the courts have decided that many types of punishment should be discontinued as *"cruel and unusual"* because they shock the moral sense of the community.

Cruelty   In the law of **divorce,** *cruelty* is that treatment by a husband or wife that gives the other **grounds** for a divorce. Its definition is different in each state. Each state's official phrase for *cruelty* varies widely and has no strong connection to what it actually takes to get a divorce based on it. Some states' words for cruelty are: *"extreme cruelty," "intolerable cruelty," "cruelty," "willful cruelty,"* and *"intolerable severity."*

Culpable   Blamable; at fault. A person who has done a wrongful act (whether **criminal** or **civil**) is called *"culpable."*

Culprit   A person who has committed a crime, but has not yet been tried. This is not a technical legal word.

Cum   (Latin) With.

Cum onere   (Latin) "Burdened by an **encumbrance**" (see that word).

Cum rights   A **stock** that comes "with rights" to buy other stock at a specified price.

Cum testamento annexo   (Latin) "With the **will** attached." An **administrator** who is appointed by a court to supervise handing out the property of a dead person whose will does not name **executors** (persons to hand out property) or whose executors cannot or will not serve.

Cumulative evidence   **Evidence** that is offered to prove what has already been proved by other evidence.

Cumulative sentence   An additional prison term given to a person who is already **convicted** of a crime, the additional term to be served after the first one is finished.

Cumulative voting   The type of voting in which each person (or each share of **stock,** in the case of a **corporation**) has as many votes as there are positions to be filled. Votes can be either concentrated on one or a few candidates or spread around.

Curator   A person appointed by a court to take care of a person (and that person's property) who cannot take care of him or herself (such as a child or someone mentally **incompetent**), or to take care of the property only (for example, for a **spendthrift**).

Cure   **1.** It is a *cure* when a seller delivers goods, the buyer rejects them because of some defect, and the seller then delivers the proper goods within the proper time.   **2.** An error in the course of a trial is *cured* if the **judgment** or **verdict** is in favor of the side complaining about the error. See also **aider.**

Curia   (Latin) Old European word for court.

Current   **1.** *Current* has many meanings; for example: immediately, within the same **accounting** period, within a year, within a few months, easily converted to cash, etc.   **2.** *Current assets* are a company's cash plus those things such as short-term **secu-**

rities, accounts receivable, and **inventory** (see those words) that will probably be turned into cash in the next few months. **3.** *Current liabilities* are a company's debts, such as **accounts payable** (see that word), wages, short-term borrowing, and taxes that must be paid within the next few months. **4.** The *current ratio* is a company's *current assets* divided by its *current liabilities*. It is a measure of a company's relatively short-term financial strength. See also **working capital** and **quick assets.**

Curtesy A husband's right to part of his dead wife's property. This right is now defined by state law and varies from state to state, but is the same within each state as a wife's rights. See **dower.**

Curtilage An area of household use immediately surrounding a home. It is usually fenced in.

Cusip number A number given by the Committee on Uniform Securities Identification Procedures of the American Bankers Association to identify each **issue** of **securities.**

Custodial interrogation Questioning by police after a person has been deprived of freedom in any way. Even if there has been no formal **arrest,** a person may have the right to a **Miranda warning** (see that word), the right to a lawyer, etc.

Custody A general term meaning various types of care and keeping. For example, parents normally have legal *custody* of their children, a warden has *custody* of prisoners, and a person has *custody* of a book loaned by another.

Custom Regular behavior of persons in a geographical area or in a particular type of business that gradually takes on legal importance so that it will strongly influence a court's decision. **Unwritten law.**

Custom house The office where goods going into or out of a country are inspected and registered, and where taxes are paid.

Customs **1.** Taxes payable on goods brought into or sent out of a country. (Also called "**duty.**") **2.** The branch of government that oversees and taxes goods brought in and out of a country.

Cut throat pricing See **predatory intent.**

Cy-pres (French) "As near as possible." When a dead person's **will** can no longer legally or practically be carried out, a court may (but is not obligated to) order that the dead person's **estate** be used in a way that most nearly does what the person would have wanted. If the court does not use its *cy-pres powers,* the will may be held **void** and no longer binding. The **doctrine** of cy-pres is now usually applied only to **charitable trusts.** [pronounce: see-pray]

Dd

D **Defendant; dictum; digest; district;** doctor; and many other law-related words.

D.b.a. Doing business as.

D.b.n. **De bonis non** (see that word).

D.C. District court; District of Columbia.

D.E.A. Drug Enforcement Administration. The branch of the U.S. Department of **Justice** that enforces narcotic and drug laws.

D.I.S.C. **Domestic International Sales Corporation** (see that word).

D.J. District judge.

D.O.D. Department of Defense. The U.S. cabinet department that runs the Army, Navy, etc.; also called "the Pentagon."

D.O.T. Department of Transportation. The U.S. cabinet department that **regulates** interstate transportation through agencies such as the Federal Aviation Administration, Federal Highway Administration, etc. It also supervises the Coast Guard in peacetime.

D.W.I. **1.** Driving while intoxicated. **2.** Died without issue (children).

Dactylography The study of fingerprint identification.

Damages **1.** Money that a court orders paid to a person who has suffered a loss or injury by the person whose fault caused it. **2.** A **plaintiff's** claim in a legal **pleading** for the money defined in no. 1. *Damages* may be **actual** and **compensatory** (directly related to the amount of the loss) or they may be, in addition, exemplary and **punitive** (extra money given to punish the **defendant** and to help keep a particularly bad act from happening again). Also, merely **nominal** damages may be given (a small sum when the loss suffered is either very small or of unproved amount).   **3.** For other types of damages (such as **consequential, incidental, liquidated,** or **treble**), see the individual words.

Damnum   (Latin) A loss. For example, *"damnum absque injuria"* means a loss without a legal injury or without any way of suing for it in court.

Dangerous instrumentality   Things that are supposedly harmful in and of themselves or are designed to be harmful, such as guns.

Date of issue   The day a document is formally put out or takes effect. The day that shows on the document itself; *not necessarily* the day it actually appears. For example, the *date of issue* of an **insurance** policy is the first day the policy says it will take effect, *not* the day the insurance is agreed to or the day the document is delivered.

Davis   *Administrative Law Treatise* by Davis.

Davis-Bacon Act   A federal law about wages on **public works** and building projects.

Day book   A book in which a merchant records each day's business as it happens.

Day certain   A specific future date.

Day in court   The right to be notified of a court proceeding involving your interests, and the right to be heard when the case comes up in court.

Day order   See **order.**

De   (Latin) Of, by, from, affecting, concerning, etc. Often the first word of an old English **statute** or **writ.**

De bene esse   (Latin) "As well done (as possible)." Provisional, temporary, subject to later challenge or change. For example, a **deposition** *de bene esse* is pretrial **testimony** that may be used only if the witness is not available for the trial.

De bonis non   (Latin) "Of the goods not (already taken care of)." An **administrator** appointed to hand out the property of a dead person whose **executor** (person chosen to hand it out) has died.

De bonis propriis   (Latin) "From his or her own goods." When a person managing another's property, **trust,** or **estate** has committed **waste** (see those words), repayment may be required.

De facto   In fact; actual; a situation that exists in fact whether or not it is lawful. For example, a *de facto corporation* is a company that has failed to follow some of the technical legal requirements to become a legal **corporation,** but carries on business as one in good faith, and a *de facto government* is one which has at least temporarily overthrown the rightful, legal one. See also **de jure** (segregation) for another illustration.

De jure   Of right; legitimate; lawful, whether or not true in actual fact. For example, a president may still be the *de jure* head of a government even if the army takes actual power by force. *De jure*, however, doesn't necessarily mean good. For example, *de jure segregation* is separation of races between schools that is the result of government action and is worse than **de facto** (see that word) segregation, which is caused by social and economic conditions only. [pronounce: de joo-re]

De minimis   Small, unimportant. Also, short for "*de minimis non curat lex*" (the law does not bother with trifles).

De novo   New; completely new from the start. For example, a *trial de novo* is a completely new trial ordered by the judge or by an **appeals** court.

De son tort   (French) "Of his own wrong." A person who takes on a duty, such as being **executor** of a **will,** without any right to take on the duty, will be held responsible for all actions he or she takes. In the case of a will, the person would be called an *executor de son tort.*

Dead   Worthless, unused, or obsolete.

Dead freight   Money paid by a shipper for that part of a ship's or vehicle's capacity that is not filled.

Dead man's acts   Laws, now mostly abolished, that prevented a person from **testifying** in a civil lawsuit, against a dead person's representative, about things that the dead person might have testified to.

Dealer   **1.** A person who buys and sells things as a business. **2.** Under **S.E.C.** law, a *dealer* is a person who buys and sells **securities** for him or herself, rather than for customers (a **broker**).

Death   The end of life. The medical definition of the exact moment of death is not agreed upon, but see **brain death rule.** *Presumptive death* is "legal" death resulting from an unexplained absence for a length of time set by state law, often seven years. See also **civil death.**

Deathbed declaration   See **dying declaration.**

Debarment   Exclusion of a person from doing something; for example, from doing government contract work. This is different from *disbarment* (see **disbar**).

Debauchery   Wrongful or illegal sexual intercourse, but not necessarily **rape**.

Debenture   A corporation's obligation to pay money (usually in the form of a **note** or **bond**) that is not **secured** (backed up) by any specific property. The common use of the word includes only long-term bonds. [pronounce: de-ben-chur]

Debit card   A plastic card, like a credit card but that allows a person to make a purchase that is paid for by a direct subtraction from the person's bank account.

Debits   Records in an **account** book of money you owe or of money paid to you. (The opposite of **credits**.)

Debt   **1.** A sum of money owed because of an agreement (such as a sale or loan).   **2.** Any money owed.

Debt financing   A company's raising money by **issuing bonds** or **notes** rather than by issuing **stock,** which is called **equity financing.**

Debt poolers (or debt adjusters or debt consolidators)   Persons or organizations who take a person's money and pay it out to **creditors** by getting the creditors to accept lower monthly payments. Unless these services are nonprofit credit counselling organizations, the chances are that the debtor will wind up paying much more than by making the arrangements him or herself.

Debt service   Regular payments of **principal,** interest, and other costs such as insurance made to pay off a loan.

Debtor   A person who owes money.

Debtor's position   The part of a property's sale price that is put up by the person buying the property, rather than by the **mortgage** lender.

Decedent   A person who has recently died.

Deceit   An intentionally false statement that misleads another person and causes that person harm.

Decennial Digest   Abbreviated "Dec. Dig." See **American Digest System.**

Decision   Any formal deciding of a dispute, such as a judge's resolution of a lawsuit.

Decision on the merits   A final decision that fully and properly decides the subject matter of a case, with the effect that other lawsuits may not be brought by the same person on the same subject against the same opponent.

Declarant

Declarant   A person who makes a statement or **declaration**, whether formal or informal.

Declaration   **1.** An unsworn statement made out of court. For example, a *dying declaration* about how a person was killed may be admitted as good **evidence,** as may a *declaration against interest* (a statement that proves a fact that hurts the person speaking).   **2.** A formal statement of fact. For example, a *declaration of intention* is a preliminary statement made by a person who wants to become a U.S. **citizen.**   **3.** A public proclamation; for example, the Declaration of Independence.   **4.** An old form of the first paper filed in a lawsuit. It was a **common law** (see that word) **pleading** and corresponds to the modern **complaint.** **5.** An announcement of a set-aside of money. For example, a *declaration of dividends* is a corporation's setting aside part of its profits to pay stockholders; and a *declaration of estimated tax* is a statement and set-aside of money required by the **I.R.S.** of persons who have income from which taxes have not been withheld.

Declaration of Paris   An 1856 agreement that abolished **privateering** and agreed to other protections of merchant shipping during time of war.

Declaration of trust   A written statement by a person owning property that it is held for another person. This is one way of setting up a **trust.**

Declaratory judgment   A **judicial** action that states the rights of the **parties** or answers a legal question without awarding any **damages** or ordering that anything be done. A person may ask a court for a *declaratory judgment* only if there is a real, not theoretical, problem that involves real legal consequences.

Declaratory statute   A law that is passed to clarify prior law. It may be to explain the meaning of a prior **statute** or to clear up uncertainty in judge-made or traditional law.

Decree   **1.** A **judgment** (see that word) of a court that announces the legal consequences of the facts found in a case and orders that the court's decision be carried out; for example, a *divorce decree.* Specialized types of decrees include a *consent decree* (agreed to by the parties) and a *decree nisi* (one that takes effect only after a certain time and only if no person shows the court a good reason why it should not take effect). Decrees are given by a court under its **equity** (see that word) powers.   **2.** A proclamation or **order** put out by a person or group with **absolute** authority to give orders.

Decrement   The amount of decrease in a property's value.

Decriminalization   An official act (usually passing a law) that makes what was once a crime no longer a crime.

Dedi et concessi   (Latin) "I give and grant." Old formal words for a transfer of land or property.

Dedication   **1.** The gift or other transfer of land or rights in land to the government for a specific public use, such as a park, and its acceptance for that use by the government.   **2.** Publishing a work without getting a formal **copyright** may be a *dedication* of that work to the public, and anyone may then publish, perform, duplicate, etc.

Deductible   **1.** That which may be taken away or subtracted. Something that may be subtracted from income for tax purposes.   **2.** That part of a loss that must be borne by a person with **insurance** before the insurance company will pay the rest. For example, a **policy** with a "$100 deductible" **clause** will pay nothing on a $100 loss, and pay $200 on a $300 loss.

Deduction   **1.** A conclusion drawn from principles or facts already proved.   **2.** Any subtraction of money owed.   **3.** Subtractions from income for tax purposes. *Itemized deductions* are those nonbusiness expenses that may be subtracted (from **adjusted gross income** [see that word]) by listing the amounts in the proper categories. These include certain medical payments; taxes; interest payments, such as home mortgages; charitable contributions; professional expenses; etc. There are detailed tax rules for deducting each. The *standard deduction* was the choice of subtracting a specific percentage of income from what is taxed instead of itemizing deductions. This has been replaced by the **zero bracket amount**. See also **credits, exclusions,** and **exemptions.**

Deed   A document by which one person transfers the legal ownership of land and what is on the land to another person.

Deed of trust   **1.** A document by which a person transfers the legal ownership of land to independent **trustees** to be held until a debt on the land (a **mortgage**) is paid off.   **2.** A document that creates a **trust** of any kind.

Deem   **1.** Treat as if. For example, if a fact is *"deemed true,"* it will be treated as true unless proven otherwise.   **2.** Held to be; determined to be. For example, if a **statute** says that certain acts are "deemed to be a crime," they are a crime.

Deep pockets   The one person (or organization), among many possible **defendants**, best able to pay a **judgment** has *deep pockets*. This is the one a **plaintiff** is most likely to sue.

Deep Rock Doctrine   The principle that even if an **insider** has a better claim to the property of a company that is going out of business, a court may give the property to **creditors** if that is fairer.

Deface   **1.** Make illegible or unreadable by erasing, scrawling over, or other means.   **2.** Deliberately destroy or mar a building, monument, public display, or public symbol such as a flag.

Defalcation   **1.** Failure of a person to account for money trusted to his or her care. There is the assumption that the money was misused.   **2.** Setting off one claim against another; deducting a smaller debt due to you from a larger one you owe to someone.

Defamation   Injuring a person's character or reputation by false and **malicious** statements. This includes both **libel** and **slander.**

Default   **1.** A failure to perform a legal duty, observe a promise, or fulfill an obligation. For example, the word is often used for the failure to make a payment on a debt once it is due.   **2.** Failure to take a required step in a lawsuit; for example, to file a paper on time. This *default* leads to a default **judgment** against the side failing to file the paper.

Defeasance clause   The part of a **mortgage** contract that says that the mortgage is ended once all payments have been made or once certain other things happen.

Defeasible   Subject to being defeated, ended, or undone by a future event or action.

Defect   The absence of some legal requirement that makes a thing legally insufficient or nonbinding. For example, a *defective title* is one that is improperly drawn up, inaccurate, fails to comply with a law, or is obtained by unlawful means.

Defendant   The person against whom a legal action is brought. This legal action may be **civil** or **criminal.**

Defendant in error   An **appellee.**

Defense   **1.** The sum of the facts, law, and arguments presented by the side against whom legal action is brought.   **2.** Any counter-argument or counter-force.   **3.** In **negotiable instrument** law, a *real defense* is good against any holder, and a *personal defense* is good against anyone except a **holder in due course** (see that word).

Deferred charges   A company's current spending for long-term needs such as research. It will be deducted from taxes over several years, not all at once.

Deferred compensation   Payments to employees, such as those made under a **pension plan** (see that word) that satisfies I.R.S. rules, that will not be taxed until the employee actually gets the money. I.R.S. *qualified* plans also allow the employer to take a tax **deduction** when the money is paid into the plan, while *nonqualified* plans make the employer wait for the deduction until the employee is taxed.

Deficiency   A lack or shortage. For example, a *deficiency* in a legal paper means that it lacks something to make it proper or able to take legal effect. Also, the difference between a tax owed and a tax paid is a *deficiency.*

Deficiency judgment (or decree)   A court's decision that a person must pay more money owed than the amount **secured** by property. For example, when an auto dealer repossesses (takes back) a car for failure to make payments and then sells the car for eight hundred dollars, if the debt owed is one thousand dollars, some states will allow the car dealer to sue for a two hundred dollar *deficiency judgment.* The same thing can happen in a mortgage **foreclosure.**

Deficit   Something missing or lacking; less than what should be; a "minus" **balance.** For example, if a city takes in less money than it must pay out in the same time period, it is called *"deficit financing"* or *"deficit spending."*

Definite sentence   See **determinate sentence.**

Definitive   Capable of finally and completely settling a legal question or a lawsuit.

Deflator   A numerical figure used to change current cost figures to past **constant dollars** by removing increases due to inflation.

Deforcement   Old word for holding on to land or buildings and keeping out persons who now have a right to them.

Defraud   To cheat.

Degree   A step, grade, or division; for example, a "step removed" between two relatives (brothers are related in the *first degree,* grandparent and grandchild in the second). Also, a *degree* is a division of a crime into different levels of severity (*first degree* murder carries a more severe maximum punishment than *second degree* murder).

Del credere

Del credere (Italian) An **agent** who sells goods for a person and also **guarantees** to that person that the buyer will pay in full for the goods. [pronounce: del <u>cred</u>-er-e]

Delectus personae (Latin) "Choice of person." The right of a **partner** to choose, approve, and disapprove of other partners.

Delegate **1.** A person who is chosen to represent another person or group of persons. **2.** To choose a person to represent you or to do a job for you.

Delegation **1.** The giving of authority by one person to another. For example, a boss often *delegates* responsibility to employees. **2.** An entire group of **delegates** or representatives. **3.** An old word for a person taking over the debt of another person with the agreement of the person owed the debt. **4.** *Delegation of powers* is the **constitutional** division of authority between branches of government and also the handing down of authority from the president to **administrative agencies.**

Deliberate **1.** To carefully consider, discuss, and work towards forming an opinion or making a decision. **2.** Well advised; carefully considered; thoroughly enough planned. **3.** Planned in advance; premeditated; intentional.

Delictum (Latin) A crime, **tort,** or wrong. ("Delict" also means criminal or wrong.)

Delinquency Failure, omission, or violation of duty; misconduct. For example, a debt that has fallen behind in payment is called a *delinquency.*

Delinquent **1.** Overdue and unpaid. **2.** Willfully and intentionally failing to carry out an obligation. **3.** Short for "*juvenile delinquent*," a **minor** who has done an illegal act or who has been proved in court to misbehave seriously.

Delist Remove a **stock** (or other **security**) from a stock (or other) exchange. This is more than a suspension of trading.

Delivery **1.** The transfer of property other than land from one person to another. (Usually the transfer of goods that have been sold.) **2.** An act other than physically handing over an object that has the legal effect of a physical transfer.

Demand **1.** A forceful claim that presupposes that there is no doubt as to its winning. **2.** The assertion of a legal right; a legal obligation asserted in the courts. **3.** "On demand" is a phrase put on some **promissory notes** or other **negotiable instruments** to mean that the money owed must be paid immediately when the **holder** of the note requests payment. These are called *"demand notes."* A *demand deposit* is money given to a bank that may be taken out at any time; for example, a checking account. **4.** The strength of buyer desire for and willingness to pay for a product.

Demeanor   Physical appearance and behavior. The demeanor of a witness is not what the witness says, but how the witness says it, including, for example, tone of voice, hesitations, gestures, apparent sincerity, etc.

Demense   An old word for **domain**.

Demise   **1.** A lease. **2.** Any transfer of property (especially land). *Not* **"devise."** **3.** Death.

Democracy   Government by the people, either directly in meetings or indirectly through representatives, usually as a basis for a system in which the highest political good is the protection of individual liberties.

Demonstrative evidence   All evidence other than **testimony;** evidence addressed directly to the senses; for example, a gun shown to the jury.

Demonstrative legacy   A gift in a **will** that is to be paid out of a particular part of the dead person's property.

Demur   To make a **demurrer** (see that word).

Demurrage   The money paid to the owner of a ship or railroad car by a person who holds it beyond the contract time.

Demurrer   A legal **pleading** that says, in effect, "even if, for the sake of argument, the facts presented by the other side are correct, those facts do not give the other side a legal argument that can possibly stand up in court." The *demurrer* has been replaced in many courts by making a **motion** to dismiss.

Denaturalization   The involuntary loss of citizenship previously acquired by being naturalized. This occurs when the citizenship is revoked. See also **expatriation.**

Denial   **1.** The part of a **pleading** that tries to refute the facts claimed in the other side's pleading. **2.** A refusal or rejection; for example, a *denial* of **welfare** benefits to a family that makes too much money to qualify. **3.** A deprivation or withholding; for example, a *denial* of a **constitutional** right.

Dep.   **1.** Short for **"deputy."** **2.** Short for "department" ("dep't." is more common).

Departure   See **variance.**

Dependent

Dependent **1.** A person supported primarily by another person. **2.** Conditional. For example, a *dependent contract* is one in which one side does not have to do something in the contract until the other side does something it is required to do.

Dependent relative revocation The legal principle in some states that if a person **revokes** (takes back or cancels) a **will** with the intention of making a new one, and that new one is either never made or is defective, there is a **rebuttable** presumption (an assumption) that he or she would have preferred the old will to no will at all.

Depletion **Amortization** (see that word) of a natural resource. See also **depletion allowance**.

Depletion allowance A tax **deduction** for extractors of oil, minerals, and other natural resources because they are being used up.

Deponent Person who gives sworn **testimony** out of court. See **deposition**.

Deportation Expelling a foreigner from a country and sending that person to another.

Depose **1.** Give sworn **testimony** out of court. See **deposition**. **2.** Ask the questions of the person in no. 1. For example, a lawyer might say "I *deposed* Mr. Smith today." **3.** Take away a person's public office against his or her will. This usually applies to a head of state's forcible removal.

Deposit **1.** Place property in another's hands for safekeeping. **2.** Give someone money as part payment, **earnest money** (see that word), or **security** for a purchase. **3.** Money placed in a bank or similar financial institution, often to earn interest. *Demand deposits* may be taken out at any time and *time deposits* must be left in a certain time.

Deposit in court **1.** A person who admits a debt or **liability**, but does not know exactly to whom it is owed, may *deposit* money with a court to be held for the person whom the court finally decides is owed the money. **2.** Money may also be deposited in court when the amount owed or the question of owing is in doubt; for example, during an **eviction** or a **rent strike** (see that word).

Depositary The person who receives a **deposit** (see that word). See also **depository**.

Deposition **1.** The process of taking a witness's sworn **testimony** out of court. It is usually done by a lawyer, with the lawyer from the other side given a chance to attend and participate. **2.** The written record of no. 1.

Depository   The place (such as a bank) where a **deposit** (see that word) is kept. See also **depositary.**

Depreciation   **1.** A fall in value or reduction in worth (usually due to deterioration or the passing of time).   **2.** The amount of the fall in value in no. 1 that is "written off" or charged to a particular time period for tax **deduction** purposes. If an equal amount of depreciation is taken in each year of a property's useful life, it is called *straight line* depreciation. If more of the depreciation is taken early, it is called *accelerated* depreciation. Depreciation is a type of **amortization** (see that word) of physical objects used in a business.

Deputy   An official authorized to act for another person; usually the second-in-command of an organization who may act in place of the head.

Deraign   Prove; vindicate; disprove things said against you.

Derelict   **1.** Property that is thrown away or **abandoned** intentionally.   **2.** An abandoned boat, whether or not abandoned intentionally.

Dereliction   **1.** The receding of water from a shore or bank, and the creation of new land due to a lower water level.   **2. Abandonment** of property.   **3.** A refusal or failure to perform a public office or duty.

Derivative action   A lawsuit by a stockholder of a **corporation** against another person (usually an officer of the company) to enforce rights the shareholder thinks the corporation has against that person.

Derivative evidence   **Evidence** that is collected by following up on evidence gathered illegally is *derivative* and may not be used in a trial.

Derivative tort   **1.** A **tort** lawsuit based on harm done by a person committing a crime.   **2.** A tort lawsuit against a **principal** for action by an **agent.**

Derivative work   Under **copyright** law, a work is *derivative* if it is a new form of a work (if it is a translation of a novel, a movie version of a play, etc.), but is still an *original* work if it is merely revised, edited, illustrated, etc.

Derogation   Partial **repeal** or abolishing of a law by a later law that limits it.

Derogation clause

Derogation clause   A phrase inserted in a **will** with instructions that no later will lacking this phrase should be treated as valid. It is an attempt to protect against later wills being fake or extracted by pressure, but courts will usually treat such a clause as **evidence** only and not automatically enforce it.

Descent   **1. Inheritance** from parents or other ancestors. **2.** Getting property by inheritance of any type, rather than by purchase or gift.

Descriptive word index   A large set of books in dictionary form that allows you to find which cases have discussed a topic by tracing down exact words or catchphrases. For example, if you are interested in cases involving tires that blow out during a skid, you might look up "tires," "blowouts," or "skidding."

Desecrate   **Deface** or otherwise damage a public building, church, graveyard, etc.

Desertion   **1.** Abandoning a military post and duty without permission and with no intention of returning.   **2.** Abandoning wife, husband, or child with no intention of either returning or of reassuming the financial and other duties of marriage or parenthood.   **3.** Any abandonment of a job or duty. For example, if a sailor deserts a merchant ship, all wages may be lost.

Design   A purpose plus a plan to carry it out.

Desire   When used in a **will,** the word *desire* can mean anything from a small preference to a total command. For example, "I leave all my jewelry to Tom and desire that Joe get my gold ring" could give an **executor** fits because words far clearer than "desire" can cause fights when used in a will.

Desk audit   **1.** A review of a job or jobs in the **civil service** (see that word) to see if the duties fit the pay and rank and to see if the person filling the job has the right qualifications.   **2.** The review of a federal tax return by an I.R.S. employee who needs no additional information from the taxpayer.

Desk jobbing   **Wholesaling** by **drop shipping** (see those words).

Despoil   Take something away from a person illegally and usually by violence.

Destination contract   A deal in which the risk of loss or of damage to a shipment of goods passes from seller to buyer once the goods are offered up at their destination.

Destroy   **1.** With regard to wills, contracts, or other legal documents, *"destruction"* does not necessarily mean total physical destruction. You can *destroy* a document's *legal effect* by less extreme methods, such as tearing it in half or writing over it. **2.** *Destruction* may mean many different things. For example, in an **insurance** contract, "destruction" may mean a total wreck or merely harm that makes something useless for its intended purpose.

Detainer   1. The unlawful keeping of another person's property even if keeping that property was originally lawful.   **2.** Holding a person against his or her will.   **3.** A **warrant** or court **order** to keep a person in **custody** when that person might otherwise be released. This is often used to make sure a person will serve a **sentence** or attend a trial in one state at the end of a prison term in another state or in a federal prison.

Detention   Holding a person against his or her will. *Detention for questioning* is the holding of a person, by a policeman or similar public official, without making a formal **arrest.**

Determinable   1. Possibly ended; subject to being ended if a certain thing happens.   **2.** Can be found out or decided upon.

Determinate sentence   An exact prison term that is set by law, rather than one that may be shortened by good behavior or the actions of a **parole** board.

Determination   1. A final decision (usually of a court or other formal decision-maker such as a **hearing examiner**).   **2.** Any formal decision. For example, the **I.R.S.** puts out *determination letters* to explain whether or not an organization has been given **tax exempt** status.   **3.** The ending of a right or interest in property. When this happens, the right *determines*.

Determine   1. Decide.   **2.** End.

Detinue   A legal action to get back property held unlawfully by another person, plus **damages** for the wrongful withholding. [pronounce: det-i-new]

Detournement   An old word for taking money or financial documents entrusted to your care and cashing them or using them for your own purposes. Similar to **embezzlement.**

Detraction   Removing inherited property from a state and transferring **title** to a new state.

Detriment   1. Any loss or harm.   **2.** Giving something up (a right, a benefit, some property, etc.).

Detrimental reliance   The legal principle that if person A promises person B to do something once B takes a certain action, and

Devaluation

B takes that action, B has *relied* on the promise to his or her *detriment* and, thus, has certain legal rights against A.

Devaluation   Reducing the value of a country's money relative to other countries' money.

Devastavit   (Latin) "He has wasted." An old word for mismanagement of property by the **administrator** of a dead person's **estate.** The administrator could be held personally **liable** for any loss. See also **"de bonis propriis"** and **waste.**

Development   **1.** A piece of land subdivided into building lots and sold, or built upon and then sold.   **2.** Preparation of a mining site to make the minerals accessible by stripping, blasting, tunneling, etc.

Devest   See **divest.**

Deviance   Noticeable differing from average or normal behavior. The word is usually applied to things society in general does not like, such as drug use.

Deviation   **1.** A departure from usual conduct, such as an employee's use of work time for personal business.   **2.** A change from original terms or plans, such as a **contractor's** substituting one type of wood for another specified in building plans. **3.** Allowing the specific terms of a **will** or **trust** to be ignored in order to accomplish its general purposes. See also **cy-pres.**

Devise   **1.** The gift of land or things on land by **will.**   **2.** Any gift by will. *Not* "**demise.**" [pronounce: de-vize]

Devisee   Person to whom land is given by **will.**

Devisor   Person who makes a **will** to give away land.

Devolution   **1.** The transfer or transition by process of law from one person to another of a right, **liability, title,** property, or office (often by death).   **2.** In England, this also means the decentralization of government.

Devolve   To go by **devolution** (see that word).

Dewey decimal system   A library reference system that classifies all subjects by number. For example, the numbers in the 340's are for law, 343 is for criminal law, and 343.2 is for a special subject under criminal law. Each new number after the decimal point subdivides the previous number (and its subject) further. Compare with **Library of Congress system.**

Dicta   Views of a judge that are not a central part of the judge's decision, even if the judge argues them strongly and even if they look like conclusions. One way to decide whether a particular part of a judge's **opinion** is *dicta* is to examine whether it was necessary to reach the result. If it could be removed without changing the legal result, it is probably dicta. If it is dicta, it is not binding **precedent** (see that word) on later court decisions, but it is probably still worth quoting if it helps your case.

Dictum (Latin) **1.** Singular of **dicta** (see that word). **2.** Short for "*obiter dictum*" (a remark by the way, as in "by the way, did I tell you . . ."); a digression; a discussion of side points or unrelated points.

Dies (Latin) **1.** A day; days; court day. **2.** *Dies gratiae* are **grace** days.

Diet A word used in various countries for **legislature.**

Digest A collection of parts of many books, usually giving not only summaries, but also excerpts and condensations. For example, the **American Digest System** covers the decisions of the highest court of each state and of the Supreme Court. It is divided into volumes by time periods. It collects "**headnotes**" or summaries given at the top of each case and is arranged by subject categories.

Dilatory Tending or intending to cause delay or gain time.

Diligence Carefulness or prudence.

Dilution **1.** The use of a **trademark** by a product so unlike the original that, while it will cause no confusion, it may still lower the trademark's value. **2.** *Dilution* of **stock** occurs when the stock is **watered** or when more stock is sold than the value of the company can support.

Diminished responsibility A state of mind, less than complete **insanity,** that may lower a person's punishment for a crime. For example, mental retardation is often accepted as a reason to lower the **degree** of a crime or lessen the punishment.

Diminution **1.** Reduction. For example, *diminution* in value is one way to measure **damages** for property or rights that have been injured or taken. **2.** Incompleteness.

Diplomatic immunity A diplomat's freedom from **prosecution** under most of the host country's criminal laws.

Diplomatic relations Ongoing, formal country-to-country communications and the permanent exchange of **ambassadors** and other officials.

Direct Immediate or straight. This word, in different settings, may be the opposite of **indirect** (not direct), **collateral** (on the side), or **cross** (opposing) (see these words).

Direct action

Direct action **1.** A lawsuit by a person against his or her own **insurance** company instead of against the person who did the harm or against that person's insurance company. **2.** A lawsuit by a stockholder to enforce his or her own rights against a company or its officers rather than to enforce the **corporation's** rights in a **derivative action** (see that word).

Direct attack An attempt to have a judge's decision overturned (**annulled, reversed, vacated, enjoined,** etc.) by a proceeding started for that specific purpose (an **appeal,** an **injunction** hearing, etc.). The opposite of **collateral attack** (see that word).

Direct cause See **proximate cause.**

Direct evidence Proof of a fact without the need for other facts leading up to it. For example, *direct* evidence that dodos are not extinct would be a live dodo. For the difference between direct and **circumstantial evidence,** see that word for examples.

Direct examination The first questioning in a trial of a **witness** by the side that called that witness.

Direct line Grandparents, parents, children, grandchildren, etc., rather than brothers, uncles, nieces, etc.

Direct placement A company selling its **stock** or **bonds** directly to a buyer, rather than to the public through underwriters. This is also called *private placement.*

Direct reduction mortgage A type of mortgage in which the payment size decreases with each payment because **interest** is paid on only the principal still owed. Contrast this with a **constant payment mortgage** (see that word).

Direct selling A manufacturer selling directly to a customer rather than through a wholesaler or retailer.

Direct tax **1.** A tax that is paid directly to the government by the person taxed. For example, income tax is direct, but a manufacturing tax is not because it is passed on to the buyer in the form of higher prices. **2.** An **ad valorem** tax (see that word). **3.** The opposite of an **indirect tax** (see that word).

Direct trust An *express* **trust.**

Direct writer An insurance **agent** who generally deals with only one insurance company.

Directed verdict A **verdict** in which the judge takes the decision out of the jury's hands. The judge does this by telling them what they must decide or by actually making the decision. The judge might do this when the person suing has presented facts which, even if believed by a jury, cannot add up to a successful case.

130

Director **1.** Head of an organization, group, or project. **2.** A person elected by the shareholders (owners) of a **corporation** to make all **corporate** decisions such as the hiring of the persons who actually run the day-to-day operations. **3.** Directors as a group are a *board of directors*. Those who are also major stockholders, officers, or employees of the company are called *inside directors*, and those with no such interests are *outside directors*.

Directory **1.** *Not mandatory.* Merely advisory, instructing, or procedural. For example, *directory language* in a **statute** merely instructs an official and may not invalidate (overturn) actions of an official who fails to follow instructions. But see no. 2. **2.** *Mandatory.* For example, a *directory trust* has specific instructions and leaves no **discretion** to the **trustee.** But see no. 1. You cannot tell what *directory* means unless you already know exactly how it has come to be used in a particular area of the law.

Disability **1.** A *legal disability* is the lack of legal capacity to do an act. For example, a married person is disabled from remarrying until the marriage ends in an **annulment,** in **divorce,** or by the spouse's death. **2.** A *physical or mental disability* is the absence of adequate physical or mental powers or the lowering of earning ability due to this absence. *Disability* is defined differently under **workers' compensation laws** (see that word) and social security laws, but it always includes the inability to perform the person's usual job.

Disaffirm Repudiate; take back consent once given; refuse to honor former promises or stick by former acts (usually used in situations where the person has a legal right to do so).

Disallow Refuse, deny, or reject.

Disaster loss A loss (such as a building damaged in a flood) that takes place in a *disaster area* designated by the president. The persons who suffer these losses are given special loan benefits.

Disbar Take away a lawyer's right to practice law.

Disburse Pay out of a fund of money.

Discharge **1.** Release; remove; free; dismiss. For example, to *discharge* a **contract** is to end the obligation by agreement or by carrying it out; to *discharge* a prisoner is to release him or her; to *discharge* a court **order** is to cancel or revoke it; to *discharge* a person in **bankruptcy** is to release him or her from all or most debts; to *discharge* a person from the army is to release him or her from service; and to *discharge a bill* is force it out of a **com-**

Disciplinary rules

mittee by a vote of the **house** of the **legislature.** **2.** The documents showing that no. 1 has taken place; for example, *discharge papers* from the army. **3.** Do or perform a duty.

Disciplinary rules Rules listing and explaining specific things that a lawyer is prohibited from doing. They appear in the **Code of Professional Responsibility.**

Disclaimer **1.** The refusal, rejection, or renunciation of a claim, a power, or property. **2.** The refusal to accept certain types of responsibility. For example, a *disclaimer clause* in a written sales contract might say "we give you, the purchaser, promises A, B, C, etc., but *disclaim* all other promises or responsibilities."

Disclosure Revealing something that is secret or not well understood. For example, the *disclosure* in a **patent** application is the statement of what the invention is, what it does, and how it works. In **consumer** law, *disclosure* refers to what information must be made available in a loan or other **credit** deal and how that information must be presented to make it clear.

Discontinuance Another word for either **nonsuit** or **dismissal** (see these words).

Discount **1.** A deduction or lowering of an amount of money; for example, a lower price. **2.** Paying interest in advance. **3.** See **discounting.**

Discount rate **1.** The percentage of the **face** value of a commercial **note, bill, mortgage,** etc., that is deducted from the payment by a buyer such as a bank. See also **rediscount rate.** **2.** The rate set by the Federal Reserve Board for the charge made by Federal Reserve Banks to other banks borrowing money from them. **3.** See **discounting.**

Discounting Calculating the present value of money to be paid or collected in a future payment or a series of future payments. The process involves answering the question: "How much money would I need to invest today at a certain interest rate to equal what is changing hands in the future?" The calculation is the reverse of compounding interest, and the interest rate used is called the "**discount rate**" (see that word) or the "capitalization rate."

Discovered peril doctrine When a **plaintiff** suing for an injury based on **negligence** is also negligent, and when the **defendant** saw the plaintiff's danger and could have avoided it, the plaintiff may still win even though he or she may have been guilty of **contributory negligence** (see these words).

Discovery   1. The formal and informal exchange of information between sides in a lawsuit. Two types of *discovery* are **interrogatories** and **depositions** (see these words).   2. Finding out something previously unknown. For example, in **patent** law, a *discovery* is finding out something rather than inventing a device or process. Also, the *discovery* of a **fraud** or of medical **malpractice** comes when the person harmed finds out the problem (or should have found out if careful).

Discredit   Damage a person's believability or a document's genuineness.

Discretion   1. Intelligent, prudent conduct; the capacity to act intelligently and prudently.   2. The power to act within general guidelines, rules, or laws, but without either specific rules to follow or the need to completely explain or justify each decision or action. For example, a *discretionary account* occurs when a customer gives a stockbroker great leeway in deciding what stocks to buy and sell, when to buy, etc.

Discretionary review   See **certiorari**.

Discretionary trust   A **trust** (see that word) that allows some leeway in carrying out its terms.

Discrimination   1. The failure to treat equals equally. The setting up of sham or irrelevant categories to justify treating persons unfairly.   2. Illegally unequal treatment based on race, religion, sex, age, etc.

Disfranchise (or Disenfranchise)   Take away the rights of a free citizen, such as the right to vote.

Dishonor   Refuse to accept or pay a **negotiable instrument** (see that word) when it comes due.

Disinterested   Impartial; not biased or prejudiced; not affected personally or financially by the outcome. (The word, however, does *not* mean "uninterested" and does *not* mean lacking an opinion.)

Disintermediation   The process that occurs when large numbers of people take their money out of savings and similar accounts and put the money directly into investments that pay higher rates of interest (and that the savings banks might have invested in with the same money).

Disjunctive   An "or" statement which, if one part is true, the oth-

Dismissal

er part is false; for example, "John was in New York yesterday at noon or he was in Boston yesterday at noon."

Dismissal   A court **order** or **judgment** that puts a lawsuit out of court. It may be "with **prejudice**" (no further lawsuit may be brought by the same persons on the same subject) or "without prejudice."

Disorderly conduct   A vague term for actions that disturb the peace or shock public morality. The term may be more closely defined by state laws, but usually is not.

Disorderly house   A building with occupants who behave in a way that creates a neighborhood **nuisance**. These often include places for gambling or prostitution.

Disparagement   The discrediting, belittling, or "talking down" of something or someone. Under some circumstances, you can be sued for doing it; for example, *disparagement* of **title** and *disparagement* of **property**. Also, a seller's disparagement of an advertised item may be part of prohibited **bait and switch** (see that word) sales tactics.

Dispatch   A speedy sending off or completion.

Dispensation   An exemption from a law or permission to do something usually forbidden.

Disposable earnings   **Gross** or "total" pay, minus **deductions** required by law. This is not exactly the same as take home pay, since voluntary deductions may further reduce "take home."

Dispose   **1.** Sell, give, or otherwise transfer something away. **2.** See **disposition.**

Disposition   **1.** Final settlement or result. A court's *disposition* of a case may be to give a **judgment,** dismiss the case, pass sentence on a criminal, etc.   **2.** Giving something up or giving it away.

Dispositive facts   Facts that clearly settle a legal question in court.

Dispossession   **1. Ouster**. Wrongfully putting a person off his or her property by force, trick, or misuse of the law.   **2.** A legal proceeding by a **landlord** to evict a **tenant.**

Dispute   A disagreement between persons about their rights and their legal obligations to one another.

Disqualify   Make ineligible. For example, a judge may be *disqualified* from deciding a case involving a company if the judge owns **stock** in that company.

Disseisin An old word for **dispossession** or for wrongfully putting another person off land owned by that person.

Dissent A judge's formal disagreement with the decision of the majority of the judges in a lawsuit. If the judge puts it in writing, it is called a *dissenting opinion*.

Dissolution **1.** Ending or breaking up. For example, *dissolution* of a **contract** is a **mutual** agreement to end it and *dissolution* of a **corporation** is ending its existence. **2.** *Dissolution of marriage* is ending a marriage because there are "irreconcilable differences" between husband and wife. This is a **"no fault"** divorce. Sometimes, "dissolution" applies to any legal ending of a marriage, including a regular **divorce.**

Distinguish Point out basic differences. To *distinguish* a **case** is to show why it is irrelevant (or not very relevant) to the lawsuit being decided.

Distrain To take another person's personal **property** either lawfully or unlawfully. For example, a landlord might *distrain* a tenant's property to make sure that back rent will be paid.

Distress **1.** The process of **distraining** (see that word) property. **2.** Forced. A *distress sale* of goods might be a "going out of business" sale in which prices are low, and a distress sale of land might be due to a mortgage **foreclosure.**

Distributee **Heir**; person who inherits.

Distribution Division by shares; for example, giving out what is left of a dead person's **estate** after taxes and debts are paid.

Distributive finding A **finding** in which a jury decides part of a case in favor of one side and part in favor of the other side.

Distributor Wholesaler.

District A subdivision of many different types of areas (such as countries, states, or counties) for judicial, political, or administrative purposes. "*Districting*" is the process of drawing a district's boundary lines for purposes of **apportionment** (see that word).

District attorney The top **criminal** prosecuting lawyer of each federal **district** (called the "U.S. attorney") and of each state district. On low-levels, this person may also be called the "*county attorney*" or "*state's attorney.*"

District court **1.** Trial courts of the U.S., one in each *federal district* that may be a whole state or part of a state. **2.** In some states, low-level state courts (or even **appeals** courts).

Disturbing the peace

Disturbing the peace A vague term, defined in different ways in different places, for interrupting the peace, quiet, or good order of a neighborhood.

Divers 1. Many; several. **2.** Different; many different. [pronounce: <u>dive</u>-ers]

Diversification 1. A company's adding new product lines or going into an entirely new business. **2.** An investor's buying new types of **stock** or other **securities**, usually to reduce the risk of one stock's sudden fall in price.

Diversion A turning aside; for example, the unauthorized changing of the course of a river; the unauthorized use of a company's funds or of **trust** funds; or the turning aside of criminals or juvenile delinquents from jail into special **rehabilitation** programs.

Diversity of citizenship The situation that occurs when the persons on one side of a case in federal court come from a different state than the persons on the other side. This allows the court to accept and decide the case based on the court's *diversity jurisdiction*.

Divest Deprive, take away, withdraw, or cast away. For example, you can *divest* yourself of a car by selling it.

Divestiture The court **order** to a company that it get rid of something (another company, **stock**, property, etc.) because of **antitrust** laws. The company's carrying out of the court order is also called divestiture (or divestment).

Dividend A share of profits or property; usually a payment per **share** of a **corporation's stock** (see those words). A few of the many different types of dividends include: *asset (or property) dividend* (paid in the form of property instead of cash or stock; for example, a blivit manufacturer might give each owner a blivit); *consent dividend* (declared to avoid a personal **holding company** or **accumulated earnings tax**, but never actually paid; this dividend is then taxed to the owners as if paid and increases their **basis** of ownership); *constructive dividend* (unreasonable compensation paid to an owner that will be taxed like a dividend; this could be unusually high wages, bargain purchases of company property, etc.); *cumulative dividend* (if not paid regularly, usually on *preferred* **stock**, it accumulates and must be paid before any **common stock** dividends are paid); *deficiency dividend* (paid to make up for a missed one; often to avoid paying a personal holding company tax); *scrip dividend* (paid in **scrip**, in **certificates** of ownership of stock not yet issued, or in short-term loan **notes**; done to divide profits but delay paying them out); and *stock dividend* (not a real dividend, but a dividing up of the increased worth of a company by **issuing** more stock).

Divisible   Something that can be divided into separate parts that do not depend on each other. For example, a *divisible contract* has parts that will be enforced by a court even if other parts are not legally valid; and a *divisible offense* is a crime that includes other lesser crimes (**murder** includes **assault**, **battery**, etc.). See also **severable**.

Divorce   The ending of a marriage by court order. It is different from an **annulment** (which wipes out the marriage from the beginning as if it never existed in law) and from a limited divorce (also called "legal **separation**," "divorce a **mensa et thoro**," and "from bed and board") in that a *limited divorce* separates the couples legally, but does not allow either one to remarry.

Do, lego   (Latin) "I give and **bequeath**." Old words introducing a gift in a **will**.

Dock   A name sometimes used for the place in the courtroom where the prisoner stays during a trial.

Docket   **1.** A list of cases, usually with file numbers, set down for trial in a court.   **2.** A list of specific actions taken in a court. For example, an *appearance docket* lists all lawyers appearing in cases and may list the formal steps taken; and a *judgment docket* is a list of all final actions taken by a court (often used to give notice to the public of new **liens** on property).   **3.** Any book of brief entries or summaries.

Doctor–patient privilege   The right of a patient in some states to keep his or her doctor from **testifying** about what the patient said.

Doctrine   A legal principle or rule.

Document   Anything with a message on it; for example, a **contract**, a map, a photograph of a message on wood, etc. An *ancient document* is an old document, produced from proper **custody** (safekeeping), that is presumed to be genuine if it is over a certain age. And a *public document* is a document that is, or should be, open for public inspection.

Document of title   A piece of paper that is normally accepted in business as proof of a right to hold goods; for example, a **bill of lading** or a **warehouse receipt**.

Documentary evidence

Documentary evidence   Evidence supplied by writings and all other **documents** (see that word).

Documentary originals rule   See **best evidence** rule.

Documentary stamp   A stamp that must be purchased and put on a **document** before it can be **recorded** in the public records of some cities or states.

Doing business   A general, flexible term meaning carrying on enough business for profit within a state so that another person can sue the company in that state. "Doing business" also means that the state itself can tax the company or otherwise claim **jurisdiction** (see that word) over it.

Doli capax   (Latin) "Capable of crime"; for example, old enough to know right from wrong and not insane.

Dollar averaging   Buying a fixed dollar amount of a **stock** (or other **security**) at regular intervals (usually getting a different number of **shares** each time).

Dolus   (Latin) **Fraud**, **deceit**, or crime.

Domain   Ownership and control (usually by the public). For example, national forests are in the *public domain* (owned and controlled by the U.S.). Some writings are also in the *public domain*, but the meaning is different (available for use and reprinting by anyone). Also see **eminent domain**.

Dombrowski doctrine   The rule that a federal court will stop state officials from **prosecuting** a person under a state law that is so broad or vague that it affects rights guaranteed by the **Fifth Amendment** to the **U.S. Constitution**.

Dome   See **doom**.

Domestic   **1.** Relating to the home. For example, *domestic relations* is the branch of law that deals with **divorce, custody, support, adoption,** etc.   **2.** Relating to the state. For example, a *domestic corporation* is a corporation created under the laws of the state in question.   **3.** Relating to the country.

Domestic International Sales Corporation   A U.S. company whose income comes primarily from foreign sales. A D.I.S.C. may get special tax breaks.

Domicile   A person's permanent home, legal home, or main residence. The words "abode," "citizenship," "habitancy," and "residence" sometimes mean the same as *domicile* and sometimes not. A *corporate domicile* is the **corporation's** legal home and usually its central office; an *elected domicile* is the place the persons who make a **contract** specify as their legal homes in the contract. [pronounce: dom-i-sill]

Domiciliary   Relating to a person's permanent home. For example, a *domiciliary administration* is the handling of a dead person's **estate** (property) in the state of the person's legal **domicile**, the primary or central place where this is done.

Dominant   Possessing rights against another thing. For example, a *dominant estate* has rights (such as an **easement**) in another piece of land.

Dominant cause   See proximate cause.

Dominion   Legal ownership plus full actual control over something.

Donated stock (or surplus)   **Stock** given back to a **corporation** by its shareholders.

Donatio   (Latin) A gift. For *donatio mortis causa*, see **causa mortis.**

Donative   As a gift. For example, a *donative trust* is a **trust** set up as a gift for another person.

Donee   A person to whom a gift is made or a **power** is given.

Donee beneficiary   If David and Paul have a contract that benefits Jonah, Jonah is the *donee beneficiary.*

Donor   A person making a gift to another or giving another person power to do something.

Doom   Old word for a law or for a judge's decision.

Dormant   "Sleeping," inactive, silent or concealed. For example, a *dormant partner* is a partner who has a financial interest, but takes no control over the business and is usually unknown to the public; and a *dormant judgment* is a **judgment** that can no longer be enforced because too much time has gone by, because the person who originally got it died, etc. Some *dormant judgments* can be "**revived**" by taking the proper legal steps. See also **lapse**.

Double entry   A method of **bookkeeping** that shows every transaction as both a **debit** and a **credit** (see those words) and by using both horizontal rows and vertical columns of numbers. If the total of the horizontal rows and the vertical columns is not the same, it is easier to find out where mistakes are than if the records were kept with only one "entry" for each item.

Double hearsay   It would be *double hearsay* if John testified in court that he heard Mary say something that Mary heard from someone else.

Double indemnity A double insurance payoff if something happens in a certain way; for example, a ten thousand dollar payment for a person's death and twenty thousand for an accidental death.

Double insurance Insurance from more than one company on the same **interest** in the same thing. It is usually not possible to collect more than a thing is worth.

Double jeopardy A second prosecution against the same person for the same crime once the first one is totally finished and decided. This is prohibited by the U.S. **Constitution**.

Double taxation **1.** Two taxes imposed on the same property by the same government during the same time period for the same purpose. This is not legal. **2.** Any time the same money is taxed twice. A legal form of *double taxation* is taxing a **corporation** on its profits, then taxing its stockholders on their **dividends** from the corporation.

Double will See **reciprocal** will.

Doubt Uncertainty of mind about proof in a trial. For example, *"beyond a reasonable doubt"* is the standard for proof to convict a person as guilty of a crime. It is the highest standard of proof required in any type of trial, but does not mean "beyond *all* doubt."

Doubtful title The opposite of **marketable** title.

Dow Jones (Industrial Average) The average price of stocks of a selected number of the largest U.S. industrial **corporations**.

Dower A wife's right to part of her dead husband's property. This right is now **regulated** by **statute** and varies from state to state, but is the same within each state for either husband or wife (see **curtesy**). Note: This is *not "dowry,"* a nonlegal word for property a bride brings into a marriage.

Down payment The cash that must be paid at the time that something is bought by **installments** (on time).

Draconian law A law that is especially harsh or severe.

Draft A **bill** of exchange or any other **negotiable instrument** (see those words) for the payment of money *drawn* by one person on another. To use an ordinary personal **check** as an example: one person (the **drawer**) writes the check to pay money from a bank (the **drawee**) to another person (the **payee**). An *overdraft* is writing a check for more money than there is in the account; a *sight draft* is payable on demand; and a *time draft* is payable after a certain number of days.

Draftsman (or drafter) A person who writes a legal document (especially the person who creates an original document) such as a **contract** or a legislative bill.

Dragnet clause A provision in a **mortgage** or similar document in which **security** is given not only for the present debt, but for past and future debts.

Drago doctrine The principle that one country should not intervene militarily in another country to force or secure payment of debts owed by the second country to citizens of the first.

Dram shop acts Laws that make bars and stores **liable** for some acts caused by persons who got drunk or bought liquor there.

Draw **1.** Prepare a legal document. **2.** Write out and sign a **bill** of exchange or make a **note** (see those words). **3.** Take money out of a bank account. **4.** Money a salesperson may take to cover expenses. The money is then subtracted from later sales. The fund this comes from is called a *drawing account*. **5.** Choose a **jury.**

Drawee **1.** A person to whom a **bill** of exchange (see that word) is addressed, and who is requested to pay the amount of the bill. **2.** A bank that has a **deposit** withdrawn from it.

Drawer The person drawing a **bill** of exchange (see that word) or signing a check.

Dred Scott case The pre-Civil War case that said black slaves were not **citizens** and had few rights.

Droit **1.** Right or justice. **2.** A law or the law. For example, *droit international* is **international law.** [pronounce: drwah]

Drop shipment The delivery of goods directly from manufacturer to retailer or to **consumer**, even though a **wholesaler** earns a profit for placing the order.

Dry **1.** **Passive**; inactive; **formal** or **nominal** only. For example, a *dry* **trust** is one in which the **trustee** is legal owner of property, but has no duties to perform other than the passive act of having the property in his or her name, and gains no profits from the trust. **2.** A state, country, or city where alcoholic beverages cannot be sold (or served).

Dual citizenship Holding citizenship in two countries. This can occur because a person was born in one country to parents who are citizens of another or because a country of which a person is a citizen still recognizes that citizenship after the person becomes a citizen of another country.

Dual court system   The American system of federal and state courts.

Dual purpose doctrine   The rule that in most cases if an employee is on a business trip, he or she is acting within the normal **course of employment** (see that word) even if doing something personal.

Duces tecum   (Latin) "Bring with you." The name for a type of **subpoena** (see that word) that commands a person to come to court and bring documents or other pieces of **evidence**.

Due   1. Owing; payable.   2. Just, proper, regular, lawful, sufficient, or reasonable. For example, "due care" means proper or reasonable care for the situation.

Due-bill   An "**I.O.U.**," especially a company's I.O.U., that can be sold by the person to whom money is owed to another person, and then cashed in for goods or services.

Due date   Day a tax or debt must be paid.

Due notice   Reasonable notice (varies with the situation).

Due process of law   The *Due Process Clause* of the U.S. **Constitution** requires that no person shall be deprived of life, liberty, or property without due process of law. The requirements of due process are regularly changed by the Supreme Court. They vary in detail from situation to situation, but the central core of the idea is that a person should always have **notice** and a real chance to present his or her side in a legal dispute and that no law or government procedure should be **arbitrary** or unfair. Some of the specifics of *due process* include the right to a **transcript** of court proceedings, the right to question adverse witnesses, etc.

Dummy   Sham; make believe; set up as a "front." For example, *dummy* incorporators are persons who initially set up a corporation to meet the formal requirements of a state's corporation laws and then drop out. It is perfectly proper in most cases.

Dump   1. Sell something in other countries for less than it is sold at home. Federal law prohibits some sales of this sort by foreign companies, and international trade agreements prohibit others.   2. Unload large quantities of goods regardless of price.

Dun   Demand payment on an overdue debt.

Dun and Bradstreet   A major supplier of business credit ratings.

Duplicate   1. A copy.   2. A new document made to take the place of an original.

Duplicity   1. Joining two or more separate reasons for a lawsuit in one paragraph, two or more subjects in one **legislative act,** etc. This is now usually permitted. Charging two or more unrelated crimes in one **indictment**, however, is usually not permitted.   **2.** Deception or "double dealing."

Duress   Unlawful pressure on a person to do what he or she would not otherwise have done. It includes force, threats of violence, physical restraint, etc.

Durham Rule   In states that use the *Durham Rule,* a **defendant** is not guilty of a crime because of **insanity** (see that word) if he or she was "suffering from a diseased or defective mental condition" at the time of the act and "there was a causal connection between the two."

Duty   1. An obligation to obey a law.   **2.** A legal obligation to another person. In this sense, when one person has a *"right"* to something, another person must have a *"duty"* to avoid interfering with that right.   **3.** Any obligation, whether legal, moral, or ethical.   **4.** A tax on imports or exports.

Duty of tonnage   Governmental port charges or port taxes on a boat.

Dwelling defense   The **castle doctrine** (see that word).

Dyer Act   A 1919 law making it a federal crime to take a stolen motor vehicle across a state line.

Dying declaration   Out-of-court words of a dying person about who killed him or her and how it happened. Normally, other persons' words are not good **evidence**, but here they are usually allowed.

Dynamite instruction   An **Allen charge** (see that word).

E.B.I.T.   Earnings before interest and taxes.

E.B.T.   *Examination before trial* of a **party** to a lawsuit. It is a part of the **discovery** process.

E.E.O.C.   **Equal Employment Opportunities Commission.**

E.F.T.S.   Electronic fund transfer system.

E.g.

E.g. Abbreviation for the Latin "exempli gratia" (for the sake of example). It is used in most law books to take the place of "for example."

E.I.S. Environmental Impact Statement.

E.O. Executive order.

E.P.A. Environmental Protection Agency. A U.S. agency that enforces pollution control, does environmental research, etc.

EPS Earnings per **share.**

E.R.I.S.A. Employee Retirement Income Security Act (see that word).

E.S.O.P. Employee stock ownership plan.

E.S.O.T. Employee stock ownership trust. A **trust fund** set up to fund an employee stock ownership plan, giving tax benefits to employer and employee.

Earlier maturity rule **Bonds** that come due first get paid off first even when the company must make unusual debt payments.

Earmarked Set aside for a particular purpose; money or property that is easily identified so that it can be separated from similar things.

Earned income **1.** Money or other compensation received for work. It does not include the profits gained from owning property. **2.** The *earned income credit* is a tax break given to some low-income workers.

Earned surplus **Retained earnings** (see that word).

Earnest money A **deposit** paid by a buyer to hold a seller to a deal and to show the buyer's **good faith** (see that word).

Earnings multiple The number by which an annual stock **dividend** must be multiplied to equal the stock's selling price.

Earnings per share A company's profits available to pay **dividends** on its **common stock** divided by the number of **shares** of stock owned by investors. *"Primary" earnings per share* and *"fully diluted" earnings per share* divide the available profits by not only the shares of common stock, but by everything that can be turned into common stock (**convertible** stock and bonds, **options, warrants,** etc.).

Earnings report See **statement** of income.

Easement An *easement* on a piece of land is the right of a specific nonowner (such as a next-door neighbor), the government, or the general public to use part of the land in a particular way. This right usually stays with the land when it is sold. Typical *easements* include the right of the owner of a piece of land with no streetfront to use a specific strip of another person's land to reach the street, or the right of a city to run a sewer line across a specific strip of an owner's land. The word for the land that gives up an easement is "**servient**" and, if there is one particular property that benefits from the easement, it is called "**dominant.**" Easements may be *affirmative* (where the landowner must permit something) or *negative* (where the landowner is prohibited from doing something). A *reciprocal negative easement* may be created when a landowner sells part of a property and places a negative easement on it. That easement may then also restrict the part kept by the owner.

Ecclesiastical courts   Religious courts that used to be powerful in England, and that affected the development of the law. Religious law was called **canon law.**

Economic rent   **Ground rent.**

Economic strike   A refusal to work because of a dispute over wages, hours, working conditions, etc. It is different from an **unfair labor practice** (see that word) strike and may result in loss of job.

Edict   A major law put out by a king or other head of state.

Educational expenses   Employee expenses to gain skills for a current job or to meet an employer's educational requirements may be tax **deductible,** but expenses to gain skills for a new job or to meet minimum educational requirements are not deductible. "*Educational expenses*" sometimes mean only the deductible ones.

Effect   **1.** To do, produce, accomplish, or force.   **2.** A result.   **3.** This is *not* "**affect.**" A handy sentence to remember the difference is "When you *effect* a change, you *affect* something and cause an *effect.*

Effective rate   See **tax rate.**

Effects   **1. Personal property.**   **2.** Personal property of a person making a will or of a dead person.

Efficient cause   See **proximate cause.**

Efficient market   A **stock, commodity,** etc., trading place or method that immediately gets and uses all available information, so that prices reflect full and current information.

Eight-hour laws   The federal laws that established the eight-hour workday and required payment for overtime.

Eighteenth Amendment

Eighteenth Amendment The 1919 **constitutional amendment** (see each word) that prohibited all alcoholic beverages until the amendment's **repeal** in 1933 by the Twenty-first Amendment.

Eighth Amendment The U.S. **constitutional** prohibition against excessive **bail** or **fines** and **cruel and unusual punishment**.

Eire See **eyre**.

Ejectione firmae (Latin) A **writ** of **ejectment** for a tenant who was wrongfully thrown out.

Ejectment The name for an old type of lawsuit to get back land taken away wrongfully. It was used primarily to establish **title** to land and was brought against a fictitious **defendant** called the *"casual ejector."*

Ejusdem generis (Latin) Of the same kind or type. Under the *ejusdem generis rule,* when a list in a document is followed by general words, those words should apply only to things of the same kind as the things on the list.

Election **1.** Any act of choosing. **2.** Choosing from among legal rights. For example, a husband or wife may have to *elect* (choose) between what was left in a **will** by the other one and what state law reserves as a minimum share of a husband's or wife's **estate.** (A husband might leave a wife "the house and ten thousand dollars" and state law may allow the wife to take one-third of the husband's total estate. The wife can have one but not both of these.) In the same sense, *election of remedies* is the choice of legally contradictory courses of action to protect a right. **3.** The choosing of an official by voting. A *general election* is one held regularly to choose public officials; a *primary election* is to choose the **candidates** of political parties; and a *special election* is to fill a vacancy at other times than those of a general election.

Election contest A challenge to the accuracy or validity of **election** results made by a loser. **Ballots** are usually recounted and their validity is examined.

Elector **1.** A voter. **2.** Member of the **electoral college** (see that word).

Electoral college A name for the persons chosen by voters to elect the president and vice-president. The *electoral college* is now almost a formality, and the vote of the general public in each state directly controls the election, though in a close election an *elector* might decide to vote differently from the way he or she was instructed.

Eleemosynary   Charitable. [pronounce: el-e-<u>mos</u>-e-nary]

Eleganter   Correctly, formally, and accurately.

Element   A basic part. For example, some of the *elements* of a **cause of action** for **battery** (see these words) are an intentional, unwanted physical contact. Each of these things ("intentional," "unwanted," etc.) is one *"element."*

Eleventh Amendment   The **constitutional** provision that prohibits the federal courts from handling a lawsuit against one of the states by a noncitizen of that state.

Eligibility   Being legally qualified. For example, *eligibility* for social security benefits means meeting all the legal requirements to get them.

Elisor   A person who is appointed by a court to take the place of a **sheriff** when the sheriff is not available or cannot act.

Eloignment   An old word for taking or concealing something away from the reach of a court.

Emancipation   Setting free. For example, a child is *emancipated* when the child is old enough so that the parents have no further right to control or obligation to support him or her.

Embargo   1. A government's refusal to allow the transportation of certain things in or out of the country.   2. A government's stopping the ships or planes of another country from coming in or going out.

Embedded   Not broken out as a separate item. Part of a larger statistic.

Embezzlement   The **fraudulent** and secret taking of money or property by a person who has been trusted with it. This usually applies to an employee's taking money and covering it up by faking business records or **account** books.

Emblements   Crops growing on a person's property.

Embracery   An old word for an attempt to bribe a jury.

Emergency doctrine   1. A person (such as a driver) is not required to take the same action in an emergency that would be required at other times, as long as the person used proper care before the emergency and did nothing reckless during the emergency.   2. If no proper person is available to give consent for emergency medical treatment for an unconscious adult or for a child, absolutely necessary treatment may be given anyway.   3. See also **Good Samaritan Doctrine** and **Rescue** Doctrine.

Eminent domain   The government's right and power to take private land for public use by paying for it.

Emit

Emit   Put out, **issue,** put into circulation.

Emolument   Any financial or other gain from employment.

Empanel   See **impanel.**

Emphyteutic lease   A lease on land that is long term and can be passed on to another person as long as the rent is paid.

Empirical   Based on observation or experiment.

Employee Retirement Income Security Act   A federal law that established a program to protect employees' pension plans. The law set up a fund to pay pensions when plans go broke and regulates pension plans as to *vesting* (when a person's pension rights become permanent), nondiversion of benefits to anyone other than those entitled, nondiscrimination against lower-paid employees, etc. See **pension plan, vested,** and **annuity.**

Employers liability acts   Federal and state laws defining under what circumstances an employer must pay for an employee's injuries and illnesses. These laws commonly **abolish** employers' **defenses** such as the **fellow servant rule** and **contributory negligence.** Many of these laws are now called **workers' compensation laws** (see that word), especially when they set up a fund for payments.

En   (French) In. For example, *en ventre sa mere* means "in its mother's womb." [pronounce: ahn <u>vahnt</u> sa mare]

En banc   (French) All the judges of a court participating in a case all together, rather than individually or in panels of a few.

En gros   (French) In **gross;** total; **wholesale.** [pronounce: ahn grow]

Enabling clause   The part of a **statute** that gives officials the power to put it into effect and enforce it.

Enabling power   **Power of appointment** (see that word).

Enabling statute   A law that grants new powers, usually to a public official, a county, or a city.

Enact   Put a **statute** into effect; pass a statute through a **legislature;** establish by law.

Encroachment   Unlawfully extending property to take over another person's property; for example, putting a fence too far over a boundary line.

Encumber   Make property subject to a **charge** or **liability.** See **encumbrance.**

Encumbrance   A **claim, charge,** or **liability** on property, such as a **lien** or **mortgage,** that lowers its value.

End balance method   Charging a full month's **interest** on all bills unpaid at the end of each monthly billing period. (If a purchase is made on the last day of the month and payment made one day later, "1 percent interest" could turn into a true **annual percentage rate** (see that word) of over 300 percent by this method.)

End position   The legal and financial status of a person at the end of a **contract,** such as the options available to someone who has **leased** equipment (renew the contract, return the equipment, pay for damages, etc.).

Endorsement   See **indorsement.**

Endowment   **1.** Setting up a fund, usually for a public institution such as a school.   **2.** The fund in no. 1.   **3.** An **insurance** policy that pays a set amount at a set time or, if the person insured dies, pays the money to a **beneficiary.**

Enfeoffment   See **feoffment.**

Enforcement   **1.** Carrying out the commands of a law. For example, the *enforcement* powers of several U.S. **constitutional amendments** give Congress the power to **enact** laws to carry out the amendments' purposes.   **2.** Putting something into effect. For example, the *Enforcement of Foreign Judgments Act,* adopted by many states, gives persons who hold money **judgments** in other states the same right to collect on them (by **levy** and **execution**) that a citizen of the state would have to collect on a judgment in the state.   **3.** Short for *law enforcement* or police.

Enfranchise   **1.** Make free.   **2.** Give the right to vote.

Engage   Take part in or do. To *"engage"* in a particular activity is to do it more than once, and probably regularly.

Engagement   **Contract** or obligation.

Engrossment (or engrossing)   **1.** Making a final or "good" copy of a document, often just prior to using it for some formal purpose, such as voting on a **bill** or executing a **deed.**   **2.** **Cornering** a market.

Enhancement   Increasing or making larger. For example, a criminal penalty may be *enhanced* (made longer or worse), even though "enhancement" is usually thought of as being good, as increasing value or attractiveness, etc.

Enjoin   Require or command. A court's issuing of an **injunction** (see that word) directing a person or persons to do or, more likely, to refrain from doing certain acts.

Enjoyment   The exercise of a right; the ability to use a right.

Enlarge

Enlarge **1.** Make larger. **2.** Extend a time limit. **3.** Release a person from **custody.**

Enoch Arden laws Laws on presumed **death** after a long absence.

Enroll **Register** or **record** a formal document in the proper office or file.

Enrolled bill **1.** A **bill** that has gone through the steps necessary to make it a law. **2.** The *enrolled bill rule* is that once a law has been fully formalized, its wording may not be challenged by referring to previous versions.

Ensue Follow later, especially follow later as a logical result.

Entail Restrict an **inheritance** in land so that it can be passed on only to children, then children's children, etc.

Enter **1.** Go into. **2.** Go onto land in order to take possession. **3.** Become a part of. **4.** Place formally on the **record;** write down formally in the proper place. For example, to *"enter an appearance"* is to submit a piece of paper to a court saying that you are now formally a part of a case, either as a **party** or as a lawyer.

Entering judgment The formal act of recording a court's **judgment** in the court's permanent records after the judgment has been given or announced.

Enticement **1.** An old form of lawsuit brought because of the seduction or taking away of a wife. **2.** Trying to persuade a child to come to a secluded place with the intent to commit an unlawful sexual act.

Entirety As a whole; not divided into parts.

Entitlement **Absolute** (complete) right to something (such as social security) once you show that you meet the legal requirements to get it.

Entrapment The act of government officials or agents (usually police) of inducing a person to commit a crime that the person would not have committed without the inducement. This is done for the purposes of prosecuting the person. It is not lawful in most cases, and a criminal charge based on *entrapment* should fail. *Entrapment* is an **affirmative defense** (see that word).

Entry **1.** The act of making or *entering* a formal record by writing it down. **2.** The thing written down in no. 1. **3.** Going into a building unlawfully to commit a crime.

Enumerated   Mentioned specifically; listed.

Enumeratio unius   (Latin) **Expressio unius** (see that word).

Enure   See **inure.**

Environmental Impact Statement   Documents required by federal and state laws to accompany proposals for projects or programs that might harm the environment.

Envoy   An **ambassador** or special government **minister.**

Eo   (Latin) *"That,"* as in the phrases *eo die* (on that day); *eo instanti* (at that instant); *eo intuitu* (with that intent); and *eo nomine* (by that name).

Equal Credit Opportunity Act   A federal law prohibiting discrimination based on race, color, religion, sex, national origin, or age in any **credit** transaction.

Equal degree   An equal number of steps or **degrees** (see that word) away from a common ancestor.

Equal Employment Opportunity Commission   A federal agency that works toward ending discrimination based on race, color, sex, age, or national origin in all work-related activities such as hiring, promotion, etc.

Equal protection of laws   A **constitutional** requirement that the government shall in no way fail to treat equals equally, set up illegal categories to justify treating persons unfairly, or give unfair or unequal treatment to a person based on that person's race, religion, etc. This is found in the *Equal Protection Clause* of the **Fourteenth Amendment.**

Equal Rights Amendment   A proposed constitutional amendment to ban sex discrimination.

Equal Time Act   A federal law that requires radio and television stations that give (or sell) time to candidates for public office to also give (or sell) time to qualified opponents.

Equalization   The process of adjusting **assessments** and taxes on real estate in order to make sure that properties are properly valued and are taxed fairly according to value.

Equipment trust   The method of financing business equipment in which **title** to the property is held by **trustees** until paid for.

Equitable   1. Just, fair, and right for a particular situation. For example, *equitable election* is choosing between two things when it is not fair to have both. The *doctrine of equitable election* is the rule that a person cannot accept something given in a **will** and also challenge the validity of the will for other purposes. Also, whenever something *should* exist but does *not* exist under a strict interpretation of the law, a court may decide in fairness that it *does* exist. Thus, there can be such things as *equitable* **adoptions, mortgages, liens,** etc. An *equitable adoption* is a court's allowing a person to **inherit** property from someone who promised to **adopt** him or her and who acted as if the adoption really took place. An *equitable mortgage* is a court's deciding that a **deed** transferring property was really given to **secure** a debt, so that a **mortgage,** not a complete transfer of property, exists. In each case, *"equitable"* can be read as "not strictly according to law, but we'll enforce it because of fairness." **2.** An *"equitable action"* is a lawsuit based on a court's **equity** (see that word) powers, often to enforce rights like those in no. 1.

Equity **1.** Fairness in a particular situation. **2.** The name for a system of courts that originated in England to take care of legal problems when the existing laws did not cover some situations in which a person's rights were violated by another person. **3.** A court's power to "do justice" where specific laws do not cover the situation. **4.** The value of property after all charges against it are paid. This is also called *net worth* or *net value.* **5. Stock.** Sometimes **common stock** only.

Equity financing A corporation raising money by selling **stock** rather than by *debt financing,* which is selling **bonds** or borrowing. Stocks, and other stocklike **securities,** are called *equity security* or *equity shares.*

Equity investor If Jay borrows money from Elizabeth to buy equipment that is then **leased** to Charles in a deal with special tax advantages, Jay is called the *equity investor.*

Equity of redemption The right of a person who has lost property through a mortgage **foreclosure** to get it back by paying all money owed, interest, and costs within a state-specified time period.

Equivalents doctrine The rule in **patent** law that if two devices do the same thing in the same basic way, they are the same even if different in name or form.

Erasure of record The procedure by which a person's **criminal record** (see those words) or juvenile delinquency record may be destroyed, or at least sealed and made unavailable for public access.

Ergo (Latin) Therefore.

Erie v. Tompkins The case establishing the principle that (except for situations involving the Constitution and federal laws) the law used to decide a case in federal court should be state law. This case ended the idea that there was a separate body of federal **common law** (see that word) for all cases.

Erratum (Latin) Mistake.

Error A mistake made by a judge in the procedures used at trial, or in making legal **rulings** during the trial, that allows one side in a lawsuit to ask a higher court to review the case. If the error is substantial, it is called *reversible error* by the higher court. If it is trivial, it is called *harmless error*.

Escalator clause **1.** A **contract term** (see those words) that allows a price to rise if costs rise. Or, in the case of a maximum payment **regulated** by the government (such as rent controls), for the price to rise if the maximum is raised or eliminated. **2.** See **cost of living clause.**

Escape clause A **contract** provision that allows a person to avoid doing something or to avoid **liability** if certain things happen.

Escheat The state's getting property because no owner can be found. For example, if a person dies and no person can be found who can legally inherit that person's property, the government gets it.

Escobedo rule When a suspect in police **custody** has asked for and been denied a lawyer, nothing the suspect says after that can be used in a criminal trial. See **Miranda** rule for even broader protections.

Escrow Money, property, or documents belonging to person A and held by person B until person A takes care of an obligation to person C. For example, a mortgage company may require a homeowner with a **mortgage** to make monthly payments into an *escrow* account to take care of the yearly tax bill when it comes due.

Esq. Short for "Esquire"; a title given to lawyers.

Essence Indispensable basis or core. See **"time is of the essence."**

Essoin An old English excuse for being absent from court, presented by a person called an *essoiner* sent for the purpose.

Establish **1.** Settle or prove a point. **2.** Set up, create, or found.

Establishment clause That part of the U.S. Constitution that states "Congress shall make no law respecting an *establishment* of religion, etc."

Estate **1.** The **interest** a person has in property; a person's right or **title** to property. For example, a "*future estate*" is a property interest that will come about only in the future if an uncertain event takes place. **2.** The property itself in which a person has an interest; for example, *real estate* (land) or a *decedent's estate* (things left by a dead person). **3.** For types of *estates*, such as **absolute, conditional, executed, executory, contingent, dominant, servient, vested,** at **will,** in **common,** in **expectancy,** in **fee simple,** in **fee tail,** etc., see those words.

Estate planning Carrying out a person's wishes for property to be passed on at his or her death and gaining maximum legal benefit from that property by best using the laws of **wills, trusts, insurance, property,** and **taxes.**

Estate tax A tax paid on the property left by a dead person. It is paid on the property as a whole before it is divided up and handed out. This is the opposite of an **inheritance** tax, which is based on the money each individual inherits and is paid by each **heir** separately.

Estate trust A **trust,** used to qualify property for the **marital** deduction from **estate** taxes, that puts property into a trust for a surviving spouse with the remaining trust property going into that spouse's estate at death for federal estate tax purposes.

Estimated tax Some persons with income other than salaries must estimate, "report," and pay income tax four times a year.

Estin doctrine The rule that while one state must recognize (give effect to) a **divorce** granted in another state, there is no need to recognize a **support** order unless the other state had **jurisdiction** over the spouse ordered to pay support.

Estoppel **1.** Being stopped by your own prior acts from claiming a right against another person who has legitimately relied on those acts. For example, if a person signs a **deed,** that person may be *estopped* from later going to court claiming that the deed is wrong. **2.** Being stopped from proving something (even if true) in court because of something you said before that shows the opposite (even if false).

Estoppel by judgment The inability to raise an issue against a person in court because a judge has already decided that precise issue between the persons.

Estoppel certificate   A **mortgage** company's written statement of the amount due on a mortgage as of a particular date.

Estover   **1.** An allowance for basics such as food, shelter, and clothing.   **2.** A tenant's right to cut timber for basic property maintenance (and sometimes for fuel).

Et al.   (Latin) Abbreviation for *et alia* ("and others"). For example, "*Smith et al.*" means Smith plus a list of other persons.

Et non   (Latin) "And not"; has the same use as **absque** hoc.

Et seq.   (Latin) Abbreviation for *et sequentes* ("and the following"). For example, "*page 27 et seq.*" means "page twenty-seven and the following pages."

Et ux.   Abbreviation for *et uxor* ("and wife") seen on old legal documents. For example, "This deed made by John Smith *et ux.*"

Et vir.   (Latin) "And husband." See **et ux.** for use.

Ethical considerations   General guidelines for proper behavior as a lawyer. These appear in the **Code of Professional Responsibility.**

Ethics   **1.** Professional standards of conduct for lawyers and judges.   **2.** Standards of fair and honest conduct in general.

Euclidian zoning   **Zoning** laws that keep all apartment houses, shops, businesses, etc., out of single-home residential areas.

Eurodollar   A U.S. dollar deposited with a bank in Europe (or anywhere outside the U.S.).

Euthanasia   **Mercy killing** (see that word).

Evasion   Eluding or dodging. *Tax evasion* is the illegal nonpayment or underpayment of taxes due (while *tax avoidance* is the legal reduction or nonpayment of taxes by using **deductions, exemptions,** etc.).

Evasive   Elusive or shifty. If a **pleading** is *evasive,* the other side in the lawsuit may demand a *more definite statement.* If an answer to a question asked in **discovery** is *evasive,* the other side may get a court **order** compelling a proper answer.

Evergreen contract   An agreement that automatically renews itself each year unless one side gives advance notice to the other side that it will end.

Eviction   A landlord putting a tenant out of property, either by taking direct action (a "*self-help*" *eviction*) or, more often, by going to court.

Evidence   **1.** All types of information (observations, recollections, documents, concrete objects, etc.) presented at a trial or other hearing.   **2.** Any information that might be used for a future trial. **3.** For types of evidence, such as **circumstantial, demonstrative, direct, hearsay, parol, probative, real, state's,** etc., see those words.

Evidence law The rules and principles about whether evidence can be admitted (accepted for proof) in a trial and how to evaluate its importance.

Evidentiary fact A fact that is learned directly from **testimony** or other **evidence.** Conclusions drawn from *evidentiary facts* are called *"ultimate facts."*

Ex (Latin) A prefix meaning many things including: out of, no longer, from, because of, by, and with.

Ex aequo et bono (Latin) By **equity** and **good faith;** in justice and fairness.

Ex arbitrio judicis (Latin) By the judge's **discretion.**

Ex assensu curiae (Latin) By leave of the court; with the judge's consent.

Ex cathedra (Latin) "From the chair"; authoritative.

Ex contractu (Latin) "From a **contract.**" A lawsuit based on a contract, rather than on a **tort** (see that word).

Ex curia (Latin) Out of court.

Ex debito justitiae (Latin) "From a debt of justice." Something that may be done as of right.

Ex defectu sanguinis (Latin) "From a defect of blood"; because there are no children.

Ex delicto (Latin) "From wrongdoing." A lawsuit based on a **tort** (or **crime**) rather than on a **contract** (see those words).

Ex dividend A **stock** sold without the right to collect a **dividend** that has been declared but not yet paid.

Ex facie (Latin) **1.** "From the **face**" of a document. **2.** Apparently.

Ex facto (Latin) As a matter of fact; happening because of a fact, a person's actions, or an occurrence.

Ex gratia (Latin) From **grace** or as a favor and not as a right.

Ex integro (Latin) New.

Ex lege (Latin) As a matter of law; as a result of a law.

Ex mero motu (Latin) "On his own **motion** or motive"; voluntarily.

Ex necessitate legis (Latin) "From legal necessity"; **implied** by law.

Ex necessitate rei   (Latin) "From the necessity of the case or matter"; **implied** from the facts.

Ex officio   **1.** By the power of the office (official position) alone. **2.** Acting as a private citizen, not as an official. (This is a popular, not legal, meaning.)

Ex parte   (Latin) With only one side present. For example, an *ex parte order* is one made on the request of one side in a lawsuit when (or because) the other side does not show up in court (because the other side failed to show up, because the other side did not need to be present for the order to **issue,** or because there *is* no other side). [pronounce: ex par-tee]

Ex post facto   (Latin) After the fact. An *ex post facto law* is one that attempts to make an action a crime that was not a crime at the time it was done, or a law that attempts to reduce a person's rights based on a past act that was not subject to the law when it was done. *Ex post facto* laws are prohibited by the **Constitution.**

Ex rel.   When a case is titled *"State ex rel. Doe v. Roe"* it means that the state is bringing a lawsuit for Doe against Roe. The phrase is short for the Latin *ex relatione,* "on relation," or "from the information given by."

Ex rights   A **stock** sold without its special right to buy a new stock **issue.**

Ex tempore   (Latin)   **1.** Without preparation.   **2.** Because of the passage of time.

Ex vi termini   (Latin) "From the force of the word (or phrase)"; explained by itself with no need to refer to other words.

Exaction   An official wrongfully demanding payment of a fee for official services when no payment is due.

Examination   **1.** An investigation; for example, the search through **title** records for any problems before buying property or the inquiry by the **patent** office into the novelty and usefulness of an invention.   **2.** A questioning; for example, the questioning of a witness under **oath** or the questioning in a hearing of a **bankrupt** about his or her full financial situation.   **3.** The order of questioning a witness is usually *"direct examination"* (by the side that called the witness), *"cross examination"* (by the other side), *"redirect," "recross,"* etc.

Examiner   **1.** The name for a type of **hearing examiner** or **administrative** judge.   **2.** A person authorized to conduct an official examination; for example, a *bank examiner* (to look into a

Exceptio

bank's dealings); a *bar examiner* (to test law students who apply for **bar** admission); etc.

Exceptio (Latin) An **exception** or **objection.**

Exception **1.** Leaving something or someone out intentionally; an **exclusion.** **2.** A formal disagreement with a judge's refusal of a request or **overruling** of an **objection.** It is a statement that the lawyer does not agree with the judge's decision, but will save the objections until later (usually for an **appeal**). It is not necessary to take *exceptions* to appeal the decision in most courts.

Excess Too much. For example, *"excess of jurisdiction"* refers to a judge's actions that go beyond the proper actions he or she can take under the court's powers.

Excess policy **Insurance** that pays for only losses greater than those covered by another policy.

Excess profits tax A tax on business profits over what is considered reasonable (calculated by return on investment or past yearly averages) and usually imposed in time of war.

Excessive bail, fine, or punishment These are all forbidden by the **Eighth Amendment** to the U.S. **Constitution.** "Excessive" is usually defined as "disproportionate to the offense."

Exchange **1.** A swap or **barter**; a transaction that involves no money and in which no price or value is set for any item involved. **2.** An organization set up to buy and sell **securities** such as **stocks.** **3.** The payment of debts in different places by a transfer of **credits** such as by **bill** of exchange.

Exchequer The English treasury department.

Excise A tax on the manufacture, sale, or use of goods or on the carrying on of an occupation or activity.

Excited utterance A statement made about an event while still excited or under stress. It is an exception to the **hearsay rule**, and may be used as **evidence** in federal court.

Exclusion **1.** Keeping someone or something out. **2.** Not counting something. For example, a certain amount of money may be given away each year without paying a tax on giving it away. This is called an *exclusion.* See also **deduction, exemption,** and **credit.**

Exclusionary clause A part of a **contract** that tries to restrict the legal **remedies** available to one side if the contract is broken.

Exclusionary rule **1.** A reason why even **relevant** (see that word) **evidence** will be kept out of a trial. **2.** *"The exclusionary rule"* often means the rule that illegally gathered evidence may not be used in a **criminal** trial.

Exclusive   **1.** Shutting out all others; sole; one only. For example, if a court has *exclusive jurisdiction* over a subject, no other court in the area can decide a lawsuit on that subject, and if a **union** has *exclusive recognition* or *exclusive bargaining rights*, the employer may not even consult with another union. **2.** For *exclusive agency* or *exclusive authorization*, see **listing**. **3.** For *exclusive contract*, see **output contract**.

Exculpate   Provide an **excuse** or **justification**; show that someone has not committed a crime or a wrongful act.

Exculpatory clause   A provision in a **trust** arrangement by which the **trustee** is relieved of all responsibility for things that go wrong or for losses if the trustee acts in good faith.

Excuse   A reason that will stand up in court for an unintentional action. For example, if you kill someone by accident and it was not your fault, it is *excusable homicide*.

Execute   Complete, make, perform, do, or carry out. For example, to *execute a* **contract** is to sign it and make it valid, but to *execute an obligation* created by the contract is to carry it out or perform it. If something is *executed*, nothing more needs to be done. This is the opposite of **executory**.

Execution   **1.** Carrying out or completion (see **execute**). **2.** Signing and finalizing (and handing over, if needed) a document such as a **deed**.   **3.** The government's putting a person to death.   **4.** An official carrying out of a court's **order** or **judgment**. For example, a *body execution* is a court order to a **sheriff** or other official to bring a person to court; and a **writ** of *execution* orders a court official to take a **debtor's** property to pay a court-decided debt, usually by then holding an *execution sale*.

Executive   **1.** The branch of government that carries out the laws (as opposed to the **judicial** and **legislative** branches). The **administrative** branch.   **2.** A high official in a branch of government, a company, or other organization.

Executive agreement   A document, similar to a **treaty**, that is signed by the president and that does not require the approval of the **Senate** as a treaty does.

Executive Office of the President   The organizations that give the U.S. president most of the direct staff help on national issues. These organizations include the *Office of Management*

Executive officer

and Budget, the National Security Council, the Council on Environmental Quality, etc.

Executive officer   One of several top officials of a company or one particular official.

Executive order   A law put out by the president or a governor that does not need to be passed by the **legislature.**

Executive privilege   The right of the president and subordinates to keep some information (primarily documents) from public disclosure. This includes more than military and diplomatic secrets, but far less than whatever the executive branch might want to keep secret. See also **Freedom of Information Act**.

Executive session   A closed meeting of a **committee**, a **board**, etc.

Executor   A person selected by a person making a will to **administer** the will and to hand out the property after the person making the will dies.

Executory   Still to be carried out; incomplete; depending on a future act or event. The opposite of **executed.**

Exemplars   Physical identification such as fingerprints, voiceprints, blood samples, handwriting samples, **lineup** identifications, etc.

Exemplary damages   See **punitive damages.**

Exemplification   An official copy of a public document used as **evidence.**

Exemption   **1.** Freedom from a general burden, duty, service, or tax.   **2.** The subtraction from income for tax purposes of a certain amount of money for each family member. Each *exemption* lowers the income on which a person must pay taxes. See also **credit, deduction,** and **exclusion. 3.** Property that may be kept by a **debtor** when property is taken away from the debtor by a court order such as in a **judgment** debt or **bankruptcy.**

Exequatur   Having an American lawsuit *"clothed with an exequatur"* means having it validated by the local court in order to have it recognized and enforced overseas.

Exercise   Make use of. For example, to *"exercise a purchase option"* is to make use of a right to buy something by buying it.

Exercise price   See **striking price.**

Exhaustion of remedies   A person must take all reasonable steps to get satisfaction from an **administrative agency** before taking a problem with that agency to court (and to get satisfaction from a state government before going into federal court). This is called "exhaustion of administrative (or state) remedies."

Exhibit **1.** Any object or document offered as **evidence** (in a trial, **hearing, deposition, audit,** etc.). If accepted, it is marked to identify it. **2.** Any document attached to a **pleading, affidavit,** or other formal paper.

Exigence A sudden event that requires immediate attention; an urgent need.

Eximbank The U.S. Export-Import Bank that finances some purchases of American goods in foreign countries.

Exoneration **1.** Clearing of a crime or other wrongdoing; exculpation. **2.** Removal of a burden or a **duty.** **3.** The right of a person who pays a debt for another person to be reimbursed by that person. **4.** The right to be paid off on a **negotiable instrument.**

Exordium The introductory clause of a **will,** stating that it is a valid will.

Expatriation The voluntary giving up of a country's **citizenship.** This includes doing a voluntary act, such as joining another country's army, that the person does not consider as "voluntarily" giving up citizenship, but that the country stripping the citizenship does.

Expectancy Something hoped for. For example, an **inheritance** under a **will** is an *expectancy* because the person making the will might change his or her mind. A right is "expectant" if a change in circumstances can end it.

Expensing Taking a tax **deduction** for the cost of an **asset** rather than taking **depreciation** for that cost.

Experience rating A change in an **insurance** policy's cost due to an unusually high or low number of claims made.

Expert witness A person possessing special knowledge or experience who is allowed to **testify** at a trial not only about facts (like an ordinary witness) but also about the professional conclusions he or she draws from these facts.

Exploit **1.** Make use of; use a natural resource; take advantage of an opportunity. **2.** Take unfair advantage; use illegally.

Exports clause A U.S. **constitutional** ban on individual states imposing import or export taxes.

Expository statute A law that is **enacted** to explain the meaning of a previously enacted law.

Express

Express Clear, definite, direct, or actual (as opposed to **implied**); known by explicit words.

Expressio unius (Latin) Short for "expressio unius est exclusio alterios" (the mention of one thing rules out other things not mentioned). This is a rule for interpreting documents. Most rules of this sort have their opposites, however, and are used by judges to justify decisions rather than to make them.

Expropriation The taking of private property for public use.

Expulsion The power of each house of a **legislature** to vote to throw out its members for prohibited conduct.

Expunge Blot out, obliterate, or strike out. For example, to *expunge* an **arrest record** is to wipe it completely and physically "off the books."

Extension 1. A lengthening of time; for example, in the **term** of a **lease** or in the time a person may pay a debt without extra payment. 2. *"Extending a case"* means a judge's applying the rule that decided a case to another case that is only somewhat similar. 3. *"Extension of remarks"* is the inclusion of speeches and materials in the **Congressional Record** that were not actually presented orally in a **House** or **Senate** session.

Extenuating circumstances Surrounding facts that make a crime less evil or blameworthy. They do not lower the crime to a less serious one, but do tend to reduce punishment.

External financing A corporation's raising money by selling **stock** or by borrowing.

Exterterritoriality The freedom from a foreign country's local laws enjoyed by **ambassadors** and many subordinates when living in that country. (*Not* **extraterritoriality**; see that word.)

Extinguishment The ending of a right, power, contract, or property interest. It may end because of a merging with a bigger thing. For example, a right of **tenancy** *extinguishes* not only if the tenant moves out, but also if the tenant buys the house.

Extort 1. To compel or coerce; for example, to get a confession by depriving a person of food and water. 2. To get something by illegal threats of harm to person, property, or reputation.

Extortion Any illegal taking of money, property, services, etc. by using threats, force, or the power of public office.

Extra 1. Outside of. 2. In addition to.

Extra legem (Latin) "Outside of the law." Something that is illegal or, while not illegal or even "wrong," is outside the law's protection.

Extradition   One country (or state) giving up a person to another one when the second country requests the person for a trial on a **criminal** charge or for punishment after a trial.

Extrajudicial   Unconnected with court business, outside of court.   **2.** Beyond the proper scope of court business.   **3.** Not having legal effect, though said or done by a judge. See **dictum.**

Extralateral right   See **Apex rule.**

Extraneous evidence   **Evidence** about a **contract** or other document that comes from other than the document itself. Also called evidence **aliunde.**

Extraordinary remedy   A group of actions a court will take only if more usual legal remedies will not suffice. These include **habeas corpus** and **mandamus** (see those words).

Extraterritoriality   The operation of a country's laws outside of its physical boundaries; for example, the U.S.'s right to bring to trial and punish its soldiers in another country for crimes committed on a U.S. base there. (*Not* **exterterritoriality**;   see   that word.)

Extremis   (Latin) Last illness or mortal injury.

Extrinsic evidence   Facts drawn from things outside the **contract** or other document in question. For example, the fact that a person was forced to sign a contract is *extrinsic* to the "**face**" (words) of the contract itself.

Eyewitness   A person with firsthand knowledge of an event. Someone who can testify as to what he or she saw or heard or smelled, etc.

Eyre   A court of traveling judges in old England.

F   **1.** Federal Reporter (see **National Reporter System**). "F.2d." is the second **series** of the Federal Reporter.   **2.** Following; for example, "26f." means "page 26 and the next page," and 26ff. means page 26 plus the next pages.

F.A.A. Federal Aviation Administration; the branch of the U.S. Department of Transportation that regulates all air travel safety matters. See also **C.A.B.**

F.A.S. Free along side. A price that includes shipping costs and delivery along side the ship.

F.A.S.B. Financial Accounting Standards Board.

F.B.I. Federal Bureau of Investigation. The U.S. Justice Department branch that investigates violations of federal law not specifically handled by other agencies.

F.C.C. Federal Communications Commission. The U.S. agency that **regulates** television, telephone, radio, etc.

F.C.I.A. Foreign Credit Insurance Association.

F.C.I.C. Federal Crop Insurance Corporation.

F.D.A. Food and Drug Administration. The federal agency that **regulates** the safety of food, drugs, cosmetics, etc.

F.D.I.C. Federal Deposit Insurance Corporation. It insures bank **deposits** for individual depositors.

F.E.P.C. Fair Employment Practice Commission. A state or local government agency that administers employment anti**discrimination** laws.

FHA 1. Federal Housing Administration. It insures housing loans through approved lenders on approved homes. **2.** Farmers Home Administration. A federal agency that provides rural housing and other loans.

F.H.L.B. Federal Home Loan Bank. Savings banks and other financial institutions that may borrow from a regional federal bank to make home loans.

F.H.L.M.C. Federal Home Loan Mortgage Corporation. A federal agency that buys **first mortgages** (see that word) from members of the Federal Reserve System and other approved banks. Also called "*Freddie Mac.*"

F.I.C.A. "Federal Insurance Contributions Act." The social security tax.

FIFO "First in, first out," a method of calculating the worth of **inventory**. Under this accounting method, if a merchant buys a blivit for a dollar, then buys another for two dollars, then sells either blivit, the remaining blivit is worth two dollars. See also **LIFO** and **NIFO.**

F.L.R.A. Federal Labor Relations Authority. It handles labor problems with unions representing federal employees.

F.L.S.A. **Fair Labor Standards Act** (see that word).

F.M.C.S.   Federal Mediation and Conciliation Service. It helps resolve labor disputes.

F.M.V.   Fair market value.

F.N.M.A.   Federal National Mortgage Association. A government sponsored, but privately owned, purchaser of home **mortgages.** Also called "*Fannie Mae.*"

F.O.B.   "Free on board." The selling price of goods includes transportation costs to the F.O.B. point, which is a specific place named in the contract.

F.O.I.A.   Freedom of Information Act (see that word).

F.P.C.   Federal Power Commission. It **regulates** the interstate transportation, production, and use of electric power and natural gas.

F.P.R.   Federal procurement regulations. Rules for federal government buying.

F.R.A.P.   Federal Rules of Appellate Procedure.

F.R.B.   Federal Reserve Board.

F.R.C.P.   Federal Rules of **Civil Procedure** (see that word).

F.R.D.   Federal Rules Decisions (see that word).

F.T.C.   Federal Trade Commission. It enforces prohibitions against "**unfair competition**" in business and "unfair or deceptive acts or trade practices"; it also enforces federal laws such as **Truth-in-Lending.**

F.Y.   Fiscal year.

F.Supp.   Federal Supplement.

Fabricated evidence   Facts that have been created or changed to use as false **evidence** in a trial or facts that have been faked to mislead officials.

Face   The language of a document including everything in it (not just the front page), but excluding things about the document that do not appear in it. For example, a **contract** can be valid "*on its face*" even though a person was forced to sign it at gunpoint and no court would uphold it.

Face value   The formal cash-in value written on a **note** or other financial document, not anything more for **interest** or other charges normally added on and not its fluctuating value in the marketplace.

Facilitation   Doing something intentionally to make it easier for another person to commit a crime.

Facility of payment clause   An agreement in an **insurance** contract allowing the insurer to make payments to a particular person to hold for the person ultimately entitled to the money.

Facsimile   Exact copy.

Fact   **1.** An act; a thing that took place; an event.   **2.** Something that exists and is real as opposed to what should exist. For example, a *"question of fact"* is about what is or what happened, while a *"question of law"* is about how the law affects what happened and what should have happened according to law. **3.** Something that exists and is real as opposed to opinion or supposition.

Fact situation   A summary of the facts of a case without any comments or legal conclusions.

Facto et animo   See **animus et factum.**

Factor   A person who is given goods to sell and who gets a **commission** for selling them.

Factor's (or agent's) acts   State laws that protect buyers of goods sold by **agents,** whether or not the owner approved the sale.

Factum   **1.** (Latin) Act; fact; central fact or act upon which a question turns.   **2.** Old word for an appeal **brief** or, for a statement of facts.   **3.** *Factum probandum* is a "fact to be proved" or one in issue in a case, and *factum probans* is an **evidentiary fact** (see that word) used to prove the main issues.

Failure of consideration   The situation that exists when something that is offered as part of a deal becomes worthless or ceases to exist before the deal is completely carried out.

Failure of issue   Dying without children.

Faint pleader   A **pleading** in a lawsuit that is false or that has false or misleading information, usually to trick someone not participating in the lawsuit.

Fair comment   The **common law** (pre**constitutional**) right to comment, within limits, upon the conduct of public officials without being **liable** for **defamation** (see that word). It is the right to be "honestly wrong" in public.

Fair Credit Billing Act   A federal law **regulating** billing disputes and making credit card companies partially responsible for items bought by **consumers.**

Fair Credit Reporting Acts   Federal and state laws **regulating** the organizations that investigate, store, and give out **consumer credit** (see that word) information, organizations that collect bills, etc. Consumers are given rights to know about investigations, see and dispute their files, etc.

Fair hearing   The word many **administrative agencies** use for their trial-like decision-making process, which is used when a person **appeals** an administrative decision. The **hearing** does not have to use full trial rules or procedures and is "fair" because it follows rules, not because persons always get what they need or deserve.

Fair Labor Standards Act   The federal law that set minimum wages and maximum hours for workers in industries engaged in **interstate commerce,** prohibited the labor of children under sixteen, etc.

Fair market value   See **market value.**

Fair trade   The fixing of a retail price for an item by the manufacturer. This is now illegal in most cases where the manufacturer is not the retailer.

Fair trial   A trial before a competent, **impartial** judge and an impartial jury in an atmosphere of judicial calm.

Fair use   The limited use that may be made of something **copyrighted** without infringing the copyright.

Fairness doctrine   The rule that broadcasters must present, or give others a chance to present, all sides of major public issues if they present one side. See also **Equal Time Act.**

False   **1.** Intentionally or knowingly untrue.   **2.** Untrue.

False arrest   Any unlawful restraint or deprivation of a person's liberty by a public official. It is a **tort.**

False imprisonment   See **false arrest.**

False pretenses   A lie told to cheat another person out of his or her money or property. It is a crime in most states, though the precise definition varies.

False representation   Similar to **false pretenses,** but the basis for a lawsuit rather than a crime. To sue for *false representation,* you must prove that a person told a lie to cheat you and that you were hurt financially by relying on that lie.

False return   **1.** A **sheriff's** or other court officer's certification that something is true (or was done) that is false (or was not done). See **sewer service** for an example.   **2.** A **tax return** that is intentionally (or grossly, negligently) wrong.

False swearing (or oath)   Lying on an **affidavit** or under **oath** in an official proceeding other than a court proceeding. A less serious form of **perjury** (see that word).

False verdict

False verdict A **jury's verdict** that is so unjust or out-of-line from the facts that the judge may set it aside. See judgement **non obstante veredicto.**

Falsus in uno (Latin) The rule that if a jury believes that any part of what a witness says is deliberately false, the jury may disregard it all as being false.

Family A broad word that can mean, among other things: **1.** Any household or group of persons living together as a single group. **2.** Parents and children. **3.** Persons related by blood or marriage. *"Family"* is usually defined differently for different purposes. For example, it might mean different things under a state's zoning laws and its tax laws.

Family car doctrine (or family purpose doctrine) The rule that the owner of a car will usually be **liable** for damage done by a family member driving the owner's car. This rule has been limited or rejected by most states.

Family corporation (or partnership) A **corporation** (or **partnership**) set up to spread income among family members, reducing the total tax bill.

Family court **1.** A court that may handle proceedings for child **abuse** and **neglect, support, paternity, custody,** juvenile delinquency, etc. **2.** A **domestic** relations court that handles **divorces, separations,** etc.

Family law See **domestic** relations law.

Fannie Mae See **F.N.M.A.**

Farm Credit Administration A federal agency that supervises the Farm Credit System of federal land banks and associated banks and **cooperatives.**

Fascism **Absolutism** (see that word) as practiced by a central state that allows private ownership of property, but makes all economic and social decisions from the top. Under *fascism,* individuals exist to serve the state.

Fatal A mistake in legal procedure is *"fatal"* if it is serious enough to unfairly hurt the side that complains about it. For example, a fatal **error** (see that word) could cause a new trial.

Fault **1.** Negligence; lack of care; failure to do a duty. **2.** Defect or imperfection. **3.** According to the **Uniform Commercial Code,** *fault* means a "wrongful act, omission, or breach."

Fauntleroy doctrine The rule that a state must enforce a **judgment** of a court in another state even if it is based on a lawsuit that would not be legal or valid in the state asked to enforce it. See also **full faith and credit**.

Favored beneficiary A person who has a hand in preparing a **will** and is favored in the will over others who have an equal claim to inherit. This favored **beneficiary** may have **undue** influence over the **testator** (the person whose will it is).

Feasance Doing an act; performing a duty.

Featherbedding A popular name given to the practice of employees demanding that more people be employed (or more work be done) than the job requires.

Fed 1. Federal Reserve System. The central U.S. bank that sets money-supply policy. 2. Short for Federal.

Federal 1. A *federal* union is a uniting of two or more states into one strong central government with many powers left to the states. 2. The U.S. federal government is the national, as opposed to state, government. 3. For the various federal **agencies** that are not listed here or by name, look under their initials at the start of the letter.

Federal common law Federal judge-made law restricted to those areas, such as **interstate commerce** and federal **labor** and **antitrust** law, that are governed by the federal Constitution and federal statutes and need not follow state court **decisions**.

Federal courts The courts created by the U.S. Constitution and by Congress. These are all integrated into one system which has federal **jurisdiction** based on such things as **diversity of citizenship** and **federal question**.

Federal question Cases directly involving the U.S. **Constitution**, U.S. **statutes**, or **treaties**.

Federal Register The first place that the rules and **regulations** of U.S. **administrative agencies** are published. Abbreviated "Fed. Reg."

Federal Reporter A publication with the **opinions** of many federal courts below the Supreme Court level. Those lower federal courts not published here are covered by the **Federal Supplement**.

Federal Reserve Act The law that created the *Federal Reserve banks*, supervised by the *Federal Reserve Board* to maintain money reserves; issue *Federal Reserve notes* (dollar bills, fives, etc.); lend money to banks; and supervise banks. The central banks of the system, one in each region of the country, are the working centers of the *Federal Reserve System*.

Federal rules

Federal rules The federal rules of **civil procedure**, **criminal** procedure, **appellate** procedure, and **evidence**.

Federal Rules Decisions A **reporter** that publishes federal court decisions having to do with the court's procedural rules.

Federal Supplement A publication with the **opinions** of many federal courts below the Supreme Court level. Those lower federal courts not published here are covered by the **Federal Reporter**.

Federal Tort Claims Act The federal law that abolished the federal government's **immunity** from lawsuits based on **torts**. Suits based on some kinds of intentional torts, or on some kinds of discretionary acts by federal officials, are still not permitted.

Federalism Several different levels of government (for example, city, state, and national) existing side-by-side in the same area with the lower levels having some independent powers.

Federation A formal group of persons, organizations, or governments loosely united for a common purpose.

Fee **1.** A charge for services. **2.** An **inheritance** without any limitations placed on it or an **estate** with no restrictions on disposing of it and which will go, upon death, to a person's **heirs**.

Fee simple The same as **fee** (see the **inheritance** part of that definition). For *types* of *fee simple*, such as **conditional** or **defeasible**, see those words.

Fee tail An **estate** that can be passed on only to children (or only to some other set line of **inheritance**).

Feint pleader **Faint pleader** (see that word).

Fellow servant rule A rule (not much used now) that an employer is not responsible for the injuries one employee does to another employee if the employees were carefully chosen.

Felon A person who commits a **felony** (major crime) and is still serving time for it.

Felonious **1.** Done with the intent to commit a major crime. For example, "*felonious assault*" is an **assault** which, if successful, would have been a **felony**. **2.** Evil; malicious; unlawful.

Felony **1.** A serious crime. **2.** A crime with a **sentence** of one year or more.

Felony–murder rule An accidental killing committed while committing a **felony** may make that killing a **murder**.

Feme couvert (French) A married woman; one who in the past had legal disabilities, such as an inability to make **contracts**.

Feme couvert was used in comparison to *feme sole* (alone or unmarried). [pronounce: fem cov-er]

Feoffment   The old method of transferring full ownership of land in England. [pronounce: feef-ment]

Ferae naturae   (Latin) "Of wild nature." Naturally wild animals. (Naturally tame animals are *dometae naturae*.)

Fertile octogenarian rule   The rule that you cannot assume that merely because persons are beyond childbearing age that there will be nobody new to **inherit** from them.

Feudal law   The law of property from the Middle Ages in England. It was based on the *feudal system* of rights and duties tying people to the land in a rigid **hierarchy** from the king on down to the serfs.

Ff   An expression such as "p. 26ff" means "found on page 26 and on the pages immediately following."

Fi. fa.   Abbreviation for **fieri facias** (see that word).

Fiat   (Latin) "Let it be done"; a command.

Fictio   (Latin) A legal **fiction** (see that word).

Fiction   A *legal fiction* is an assumption that something that is (or may be) false or nonexistent is true or real. Legal fictions are assumed or invented to help do justice. For example, bringing a lawsuit to throw a nonexistent "John Doe" off your property used to be the only way to establish a clear right to the property when legal **title** was uncertain.

Fictitious   **1.** Fake (and usually in bad faith).   **2.** Nonexistent; made up.

Fidelity bond   Insurance on a person against that person's dishonesty. A company must often buy this type of insurance when an employee is in a position of trust, handles large sums of money, and is seldom checked on by others.

Fides   (Latin) Faith, honesty.

Fiduciary   **1.** A person who manages money or property for another person and in whom that other person has a right to place great trust.   **2.** A relationship like that in no. 1.   **3.** Any relationship between persons in which one person acts for another in a position of trust; for example, lawyer and client or parent and child.

Field warehousing   An arrangement by which a lender takes formal control of goods stored in the possession of a borrower.

Fieri facias

The borrowing merchant, wholesaler, or manufacturer gets access to the goods, and the lender gets a **security** interest and close watch over the goods.

Fieri facias   (Latin) An old **writ** of **execution** commanding a **sheriff** to take goods to pay off a debt. [pronounce: fie-er-e fay-she-as]

Fifteenth Amendment   The U.S. constitutional amendment that guarantees the right to vote regardless of race, color, or prior slavery.

Fifth Amendment   **1.** The **constitutional** amendment that guarantees an **indictment** or grand jury **presentment** for persons accused of major crimes; **due process of law** (see that word) in depriving a person of life, liberty, or property; and just compensation in taking private property for public use. The amendment also prohibits **double jeopardy** (see that word) and forcing a person to be a **witness** against him or herself. **2.** *"Taking the Fifth"* means refusing to answer a question because it might implicate you in a crime.

Fighting words   Speech that is *not* protected by the **First Amendment** to the U.S. **Constitution** because it is likely to cause violence by the person to whom the words are spoken.

File   **1.** The complete court record of a case.   **2.** "To file" a paper is to give it to the court clerk for inclusion in the case record.   **3.** A folder in a law office (of a case, a client, business records, etc.).

Filiation proceeding   Same as **paternity suit** (see that word).

Filibuster   A procedure in the U.S. Senate by which long, often irrelevant speeches are made to kill a proposed bill. *Filibusters* can be cut off by a **cloture** vote or by outlasting the talker.

Final argument   A last statement given to the jury by each side in a trial. Each side presents what it thinks the facts are and how it thinks the law applies to these facts.

Final decision   This word has opposite uses: **1.** The last action of a court; the one upon which an **appeal** can be based.   **2.** The last decision of a court or a series of courts from which there are *no more* appeals.

Final passage   The last affirmative vote on a **bill** in one **house** of a **legislature** after it has gone through all preliminary procedures.

Final submission   The time when an entire case (**testimony**, each side's in-court **arguments** and written materials, etc.) is finished and the judge can make a **decision**.

Finance charge   The interest or other payment made in addition to the price of goods or services paid off in installments or "on time." This does not include late charges, collection expenses, etc. It must often be expressed as an **annual percentage rate** (see that word).

Finance committee   1. A U.S. **Senate committee** (see those words) that handles taxation and related matters. It is comparable to the House Ways and Means Committee.   **2.** A committee of a company's **board** of directors that makes major financial decisions.

Financial institution   Any **bank, trust company, credit union, savings and loan association,** or similar organization **licensed** by a state or the U.S. government to do financial business.

Financial lease   A long-term property **lease** that cannot be cancelled and that provides no maintenance or other services.

Financial responsibility acts   State laws requiring **insurance,** posting a **bond,** or a cash payment by applicants for a motor vehicle **license** or **registration.**

Financial statement   A summary of what a company or other organization owns and what it owes. It may be in the form of a **balance sheet,** a profit and loss statement, or an **annual report.** This is *not* a "financing statement."

Financing statement   A paper, filed on the proper public records, that shows a **security** interest in goods. This is *not* a "financial statement."

Finder   A person who brings together two companies for a **merger,** who secures a **mortgage** for a borrower, who locates an **underwriter** for a company issuing **stock,** etc., usually for a fee.

Finding   A decision (by a judge, jury, **hearing examiner,** etc.) about a question of fact; a decision about **evidence.** It is often called a *"finding of fact"* upon which a *"conclusion of law"* may be based.

Fine   The punishment of payment of a sum of money imposed by a court. It may be a **civil** or a **criminal** penalty.

Fire sale   A sale at reduced prices due to fire or water damage or, sometimes, any emergency. Fire sales often require special **licenses** and are **regulated** to protect **consumers.**

Firm offer   A written **offer** (see that word), by a merchant, that will be held open for a certain length of time. It is a type of **option** that requires no **consideration** (see that word) to be valid.

First Amendment   The U.S. **constitutional amendment** that guarantees *freedom of speech, religion, press, and assembly* as well as the right to **petition** the government.

First degree murder   **Murder** that includes **premeditation** or extreme atrocity or cruelty, or one that is done in the commission of a major **felony.**

First impression   New. A case or a question is *"of first impression"* if it presents an entirely new problem to the court and cannot be decided by **precedent.**

First instance   A *court of first instance* is a **trial** court as opposed to an **appeals** court.

First mortgage (or lien)   The **mortgage** (or **lien**) that has the right to be paid off before all others. This is not necessarily the first in time.

First offender   A person who has never before been convicted of a crime and who may be entitled to more lenient treatment.

Fiscal   Financial. The *fiscal* year is a period of time, equal to a calendar year, but starting on the day that the state or company uses as "day one" for its business records. This is often January, April, July, or October first.

Fishing trip (or expedition)   **1.** Using the courts to find out information beyond the fair scope of the lawsuit.   **2.** The loose, unfocused questioning of a **witness** or the overly broad use of the **discovery** process.

Fitness for a particular purpose   The rule that if a merchant knows or should know that an item is used for a particular purpose, the merchant is responsible to buyers for that item's fitness for the purpose. This is an **implied warranty.**

Fixation   See **fixed work.**

Fixed assets   Property such as land and machinery used in a company's business. It is not part of the company's merchandise; is used up slowly, if at all; and is sometimes summarized as "property, plant, and equipment."

Fixed charges (or fixed costs)   Business costs that continue whether or not business comes in; for example, rent.

Fixed opinion   A **juror's bias** or prejudgment about a person's guilt or **liability** that disqualifies the juror due to lack of impartiality.

Fixed trust   A *non*discretionary trust (see that word).

Fixed work   Under **copyright** law, a new work is *"fixed"* or *"cre-*

ated" when it is put in stable, tangible form, such as written on paper, recorded on film, sculpted in clay, etc. This "fixation" gives the work an automatic copyright, whether or not the formalities of copyright are followed (although registering the work with the Copyright Office and putting a copyright notice on it gives the work many added protections).

Fixture Anything attached to land or a building. The word is sometimes used to mean those attached things that, once attached, may *not* be removed by a tenant and sometimes means those things attached that *may* be removed.

Flag of convenience A merchant ship **registered** in a country that has low fees, low safety requirements, etc., rather than in the country where it is owned or does most of its business, flies a "flag of convenience."

Flagrante delicto (Latin) **1.** In the act of committing the crime. **2.** Popularly used to mean lovers caught together in bed.

Flat-benefit plan A **pension plan** (see that word) or other employee **benefit** plan that is unrelated to salary level (pays the same to everyone, pays more by years of service, etc.).

Flat rate A fixed amount of money paid each time period rather than paying at fluctuating levels (for electricity used, for services used, for changeable prices, etc.).

Flee to the wall doctrine The "rule" that a person must try every reasonable way of escape before killing an attacker. Contrast this with the **true person doctrine**.

Flipping Popular word for refinancing **consumer** loans, often at higher rates of interest.

Float **1.** The time between the deposit of a check in one bank and its subtraction from an account in another bank. This is "free" use of the money by the person who wrote the check. **2.** To let a national currency's value against other currencies change freely depending on supply and demand rather than by one or both countries' fixing or "**pegging**" the "exchange rate" by law or otherwise. **3.** See the various "**floating**" words, in most of which "floating" means "changeable."

Floating debt (or capital) Short-term debt (or money available to *pay* short-term debt and other current expenses).

Floating interest An interest rate that varies with the general interest rate market.

Floating lien An arrangement in which later property purchased by someone with a **secured** debt or **lien** (see these words) on property becomes **subject to** that debt or lien, and the original property remains subject to the lien until all debts are paid.

Floating (or floater) policy   A supplemental **insurance** policy to cover items such as jewelry that frequently change location or quantity.

Floating stock (or bonds)   Issuing and selling **stock** (or **bonds**).

Floor   **1.** The right to speak in a meeting or **legislature** is called "holding the floor."   **2.** The central meeting place of a legislature or **stock** (or similar) **exchange**.   **3.** A lowest limit.

Floor plan financing   A loan to a retail seller that is **secured** by the items to be sold and that is paid off as each sells.

Flotsam   The wreckage of a ship or its goods found floating in the water. See also **jetsam.**

Fluctuating clause   See **escalator clause**.

Followed   A **case** is *followed* by a later case if it is relied upon as **precedent** to decide the later case.

For cause   For a sound legal reason, as opposed to merely a stated reason. To remove an official from a job *for cause* may require a better reason than "because we didn't like certain actions he took or like the way he handled his job." It usually requires proof that the official lacked the ability or fitness to do the job right.

Forbearance   **1.** Refraining from action (especially action to enforce a right).   **2.** Holding off demanding payment on a debt that is due.   **3.** The *"forbearance rule"* or *"patient forbearance rule"* is the principle that, in most circumstances, a person does not lose a right merely because the person did not enforce the right quickly. For example, if a wife puts up with abuse, this does not automatically stop the wife from getting a **divorce** based on that abuse.

Force   **1.** Unlawful or wrongful violence. For example, *forcible entry* is taking possession or entering another person's property against that person's will or by using "force" in its ordinary meaning.   **2.** "In force" means in effect and valid.

Force majeure (or majestire)   (French) Irresistible, natural, or unavoidable force; for example, an earthquake.

Forced heir   A person who cannot be deprived of a share of an **estate** unless the **testator** (person making a will) has a recognized legal cause for disinheriting the person.

Forced sale   A sale made to pay off a court's **judgment,** ordered by that court, and done according to rules set by that court.

176

Forcible detainer **1.** The act of a person who originally had a right to occupy land or a building and then refuses to give up the property when that right is ended. **2.** The summary (quick) court process for getting back land or a building held as in no. 1.

Foreclosure An action by a person who holds a **mortgage** to: 1) take the property away from the mortgagor (such as the homeowner); 2) end that homeowner's rights in the property; and 3) sell the property to pay off the mortgage debt. Both the process (which is usually but not always done by lawsuit) and the result are called "*foreclosure.*"

Foreign Belonging to, coming from, or having to do with another country or another state. For example, a Maine court would call a **corporation** incorporated in and based in Ohio a *foreign* corporation.

Foreign agent **1.** A person who must register with the federal government as a lobbyist, advertising agency, or other representative of a foreign country or company. See also **lobbying acts.** **2.** A spy or other person who works for a foreign country.

Foreign exchange Changing the money of one country into that of another.

Foreign service **Ambassadors** and lower-ranking officials who represent the U.S., usually overseas, through the State Department.

Foreign situs trust A **trust** that exists because of foreign laws.

Foreign substance Something not naturally occurring, such as a sponge left behind by a doctor in a patient's body or a nail in a can of beans.

Foreign trade zone An area of a country where component parts and raw materials may be imported tax-free until the finished product enters that country's market or is re-exported. See also **free port.**

Foreman The leader of a **jury** who speaks for it.

Forensic Having to do with courts and law. For example, *forensic medicine* is medical knowledge or medical practice involved with court **testimony** or other legal matters.

Foreseeability What a reasonably careful and thoughtful person would expect and plan for at the time of an occurrence and under the same circumstances. *Not* hindsight.

Forfeit

Forfeit To lose the right to something due to neglect of a duty, due to an offense, or due to a **breach** of **contract**. For example, if a **defendant** fails to show up for trial, he or she may *forfeit* the bail bond.

Forgery **1.** Making a fake document (or altering a real one) with intent to commit a **fraud.** **2.** The document itself in no. 1.

Foris (Latin) On the outside; put out. For example, *forisfactura* is a "putting out" or forfeiture.

Form **1.** A model to work from (or a paper with blanks to be filled in) of a legal document such as a **contract** or a **pleading.** **2.** The language, arrangement, conduct, procedure, or legal technicalities of a legal document or a legal **proceeding,** as opposed to the "**substance**" or subject of the document or proceeding.

Forma pauperis **In forma pauperis** (see that word).

Formal **1.** In form only. For example, a *formal party* is a person who is involved in a lawsuit in name only and has no real interest in the proceedings. The opposite of real, substantial, etc. **2.** Fully formalized. For example, a formal contract is written, as opposed to oral, and contains all the necessary legal language, signatures, etc. The opposite of informal.

Formbook A collection of legal forms with summaries of relevant law and information on how to use the forms.

Formed design A deliberate and set intention to commit a crime (particularly a killing).

Former jeopardy **Double jeopardy** (see that word).

Forms of action The special, individual, technical ways each different type of lawsuit formerly was brought in court. If a legal problem did not fit into one of these pigeonholes (such as **assumpsit, debt, detinue, ejectment, replevin, trespass,** trespass on the **case,** and **trover**), it could not be brought to court. These have all been replaced under the Rules of Civil Procedure by **civil actions.**

Fornication Sexual intercourse between unmarried persons.

Forswear Swear to something you know is untrue. This is broader than **perjury** (see that word), but not as serious.

Forthwith An unnecessarily formal word meaning immediately; as soon as possible.

Fortiori (Latin) See **a fortiori.**

Fortuitous Happening by chance or accident; unexpected; unforeseen; unavoidable. It does *not* mean "lucky."

Fortune 500   A ranked list of the 500 largest U.S. industrial corporations.

Forum   (Latin) A court. For example, *forum domicilii* is a court in the place where a person lives, and *forum rei* is a court where either the thing involved with the suit is or where the **defendant** lives.

Forum non conveniens   (Latin) "Inconvenient court." If two or more courts both have proper **venue** (see that word) for a case, a judge may rule that a lawsuit must be brought in the *other* court for either the convenience of or fairness to the parties.

Forum shopping   Choosing the one court, among many that may legally handle a lawsuit, that you think may look most favorably at your side.

Forward   **1.** Set a rate (such as an **interest** or exchange rate) today for a future transaction.   **2.** Send on. For example, a *forwarding fee* is money paid to a lawyer who **refers** a client to another lawyer. The money is paid by the lawyer who receives the client. Some forms of this type of arrangement are unethical.

Forward contract   **Futures** (see that word).

Foster child   A child living with, cared for, and under the control of someone other than his or her own parents, but not **adopted** by this other person. A *foster home* is a home for children without parents or who have been taken away from parents by a court.

Foul bill   A **bill of lading** that says that the goods are damaged or partly missing.

Foundation   **1.** Basis. For example, the *foundation* of a trial is the group of issues in dispute between the sides (as set out in the **pleadings**).   **2.** The preliminary questions to a **witness** that establish the admissibility (legal usability) of that person's **testimony** as **evidence** in a trial are called "*laying the foundation.*"   **3.** An organization maintained by contributions and set up to give money to charitable, educational, and other nonprofit organizations and projects. However, *any* organization may legally call itself a "foundation" without meeting the actual definition, and a "private foundation," according to the I.R.S., is one that does *not* meet several technical requirements for the *most* favorable charitable organization tax treatment.

Four corners   Same as **face** (see that word) of a document; that is, the document itself without outside information about it.

Four corners rule   **1.** The meaning of a document should be read from the document alone, not from oral **testimony** about what the writer "really" meant. (As with most rules, this one is riddled with exceptions.) **2.** The meaning of a phrase should be read from the entire document, not from the phrase in isolation.

Fourteenth Amendment The U.S. constitutional amendment that forbids the states from enforcing laws that *"abridge the privileges and immunities"* of U.S. citizens, forbids the states from depriving any person of **due process** or **equal protection** under law, and changes the **apportionment** of congressional **representatives.**

Fourth Amendment The U.S. constitutional amendment that forbids unreasonable searches and seizures and requires **probable cause** for search **warrants.**

Frame 1. Popular word for incriminating someone on false **evidence. 2.** Draw up; put into words. For example, to *frame* a **complaint** is to choose the legal form it will take, fit the facts to the form, and choose the actual wording.

Franchise 1. A business arrangement in which a person buys the right to sell, rent, etc., the products or services of a company and use the company's name to do business. **2.** A special right given by the government, such as the right to vote or to form a **corporation. 3.** A sports team granted a particular territory by the league.

Franchise tax A tax on the right of a company to do business. It may be based on a fixed fee, on the amount of business done, on **assets,** etc.

Frank 1. The right to mail things without charge. Also called a *franking privilege.* **2.** An old English word for *free.* For example, a *frank-pledge* was the responsibility of all free persons (the community as a whole) for the good conduct of each adult in the community.

Fraternal benefit association A group of persons, often in the same line of work, who band together for such things as **group insurance** coverage.

Fraud Any kind of trickery used by one person to cheat another. For different types of *fraud,* such as **tax fraud,** see those words.

Fraud order A decision by the postmaster general to deny, as much as possible, the use of the mails to obtain money fraudulently.

Frauds, statute of See **statute of frauds.**

Fraudulent   Cheating. For example, a "fraudulent conveyance" is a **debtor's** transfer of property to someone else in order to cheat a **creditor** who might have a right to it.

Freddie Mac   See **F.H.L.M.C.**

Free and equal election   *Free* means that each person has a reasonable chance to qualify as a voter and, once qualified, a reasonable chance to vote without coercion of any kind. *Equal* means that each voter has the same rights as any other voter to have his or her vote count equally in the election.

Free exercise clause   See **freedom of religion**.

Free on board   See **F.O.B.**

Free port   An area of a country (usually of a marine port, but sometimes a railroad crossover, airport, etc.) set aside for bringing in and selling foreign goods without paying import taxes. See also **foreign trade zone.**

Free ride   The possibility of a riskless profit.

Free trade zone   **Foreign trade zone** (see that word).

Freedom of association   The **First Amendment** right to gather together in groups for any lawful purpose.

Freedom of choice   The right to attend the school of your choice within a school district so long as there is no **de jure** segregation. This "right" often produces **de facto** segregation.

Freedom of contract   The constitutionally protected right to make and enforce **contracts,** limited only by reasonable health, safety, and consumer protection laws.

Freedom of expression   The **First Amendment** freedoms of religion, speech, and press combined.

Freedom of Information Act   A law that makes all records held by the federal government, except for certain specific types of records (such as certain military secrets), available to the public. Procedures are set up to get these records and to **appeal** decisions to withhold them, but these procedures are often slow and cumbersome.

Freedom of religion   The **First Amendment** right to believe any religion and to practice it in any way that does not infringe on public safety or on the equally important rights of others. Also, the right of all citizens to be free of the exercise of religious control by or through the government. See **establishment clause.**

Freedom of speech   The constitutional right to say what you want as long as you do not interfere with others' rights. These

Freedom of the press

other rights are protected by the laws of **defamation,** public safety, etc.

Freedom of the press   The First Amendment right to publish most things without prior **censorship** or restraint, to be free from unreasonable attempts to punish what has already been published, and other rights.

Freehold   Ownership of land, either unrestricted or restricted by no more than a time limit.

Freeze   A halt to changes in prices, wages, hiring, etc.

Freeze-out   The use of **corporate** power by a majority of the shareholders (owners) or of the **board** of directors to either get rid of **minority** shareholders and board members or to strip them of all power. See also **squeeze-out.**

Fresh complaint rule   The idea, used less and less now, that a rape or other sexual assault victim may not be believable unless she complained and went for help within a short time.

Fresh (or hot) pursuit rule   **1.** The right of a police officer to cross state (or county or other) lines to continue an unbroken chase of a suspected criminal. This right is limited to those states which allow it.   **2.** The right of a person who has had property taken to use reasonable force to get it back after a chase that takes place immediately after it was taken.

Friend of the court   See **amicus curiae.**

Friendly fire   A fire that remains contained where intended, but may do damage anyway.

Friendly suit   A lawsuit brought by agreement to settle a point of law that affects opposing persons.

Friendly takeover   One company gaining control of another with the approval of the second company's **board** and officers.

Fringe benefits   Things besides salary that either compensate a person for working (such as paid medical insurance or profit-sharing plans) or make it pleasant to work (such as on-site recreational facilities).

Frisk   A superficial running of hands over a person's body in order to do a quick search, especially for weapons.

Frivolous   Legally worthless. For example, a **pleading** that clearly has no legal leg to stand on, even if every fact it claims is true, is *frivolous.* Also, an **appeal** that presents no legal question or is so lacking in substance that it could not possibly succeed is *frivolous.*

Frolic   An employee's turning aside from a mission to do something for him or herself.

Front name   **Street name** (see that word).

Front wages   Prospective payments made to a victim of job **discrimination** who cannot yet be given the job to which he or she is entitled. These payments, made until the job comes through, make up the difference between money earned now and money that would be made now if the new position were immediately available.

Frontage assessment   A tax to pay for improvements (such as sidewalks or sewer lines) that is charged in proportion to the frontage (number of feet bordering the road) of each property.

Front-end load   Charging a large part of the administrative costs, of commissions, etc., at the start of a deal to buy insurance, to lease property, etc.

Frozen account   An **account** (usually a bank account) from which no money may be removed until a court **order** is lifted.

Frozen assets   The property of a business that cannot be easily sold without damaging the business. This includes financial assets which, if sold, will hurt the company's financial structure. The opposite is liquid assets.

Fructus   (Latin) **Fruit** or profit.

Fruit   Product of; material result. For example, rental income is the *fruit* of renting land out and stolen money is the "fruit of crime."

Fruit and tree doctrine   The rule that income tax cannot be avoided by assigning the income to another person. The only way to transfer the income tax to another person is to give away the income-producing property itself (such as by giving it to a child who pays lower taxes).

Fruit of the poisonous tree doctrine   **Evidence** that is a result of an illegal search or questioning cannot be used against the person searched or questioned even if the evidence was obtained only indirectly.

Frustration   *"Frustration of contract"* occurs when carrying out a bargain has become impossible because of some change or occurrence that is not the fault of the persons making the deal. The change must remove something (or change some condition) that the persons who made the contract knew from the beginning was necessary for the contract to be carried out. *"Frustration of purpose"* occurs when, even if a bargain can be carried out, some change has wiped out the real reasons for the contract. In some cases, promises need not then be carried out.

Fugitive Felon Act   A law that makes it a federal crime to cross state lines to avoid a state **felony** prosecution, a state felony punishment, or giving **testimony** in a state felony case.

Fugitive from justice   A person who commits a crime and either leaves the area or hides to avoid prosecution.

Full coverage   Insurance that pays for every dollar of a loss with no maximum and no **deductible** amount.

Full faith and credit   The constitutional requirement that each state must treat as valid, and enforce where appropriate, the laws and court decisions of other states. There are exceptions to this rule, especially those cases where the other state lacked proper **jurisdiction.**

Functus officio   (Latin) A person whose official job is finished and who has no further authority to act.

Fund   **1.** A sum of money set aside for a particular purpose. **2.** Money and all other **assets** (such as stocks or bonds) on hand.

Fundamental analysis   Deciding whether to buy or sell a particular **stock** or other **security** based on the company itself, the industry in general, etc. See also **technical analysis.**

Fundamental law   A country's **constitution** or basic governing principles.

Funded debt   **1.** State or local debts that have either a fund of money or a specific tax plan set aside for payment.   **2.** A company's long-term debt, such as a **bond issue,** replacing other short-term debts.

Fungible   Things that are easily replaced one for another. For example, pounds of identical rice are *fungible* because one may be substituted for another, but different paintings are not fungible. [pronounce: <u>fun</u>-jible]

Furandi animus   (Latin) See **animo.**

Furtum   (Latin) A theft or the item stolen.

Future acquired property   Property that is made part of a **mortgage** on presently owned property.

Future advances   Money lent on the same **security** as a previous loan. Some open-ended **credit** and **mortgage contracts** allow additional loans like this.

Future earnings   Estimated money that would have been made in the future if an injury had not occurred.

Future interests Present rights in property that give the right to future possession or use; for example, the right to own property and use it after ten years go by.

Futures Contracts promising to buy or sell standard commodities (rice, soybeans, etc.) or **securities** at a future date and at a set price. These are "paper" deals and involve profit and loss on promises to deliver, not possession of the actual commodities.

G.A.A.P. *Generally Accepted Accounting Principles,* put out by the Financial Accounting Standards Board.

G.A.A.S. *Generally Accepted Auditing Standards,* put out by the American Institute of **Certified Public Accountants.**

G.A.O. General Accounting Office. It assists the U.S. Congress in financial matters; **audits** and investigates federal programs; settles claims against the U.S., etc.

G.A.T.T. *General Agreement on Tariffs and Trade.* An international agreement that lowers import taxes and otherwise makes international trade flow more smoothly.

G.N.M.A. Government National Mortgage Association. A government organization that operates special programs in which housing **mortgages** are bought and sold to encourage private lending in certain types of housing. Also called *"Ginnie Mae."*

G.N.P. **Gross national product** (see that word).

G.P.M. **Graduated payment mortgage.**

G.P.O. Government Printing Office. It publishes all the laws, **regulations,** etc., of the federal government.

G.S. General schedule or government service. Rank levels in the federal **bureaucracy,** ranging from G.S. 1 to G.S. 18.

G.S.A. General Services Administration. It manages all U.S. property.

Gag order 1. A judge's **order** that a wildly disruptive **defendant** be bound and gagged during a trial. 2. A judge's order to lawyers and **witnesses** that they discuss the trial with no outsiders, reporters in particular. **3.** A judge's order, usually held **unconstitutional,** to reporters that they not report certain court proceedings.

Gage An old word for **pledge,** pawn, or **security.**

Gambling policy An insurance policy issued to a person who has no **insurable interest** in the person or property insured. These are often illegal.

Gaol Jail.

Garnishee A person who holds money or property belonging to a **debtor** and who is subject to a **garnishment** (see that word) proceeding by a **creditor.**

Garnishment A legal proceeding taken by a **creditor** after a **judgment** is received against a **debtor.** If the creditor knows that the debtor has money or property with someone else (such as a bank account or wages paid by an employer), the creditor first has the money tied up by legal process and then takes as much of it as state laws allow to pay off the debt. The amount of wages that may be garnished also is limited by the *Federal Wage Garnishment Act* which, in addition, gives some protection from dismissal due to garnishment.

Gault The Supreme Court case (in the matter of Gault) that gave juvenile **defendants** the rights of adult criminal defendants (such as the right to **counsel,** the privilege against **self-incrimination,** etc.).

Gearing See **leverage.**

Gele An old word for a rent or a public license similar to a **royalty** payment for mining.

Gen. General.

General **1.** A whole group, as opposed to only a part of the group or only one individual in the group; applying to all, as opposed to only some or only one; broad or unlimited. The opposite of *"general"* is often **"special"** or **"limited."** **2.** For those "general" words (such as *general election, general partner, general verdict,* etc.) that are not listed among the following words, see the main word (**election, partner, verdict,** etc.).

General appearance Coming before a court and submitting to its **jurisdiction** in a case. The opposite of **special appearance** (see that word).

General assembly **1.** The entire **legislature** of many states.

2. The lower **house** of many state legislatures. **3.** The meeting of representatives of all the member nations of the United Nations.

General assignment for creditors A transfer of all rights to a **debtor's** property to a **trustee** who settles the debtor's affairs and distributes money to the **creditors.**

General assistance (or general relief) A local form of aid to the poor that sometimes has state backing, but involves no federal funds. It is usually temporary.

General average loss A loss at sea that will be shared by the shipowner and all owners of cargo shipped. This happens if the lost or damaged items (often thrown overboard) were intentionally lost to save the ship and the rest of the cargo.

General building scheme The division of a piece of land into separate building lots that are sold with identical restrictions on each as to how the land may be used.

General cash issue (or offer) A sale of **stock** or other **securities** open to all buyers.

General (or prime) contractor A person who **contracts** for a whole project (such as a building job) and hires subcontractors (such as plumbers) to do specialized work.

General creditor A person who is owed money, but who has no **security** (for example, a **mortgage**) for the debt.

General digest See **American Digest System.**

General execution A court **order** to a sheriff or another court official to take any personal **property** of a **defendant** in order to pay off a **judgment** against that person.

General jurisdiction The power of a court to hear and decide any type of case that comes up within its geographical area.

General lien A right (arising from a **contract**) to hold personal **property** of another person until payment of a debt is made.

General strike A work stoppage by a large part of the workers in a geographic area. It is usually political rather than economic.

General warranty deed A transfer of land that includes the formal, written promise to protect the buyer against all claims of ownership of the property.

General welfare clause The U.S. **constitutional** provision that Congress may tax and pay debts to provide for the country's *"general welfare."*

Generation-skipping trust A **trust** in which, for example, a grandmother gives the income from the trust property to her children and then the trust **assets** to her grandchildren. By not passing the trust assets directly to her children, then on to the grandchildren, one *transfer tax* is avoided, but there are now tax rules that impose a special *generation-skipping tax* on this.

Generic name The non**trademark** name of a product.

Geneva Convention An international agreement for the conduct of war that includes the proper care of enemy wounded, the safety of hospitals and medical crews, etc.

Gentlemen's agreement A deal that cannot be enforced in court and that depends solely on the good faith of the persons making it. *Informal agreement* is a more general word for this type of deal.

Germane Close on point, relevant, pertinent.

Gerrymander Create unusually shaped political boundaries or districts in a state or country in order to accomplish an improper purpose, such as to give a voting advantage to one political party.

Gideon v. Wainwright The **Supreme Court** case that gave **criminal defendants** in state **felony** trials the right to **counsel**.

Gift **1.** Any willing transfer of money or property without payment close to the value of the thing transferred. **2.** Any willing transfer of money or property without payment and with no thought of any possible financial benefit to the giver. **3.** For *gift causa mortis*, see **causa mortis**.

Gift over A property transfer that takes effect automatically when another ends; for example, a gift "to Linda for life, then to David."

Gift schedule A regular, annual giving away of money or property to several persons, each amount within the yearly tax-free limit.

Gift tax A tax on **gifts** (see that word) that is paid by the giver (federal and some state taxes) or by the person receiving the gift (some states). See **Unified Transfer Tax** (and see **inheritance** tax for a contrast).

Gifts to Minors Act A **uniform act**, adopted by most states, that simplifies the transfer of property. An adult has **title** to and control over the property, and the child gets the **interest** or **dividends**, which may be used for the child's support.

Gilt edge A popular term for a **stock**, **bond**, or other **security** with the highest rating (for safety of investment) or for a **negotiable instrument** with similar safety.

Ginnie Mae   See **G.N.M.A.**

Gist   The main point, issue, or argument.

Giveback   A union negotiating a new contract with lower salaries or benefits, usually to preserve jobs.

Gloss   An explanation of a passage in a book or document that is usually put on the same page.

Glossary   **1.** Dictionary.   **2.** Small dictionary; specialized dictionary.

Go to protest   See **protest**.

Going and coming rule   A person going to or from work is usually not covered by **workers' compensation** laws.

Going concern   A company that is transacting its usual business in its usual way (even if in a weak financial condition).

Going private   **1.** A company's taking its **stock** off a stock **exchange**.   **2.** A company's rebuying of its own stock or otherwise rearranging its financial affairs so that it is no longer owned by many persons (for example, by merging with or being bought by a larger company).

Going public   Selling **shares** in a **corporation** to the general public for the first time.

Goldberg v. Kelly   A 1970 Supreme Court case that called **welfare** a **right**, not a **privilege**, and required a **hearing** before termination of benefits.

Goldbricking   **1.** An organized work slowdown.   **2.** Shirking work and general laziness.

Golden rule argument   A request by a lawyer (or instructions by a judge) that **jurors** put themselves or family members in the place of the person hurt (who is suing), and then make a decision. This request is no longer permitted in any trial.

Good   Valid; legally sufficient.

Good behavior   A vague term, applied differently to the conduct required for public officials to keep their jobs, for criminals to get out of jail early, etc.

Good cause   Legally sufficient; not arbitrary.

Good faith   **1.** Honest; honesty in fact.   **2.** For a merchant, *good faith* also means "the observance of reasonable commercial standards of fair dealing in the trade" according to the **Uniform Commercial Code.**   **3.** *Good faith bargaining* is the obligation of an employer to hold honest negotiations about wages, hours,

Good Samaritan doctrine

and employment conditions with a **union** that has been **certified** to represent its employees.   **4.** A *good faith purchaser* is a person who buys something (usually a **negotiable instrument**) without knowing any facts that should make a person suspicious of the seller's **title** to the thing.

Good Samaritan doctrine   **1.** A person who helps another in great danger cannot be held **liable** for that person's injuries unless the help was **negligent** and definitely worsened the person's condition.   **2.** See also **emergency doctrine** and **rescue** doctrine.

Good title   Marketable title (see **marketable title acts**).

Goods   A general word that can have a meaning as broad as all property (excluding land) or as narrow as items for sale by a merchant. *Durable goods*, such as refrigerators, have a long life; *fungible goods*, such as a pound of rice, are interchangeable; *hard goods* are durable goods sold to consumers; and *soft goods* are things like clothing.

Goodtime   The reduction of a prison sentence for **good behavior**.

Goodwill   The reputation and built-up business of a company. It can be generally valued as what a company would sell for over and above the value of its physical property, money owed to it, and other **assets**.

Government instrumentality doctrine   A legal rule that any organization run by a branch of government may not be taxed. This rule is also called "*governmental immunity.*" See also **sovereign immunity.**

Governmental trust   A **charitable trust** for things like maintenance of historic government buildings and city playgrounds.

Grab law   Aggressive collection (see that word).

Grace   **1.** A favor.   **2.** A holding off on demanding payment of a debt or enforcing some other right. Often called "*grace days.*" These days may be truly a favor or they may be a legal requirement.   **3.** A permission to do something in a lawsuit is "*of grace*" if it is not automatic, but given because the judge thinks it is the fair and right thing to do.

Grace period   A short period of time an **insurance** policy stays in effect after the **premium** payment is due.

Graded offense   A criminal offense divided into **degrees** (see that word).

Graduated lease   A commercial **lease** with payment that varies according to the money made by the renter or by some other standard such as the number of people who enter the store.

Graduated payment mortgage   A **mortgage** in which payments go up by a set formula over the years. See also **variable rate mortgages.**

Graduated tax   See **tax rate.**

Grand jury   See **jury.**

Grand larceny   A **theft** of money or property worth above a certain amount which is set by law.

Grandfather clause   An exception to a restriction or requirement that allows all those already doing something to continue doing it even if they otherwise would be stopped by the new restriction or obligated to meet the new requirement.

Grant   **1.** Give or confer.   **2.** A transfer of land, usually by **deed. 3.** A gift or subsidy.

Grantee   A person to whom a **grant** is made or land is deeded.

Grant-in-aid   A sum of money given for a particular purpose and with some strings attached.

Grantor   Person making a **grant** or deeding over land.

Grantor trust   A **trust** with income that is taxed to the person who created it because he or she kept certain rights to the **assets.**

Grantor–grantee index   County records with the volume and page numbers of all recorded documents such as land **deeds** and **negotiable instruments**. The records are kept by the names of the person transferring the property and the person to whom it was transferred. See also **tract index.**

Gratis   (Latin) Free, as in *"gratis dictum"*; a voluntary statement to which a person may not be strictly held.

Gratuitous   Without payment or other real **consideration.**

Gratuitous licensee   A nonbusiness visitor; a social guest.

Gravamen   The basis, gist, "heart," or material part of a **charge, complaint**, etc.

Green river ordinance   A local law that protects residents against peddlers and door-to-door salespersons.

Grievance procedure   An orderly, regular way of handling problems between workers and employers, prisoners and guards, etc.

Gross   **1.** Great or large.   **2.** Flagrant or shameful.   **3.** Whole or total.

Gross estate

Gross estate   The total value of a dead person's property from which **deductions** are subtracted to determine the amount on which federal **estate taxes** will be paid.

Gross income   1. Money taken in (as opposed to "**net**" income, which is money taken in minus money paid out).   2. Under the federal tax laws, *gross income* is money taken in minus "**exclusions**" (such as gifts or interest on tax-free **bonds**). It is formally defined as "all income from whatever source derived" in the Internal Revenue Code.

Gross lease   A **lease** in which the landlord pays all ownership and maintenance expenses, and the tenant pays rent. Contrast this with a **net lease**.

Gross national product   A single figure that sums up the value of goods and services produced by a country, plus breakdowns on these and on income, investment, savings, prices, etc.

Gross up   Add back into the value of property or income the amount that has already been deducted or paid out (usually for taxes).

Ground rent   Rent paid for land when the tenant has put up the building.

Grounds   Basis, foundation, or points relied on. For example, "grounds" for a **divorce** may include **adultery, cruelty,** etc.

Group legal services   Legal help given to members of an organization or employees of a company. It is paid for in advance on a group basis, often similar to health insurance.

Group insurance   1. Insurance for employees paid by or through the employer.   2. Any insurance bought through an organization, rather than directly from the insurance company, with the organization holding the "*master policy.*"

Growth stock   A stock invested in primarily for an increase in value (**capital** gains) rather than for income payments (**dividends**).

Guarantee   Same as **guaranty** (see that word).

Guarantee clause   The U.S. constitutional provision promising the states a republican form of government and protection from invasion and domestic violence.

Guaranteed mortgage   A **mortgage** made by a mortgage company that then sells the mortgage to an investor, guarantees payments to the investor, and manages the mortgage for a fee.

Guaranty   **1.** The same as a merchant's **warranty** (promise) that goods are of a certain quality, will be fixed if broken, will last a certain time, etc.   **2.** A promise to fulfill an obligation (or pay a debt) if the person who has the obligation fails to fulfill it. For example, John contracts with Ron that if Ron lends Don five dollars and Don fails to pay it back in a week, John will pay it.   **3.** Any promise.

Guardian   A person who has the legal right and duty to take care of another person or that person's property because that other person (for example, a child) cannot legally take care of himself or herself. The arrangement is called *"guardianship."*

Guardian ad litem   A **guardian** (see that word), usually a lawyer, who is appointed by a court to take care of the interests of a person who cannot legally take care of himself or herself during a lawsuit involving that person.

Guest statute   Laws in some states that do not permit a person who rides in another person's car as a *guest* (without payment or other business purpose) to sue that person if there is an accident, unless the accident involves more than ordinary **negligence.**

Guilt by association   Being penalized (by loss of job, prosecution for a crime, etc.) merely for belonging to a particular group or by being personally associated with certain people. Except in cases of a **conspiracy,** criminal prosecutions of this type are not permitted.

Guilty   **1.** Responsible for a crime.   **2.** Convicted of a crime.   **3.** Responsible for a civil wrong, such as **negligence.**

H.B.   *"House Bill."* A **bill** in the process of going through the House of Representatives on its way to becoming a law.

H.D.C.   **Holder in due course.**

H.L.   House of Lords.

H.O.W.   **Home owners warranty** (see that word).

H.R.   House of Representatives.

H.U.D.   Department of Housing and Urban Development. The

U.S. **cabinet** department that coordinates federal housing and land use policy and funds housing construction through a variety of programs.

Habeas corpus   (Latin) "You have the body." A judicial **order** to someone holding a person to bring that person to court. It is most often used to get a person out of unlawful imprisonment by forcing the captor and the person being held to come to court for a decision on the legality of the imprisonment or other holding (such as keeping a child when someone else claims **custody**). [pronounce: hay-bee-as core-pus]

Habendum   The part of a **deed** that describes the ownership rights being transferred.

Habitability   The requirement that a rented house or apartment be fit to live in, primarily that it pass building and sanitary code inspections.

Habitual   Regular, common, and customary; more than just frequent. Some states have "*habitual criminal*" laws that may apply to a person who has been convicted of as few as two prior crimes and that greatly increase the penalties for each succeeding crime.

Habitual intemperance   Regular drunkenness that is serious enough to interfere with a normal home or job. This is grounds for a **divorce** in many states. Also, some states include drug addiction under the label.

Haeres/haereditas   (Latin) **Heir/inheritance.** Also, *haeredes proximi* are "nearest heirs" or **next of kin;** *haereditas testimentaria* is inheritance by **will;** and *haereditas legitima* is **intestate** (by law) inheritance.

Hague Tribunal   See **International Court of Justice.**

Hallmark   A stamp put on gold, silver, and other items to prove their genuineness. The word is used in a legal sense to mean any official mark of genuineness.

Hammer   A **forced sale**; any sale by auction.

Hammurabi, code of   One of the oldest sets of laws, prepared in Babylonia almost four thousand years ago.

Hand down   Decide. A judge *hands down* an **opinion** or a **decision** (usually in a case that has been appealed or one in which the judge has delayed a decision) by announcing it or filing it.

Harassment   Words and actions that unlawfully annoy or alarm another. Harassment may include anonymous, repeated, offensively coarse, or late-night phone calls; insulting, taunting, or physically challenging approaches; words or actions by a debt collector that serve no legitimate purpose; etc.

Harbor 1. Shelter, house, keep, or feed. 2. Shelter or conceal a person for an illegal purpose, such as to protect a criminal from the police.

Hard cases Cases where fairness requires being loose with legal principles. The phrase "hard cases make bad law" comes from this idea.

Harmless error See **error.**

Harter Act A federal law prohibiting **bills of lading** that relieve shipowners of **liability** for lost or damaged cargo merely because they used care in operating the ship.

Hatch Act A federal law to prevent certain types of political activity.(such as holding public office) by federal employees and by certain federally-funded state employees.

Have and hold A common formal phrase in a **deed** that is no longer necessary to make the deed effective.

Hazard Any risk or danger of loss or injury. In **insurance** law, *hazard* is the probability that something may happen, and *moral hazard* is the risk of fire or similar destruction as measured by the carefulness, integrity, etc., of the person whose property is insured plus the loss (or gain!) the person would suffer from the destruction of the insured property.

Head of family A person who financially supports a group of related persons living together.

Head of household A special category of federal taxpayer. To be allowed to pay at "head of household" rates, you must meet several tests; for example, unmarried or legally separated, pay over half the support of your **dependents,** etc.

Head money 1. A tax based on each person counted. A "head tax," "**capitation tax,**" **poll tax,** immigration tax, etc. 2. A bounty or reward for enemies or outlaws killed or brought in alive.

Head tax **Capitation tax** (see that word).

Headnote A summary of a **case** placed at the beginning of the case when it is collected and published.

Hearing 1. A court proceeding. 2. A trial-like proceeding that takes place in an **administrative agency** or other noncourt setting. **3.** A meeting of a legislative **committee** to gather information. **4.** A *"public hearing"* may involve an agency's showing a new plan or proposed action to the public and allowing public comment and criticism.

Hearing examiner (or hearing officer) A judgelike official in an **administrative agency.** Also called "administrative law judge."

Hearsay Secondhand **evidence.** Facts not in the personal knowledge of the witness, but a repetition of what others said, that are used to prove the truth of what those others said. Oral or written evidence that depends on the believability of something or someone not available to the court.

Hearsay exception **Evidence** that will be admitted as evidence in a trial because it fits under a special rule, even though it is **hearsay** (see that word) and would normally be kept out because of this. For example, **dying declarations** are a *hearsay exception* in some situations. There are many such exceptions, and the rules for whether or not *hearsay* may be used are among the more complex in the law.

Heart-balm act State laws either eliminating or restricting lawsuits based on **breach of promise** to marry.

Heat of passion A state of violent and uncontrollable provoked anger that may reduce the legal definition of a killing from **murder** to **manslaughter.**

Hedging Safeguarding a deal or speculation by making counterbalancing arrangements. For example, if a dealer **contracts** to deliver a hundred ounces of gold at a future time, then thinks that the price of gold may go up, the dealer might contract to *buy* fifty, or even a hundred, ounces of gold for that same future delivery date.

Height density controls Control of an area's population density by limiting the maximum height of buildings through **zoning** laws.

Heir A person who **inherits** property; a person who has a *right* to inherit property; or a person who has a right to inherit property only if another person dies without leaving a valid, complete **will.**

Held Decided; as in "the court held that"; (see definition no. 2 of **hold**).

Henceforth An unnecessarily formal word meaning "now and in the future."

Hepburn Act A change in the *Interstate Commerce Act* to include pipelines under the act and to impose certain restrictions on common **carriers** (such as a prohibition on carrying most products in which the carrier has a financial interest).

Hereafter An unnecessarily formal word meaning "in the future."

Hereditaments Anything that can be inherited. Objects that can be inherited are called *"corporeal hereditaments"* and rights that can be inherited are called *"incorporeal hereditaments."*

Herein A vague word meaning "in this document." (*"Hereinabove"* and *"hereinafter"* are just as vague, adding only "before this" and "after this" to the definition.)

Heresy Holding or advocating opinions contrary to established religion. This used to be punishable by the government, but the **Constitution** prohibits governmental involvement in religion.

Hereto An unnecessarily formal word meaning "to this."

Heretofore A vague and unnecessary word meaning "before" or "in times past."

Hereunder A vague word meaning either "later in this document" or "somewhere in this document."

Herewith An unncessarily formal word meaning "in this" or "with this."

Hermeneutics Legal hermeneutics is the art of the **construction** and **interpretation** of legal documents and the rules and **doctrines** so used.

Hidden asset An **asset** with a much higher value than the value stated in the company's financial records.

Hierarchy An ordering of persons, things, or ideas by rank or level, with more at the bottom than at the top. A typical *hierarchy* is the army (many privates, some majors, very few generals, etc.). Most **bureaucracies** are arranged this way.

High crimes and misdemeanors The basis for **impeachment** in the U.S. **Constitution**. Opinions differ as to the exact meaning of the phrase. It may include **felonies**; it may include offenses against the U.S. that have serious governmental or political consequences; or it may be whatever the U.S. **Congress** decides it is.

Highest and best use The use of land that would bring in the most money. For example, a real estate **assessor** valuing a piece of farm land inside an urban area might say that it should be taxed as if an office building could go up on the site.

Hijacking Stealing goods (or goods plus the vehicle) while they are in transit.

Hilton doctrine The principle that in a lawsuit over an oil or gas **lease,** persons entitled to **royalty** payments must be brought in as **parties** if they would lose their rights upon termination of the lease.

Hitherto An unnecessarily formal word that means "in the past."

Hobbs Act **Anti-Racketeering Act** (see that word).

Hobby loss A non**deductible** loss from a hobby, rather than a loss from a profit-making activity. One test of a *hobby loss* is whether or not the activity made a profit in two of the last five years.

Hoc (Latin) This.

Hold **1.** To possess or own something lawfully and by good **title.** **2.** To decide. A judge who decides how law applies to a case or "declares **conclusions of law**" is said to *"hold that . . . ."* **3.** Conduct or have take place; for example, to *"hold court."*

Hold harmless Agree to pay claims that might come up against another person.

Hold over **1.** Keep possession as a **tenant** after the **lease** period ends. **2.** Stay in office after the **term** of office is up.

Holder A person who has legally received possession of a **negotiable instrument** (see that word), such as a **check,** and who is entitled to get payment on it.

Holder in due course A **holder** (see that word) who buys a **negotiable instrument** thinking that it is **valid,** and having no knowledge that any business involving it is shady. The Uniform Commercial Code defines it as "a holder who takes the instrument for value, in good faith and without notice that it is overdue or has been dishonored or of any defense against or claim to it." But this definition is limited to the "usual course of business" and does not usually include *judicial sales,* **inheritance,** etc. A *holder in due course* has more rights than a mere holder. For example, except in **consumer** sales and credit, a holder in due course cannot be sued for defective goods by a buyer of merchandise involving the negotiable instrument.

Holding The core of a judge's **decision** in a case. It is that part of the judge's written **opinion** that applies the law to the facts of the case and about which can be said "the case means no more and no less than this." When later cases rely on a case as **precedent,** it is only the *holding* that should be used to establish the precedent. A *holding* may be less than the judge said it was. If the judge made broad, general statements, the holding is limited to only that part of the generalizations that directly apply to the facts of that particular case. "Holding" is the opposite of "**dicta.**"

Holding company   A company that exists primarily to control other companies by owning their **stock.** A *personal holding company* is formed by a few persons to avoid taxes. This type of company is subject to a special federal income tax.

Holding period   The length of time a **capital** asset must be owned to make the federal taxation more favorable as a **capital** *gain.*

Holograph   A **will, deed,** or other legal document that is entirely in the handwriting of the signer. Some states require a *holographic* **will** to be signed, witnessed, and in **compliance** with other formalities before it is valid. Other states require less.

Home owners warranty   The protection of a new home against major defects for several years either under a **warranty/insurance** program run by a national builders' association or under state laws.

Home relief   See **general assistance.**

Home rule   Local self-government.

Home port doctrine   **1.** A ship in interstate or foreign commerce may be taxed only in its home port.   **2.** A provider of repairs for a ship anywhere other than in the home port can get a **lien** for these repairs, but in the home port, local law decides whether a lien is allowed.

Homeowners policy   A standard type of **insurance** that covers fire, water, theft, **liability,** and other losses.

Homestead exemption   State laws allowing a head of a family to keep a home and some property safe from **creditors** or to allow certain persons (such as those over a certain age) to avoid paying real estate or inheritance taxes on their homes.

Homicide   Killing another person (not necessarily a crime).

Homo   (Latin) A man; a human being.

Homologation   **1.** Approval by a court.   **2. Estoppel.**

Hon   Short for "honorable," often placed before a judge's name.

Honor

Honor To **accept** (or pay) a **negotiable instrument,** such as a **check,** when it is properly presented for acceptance (or payment).

Honorarium A free gift; a free payment as opposed to a payment for services. But merely calling a payment (for example, for a speech) an *honorarium* does not necessarily make it nontaxable. There are specific tax rules.

Honorary trust A **trust** that gets no special tax advantages, but is not quite a private, ordinary trust; for example, to "feed the pigeons in Clark Park." Some states allow these trusts, but most do not.

Horizontal merger One company acquiring another that produces the same or similar products for sale in the same geographic area.

Horizontal price-fixing An agreement among competing producers, wholesalers, or merchants to set the price of goods. These agreements are prohibited by law.

Horizontal property acts Laws dealing with **cooperative** housing or **condominiums.**

Hornbook A book summarizing the basic principles of one legal subject, usually for law students.

Hose and spray An expression for the power of some **trustees** to decide how much each person named in a will should get.

Hostile fire A fire that either escapes from where it was contained or a fire that was never intended to exist at all.

Hostile possession Claiming ownership of land against the whole world (including the person whose name appears on the land records as owner), but not necessarily in an angry, aggressive, or emotionally "hostile" way.

Hostile witness A **witness** called by one side in a trial who shows so much **prejudice** or hostility to that side that he or she can be treated as if called by the other side. This allows **cross-examination** of your own witness.

Hot blood **Heat of passion** (see that word).

Hot cargo **1.** Goods produced or handled by an employer with whom a **union** has a **labor dispute.** "*Hot cargo agreements*" in which a company promises to put pressure on another company with which a union has a dispute are now illegal. **2.** Stolen goods.

Hot pursuit **Fresh pursuit** (see that word).

Hotchpot **1.** The mixing of property belonging to several persons in order to divide it equally. **2.** Taking into account money or property already given to children when dividing up the property of a dead person in order to equalize shares.

House **1.** One of the branches of a legislature; either the *"upper house"* or the *"lower house."* **2.** The lower branch of a two part **legislature** such as Congress is called "the House."

House counsel A lawyer who is an employee of a business and does its day-to-day legal work.

House of representatives **1.** The lower **house** of the U.S. **Congress** with members elected according to state population to two-year terms. **2.** The name for the lower chamber of several other **legislatures.**

Housebreaking Breaking into and entering a house to commit a crime. Some states call it **burglary** if done at night.

Household A **family** (see that word) living together (plus, sometimes, servants or others living with the family).

Hung jury A **jury** that cannot reach a **verdict** (decision) because of strong disagreement among jurors.

Humanitarian doctrine **Last clear chance** (see that word).

Hurdle rate The minimum acceptable rate of profit expected on a project for it to be started. See **opportunity cost.**

Husband-wife privilege **Marital communications privilege** (see that word).

Hybrid state (or hybrid theory jurisdiction) A state in which a **mortgage** is considered a cross between a **lien** and a transfer of **title.** In a *hybrid state* the **creditor** must use **foreclosure.** One example is a state in which **trustees** hold title to the property during the mortgage.

Hypothecate **1.** To **pledge** or **mortgage** a thing without turning it over to the person making the loan. **2.** Securing repayment of a loan by holding the **stock, bonds,** etc., of the **debtor** until the debt is paid, with the power to sell them if it is not paid.

Hypothesis A theory or working assumption.

Hypothetical question A process of setting up a series of facts, assuming that they are true, and asking for an answer to a question based on those facts. In a trial, *hypothetical questions* may be asked of **expert witnesses** only. For example, a gun expert might be asked "If this gun had a silencer, could a shot be heard from a hundred feet away?"

Ii

I.C.C. **1.** Interstate Commerce Commission. A federal agency that **regulates** interstate railroads, trucking companies, etc. **2. Indian Claims Commission.**

I.e. (Latin) That is. Short for *id est*.

I.L.P. Index of Legal Periodicals.

I.M.F. International Monetary Fund. A United Nations agency that helps stabilize international exchange rates and promotes world trade.

I.N.S. **Immigration and Naturalization Service** (see that word).

I.O.U. "I owe you." A written acknowledgment of a debt.

I.R.A. **Individual retirement account.**

I.R.C. **Internal Revenue Code** (see that word).

I.R.S. Internal Revenue Service. The U.S. tax collection agency.

I.T.C. Investment tax credit.

Ibid. (Latin) The same; in, from, or found in the same place (same book, page, case, etc.). Short for *ibidem*.

Id (Latin) The same; exactly the same thing. Short for *idem*.

Identity **1.** In **patent** law, *identity of invention* means exact sameness as to looks, parts, method of operation, and results. **2.** In **civil procedure,** *identity of interest* means two persons joined so closely (usually in a business sense) that suing one serves as **notice** of the lawsuit on the other, and a **judgment** against one **bars** another judgment against the other. **3.** In **evidence** law, *identity* means that something or someone is authentic, that it is the thing or person it is represented to be.

Ignoramus (Latin) *"We are ignorant" (of a reason).* The formal words that used to be said by a grand **jury** that failed to find a reason to charge someone with a crime. Now they say *"No bill," "not found,"* or something similar.

Ignorantia legis neminem excusat (Latin) Ignorance of the law is no excuse.

Illegal Contrary to the criminal law; breaking a law (not just improper or civilly wrong).

Illegal entry A foreigner is guilty of *illegal entry* into the U.S. if he or she comes in at the wrong time or place, avoids examination by immigration officials, or gets in by **fraud.**

Illegal purpose doctrine The rule that an otherwise legal act is illegal if done to further an illegal purpose. This rule is **constitutional** only in certain limited situations.

Illegally obtained evidence **Evidence** obtained by violating a person's **constitutional** or **statutory** rights; by searching without a **warrant,** with a legally defective warrant, or no **probable cause** to arrest and search; etc. This evidence cannot be used in a **criminal** trial.

Illegitimate **1.** Contrary to law; lacking legal authorization. **2.** A child born to unmarried parents. The law in many states is changing as to who may be defined as *illegitimate,* as to **inheritance** and other rights of illegitimate children, and as to use of the word itself to describe *any* child.

Illicit Prohibited; unlawful.

Illusory promise A statement that looks like a promise that could make a **contract,** but, upon close examination of the words, promises nothing real or legally binding.

Imbargo See **embargo.**

Imbezzle See **embezzlement.**

Imitation Something made intentionally to resemble something else. In **trademark** law, if a use of words, letters, signs, etc., is close enough to a trademark to fool the general public (not necessarily when placed side by side, but when there is no chance to compare the two), it is an *imitation* and usually forbidden.

Immaterial Not necessary; not important; without weight; trivial.

Immediate cause **1.** The last event in a series of events, which, without any further events, produced the result in question. This may be different from "**proximate cause.**" **2.** Proximate cause (see that word).

Immediate issue Children.

Immemorial See **time immemorial.**

Immigrant **1.** A foreigner who comes into a country. **2.** A foreigner who comes into a country with the intention of living permanently. **3.** In U.S. law, a foreigner who comes to the U.S. to live permanently and who meets several specific requirements of the Immigration and Naturalization Act.

Immigration act of 1965   A federal law that eliminated the immi-gration quota preference given to Europeans and set new stan-dards, such as "possessing special skills," for preference.

Immigration and Naturalization Service   A U.S. government agency that handles the admission, **naturalization,** and **depor-tation** of foreigners. It also guards against the illegal entry of **aliens.** The *Immigration Appeals Board* handles mostly **appeals** from deportation orders.

Imminent   Just about to happen; threatening.

Immoral   A vague word that can mean anything from "contrary to the accepted conduct of one religious sect" to "flagrant and shameless disregard for the welfare of the community or the opinions of most of its members" to "violating community stan-dards as expressed by law." For a **contract** to be **invalid** or **void** due to *immoral* **consideration** or for a lawyer to be disbarred due to *immoral conduct,* immorality usually means serious illegality.

Immovables   Land and things naturally and permanently a part of the land.

Immunity   **1.** Any exemption from a duty that the law usually requires.   **2.** Freedom from a duty or a penalty of any kind. **3.** The freedom from prosecution (based on anything the **wit-ness** says) that is given by the government to a witness who is forced to **testify** before a grand **jury,** a **legislature,** etc. *Use im-munity* is a witness's freedom from prosecution for any crime involved with the compelled testimony or any "leads" from it. *Transactional immunity* is freedom from prosecution for only the crime inquired about. The federal government and most states give full *use* immunity.   **4.** The freedom of a national, state, or local government from all taxes and from most **tort** lawsuits. See **governmental instrumentality** and **sovereign immunity.**

Immunity bath   Automatic **immunity** (see that word) from pros-ecution when you testify, whether or not you request it.

Impact rule   The rule (used today in very few states) that **dam-ages** for emotional distress cannot be had in a **negligence** law-suit unless there is also a physical blow.

Impair   Weaken, make worse, lessen, or otherwise hurt.

Impanel   Make up a list of **jurors** for a trial or select those who will actually serve.

Imparl   Delay proceedings in a lawsuit so that the two sides can discuss settlement of the dispute. Both the delay and the discussion are called an *imparlance.*

Impartial   To be *impartial,* an **expert witness** or a **jury** must not favor one side over the other or prejudge any of the facts or theories involved in the case. A **juror** in particular must be fair, open-minded, unbiased, and just, so that decisions are based only on legally-produced **evidence.**

Impeach   1. See **impeachment.**   2. Show that a **witness** is untruthful, either by **evidence** of past conduct, or by showing directly that the witness is not telling the truth.

Impeachment   1. See **impeach.**   2. The first step in the removal from public office of a high public official such as a governor, judge, or president. In the case of the U.S. president, the House of Representatives makes an accusation by drawing up *"articles of impeachment,"* voting on them, and presenting them to the Senate. This is *impeachment.* But impeachment has popularly come to include the trial of the president in the Senate and conviction by two-thirds of the senators.

Impediment   The legal inability to make a contract. For example, an *impediment to marriage* might be a prior marriage that is still **valid.**

Imperfect trust   An **executory trust** (see each word).

Impersonation   Pretending to be a police officer, a public official, or a person (such as a doctor or lawyer) whose occupation requires a state license. This may be a crime in many situations.

Impertinence   Irrelevance in the sense that the proof offered may be relevant to an issue, but the issue itself is irrelevant to the trial.

Implead   Bring into a lawsuit. For example, if A sues B and B sues C in the same lawsuit, B **impleads** C.

Implied   Known indirectly. Known by analyzing surrounding circumstances or the actions of the persons involved. The opposite of **express.** For example, *implied authority* is the authority one person gives to another to do a job even if the authority is not given directly (such as the authority to buy and charge gas if you run out while making a delivery for your boss). And *implied terms* are parts of a **contract** that do not exist on paper, but are part of the contract nonetheless (because the law requires them, because usual contracts in that business have them, etc.).

Implied powers

Implied powers   See **necessary**.

Implied remedies   A private lawsuit to protect a **constitutional right** may be permitted by a court even if no particular lawsuit is specifically provided for by law. This lawsuit (a **remedy**) is **implied** in the right itself.

Implied warranty   The legal conclusion that a merchant promises that what is sold is fit for normal use, or, if the merchant knows what the buyer wants the thing for, that it is fit for that particular purpose. Unless these *implied warranties* are expressly excluded (for example, by clearly labeling the thing sold "**as is**"), a merchant will be held to them.

Import–export clause   The **constitutional** provision that no state may tax imports and exports unless the tax is absolutely necessary for inspection laws or otherwise permitted by Congress.

Impossibility   That which cannot be done. A contract is not binding and cannot be enforced if it is *physically impossible* (for example, to be in two places at once); *legally impossible* (for example, to make the contract at age four); or *logically impossible* (for example, to sell a car for one thousand dollars when the buyer pays two thousand for it). These are all examples of "*objective impossibility.*" However, "*subjective impossibility*" (such as not having enough money to pay for something you have contracted to buy) will not get you out of a contract.

Imposts   Taxes; import taxes.

Impound   **1.** Take a thing into the **custody** of the law until a legal question about it is decided.   **2.** *Impoundment* is an action by a president or governor to prevent the spending of public money that the **legislature** has ordered spent.

Impracticability   Less than an **impossibility** and more than a big inconvenience; difficult, to the point where it would be unreasonable or unfair to require something. "*Impracticability*" is another example of legal language run wild.

Impressment   The power (not available in the U.S.) of a government to take merchant seamen (or even merchant ships and crew) to add to the navy.

Imprest   **1.** A loan or advance.   **2.** An *imprest fund* is petty cash.

Imprimatur   (Latin) "Let it be printed." Official government permission to publish a book. This is not needed in the U.S.

Imprisonment   **1.** Putting a person in prison.   **2.** Depriving a person of personal liberty in any physical way.

Improper accumulation   Too much profit that is kept by a business to shield the owners from personal taxes. See **accumulated earnings tax**.

Improvement   An addition or change to land or buildings that increases the value. More than a repair or replacement. See **repair** for the *tax* difference.

Improvident   A judge's **decision, judgment,** or **order** is "*improvidently granted*" if the judge later thinks that he or she made a mistake.

Imputed   Something is "*imputed*" to a person if, even though that person does not know a fact, he or she *should* have known it (both legally and actually) or if, even though that person is not physically responsible for something, he or she is legally responsible. For example, if a person does certain kinds of activities, **income** will be imputed to him or her for tax purposes whether or not money was actually paid. See the words following for examples.

Imputed knowledge   If the facts are available to a person and if it is that person's duty to know those facts, knowledge may be *imputed* to that person, and he or she is treated legally as if the facts are known.

Imputed negligence   If David is **negligent** and Paul is responsible for David's actions, David's negligence is *imputed* (carried over or attributed) to Paul.

Imputed notice   If Linda is given **notice** of something (a fact, a lawsuit, etc.) and Linda is Ruth's **agent** (lawyer, manager, etc.), then notice to Linda can be *imputed* as notice to Ruth.

In autre droit   (French) "In another's right." Representing someone else (as an **executor, trustee,** etc.) in a legal proceeding.

In banc   See **banc**.

In being   Existing now. An unborn child may sometimes be considered a "life in being," but usually not.

In blank   Without restriction. Signing a **negotiable instrument,** such as a **check,** without making it **payable** to anyone in particular (leaving the "pay to" space empty).

In camera   (Latin)   **1.** "In chambers"; in a judge's private office. **2. A hearing** in court with all spectators excluded.

In common   More than one person sharing something whole. For example, if two people own a house "*in common,*" they both own all of it.

In eadem causa   (Latin) In the same condition.

In esse   (Latin) In being; now existing.

In evidence   **1.** Facts or things that are already before the court as **evidence**.   **2.** "*Facts in evidence*" may be those facts already fully proved (but not necessarily believed, or believed to be important, by the jury).

In extremis   (Latin) In the last illness before dying.

In faciendo   (Latin) While doing something.

In fieri   (Latin) Incomplete. In the process of happening or being made.

In forma pauperis   (Latin) "As a pauper." Permission to sue in court without paying any court costs.

In futuro   (Latin) In the future; at some future time.

In haec verba   (Latin) In these (same) words.

In hoc   (Latin) In this; concerning this.

In integrum   (Latin) To the original or former state.

In invitum   (Latin) Against an adversary.

In jure   (Latin) In law or by right. *In jure alterius* means "by another's right."

In kind   The same type of thing. For example, a loan is returned "*in kind*" when a closely similar, but not identical, object is returned.

In lieu of   Instead of; in place of.

In limine   (Latin) "At the beginning"; preliminary. A **motion** *in limine* is a pretrial **protective order** (see that word).

In litem   (Latin) See **ad litem**.

In loco parentis   (Latin) In the place of a parent; acting as a parent with respect to the care and supervision of a child; the power to discipline a child as a parent can.

In medias res   (Latin) Into the heart or middle of a subject without introduction or preface.

In pais   (French)   **1.** An act done informally, as opposed to being done by taking legal action, or by making a formal document.   **2.** Outside of the courtroom. See **pais**. [pronounce: in pay]

In pari delicto   (Latin) In equal fault; equally guilty.

In pari materia   See **pari materia**.

In perpetuity   Forever.

In personam   (Latin) A lawsuit brought to enforce rights against another person, as opposed to one brought to enforce rights in a thing against the whole world (**in rem**). For example, a suit for automobile accident injuries is in *personam* because it is against the driver or owner only. A suit to establish **title** to land is *in rem* because, even if there is a person fighting the claim on the other side, a victory is binding against the whole world and a "thing" is primarily involved.

In pleno lumine   (Latin) "In daylight"; common knowledge.

In posse   (Latin) "In possibility"; not now or yet existing.

In praesenti   (Latin) Right now.

In principio   (Latin) At first; at the start.

In promptu   (Latin) **1.** Now ready; in readiness. **2.** Without preparation.

In propria causa nemo judex   (Latin) No one can be a judge in his or her own case.

In re   (Latin) "In the matter of." This is a prefix to the name of a case concerned with a thing, rather than a lawsuit directly between two persons. For example, *"in re Brown's Estate"* might be the title of a proceeding in **probate** court to dispose of the property of a dead person. The words are also used when a child is involved. For example, *"in re Mary Smith"* might be the title of a child **neglect** proceeding even though it is really against the parents. *"In re"* should *not* be used in an ordinary sentence as a substitute for "concerning." [pronounce: in ray]

In rem   (Latin) A lawsuit brought to enforce rights in a thing against the whole world as opposed to one brought to enforce rights against another person. For an example of each type of suit, see **in personam**. Also, there is a type of lawsuit in between *in rem* and *in personam* called *"quasi in rem"* or "sort of concerning a thing." These are **actions** that are really directed against a person, but are formally directed only against property (or vice versa); for example, a mortgage **foreclosure.**

In solido   (Latin) "As a whole." Each of several persons who own (or owe) something all together also owning (or owing) the whole thing individually.

In specie   (Latin) **1.** In the same or similar form or way. **2.** Exactly the same; specific **performance** (see that word).

In terrorum   (Latin) "In threat." The name given to language in a **will** that requires any person taking money or property under the will to refrain from contesting the will to get a bigger share.

In testimonium

In testimonium (Latin) As a **witness** to; as **evidence** of.

In the black (red) Making a profit (taking a loss).

In toto (Latin) In whole; completely.

In transitu (Latin) While in transit.

Inadmissible Facts or things that cannot be admitted into **evidence** in a trial; for example, evidence from an illegal search or most types of **hearsay** (secondhand) **testimony**.

Inadvertence **1.** Lack of attention or carelessness. **2.** Excusable mistake or oversight.

Inalienable Something that cannot be given away, taken away, or sold. For example, *"inalienable rights"* are those basic **constitutional** rights that cannot be taken away.

Inc. Incorporated; for example: "Pink Ink, Inc." is the Pink Ink Corporation.

Incapacity **1.** Lack of legal ability or power to do something. For example, a child has a legal *incapacity* to vote or make **contracts**. **2.** An injury bad enough to prevent working.

Incarceration Confinement in a jail or prison.

Incest Sexual intercourse between a man and woman who, according to state law, are too closely related by blood.

Inchoate Partial, unfinished, unripened. For example, an *"inchoate instrument"* is a document, such as a **deed**, that is **valid** between the **parties**, but is not "complete" and valid against anyone else until it is registered or recorded with the proper officials. [pronounce: in-ko-ate]

Incidental Depending upon something else more important. For example, *"incidental damages"* are the "side costs" of a broken contract, such as storing the goods you thought were sold, and a search is *incidental* to an arrest only if it is at the same time, limited in scope, and for a definite purpose.

Incident of ownership An indication that a right or some property has been kept rather than fully given away; some measure of control kept over something.

Incite Urge, provoke, strongly encourage, or stir up.

Included offense A crime that is part of another crime and that requires less proof. For example, **battery** is usually included in *manslaughter*. Also called "lesser included offense."

Income **1.** Money gains from business, work, or investments. **2.** All financial gain. **3.** *Accrued income* is earned, but not yet received. *Earned income* is from work or a business, rather than from investments; *gross income* is what is taken in before **deductions**; *imputed income* is a benefit that will be taxed as income even though it doesn't look like income; and *ordinary income* is from wages, interest, etc. (everything except **capital** gains, such as stocks that go up, etc.).

Income averaging   Reducing your taxes by showing that your income in prior years was far lower and by paying tax on the basis of your average income for several years.

Income basis   A way of figuring out the *rate of return* (payoff) of a **security** (such as a stock or bond) by dividing the price paid for it by the income (**interest** or **dividends**) paid that year.

Income splitting   Reducing total family taxes by giving income-producing property (such as **stocks**) to a family member who pays taxes at a lower rate.

Income statement   See **statement** of income.

Income tax   A tax on profits from business, work, or **investments**, but not on the growth in value of investments or property. For income tax **return**, see **tax return**.

Incompatibility   1. Two or more things incapable logically, physically, or legally of existing together.   2. The inability of a husband and wife to live together in marriage. "*Incompatibility*" is "**grounds**" for a **divorce** in some states. In these states, a divorce may be granted without either person being at fault.

Incompetency   The lack of ability or of a legal right to do something. This word often refers to the condition of persons who lack the mental ability to manage their own affairs and who have someone appointed by the state to manage their finances.

Incompetent evidence   Facts, objects, **testimony**, etc., that may not be admitted into (used as) **evidence** in a legal proceeding.

Incomplete transfer   A gift or other transfer of property made by a person who keeps some of the control or benefits. If the person then dies, the value of that property may be included in his or her **estate** for tax purposes. See also **incidents of ownership**.

Inconsistent   Contradictory, so that if one thing is **valid**, another thing cannot be valid. Or, if one thing is allowed to happen, another thing cannot be.

Incontestability clause   A provision in a life or health **insurance** policy that after a certain number of years the insurance company cannot get out of the contract by claiming that statements made in the original application were wrong.

Inconvenience

Inconvenience   A broad word meaning anything from trivial problems to serious hardship or injustice.

Incorporate   Formally create a **corporation**. The persons who do this initially are called "incorporators."

Incorporate by reference   Make a part of something by mere mention; for example, in document A, say that document B is a part of document A, just as if document B were actually written out in document A. This is a space-saving technique.

Incorporation doctrine   The principle that most of the safeguards in the **Bill of Rights** must be followed by the states, as well as by the national government, because the Fourteenth Amendment requires it.

Incorporeal   Without body. The opposite of **corporeal** (see that word).

Incorrigible   Cannot be corrected. An *incorrigible* **juvenile** is a child who cannot be managed or controlled by parents or **guardians.**

Increment   **1.** One piece or part of a piece-by-piece increase. **2.** Anything gained or added. **3.** The process of gaining or adding to something.

Incriminate   Expose yourself or another person to the danger of prosecution for a crime.

Incriminatory   Tending to show guilt.

Incroachment   See **encroachment**.

Inculpate   **1.** Accuse of guilt or crime. **2.** Involve in guilt or crime.

Incumbent   A person who presently holds an office (usually an elected public office).

Incumber   See **encumber**.

Incumbrance   See **encumbrance**.

Incur   Get. Get something bad, such as a debt or **liability**, because the law places it on you. For example, you *incur a liability* when a court gives a money **judgment** against you.

Indebitatus assumpsit   See **assumpsit**.

Indecent   A general term meaning "offensive to public morality." *Indecent* is well defined in: *indecent assault* (fondling or otherwise touching an unwilling person, but with no intent to commit **rape**); *indecent exposure* (showing genitals in a public place); and *indecent liberties* (fondling or otherwise taking sexual advantage of a child). *Indecent* is not well defined in the field of obscenity.

Indefeasible   A right that cannot be defeated, **revoked**, or taken away in any way is called *"indefeasible."*

Indefinite term   A jail or prison sentence for an unfixed length of time up to a certain maximum. See also **indeterminate**.

Indemnify   Compensate or reimburse a person who has suffered a loss.

Indemnity   A contract to compensate or reimburse a person for possible losses of a particular type; a type of **insurance**. For *indemnity bond*, see **bond** and for *indemnity policy*, see **insurance**.

Indenture   1. An old word for a formal paper, such as a **deed**, with identical copies for each person signing it.   2. The written agreement of sale for **bonds** that contains the **maturity** date, interest rate, etc.   3. Any **mortgage** or similar agreement in which there is a **lien** or similar **security interest**.   4. An apprenticeship agreement.

Independent agency   A federal **agency, board** or **commission** that is not a part of one of the **cabinet** departments. These include the *Veterans Administration, Environmental Protection Agency, Federal Trade Commission, Federal Reserve Board*, and many others.

Independent contractor   A person who contracts with an employer to do a particular piece of work by his or her own methods and under his or her own control.

Independent source rule   If evidence can be traced to a source completely apart from illegally gathered **evidence**, it may be used by the government in a criminal trial. See also **fruit of the poisonous tree**.

Indestructible trust   A **Claflin trust** (see that word).

Indeterminate   With the exact time period not set. For example, an *indeterminate sentence* is a criminal sentence with a maximum or minimum set, but not the exact amount of time. Some states allow judges to set only indeterminate sentences, and have special **boards** to decide the exact sentence later.

Index offenses   The types of crime reported to the **F.B.I.**, such as **murder, rape, robbery**, etc.

Indexing   Linking the level of payments (on **bonds**, wages, pension benefits, etc.) to an index such as the **consumer price index.**

Indian Claims Commission A government agency that handles claims against the U.S. by groups of American Indians.

Indian reservation See **reservation.**

Indicia Indications; pointers; signs; circumstances that make a certain fact probable, but not certain. For example, *indicia of partnership* are those facts that would make you believe that a person was a partner in a business even if it doesn't seem so on the surface, and *indicia of title* are documents, other than original legal proofs, that something is owned (a copy of a bill of sale, etc.). [pronounce: in-dish-i-a]

Indictment A formal accusation of a crime, made against a person by a grand **jury** upon the request of a **prosecutor.** [pronounce: in-dite-ment]

Indigent A poor person. A person entitled to a free lawyer in **criminal** cases and in some **civil** cases.

Indignity In **divorce** law, indignities such as abusive vulgarity or disdain are a type of mental **cruelty.**

Indirect cost **Fixed charges (or fixed cost)** (see that word).

Indirect evidence **Circumstantial evidence** (see that word).

Indirect tax 1. A tax on a right, privilege, or event (such as the granting of the right to **incorporate**) rather than a tax on a thing, on income, etc. 2. The opposite of a **direct tax** (see that word).

Indispensable party A person who has such a stake in the outcome of a lawsuit that the judge will not make a final decision unless that person is formally joined as a **party** to the lawsuit.

Individual Retirement Account A **trust**like bank account or other plan into which employees who are not part of tax-deferred **pension** or profit-sharing plans may set aside a certain amount of money each year and have the money and all interest taxed only later when withdrawn. See also **Keogh plan.**

Indorse Sign a paper or document.

Indorsement 1. Signing a document "on the back" or merely signing it anywhere. 2. Signing a **negotiable instrument,** such as a check, in a way that allows the piece of paper, and the rights it stands for, to transfer to another person. A *qualified indorsement* limits rights (for example, signing "without recourse") and a *restrictive indorsement* limits its purpose or the person who may use it (for example, signing "for deposit"). For **accommodation, blank,** and **conditional** indorsements, see those words.

Inducement **1.** That thing, statement, or promise by a person that convinces another person to make a deal. A benefit or advantage of a deal. **2.** The thing that convinces someone to do something. The motive for an action.

Industrial relations All employer-employee matters, such as safety, **benefits,** union recognition and bargaining, etc.

Industrial union A labor union whose members may have different skills, but who work for the same type of industry (printing, clothing manufacture, etc).

Industry Any type of trade or business.

Infamy The loss of a good reputation because of **conviction** of a major crime, and the loss of certain legal rights that accompanies this loss.

Infancy A general word for being a very young child. In some states, however, this means the same as **minority** (see that word).

Infant **1.** A person under the age of adulthood. **2.** A very young child.

Inference A fact or proposition that is shown to be probably true because it is the logical result of another fact or proposition that has already been proved or admitted to be true. For example, if the first four books in a set of five have green covers, it is a logical *inference* that the fifth book has a green cover.

Inferior court **1.** Any court but the highest one in a court system. **2.** A court with special, limited responsibilities, such as a **probate** court.

Infirmative Something that weakens the impact of other **evidence** is *infirmative*. In **criminal** law, infirmative evidence weakens either the facts or theories upon which the government bases its case. Evidence that **exculpates**.

Infirmity A defect. For example, if the papers that transfer a **title** are defective, the title transferred has an *infirmity*.

Information **1.** A formal accusation of a crime made by a proper public official such as prosecuting attorney. **2.** A sworn, written accusation of a crime that leads to an **indictment**. **3.** Personal knowledge of something. (But *"information and belief"* may mean no more than a person's opinion.)

Informed consent A person's agreement to allow something to happen (such as surgery) that is based on a full disclosure of the facts needed to make the decision intelligently.

Informer's privilege The government's right in some situations to withhold the identity of persons who give information on illegal activity.

Infra (Latin) **1.** Below or under. **2.** Within. **3.** Later in this book. For example, *"infra p. 236"* means "look at page 236, which is further on."

Infraction **1.** A violation of a minor law. **2.** A violation or **breach** of a contract or a duty.

Infringement **1.** A **breach** or violation of a right. **2.** The unauthorized making, using, selling, or distributing of something protected by a **patent, copyright,** or **trademark.**

Infuedation An old English word for granting a person a **freehold** (full and complete) **estate** in land.

Ingross See **engrossment.**

Inherent Derived from and inseparable from the thing itself. For example, *"inherent danger"* is the danger some objects have by merely existing. A bomb is probably inherently dangerous, while a hammer is probably not.

Inherent vice Basic defect.

Inherit To receive property from a dead person, either by the effect of **intestacy** laws or from a **will.**

Inheritance Property received from a dead person, either by the effect of **intestacy** laws or from a **will.** An *inheritance tax* is the tax that the person who inherits pays. This is not an **estate tax** (see that word).

Initiative The power of the people to enact laws by voting, without the need for passage by the **legislature.**

Injunction A judge's order to a person to do or to refrain from doing a particular thing. For example, a court might *issue an injunction* to or "**enjoin**" a company from dumping wastes into a river. An injunction may be *preliminary* or *temporary* until the issue can be fully tried in court, or it may be *permanent* or *final* after the case has been decided.

Injure **1.** Hurt or harm. **2.** Violate the legal rights of another person.

Injuria (Latin) A wrong or injury. For example, *injuria absque damno* is an **injury** without **damages** (one that cannot be the basis of a lawsuit), and *injuria non excusat injuriam* means "one wrong does not excuse another." [pronounce: in-joo-ri-a]

Injurious falsehood   A false statement that causes intentional injury is an *injurious falsehood* even if it is not **defamation** (see that word).

Injury   Any wrong, hurt, or damage done to another person's rights, body, reputation, or property.

Innocent   **1.** Not guilty.   **2.** Not responsible for an action or event.   **3.** In good faith, or without knowledge of legal problems involved.

Inns of court   Associations that govern the education and **admission** to the **bar** of prospective trial lawyers (called "**barristers**") in England.

Inoperative   Not now in effect.

Inquest   **1.** A **coroner's hearing** (see each word) into the cause of a person's death, when that death was either violent or suspicious.   **2.** Any formal inquiry; for example, into a person's sanity or into the validity of a **title**.

Inquisitorial system   A system in which the judge acts to dig out facts and also to represent the state's interest in a trial. It is the opposite of the **adversary system** (see that word) we have in U.S. trials.

Insane   See **insanity.**

Insanity   **1.** *Insanity* is a legal, not a medical word, but it is no more precise or useful than "crazy" or "nuts." It has different meanings in different situations.   **2.** In various state proceedings to put a person into a mental hospital against his or her will because of *insanity*, the person may have to be "a danger to himself or others," "incapable of caring for himself and his property," or "a fit subject for treatment." The definitions are often circular, allowing the locking up of "insane persons" and defining "insane persons" as those who need locking up!   **3.** In a test of **capacity** to stand trial on a **criminal** charge, the definition of *insanity* is usually "an inability to understand the **charge** or to help in the **defense.**"   **4.** There are several different definitions of *insanity* when deciding whether a person is "not guilty (of a crime) by reason of insanity" (at the time it was committed). These include the **M'Naghten Rule** and the **Durham Rule** (see these words). The *Model Penal Code* says, "A person is not responsible for criminal conduct if at the time of such conduct, as a result of mental disease or defect, he lacks substantial capacity either to appreciate the criminality (wrongfulness) of his conduct or to conform his conduct to the requirements of law." **5.** When deciding the **capacity** of a person to make a valid **will**, some of the signs of *insanity* are "inability to understand the property being given away, the purpose and manner of its distribution, and the persons who are to receive it." **6.** Other areas of law that may involve definitions of *insanity* include: **defenses** to a **contract, annulment** of a marriage, **divorce,** appointment of a **guardian,** etc.

Inscription **1.** Placing a document, such as a mortgage, into the public records; **record** a document. **2.** Anything written on a durable surface such as a ring, a tombstone, etc.

Insecurity clause A section of a **contract** that allows a **creditor** to make an entire debt come due if there is a good reason to think that the **debtor** cannot or will not pay.

Insider A person who has business knowledge not available to the general public. This could be anyone from a **corporate officer** to the brother-in-law of a company's outside **accountant** (see "**tippee**"). There are federal rules about **stock** trading and other actions by *insiders* and monthly reports required on *insider trading* (usually by those owning 10 percent or more of a company).

Insolvency The condition of being **insolvent** (see that word).

Insolvent The condition of some persons (or organizations) who either cannot pay debts as they come due or whose **assets** are less than **liabilities.**

Inspection **1.** The right to see and copy documents, enter land, or do other things in order to gather **evidence** through the **discovery** process. **2.** *Inspection* laws include such subjects as on-site examinations of cleanliness in serving, storing, or shipping food; safety of medical machines, building, work conditions, etc.

Installment **1.** A separate delivery or payment. For example, an *installment contract* usually includes the delivery of goods in separate lots with payment made for each. **2.** A regular, partial payment of a debt. *Installment credit* is an arrangement where a buyer pays the price (and, usually, interest and other finance charges) in regular (usually monthly) payments. *Installment* sales, loans, etc., are usually subject to laws such as interest rate maximums and the **Truth-in-Lending Act** (see that word).

Instance **1.** Forceful request. **2.** Situation or occurrence.

Instant Present or current.

Instanter (Latin) Immediately.

Instigate Push into action (especially a bad action or a crime); **abet**.

Institutes An old word for various textbooks about the law.

Institution **1.** A public organization such as a college or a prison. **2.** The start of anything; for example, the commencement of a lawsuit. **3.** A basic system of laws.

Instructions Directions given by the judge to the jury explaining how they should go about deciding the case. This may include a summary of the questions to be decided, the laws that apply, and the **burden of proof**.

Instrument **1.** A written document; a formal or legal document such as a **contract** or a **will**. **2.** Short for "**negotiable instrument**" (see that word).

Instrumental trust A **ministerial** trust.

Instrumentality A **corporation** that is totally controlled by another corporation.

Insurable interest A person's real financial interest in another person or in an object. The "interest" is the fact that a person will suffer financially if the insured person dies or the insured object is lost. An **insurance** contract must involve an *insurable interest*, or it may be a form of gambling and unenforceable.

Insurance **1.** A **contract** in which one person pays money and the other person promises to reimburse the first person for specified types of losses if they occur. The person agreeing to compensate for losses is usually called the *"insurer"* or *"underwriter"*; the person who pays for this protection is the *"insured"*; the payment to the insurer is a *"premium"*; the written contract is a *"policy"*; the thing or person being protected is the *"insurable interest"*; and the types of harm protected against are *"risks"* or *"perils."* **2.** A few of the more common types of insurance (and the situations they cover) are as follows: *automobile liability* (injury to other persons or their property from an accident involving a car you own or drive); *casualty* (accidents and injuries); *credit life* (to pay off a car or other major purchase in case of death while installments are still owed); *group* (insurance provided at lower rates through an employer or other defined group of people); *homeowners* (a set of different types of insurance that usually include fire, theft, and liability); *self* (putting aside money into an account that will be used to pay claims if they come up or merely being *prepared* to pay for possible losses or claims); *straight life* (life insurance with continuing payments); *term* (insurance that ends at the end of a certain time period); *title* (protection against claims made on the title of land you own); *unemployment* (a government program through your job) and **workers' compensation. 3.** There are hundreds of types of insurance and dozens of ways of arranging it. Some of these are defined under their own words, but many are too technical or too little used to be included here.

Insured 1. A person who buys insurance on property or life. **2.** A person whose life is insured.

Insurer The person or company that provides insurance.

Insurrection A violent rebellion. (This is a federal crime.)

Intangibles Property that is really a right, rather than a physical object; for example, bank accounts, **stocks, copyrights, "goodwill"** of a business, etc.

Integrated Made whole or complete.

Integrated agreement An agreement is *integrated* when the persons making it agree on a document or documents as the final and complete expression and explanation of the agreement. This complete and written document is called an "**integration.**"

Integrated bar A system in which all lawyers who practice before the courts of a geographical area must belong to one organization, which is supervised by the highest court of that area.

Integration 1. The process of making something whole or complete. See "**integrated**" and the words following it. **2.** Bringing together two different groups (such as races) as equals. **3.** The combination of different businesses.

Intelligibility Clearness. (This word is a typical case of legal language run wild.)

Intemperance See **habitual intemperance.**

Intended use doctrine In **product liability** cases, a manufacturer is responsible for harm done by a product if the advertising and marketing indicates that the product can be used a certain way and if the harm done is a foreseeable result of such use.

Intendment True, correct meaning; intention.

Intent 1. The resolve or purpose to use a particular means to reach a particular result. "*Intent*" usually explains *how* a person wants to do something and *what* that person wants done, while "**motive**" explains *why*. These words often get confused. **2.** In **criminal** law, *intent* is divided into two types: *general* (intent to do something that the law prohibits); and *specific* (intent to do the exact thing **charged**). Also, if a person does something knowing that a certain result is likely, there is an *intent* to cause that result whether or not the person *desires* it.

Intention   Determination to do a certain thing (see **intent**).

Inter   Among or between.

Inter alia   (Latin) "Among other things." The phrase is usually used when what is being mentioned is only part of what there is; for example, "We found in the box, *inter alia,* a book."

Inter se   (Latin) Among or between themselves only. [pronounce: in-ter <u>say</u>]

Inter vivos   (Latin) "Between the living." The phrase describes an ordinary gift, as opposed to a gift made shortly before dying to avoid **estate** taxes. It also describes an *ordinary* **trust** as opposed to one set up under a **will**.

Interdict (or interdiction)   **1.** A prohibition; a **decree** prohibiting something.   **2.** A guardianship.

Interesse   (Latin) A legal interest or right. For example, an *interesse termini* is a **lease** held by a **tenant** who has not yet taken possession of the property.

Interest   **1.** A broad term for any right in property. For example, both an owner who **mortgages** land and the person who lends the owner money on the mortgage have an *interest* in the land.   **2.** The extra money a person receives back for lending money to another person; money paid for the use of money.   **3.** For the various types of interest, such as: **compound, future, public,** or **security** interest, see those words.

Interest equalization tax   A U.S. tax on long-term investment interest earned by U.S. citizens on foreign stocks, bonds, etc.

Interference   The state of affairs when two different persons claim a **patent** on what may be the same discovery or invention.

Interim   Temporary; meanwhile. For example, *interim financing* is a short-term construction loan, with final financing provided later by a **mortgage.**

Interior   Department of the Interior. The U.S. **cabinet** department that manages public lands, Indian affairs, natural resources, etc.

Interlineation   Writing between the lines.

Interlocking directorate

Interlocking directorate   Several of the same persons serving on the **boards** of directors of more than one company.

Interlocutory   Provisional; temporary; while a lawsuit is still going on. The *Interlocutory Appeals Act* is a federal law that provides for an **appeal** while a trial is going on if the trial judge states in writing: 1) A legal question has come up that directly affects the trial.   2) There are major questions as to how that point of law should be resolved.   3) The case would proceed better if the appeals court answers the question.

Intermediation   Investing through a bank or other financial institution.

Internal financing   Raising money for projects by keeping earnings, by getting back money from taxes due to **depreciation**, and other methods that do not involve selling **stock** or borrowing.

Internal law   The law of a country (or state) that applies to disputes wholly within that country; a country's laws excluding its **conflict of laws** rules.

Internal Revenue Code   The United States **tax** laws.

Internal security acts   Federal laws controlling the subversive activities of communist organizations and others whose purpose it is to overthrow or disrupt the government.

International Court of Justice   A branch of the United Nations that settles voluntarily submitted disputes between countries and also gives **advisory opinions** to the branches of the U.N.

International law   **1.** *Public international law* is the customary law that applies to the relationships and interactions between countries.   **2.** *Private international law* is the set of principles that determines which country's courts should hear a dispute and which country's laws should apply to each situation. It is sometimes called **conflict of laws**.

International Shoe Doctrine   The principle that a corporation must have at least minimal contacts with a state (carry on at least some activity there) for it to be sued in that state.

Internment   The confining of enemy foreigners or persons suspected of disloyalty during war.

Interpellation   **1.** Questioning.   **2.** A short-term agreement.   **3.** *Not* "interpolation."

Interpleader   **1.** A procedure in which persons having claims against another person may be forced to enter into a lawsuit or risk losing their claim. For example, if A is sued by B for a debt and A thinks that C might have a legitimate claim against A for the same debt, A may *interplead* C (join C as a **party**) to the suit. **2.** *Interpleader* also refers to the settling or deciding of claims between **defendants** in order to then settle or decide claims between the **plaintiff** and the defendants.

Interpol International criminal police organization, a coordinating group for law enforcement.

Interpolation **1.** The insertion of words into a completed document. **2.** *Not* **interpellation.**

Interposition The principle, now dead, that a state may reject a federal government demand if the state considers the demand **unconstitutional.**

Interpretation **1.** The process of discovering or deciding the meaning of a written document by studying only the document itself and not the circumstances surrounding it. **2.** Deciding what a document means as opposed to what it should mean.

Interrogation The questioning by police of a person suspected or accused of a crime.

Interrogatories **1.** Written questions sent from one side in a lawsuit to another, attempting to get written answers to factual questions or seeking an explanation of the other side's legal contentions. These are a part of the formal **discovery** process in a lawsuit and usually take place before the trial. **2.** Written questions addressed to any **witness.**

Interstate Commerce Act A federal law that **regulates** the surface transportation of goods and persons between states; regulates rates for railroads, pipelines, etc. all through the *Interstate Commerce Commission.*

Interstate compact An agreement between or among states that has been passed as law by the states and has been approved by Congress.

Intervening cause A cause of an accident or other injury that will remove the blame from the wrongdoer who originally set events in motion. It is also called an *"intervening act," "intervening agency,"* or *"intervening force,"* not to mention *"superseding cause," "supervening negligence,"* etc.

Intervenor A person who voluntarily **enters** (becomes a **party** in) a lawsuit between other persons (see **intervention**).

Intervention A proceeding by which a person is allowed to become a **party** to a lawsuit by joining the **plaintiff**, joining the **defendant,** or making separate claims.

Intestacy

Intestacy   See **intestate**.

Intestate   **1.** Dying without making a **will**; dying without making a valid will; dying and leaving some property that is not covered by a will.   **2.** A person who dies without making a valid will.

Intestate succession   **Inheritances** distributed to **heirs** according to a state's laws about who should collect. This is done when there is no valid **will** or when the will does not cover some of a dead person's property.

Intolerable cruelty   Same as **cruelty** (see that word).

Intoxication   A greatly lessened ability to function normally caused by alcohol or drugs. *Involuntary* (caused by others against your will) *intoxication* is a defense against **criminal** charges and **negligence** suits, while *voluntary intoxication* is only relevant in determining a state of mind when proving a particular state of mind as part of a criminal charge.

Intra   "Within." For example, *intrastate commerce* is business carried out entirely within one state, as opposed to **interstate commerce** (see that word).

Intrinsic evidence   Facts learned from a **document** itself, not from outside information about it.

Introduction of evidence   The submission of **evidence** for possible acceptance in a trial.

Inure   Take effect; result. For example, if "benefits *inure* to Mr. Smith," they will come to him and take effect for him. "*Inurement*" usually means taking effect by **operation of law**, rather than by a person's actions.

Invalid   **1.** Inadequate; useless.   **2.** Not binding; lacking legal force.

Invasion of privacy   Publicizing someone's private affairs that are of no legitimate public concern; using a person for publicity without permission; eavesdropping; or violation of the right to be left alone. This may be a **tort**.

Invention   In **patent** law, this is the process of producing (not merely discovering) by independent work something not previously known or existing.

Inventory   **1.** A detailed list of articles of property.   **2.** Goods or materials held for sale or lease; sometimes also work in process or materials used in a business.

Inverse condemnation   A lawsuit against the government to demand payment for an informal or irregular taking of private property.

Inverse order of alienation doctrine The rule that when a piece of land has been sold off in separate parcels and a person must collect on a **mortgage** or **lien** on the original land, the person must now collect first on the piece still held by the original owner, then on the piece sold last, then next to last, and so on until paid off.

Investment Using money to make money (buying **stocks,** putting cash in a savings account, etc.).

Investment Advisors Act A federal law that regulates all persons who give professional investment advice. It is administered by the *Securities Exchange Commission.*

Investment banker An underwriter or middleman between a **corporation** putting out new **stocks** and **bonds** and the buying public. The *investment banker* may form a group of bankers to buy the stocks outright and then resell them or merely buy some and act as **agent** for the rest.

Investment Company Act A federal law that **regulates** persons and companies that trade in **securities** such as **stocks, bonds,** and **commodity options** (or claim to trade in them); that invest in large blocks of securities; that invest in other companies, etc.

Investment contract Under federal law an *investment contract* is any deal that involves an investment of money pooled with others' money to gain profits solely from the efforts of others.

Investment credit A tax break on some property bought for business purposes. This *investment tax credit* is more than a **deduction**. It is a direct subtraction from income of a percentage of the purchase price of major machines, buildings, etc.

Investment securities **Stocks, bonds,** etc.

Investment trust A company that sells its own stock and invests the money in stocks, real estate, etc. A **mutual fund** is one example.

Invitation **1.** Asking someone to come onto your property. **2.** Keeping land or a building in such a way as to make persons think that you want them to come in. For example, a store owner *"invites"* the public to come in. In the law of **negligence,** a person must be more careful for the safety of any person *"invited"* in than for the safety of a person who is merely *allowed* onto the property.

Invited error The rule that when one side in a lawsuit gets away with using **inadmissible evidence,** the other side may use similar evidence to refute it.

Invitee   A person who is at a place by **invitation** (see that word). Note: a social caller may not be an "*invitee*," but a "**licensee**" (see that word).

Invoice   A list sent by a merchant that details goods sent to another person (often a purchaser) and usually gives prices item by item.

Involuntary confession   A confession of a crime may be thrown out as *involuntary* not only if it is gained by force or threats, but also sometimes when it is gained by promises, improper influence, etc.

Involuntary conversion   Loss of property by theft, casualty, or public condemnation. Any financial gain (from insurance on the lost property, payment for the condemnation, etc.) can be treated as unrecognized for tax purposes (and no tax paid at the time) if property similar to what was lost is bought soon after.

Involuntary manslaughter   The unintentional, but still illegal, killing of another human being. This is defined differently in different states.

Involuntary servitude   The forcing of one person to work for another.

Involuntary trust   A **constructive trust** (see that word).

Ipse dixit   (Latin) "He himself said it." A statement that depends for its persuasiveness on the authority of the person who said it.

Ipso facto   (Latin) "By the fact itself"; "by the mere fact that."

Ipso jure   (Latin) By **operation of law** alone.

Irreconcilable differences   **Grounds** for a **divorce** in a **no-fault** divorce state.

Irrecusable   "Unrefusable."

Irregularity   The failure to proceed properly. The failure to take the proper formal steps in the proper way while involved in a lawsuit or doing some official act. An *irregularity* is not an illegal act, but it may be serious enough to invalidate or otherwise harm what a person is trying to accomplish.

Irrelevant   Not related to the matter at hand. For example, *irrelevant evidence* is **evidence** that will not help to either prove or disprove any point that matters in a lawsuit.

Irreparable injury   Probable harm that cannot be properly fixed by money alone, and that is serious enough to justify an **injunction** (see that word).

Irresistible impulse   The loss of control due to **insanity** that is so great that a person cannot stop from committing a crime. This is one of many vague "*tests*" to decide whether a person will be treated as a criminal (and put away in jail) or treated as a mental patient (and put away in a mental hospital).

Irrevocable Incapable of being called back, **revoked** (see that word), stopped, or changed.

Issuable Something that leads to an **issue** being joined (that describes a dispute clearly enough that a trial can proceed).

Issue **1.** To send forth, put out, or **promulgate** officially. For example, when a court *issues* a **writ** or other legal paper, it gives it to a court officer to be served on (delivered to) a person. **2.** One single point in dispute between two sides in a lawsuit. An issue may be "*of law*" (a dispute about how the law applies to the case) or "*of fact*" (about the truth of a fact). **3.** Descendants (children, grandchildren, etc.). **4.** A group of **stocks** or **bonds** that are offered or sold at the same time. **5.** The first transfer of a **negotiable instrument** such as a check.

Issue preclusion **Collateral estoppel** or **res judicata** (see those words).

Ita est (Latin) "So it is." A formal statement put on a copy of a document by a **notary public** when the document was notarized by an earlier notary.

Item **1.** A separate **entry** in an **account** or list. **2.** One single sum of money for a particular purpose in an **appropriation.**

Itemize **1.** List by separate articles or items; break down something by listing its separate parts. **2.** For *itemized deductions*, see **deduction.**

Iter (Latin) A right of way.

J **1.** Judge. For example, "*Johnson, J.*" means Judge Johnson. **2.** Journal.

J.A.G. *Judge advocate general.* See **military law.**

J.D. Short for "Juris Doctor" or "Doctor of Jurisprudence." This is now the basic law degree, replacing the "LL.B." in the late

1960s. There are many other law degrees offered in other countries and many advanced law degrees offered here and elsewhere. These include the LL.M., LL.D., B.L., J.C.D., D.C.L., etc. Their exact names are not important; you need to know who gives the degree and what that school says it means.

J.N.O.V.   Judgment **non obstante veredicto** (see that word).

J.P.   Justice of the peace. A low-level local judge.

Jactitation   False boasting or false claims.

Jail   A place of confinement that is more than a police station lockup and less than a **prison.** It is usually used to hold persons either convicted of **misdemeanors** (minor crimes) or persons who cannot get out on **bail** while awaiting trial.

Jailhouse lawyer   A popular name for a prisoner who helps other prisoners with legal problems, such as getting **sentences** reduced.

Jason clause   A provision in a **bill of lading** that requires a cargo owner to contribute to the **general average loss** (see that word), even if the loss was caused by **negligence,** as long as the shipowner was careful in outfitting and crewing the ship.

Jay walking   Crossing a street in any but a safe, legal way.

Jencks rule   A federal criminal **defendant** must be given government documents needed to **cross-examine witnesses** (for prior statements inconsistent with current **testimony,** etc.).

Jeofaile statute   A law that allows **pleadings** to be freely corrected.

Jeopardy   1. Danger; hazard; peril.   2. The risk of **conviction** and punishment faced by a **defendant** in a criminal trial. [pronounce: jep-er-dee]

Jeopardy assessment   The right of the **I.R.S.** to **assess** and collect a tax immediately if tax **evasion** is probable (for example, if the taxpayer plans to leave the country).

Jetsam   1. Goods thrown off a ship to lighten it in an emergency.   2. Any goods jettisoned (thrown off). See also **flotsam.**

Job action   A **strike** or work slowdown, usually by public employees.

Jobber   1. A person who buys and sells for other persons.   2. A wholesaler.

John Doe   A made-up name used in some types of lawsuits where there is no real **defendant,** in a legal proceeding against a person whose name is not yet known, to protect a person's identity, etc., or as a name for a person in an example used to teach law. (He tends to have many legal dealings with Richard Roe, the owner of Whiteacre.)

Joinder   Joining or uniting together. For example, *joinder of parties* is the bringing in of a new person who joins together with the **plaintiff** as a plaintiff or the **defendant** as a defendant; *joinder of issue* is when a lawsuit gets by the preliminary stages and issues are clearly laid out, with one side asserting the truth of each point and the other side asserting its falsity; *nonjoinder* is the failure to bring in a person who is necessary as a **party** to a lawsuit; *misjoinder* is improper or mistaken joinder; *collusive joinder* is bringing in an unnecessary party from another state in order to have the case brought in federal court; and *permissive joinder* is the right of several persons to join together as plaintiffs if the suit is based on the same occurrences and if some of the legal issues overlap.

Joint   Together; as a group; united; undivided. For example, a "*joint return*" is a combined reporting of income taxes by a husband and wife, and a *joint work* in **copyright** law is written by two or more authors and merged into one whole.

Joint adventure (or joint venture)   A "one-shot" grouping together of two or more persons in a business. If they have a continuing relationship, it may be a **partnership** (see that word).

Joint and several   Both together and individually. For example, a **liability** or debt is *joint and several* if the **creditor** may sue the **debtors** either as a group (with the result that the debtors would have to split the loss) or individually (with the result that one debtor might have to pay the whole thing).

Joint authorship   Work together on a common design. Mere additions or improvements do not give a person the right to claim *joint authorship* of a book, a song, etc.

Joint bank account   A bank account held in the names of two or more persons, each of whom has full authority to put money in or take it out, and all of whom share equally.

Joint debtors acts   **1.** State laws that allow a judge to grant a **judgment** for or against some **defendants** who owe money and allow the trial to go on against the others.   **2.** State laws that allow a **plaintiff** to go ahead with a lawsuit when only some of the defendants who owe money have been served with **process**

Joint enterprise

(formally told to show up in court), and to get a judgment against all of them.

Joint enterprise A **joint adventure** (see that word).

Joint estate The ownership of property by more than one person where, when anyone dies, the others get that person's share.

Joint lives A right that lasts only as long as all the persons who share it live.

Joint stock company A company that is more than a **partnership**, but less than a **corporation** (see these words). It is similar to a corporation in most ways, but all owners are **liable** for company debts.

Joint tenancy See **tenancy**.

Joint through rate The charge for shipping something from a point on one transportation line to a point on another.

Joker A clause or phrase inserted in a **legislative bill** (or a contract or other document) that is superficially harmless, but actually destroys the bill's effectiveness.

Jones Act A federal law that permits ship employees (such as merchant seamen) to sue for **damages** if injured.

Journal 1. A book that is written in regularly, such as an **account** book, in which all expenses and all money taken in are written down as it happens. 2. A periodical magazine such as a *law journal*.

Journalists' privilege 1. The right of a publisher or writer to make "**fair comment**" upon the actions of public officials without being **liable** for **defamation**. This privilege exists so long as the writer and publisher didn't know (and didn't recklessly disregard their obligation to find out) that the statements were false. 2. See **shield laws**.

Journey worker (or journeyman) 1. A person who has completed apprenticeship training in a trade or craft. *Journey worker's pay* (or "union scale") is the minimum wage paid to an experienced worker in a particular job in a geographic area. 2. A day worker or hired hand.

Joyriding Stealing a car to ride around, rather than to keep it.

Judex (Latin) A judge.

Judge 1. The person who runs a courtroom, decides all legal questions, and sometimes decides entire cases. 2. To decide.

Judge advocate A military legal officer who may act as a judge or a lawyer.

230

Judgment **1.** The official decision of a court about the rights and claims of each side in a lawsuit. *"Judgment"* usually refers to a final decision that is based on the facts of the case and made at the end of a trial. It is called a *judgment on the merits*. **2.** There are, however, other types of judgments. For example, a *consent judgment* is the putting of a court's approval on an agreement between the sides about what the judgment in the case should be; a *default judgment* is one given to one side because the other side does not show in court or fails to take proper procedural steps; and an *interlocutory judgment* is one given on either a preliminary or a side issue during the course of a lawsuit. For other types of *judgments*, such as **cognovit note, confession of, declaratory, default, deficiency, non obstante veredicto,** etc., see those words.

Judgment book (or docket) A list of court **judgments** kept for public inspection. Also called a civil docket or criminal docket, depending on the type of case.

Judgment creditor A person who has proven a debt in court and is entitled to use court processes to collect it. The person owing the money is a *judgment debtor*.

Judgment note The paper a debtor gives to a creditor to allow **confession of judgment.**

Judgment-proof Persons against whom a money **judgment** will have no effect (persons without money, persons protected by wage-protection laws, etc.).

Judicare Publicly financed legal services (often allowing a person the choice of a lawyer).

Judicature Relating to the **judicial** branch of government; the judicial branch of government itself. For example, in England, the *Judicature Acts* set up their modern system of courts.

Judicia (Latin) **Trials, judgments,** or **decisions.**

Judicial **1.** Having to do with a court. **2.** Having to do with a judge. **3.** The branch of government that interprets the law and that judges legal questions.

Judicial activism A judge's decision that ignores strict **precedent** in order to bring about a result the judge thinks is just and that is in keeping with the judge's view of how society as a whole should operate.

Judicial discretion The right of a judge to have great leeway in making decisions, so long as he or she follows the law and proper procedures and refrains from arbitrary action.

Judicial immunity

Judicial immunity   A judge's complete protection from personal **liability** in lawsuits based on the judge's official duties, even in situations where the judge acted in bad faith.

Judicial notice   The act of a judge in recognizing the existence or truth of certain facts without bothering to make one side in a lawsuit put them in **evidence**. This is done when the facts are either common knowledge and undisputed (such as the fact that Argentina is in South America) or are easily found and cannot be disputed (such as the text of the Constitution).

Judicial question   An issue that the courts may decide, as opposed to one that only the **executive** branch may decide (a **political question**) or that only the **legislature** can decide (a *legislative question*).

Judicial review   **1.** A court's power to declare a **statute unconstitutional** and to interpret laws.   **2.** An **appeal** from an **administrative agency** decision. In the federal government the general rules governing this are in the *Judicial Review Act.*

Judicial sale   A sale held under a court **judgment** or **order** or held under court supervision. See also **execution**.

Judiciary   The branch of government that interprets the law; the branch that judges. For example, the Judiciary Act of 1789 set up the system of federal courts.

Jump bail   **1.** Leave the area or hide to avoid going to court while out on **bail**.   **2.** Fail to show up in court while on bail.

Junior   An interest or a right that collects after, or is subordinate to, another interest or right.

Jura   (Latin) Rights or laws.

Jural   **1.** Having to do with the basic or fundamental law of rights and obligations.   **2.** Legal rather than moral rights and obligations.

Jurat   Name for the statement on an **affidavit** about where, when, and before whom it was sworn to.

Jure   (Latin) By right; by the right or law of. See **de jure**.

Juridical   **1.** Having to do with the court system or with a judge.   **2.** Regular, conforming to law and court practice.

Juris   (Latin) Of right, of law.

Juris doctor   *Doctor of laws.* The basic law degree, replacing the Bachelor of Law degree or LL.B. It is abbreviated "**J.D.**"

Juris et de jure   (Latin) "By law and right." A **conclusive** presumption.

Jurisdiction **1.** The geographical area within which a court (or a public official) has the right and power to operate. **2.** The persons about whom and the subject matters about which a court has the right and power to make decisions that are legally binding. For types of jurisdiction, such as **ancillary, appellate,** etc., see those words.

Jurisdictional **1.** Having to do with **jurisdiction** (see that word). **2.** Essential for jurisdiction. For example, the "*jurisdictional amount*" is the value of a claim being made in a case. Some courts take only those cases that have jurisdictional amounts above or below a certain money limit. *Jurisdictional facts* are those things a court must know before taking and keeping a case (such as whether the **defendant** has been properly served, etc.).

Jurisdictional dispute A conflict between unions, either as to which union should represent certain workers or as to which union's members should do a certain type of work. Strikes based on these disputes are generally illegal.

Jurisprudence The study of law and legal philosophy.

Jurist **1.** A judge. **2.** A legal scholar.

Juristic act Sonething done that is intended to have (and capable of having) a legal effect.

Juristic person A person for legal purposes. This includes both natural persons (individuals) and **artificial persons (corporations).**

Juror A person who is a member of a **jury.**

Jury A group of persons selected by law and sworn in to look at certain facts and determine the truth. The two most common types of juries are a *grand jury* (persons who receive complaints and accusations of crime, hear preliminary evidence on the complaining side, and make formal accusations or **indictments**) and a *petit jury* or *trial jury* (usually twelve, but sometimes as few as six persons who decide questions of **fact** in many trials). There are also **coroner's** juries, **advisory juries,** and other types.

Jury box The enclosed place where the jury sits in a trial.

Jury commission A committee of private citizens that picks **jurors.** In some places, this job is done by a jury **clerk.**

Jury list **1.** A list of those **jurors** selected to try a case. **2.** A list of all jurors commanded to be in court to be selected for various cases. **3.** A list of all possible jurors.

Jury trial

Jury trial   A trial with a judge and jury, not just a judge. This is a **constitutional** right which need only be requested in all **criminal** cases and in **civil** ones involving over twenty dollars.

Jury wheel   A device for randomly selecting jurors from a list of eligible citizens.

Jus   (Latin)   **1.** Right or justice.   **2.** Law, or the whole body of law. For example: *jus belli* (the law of war, wartime rights); *jus civile* (**civil** law, Roman law, or the law of one country); *jus commune* (**common** law); *jus gentium* (the law of nations or **international law**); *jus naturae* (the "law" of nature); *jus naturale (*natural law*)*; *jus privatum* (the law of private rights); *jus publicum* (public or governmental law); and *jus soli* (the law of a person's birthplace; also, citizenship in a country because you are born there).   **3.** A particular right. For example: *jus disponendi* (the right to do what you want with your own property or the right of a seller to let **title** pass or keep it until all payments are made); *jus dividendi* (the right to give property by **will**); *jus habendi* (the right to possess something); *jus sanguinis* ("law of the blood"; citizenship in a country because your parents are citizens); and *jus tertii* (the right of someone not involved in a lawsuit to property that is involved in the suit).

Just   **1.** Legal or lawful.   **2.** Morally right; fair. Words like "*just cause*" and "*just compensation*" include both meanings (no. 1 and no. 2) of "just."

Justice   **1.** Fairness in treatment by the law.   **2.** *Department of Justice.* The U.S. **cabinet** department that manages the country's legal business. It represents the U.S. in both **civil** and **criminal** matters, runs the federal prison system, and has specialized departments that handle **antitrust, civil rights,** the Federal Bureau of Investigation, Immigration and Naturalization, etc.   **3.** A judge of many types of courts, such as the U.S. Supreme Court.

Justice of the peace   One type of low-level local judge.

Justiciable   Proper to be decided by a court. For example, a "*justiciable controversy*" is a real, rather than hypothetical, dispute that a court may handle. [pronounce: jus-<u>tish</u>-able]

Justification   A reason that will stand up in court for an intentional action that would otherwise be unlawful. A just cause. For example, self-defense may be *justification* for a killing.

Juvenile   **1.** Not yet an adult for the purpose of the criminal law.

2. Not yet an adult. A minor. This may be a different age than no. 1.

Juvenile court A court set up to handle cases of either **delinquent** or neglected children.

Kk

K Abbreviation for **contract.**

K.B. **King's Bench** (see that word).

Kangaroo court A popular expression for a mock court with no legal powers.

Keep To carry on or manage (a hotel); to tend or shelter (a dog); to maintain continuously (a record book); to store (a box); to continue without change (a ship's course); or to protect (a child).

Kefauver-Cellar Act A federal law prohibiting a takeover of a company by one in the same business if the effect is to lessen competition.

Kentucky rule The principle that all **dividends** (except for some **stock dividends**) are **income** to a **trust**, not an addition to **principal.**

Keogh Plan ("H.R.10 Plan") A tax-free retirement account for persons with self-employment income that is similar to an **individual retirement account** (see that word). [pronounce: key-oh]

Key numbers A reference system that classifies legal subjects by specific topics and subtopics, with a "Key number" ( ) attached to each topic. It allows you to find cases by subject in the **American Digest System** and the **National Reporter System** (see these words), and was developed by West Publishing Company.

Kickback Something given to a company (or government) employee for doing a favor for another company. This may be a crime if done, for example, by a federal **contractor.**

Kicker **1.** Loan charges in addition to the interest. **2.** Any extra charge or penalty.

Kidnapping Taking away and holding a person illegally, usually by force.

Kilberg doctrine The principle that a court is not bound by the law of the place where a person died for a limit on **wrongful death action damages** (because that limit is **procedural law** and governed by the law of the place where the court is).

Kin (or kindred) **1.** Blood relationship. **2.** Any relationship.

Kind See **In kind.**

King's Bench (or Queen's Bench) An English court that developed most of the "**common law**" (see that word) that has become the basis for American law.

Kiting Writing checks on an **account** before money is put in to cover them.

Knock and announce rule A police officer making a legal arrest or search may break down a door only after first stating his or her authority and purpose for being there and after entrance is refused or avoided.

Knock down An auctioneer's acceptance of a **bid** as final. This gives the property to the bidder once it is paid for.

Knowingly With full knowledge and intentionally; **willfully.**

LIFO "Last in, first out." A method of calculating the worth of a merchant's **inventory.** Under this method if a merchant buys a blivit for a dollar, then buys another for two dollars, then sells either blivit, the remaining blivit is worth one dollar. See also **FIFO** and **NIFO**.

L.J. **1.** Law journal. **2.** Law judge.

LL.B. "Bachelor of Laws." The basic law degree up until the late 1960s. Replaced by "**J.D.**"

LL.M and LL.D. Advanced law degrees (masters and doctorate). Other initials are also used for some advanced law degrees (see **J.D.** for a list of examples).

L.M.R.A. Labor Management Relations Act (see **Taft-Hartley Act**).

L.M.R.D.A. Labor Management Reporting and Disclosure Act (see **Landrum-Griffin Act**).

L.R. **1. Law Reports.** **2.** Law Review (see **Law Journal**).

L.R.I. Legal Resources Index. A large, computerized and micro-filmed listing of law review articles and law-related articles in general newspapers and magazines.

L.S. Short for "locus sigilli" or "the place of the seal." These letters once were placed next to a signature to make a **contract** formally binding.

L.S.A.T. Law School Aptitude (or Admissions) Test; "the law boards."

L.Ed. *Lawyer's Edition* of the U.S. Supreme Court Reports.

Label **1.** Any writing added onto a larger document. **2.** Product and package labels are **regulated** for honesty by the Federal Fair Packaging and Labeling Act and for content by various food and drug laws.

Labor Department of Labor. The U.S. cabinet department that **regulates** working conditions, labor–management relations, manpower development, etc. However, the National Labor Relations Board (**N.L.R.B.**) is an independent agency.

Labor contract A **collective bargaining agreement** (see that word).

Labor dispute A controversy between an employer and employees or an employer and a union involving wages, hours, working conditions, or the question of who has the right to speak for the employees.

Labor Management Relations Act The **Taft-Hartley Act** (see that word).

Labor Management Reporting and Disclosure Act The **Landrum-Griffin Act** (see that word).

Labor organization Any group, whether or not a labor **union,** and whether or not it is formally organized, that deals with pay, hours, or any other working conditions.

Labor union A formal organization of employees formed to improve compensation and working conditions. See **union** for types.

Laborer's lien See **mechanic's lien.**

Laches A delay (in pursuing or enforcing a claim or right) that is so long that the person against whom you are proceeding is unfairly hurt or **prejudiced** by the delay itself. This will keep you from winning. [pronounce: latch-es]

Laden in bulk   Carrying loose cargo such as grain rather than carrying containers of grain or individual items such as chairs.

Lading   See **bill of lading**.

Laesa majestas   Treason.

Laissez faire   (French) The theory of a free economy in which the government does not meddle with private economic decisions. [pronounce: lay-say fair]

Lame duck   **1.** An elected official who is serving out the end of a **term** after someone else has been elected to take his or her place. A *lame duck session* is a **legislative** session held after an election and before new members of the legislature are to begin their terms. The **Twentieth Amendment** to the U.S. **Constitution** is called the *Lame Duck Amendment* because it abolished the short congressional term that allowed defeated representatives a chance to act irresponsibly.   **2.** An investor in **stock** who has overbought and cannot meet his or her financial commitments.

Land   In the law, land is not just the surface. It includes everything underneath plus the airspace above and means the same thing as **real estate** or property.

Land bank   **1.** A federal program in which land is taken out of agricultural production and used for conservation or trees. Also called *soil bank*.   **2.** A federally created bank that makes low-interest farm loans.

Land grant (or land patent)   A gift (usually with conditions attached) of land from the government to a private person, organization, business, or another government. Many state colleges are *land grant* institutions.

Land sales contract   A **contract** for the sale of real estate, not recorded in the land records, in which the seller keeps **title** to the property until an agreed future time. This is often done to keep a low interest rate on an existing **mortgage.** Also called a *contract for deed* and *installment contract.*

Land use planning   A general term that can mean **zoning** laws, real estate development and use laws, environmental impact studies, state and local master plans, etc.

Landlord   The owner of land or a building that is rented or leased to a **tenant.**

Landmark case   A court case that makes major changes in the law.

Landrum-Griffin Act   A federal law, passed in 1959, that gave several new rights to individual union members (such as the requirement that unions must have a fair **constitution**). It also changed the **Taft-Hartley Act** in several ways; some prounion, some proemployer. See also **secondary boycott** and **hot cargo.**

Lanham Act   A 1947 revision of **trademark** law.

Lapping   Stealing or "borrowing" from an employer by taking money paid by a customer, not recording the payment, then covering the theft by putting the next customer's payment into the first's account, and so on.

Lapse   **1.** The end or failure of a right because of the neglect to enforce or use it within a time limit.   **2.** The failure of a gift by **will.**   **3.** For *lapse statute*, see **anti-lapse statute.**

Larceny   Stealing of any kind.

Larger parcel rule   When a piece of land taken by **eminent domain** (see that word) is part of a larger piece of land, the price paid by the government may be higher than it would have been for an identical piece of land standing alone.

Lascivious   Tending to excite lust; impure; obscene; immoral. [pronounce: las-<u>siv</u>-i-us]

Last antecedent rule   A word or phrase in a law that might refer either to the immediately preceding words or also to earlier words should be read as referring only to the words right before it unless the law clearly means otherwise.

Last clear chance doctrine   A legal principle that a person injured in (or having property harmed by) an accident may win **damages** even when **negligent** if the person causing the damage could have avoided the accident after discovering the danger and if the person injured could not have. This rule is not accepted in every state and, where accepted, has many different forms (and names).

Last resort   A *court of last resort* is one from which there is no **appeal.**

Last will and testament   **Will.**

Latent   **1.** Hidden. For example, a *latent defect* is something wrong (with an article sold or with the validity of a legal document) that cannot be discovered by ordinary observation or care. In this sense, its opposite is **patent.**   **2.** Dormant, **passive,** or "put away." For example, a *latent deed* is one kept for twenty (or thirty) years in a secret place.   **3.** *"Latents"* is police slang for fingerprints.

Lateral support   The right to have land supported by adjoining land. For example, digging that causes a cave-in on the property next door violates this right.

Laudum   (Latin) A **judgment** or **award.**

Law   **1.** That which must be obeyed.   **2.** A **statute;** an act of the **legislature.**   **3.** The whole body of principles, standards, and rules put out by a government.   **4.** The principles, standards, and rules that apply to a particular type of situation; for example, *"juvenile law."*   **5.** The opposite of **fact** (see that word).   **6.** For the many different types of law, such as **caselaw, constitutional law, military law, substantive law,** etc., see those words.

Law day (law date)   **1.** A court-set day after which a **mortgagee** can no longer pay off a debt on real estate and get the land back from **foreclosure.**   **2.** May First. A day for special school and public programs honoring the American legal system.

Law directory   A **law list** (see that word).

Law enforcement officer   Police, **F.B.I.** agents, **sheriffs,** etc.

Law French   The Norman French language used in the law in England for several centuries. Many words survive.

Law journal (or law review)   A publication put out by a law school with articles on legal subjects such as court decisions and legislation.

Law Latin   The changed form of Latin evolved in the English courts. Many words survive.

Law list   A directory of lawyers practicing in a particular area. The *Martindale-Hubbell Law Directory* is the largest.

Law merchant   The generally accepted customs of merchants. These customs have standardized over the years and become a part of the formal law.

Law of nations   See public **international law.**

Law of nature   **1.** **Natural law** (see that word).   **2.** The "law" of brute survival in a state of nature.

Law of the case   Any **decision** or **ruling** on a case by a trial or **appeals** court becomes the *"law of the case"* in any subsequent case on the subject between the same persons.

Law of the land   **1.** A law or rule that is in force throughout the country or, sometimes, throughout a geographical area.   **2.** A country's customs, which gradually become as important legally as written law. **3.** Basic ground rules of **due process** and **equal protection** (see those words) that give rights to every person.

Law of the road Safety customs, such as "keep to the right," that have become law.

Law reform Using the courts to make basic changes in the laws, often by bringing **test cases.**

Law reports Published books in a series that contain cases decided by a court.

Law week *U.S. Law Week* is a **loose-leaf service** with "hot off the press" news from the Supreme Court, other courts, and some **legislatures.**

Lawful Legal; authorized by law; not forbidden by law.

Lawsuit A **civil action.** A court proceeding to enforce a right between persons (rather than to **convict** a **criminal**).

Lawyer A person licensed to practice law. Other words for "lawyer" include: **attorney, counsel, solicitor,** and **barrister.**

Lay Nonprofessional. For example, a lawyer would call a nonlawyer a layperson and a doctor would call a nondoctor a layperson.

Lay advocate A **paralegal** who specializes in representing persons in administrative **hearings.**

Layaway Putting down a deposit to hold a purchase for later pickup. (This is *not* necessarily an "**installment** sale" involving **credit.**)

Laying foundation Establishing the preliminary **evidence** needed to make later, more important evidence **relevant** and **admissible.**

Layoff A temporary or indefinite loss of a job due to a reduction in work to be done. **Seniority** rights are usually kept.

Leading case A case that either established a legal principle or is otherwise very important in an area of law.

Leading object rule The **main purpose doctrine** (see that word).

Leading question A question that shows a **witness** how to answer it or suggests the preferred answer; for example, "Isn't it true that you were in Boston all last week?" *Leading questions* are generally permitted on **cross examination** of the other side's witness in a trial, but not on **direct examination** of your side's witness.

Lease

Lease   1. A **contract** for the use of land or buildings, but not for their ownership. The **lessor** is called the **landlord** and the **lessee** is the **tenant.   2.** A contract for the use of something, but not for its ownership.   **3.** A long-term loan of something in exchange for money. Also, a *sublease* is a lease made to another person by a person to whom something is leased.   **4.** For special types of *leases* such as a **mineral lease** and **percentage lease,** see those words.

Leaseback   A sale of property with a **lease** of the same property from the buyer back to the seller. This is often done with land or industrial equipment for tax purposes.

Leasehold   Land or buildings held by **lease.**

Least and latest rule   Pay the least amount of taxes legally possible as late as legally possible.

Least fault divorce   Comparative rectitude (see that word).

Leave   1. To give by **will.   2.** Permission. For example, "*leave of court*" is permission from a judge to take an action in a lawsuit that requires permission (to file an amended pleading, for example).

Ledger   A business **account** book, usually recording the day-to-day transactions, and usually showing **debits** and **credits** separately.

Legacy   1. A gift of money by **will.   2.** A gift of personal property (anything but real estate) by will.   **3.** A gift of anything by will.

Legacy tax   A tax on the privilege of inheriting something. This may be an **inheritance tax** based on the value of the property or it may be a flat fee.

Legal   1. Required or permitted by law.   **2.** Not forbidden by law.   **3.** Concerning or about the law.   **4.** Having to do with an old *court of law* as opposed to a court of **equity** (see that word).   **5.** See the long list of *legal* words that follows for various examples and other meanings. Also, many words preceded by the word "legal" will be found only under the word itself.

Legal acumen doctrine   The rule that, if it takes special legal skills to figure out that there may be something wrong with the **title** to a piece of land, a court may be asked to use its **equity** power to clear up the problem.

Legal age   The age at which a person becomes old enough to make contracts. This is generally eighteen to twenty-one in most states, but it may be lower for specific purposes. The phrase is sometimes used to mean the age at which a person can legally buy alcoholic beverages or legally consent to sexual intercourse.

Legal aid   A place that provides free legal help to poor persons.

Legal assistant   See **paralegal.**

Legal cap   Long legal stationery with a wide left-hand margin and a narrow right-hand margin.

Legal capital   **1.** The **par** or stated value of a company's **stock. 2.** The amount of money a company must keep to protect its **creditors. 3.** Property with enough value to balance a company's **stock liability.**

Legal cause   See **proximate cause.**

Legal cruelty   See **cruelty.**

Legal death   See **brain death, civil death,** and **death** for various uses of the word.

Legal description   The identification of a piece of land that is precise enough to locate it without ambiguity and to show any **easements** or **reservations.** This may be done by government survey, recordation of precise measurements, lot numbers on a recorded **plat,** or similar formal means.

Legal detriment   A person acquires a *"legal detriment"* when making a **contract** by taking on **liabilities** or duties that are enforceable in court or by changing financial position in some way. This *detriment* allows the person to enforce corresponding *rights.*

Legal entity   A living person, a **corporation,** or any organization that can sue and be sued or otherwise function legally.

Legal ethics   **1.** The moral and professional duties owed by lawyers to their clients, to other lawyers, to the courts, and to the public. **2.** The study of no. 1. **3.** The **Code of Professional Responsibility** of the **A.B.A.**

Legal executive   A highly trained English **paralegal.**

Legal fiction   See **fiction.**

Legal heirs   **1.** Persons who will inherit if a person dies without a will. **2.** Any **heirs.**

Legal holiday   A day on which normal legal business may not be transacted. This varies widely from state to state, but the businesses may include **service** of **process,** court proceedings, banking, etc.

Legal investments

Legal investments (or legal list) See **prudent person rule**.

Legal proceedings Any actions taken in court or connected with a lawsuit.

Legal realism A philosophy of law that takes psychology, sociology, economics, politics, etc. into account in order to explain how legal decisions are made.

Legal representative **1.** A person who takes care of another person's business involving courts, especially **executors** or **administrators** of **wills**. **2.** A family member entitled to bring a **wrongful death action**.

Legal reserve The percentage of total funds that an insurance company or a bank must set aside to meet possible claims.

Legal residence Actually living in a place and intending to stay there. See **domicile**.

Legal Services Corporation The organization that runs the federally funded program of legal aid.

Legal tender Official money (dollar bills, coins, etc.).

Legal value See **par** value, **book value**, and **face value**.

Legal worker See **paralegal**.

Legalese Legal jargon or overly complicated language in laws and **regulations.**

Legalism A decision that pays more attention to the exact wording of a law than to what would be fair or to what was probably intended by the law's passage.

Legalized nuisance A **nuisance** that may not be objected to as a nuisance because it exists due to specific laws. If, for example, a hospital is a **nuisance,** the only way a private citizen might object to the neighborhood problems it causes is through the environmental protection laws, not the **zoning** laws.

Legatee A person who **inherits** something in a **will.**

Legation All the persons making up one country's embassy in another country.

Leges (or legis, legem) (Latin) Laws.

Legislate To enact or pass laws. A *legislator* (person who makes laws) works in the *legislature* (lawmaking branch of government) on *legislation* (laws, **statutes, ordinances,** etc.). This work of *legislation* (passing laws) is a *legislative* function (lawmaking, as opposed to "**executive**," which is carrying out laws, or "**judicial**," which is interpreting laws).

Legislation   **1.** The process of thinking about and passing or refusing to **pass bills** into law (**statutes, ordinances,** etc.).   **2.** Statutes, ordinances, etc.

Legislative   Lawmaking, as opposed to "**executive**" (carrying out or enforcing laws), or "**judicial**" (interpreting or applying laws).

Legislative council   A group of officials that studies state laws, **legislative** problems, etc.

Legislative counsel   A person or office that helps **legislators** and **legislative committees** research and write **bills,** as well as help with other technical aspects of lawmaking.

Legislative courts   Courts that have been set up by **legislatures** (Congress, state legislatures, etc.), rather than those set up originally by the U.S. **Constitution** or by state constitutions.

Legislative facts   General facts that help an **administrative agency** to decide general questions of law and policy and to make rules. They are the opposite of **adjudicative facts** (see that word).

Legislative history   The background documents and records of **hearings** held on a **bill** as it became a law.

Legislative immunity   The constitutional right of a member of Congress to say almost anything for almost any reason while performing an official function (speeches, debates, newsletters, etc.), and to be free from **defamation** lawsuits based on what was said.

Legislative intent rule   A court should decide what the lawmakers meant or wanted when they passed a law by looking at the **legislative history.** This is one of several possible ways of interpreting statutes. It is different from the **legislative purpose rule** (see that word).

Legislative purpose rule   A court should look at what the law was before the present law was passed and decide by looking at the law itself what the law was trying to change. This is one of several possible ways of interpreting statutes. It is different from the **legislative intent rule** (see that word).

Legislator   A lawmaker, such as a U.S. Senator, a member of a city council, etc.

Legislature   A lawmaking body such as the U.S. Congress, a city council, etc.

Legitimate   **1.** Lawful or legal (also, a child born to a married couple is called *legitimate*).   **2.** To make lawful.

Legitime   An **inheritance** that must go to a **forced heir** (see that word).

Lese majesty   (French) **Treason** (see that word) or **rebellion.**

Lessee   A person who **leases** or rents something from someone. A lessee of land is a **tenant.**

Lesser included offense (lesser offense)   A crime that is a part of a more serious crime. For example, **manslaughter** is a lesser crime included in the description of **murder.**

Lessor   A person who **leases** or rents something to someone. A *lessor* of land is a landlord.

Let   1. To **award** a contract (such as a building job) to one of several bidders.   **2.** To **lease.**

Letter   1. The strict, precise, literal meaning of a document. The exact language (of a law, for example) rather than the spirit or broad purpose.   **2.** A formal document. For example, a *"letter of attorney"* is a document giving a person **power of attorney** (see that word).

Letter of advice   A **drawer's** (for example, a person who makes out a check) notice to a **drawee** (for example, a bank) that a **draft** (a check for a certain amount to a certain person) has been *drawn* (made out).

Letter of attornment   A letter from a landlord to a tenant saying that the property has been sold and telling who now should get the rent payments.

Letter of comment   A letter from the **S.E.C.** to persons registering a proposed sale of **securities** (**stocks,** etc.) that the **registration** statement does not comply with law and must be changed.

Letter of credence   The document that **accredits** a new **ambassador** or other foreign **minister** (recommends and certifies him or her to another country).

Letter of credit   A statement by a bank or other financer that it will back up or pay the financial obligations of a merchant involved in a particular sale. It may be a **negotiable instrument** to pay a certain sum, a letter that the person's **credit** is good to a certain amount, or something in between. *Import, export* and *travelers' letters* authorize a foreign bank to cash checks or make other payments in local currency to be reimbursed by the bank that writes the letter.

Letter of intent   1. A preliminary understanding that forms the basis of an intended **contract.   2.** A letter (often from a government **agency**) to a **contractor** stating that a contract **award** will be made. This gives the contractor some, but not all, the rights of a signed contract.

Letter ruling   A written answer by the **I.R.S.** to a taxpayer about how the tax laws apply to a specific set of facts (often a proposed transaction). Sometimes this is called a "private letter ruling" because it is advice for one specific situation and one specific person only.

Letter stock   **Stock** that does not need to be **registered** with the **S.E.C.** because buyers give the seller a letter saying that the stock will be held for investment and not resold for a long time.

Letters   Formal, written permission to do something. See the following words for examples.

Letters of administration (or letters testamentary)   Court papers allowing a person to take charge of the property of a dead person in order to distribute it.

Letters of marque and reprisal   See **marque and reprisal.**

Letters patent   A government document giving a person exclusive rights to a piece of land or to a **patent.**

Letters rogatory   A request made by one court to another in a different **jurisdiction** that a **witness** answer the **interrogatories** sent with the letter.

Lettres de cachet   (French) Documents signed by the king that allowed persons to be imprisoned or excused persons from crimes for no reason at all. These were abolished during the Revolution of 1789.

Leverage   **1.** Any borrowing (especially for investment purposes).   **2.** Putting down a small investment (usually as a down payment) to control a large amount of **stock** (and usually borrowing the rest). This makes the eventual profit or loss quite large when compared to the money actually put up if the price of the stock changes.   **3.** The proportion of a company's **bonds** and **preferred stock** compared to its **common stock.** The common stock is called *"highly leveraged"* if there is proportionately little of it, because small changes in the company's income can result in big changes in the stock's value, since payments that must be made on bonds and preferred stock are large, but unchanging.   **4.** A *"leveraged lease"* is a deal in which leased items are financed by a third person. This is often done to shift tax benefits from users of the property to the owners who gain more. See **equity investor.**

Levy

Levy   **1.** To **assess,** raise, or collect. For example, to *levy a tax* is to either **pass** one in a **legislature** or to collect one.   **2.** To seize or collect. For example, to *levy on a debtor's property* is to put it aside by court **order** in order to pay **creditors.**   **3.** The **assessment** or seizure itself in no. 1 and no. 2.

Lewd   Morally impure in a sexual sense; **lascivious.**

Lex   (Latin)   **1.** Law (or a collection or body of laws). For example: *lex mercatoria* (**law merchant**); *lex naturale* (**natural law**); *lex ordinandi* (**procedural,** as opposed to **substantive, law**); *lex scripta* (written law; **statutes**); *lex talionis* (law of retaliation; "eye for an eye"); and *lex terrae* (law of the land; **due process**). **2.** *Lex loci* is the "law of the place." For example, *lex loci actus* (law of the place where the act was done); *lex loci contractus* (law of the place where the **contract** was made or the place with the most important legal connections to the contract); *lex loci criminis or delictus* (law of the place where the crime was committed); *lex loci domicilii* (law of the **domicile** or permanent home of the person involved); *lex loci rei sitae or situs* (law of the place where the thing, usually land, is); etc. Many of these are abbreviated without the "*loci,*" but that changes the Latin ending of the words. See no. 3 for contrast.   **3.** *Lex fori* is the "law of the **forum**" or court; the law of the state or country where the case is decided. Judges must often choose whether *lex fori* or *lex loci* (see no. 2) is the law that decides a case. See also **conflict of laws.**

Lexis   A computerized legal research source.

Leze majesty   (French) **Treason** (see that word) or **rebellion.**

Liability   A broad word for legal obligation, responsibility, or debt.

Liable   Responsible for something (such as harm done to another person); bound by law; having a duty or obligation enforceable in court against you by another person. (*Not* **libel.**)

Libel   **1.** Written **defamation** (see that word); published false and **malicious** written statements that injure a person's reputation. **2.** Formerly the first **pleading** in an admiralty (maritime or ocean–ship) court, corresponding to the **complaint** of an ordinary **civil** lawsuit. Also, the name for some specialized complaints in some places, such as a "*divorce libel.*" (*Not* **liable.**)

Libelant   **Plaintiff** (see that word).

Libelous   Defamatory; tending to injure a reputation.

Liberty **1.** Freedom from illegal personal restraint. **2.** Personal rights under law.

Library of Congress system A method of finding books, first by subject area (law is "K") and then by a number assigned in time order by the Library of Congress. Compare with the **Dewey decimal system**.

License **1.** Formal permission to do something specific; for example, a state driver's license or the license given by one company to another to manufacture a patented product. **2.** The document that gives the permission in no. 1. **3.** Acting without any legal restraint; disregarding the law entirely.

Licensee **1.** A person who holds a **license**. **2.** A person who is on property with permission, but without any enticement by the owner and with no financial advantage to the owner; often called a *"mere licensee"* as opposed to an **"invitee"** in **negligence** law. In some situations, an invited personal guest is a *licensee, not* an *invitee*.

Licentiousness **1.** Doing what you want with total disregard for ethics, law, or others' rights. **2.** Lewdness or lasciviousness; moral impurity in a sexual context.

Lie Exist; be supported by. For example, the phrase "the action *lies* in **tort**" means that the right way to bring a lawsuit based on a particular subject is as a tort case.

Lie detector A machine that reads blood pressure, perspiration rate, and other body signs (such as the skin's electrical resistance) and gives a rough indication of whether or not a person is telling the truth while questions are asked. Lie detector (also called *polygraph*) tests are not admitted as evidence, except in some states that allow them when both sides of a case agree to use the results. (Other machines, such as "voice stress analyzers," have also been used as lie detectors.)

Lien A claim, charge, or liability against property that is allowed by law, rather than one that is part of a **contract** or agreement. For example, a *mechanic's lien* is the right of a workman to hold property worked on until paid for the services, and a *tax lien* is the government's placing of a financial obligation on a piece of property that must be paid because taxes have not been paid. Other types of *liens* include **judgment, landlord's,** maritime, etc. [pronounce: leen]

Lien creditor See **secured creditor**.

Lien theory state

Lien theory state (or jurisdiction)   A state in which a **mortgage** is considered a **lien** on property, and the **title** does not transfer to the lender.

Lieu   (French) "Place." "*In lieu of*" means "instead of."

Lieutenant   **1.** A **deputy,** substitute, or second in command, such as a *lieutenant governor.*   **2.** A military or police middle rank; closer to the bottom than the top in the military, about the middle for the police.

Life   **1.** Human *life* begins at different times for different legal purposes. It may begin at conception, at the time when a child is capable of living outside the womb, at the moment of birth and first breath, etc. For definitions of the end of life, see **death.** **2.** *Life* is also short for "*for life*" or "*for the duration of life.*" For example, a *life* **estate, interest,** or **tenancy** is limited to the life of the person holding it or the life of another named person. And a *life* **annuity** is a type of **insurance** or **pension plan** (see that word) that pays from a certain point until the end of the person's life.

Life care contract   An agreement (usually between an elderly person and a nursing home) in which the person turns over all property in return for all support from then on.

Life estate   A property right that is good until someone dies, but that cannot be passed on to an **heir.**

Life expectancy   The length of time a person of a given age, sex (and sometimes health) is expected to live. This is computed from life (or actuarial) tables and used in figuring **insurance** rates, **damages** for injuries, etc.

Life in being   The remaining length of time a specific person already born has to live, or the length of time a person who *will* be alive when a **deed** or **will** takes effect will live. A *life in being* is used in the calculations used in the **rule against perpetuities.**

Lift   Remove an obstacle or obligation. Stop the effect of something, such as a court **order.**

Like-kind exchange   A trade of certain types of business property that will not be taxed. There are detailed **I.R.S.** rules.

Limine   (Latin) See **in limine.**

Limit order   See **order.**

Limitation   **1.** A restriction.   **2.** A time limit. For example, a "*statute of limitations*" is a law that sets a maximum amount of time after something happens for it to be taken to court, such as

250

a *"three year statute"* for lawsuits based on a contract, or a*"six year statute"* for a criminal prosecution. **3.** *Limitation* of a **case** is a judge's refusing to apply the rule that decided it to deciding another case.

Limited   **1.** Partial or restricted. For example, *limited liability* is the legal rule that the owners (shareholders) of a **corporation** cannot usually be sued for **corporate** actions and, thus, the most they can usually lose is the value of their investment. But see **piercing the corporate veil**. **2.** *"Limited"* is the British and Canadian word for "corporation." It is abbreviated "Ltd." **3.** For other examples, see the words following.

Limited admissibility   A judge may allow some types of **evidence** to be used for one purpose, but not another, and must then instruct the **jury** carefully about what the evidence may and may not prove and how the jurors may consider it.

Limited divorce   See legal **separation**.

Limited fee simple   See **fee simple** and **determinable**.

Limited partnership   A special form of unincorporated business ownership, available under some state laws, that allows the business to be run by *general partners* and financed partly by *limited partners*, who may take no part in running the business and have no **liability** for business losses, lawsuits, etc., beyond the money they put in.

Limited trust   A **trust** set up for a specific time period.

Lindberg Act   A federal law prohibiting the transportation of a kidnapped person across a state line.

Line of credit   The promise of credit up to a certain maximum that a merchant or bank will give to a customer, usually for an ongoing series of loans and paybacks.

Line of descent   A **direct** *line of descent* includes grandparents, parents, children, etc., and a **collateral** *line of descent* includes brothers, aunts, nieces, etc.

Lineal   In a line. For example, *lineal relationships* are those of father and son, grandson and grandmother, etc.

Lineup   Showing a witness several persons in a line and asking the witness to identify the person who committed a crime. A *lineup* must not be staged so that it is suggestive of one person.

Link financing   One person depositing a **compensating balance** in a bank for another person's loan.

Link-in-chain

Link-in-chain The **constitutional** privilege against **self-incrimi-nation** (see that word) includes protection against questions that could lead even indirectly to a linking of the person and criminal activity.

Liquid **1.** Having enough money to carry on normal business. A "live" business is *liquid,* but a "dead" business is *liquidated* (made *liquid* in the totally different sense of being turned entirely into cash). **2.** Easily turned into cash.

Liquidate **1.** Pay off or settle a debt. **2. Adjust** or settle the amount of a debt. **3.** Settle up affairs and distribute money, such as the money left by a dead person or by a company that goes out of business.

Liquidated **1.** Paid or settled up. **2.** Determined, settled, or fixed. For example, a *"liquidated claim"* is a claim or debt with a definite amount fixed either by agreement or by a court's action.

Liquidation **1.** See **liquidate.** **2.** Winding up business and ending a company.

Liquidity **1.** See **liquid.** **2.** The ability to turn **assets** easily into cash.

Lis pendens **1.** A pending lawsuit. **2.** A warning notice that **title** to property is in **litigation** and that anyone who buys the property gets it with legal strings attached.

List **1.** See **listing.** **2.** See **docket.** **3.** *List price* is the price of goods set by the manufacturer. It may be reduced for many reasons.

Listed security A **stock** or other **security** that has met the requirements of an **exchange** (financial reports, supervision, etc.) and is traded on that exchange.

Listing **1.** A **real estate agent's** right to sell land. An *open* or *general listing* is the right to sell that may be given to more than one agent at a time. An *exclusive agency listing* is the right of one agent to be the only one other than the owner who may sell the property during a period of time. An *exclusive authorization to sell listing* is a written **contract** that gives one agent the sole right to sell the property during a time period. This means that even if the owner finds the buyer, the agent will get a **commission.** *Multiple listing* occurs when an agent with an exclusive listing shares information about the property sale with many members of a real estate association and shares the sale commission with an agent who finds the buyer. And, a *net listing* is an arrangement in which the seller sets a minimum price he or she will take for the property, and the agent's commission is the amount the property sells for over that minimum selling price. **2.** See **listed security**.

Literacy test   A reading test that must be passed to vote in some states. These have been mostly suspended by the *Federal Voting Rights Act.*

Literal construction   Interpreting a document by the exact meaning of the words, and by the words alone, without considering outside facts such as the intent of the persons writing it.

Literary property   The right of an author (and those to whom the author has transferred the right) to all control of and profits from a literary work such as a book, a letter, etc. This right is primarily protected by **copyright** law.

Literary work   Under **copyright** law, any work (except audiovisual) expressed in words, numbers, or symbols, regardless of its physical form (books, manuscripts, tapes, etc.).

Litigant   A **party** to (participant in) a lawsuit.

Litigate   **1.** Actively carry on a lawsuit.   **2.** Carry on the **trial** part of a lawsuit.

Litigation   A lawsuit or series of lawsuits.

Litigious   **1.** Fond of bringing lawsuits; bringing too many lawsuits.   **2.** Disputable; subject to disagreement.

Littoral   Having to do with a shore, bank, or side of a body of water.

Live storage   The temporary parking of a car in a garage.

Livery   An old word for the formal transfer and delivery of something (especially land).

Living trust   A **trust** that will take effect while the person setting it up is still alive, as opposed to one set up under a **will**. It is also called an "**inter vivos** trust."

Living will   A document in which a person states the desire to be allowed to die naturally if unconscious from a terminal disease or injury.

Lloyd's of London   The world's largest association of **insurance** underwriters (persons and companies that insure things).

Load   That part of **insurance, mutual fund,** or other business charges that represents **commissions** and selling costs.

Loan commitment   A promise by a bank, **mortgage** company, etc., that it will lend a buyer a certain amount of money at a certain rate for a certain length of time on a particular piece of property and hold the loan open for a certain length of time for the buyer to complete the **real estate** purchase.

Loan for consumption   A loan such as a cup of sugar that gets returned as a different cup of sugar. See **loan for use.**

Loan for use   A loan such as a lawnmower that gets returned as exactly the same lawnmower. See **loan for consumption.**

Loan ratio   A comparison of the amount of a loan to the value of the property on which the loan is made. The closer together the two numbers are, the higher the interest a bank is likely to charge for the loan.

Loan shark   A person who lends money at an **interest** rate higher than the legal maximum or who uses **extortion** to get repaid.

Loan value   The highest amount a lender will lend (or can safely lend) on a piece of property, on a life **insurance** policy, etc.

Loaned servant doctrine   The legal principle that in most cases when an employer lends a person to another employer, that person becomes an employee of the second employer for many purposes, such as **liability** to others.

Lobbying   Attempting to persuade a **legislator** (congressman, etc.) to vote a certain way on a bill or to introduce a bill.

Lobbying acts   Federal and state laws requiring the **registration** of *lobbyists,* the reporting of money spent by lobbyists, and other things. See also **foreign agent.**

Local action   A lawsuit that may be brought in only one place.

Local agent   A person who takes care of a company's business in a particular area. Many states require a company doing business in the state to **register** a *local agent* for the **service** of **process** for lawsuits against the company.

Local assessment (or local improvement assessment)   A tax on only those properties benefiting from an improvement such as a sidewalk or sewer.

Local court   A vague term meaning a state rather than a **federal** court, a **municipal** court, a particular **foreign** court, etc.

Local law   A vague term for a law that operates only in one geographical area, that affects only one type or group of persons or things, that operates "here" rather than "there," etc.

Local option   **1.** The choice given to a city, county, etc., under state law to choose whether to allow the sale of alcoholic beverages, to allow racetracks, etc.   **2. Home rule** (see that word).

Location Marking the boundaries of land in which you have made a mineral discovery and want to make a mining **claim.** There are detailed rules for this.

Locative calls The description of land in a **deed** or other document by using landmarks, physical objects, and other things by which the land can be precisely located and identified.

Lockbox system First a company's customers send payments to a local post office box, then a local bank collects the payments and sends them on to the company's main bank. This is the most common form of *concentration banking,* in which local payments feed into local banks for transfer.

Locked in **1.** A person is *"locked in"* who has profits on **stocks** or other **securities,** but who will have to pay a high tax on them if he or she sells them now. **2.** A person may also be *"locked in"* who owns an **option** to purchase something at a certain price even if the price goes up.

Lockout An employer's refusal to allow employees to work. This is not an individual matter between an employer and a single employee, but a tactic in employer–union disputes.

Lockup A place of detention in a police station or courthouse.

Loco parentis See **in loco parentis.**

Locus (Latin) **1.** Place. For example, *locus contractus* (the place where the contract was made); *locus criminis or delicti* (the place where the crime was committed); *locus regit actum* (the place where the act is done); etc. See *lex loci* (**lex** no. 2) for more examples. **2.** *Locus sigilii* is "the place of the seal." See **L.S.** **3.** *Locus poenitentiae* is the "place of repentance," a final chance to change your mind before making a deal or committing a crime.

Lodger A person who lives in a part of a building run by another and who does not have total control over the rooms lived in.

Log rolling **1.** Including many different things in one **legislative bill** to get many different people to vote for it, thus voting for things they might have voted against if they were separate. **2.** Legislative favor-trading in general.

Logging in An initial record (a "log") of the name of persons brought to a police station. The *logging in* process may be combined with **booking** (see that word).

Long (or long position) A person who has large amounts of **stock** or who has contracted to buy large amounts of a stock for future delivery in expectation of a price rise is called *long* and has *a long position.*

Long-arm statute   A state law that allows the courts of that state to claim **jurisdiction** over (decide cases directly involving) persons or property outside the state. Even with a *long-arm statute,* a person cannot be sued unless he or she has certain minimal contacts with the state.

Loophole   Someone else's way of legally avoiding taxes. (See **deduction, credit exclusion**, etc., for your way.)

Loose-leaf service   A set of books in loose-leaf binders that gives up-to-the-minute reports on one area of law, such as federal taxes. As the law changes, new pages replace old ones. Three big publishers of these are Prentice-Hall, Commerce Clearing House, and Bureau of National Affairs.

Lord Campbell's Act   **1.** A law that sets the maximum amount that can be recovered in a **wrongful death action** (see that word).   **2.** The first law that allowed truth and public benefit to be a **defense** to **libel.**

Lord Mansfield's Rule   A law, used in only some states, that **bars testimony** about whether a husband could have fathered a child during a marriage.

Loss   A broad word that can mean anything from *total loss* (dropping a coin accidently in the ocean) through *partial loss* (a drop in the value of a **stock**) to *technical loss* ("loss" of an eye might mean the loss of use of the eye for practical purposes). In general, the legal use of the word is close to its ordinary use. For various types of *loss,* such as **capital, casualty, general average, hobby,** etc., see those words.

Loss leader   Merchandise sold below cost to attract customers who may buy other items. When this is done with no intention of selling the promised items, it is called **bait and switch** (see that word).

Loss payable clause   A provision in an **insurance** policy that lists the order of payments if the insurance is not enough to pay everyone involved.

Loss ratio   The proportion between **insurance** premiums collected and loss claims paid.

Lost grant doctrine   The principle that if a person holds land as the owner and the previous owner knew about it for a long time, there must have been a document transferring ownership even if it cannot be found now.

Lost will   In some states, a *lost will* can be proved by **evidence** about it, but in other states it is **void.**

Lot   **1.** An individual piece of land.   **2.** A thing or group of things that is part of one separate sale or delivery.   **3.** The number of shares of a **stock** or other **security** that is the normal minimum trading size. See **odd lot** and **round lot.**

Loyalty oath   A pledge of allegiance required of many public employees, mostly in jobs having access to secrets, but also in some others. If the oath is vague or requires swearing to things that violate **civil liberties**, it is usually held **unconstitutional.**

Ltd.   Limited.

Lucrative title   Rights to property received by gift or **inheritance.**

Lucri causa   (Latin) In order to gain or profit.

Lump-sum settlement   **1.** Payment of an entire amount of money owed at one time, rather than in payments. This may be less than the entire amount owed or in dispute.   **2.** Payment of a fixed amount of money to take care of an obligation that might otherwise have gone on forever. For example, *"lump-sum alimony"* might be a payment of one large sum to avoid the possibility of having to pay a changeable, potentially greater, amount of money on a regular basis for a long time.

Lunacy   See **insanity.**

Luxury tax   A tax on things considered unnecessary, such as cigarettes, liquor, or jewelry over a certain price. It is a type of **excise.**

Lying by   A person who remains silent during a transaction that affects his or her interests is "lying by" and may not be able to protest it later. See also **estoppel.**

M.D.   Middle **district.**

M.J.   Military Justice Reporter.

M.O.   **Modus** operandi (see that word).

Magisterial precinct (or district) The part of a county in which a **magistrate, constable,** or **justice of the peace** has official power.

Magistracy 1. All public officials. 2. All judges and law enforcement officials. 3. All judges. 4. All low-level judges such as **justices of the peace.** 5. The office of **magistrate** (see that word).

Magistrate A low-level judge, usually with limited functions and powers; for example, a police court judge. U.S. magistrates perform this job for the federal courts. They can conduct pretrial proceedings, try minor criminal matters, etc.

Magna Charta A document, signed by the English king in 1215, that defined and gave many basic rights for the first time in England. These included personal and property rights, limits on taxation and religious interference, etc. (Also spelled Magna Carta.)

Magnuson–Moss Act A federal law that set standards for **warranties** on **consumer** products. The act requires clear, simple written warranties, defines what "full warranty" means, etc.

Mail fraud The federal crime of using the mails in any way to deliberately cheat another person.

Mail order divorce A **divorce** granted by a country in which neither person lives and to which neither person has traveled to get the divorce. These are not valid in the United States.

Mailbox rule The rule that an **acceptance** of an **offer** is made (and forms a valid **contract**) when it is mailed, so neither the person making the offer nor the person accepting it can take it back after the acceptance is in the mail. This rule applies only in situations where mailing is a reasonable practice. The general principle (that sending, not receipt, makes an acceptance) applies to other ways of communicating also.

Maim Seriously wound, disfigure, or disable a person.

Main purpose doctrine The principle that if the *main purpose* of a person's promise to pay another's debt is the person's own benefit, that promise need not be in writing to be enforceable. (This is an exception to the general rule that the promise to pay another's debts must be in writing because it comes under the **statute of frauds.**)

Maintain Carry on; keep from **lapse** or failure; support; keep in good shape; continue; do repeatedly. See also **maintenance.**

Maintenance 1. To **maintain** (see that word). 2. Meddling with a lawsuit that doesn't concern you; for example, by paying a person to continue a lawsuit he or she would have dropped. See also **champerty**.   **3.** Supply the necessities of life. See also **separate maintenance**.

Major and minor fault rule   The rule that when one ship's fault is uncontradicted and clearly could have caused the collision, any doubts about the other ship's possible fault should be resolved in its favor.

Major dispute   A *major dispute* in transportation *labor law* concerns the creation or change of a labor contract, while a *minor dispute* concerns the meaning of an existing contract as it applies to specific situations.

Majority   **1.** Full legal age to manage your own affairs. **2.** More than half. Fifty-one is *a majority* of votes when one hundred persons vote. A distinction is sometimes made between an *absolute majority* (more than half of the voters who come to vote) and a *simple majority* (more than half of the voters who actually vote on one particular issue or election contest).

Make whole   Put a person who has suffered legal **damages** back into the financial position he or she was in before the wrong was done.

Maker   **1.** A person who initially signs a **negotiable instrument**, such as a **note**, and by doing so promises to pay on it.   **2.** A person who signs, creates, or performs something.

Mala fides   (Latin) Bad faith. [pronounce: mal-a fee-dez]

Mala in se   See **malum in se**.

Mala praxis   **Malpractice**.

Malefactor   A person who is guilty of a crime.

Malfeasance   **1.** Wrongdoing.   **2.** Doing an illegal act (especially by a public official).

Malice   **1.** Ill will.   **2.** Intentionally harming someone; having no moral or legal justification for harming someone.

Malice aforethought   An intention to seriously harm someone or to commit a serious crime.

Malicious   Done intentionally, from bad motives and without excuse. For example, "*malicious prosecution*" is bringing criminal **charges** against someone in order to harm that person and with no legal justification for doing it. If the person prosecuted wins, that person can sue the person who brought the charges for *malicious prosecution*.

Malicious mischief The criminal offense of intentionally destroying another person's property.

Mallory rule The **McNabb–Mallory rule** (see that word).

Malo animo (Latin) "With evil mind"; **malice.**

Malo grato (Latin) Unwillingly.

Malpractice Professional misconduct or unreasonable lack of skill. This word usually applies to bad or unfaithful work done by a doctor or lawyer.

Malum (or mala) in se (Latin) "Wrong in and of itself"; morally wrong; **common law** crimes.

Malum (or mala) prohibitum (Latin) "Prohibited evils"; **statutory** crimes.

Manager **1.** A person chosen to run a business or a part of one. **2.** A member of the House of Representatives who is chosen to prosecute an **impeachment** trial in the Senate.

Mandamus (Latin) "We command." A court **order** that tells a public official or government department to do something. It may be sent to the **executive** branch, the **legislative** branch, or a lower court. [pronounce: man-<u>day</u>-mus]

Mandate **1.** A judicial command to act; see **mandamus. 2.** An authorization to act.

Mandatory Required; must be followed or obeyed.

Mandatory authority **Binding authority** (see that word).

Manifest **1.** Clear, visible, indisputable, or requiring no proof. **2.** A written document that lists goods being shipped or stored, giving descriptions, values, shipping information, etc. **3.** A list of passengers or cargo carried by a ship or a plane.

Manifesto **1.** A formal written statement by the head of a country concerning a major international action. **2.** A public declaration of political principles.

Man-in-the-house rule Some states used to deny **welfare benefits** (see those words) to poor families solely because a man lived with them. This is now **unconstitutional** (see that word).

Manipulation A series of **stock** (or other **securities**) transactions intended to raise or lower the price of the stock or to convince others to buy or sell. This is usually done by creating a false impression of active trading or by trying to trigger a major trading trend.

Mann Act A federal law against transporting women across state lines for immoral purposes (especially prostitution).

Manslaughter   An unlawful killing of a person without **malice** (see that word). There are various types of *manslaughter*. In some states *voluntary manslaughter* is a killing in a sudden rage such as occurs during a quarrel and fight, and *involuntary manslaughter* is a killing with no intention to cause serious bodily harm, such as by acting without proper caution.

Manufacturer's liability   See **strict liability**.

Manumission   Freeing a person from another's control.

Mapp rule   The **constitutional** principle that illegally obtained **evidence** may not be used in a state criminal trial. It comes from the 1961 Supreme Court case *Mapp v. Ohio*. It is an **exclusionary rule**.

Marbury v. Madison   The **Supreme Court** case that established the right of the **judiciary** to decide whether an act of **Congress** is **constitutional**. This is also called **judicial review**.

Margin   **1.** A boundary or boundary line.   **2.** The percentage of the cost of a **stock** (or other **security**) that must be paid in cash by the buyer. A **broker** who offers such a *margin* transaction then makes a loan for the balance of the cost, keeping the stock as **collateral** in the *margin account*.   **3.** For *margin of profit*, see **profit margin.**

Margin call   **1.** A **stock broker's** (see that word) demand for more cash or more **collateral** for a stock bought on **margin** because the stock has gone down in value. This is also called *remargining* and is done by others, such as **commodity** dealers.   **2.** A stock broker's notice to a buyer that a certain stock has been bought and that the purchase price must now be paid.

Marginal cost   The cost of adding one more identical item to a bulk purchase, of manufacturing one more item in a production run, of borrowing one more dollar in a loan, etc.

Marginal rate   See **tax rate.**

Marital   Having to do with marriage. For example, the *marital deduction* is the amount of money a wife or husband can inherit from the other without paying **estate** or gift taxes; and *marital property* is anything acquired during a marriage.

Marital agreements   **1.** All **contracts** between persons married to each other.   **2.** Contracts between persons about to get married or about to separate. These usually concern the division of property and are also called *premarital agreements* and **antenuptial agreements.**

Marital communications privilege **1.** The right of a husband and wife to keep things secret between them. **2.** The right of a husband or wife to keep the other from testifying against him or her in a **criminal** trial. This right is often limited when the person harmed is the spouse.

Maritime (or marine) belt See **territorial** waters.

Maritime law The law of ships, ocean commerce, and sailors.

Mark **1.** A sign, such as a cross-mark (X), used by a person who cannot sign a name. To be valid, it usually requires signing **witnesses.** **2.** Same as **marque.** **3.** An indication; proof or evidence. For example, a *mark of fraud* is a sign or indication that something is phony. **4.** A **trademark, service** mark, **collective mark** or **certification mark** (see those words) that can be **registered** under federal law because it is "used in commerce" by being displayed on or with a product or service sold or advertised in more than one state or country.

Market **1.** The geographical region in which a product can be sold, or the economic and social characteristics of potential buyers. **2.** An abbreviation for stock market or commodities market. **3.** The demand for something or the price it will sell for if sold. **4.** The range of **bid and asked** (see that word) prices for **over-the-counter** stocks.

Market making Establishing a sales price for **over-the-counter stocks** and other **securities** by placing **bid and asked** (see that word) quotations.

Market order See **order.**

Market price **1.** The price at which something has just sold in a particular market. **2.** **Market value** (see that word).

Market share The percentage of sales of a particular item in a particular market that one company controls.

Market value The price to which a willing seller and a willing buyer would agree for an item in the ordinary course of trade. It is also called "actual market value," "actual value," "cash market value," "clear market value," "current market value," "fair cash value," "fair market value," "fair value," "just compensation," etc.

Marketable **1.** Easily sold for cash. For example, a *marketable security* is a **stock, bond,** etc., that can be sold in the proper **exchange** or through normal business channels. *Marketable securities* also refers to a company's temporary investments of extra cash in such short-term, low-risk things as **treasury bills** and

commercial paper. **2.** Commercially valid. For example, a *marketable title* to land is ownership that can be freely sold because it is clear of any reasonable doubts as to its validity.

Marketable title acts   State laws that make it possible to determine whether or not a **title** to land is good by searching the public records for a limited time only (for example, back to forty years ago).

Marketing contract   **1.** Any agreement between an **agent,** a **broker,** or a merchant and a producer in which goods, **securities,** etc., are sold. **2.** An agreement between a producers' **cooperative** and its members in which the members promise to sell through the co-op and the co-op promises to get the best possible price. **3.** An **output contract** or a **requirements contract.**

Marketing order   A federally approved limit on the amount of a particular vegetable or other argicultural commodity that can be sold by farmers in a particular area.

Markup   **1.** The meeting in which a **committee** of a **legislature** goes through a **bill** section-by-section to revise it. **2.** An amount of money added to the cost of an item to give the merchant selling costs plus a profit. If a merchant buys a shirt for ten dollars and sells it for fifteen, it has a "50 percent markup," or a "five dollar markup."

Marque and reprisal   The request made to the ruler of one country to seize the citizens or goods of another country until some wrong done by that other country is straightened out. It is prohibited by the U.S. **Constitution.**

Marriage   Legal union as husband and wife. For **ceremonial marriage,** see that word. For *informal, consensual,* or *common-law* marriage, see **common-law marriage.**

Marriage settlement   **1. Marital agreement** (see that word). **2.** A transfer of **title** to property that firmly fixes the right of **succession** and that is made because of a marriage. For example, an aunt might *settle* the title to a house on the bride and her children as of the date of the proposed marriage.

Marshal   A person employed by federal courts to keep the peace, deliver legal orders, and perform duties similar to those of a state **sheriff.**

Marshaling   **1.** Arranging, ranking, or disposing of things in order. For example, *marshaling assets and claims* is collecting them up and arranging the debts into the proper order of priority and then dividing up the **assets** to pay them off. This is done by a **trustee** when someone goes **bankrupt** and by an **executor** or **administrator** during the **probate** of a dead person's **estate**. **2.** In general, if one **creditor** could collect from either of two pots of a **debtor's** money and a second creditor can collect from only one of them, the first creditor will be required to take from the singly-claimed pot first. This is called the *rule of marshaling assets*, the *rule of marshaling remedies*, and the *rule of marshaling securities*. For the *rule of marshaling liens*, see **inverse order of alienation**.

Martial law Government by the military. [pronounce: <u>mar</u>-shall]

Martindale-Hubbell A set of books that lists many lawyers by location and type of practice. It also has one volume that gives summaries of each major area of the law in each state.

Massachusetts trust A **business trust** (see that word).

Master **1.** An employer who has the right to control the actions of an employee. **2.** A *"special master"* is a person appointed by a court to carry out the court's orders in certain types of lawsuits. A *special master* might, for example, supervise the sale of property under a **decree (order)** that it be sold. Federal courts, and many state courts, have *masters* to perform a wide variety of information gathering jobs for a trial. **3.** Overall or controlling; for example: a *master agreement* is an agreement between a large **union** and the leaders of one industry. This becomes a model for **labor contracts** with each individual company; a *master plan* is the overall plan of a city for housing, business, etc., as laid out in a map and in materials on **zoning** laws, **environmental impacts**, etc.; a *master policy* is an **insurance** policy for persons in a **group insurance** plan; and a *master contract* is a basic agreement to buy or lease equipment as needed, each time under the same general terms.

Material Important; probably necessary; having effect; going to the heart of the matter. For example, a *material allegation* in a legal **pleading** is a statement that is essential to the **claim** or **defense** being used and without which the pleading would have little or no legal effect, and a *material alteration* is a change in a document that affects its meaning or legal effect. For other examples, see the words following.

Material evidence See **relevant** evidence.

Material fact **1.** A basic reason for a contract, without which it would not have been entered into. **2.** A fact that is central to winning or deciding a case. **3.** A fact which, if told to an **insurer,** would have influenced the insurer to refuse insurance, cancel insurance, or raise its cost.

Material issue A question that is formally in dispute between persons properly brought before the court and is important to determining the outcome of the lawsuit.

Material witness A person who can give **testimony** no one else can give. In an important **criminal** case, a *material witness* may sometimes be held by the government against his or her will in order to assure that person's availability for testimony.

Materialman A person who supplies building materials for a construction or repair project. A more general word is *"supplier."*

Mathematical evidence A phrase sometimes misused to mean **demonstrative evidence** (see that word).

Matrimonial actions Annulments, divorces, legal **separations,** etc.

Matter **1.** A central, necessary, or important fact. **2.** An event, occurrence, or transaction. **3.** The subject of a lawsuit. **4.** The name for certain special types of legal proceedings. For example, *"In the matter of John Jones"* might be the name for a child **neglect** case.

Matter of fact A question that can be answered by using the senses or deduced from the **testimony** of **witnesses** or other **evidence.**

Matter of law A question that can be answered by applying the law to the facts of a case.

Matter of record Anything that can be proved by merely checking in a court record. The word is sometimes broadened to include anything that can be proved by checking any official record.

Matured **1.** See **liquidated.** **2.** See **maturity.**

Maturity The time when a debt or other obligation becomes due or a right becomes enforceable.

Maxim A general statement about the law that works when applied to most cases.

Mayhem The crime of violently giving someone a serious permanent wound.

Mayor The head of a city, town, or other local government. Mayors may be elected or appointed, important or ceremonial. A *mayor's court* is usually a police or traffic court in a small town, with the mayor serving as judge.

McCarran Act **1.** See **internal security acts.** **2.** A federal law that permits states to tax and **regulate** out-of-state **insurance** companies with in-state customers.

McCormick *McCormick on Evidence;* a **treatise.**

McNabb-Mallory rule The rule that if someone has been held too long by the police before bringing the person before a judge, no **confession** obtained may be used against that person.

McCulloch v. Maryland The 1819 Supreme Court case that upheld the **implied** power (not stated directly in the **Constitution**) of the federal government to take actions, such as establishing banks, and denied the states the right to tax any part of the federal government, confirming that the national government was supreme in all matters allowed it by the Constitution.

Mean high tide The long-term average, furthest line that the tide reaches on oceanside land. This is often considered the private property line; anything on the seaward side may be used by the public.

Means **1.** Money, property, or income available to support yourself, to support your family, to pay a debt, etc. **2.** Laws, **acts,** and **initiative** and **referendum** measures (the *means* to accomplish what the people want the government to accomplish). **3.** A cause; an agent of change; a method of accomplishing something.

Means test **1.** A financial requirement that a person have or make either more or less than a certain amount of money to qualify for something. **2.** The requirement that if a company makes choices that are potentially *discriminatory* (see **discrimination**), the company's purpose must be legally justified and the *means* it uses to accomplish that purpose (or "end") must be the least drastic possible.

Mechanical equivalents Two things that do the same work in the same basic way and produce the same result.

Mechanic's lien A worker's legal claim to hold property (such as a car) until repair charges are paid or to file formal papers securing a right to property (such as a car or a house) until charges for work done are paid.

Mediate   1. "In between"; secondary; incidental.   2. See **mediation.**

Mediation   Outside help in settling a dispute. The person who does this is called a mediator. This is different from **arbitration** (see that word) in that a *mediator* can only persuade, not force, people into a settlement. The Federal Mediation and Conciliation Service (**F.M.C.S.**) helps to settle **labor disputes.**

Medicaid   Medical assistance payments for low-income persons who meet federal and state requirements.

Medical examiner   A public official who investigates all violent or unexplained deaths, performs autopsies, and helps **prosecute homicide** cases. This is the modern version of a **coroner.**

Medical jurisprudence   **Forensic** medicine (see that word).

Medicare   Federal medical payments for elderly persons.

Meeting of creditors   In the *first* meeting of **creditors** under **bankruptcy** law, the **bankrupt** person is questioned, and claims are made (and allowed or disallowed by the **trustee**). *Interim* meetings may do more of the same, and a *final* meeting closes the bankrupt's affairs prior to a final court hearing.

Meeting of minds   Agreement by each person entering into a deal on the basic meaning and legal effect of the **contract.**

Melioration   Improvements, rather than repair to property.

Member   1. One of the persons in a family, **corporation, legislature, union,** etc.   2. A bank that is **affiliated** with one of the federal reserve banks, or a **brokerage** firm that is affiliated with a **stock** or other **securities exchange.**   3. Short for member of the **House of Representatives.**   4. An external part of a body, such as an arm.

Membership corporation   A nonprofit, non**stock corporation** created for social, charitable, political, etc., purposes.

Memorandum   1. An informal note or summary of a meeting, a proposed agreement, etc.   2. A note from one member of an organization to another.   3. A written document that proves a **contract** exists.   4. A **brief** (see that word) of law submitted to a judge in a case.

Memorandum decision   A court's *decision* that gives the **ruling** (what it decides and orders done), but no **opinion** (reasons for the decision).

Memorial   1. A **petition** or written statement presented to a **leg-**

Men of straw

islature or to the head of a country or state. **2.** A rough draft, **abstract,** or **memorandum** of a court's **order,** setting it down in writing until it can be put into the public records in final form.

Men of straw   See **straw man.**

Mens rea   (Latin) Guilty mind; wrongful purpose; criminal intent. *Mens rea* is a state of mind which (when combined with an **actus** reus, or "criminal act") produces a crime. This state of mind is usually to *intentionally* or *knowingly* do something prohibited, but is occasionally to *recklessly* or *grossly negligently* do it. See also **strict liability** for crimes that do not require *mens rea.*

Mensa et thoro   (Latin) "Bed and board." A type of limited **divorce** (see that word); a legal separation.

Mental anguish (or mental suffering)   In deciding payment for harm done, "mental anguish" may be as limited as the immediate mental feelings during an injury or as broad as prolonged grief, shame, humiliation, despair, etc.

Mental cruelty   See **cruelty.**

Mercantile   Commercial; having to do with buying and selling, etc.

Merchantable   **1.** Fit to be sold; of the general type and quality described and fit for the general purpose for which it was bought. **2.** For *merchantable title,* see **marketable title acts.**

Mercy killing   Causing the death of a person who is near death from a terminal disease and who is thought to desire death. Also called *euthanasia.* See also **death, brain death,** and **natural death acts.**

Merger   **1.** The union of two or more things, usually with the smaller or less important thing ceasing to exist once it is a part of the other. Companies, rights, contracts, etc., can *merge.* The following definitions divide these mergers by type. **2.** When **corporations** merge, it is a *horizontal merger* if business competitors selling the same product in the same area join; a *vertical merger* is if a company joins with its customers or suppliers; and a *conglomerate merger* is if unrelated companies join. *Conglomerate mergers* are of three types: when two totally unrelated companies join, it is a *pure merger;* when companies selling similar products in different **markets** join, it is a *geographical extension merger;* and when two compaines selling related, but different products join, it is a *product extension merger.* Finally, when a *subsidiary* merges with its parent company, many states allow a quick, cheap *short-form merger*. **3.** In **contract** law, if the persons who make a contract intend it, one contract may end and become a part of another through *merger*. Also, all prior oral agreements may be ended by establishing a written contract as the entire agreement by including a *merger clause*. **4.** Two rights or **estates** can merge. For example, if a tenant buys the house, the right of **tenancy** *merges* and is ended with the start of the right of ownership. Merging of rights occur in many other areas of the law, such as **divorce** law, **judgment** law, etc. **5.** *Merger* also occurs in **criminal** law when a person is charged with two crimes based on the exact same acts. The lesser crime *merges* with the greater, and the person may only be **sentenced** on one.

Merit system   A method of hiring, firing, and promoting used by governments and based on specific rules. It is meant to ensure competence in the **civil service** and to eliminate **patronage** from most positions.

Merits   **1.** The central part of a case; the "meat" of one side's legal position.   **2.** The substance or real issues of a lawsuit, as opposed to the form or the legal technicalities it involves. *Judgment on the merits* is a final resolution of a lawsuit after hearing all **evidence.**

Mesne   Middle; intermediate. For example, "*mesne process*" includes the legal papers and court **orders** *in between* the start and finish of a lawsuit. [pronounce: men]

Messuage   A home plus its surrounding land and outbuildings. See also **curtilage.**

Metes and bounds   Measuring land by boundary lines and fixed points and angles.

Metropolitan district   An area that includes more than one city, a city and its suburbs, etc., and that is set up by state law to handle regional problems such as public transportation, water supply, and sewage disposal. It may be a *general* district, headed by a *metropolitan council*, or a *specific* district such as "transportation district" run by a transportation **board.**

Middleman   **1.** A person who brings others together and helps them make deals.   **2.** A person who buys from one person and sells to another.   **3.** An **agent** or **broker.**

Migratory divorce   A **divorce** gained by a person who has moved (often temporarily) to another place in order to get the divorce.

Military law

Military law   The law that **regulates** the armed forces and its members. This is different from *military government* (government by the military of territory outside the U.S. or of territory inside the U.S. occupied by rebels) and from *martial law* (government by the military, usually when **civil** government breaks down). U.S. *military law* is contained in a comprehensive **Code of Military Justice,** administered by military officers under the supervision of the **judge advocate** general of each service and decided by a system of *military courts* (**courts martial** for trials, *courts of military review* for major cases on **appeal,** and the U.S. *Court of Military Appeals* for **civilian** review of the most major cases). There are also *military boards,* which act as fact finders, advisory boards, and courts in cases involving personnel matters such as promotion and in matters such as property damage, loss of funds, etc. Typical *military offenses* (in addition to those which would also be civilian crimes) include **desertion,** *insubordination,* or sleeping while on guard.

Militia   A part-time military force, called to active duty during a crisis. This job is now primarily performed by the National Guard and the Reserves.

Mill   One-tenth of a cent. Some property taxes are expressed in mills. A mill rate of "one" would be a dollar for each thousand dollars of assessed property.

Miller v. California   The 1973 Supreme Court case that listed several standards for obscenity prosecutions (community standards, appealing to prurient interest, no redeeming merit, etc.).

Mind and memory   A phrase describing adequate mental **capacity** to make a **will** (know what you're doing, know what you're giving away, and to whom).

Mineral   As defined in land laws, *mineral* may mean any nonanimal, nonvegetable substance found on or in the ground, any commercially valuable mineral, or one specific type of mineral.

Mineral lease   An agreement giving a right to explore for **minerals** and then to take out those found upon payment of rent for use of the land or **royalties** based on what is taken.

Mineral right   A right to either take minerals out of the ground or to receive payment for minerals taken out.

Minimal (or minimum) contacts doctrine   The rule that a person must carry on a certain minimum amount of activity within a state, or have formal ties to the state, before that person can be sued in the state.

Minimum fee schedules   The lowest fee for a particular service that a **bar association** will permit a lawyer to charge. *Minimum fees* have been abolished because they violate **antitrust** laws.

Minimum wage   The lowest wage that may be paid to employees as set by federal law.

Mining lease   A type of **mineral lease** (see that word).

Mining location   See **location**.

Minister   1. A person acting for another person or carrying out that person's orders.   2. A diplomatic representative such as **ambassador** or **envoy**.   3. The head of a **cabinet** department or government organization in many countries. The job is similar to that of a **secretary** (of defense, of labor, etc.) in the United States.

Ministerial   1. Done by carrying out orders, rather than by making many choices of how to act. In this use of the word, a police *chief's* actions would be "discretionary" and a police *officer's* actions *"ministerial."*   2. Done by carrying out a general policy (whether or not there is much choice of action) rather than by setting or making **policy**. In this sense of the word, a police *chief's* actions would be *ministerial* and the police *board's* would be discretionary.

Minor   1. A person who is under the age of full legal rights and duties.   2. Less or lower.

Minor dispute   See **major dispute**.

Minority   1. Being a **minor** (see that word).   2. Less than half.   3. Groups with only a small percentage of the total population.

Minority opinion   A *dissenting opinion*. See **opinion** (or **dissent**).

Minority stockholder   A person who holds too few **shares** of **stock** to control the way the **corporation** is managed (or to elect any **directors**).

Minor's estate   Property that must be looked after by a **trustee** because its owner is not yet of legal age to manage it.

Minute book   The record book kept by the **clerk** of some courts that lists a summary of all **orders** in each case by case number.

Minutes   Written notes of a meeting.

Miranda warning   The warning that must be given to a person **arrested** or taken into **custody** by a police officer or other official. It includes the fact that what you say may be held against you and the rights to remain silent, to contact a lawyer, and to have a free lawyer if you are poor. If this warning is not given proper-

Misadventure

ly, no statements made by the **defendant** may be used by the police or by the **prosecutor** in court because of the constitutional right to avoid self-incrimination.

Misadventure   An accident; an unintentional injury, often with no one legally at fault.

Misappropriation   Taking something wrongfully, but not necessarily illegally.

Misbranding   Any intentionally false information on a product label.

Miscarriage of justice   A legal proceeding or other official action that does unfair harm to a person.

Mischief   **1.** Intentionally or recklessly done harm.   **2.** The problem or danger that a **legislative act** is designed to correct.

Misconduct   **1.** Doing a forbidden act intentionally or willfully. *Official misconduct* includes **malfeasance, misfeasance,** and **nonfeasance.**   **3.** The act done in no. 1.

Misdemeanant   A person who commits a **misdeameanor** (see that word).

Misdemeanor   A criminal offense less than a **felony** that is usually punishable by a **fine** or less than a year in jail.

Misfeasance   The improper doing of an otherwise proper or lawful act.

Misfortune   A truly "accidental" accident; one which could not have been guarded against.

Misjoinder   See **joinder.**

Mislaid   Put somewhere by someone who then forgets where. For some legal purposes *mislaid property* is not technically "lost," and different legal rules for return apply to the finder.

Misprision   **1.** The failure to carry out a public duty, such as the duty to properly carry out a high public office.   **2.** The failure to prevent or report a crime.   **3.** Concealing another's crime.   **4.** An old meaning of *misprision* included **contempt** of court, **sedition,** and other open rejections of proper authority.

Misrepresentation   **1.** A false statement that is not known to be false is an *innocent misrepresentation.*   **2.** A false statement made when you should have known better is a *negligent misrepresentation.*   **3.** A false statement known to be false and meant to be misleading is a *fraudulent misrepresentation.*

Mistake   An unintentional error or act. A *"mistake of fact"* is a mistake about facts that is not caused by a **negligent** failure to find out the truth. A *"mistake of law"* is knowledge of the true

272

facts combined with a wrong conclusion about the legal effect of the facts.

Mistrial A trial that the judge ends and declares will have no legal effect because of a major defect in procedure or because of the death of a **juror,** a deadlocked **jury,** or other major problem.

Mitigating circumstances Facts that do not justify or **excuse** an action, but that can lower the amount of moral blame, and thus lower the **criminal penalty** or **civil damages** for the action.

Mitigation of damages **1.** Facts showing that the size of a claim for **damages** is unjustified. **2.** The rule that a person suing for damages must have done everything reasonable to minimize those damages, or the amount of money awarded will be lowered.

Mittimus The name for a court **order** sending a convicted person to prison, or transferring records from one court to another.

Mixed questions Legal questions involving both **fact** and **law** or involving both **local** and **foreign** law.

Mixed trust A trust set up for both charities and private persons.

M'Naghten's rule One of many rules, proposed over the years in different cases, to determine whether a person will be held criminally responsible for an act. According to the *"Rule in M'Naghten's Case,"* a person is "not guilty because of **insanity**" if, at the time of the offense, "a defect of reason produced by a disease of the mind" caused the person to "not know the nature of the act" or to "not know right from wrong."

Model acts Proposed laws put out by the National Conference of Commissioners on Uniform State Laws (but not those proposed as "uniform laws"); for example; the *Model Public Defender Act.*

Modification A change or alteration (usually a minor one).

Modus (Latin) Method, means, manner, or way. For example, *"modus operandi"* is a method of operation (that usually refers to criminal behavior).

Moiety **1.** Half. *Moiety acts* are criminal laws that give half the **fine** paid by a convicted person to the informer who started the prosecution. **2.** A part; a fractional part. [pronounce: <u>moy</u>-ity]

Monarchy A government by a king, queen, or other royal head. Monarchies may be **absolute** or **constitutional.**

Monetary aggregates Subcategories of the **money supply** (see that word).

Money market The institutions that deal with short-term loans and near-term transfers of funds. Also short for **money market fund** or **money market certificate**.

Money market certificate   A savings certificate, sold by banks and other savings institutions, that is usually held for six months and is based on the interest rate paid by U.S. **Treasury Bills**.

Money market fund   A **mutual fund** that invests in safe short-term **securities** such as **treasury bills**.

Money order   A type of **draft** sold by banks, post offices, and other companies to persons who want to make payments in check form, but who do not use their own checks.

Money supply   The amount of money in circulation as defined by the **Federal Reserve**. For example, "M-1A" is all paper money and coins plus all **demand** deposits held in banks.

Money-purchase plan   A **pension plan** in which an employer contributes a fixed amount each year. The ultimate value of the **benefits** paid will vary, depending on how much the invested sums earn.

Monition   A judge's order or warning.

Monopoly   The ability of one or a few companies to control the manufacture, sale, distribution, or price of something. A *monopoly* may be prohibited if, for example, a company deliberately built its power to fix prices, exclude competition, etc.

Monroe doctrine   The assertion that the U.S.A. will oppose any European interference in the affairs of any Western Hemisphere country.

Monument   A post, pile of stones, natural boundary, marked tree, etc., used to give land boundaries.

Moore   *Moore's Federal Practice Manual.* A **treatise**.

Moot   *Moot* has several conflicting and overlapping definitions, including: **1.** No longer important or no longer needing a decision because *already decided*. For example, a federal court will not take a case if it is *moot* in this sense. **2.** For the sake of argument or practice. For example, *moot court* is a mock court in which law students practice arguing cases. **3.** Abstract. Not a real case involving a real dispute. **4.** A subject for argument; undecided; unsettled. In this sense, moot means the opposite of the prior definitions.

Moral   **1.** Having to do with the conscience and principles of good conduct. **2.** Having to do only with the conscience and not enforceable by law, as in "only a moral obligation." **3.** Depending upon a belief, rather than positive proof. In this sense, testimony is *moral evidence,* and *moral certainty* is a very strong likelihood of something's being correct.

Moral turpitude   Immoral conduct. A criminal act involving more than a technical breaking of the law.

Moratorium   **1.** An enforced delay. For example, a city may impose a suspension or temporary delay in giving out building permits if it is necessary to protect the environment.   **2.** Any deliberate delay, whether or not enforced, required, or agreed to.

More favorable terms clause   A labor contract provision in which a **union** promises not to give more favorable terms (as to wages, benefits, hours, working conditions, etc.) to competitors of the company.

More or less   A **contract term** meant to keep the delivery of small variations in quantity from being a **breach.** What is *"more or less"* the right amount varies with what is customary in the trade and between the persons.

Morgue   The place where unidentified or as yet unclaimed dead bodies are taken for identification. [pronounce: morg]

Mortality tables   Actuarial tables (or mathematical formulas) that predict how many persons from a group of a certain age, sex, and other characteristics will die in each succeeding year.

Mortgage   **1.** One person putting up land or buildings (or, in the case of a "chattel mortgage," personal **property**) in exchange for a loan. A mortgage usually takes one of three forms: A. The ownership of the property actually transfers in whole or in part to the lender.   B. The ownership does not change at all, and the mortgage has the same effect as a **lien** (see that word).   C. The property is put into **trust** with an independent person until the debt is paid off.   **2.** For various types of mortgages, such as amortized, **blanket, closed-end, conventional, FHA, first, junior, purchase-money, second, wraparound,** etc., see those words.   **3.** Some "mortgage" words include the following: A *mortgage banker* makes mortgage loans with its own or others' money, usually of a short-term type. A *mortgage bond* is a **bond** with property put up for **security.** A *mortgage certificate* is a document showing a share owned in a mortgage. A *mortgage commitment* is a letter agreeing to a specific loan on specific terms. A *mortgage company* makes mortgage loans, then sells them to others. A *mortgage contingency clause* makes a sale depend on finding mortgage money. A *mortgagee* is a lender who takes a mortgage. *Mortgaging out* is 100 percent financing, or buying property without using any of your own money. A *mortgagor* is someone who borrows on a mortgage.

Mortis causa   See **causa mortis.**

Mortmain   **1.** An old word for giving or selling land to a **corporation** or to a religious organization.   **2.** Modern *mortmain* **statutes** limit deathbed gifts to charity because these gifts can cause last-minute disinheritances. Many of these laws have been invalidated by state courts.

Most favored nation   **1.** An agreement between two countries that says that each will treat the other as well as it treats the country it treats best. The main effect of "most favored nation" status is lowered **import** taxes.   **2.** For a *most favored nation* **clause** in a **labor contract**, see **more favorable terms clause.**

Most suitable use   **Highest and best use** (see that word).

Motion   **1.** A request that a judge make a **ruling** or take some other action. For example, a *motion to dismiss* is a request that the court throw the case out; a *motion for more definite statement* is a request that the judge require an opponent in a lawsuit to file a less vague or ambiguous **pleading;** a *motion to strike* is a request that **immaterial** statements or other things be removed from an opponent's pleading; and a *motion to suppress* is a request that illegally gathered **evidence** be prohibited. *Motions* are either *granted* or *denied* by the judge.   **2.** The formal way something is proposed in a meeting.

Motive   The reason why a person does something. *Not* **intent** (see that word for the difference).

Motor Carrier Act   The federal law that gives the Interstate Commerce Commission (**I.C.C.**) power to **regulate** routes and rates of cars, buses, trucks, etc., that carry things or people in interstate commerce.

Mouthpiece   Slang for "lawyer."

Movables   Personal property.

Movant   Person who makes a **motion** (see that word).

Move   To make a **motion** (see that word).

Moving cause   See **proximate cause.**

Moving papers   Court papers to make or support a **motion** or a lawsuit.

Mugging   A street robbery, particularly one using physical violence.

Mugshot   A picture taken for an official police record during a

booking. These pictures are collected in *mugbooks* to help identify criminals in the future.

Mulct   A **fine** or **penalty.**

Mulier   An old word for a **legitimate** child.

Multidistrict litigation   Lawsuits involving the same facts that come up in several different **federal district courts** may all be transferred to one court by a special federal panel according to special rules. The types of complex cases to get transferred this way often include **antitrust** cases, airplane crash suits, **patent, trademark**, and **securities** cases, etc.

Multifariousness   Lumping several unconnected claims in one lawsuit or several unconnected subjects in one **legislative bill.**

Multilateral agreement   An agreement among several persons, companies, or governments.

Multilevel distributorship   A **pyramid sales scheme** (see that word).

Multinational   **1.** A company with major centers of operation or **subsidiaries** in several countries.   **2.** A company that merely does business in several countries.

Multiple access   The **defense** to a **paternity** action that the woman had several lovers.

Multiple evidence   Facts that may be used in a trial to prove only certain things and no others.

Multiple listing   See **listing.**

Multiple offense   An act that violates more than one law and in ways that do not totally overlap.

Multiple party account   A bank **account** such as a **joint** account or a **trust** account, but not an account for an organization.

Multiple sentences   See **cumulative sentences.**

Multiplicity of actions   Improperly bringing more than one lawsuit on the same subject when one would do.

Mun.   Municipal.

Municipal   **1.** Having to do with a local government. For example, *municipal bonds* are **bonds** issued by a local government to raise money, and a *municipal ordinance* is a local law or regulation.   **2.** Having to do with any one government, whether city, state, county, etc.

Municipal corporation   A city or other local government unit that has been set up according to state requirements.

Municipality   A **municipal corporation** (see that word).

Muniments   Documents that are **evidence** of **title,** such as **deeds.**

Murder   The unlawful killing of another human being that is premeditated (planned in advance) or has **malice aforethought** (see that word). Most states divide murder into first and second **degrees.** *First degree murder* usually involves **willful** and deliberate killings, such as by torture or lying in wait, or killing during the commission of another **felony** such as **arson, rape, robbery,** and **kidnapping.** *Second degree murder* is less serious, but still worse than **manslaughter.**

Mutatis mutandis   (Latin) With necessary changes in detail.

Mutilation   **1.** Cutting, tearing, erasing, or otherwise changing a document in a way that changes or destroys its legal effect. **2. Mayhem** (see that word).

Mutiny   **1.** A revolt in the armed services.   **2.** A revolt of sailors aboard any ship.

Mutual   Done together; **reciprocal.** For example, *mutual wills* are separate **wills** that were made out as part of a deal, each one done because of the other one.

Mutual company   A company in which the customers are the owners who get the profits.

Mutual fund   An investment company that pools investors' money and buys **shares** of **stock** in many companies. It does this by selling its own shares to the public.

Mutual strike aid   Companies in an industry agreeing to give financial help to those that are struck by a union.

Mutuality of contract (or obligation)   The principle that each side must do something, or promise to do something, to make a **contract** binding and valid.

Nn

N.A.   Nonacquiescence; not allowed; not available; not applicable; etc.

N.A.A.C.P.   National Association for the Advancement of Colored People. A group that brought many landmark civil rights cases.

N.A.L.A.   National Association of Legal Assistants.

N.A.L.S.   National Association of Legal Secretaries. A group that provides information and professional **certification** for legal secretaries.

N.A.R.   National Association of Realtors.

N.A.S.A.   National Aeronautics and Space Administration.

N.A.S.D.   National Association of Securities Dealers. An association of dealers in **over-the-counter stocks** and other **securities.**

N.B.   (Latin) "Nota bene." Mark well, note well, or observe. The phrase is used to single out one thing for special emphasis.

N.C.D.   (Latin) "Nemine contra dicente." No one dissenting.

N.D.   Northern district.

N.E.   North Eastern Reporter (see **National Reporter System**).

NIFO   "Next in, first out." Valuing current **inventory** by its replacement cost. Under this accounting method, if a merchant buys a blivit for a dollar, but knows that once it is sold a replacement blivit will cost two dollars, the owned blivit is worth two dollars. See also **FIFO** and **LIFO.**

N.L.A.D.A.   National Legal Aid and Defender Association.

N.L.R.A.   **National Labor Relations Act** (see that word).

N.L.R.B.   National Labor Relations Board. A federal agency that **regulates** labor–management activities such as **collective bargaining,** union elections, **unfair labor practices,** etc.

N.O.V.   See **non obstante veredicto.**

N.O.W.   *Negotiable order of withdrawal.* A type of checking account that pays interest.

N.P.   **Notary public.**

N.R.   New reports; not reported; nonresident.

N.R.C.   Nuclear Regulatory Commission.

N.S.   New series.

N.S.F.   National Science Foundation; not sufficient funds.

N.Y.S.E.   New York **stock exchange** (see those words).

Naked   Incomplete; without force.

Napoleonic Code   **Code Civil** (see that word).

Narcotic   **1.** Any substance that dulls senses, induces sleep, or becomes addictive.   **2.** A substance like those in no. 1, that either federal or state law prohibits or regulates as possibly harmful to public health or safety. However, substances such as caffeine and nicotine are not defined as *narcotics.*

Narr Abbreviation for the Latin "narratio" (a **declaration** in a lawsuit) and used in the phrase "narr and **cognovit**," which means **confession of judgment** (see that word).

Narrative evidence A **witness's testimony** that is given without interruption or the usual questions by a lawyer.

National bank A bank incorporated under the laws of the U.S., rather than state laws, even though it does business primarily in one state only. It is usually a member of the **federal reserve** system and the **F.D.I.C.**

National consultation rights The right of certain large unions of federal employees to suggest changes in federal personnel policies.

National Environmental Policy Act The federal law requiring **environmental impact statements** (see that word) on major projects and setting out the major environmental goals of the U.S.

National Labor Relations Act The federal law that set up the National Labor Relations Board (N.L.R.B.) and established rules for all types of employer–employee contact (union **recognition**, strikes, secret ballots for selection of a union, union elections, "**unfair labor practices**," etc.). It is a combination of the **Wagner, Taft-Hartley** and **Landrum-Griffin Acts.**

National Reporter System A system of sets of books that collects all cases from state supreme courts by region. (For example, the North Eastern Reporter has Illinois, Indiana, Massachusetts, New York, and Ohio. It is abbreviated "N.E." and its more recent books are N.E.2d or "second.") The Reporter System also has sets for all federal cases, some lower court cases state-by-state, and a **digest** for each region. It has become the official place for some states to publish their decisions, and is put out by West Publishing Company.

Nationality The country of which a person is a citizen. (In some cases, a person could be an American "*national*" without being a citizen; for example, the residents of an American **territory**.) Nationality gives a person a political base, while **domicile** gives the person a **civil** base (a place to sue and be sued, pay taxes and claim benefits, etc.). A person gains nationality by birth or **naturalization.** The *U.S. Nationality Act* is the shortened name for the U.S. law dealing with immigration, naturalization, and entry to the country of foreigners.

Nationalization A country taking over a private industry, owning and running it, with or without payment to the ex-owners.

Native   A **citizen** by birth (including persons born overseas to parents who are citizens).

Natural affection   Love or family ties between persons directly related (parent–child, husband–wife, sister–brother). *Natural affection* alone may be **consideration** for a promise.

Natural born citizen   A person born in the United States or, perhaps, a person born *to* American citizens.

Natural death acts   State laws that allow a person to give written instructions that doctors should not prolong the person's life by artificial means if he or she is near death from a terminal condition. See also **mercy killing**.

Natural heir   **1.** Child.   **2.** Close relative.   **3.** Anyone who would **inherit** if there were no **will**.

Natural law   **1.** Rules of conduct that are thought to be the same everywhere because they are basic to human behavior.   **2.** Basic moral law.

Natural monument   See **monument**.

Natural object   In the law of **wills**, a *natural object* of a person's gift is a person who would have inherited property if no will existed.

Natural resources   **1.** Materials still in their original state that would have economic value if extracted (timber, oil, minerals, etc.).   **2.** Any natural place or product that is of benefit to people (those things in no. 1 plus lakes, parkland, etc.).

Naturalization   Becoming a **citizen** of a country.

Navigable waters   Water in or adjacent to the U.S. that forms a continuous passage for commercial ships from the sea.

Ne exeat   (Latin) A court paper forbidding a person from leaving the area.

Ne varietur   (Latin) "Do not alter it." Words written by a **notary** after authenticating a document.

Near v. Minnesota   A 1931 Supreme Court case forbidding most prior restraint of the press.

Near-money   **Quick assets**.

Necessaries doctrine   The rule that a seller may collect from a spouse or parent the price of goods sold for the basic support of a spouse or child.

Necessarily included offense   **Lesser included offense** (see that word).

Necessary

Necessary   **1.** Physically or logically inevitable. For example, a *necessary cause* is that event or action without which something would not have happened.   **2.** Legally required. For example, a *necessary party* is a person without whom a lawsuit cannot fairly proceed.   **3.** Appropriate or helpful, whether or not absolutely required. For example, the *necessary and proper clause* of the U.S. **Constitution** gives **Congress** the power to pass all laws appropriate to carry out its functions. See also **penumbra doctrine.**

Necessity   **1.** Anything from an irresistible force or compulsion to an important, but not required action. See **necessary** for the range of possibilities.   **2.** See **necessaries.**

Negative averment   Something stated in the negative form that is really a positive statement to be proved, rather than a denial of someone else's positive statement. For example, "he was not old enough to make a valid contract when he signed the papers" is a *negative averment* (because it's something he must prove), while "the signature is not his" is a simple denial (because the other side must prove the signature is his).

Negative covenant   **1.** An agreement that prohibits an employee or the seller of a business from competing in the same area with a similar product.   **2.** Any agreement in a contract to refrain from doing something.

Negative easement   See **easement.**

Negative pregnant   A denial that really admits what seems to be denied. For example, in response to the question "Did you go to New York?" "I didn't go yesterday" would be a *negative pregnant* because it implies going some other time.

Neglect   **1.** Failure to do a thing that should be done.   **2.** Absence of care in doing something.   **3.** Failure to properly care for a child.

Negligence   **1.** The failure to exercise a reasonable amount of **care** in a situation that causes harm to someone or something. It can involve doing something carelessly or failing to do something that should have been done. Negligence can vary in seriousness from **gross** (recklessness or willfulness), through *ordinary* (failing to act as a reasonably careful person would), *to slight* (not much).   **2.** *Criminal negligence* is careless conduct that is defined as a crime; for example, the extreme carelessness in driving a car that might change a noncriminal **homicide**

282

into **manslaughter.** For **comparative, concurrent, contributory, imputed, wanton, willful,** etc., negligence, see those words.

Negligent Careless (see **negligence**).

Negotiable Something that can have its ownership transferred by signing it over to someone else is "negotiable."

Negotiable instrument A signed document that contains an unconditional promise to pay an exact sum of money, either when demanded or at an exact future time. Further, it must be marked **payable** "to the **order** of" a specific person or payable "to **bearer**" (the person who happens to have it). *Negotiable instruments* include **checks, notes,** and bills of **exchange.** There is a whole branch of law concerning them and a special vocabulary of ordinary sounding words (such as "**holder**") that have specialized meanings in this area. However, if you look at a *check* and think about the bank's rules for cashing it, you have a basic idea of what *negotiable instruments* are about.

Negotiate **1.** Discuss, arrange, or bargain about a business deal. **2.** Discuss a compromise to a situation. **3.** Transfer a "**negotiable instrument**" (see that word) from one person to another.

Negotiation See **negotiate.**

Nem. con. Abbreviation for **nemine contradicente** (see that word).

Nemine contradicente (Latin) "No one dissenting." A unanimous decision or vote.

Nemo (Latin) No one; no person. *Nemo* is used in many legal phrases such as "nemo est supra leges" (no one is above the law).

Nepotism Giving jobs or contracts to relatives.

Net The amount remaining after subtractions. For example, *net assets* (or net worth) are what is left after subtracting what you owe from what you have; *net weight* is the weight of a product not counting the container; and the *net cost* of a car might be what you pay the dealer minus what you get back from the automaker as a **rebate.** For *net* **estate, income, loss, profit, yield,** etc., see those words; and for other examples, see the words following.

Net book value (or net asset value) The amount of a company's property backing each share of **stock** or **bond** it puts out. Calculating this amount is complex.

Net contract

Net contract (or listing)   A sale in which a **broker's commission** is equal to the amount by which the sale price exceeds a particular amount.

Net lease   A **lease** in which the tenant pays rent plus all the costs of ownership, such as taxes and maintenance.

Net position   The difference between **long** and **short contracts** held in one thing by a commodities or **securities** trader; more simply, the amount that a person will gain or lose by a change in a **commodity's** or a **stock's** value.

Net worth method   A way the I.R.S. proves that a person has understated taxable income by showing that the person has acquired more **assets** than could be bought by the stated income.

Neutrality laws   Laws prohibiting the U.S. government or U.S. citizens from giving military help against any country with which the U.S. is at peace.

Neutralize   Lessen the effect of harmful **testimony** by showing that the **witness** has made conflicting statements. See also **impeach.**

New and useful   In **patent** law, an invention is *new and useful* if it accomplishes a practical result in a new way.

New York Times v. Sullivan   The 1964 **Supreme Court** case that limited the right of a public official to sue a newspaper or other publication for **libel** to those cases where the publisher knew the material was false or published it with a **malicious** or **reckless** disregard for whether or not it was true.

Newly discovered evidence   Facts about something crucial to the outcome of a trial which existed at the time of the trial. The fact must have been unknown to the person asking for a new or reopened trial through no fault of that person.

Newsperson's privilege   The **constitutional** right of a reporter or similar person to keep sources of information secret. This right has been greatly limited by recent cases and is now best available under state **shield laws** (see that word).

Next cause   See **proximate cause.**

Next friend   A person who acts formally in court for a child without being that child's legal **guardian.**

Next of kin   **1.** Persons most closely related to a dead person. **2.** All persons entitled to **inherit** from a person who has not left a **will.**

Nihil   (Latin) Nothing. For example, *nihil dicit* ("he says nothing") is a **default judgment** given by a court to the **plaintiff** because the **defendant** does not answer the **complaint;** and *nihil est* ("there is nothing") is a **sheriff's** statement when a court paper cannot be formally delivered to someone.

Nil   (Latin) Nothing.

Nineteenth Amendment   The U.S. constitutional amendment that gave women the right to vote.

Ninety day letter   A notice that the **I.R.S.** claims you owe taxes. During the 90 days after receiving the notice, you must either pay the taxes (and claim a refund) or challenge the I.R.S.'s decision in **tax court.**

Ninth Amendment   The U.S. constitutional amendment that states that merely because certain rights are specifically given to the people, other rights are not denied or limited by failure to list them.

Nisi   (Latin) "Unless." A judge's **rule, order,** or **decree** (see these words) that will take effect *unless* the person against whom it is issued comes to court to "**show cause**" why it should not take effect. [pronounce: ni̲-si]

Nisi prius   (Latin) "Unless before." In American law, a trial court. [pronounce: ni̲-si pri̲-us]

Nixon v. United States   A 1974 Supreme Court case that refused to allow a claim of **executive privilege** (see that word) to keep tape recordings made by the president from being produced for an important **criminal** trial.

No action clause   A provision in many **liability insurance** policies that the insurance company need not pay anything until a lawsuit against the insured person results in a **judgment** or agreement about the amount owed.

No action letter   A letter from a government **agency** lawyer that, if the facts are as represented in a request by a person for an agency decision, the lawyer will recommend that the agency take no action against the person.

No bill   The statement made by a grand jury that finds insufficient evidence to **indict** a person on a **criminal charge.** Also called "not found," "not a true bill," or "ignoramus."

No contest   1. See **nolo contendere.**   2. A **no contest clause** is a provision in a **will** that, if a person challenges the will or anything in it, that person loses what he or she was given in the will.

No evidence   There is *no evidence* to support a contention or a lawsuit if facts to support any crucial part of the case are completely missing, are barred from **admission,** are so trivial that they amount to nothing, or are indisputably contradicted by contrary facts. (If any of these situations exist, a judge may give a judgment **non obstante veredicto**, a **summary judgment**, or a **directed verdict**.)

No eyewitness rule   The principle that if there is no **direct evidence** (see that word) of what a dead person did to avoid an accident, the **jury** may assume that the person acted with care for his or her own safety.

No fault   **1.** A type of automobile **insurance**, required by some states, in which each person's own insurance company pays for injury or damage up to a certain limit no matter whose fault it is.   **2.** The popular name for a type of **divorce** in which a marriage can be ended because it has simply broken down.

No limit order   Instructions from a client to a **broker** to buy or sell a certain amount of **stock** or other **securities** without any limits on price.

No load fund   A **mutual fund** that charges no initial sales commissions.

Nolens volens   (Latin) Willing or unwilling.

Nolle prosequi   (Latin) The ending of a criminal case because the **prosecutor** decides or agrees to stop prosecuting. When this happens, the case is *"nolled," "nollied,"* or *"nol. prossed."* (This is *not* **nolo contendere** or **non prosequitur.**)

Nolo contendere   (Latin) "I will not contest it." A **defendant's plea** of *"no contest"* in a **criminal** case. It means that he or she does not directly admit guilt, but submits to **sentencing** or other punishment. A defendant may plead *nolo contendere* only with the judge's permission because, unlike a **"guilty"** plea, this cannot be used against the defendant in a later **civil** lawsuit.

Nominal   **1.** In name only. For example, a *nominal defendant* is a person sued in a lawsuit, not to get anything but because the lawsuit would be formally defective without including that person. And a *nominal interest rate* is the interest stated on a **stock** or other **security**, rather than the actual interest earned as computed by the cost of the stock and other factors.   **2.** Not real or substantial. Slight; token.

Nominal trust   A **dry** trust (see that word).

Nominee   **1.** A person chosen as a candidate for public office.   **2.** A person chosen as another person's representative (**deputy, agent, trustee,** etc.). **3.** A *nominee* **trust** is an arrangement in which one person agrees in writing to hold land, **stock,** etc., for the benefit of another (undisclosed) person. See also **street name.**

Non **1.** A prefix meaning "no" or "not." Its use may be separate ("non contestable"), hyphenated ("non-contestable"), or together with the base word ("noncontestable"). **2.** Most English words beginning with "non" can be found by looking up the base word. (For example, to understand "Nonacceptance," look up "acceptance.") These words include: *non***access,** *non***assessable,** *non***cancelable,** *non***contribution,** *non***insurable,** *non***joinder,** *non***stock,** etc. **3.** Some English "non" words (such as **nonacquiescence, noncontestable, nonintervention,** etc.) have technical meanings not found in the base word definitions. These are separately defined after this word. **4.** A Latin word meaning "no," "not," "do not," "should not," "did not," etc. It appears in many legal phrases (such as "**non compos mentis,**" "**non obstante veredicto,**" "**non prosequitur,**" etc. These are separately defined after this word. **5.** "He did not." The first of many **defenses** to old lawsuits, such as *non acceptavit* ("he did not accept" a bill of **exchange**); *non assumpsit* ("he did not promise" to make a **contract**); *non concessit* ("he did not **grant**" a **deed**); *non demisit* ("he did not **demise**" a property lease); *non detinet* ("he did not detain" the property of another); and *non est factum* ("it is not his deed" that is being sued on).

Non compos mentis (Latin) Not of sound mind. This includes idiocy, **insanity,** severe drunkenness, etc.

Non obstante veredicto (Latin) "Notwithstanding the verdict." A judge's giving **judgment** (victory) to one side in a lawsuit even though the jury gave a **verdict** (victory) to the other side.

Non pros Abbreviation for **non prosequitur** (see that word).

Non prosequitur (Latin) "He does not follow up." A **judgment** given to a **defendant** because the **plaintiff** has stopped carrying on the case. This is now usually replaced by a "**motion** to dismiss" or a **default** judgment, but where still used is often called a *non pros.* (This is *not* **nolle prosequi** or **nolo contendere.**)

Non sui juris (Latin) "Not of his own law or right." A **minor,** an insane person, etc.

Non vult contendere **Nolo contendere** (see that word).

Nonacquiescence The **I.R.S.**'s announced disagreement with a decision of the U.S. **tax court** (see that word).

Nonage

Nonage   Not yet of legal age; still a **minor** (see that word).

Nonconforming goods   Goods that fail to meet contract specifications.

Nonconforming lot   A piece of land with a size, shape, or location that is not permitted by current **zoning** laws.

Nonconforming use   The use of a piece of land that is permitted, even though that type of use is not usually permitted in that area by the **zoning** laws. This can come about either because the use (building size, use, etc.) existed before the zoning law or because a **variance** has been granted.

Noncontestable clause   A provision in an **insurance** policy that prohibits the insurance company from refusing to pay on an insurance claim based on **fraud** or **mistake** in the original application after a certain amount of time.

Nonfeasance   The failure to perform a required duty (especially by a public official).

Nonintervention will   A **will,** valid in some states, that allows the **executor** to handle the dead person's property without court supervision and without posting a **bond.**

Nonprofit corporation   A **corporation** that has no "owners" and gives none of its income to its members, **directors,** or **officers.** It must be set up for religious, charitable, educational, or similar purposes. See also **charitable.**

Nonrecourse loan   A loan in which the lender cannot take more than the property borrowed on as repayment for the loan. This type of loan is used in surplus crop price support programs in which the crop is the only **security** for the loan. Some **mortgages** are also of this type, but most are not.

Nonsuit   The ending of a lawsuit because the **plaintiff** has failed to take a necessary step or accomplish a necessary action. In most places now, this will be a **dismissal,** a **default judgment,** or a **directed verdict.**

Nonsupport   The failure to provide financially for a wife (or, sometimes, for a husband). It is **grounds** for a **divorce** in some states.

Normal law   The law as it affects normal persons "of sound mind" who can manage their own affairs and act for themselves in legal situations.

Norris-LaGuardia Act   A federal law, passed in 1932, to prevent many types of **injunctions** against strikers and to prohibit "**yellow dog**" **contracts** (see that word).

Noscitur a sociis (Latin) "It is known from its associates." **1.** The rule that a word's meaning may be decided by looking at surrounding words or reading it "in context." **2.** A person's character may be inferred from that of his or her friends.

Not found **No bill** (see that word).

Notary public A semipublic official who can administer **oaths,** certify the validity of documents, and perform other witnessing type duties needed by the business and legal worlds.

Notation voting Voting (by a **board, legislature,** etc.) without any meeting. It is not permitted in most situations.

Note A document that says the person who signs it promises to pay a certain sum of money at a certain time.

Notes of decisions References to cases that discuss the laws printed in an **annotated statutes** book.

Notice **1.** Knowledge of certain facts. Also, *"constructive notice"* means a person *should have known* certain facts and will be treated as if he or she knows them. **2.** Formal receipt of the knowledge of certain facts. For example, *"notice"* of a lawsuit usually means that formal papers have been delivered to a person (*personal notice*) or to the person's **agent** (*imputed notice*). **3.** Various **trial** notices include *notice:* of **motion,** of **orders** of **judgments,** of **trial,** to appear, to **plead,** etc. **4.** For various types of real estate transaction *notice* laws (such as a *"notice-race" statute or act,* a *"notice" statute or act,* a *"notice recording" statute or act,* etc.), see **recording acts.** **5.** A *"notice to creditors"* is the *notice* in a **bankruptcy** proceeding that a **meeting of creditors** will be held, that claims must be **filed,** or that **relief** has been granted. **6.** A *"notice to quit"* is the written notice from a **landlord** to a **tenant** that the tenant will have to move.

Novation The substitution by agreement of a new **contract** for an old one, with all the rights under the old one ended. Usually, the substitution of a new person who is responsible for the contract and the removal of an old one.

Novelty For an invention to be *novel* enough to get a **patent,** it must not only have a new form, but also perform a new function or perform an old one in an entirely new way.

Nude Lacking something basic to be legally valid.

Nudum pactum (Latin) "Nude pact" or bare agreement. A promise or action without any **consideration** (payment or promise of something of value) other than good will or affection. [pronounce: <u>new</u>-dum <u>pack</u>-tum]

Nugatory Invalid; without force or effect.

Nuisance **1.** Anything that annoys or disturbs unreasonably; hurts a person's use of his or her property; or violates the public health, safety, or decency. **2.** Use of your own land that does anything in no. 1. **3.** A *private nuisance* is a **tort** that requires a showing of special harm to you or your property and allows the recovery of **damages** for the harm as well as an **injunction**. A *public nuisance* is a general, widespread problem that can be opposed by an **injunction** or criminal prosecution. A *nuisance* can be both public and private.

Null No longer having any legal effect or validity.

Nulla bona (Latin) "No goods." A **sheriff's return** (to the judge) when commanded to seize goods, and there are none available.

Nullity "Nothing." Of no legal force or effect.

Nunc pro tunc (Latin) "Now for then." Retroactive effect. For example, a judge may sometimes issue an **order** to have a legal effect that starts at an earlier date, in effect *backdating* the order.

Nuncupative will An oral **will.** It is valid in a few states.

O.A.S. Organization of American States.

O.A.S.D.I. **Old age, survivors, and disability insurance** (see that word).

O.M.B. Office of Management and Budget. It helps the U.S. president in financial matters, oversees the federal budget and each department's share, etc.

O.P.I.C. Overseas Private Investment Corporation.

O.P.M. The federal Office of Personnel Management.

O.R. Short for "own recognizance" or release without **bail** (see **recognizance**).

O.S.H.A. **Occupational Safety and Health Administration** (see that word).

O.T.C. **Over-the-counter** (see that word).

Oath A formal swearing that you will tell the truth (an *assertory oath*) or will do something (a *promissory oath*). Oaths of truthfulness are required of **witnesses**, and oaths of **allegiance** and faithful performance of duty are required of many public office-holders, soldiers, etc.

Obiter dictum (Latin) See **dictum**.

Object **1.** Purpose. **2.** Claim that an action by your adversary in a lawsuit (such as the use of a particular piece of **evidence**) is improper, unfair, or illegal, and ask the judge for a **ruling** on the point. **3.** Say that an action by the judge is wrong.

Objection **1.** The process of objecting (see **object**). **2.** Disapproval.

Obligation A broad word that can mean any **duty**, any legal duty, a duty imposed by a **contract**, a formal written promise to pay money, a duty to the government, a tax, etc.

Obligee Person to whom a **duty** is owed.

Obligor Person who owes another person a **duty**.

Obliteration Erasing or blotting out written words. (Sometimes lining out or writing over is *obliteration* even if the words still show.)

Oblivion An act of forgiving and forgetting such as a **pardon** or **amnesty** (see those words).

Obscene Indecent or lewd. The U.S. **Supreme Court** "test" of *obscenity* includes such things as whether a book, movie, etc., "violates community standards," "appeals primarily to prurient interest," "is without redeeming social importance," etc. If a court finds something to be *obscene*, it loses its protection under the *free speech* and *freedom of the press* clauses of the **First Amendment** to the **Constitution** and may be **banned**.

Obscenity See **obscene**.

Obstructing justice Interfering by words or actions with the proper working of courts or court officials; for example, trying to keep a **witness** from appearing in court. This can be a crime.

Occupancy **1.** Physical possession of land or buildings, either with or without legal right or **title**. **2.** Another word for **adverse possession** (see that word). **3.** Another word for federal **pre-emption**.

Occupation **1.** Physical possession. **2.** Business or profession.

Occupational disease A disease that is widespread among workers in a particular job, such as "black lung" disease among miners. **Workers' compensation** and special federal programs pay workers who contract these diseases if the disease is peculiar to the industry or if the job puts workers at a much higher risk than other workers of contracting the disease.

Occupational Safety and Health Administration   A federal agency that sets and enforces health and safety standards in many industries. The *O.S.H.A. Review Commission* handles appeals from O.S.H.A. rulings.

Occupying claimant acts   State laws giving a **good faith** occupant of land who turns out to lack legal **title** the right to collect from the land's true owner, who comes to claim it, payment for any improvements that increase the land's value.

Occupying the field   The federal government's prohibiting all state laws in a subject area because the subject (such as **treaty** making) is of major national importance. *Occupying the field* is total **pre-emption** (see that word).

Odd lot   A number of shares of **stock** less than the number usually traded as a unit. This is often fewer than one hundred shares.

Odium   Widespread community hatred or dislike.

Of age   No longer a **minor**. A person who has reached the legal age to sue, vote, drink, etc.

Of counsel   **1.** A person employed as a lawyer in a case.   **2.** A lawyer who helps the primary lawyer in a case.   **3.** A lawyer who advises a law firm or who is a temporary member.

Of course   As a matter of right. Actions that a person may take in a lawsuit, either without asking the judge's permission, or by asking and getting automatic approval.

Of grace   See **grace**.

Of record   Entered on the proper formal records. For example, *"counsel of record"* is the lawyer whose name appears on the court's records as lawyer in a case.

Off   Postponed indefinitely.

Off-board   A **stock** or other **securities** transaction that does not take place through a national securities **exchange**. *Off-board* exchanges are either between private individuals or **over-the counter**.

Offense   **Crime** or **misdemeanor**. Any breaking of the criminal laws.

Offer   **1.** To make a proposal; to present for acceptance or rejection. **2.** To attempt to have something admitted into **evidence** in a trial; to introduce evidence. **3.** An *"offer"* in contract law is a proposal to make a deal. It must be communicated from the person making it to the person to whom it is made, and it must be definite and reasonably certain in its terms.

Offer of compromise An offer to settle a dispute without admitting **liability**.

Offer of proof When a question to a witness has not been allowed by the judge, the lawyer who wanted to ask the question may tell the judge, out of the jury's hearing, what *would* have been the answer. This "offer of proof" creates a more complete **record** of the lawsuit in case the refusal to allow the question is **appealed**.

Offering A sale of **stock** (or other **securities**). A *primary offering*, also called a "new issue," is the sale of a new stock by a company. A *secondary offering* is a sale by persons who hold already-issued stock. A *private offering* is made to a small group of persons who know something about the company. It is not as strictly regulated by the **S.E.C.** as a *public offering*, a sale of stock to the general public. Private stock sales require an *offering circular*, a document similar to a **prospectus**.

Office **1.** A power to act plus a duty to act in a certain way; for example, the *office* of **executor** of an **estate**. **2.** Short for *"public office,"* the description of mid- and upper-level elected and appointed government jobs. **3.** A bureau, department, or other government **agency**. The place where this bureau works.

Office audit See **audit**.

Officer of the court **1.** The phrase includes court employees such as **judges, clerks, sheriffs, marshals, bailiffs,** and **constables** (see these words). Lawyers are also *officers of the court* and must obey court rules, be truthful in court, and generally serve the needs of justice.

Officers The persons who actually run an organization at the top (president, secretary, etc.).

Official gazette A weekly publication listing **patent** and **trademark** applications and notices.

Official notice The same as **judicial notice** (see that word), but for an **administrative agency**, not a judge.

Official records Reports, statements, data files, etc., kept by a government agency. These may be used as **evidence** in a federal trial without need for the record keeper as a **witness**. The *Official Records Act* allows this same use of government documents in federal **administrative** proceedings.

Offset **1.** Any claim or demand made to lessen or cancel another claim. When done in a lawsuit, it may be a set-off, a **counterclaim**, or a recoupment, depending on whether or not it is an entirely separate claim, whether it exceeds the original claim, and other factors. **2.** An *offset account* is a **bookkeeping** device to **balance** one set of figures against another to make the books come out even at the end.

Old age, survivors, and disability insurance Commonly known as "social security," this is the federal program funded by employer and employee payments that pays for retirement, disability, dependent, and widow/widower benefits.

Oligarchy Government by a small group of people.

Oligopoly A situation in which a few sellers dominate the market for a particular product.

Olograph See **holograph**.

Ombudsman (Swedish) A person who acts as the government's "complaint bureau" with the power to investigate official misconduct, help fix wrongs done by the government, and, sometimes, prosecute the wrongdoers.

Omnibus (Latin) Containing two or more separate and independent things. For example, an *"onmibus bill"* is a piece of **legislation** concerning two or more entirely different subjects.

Omnibus clause **1.** A provision in a **will** or **judicial distribution** of property that gives out all property not specifically mentioned. **2.** A provision in an auto **insurance** policy that extends insurance to all drivers operating with the owner's permission.

Omnis (or omne, omni, omnia, etc.) (Latin) *All*; as in the phrase *"omnis definitio in lege periculosa"* (all legal definitions are dangerous).

Omnium The total value of several different things.

On account As a part payment for something bought or owed.

On all fours See **all fours**.

On demand (or on call) Payable immediately when requested.

On or about Approximately. A phrase used to avoid being bound to a time more exact than a business deal or the law requires; for example, *"on or about July 15."*

On point   A law or prior case is "on point" if it directly applies to the facts of the present case.

One   "Someone by the name of" or "something called a." A useless word when put in front of a word that needs no number; for example, "one Marcie Evans testified that . . . "

One person, one vote   The rule, established in the case of *Reynolds* v. *Sims*, that each **house** of a state **legislature** must be apportioned (and regularly reapportioned) by population, so that each person's vote has equal power.

Onerous   **1.** Unreasonably burdensome or one-sided; for example, an *unconscionable contract* (see **unconscionability**).   **2.** In some countries *onerous* means *properly* burdensome. An *onerous contract* there is one with benefits and burdens on both sides, and an *onerous title* is the right to property that is paid for or otherwise gained in exchange for something.

Onus probandi   (Latin) **Burden of proof** (see that word).

Open   **1.** Begin.   **2.** Make visible or available.   **3.** Remove restrictions, reopen, or open up.   **4.** Visible or apparent.   **5.** With no limit as to time or as to amount.   **6.** For examples of these meanings, see the words following.

Open a judgment   Keep a **judgment** from going into effect until a court can reexamine it.

Open account (or open credit)   A "charge account" in which purchases (or loans) can be made without going through separate **credit** arrangements each time. This is often done on credit cards and "revolving charges" where you can pay a part of what you owe each month on several different purchases. See also **open-end mortgage**.

Open bid   An offer to do work or supply materials (usually in the construction business) that reserves the right to lower the bid to meet the competition.

Open court   **1.** A court that is formally open for business that day.   **2.** A court that allows public spectators.

Open listing   A **real estate** (see that word) **contract** by which any **agent** who produces a sale gets a **commission**.

Open mortgage   A **mortgage** that can be paid off without a penalty at any time before **maturity** (the time it ends). See also **open-end mortgage** and **closed-end mortgage.**

Open order   An **order** placed by a customer with a **broker** to buy **stock**, other **securities**, or **commodities** at or below a certain price. The order remains active until canceled.

Open price term

Open price term An unspecified price in a contract. For example, it is possible to have a valid **contract** without setting an exact price for something if this *open price term* depends on some standard market indicator or if the persons intend the contract to read that way and don't agree on price. In this case a reasonable price at time of delivery will be set.

Open shop A business where nonunion persons may work.

Open-end company A **mutual fund** (see that word).

Open-end contract A **requirements contract** (see that word).

Open-end mortgage A **mortgage** agreement in which amounts of money may be borrowed from time to time on the same agreement. See also **open account, open mortgage,** and **closed-end mortgage.**

Open-end settlement **Workers' compensation** payments that continue until a person can work again.

Opening statement In an *opening statement* to a **jury** at the start of a trial, lawyers for each side explain the version of the facts best supporting their side of the case, how these facts will be proved, and how they think the law applies to the case.

Operating The running of a business. *Operating expenses* are such things as rent and electricity required to keep a business running normally. *Operating profit* is sales minus the cost of the goods sold and operating expenses. *Net operating assets* are **assets** used in the ordinary course of business (after **depreciation** and **bad debts** are subtracted). These assets do not include things like **stocks** and **bonds.** *Net operating income (or loss)* is income (or loss) after subtracting for depreciation of operating assets, but not yet accounting for any interest gained or income taxes paid. *Operating margin* is *net operating income* divided by sales. Also, an *operating lease* is a short-term **lease** that can be canceled.

Operation of law The way in which rights or **liabilities** sometimes come to or fall upon a person automatically, without his or her cooperation.

Operative words (or part) That part of a document, such as a **deed**, in which rights are actually created or transferred. The legal "heart" of the document, as opposed to the introduction, explanations, etc.

Opinion **1.** A judge's statement of the decision he or she has reached in a case. **2.** A judge's statement about the conclusions of that judge and of others who agree with the judge in a case. A *majority opinion* is written when over half the judges in a case agree about both the result and the reasoning used to reach that result. A *plurality opinion* is written when a majority of the judges agree with the result, but not with the reasoning. A *concurring opinion* agrees with the result, but not the reasoning. A *dissenting or minority opinion* disagrees with the result. (Concurring, dissenting, and minority opinions are all *separate opinions*.) A *per curiam opinion* is unanimous and anonymous, and a *memorandum opinion* is unanimous and very short. **3.** A document prepared by a lawyer for a client that gives the lawyer's conclusions about how the law applies to a set of facts in which the client is interested.

Opinion evidence   Evidence of what a witness thinks, believes, or concludes about facts, rather than what the witness saw, heard, etc. *Opinion evidence* is usually accepted only from an **expert witness** (see that word).

Opportunity cost   The rate of profit you could get by investing your money, rather than putting it into a particular project. See **hurdle rate**.

Oppression   1. Unconscionability (see that word). **2.** Harm (usually bodily harm) done by a public official in excess of authority.

Opprobrium   Shame or disgrace.

Option   A **contract** in which one person pays money for the right to buy something from, or sell something to, another person at a certain price and within a certain time period. For example, a *commodity option* gives a person the right to buy (a *"call"*) or the right to sell (a *"put"*) a certain **commodity** (such as a ton of rice) at a certain price (the *"striking"* price) by a certain time. The option holder pays a fee (a *"premium"*) for this right and may use (*"exercise"*) it or not depending on **market** conditions. A combined right to either buy or sell is called a *straddle*. And an option sold by a person who owns no stocks or commodities to back it up is called a *naked option*.

Optional bond   A **callable** bond (see that word).

Optional writ   A **show cause** order (see that word).

Oral argument   The time-limited presentation of each side of a case before an **appeals court**.

Oral contract   A **contract** that is not entirely in writing or not in

Ordeal

writing at all. (Similarly, an oral **will** is either partly in writing or not in writing at all.)

Ordeal An ancient form of trial in England by which God was supposed to make the decision. Ordeals were by fire or water and uniformly nasty. The cold water ordeal, for example, involved throwing a tied-up person into a pond. Floating meant guilt (and often death); sinking meant innocence (and often death).

Order 1. A written command or direction given by a judge. For example, a *restraining order* is a judicial command to a person to temporarily stop a certain action or course of conduct. 2. A command given by a public official. 3. *"To the order of"* is a direction to pay something. These words (or "pay to the **bearer**") are necessary to make a document a **negotiable instrument** (see that word). A document with these words on it is called *order paper*. 4. For *"order nisi,"* see **nisi**; and for *"order of the coif,"* see **coif**. 5. Instructions to buy or sell something. In **stock** sales, for example, a *"day order"* is an instruction from a customer to a **broker** to buy or sell a stock on one particular day only; a *"limit order"* is an instruction to buy only under a certain price or sell only over it; a *"market order"* is an instruction to buy or sell right away at the current **market** price; a *"scale order"* is an instruction to buy or sell a certain amount of stock at each of several price levels; and a *"split order"* is an instruction to buy or sell some stock when it reaches one price and some when it reaches another. For **stop order,** see that word.

Ordinance 1. A local or city law, rule, or **regulation**. 2. A more general law, such as the *Ordinance of 1787* for the government of the Northwest Territory.

Ordinary Regular or usual. This word is the same in most legal and nonlegal uses. In tax law, however, *ordinary income* means income from business profits, wages, **interest, dividends,** etc., as opposed to **capital** gains (see that word).

Organic Basic. For example, an *organic act* is a law giving self-government to a geographical area, and *organic law* is the basic, fundamental law of a government (its basic unwritten assumptions and its **constitution**).

Organized labor Workers represented by **labor unions.**

Organization Almost any group of persons with legal or formal ties may be an organization. So may almost any business.

Original document rule The rule that the **best evidence** (see that word) of what a document says is the original document. A copy is not acceptable in court unless the original is not available.

Original jurisdiction   The power of a court to take a case, try it, and decide it (as opposed to *appellate jurisdiction*, the power of a court to hear and decide an **appeal**).

Original package doctrine   The federal rule that a state can tax an imported item only after the original package is broken because this takes the item out of interstate commerce.

Origination fee   A charge for finding, placing, or starting financing; for example, for a **mortgage** on a house.

Ostensible   Apparent or visible. For example, *ostensible authority* is the power a person seems to have (especially the power a **principal** seems to give to an **agent**).

Ouster   Throwing someone off land who has a right to possess it. [pronounce: <u>ow</u>-ster]

Out-of-court settlement   A private compromise or agreement that ends a lawsuit without official help from, or orders by, the judge. This may take place in or out of the courtroom.

Out-of-pocket   **1.** A small cash payment.   **2.** A loss measured by the difference between the price paid for an item and the (lower true) value of that item. The *"out-of-pocket rule"* allows this to be the measure of **damages** when something has been sold by **fraudulent** statements.

Outcome test   When a case is in federal court solely because of **diversity of citizenship** (see that word), the result should be the same as it would be in the proper state court. If it is not, an appeals court will decide that the trial judge used the wrong law to decide the case or otherwise acted incorrectly.

Output contract   An agreement in which a manufacturing company agrees to sell everything it makes to one buyer, and the buyer agrees to take it all. This is a valid **contract** even though the amounts are indefinite.

Outs   Conditions or promises which, if not complied with by a customer, allow a banker to get out of a deal.

Outside director   See **director.**

Outside salesperson   A person whose full-time job is making sales away from the employer's business and who may **deduct** all work expenses from taxes.

Outstanding   **1.** Still unpaid; not yet collected.   **2.** Remaining in existence; not brought in or gathered up.

Outstroke Mining through tunnels and shafts into an adjoining property.

Over **1.** Continued (on the next page or in the next session of a court). **2.** Shifting or passing on from one person, thing, or time to another; "on to the next." For example, a *"gift over"* or *"estate over"* takes place when someone leaves property in a will to one person, and then to another person (after the first one dies, after a certain number of years, etc.).

Overcapitalization **Watered stock**.

Over-the-counter **Securities,** such as **stocks** and **bonds,** sold directly from **broker** to broker or broker to customer rather than through an **exchange.** Much "O.T.C." business is done by telephone.

Overbreadth A law will be declared **void** and invalidated for *overbreadth* if it attempts to punish speech or conduct that is protected by the **Constitution** and if that punishment cannot be separated out from the law's more legitimate reach.

Overdraft (or overdraw) Taking out more money by check from a bank account than you have in the account.

Overhead **1. Fixed charges** (see that word) and all those costs that cannot be allocated to a particular department or product. **2.** An *overhead rate* is the way fixed costs are divided up and added to the cost of producing products and services.

Overissue Putting out more shares of a company's **stock** than are permitted by the company's incorporation papers or by the law.

Overlying right A landowner's right to take and use water from under his or her own land.

Overreaching Taking unfair commercial advantage by **fraud** or **unconscionability.**

Override **1.** A **commission** paid to a supervisor when an employee makes a sale. **2.** A commission paid to a **real estate** (see that word) **agent** when a landowner sells directly to a purchaser who was found by the agent before the **listing** was ended.

Overrule **1.** To reject or supercede. For example, a case is *overruled* when the same court, or a higher court in the same system, rejects the legal principles on which the case was based. This ends the case's value as **precedent.** **2.** To reject an **objection** made during a trial. This is done by the judge.

Oversubscription A situation in which more orders for **shares** of **stock** exist than there are shares of stock to fill the orders.

Overt Open; clear. For example, an *overt act* in **criminal** law is more than mere preparation to do something criminal, it is at least the first step of actually attempting the crime.

Owner A general term meaning the person who holds the legal or "paper" **title** to property, the person who has a right to property no matter what the "papers" say, or several other shades of control or rights to benefit from property.

Owners' equity statement See **statement.**

Oyer and terminer (French) "Hear and decide." Some higher state **criminal** courts are called by this name. [pronounce: oy-yay and term-i-nay]

Oyez "Hear ye." The word cried out by a court official in some courtrooms to get attention at the start of a court session. [pronounce: oy-yay]

P. 1. Pacific Reporter (see **National Reporter System**). 2. **Plaintiff.**

P.A. **Profesional association** (see that word).

P.B.G.C. Pension Benefit Guarantee Corporation. Most private **pension plans** (see that word) must pay into this federal agency to protect against insufficient pension funds through an insurancelike plan.

P.C. 1. Professional corporation. A special type of **corporation** set up by doctors, lawyers, or other professionals. 2. Also patent cases; penal code; and many British phrases such as Pleas of the Crown and Privy Council.

P.C.R. **Postconviction remedy** (see that word).

P.-H. Prentice-Hall (see **loose-leaf service**).

P.H.C. Personal **holding company.**

P.H.V. **Pro hac vice** (see that word).

P.J. Presiding judge.

P.L. Public law; public laws; pamphlet laws.

P.L.I. *Practicing Law Institute.* A nonprofit organization that publishes books and holds seminars to educate lawyers.

P.L.S. A Professional Legal Secretary who has passed the N.A.L.S. exam.

P.O.D. *"Payable on death."* A bank or other account payable to a person (or a group of persons) and, on that person's death, payable to someone else.

P.S. Public **statute.**

P.U.C. Public Utilities Commission. State agencies that **regulate** power companies, railroads, etc.

P.U.D. **Planned unit development** (see that word).

P.T.I. Previously taxed income.

Package mortgage A **mortgage** that covers things like stoves and refrigerators in addition to the building.

Package settlement The total money value of wage and **benefit** changes in a new union–employer **contract.**

Packager **1.** A **broker.** **2.** An **underwriter.** **3.** A person who puts together deals, such as group travel, a television series, etc.

Packing Trying to get a favorable decision from a jury (or a court, an agency, etc.) by improperly placing specific persons on the jury, court, etc.

Pact A bargain or agreement.

Pactum (Latin) A bargain or agreement.

Paid-in Supplied by the owners. For example, *paid-in capital* is money or property paid to a company for its **capital** stock, and *paid-in surplus* is that part of a company's **surplus** supplied by the stockholders rather than generated from profits.

Pains and penalties See **bill of pains and penalties.**

Pairing **1.** Two persons (one for and one against a **bill** in a **legislature**) agreeing to refrain from voting. This allows them both to be absent for the vote. This is also called *"pairing off."* **2.** Sending all the children from two school areas to one or the other school by grade, not by closeness.

Pais (French) Outside the court; the countryside. For example, a matter "**in pais**" (see that word) has to do with facts (that happened outside the courtroom), not with law (that is decided inside the courtroom), and is tried *"per pais"* (by the jury). [pronounce: pay]

Palimony **1.** **Alimony** (see that word) paid between persons who are not and never were married. **2.** Any payments based on an

express or **implied contract** between two persons who lived together in a sexual relationship. The law as to the validity of these contracts is still changing.

Palm off Sell goods made by one manufacturer as if they are made by another (better or more famous) manufacturer.

Palpable Plain, clear, easily seen, or notorious. (The word usually refers to an **error,** an **abuse** of authority, or something else wrong.)

Palsgraf doctrine The rule that a person is responsible for only those results of a **negligent** action that are foreseeable and not for everything that happens to follow.

Pander To pimp or solicit for prostitution.

Panel 1. A jury list. 2. A group of judges (smaller than the entire court) who decide a case. 3. *"Open panel"* legal services is a plan in which legal help is paid in advance (usually by a type of insurance), and a person can choose his or her own lawyer. *"Closed panel"* is paid in advance legal services given by a specific group of lawyers.

Paper 1. "The papers" are all the documents connected with a lawsuit. 2. "Paper" may be short for "**commercial paper**" or a **negotiable instrument** (see those words). 3. "Paper" may mean "only paper." For example, a *"paper title"* is a **document of title** (see that word) to something that may or may not be valid; and a *"paper profit"* is an increase in value (of an investment) that might be lost again if the value goes down before sale. 4. When a prosecutor *"papers"* a case, it means, in some places, that it *will* be formally prosecuted, and, in other places, that it will *not* be formally prosecuted any more.

Par 1. At **face** value. For example, if a hundred dollar **bond** sells in the bond market for one hundred dollars, it sells *"at par."* 2. *"Par items"* are things a bank will process and send on without charge to another bank.

Paralegal A paralegal is a nonlawyer who needs legal skills to do a job. Most persons who work for lawyers (such as legal secretaries or "legal assistants") are *paralegals*, and many persons who work for agencies and do legally related work are paralegals. It is a general word that takes into account the types of work done, the amount of legal knowledge needed, the work setting, and the type of supervision.

Parallel citation A case (or other legal document) that is published in more than one place.

Parallel jurisdiction

Parallel jurisdiction   **Pendent jurisdiction** (see that word).

Paramount title   **1.** A **holder in due course** (see that word) has the best right to a document (and to all the money or property it stands for) in all but a few circumstances. For example, if the property were originally stolen, the real owner has "*paramount title.*" **2.** In **real estate** law, *paramount title* originally meant original title, but has come to mean simply "better" or "superior."

Parcener   An old word for a **joint heir.** A person who inherits property along with another person's inheriting it (each person inherits the whole thing). "*Coparcener*" means the same thing as "parcener."

Pardon   A president's or governor's power to release a person from punishment for a crime.

Parens patriae   (Latin) The right of the government to take care of minors and others who cannot legally take care of themselves. The use of this power to deprive a person of freedom has been limited by recent laws and decisions. [pronounce: pa-rens pat-ri-eye]

Parent corporation   A company that fully controls another company.

Parental liability   Some state laws hold parents responsible for damage done by their children if the parents were **negligent** in their control over the child.

Parental rights   These include such things as the right to discipline and control a child, to manage the child's property, to be supported by an adult child, etc.

Pari causa   (Latin) With (or by) equal right.

Pari delicto   (Latin) Equal fault. The "*doctrine of pari delicto*" is the rule that no court will help enforce an illegal or invalid contract.

Pari materia   (Latin) "On the same subject"; interdependent. For example, laws *pari materia* must be read together to know what effect each should have.

Pari passu   (Latin) Equally; without preference.

Parish   A **county** in Louisiana.

Parity   **1.** Equality, equivalence, even-exchangeability.   **2.** Government **price support** of farm products based on a comparison with the farmer's equivalent purchasing power during a prior "base period."   **3.** *Parity* may also refer to proportional job opportunities and fair wages for minorities, to equality of pay between police and fire fighters, etc.

Parliamentary law   Rules and customs by which **legislatures** (any many other types of meetings) are run.

Parliamentary system   A government by an elected **legislature**, from which a prime minister and **cabinet** are selected by the majority party. This system, based on the one developed in England, does not have the **separation** of powers between the **legislative** and **executive** branches that exists in America.

Parol   Oral; not in writing. For example, *parol evidence* is oral **evidence** or the evidence a **witness** gives. It usually refers to evidence about an agreement's meaning that does not appear in the written **contract**.

Parol arrest   An "on-the-spot" **arrest** without a **warrant**.

Parol evidence rule   A legal doctrine that says when persons put their agreement in writing, the meaning of the written agreement cannot be contradicted by using prior oral agreements (unless there was a **mistake** or **fraud** in preparing the written contract).

Parole   A release from prison, before a **sentence** is finished, that depends on the person's "keeping clean" and doing what he or she is supposed to do while out. If the person fails to meet the *conditions of parole*, the rest of the sentence must be served. *Parole* decisions are made by a state or federal *parole board* or *corrections board*, and persons out on parole are supervised by *parole officers.*

Pars   (Latin)   **1.** A **party**; as in *pars rea* (party defendant).   **2.** A part.

Part performance   See **performance**.

Partial average   **Particular average loss** (see that word).

Partial incapacity   An injury that disables a worker from doing part of his or her job or that lowers the value of that person's labor. The word does not mean the loss of part of an arm, part of the use of an arm, part of the ability to lift things, etc. This is usually called *partial loss*.

Particeps criminis   (Latin) An **accomplice**.

Participation   **1.** An **insurance** policy in which the person insured pays a certain percentage of any loss.   **2.** A loan arrangement in which several banks combine to make a large loan.   **3.** A **mortgage** agreement in which the lender gets a

Particular average loss

share of the profits of the venture in addition to interest on the loan.

Particular average loss   A loss of property at sea that is the result of **negligence** or accident and that must be borne by the owner of the property.

Particular lien   A right to hold specific property because of a claim against that property; for example, a garage's right to hold a car until the repair bill is paid.

Particulars   **1.** The details of a legal **claim** or of separate items on an **account**. See also **bill of particulars**.   **2.** A detailed description of property to be sold at auction.

Parties   See **party**.

Partition   Dividing land owned by several persons into smaller parcels owned by each person individually.

Partner   A member of a **partnership** (see that word). A *"full"* or *"general"* partner participates fully in running the company and sharing the profits and losses. A *"dormant," "silent,"* or *"sleeping"* partner is a person who is in a partnership, but is not known as a partner by the public, does not take an active hand in the business, and, if also a *"special"* or *"limited"* partner, puts in a fixed amount of money, gets a fixed amount of profit, and is usually not **liable** for anything beyond the investment itself. Finally, a *"nominal"* or *"ostensible"* partner is *not* a partner, but only someone who *looks like* a partner to the public.

Partnership   A **contract** between two or more persons to carry on a business together and to share money and labor put in and profits or losses taken out. It is not a **corporation** (see that word). For *limited partnership* and other types, see **partner**.

Party   **1.** A person concerned with or taking part in any matter, affair, or proceeding.   **2.** A person who is either a **plaintiff** or a **defendant** in a lawsuit. A *real party* is a person who actually stands to gain or lose something from being a part of the case, while a *formal* or *nominal party* is one who has only a technical or "name only" interest.   **3.** A *third party* is a person who is not directly involved in a **contract**, but who is or might be affected by it.   **4.** Of two or more parts. For example, a *party wall* is put up between two properties.   **5.** A group of voters organized to nominate and elect persons to public office, to influence government policy, etc.

Party of the first part   A wordy and unnecessary phrase used instead of repeating the name of a **party** to a document. For example, if a **contract** is between Freeway Motors and John Driver, the contract should use "Freeway Motors," "Freeway," "seller," etc., rather than "party of the first part."

Pass **1.** Say or pronounce. For example, a judge *passes sentence* on a convicted defendant. **2.** Enact successfully. For example, a **bill** "passes" when a **legislature** votes "yes" on it. **3.** Examine and determine. For example, a jury *passes upon* the issues in a lawsuit. **4.** Transfer or become transferred. For example, when a **deed** is properly made out, property *passes* from one person to another. **5.** Approve. For example, when **account** books are examined and determined accurate, they "pass." **6.** Put out, especially to put out fraudulently; for example, "*pass*" **conterfeit** money.

Passage Enactment or approval of a **bill** by one **house** of a **legislature**; enactment by both houses; or enactment plus signature by the president or governor.

Passbook A document in which the deposits and withdrawals of savings accounts may be recorded.

Passenger **1.** Any rider other than the driver of a motor vehicle. **2.** A rider who pays, or a rider in a vehicle driven by a person who gets some benefit other than friendship from driving.

Passim (Latin) "Here and there"; found in various places; everywhere (indicating a general mention or overall reference to a book or document).

Passion Rage, anger, or terror (not love or lust).

Passive **1.** Inactive. **2.** Submissive or permissive, rather than actually agreeing to or participating in something.

Passive trust A **dry** trust (see that word).

Passport **1.** A document giving a person his or her country's permission to travel, and that country's request that other countries permit the person to pass through safely. **2.** A document issued in time of war to give a person or a ship safe conduct.

Past consideration **Consideration** (see that word) that is given or takes place before a **contract** is made. Except in the case of **negotiable instruments**, *past consideration* is usually not enough of a basis to support or enforce a contract.

Past recollection recorded See **recollection**.

Pat. Pend. "*Patent pending.*" A **patent** has been applied for and, if granted, will be valid as of the date of the original application.

Patent

Patent **1.** Open, evident, plainly visible. **2.** A right (given by the federal government to a person) to control the manufacture and sale of something that person has discovered or invented. **3.** A **grant** of land by the government to an individual.

Patent and copyright clause The U.S. constitutional provision protecting the rights of authors and inventors to exclusive use of their products for a limited time (Article I, Section 8, Clause 8).

Patent and Trademark Office A federal agency in the **Commerce** Department that decides on and keeps track of **patent** and **trademark** applications, keeps a complete public reference file, publishes related information, etc.

Patent pooling An agreement among companies (usually manufacturers) to share **patent** information and rights.

Patentable A discovery or invention that includes a new idea is "*patentable,*" or suitable to be given a patent.

Paternity suit A court action to prove a person is the father of an "**illegitimate** child" and to enforce **support** obligations.

Patient forbearance rule See **forbearance**.

Patient–physician privilege The right of a patient, under many state laws, to keep private what is said to or by a doctor. This right may extend to some or all of the doctor's records. See **privilege**.

Patrimony **1.** All rights and property that have passed or will pass to a person from parents, grandparents, etc. **2.** All of a person's property, rights, and liabilities that can be given a dollar value.

Patronage **1.** All the customers of a business; giving a company business. (A "*patronage dividend*" is the refund given to a member of a **cooperative** based on purchases made from the cooperative.) **2.** The right of some public officials to give out some jobs on their own **discretion**, without going through a **civil service** process. This right is often limited at higher levels to jobs of a "political or confidential" nature and at low levels to small governments without a full civil service system.

Pattern or practice Regular, repeated, intentional conduct.

Pauper A poor person who cannot support him or herself and who requires financial help from the government (to live, to carry on a lawsuit or defend a criminal trial, etc.).

Pawn **1.** To give personal **property** (such as a camera) to another person (usually called a *pawnbroker*) as **security** for a debt. A pawned item is held until the money loaned is paid back. If the money is not paid back within a certain time, the item is sold. **2.** The item itself in no. 1.

Payable **1.** Owing, and to be paid in the future. **2.** Owing, and due for payment now. **3.** For *payable to bearer* and *payable to order*, see **bearer** and **order**.

Payables Accounts **payable** (see that word).

Payee The person to whom a **negotiable instrument** (such as a check) is made out; for example, "pay to the **order** of John Doe."

Payout ratio The **dividend** a company pays on each share of **common stock** divided by its **earnings per share** (see that word). This percentage shows how much money a company pays its investors compared to what it can plow back into the business.

Payroll tax A tax collected by deducting it from a company's payroll. It may be paid by the employer, employee, or both.

P/E ratio **Price–earnings ratio** (see that word).

Peace bond A **bond** to guarantee good behavior for a period of time.

Peace officer Any public official (such as a **sheriff**, police officer, **marshall**, etc.) with the authority to make **arrests**.

Peaceable possession Occupying land or a building for a time during which there are no legal or forcible attempts to throw you out.

Peculation **Embezzlement** (see that word).

Pecuniary Monetary; related to money. A *pecuniary interest* is any **interest** that might have a direct financial effect on a judge and that should make the judge **disqualify** him or herself from a case.

Pederasty Anal intercourse between men. It is a crime in many states.

Peers Equals. However, a "trial by a jury of peers" does not mean by persons exactly equal to the **defendant**, but merely by citizens chosen fairly.

Pegging Officially, arbitrarily, or artificially fixing or setting the value of something. For example, a country can "*peg*" the relative value of its money or allow it to **float** relative to other countries'. Also, an underwriter selling a new stock **issue** can "*peg*" the price by placing repeated buying orders at a certain price in the stock **market**.

Peine fort et dure

Peine fort et dure (French) A punishment in ancient England involving pressing to death under a great weight a person who refused to speak when accused of a major crime.

Penal **1.** Concerning a penalty. In this sense a *penal action* is a **civil** lawsuit to make a wrongdoer pay a fine or penalty to the person harmed, and a *penal bond* is a **bond** put up as a promise to pay money if a certain thing is not done. **2.** Criminal. In this sense a *penal action* is a **criminal** prosecution, a *penal law* is a criminal law, a *penal code* is a collection of federal or state criminal laws, and *penal servitude* is imprisonment with forced labor. **3.** For *penal damages*, see **punitive damages**.

Penalty **1.** A punishment imposed by law. **2.** A sum of money promised by one person to another, to be paid if the first person fails to do something called for in a **contract** between them.

Penalty clause A **contract** provision that requires payment of an exact sum of money if something is done to vary the contract's requirements; for example, paying off a **mortgage** before it is due in order to avoid further interest payments.

Pendency **1.** While **pending** (see that word). **2.** A *notice of pendency* is a formal warning, placed on property records, that a lawsuit or claim has been placed against a property and that anyone who buys it may have to pay off a **lien**, a **judgment**, etc.

Pendent jurisdiction A federal court's right to decide a claim based on a nonfederal **issue** if this claim depends on the same set of facts as does a federal claim in the case before the court.

Pendente lite (Latin) "Pending the suit"; while a lawsuit is in progress. [pronounce: pen-den-te lee-te]

Pending As yet undecided; begun but not finished.

Penitentiary A **prison** for convicted **felons**.

Pennoyer v. Neff The 1878 U.S. Supreme Court case that established the rule that a court cannot take **jurisdiction** over a person unless the person has been **served** with **process** in the state. This rule has been greatly modified (see, for example, **long-arm statute**), but the general principle that a court must have jurisdiction over a person to give a **judgment** or **decree** against that person is still valid.

Pennsylvania rule The principle that if a person who breaks a traffic law is in a collision, that person must prove that the violation did *not* cause the accident in order to be free of fault.

Penny stock Speculative **stock** selling at less than a dollar a share.

Penology   The study of prisons and criminal punishment.

Pension Benefit Guaranty Corporation   A federal agency that sets up a fund to pay pension **benefits** to persons whose **pension plans** (see that word) go broke.

Pension plan   A plan set up by an employer to pay employees after retirement. This may be either a fund of money (called "funded" if it is fully paid-in to meet the promised pension needs) set up by the employer or payments by the employer to the employee. A *qualified plan* is one that meets **I.R.S.** requirements for the payments to be deducted by the employer and initially tax-free to the employee. A *defined-benefit plan* is one with employer *payments* varying to pay for fixed, specifically promised *benefits* (or a fixed benefit formula). A *money-purchase plan* (or *defined-contribution* plan) is one with *benefits* varying depending on the ultimate value of fixed, specifically promised regular *payments* (or a fixed payment formula) by the employer. See also **I.R.A.**, **Keogh Plan**, **Employee Retirement Income Security Act**, **vested**, and **annuity**.

Penumbra doctrine   The principle that the **necessary** and proper clause of the U.S. **Constitution** allows the federal government to take all actions to carry out legitimate government purposes, even if the powers needed to carry out these purposes are only **implied** from other powers (which themselves are not specifically mentioned in the Constitution, but only implied).

Peona   (Latin) Punishment.

Peonage   Slavery or forced labor to pay off a debt.

People   **1.** A nation or state.   **2.** All persons in a nation or state as one whole group.   **3.** Not the plural of "person" in the law.

Peppercorn   A dried pepper berry; something of **nominal** (extremely small), but real value.

Per   (Latin) By; through; by means of; during. For example, *per annum* means by the year or yearly and *per autre vie* means during the life of another person.

Per capita   (Latin) "By heads." By the number of individual persons, each to share equally. Sometimes, the opposite of "**per stirpes**" (see that word).

Per curiam   (Latin) "By the court." An **opinion** backed by all the judges in a particular court and usually with no one judge's name on it. [pronounce: per cure-i-am]

Per diem   (Latin) **1.** By the day; day by day; each day.   **2.** A fixed amount of money paid to a person each day for either a salary or expenses of employment such as food and lodging. [pronounce: per dee-em]

Per pais   See **pais**.

Per procuration   In English law, this means acting as an **agent** with only limited authority. Abbreviated "per. proc." or "p.p."

Per quod   (Latin) "By that"; "by which acts." A specification of necessary details.

Per se   (Latin) In and of itself; taken alone; inherently. For example, some types of business arrangements are called "*per se violations*" of **antitrust** laws because, even without specific proof that **monopoly** power has hurt competition, the arrangements are in and of themselves bad. [pronounce: per say]

Per stirpes   (Latin) "By roots." A method of dividing a dead person's **estate** by giving out shares equally "by representation" or by family groups. For example, if John leaves three thousand dollars to Mary and Sue, and Mary dies, leaving two children (Steve and Jeff), a *per stirpes* division would give one thousand and five hundred dollars to Sue and seven hundred and fifty dollars each to Steve and Jeff. A "**per capita**" (see that word) division would give one thousand dollars each to Sue, Steve, and Jeff.

Percentage depletion   **Depletion allowance** (see that word).

Percentage lease   A **lease** of a building with the rent based on the dollar value of sales by the tenant in the building.

Percentage order   Instructions from a customer to a **broker** to buy or sell a certain number of shares of stock after a specific number of shares have been traded on the **market**.

Perception   An old word for taking something into possession or for counting out and paying a debt.

Peremptory   **1.** Absolute; conclusive; final or arbitrary. **2.** Not requiring any explanation or cause to be shown. For example, a *peremptory challenge* to a **juror** means that one side in a trial has been given the right to throw out a certain number of possible jurors before the trial without giving any reasons.

Peremptory ruling   A judge's ruling that takes the final decision away from the jury; for example, a **directed verdict** or **judgment non obstante veredicto** (see these words).

Perfect   **1.** Complete; enforceable; without defect. Also called "perfected." **2.** To tie down or "make perfect." For example, to *perfect a title* is to **register** it in the proper place so that your ownership is protected against all persons, not just against the person who sold to you. This is called "perfection." And *perfecting bail* is meeting all the qualifications to "go **bail**" for someone and get him or her out of jail.

Perfect tender rule   The rarely-applied rule that exact **performance** of the details of a commercial **contract** is required to make the contract enforceable.

Performance   Carrying out a **contract**, promise, or other **obligation** according to its terms, so that the obligation ends. *Specific performance* is being required to do exactly (or as close to exactly as is fair) what was required. A court may require specific performance if one person fails to perform one side of a deal and money **damages** will not properly pay back the other side for harm done. *Part performance* is doing something in **reliance** upon a contract. If the contract is oral, it may not be enforceable unless part performance has been made.

Performance (or completion) bond   A **bond** that guarantees that a **contractor** will do a job correctly and finish it on time.

Peril   **1.** A **risk** or **accident** insured against in an **insurance** policy.   **2.** A natural, as opposed to human-caused danger.

Periodic   Happening after regular, fixed amounts of time. For example, *periodic alimony* is payment of a certain sum of money to an ex-spouse once a month, once a week, etc.; and *periodic tenancy* is a **lease** that continues from month-to-month or year-to-year unless ended (usually by someone giving a notice that it will be ended).

Perjury   Lying while under **oath**, primarily in a court proceeding. It is a crime. See also **false swearing**.

Perks   **Perquisites** (see that word).

Permanent   *Permanent* can mean anything from "for an indefinite time" (as in *permanent employment*), to "definitely right now" (as in *permanent residence*), to "definitely for a long time" (as in *permanent disability*), to "forever."

Permissive   **1.** Allowed or endured, as opposed to actively approved of.   **2.** By right.   **3.** Lenient or tolerant.

Permit   **1.** An official document that allows a person to do something (usually something legal that is not allowable without the permit).   **2.** A *permit card* is a document given by a union to a nonmember allowing that person to work on a job for which there are not enough union members.

Pernancy An old word for the taking or receiving of something.

Perpetrator The person who commits a particular crime.

Perpetual succession The continuous existence of a **corporation** as the same "being," even though its owners, **directors**, and managers may change.

Perpetual trust A **trust** that continues as long as the need lasts (the life of a person or a charity, etc.).

Perpetuating testimony A procedure for taking and preserving **testimony** (usually by **deposition**) of persons who are in very bad health, very old, or about to leave the state.

Perpetuation of evidence Making sure that **evidence** is available for a possible trial later.

Perpetuity 1. Forever. 2. An investment that gives equal future payments essentially forever. 3. Any attempt to control the **disposition** of your property by **will** that is meant to last longer than the life of a person alive when you die (or at least conceived by then) plus twenty-one years. Most states prevent such control by a law known as the *rule against perpetuities.*

Perquisites Benefits of a job in addition to the salary; for example, a company car for personal use.

Person 1. A human being (a "natural" person). 2. A **corporation** (an "artificial" person). Corporations are treated as persons in many legal situations. Also, the word *"person"* includes corporations in most definitions in this dictionary. 3. Any other "being" entitled to sue as a legal entity (a government, an association, a group of **trustees**, etc.). 4. The plural of person is *persons*, *not* **people** (see that word).

Persona non grata (Latin) "Persons not wanted." A person rejected as an **ambassador** or other government representative by the country to which he or she is sent.

Personal 1. Having to do with a human being. 2. Having to do with movable property, as opposed to land and buildings. *Personal effects* means anything from all movable property to only that property normally carried on the person. 3. For *personal* **holding company, jurisdiction, liability, property, recognizance**, etc., see those words. A few other "personal" words follow this word.

Personal injury 1. Any harm done to a person's rights, except for property rights. 2. **Negligence** actions such as for automobile accidents.

314

Personal representative   A general term for **executor** or **administrator** of a dead person's property.

Personal trust   A **trust** for individuals and their own families.

Personalty   **Personal** property; movable property.

Persuasive authority   All sources of law that a judge might use (but is not required to use) in making up his or her mind about a case; for example, legal encyclopedias or related cases from other states. A case may be strongly persuasive if it comes from a famous judge or a nearby, powerful court.

Pertinent   **Relevant** to an **issue** that itself is relevant to the outcome of a trial.

Perverse verdict   A **jury's verdict** that did not follow (or could not have been in accordance with) a judge's **instructions** about a **point** of law.

Petit jury (or petty jury)   "Small jury" or trial jury (see **jury**).

Petition   **1.** A written request to a court that it take a particular action. In some states the word is limited to written requests made when there is no other side in a case (**ex parte** cases, see that word), and in some states, "*petition*" is used in place of "**complaint**" (see that word) as the first **pleading** in a lawsuit. **2.** A request made to a public official.

Petition in bankruptcy   A paper filed in a **bankruptcy** (see that word) court by a **debtor** requesting **relief** from debts. It can also be filed by **creditors** asking that a person be put into bankruptcy involuntarily.

Petitioner   Same as "**plaintiff**" (see that word) in many states.

Petitory action   A lawsuit to establish **title** to land, as opposed to a lawsuit to gain physical possession of the land.

Pettifogger   An old word for a lawyer who is either incompetent or who tries to win by clouding the issue and drowning it in trivia.

Petty   Small or unimportant. For example, *petty cash* is money kept on hand to meet small expenses, and a *petty offense* is one punishable by only a **fine** or a short jail term. But for *petty jury*, see **petit jury**.

Philadelphia lawyer   Originally praise of a lawyer's skill, this phrase has come to mean a sly or tricky lawyer.

Physical   **1.** Having to do with the body, rather than the mind. **2.** Real as opposed to imaginary. **3.** See **physical fact**. **4.** Other meanings of *physical* include: *physical impossibility*

Physical fact

(practical impossibility); *physical incapacity* (impotence due to physical causes); and *physical necessity* (being compelled to do something by an irresistible force).

Physical fact   **1.** An indisputable law of nature or a scientific fact.   **2.** Something visible, audible, or otherwise "graspable" by the senses.   **3.** The "*physical fact rule*" is the principle that **evidence** contrary to a known law of nature may justify a judge's decision to take a case away from the **jury**. This evidence may also be disregarded by an **appeals** court even if the judge accepted it.   **4.** Another different "*physical fact rule*" is that a driver is **negligent** if he or she did not see what should have been seen.

Physical incapacity   **1.** Impotence.   **2.** An injury that prevents working.

Physician–patient privilege   **Patient–physician privilege** (see that word).

Picketing   Persons gathering outside a place to disturb its activities or to inform persons outside of grievances, opinions, etc., about the place. This usually takes place when a **labor union** tries to publicize a **labor dispute** with a company, influence customers to withhold business, etc. For **chain**, **common situs**, **cross**, and other types of *picketing*, see those words.

Piercing the corporate veil   A judge's holding individual owners, **directors**, **officers**, etc., **liable** for a **corporation's** debts or wrongdoing. This is done in unusual circumstances such as to punish **fraud** or when the corporation's stock is not fully paid for.

Pioneer patent   A **patent** for an invention or device that is entirely new, rather than a small improvement; or a patent that may open up a whole new area of experimentation or development.

Piracy   **1.** Attacking and looting or stealing a ship or airplane.   **2.** Reprinting all or part of a copyrighted book, movie, etc., without permission.

Pit   A **commodity exchange's** trading area.

Place   Arrange a sale or other financial transaction. *Placement* could be arranging the sale of a new **issue** of **stock**, arranging a loan or **mortgage** by matching up borrower and lender, or finding a job for a person.

Placer claim   A public land claim to mine minerals deposited in loose sand or rock, along the bank or under a river, etc.

Placitory   Having to do with **pleading** or **pleas**.

316

Placitum (Latin) An old word for a wide variety of different things including agreements, laws, court decisions, public meetings, courts, lawsuits, **pleadings**, etc.

Plagiarism Taking all or part of the writing of another person and passing it off as your own. See also **infringement** of **copyright**.

Plain error rule The principle that an **appeals** court can **reverse** a **judgment** because of an **error** in the proceedings even if the error was not objected to at the time.

Plain meaning rule If a law seems clear, take the simplest meaning of the words and do not read anything into it. This is one of several possible ways of interpreting **statutes**.

Plain view doctrine The rule that if police happen to come across something while acting within their lawful duty, that item may be used as **evidence** in a criminal trial even if the police did not have a **search warrant** (see that word).

Plaintiff A person who brings (starts) a lawsuit against another person.

Plaintiff in error An **appellant**.

Planned unit development An area of land to be developed as one unit of various housing groups plus commercial or industrial development. This development may be approved even if the **zoning** requirements for one part of the land might not allow the buildings planned for that piece.

Plat (or plot) A map showing how a piece of land will be subdivided (divided up) and built upon. A platmap gives the legal description of pieces of property by lot, street, and block numbers.

Plea 1. The **defendant's** formal answer to a criminal **charge**. The defendant says: "**guilty**," "**not guilty**" or "**no contest**" (see these words). 2. For the use of the word in most modern **civil** lawsuits, see **pleading**. 3. An older word for several types of civil motions. For example, a *plea in abatement* has been replaced in most places by a **motion** to dismiss for a technical reason, such as the suit's being brought in the wrong court. Other types of old pleas include *pleas in* **bar**, *pleas in* **discharge**, and *pleas of* **release**.

Plea bargaining Discussions between a **prosecutor** and a criminal **defendant's** lawyer in which the defense lawyer generally offers to have the defendant **plead guilty** in exchange for the prosecutor's agreeing to accept a **plea** to a less serious **charge**,

Plead

to drop some charges, or to promise not to request a heavy **sentence** from the judge.

Plead **1.** Make or file a **pleading** (see that word). **2.** Argue a case in court.

Pleading **1.** The process of making formal, written statements of each side of a case. First the **plaintiff** submits a paper with facts and claims; then the **defendant's** paper submits facts and countercharges; then the plaintiff responds; etc., until all issues and questions are clearly posed for a trial. **2.** A *pleading* is one of the papers mentioned in no. 1. The first one is a **complaint**, the response an **answer**, etc. *The pleadings* is the sum of all these papers. Sometimes, **motions** and other court papers are called *pleadings*, but this is not strictly correct. **3.** The old forms of **common-law** *pleadings* (which were so rigid that one small technical mistake could determine the entire outcome of the suit) included a *declaration, defendant's plea, replication, rejoinder, surrejoinder, rebutter, surrebutter,* etc. See **theory of pleading doctrine.** **4.** In modern legal practice under the *Rules of Civil Procedure*, pleading is no longer inflexible, and pleadings may be changed freely to fit facts as they develop. Modern *pleadings* include **complaints, answers,** (which may include **counterclaims** or **cross-claims**), replies (or **answers**) to these claims, and **third party** complaints and answers.

Plebicite A vote by the people for or against a proposed new major law or expressing an opinion on a major public issue.

Pledge Handing over physical possession of a piece of personal **property** (such as a radio) to another person, who holds it until you pay off a debt to that person.

Plenary Full; complete; of every person or every thing. For example, *plenary jurisdiction* is the full power of a court to make decisions about all the people and property involved in a case, and a *plenary session* is a meeting of all the members of a **legislature** or other large group.

Plenipotentiary Possessing full powers. *Ministers plenipotentiary* are diplomatic representatives slightly below the rank of **ambassador.**

Plessy v. Ferguson The 1896 Supreme Court case, since overturned by *Brown* v. *Board of Education*, that allowed "separate but equal" racial **segregation.**

Plottage The extra value two pieces of land may have because they are side-by-side and can be sold as a unit.

Plow back   Reinvesting profits into a business rather than paying them out to owners.

Plurality   The greatest number. For example, if Jane gets ten votes and Don and Mary each get seven, Jane has a *plurality* (the most votes), but not a **majority** (more than half of the votes).

Pluries   Many. Many interrelated things.

Pocket part   An addition to many lawbooks that updates them until a new edition comes out. It is found inside the back cover and should always be looked for and used when doing legal research.

Point   1. An individual legal proposition, argument, or question raised in a lawsuit. *Points and authorities* is the name for a document prepared to back up a legal position taken in a lawsuit (for example, to support or oppose a **motion**).   2. One percent. A term used by **mortgage** companies to describe an initial charge made for lending money.   3. One unit of measure. For example, if a **stock** goes up in price one dollar, it has gone up "one point," since stocks are usually expressed in dollar amounts; and a speeding violation might cost a driver "three points" towards the suspension of a driver's license when licenses are taken away for the accummulation of a certain number of "points" that reflect the severity of driving tickets.

Point reserved   See **reserve** ("reserving decision").

Poisonous tree   See **fruit of poisonous tree**.

Polar star rule   The rule that the intent of a document should be read from the document alone unless it violates laws or public policy. See also **four corners rule**.

Police court   A low-level local court with widely different functions in different places, but almost always the power to handle minor criminal cases.

Police power   The government's right and power to set up and enforce laws to provide for the safety, health, and general welfare of the people; for example, the power to **license** occupations such as hair cutting.

Policy   1. The general operating procedures of an organization.   2. The general purpose of a **statute** or other law.   3. A type of lottery by betting on numbers; the "numbers game."   4. *Public policy* is the general good of the state and its people. A contract is "against public policy" if carrying it out will be harmful to the public.   5. For various types of *insurance policies*, see **insurance** and the individual words.

Political crime

Political crime (or offense) A crime against the government, such as **treason** or **sedition**. It is often a crime of violence against the established order. These crimes are usually excluded from **extradition** treaties.

Political question A question that the courts will not decide because it concerns a decision properly made by only the **executive** branch of government. For example, only the executive branch has the right to decide whether or not a foreign country has become an independent nation.

Political rights Rights concerning a citizen's participation in government; for example, the right to vote.

Poll tax A tax, now illegal, on the right to vote.

Polling the jury Individually asking each member of a **jury** what his or her decision is.

Polls A *challenge to the polls* is an objection to the selection of a particular **juror**, made before the jury (often a grand **jury**) convenes.

Polygamy Having more than one wife or husband. It is a crime in the U.S.

Polygraph A **lie detector** (see that word).

Polyopsony The fewness of buyers of a particular item or commodity.

Polypoly The fewness of sellers of a particular item or commodity.

Pool **1.** A joining together of resources (by individuals or companies) in a common commercial venture. **2.** An agreement between companies to not compete and to share profits. These types of arrangements are usually illegal under **antitrust** laws. **3.** A pot of money bet on a horse race, a football game, etc.

Pooling of interest Directly combining the **balance sheets** of two companies when they merge. (This **accounting** method disregards **goodwill** as a measure of the difference in company values.)

Popular Belonging to the people.

Popular name tables Reference charts that help find **statutes** if their popular names are known. For example, you could find the official name and **citation** of the "Sherman Act" from a *popular name table*.

Popular sense The sense that persons familiar with the subject area of a **statute** would give to it. This is *not* necessarily the common-language meaning of the words.

Pornographic Obscene (see that word).

Port authority Various federal, state, or interstate agencies that **regulate** boat traffic, promote port business, and maintain other services such as airports, tollroads, etc.

Port of entry A port where immigrants and imported goods may enter the country and where **customs** offices exist.

Portal-to-portal act A federal law requiring payment for some types of employees' time getting to and from work.

Portfolio All the investments (usually **stocks** and other **securities**) held by one person or organization.

Position classification Basing salaries, duties, and authority of workers in an organization on formal job descriptions.

Positive evidence Direct evidence (see that word).

Positive law Law that has been enacted by a **legislature**.

Posse commitatus (Latin) "The power of the state." The group of citizens who may be gathered by the **sheriff** or other law officer to help enforce the law, usually on an emergency basis. It is abbreviated *"posse."*

Possession 1. Ownership and control of personal **property**. 2. Rightful control of land or buildings. For example, a **tenant** may have *possession*. 3. Simply holding something. For example, having an illegal drug in your pocket is called *possession*.

Possession is nine-tenths of the law 1. To get a court to give you something held by another person, you must have a strong legal **title** to it. 2. Court procedures are often so costly and cumbersome that it is often not worth trying to use the courts to get something held by someone else even if you have a legal title to it.

Possessory action A lawsuit to gain control of property, as opposed to one that attempts to get legal ownership to property. For example, an **eviction** is a *possessory action*.

Possibility of issue See **fertile octogenarian rule**.

Post 1. Announce something to the public by putting up signs in prominent places. 2. Put something in the mail. 3. See **posting**. 4. Put land or water off limits to trespassing or hunting by placing signs around the borders.

Postconviction remedies Procedures for prisoners to challenge their **convictions** or **sentences**. These procedures include asking the convicting court to correct the sentence, **habeas corpus**

Postdate

petitions, and other forms of court action. There are federal and state laws regulating this area.

Postdate   To put a date on a document that is later than the date the document is signed.

Posthumous   After death. For example, a *posthumous child* is one born after the death of the father, and *posthumous work* is work for which a **copyright** or **patent** is sought by persons who now possess the rights to the work of a dead writer or inventor.

Posting   **1.** Writing down an **entry** (such as money spent for a lamp) into an **account** book.   **2.** The same as no. 1, but by transferring the information from an original record or notation.

Post-mortem   (Latin) "After death." An **autopsy** or examination of a body to determine the cause of death.

Post-obit   An agreement in which a borrower promises to pay back a larger sum of money after the death of someone from whom the borrower expects an **inheritance**.

Postponement   **Subordination** of a **lien**, **mortgage**, or **judgment** when it would normally have **priority** over the lien, mortgage, or judgment now given priority.

Post-trial discovery   **Deposition** (and other information gathering) done between a trial and an **appeal** to record the **testimony** of **witnesses** in case there are further trial proceedings.

Poundage   Fees paid to a **sheriff** or other public official who conducts a court-ordered **execution** on property.

Pourover   A **will** that gives some money or property to an existing **trust** is called a *pourover will*, and a trust that does the same thing is a *pourover trust*.

Poverty affidavit   A document signed under **oath** that a person is poor enough to qualify for public assistance, a free lawyer, **waiver** of court fees, etc.

Powell   *Powell on Real Property*; a **treatise**.

Power   **1.** The right to do something.   **2.** The ability to do something.   **3.** A combination of no. 1 and no. 2.

Power of appointment   A part of your **will**, **deed**, or separate document that gives someone the power to decide who gets your money or property or how it will be used.

Power of attorney   A document authorizing a person to act as **attorney** for the person signing the document.

Power of sale The right of a **mortgage** holder or mortgage **trustee** to sell the property if payments are not made.

Pp. Pages.

Practicable A stuffy word meaning "feasible"; can be done.

Practice 1. Custom, habit, or regular repetition. 2. Formal court procedure; the way a lawsuit is taken to and through court as opposed to what it is about. For example, a *practice manual* is a book of forms and procedures to use in **pleading** and court practice. 3. Engaging in a profession, such as law. 4. Doing things that are only permitted to be done by a member of a profession. For example, giving legal advice or arguing a case in court is the *practice of law.*

Praecipe (Latin) A formal request that the court **clerk** take some action. A **motion** that does not need a judge's approval and, if done correctly, will be carried out by the court clerk. For example, in most places a lawyer can **enter** an appearance in a case by *praecipe.* [pronounce: <u>pres</u>-i-pee]

Praedial 1. "From the ground." Crops, trees, and growing things. 2. A *praedial servitude* is a requirement put on one piece of land that it may be used in some way by the owner of another piece of land. [pronounce: <u>pred</u>-i-al]

Prayer Request. That part of a legal **pleading**, such as a **complaint**, that asks for **relief** (help, specific court action, something from the other side, etc.).

Preamble An introduction (usually saying why a document, such as a **statute**, was written).

Preappointed evidence Proof that is required in advance. For example, a **statute** may say that proof of a certain crime requires proof of a specific set of facts.

Precatory Expressing a wish; advisory only; not legally binding in most situations. [pronounce: <u>prek</u>-a-tory]

Precedent 1. A court decision on a *question of law* that gives **authority** or direction on how to decide a similar question of law in a later case with similar facts. The American court system is based on judges making decisions supported by past precedent, rather than by the unsupported logic of the judge alone. See also **stare decisis.** 2. Something that must happen before something else may happen; see **condition** precedent. [pronounce: <u>press</u>-i-dent]

Precept 1. A command by a person in authority. Most often, a written **warrant** or other command from a court to someone outside the court. **2.** A rule of conduct.

Precinct A police or election district within a city.

Precipe See **praecipe**.

Preclusion order When one side in a lawsuit doesn't produce something requested by **discovery**, the judge may **issue** a *preclusion order* forbidding that side from making or opposing legal arguments based on what was not produced.

Precognition The examination of a **witness** before trial.

Precontract A **contract** that keeps you from entering into a similar contract with someone else.

Predatory intent Lowering prices solely to put a competitor out of business.

Predial See **praedial**.

Pre-emption **1.** The first right to buy something. For example, *pre-emptive rights* are the rights of some stockholders to first chance at buying any new stock the company issues. **2.** The first right to do anything. For example, when the federal government *pre-empts the field* by passing laws in a subject area, the states may not pass conflicting laws and sometimes may not pass any laws on the subject at all.

Preference **1.** A **creditor's** right to be paid before other creditors. **2.** The act of an **insolvent** (broke) **debtor** in paying off a creditor more than a fair share of what is left. For example, if John owes Mary ten dollars and Don ten dollars, but has only ten dollars left and pays it all to Mary, this is a *preference*. If a debtor gives a creditor preference shortly before going into **bankruptcy**, the bankruptcy court may be able to get that money back in to be divided fairly.

Preferential shop A place of business where **union** members will be hired first and laid off last.

Preferential voting An election in which voters may (or must) list first, second, third, etc., choices. If no one gets over half the first place votes, second place choices are added in (then, if needed, third place, etc.) until someone gets over 50 percent of the votes.

Preferred stock See **stock**.

Prehire agreement An agreement by which a **union** may **bargain** with an employer even though it has not proved that it represents a majority of the employees.

Prejudice   **1.** Bias; a preconceived opinion. Leaning towards one side in a dispute for reasons other than an evaluation of the justice of that side's position.   **2.** A judge's *prejudice* refers not to an opinion about the subject of the case, but to the judge's bias towards one of the *persons* in the dispute.   **3.** All rights are lost. For example, if a case is *dismissed with prejudice*, it cannot be brought back into court again.   **4.** Substantially harmful to rights. For example, *prejudicial error* is serious enough to be appealed, and *prejudicial publicity* is news reports that deprive a **defendant** of a fair trial.

Preliminary complaint   The process in some states by which a low-level court can conduct a **probable cause** (see that word) **hearing** for **binding over** a **criminal defendant** to a court that can hold criminal trials.

Preliminary evidence   Those facts needed to begin a hearing or trial; not necessarily those needed to ultimately win.

Preliminary hearing   **1.** The first screening of a **criminal** charge, in federal courts and many state courts, by a **magistrate** or a judge to decide whether there is enough evidence for the government to continue with the case and to require the defendant to post **bail** or be held for trial. It is also called a *preliminary examination*, **probable cause** *hearing*, and *bind over hearing*. **2.** In some states, a preliminary hearing is a court session for hearing **motions** before the actual trial.

Preliminary injunction   See **injunction**.

Premeditation   A prior determination to do something; thinking in advance about how to do something (usually a crime).

Premises   **1.** Buildings and the surrounding land under the same control.   **2.** The part of a document that explains the "who, what, where, how, and when" of a transaction before the words actually putting the transaction into effect.   **3.** The basis for a logical deduction. The facts or arguments upon which a conclusion is based.

Premium   **1.** The money paid for **insurance coverage**.   **2.** An extra amount of money paid to buy something; a bonus.   **3.** The amount by which a **stock** or other **security** sells above its **par** (**face** or **nominal**) value.

Prenuptial agreement   **Antenuptial** agreement (see that word).

Prepaid expense   Any expense or debt paid before it is due. This may have special tax consequences.

Prepaid income   Money received, but not yet earned or due to you. This may have special tax consequences.

Prepaid legal services   Legal insurance plans similar to medical insurance. The plans may be *open-panel* (choose your own lawyer) or *closed-panel* (pick from a list or have one assigned).

Prepayment penalty   Extra money that must be paid if you pay off a loan early. This compensates the lender for lost interest or extra paperwork.

Preponderance of evidence   The greater weight of evidence, not as to *quantity* (in number of witnesses or facts) but as to *quality* (believability and greater weight of important facts proved). This is a *standard of proof*, generally used in **civil** lawsuits. It is not as stringent as others such as **clear and convincing proof** or **beyond a reasonable doubt**.

Prerogative   **1.** A special privilege.   **2.** Special official power.

Prerogative writs   Actions a court will take only under special circumstances. These include, for example, **mandamus** and **habeas corpus** (see these words). These **writs** have been abolished in federal court and most state courts and have been replaced by regular **motions** for the same things.

Prescription   **1.** A method of getting legal ownership of personal **property** (everything but land) by keeping it in your possession openly, continuously, and with a claim that it belongs to you. This must be done for a length of time set by state law.   **2.** The right of access to a path, a waterway, light, open air, etc., that is gained because of longtime continuous use.   **3.** An order or direction.

Presence   A police officer may make an **arrest** without a **warrant** if the **offense** was committed in the officer's *presence*, which means "view," "earshot," or general observation. This may include hearing a disturbance at a distance or finding out in many other direct, immediate ways that there was an offense committed and that a particular person probably did it.

Present   **1.** Immediate.   **2.** See **presentment**.

Present recollection recorded   See **recollection**.

Present sense impression   A statement made during or immediately after an event by a participant or an observer. It is an exception to the **hearsay rule** and may be used as **evidence** in federal court.

Present worth (or value)   Future payments, earnings, or debts discounted to their value today (as if a sum of money were invested today to make the future payments).

Presentence investigation An investigation by court-appointed social workers, **probation** officers, etc., into a criminal's background and prospects for rehabilitation. This investigation produces a report and recommendations which are considered by a judge at a *presentence hearing.*

Presentment (or presentation) **1.** A grand **jury's** charging a person with a crime that it has investigated itself without an **indictment** given to it by a prosecutor. In some states it is an informal document; a statement, not a charge. **2.** Showing a **negotiable instrument**, such as a check, and asking for payment on it.

Presents "These presents" is an obsolete phrase for "this legal document."

Presidential electors See **electoral college**.

Presumed intent The legal rule that a person means to cause any natural or probable results of his or her **voluntary** acts. A person legally *intends* not only a crime, but its consequences.

Presumption A conclusion or inference drawn. A *presumption of fact* is a conclusion that because one fact exists (or one thing is true), another fact exists (or another thing is true). If no new facts turn up to prove the presumption wrong, it is **evidence** as good as any direct proof of the fact. A *presumption of law* is a rule of law that whenever a certain set of facts shows up, a court must automatically draw certain legal conclusions. For example, the *presumption of innocence* is that whenever a person is charged with a crime, he or she is innocent until proved guilty, so the government must make the case. Presumptions can be *rebuttable* (good until destroyed by more facts) or *conclusive, absolute, or irrebuttable* (an inference that must be drawn from a set of facts no matter what). Other *presumptions* include the *presumption of death* (if a person disappears and is gone for seven years, that person is presumed dead); the *presumption of legitimacy* (if a child is born to a married woman, the husband is presumed to be the father); and the *presumption of survivorship* (in those states that do not have **simultaneous death acts** [see that word], the younger, stronger, healthier, etc., person is presumed to have been the later one to die in an accident if it is not known who really died last).

Presumptive May be inferred. For *presumptive evidence*, see **presumption** (of fact).

Presumptive trust   A **resulting trust** (see that word).

Pretermitted heir   A child (or sometimes any descendant) either unintentionally left out of a **will** or born after the will is made. Some states have *pretermission statutes* that allow a child left out by mistake to take a share of the parent's property.

Pretrial conference   A meeting of lawyers and judge to narrow the issues in a lawsuit, agree on what will be presented at the trial, and make a final effort to **settle** the case without a trial. Procedural agreements can be put in writing in a *pretrial order*.

Pretrial diversion   See **diversion**.

Prevailing party   The person who wins a lawsuit (even if the person is **awarded** far less money than he or she sued for).

Preventive detention   Holding persons against their will because they are likely to commit a crime. This practice is **unconstitutional** in most but not all situations.

Preventive justice   A general term for **peace bonds** (see that word) and other actions taken by judges to prevent future lawbreaking.

Preventive law   Legal help and information designed to help persons to avoid legal problems before they occur.

Previous question   To "call" or "move" "the previous question" is to request that a question be voted upon immediately.

Previously taxed income   Earnings that have been taxed, but not yet distributed. (This usually happens when a **Subchapter S corporation** [see that word] holds onto earnings.) This income will not be taxed a second time when given out to the company's owners.

Price discrimination   **Predatory intent** (see that word).

Price–earnings ratio   The cost of a **share** of **stock** divided by the yearly **dividend** paid by that stock. For example, a $20 stock that paid $2 has a ten-to-one ratio. This figure is used in comparing stocks' investment potential.

Price fixing   *Horizontal price fixing* is different companies (or associations of companies) agreeing to charge similar prices for similar things. *Vertical price fixing* is controlling the resale price of something (by requiring a retailer to sell at no lower than a certain price, etc.). All of these arrangements are violations of **antitrust** laws.

Price leadership   A situation in which one large company regularly sets selling prices for something, and the rest of the industry then sets the same price. This is not a violation of **antitrust**

laws unless the companies worked together on the pricing or tried to drive other companies out of the market.

Price supports Government loan, subsidy, and buying programs designed to keep prices (usually farm prices) above a certain level.

Prima facie (Latin) At first sight; on the face of it; presumably. A fact that will be considered to be true unless disproved by contrary **evidence**. For example, a *prima facie case* is a case that will win unless the other side comes forward with evidence to dispute it. [pronounce: pry-ma fay-she]

Primary activity A **strike**, **boycott**, or **picketing** against an employer with which a **union** has a dispute. (In contrast, a boycott directed against, for example, a store that handles the employer's products is a **secondary boycott**.)

Primary authority 1. Binding authority (see that word). **2.** Laws, court decisions, regulations, and other similar sources of law rather than encyclopedias, **treatises**, etc.

Primary election An **election** in which a political **party** chooses its candidates for public office (to run in the general election).

Primary evidence The best evidence to prove a point. For example, a document itself is the **best evidence** of what it says, so it is *primary*.

Primary jurisdiction doctrine The principle that even if a court has the right and power to take a case, if the case involves issues that are better decided in an **administrative agency**, the court should keep hands off until the agency has had a chance to resolve the issue.

Primary market The place in which, or the method by which, the first sale of a **stock** or other **securities issue** is made.

Prime 1. Original. **2.** Most important. **3.** For *prime contractor*, see **contractor**. **4.** The *prime rate* is the lowest **interest** a bank will charge its best customers for short-term, unsecured loans. This is an indicator of what the bank's other interest rates will be, and the *prime rates* of **national banks** (see that word) are one major economic indicator.

Primogeniture 1. The first child born to a husband and wife. **2.** An outdated rule that the first son inherited everything.

Principal 1. Chief; most important; primary. **2.** A sum of money, as opposed to the profits made (**interest**) on that money. **3.** An employer or anyone else who has another person (an **agent**) do things for him or her. **4.** A person directly involved

Principle

with committing a crime, as opposed to an **accessory** (see that word). **5.** *Not* "**principle**."

Principle   A basic legal truth, doctrine, or generalization. *Not* "**principal**."

Printers ink statute   A state law that makes it illegal to advertise anything that is false or deceptive.

Prior act   A device or process similar enough to one in a **patent** application to justify rejecting the patent.

Prior hearing   A **hearing** by an **administrative agency** that in some situations must be given to a person before taking any action that harms the person.

Prior inconsistent statements   Out-of-court statements by a witness that contradict what he or she now says in a trial. These statements may be used to discredit the believability of the witness, but not to prove the truth of what was said.

Prior restraint   Stopping someone from publishing something. *Prior restraint* is **unconstitutional** unless the material is a "clear and present danger" to the country or a court has found that it is **obscene** or violates a person's legally recognized right to **privacy**.

Prior use doctrine   The rule that one governmental organization cannot take property for a public use if the property is already devoted to a public use by another government organization unless there are specific laws allowing it.

Priority   The right to come first. The right to have a claim paid first and completely, whether or not the deal on which the claim is based came first and whether or not the claim itself was made first. (When these claims are **liens**, the first person to perfect the lien has *priority*.)

Prison   A place for the long-term holding of persons incarcerated for a crime.

Prisoner   Anyone deprived of liberty by the government, either because of an accusation of a crime or **conviction** of a crime.

Privacy   The right to be left alone. This right is generally "balanced" against other rights, such as *freedom of the press*.

Privacy acts   Federal and state laws restricting access to personal and financial information (tax returns, mental health records, etc.) and prohibiting many types of electronic and other surveillance (wiretapping, etc.).

Private   **1.** Concerning individuals, not the general public and not the government. **2.** For *private* **foundation, letter ruling, offering,** etc., see those words. Others follow here.

Private attorney general A private individual who goes to court to enforce a public right for all citizens.

Private international law See **conflict of laws.**

Private law **1.** A **statute** passed to affect one person or group, as opposed to a **public law** (see that word). This is also called a *private bill.* **2.** The law of relationships among persons and groups (such as the law of **contracts,** divorce, etc.) as opposed to **public law,** which concerns relationships between individuals and the government or the operation of government.

Private letter ruling See **letter ruling.**

Private placement Adopting a baby or selling **stock** without going through the usual organizations that handle these transfers.

Privateer A ship owned and armed by a private individual that is empowered by a government to fight with enemy ships and capture enemy shipping in time of war. There is an international **treaty** abolishing *privateering,* but the United States never signed it.

Privies See **privity** and **privy.**

Privilege **1.** An advantage; a right to preferential treatment. **2.** An exemption from a duty others like you must perform. **3.** The right to speak or write defamatory (personally damaging) words because the law allows them in certain circumstances. For example, most words are *privileged* if spoken completely "in the line of public duty." **4.** A basic right. For example, the *privileges and immunities* guaranteed to all by Article IV and the Fourteenth Amendment of the U.S. Constitution. **5.** A special advantage, as opposed to a right; an advantage that can be taken away again. **6.** The **right,** and the **duty,** to withhold information because of some special status or relationship of **confidentiality.** These privileges include: **husband–wife, doctor–patient,** clergy, **journalist–**source, **executive,** etc.

Privileged communication See **confidentiality** and **privilege.**

Privileges and immunities The **constitutional** requirement that no state may treat a person from another state unfairly.

Privity **1.** Private or "inside" knowledge. **2.** A close, direct financial relationship. For example, both the **executor** (person who **administers** a **will** and hands out property) and an **heir** (person who gets the property) are in **privity** with the **testator** (person who wrote the will and gave away the property). Also,

Privy

privity of contract exists among those persons who actually took part in making the deal and have rights and duties because of it. For example, a manufacturer and a seller may be "in privity," but not the manufacturer and the buyer.

Privy   1. A person who is in **privity** (see that word) with another person. The plural is *privies*.   2. Private.

Prize   A ship taken by one country (or by a **privateer** from that country) from another with which it is at war. When a ship is brought in as a prize, a *prize court* determines who gets it.

Pro   (Latin) For.

Pro bono publico   (Latin) For the public good. When abbreviated to *"pro bono,"* it stands for free legal work done for some charitable or public purpose.

Pro forma   1. (Latin) As a matter of form; a mere formality. 2. Projected. A *pro forma* financial **statement** is one that is projected on the basis of certain assumptions.

Pro hac vice   (Latin) For this one particular occasion only; for example, when an out-of-state lawyer wants to appear before a state court in one case without being permanently admitted to the state **bar**. [pronounce: pro hock <u>vee</u>-chay]

Pro interesse suo   (Latin) "According to his interest." For example, a person who claims a right to property that is burdened with a **mortgage, judgment, lease**, etc., may ask a court to decide whether or not (or how much of) the property is his or hers. This is an *examination pro interesse suo.*

Pro rata   Proportionately; by percentage; by a fixed rate; by share. For example, if Tom, Dick, and Harry are owed two, four, and six dollars respectively by John, but John has only six dollars to give out, a *pro rata* sharing would be one, two, and three dollars respectively. A *pro rata clause* in an **insurance** policy says that the company will not pay a higher percentage of a loss than the percentage that company covers of the total insurance coverage from all companies. And a *pro rata distribution clause* in an insurance policy says that the amount of insurance on each piece of property is in proportion to the value of that property compared to the total value of all property covered.

Pro se   (Latin) For himself or herself; in his or her own behalf. For example, *pro se representation* means that a person will handle his or her own case in court without a lawyer. [pronounce: pro say]

Pro tanto (Latin) For that much; to the extent of; partial payment.

Pro tem (Latin) Short for "pro tempore"; for the time being.

Probable cause 1. The U.S. **constitutional** requirement that law enforcement officers present sufficient facts to convince a judge to issue a **search warrant** or an **arrest warrant**, and the requirement that no warrant should be issued unless it is more likely than not that a crime has been committed by the person to be arrested or that the objects sought will be found in the place to be searched. 2. In certain situations where an officer cannot obtain a warrant (for example, when the person to be arrested might escape or the **evidence** to be searched for might be destroyed) an officer may search or arrest if, from what the officer knows, it is more likely than not that a crime is being (or has been) committed. *Probable cause* does not depend on what the officer finds out after the search or arrest, but on what the officer knew before taking action. If there was no probable cause to search or arrest, the search or arrest was probably not proper. In each case, it depends on the nature of the suspicion, the need for immediate action, and the intrusiveness of the search.

Probate 1. The process of proving that a **will** is genuine and giving out the property in it. 2. The name in some states for a court that handles the **distribution** (giving out) of **decedents' estates** (dead persons' property) and other matters such as **insanity commitments**.

Probation 1. Allowing a person convicted of a criminal offense to stay out of jail under supervised conditions (by a *probation officer*). If the person "keeps clean" and satisfies the *conditions of probation*, he or she may never go to jail. 2. A trial period. A period during which a person's employment is still conditioned on "making good" in the job and during which the person has fewer job rights than other employees.

Probationer A person free on **probation** (see that word).

Probative Tending to prove or actually proving something.

Probative facts Facts that actually prove other facts necessary to a valid issue in a lawsuit; **evidentiary facts** (see that word).

Procedural law The rules of carrying on a lawsuit (how to enforce rights in court) as opposed to "**substantive law**" (the law of the rights and duties themselves).

Procedure The rules and methods of carrying on a lawsuit

Proceeding

(**pleading**, making **motions**, presenting **evidence**, etc.). Federal court practice is governed by the *Federal Rules of Civil Procedure* and the *Federal Rules of Criminal Procedure*.

Proceeding   **1.** A **case** in court.   **2.** The orderly progression of a case in court.   **3.** The recorded history of a case.   **4.** Any action taken by a governmental body (an **agency hearing**, a police investigation, etc.).

Proceeds   Money or property gained from a sale.

Process   **1.** A court's ordering a **defendant** to show up in court or risk losing a lawsuit without being represented; a **summons**.   **2.** Any court **order** that "takes **jurisdiction** over" (brings formally under the court's power) a person or property.   **3.** A regular, legal method of operating.

Process patent   A **patent** for a new way of making something or of bringing about a result that has commercial value.

Process server   A person with legal authority to formally deliver court papers such as **writs** and **summonses** to **defendants**.

Prochein ami   (French) **Next friend** (see that word). [pronounce: pro-shen ah-mee]

Proclamation   A formal government declaration that is made generally known.

Proctor   **1.** Someone appointed to manage another person's affairs.   **2.** A lawyer or representative.

Procuration   **1.** Making someone else your **agent**, lawyer, or representative. See **proctor**.   **2.** Doing something as someone's agent, buyer, or representative. See **proctor**.   **3.** Pimping; soliciting for prostitutes. See **procure**.   **4.** *Not* **procurement**.

Procure   **1.** Make something happen; get something for someone.   **2.** Solicit customers for a prostitute.

Procurement   **1.** Government purchasing; usually by special rules, forms, contracts, etc.   **2.** *Not* **procuration**.

Procuring cause   **1.** See **proximate cause**.   **2.** A **broker** who has started in motion a chain of events leading to the sale of real estate and who is entitled to a **commission** for this service.

Prodition   **Treason**.

Produce   Bring forward; show; yield up. For example, a *motion to produce* or a *motion for production* is a request that the judge order the other side to show you specific documents.

Producing cause   **1.** See **proximate cause**.   **2.** See **procuring cause**.

Product liability The responsibility of manufacturers (and sometimes sellers) of goods to pay for harm to purchasers (and sometimes other users or even bystanders) caused by a defective product.

Production payment An advance payment for a purchase that is really a loan to allow its production.

Profer (or profert) See **proffer**.

Professio juris A made-up Latin word for an agreement in a **contract** to have the law of one particular state or country decide all questions involving the contract.

Professional association Any group of professionals organized for social, educational, or other purposes; for example, a bar association.

Professional responsibility See **Code of Professional Responsibility**.

Proffer 1. Offer or present. 2. **Avowal** (see that word).

Profit All gains, including both money and increases in the value of property.

Profit and loss statement See **statement** of income.

Profit margin 1. Sales minus costs and expenses (and taxes). 2. Sales minus the cost of sales and **operating** expenses, that figure then divided by sales. A company's *gross profit margin* (also called *operating margin*) is its **operating** profit divided by its money made on sales. Its *net profit margin* (also called *net ratio*) is its net profit divided by its sales. These percentage figures can be used to compare the company with others and to compare efficiency and profitability with prior years.

Profit sharing A plan set up by an employer to distribute part of the firm's profits to some or all of its employees. A *qualified plan* (one that meets requirements for tax benefits) must have specific criteria and formulas for who gets what, how, and when.

Profiteering Making unreasonable profits by taking advantage of unusual circumstances; for example, by selling scarce goods at high prices during a war.

Profits a prendre (French) The right to take the growing crops of another person's land. [pronounce: a prahn-d]

Profits a rendre (French) That which must be rendered or paid; usually rent. [pronounce: a rahn-d]

Programmed costs **Fixed charges** (see that word), such as long-

Progressive tax

term research, that do not directly produce or sell goods and services. The opposite of **capacity costs** (see that word).

Progressive tax A tax that charges the rich a larger proportion of their wealth than it charges the poor. For example, federal *income tax* is progressive, at least in theory. The opposite of a progressive tax is a **regressive tax**. This hits the poor harder. An example is a sales tax. Even though everyone pays the same tax, it takes a larger part of a poor person's money to pay it.

Prohibited degrees Blood relations too close to legally marry; for example, brother and sister, grandfather and granddaughter, in most states first cousins, etc.

Prohibition **1.** An order to stop certain actions or a warning not to engage in them. For example, a *writ of prohibition* is an order from a higher court telling a lower one to stop proceeding with a lawsuit. **2.** The popular name for the period in American history from 1919 to 1933 when the manufacture or sale of alcoholic beverages was illegal.

Prolixity Using too many words, facts, theories, etc., in court papers or **evidence**.

Promise **1.** A statement that morally, legally, or some other way binds the person who makes it to do something. **2.** In legal language, a *promise* is an oral or written statement from one person to another, given for something of value in return. It binds the person making the promise to do something and gives the other person the legal right to demand that it be done.

Promissory estoppel The principle that if Person A makes a promise and expects Person B to do something in **reliance** upon that promise, then Person B does act in reliance upon that promise, the law will usually help Person B enforce the promise.

Promissory note **1.** A written promise, with no strings attached, to pay a certain sum of money by a certain time. **2.** A **negotiable** *promissory note* is a signed written promise, with no strings attached, to pay an exact sum of money immediately, when asked for, or by a certain date to either "the **order** of" a specific person or to "**bearer**" (the person who physically has it).

Promoter A person who forms a **corporation**.

Promulgate Publish; announce officially; put out formally.

Pronounce To say formally and officially. For example, a judge *pronounces* **sentence** by solemnly saying in open court what sentence a convicted **defendant** will have to serve.

Proof 1. A body of **evidence** supporting a contention. Those facts from which a conclusion can be drawn. In this sense, *proof* can be convincing or unconvincing. But see no. 2. **2.** The result of convincing **evidence**. The conclusion drawn that the evidence is enough to show that something is true or that an argument about facts is correct. There are various **standards** of *proof* including: *beyond a reasonable doubt* (how convincing evidence must be in a **criminal** trial); *by clear and convincing evidence*; and *by a preponderance* (greater weight) *of the evidence*. In this sense, proof is always convincing. But see no. 1.

Proof of claim A sworn statement in a **bankruptcy** or **probate** proceeding of how much a **creditor** is owed.

Proof of loss A sworn statement made to an **insurance** company of a loss suffered under an insurance policy.

Proper Fit, suitable, or appropriate. For example, a *proper party* to a lawsuit is a person who has a real, substantial interest in the suit's outcome, who can conveniently be added to the suit as a **party**, but without whom the suit can still be decided.

Property 1. Ownership of a thing; the legal right to own a thing. **2.** Anything that is owned or can be owned, such as land, automobiles, money, **stocks**, **patents**, the right to use a famous actor's name or picture, etc. Property is usually divided into *real* (land and things attached to or growing on it) and *personal* (everything else). Some things fall in between or are both; for example, a partly built-in bookcase or a **title** document to a piece of land.

Property tax A state or local tax based on the value of certain property (homes, cars, etc.) owned.

Proponent The person who offers something, puts something forward, or proposes something.

Proposal 1. An **offer** that can be accepted to make a **contract**. **2.** A preliminary or exploratory idea for discussion that is *not* an offer as in no. 1.

Propound To offer, propose, or put forward something. For example, to *propound a will* is to put it forward and request that it be accepted as valid by the **probate** court.

Proprietary Having to do with ownership. *Proprietary rights* or interests are the rights or interests a person has because of, or attached to, property ownership. For example, if one person has the sole right to make and sell a medicine, it is a *proprietary drug*. And the right to vote a **share** of **stock** is a *proprietary in-*

Proprietorship

terest of owning it. The *proprietary functions* of a city (as opposed to its public functions) include such things as sidewalk repair and trash pickup. And a *proprietary lease* is between tenant–owners of a **cooperative** apartment building and the owners' association.

Proprietorship   1. The running of a business.   2. **Sole** proprietorship (see that word).

Prorate   To divide or share proportionately or by shares; see **pro rata**.

Prorogation   1. An agreement in a **contract** to allow the courts of one particular state or country to decide all disputes involving the contract.   2. A delay, putting off, or **continuance**.

Prosecute   1. Begin and follow up on a **civil** lawsuit.   2. Charge a person with a crime and bring that person to trial. The process is called *prosecution*, the procedure is called a *prosecution*, the person who was harmed by the crime or who made the complaint is a *prosecuting witness*, and the public official who presents the government's case is called the **prosecutor**.

Prosecutor   1. A public official who presents the government's case against a person accused of a crime and who asks the court to **convict** that person.   2. The private individual who accuses a person of a crime is sometimes called the *private prosecutor*.

Prosecutorial discretion   The power of the **prosecutor** (see that word) to decide whether or not to prosecute a **charge** against a person, to decide how serious a charge to press, how large a penalty to request, what kind of a **plea bargaining** deal to accept, etc.

Prospective   Looking forward; concerning the future. For example, a *prospective law* is one that applies to situations that arise after it is enacted. Most laws are *prospective* only.

Prospectus   1. A document put out to describe a **corporation** and to interest persons in buying its **stock**. When new stock is sold to the public, the **S.E.C.** requires a *prospectus* that contains such things as a **statement** of income, a **balance sheet**, an **auditor's report**, etc.   2. Any offer (written, by radio or television, etc.) to interest persons in buying any **securities**, such as stock.   3. A document put out to interest persons in any financial deal (such as the offer to sell a building).

Prosser   *Prosser on Torts*; a **treatise**.

Prostitution   A person offering her (in some states, his or her)

338

body for sexual purposes in exchange for money. A crime in most states.

Protective committee   A group of stockholders appointed to protect the interests of all holders of that type of stock during the **reorganization** or **liquidation** of a **corporation**.

Protective custody   Putting someone in jail, in a mental hospital, in a secret house, etc., for the person's own safety, whether or not the person wants it. This can happen to a **witness** in a case involving dangerous **defendants**, to a drunk, to a mentally ill person, etc.

Protective order (or protection order)   **1.** A court's **order** that temporarily allows one side to hold back from showing the other side documents or other things that were properly requested.   **2.** Any court order protecting a person from harassment, **service** of **process**, or other similar problems.   **3.** A court order putting someone in **protective custody** (see that word).

Protective (or protection) theory   The legal rule that a government can **condemn** more property than is needed for a public project if a "buffer zone" is useful to protect the environment or the surrounding neighborhood.

Protectorate   A country whose international affairs are managed by another country.

Protest   **1.** A written statement that you do not agree to the legality, justice, or correctness of a payment, but you are paying it while reserving your right to get it back later.   **2.** A formal certificate of the **dishonor** of a **negotiable instrument** (see these words) you have presented for payment. It is signed by a **notary** and gives **notice** to all persons **liable** on the negotiable instrument that they may have to pay up on it.

Prothonotary   Head **clerk** of some courts.

Protocol   **1.** The first draft of an agreement between countries or the preliminary document opening an international meeting.   **2.** Formalities.   **3.** The etiquette of international diplomacy, including the ranking of officials.   **4.** A short summary of a document.   **5.** The **minutes** of a meeting (usually initialed by all to show their accuracy).

Province   Duty, or area of responsibility.

Provision   Money or property held by or sent to the **drawee** of a **bill** of exchange in order to pay it upon **presentment**.

Provisional

Provisional   Temporary or preliminary. For example, a *provisional remedy* is a court **order** or an action permitted by a court that helps to enforce the law on a temporary basis. These include temporary **injunctions** and **attachments** (see these words).

Proviso   A **condition, qualification,** or **limitation** in a document.

Provocation   An act by one person that triggers a reaction of rage in a second person. *Provocation* may reduce the severity of a crime. It may also be a **defense** to a **divorce** based on **cruelty.**

Proximate cause   The real cause of an accident or other injury. It is not necessarily the closest thing in time or space to the injury and not necessarily the event that set things in motion. It is a general word for a general idea. Some other names for the same idea are "causa causans," "causa proxima," and "dominant," "efficient," "immediate," "legal," "moving," "next," or "producing" cause.

Proxy   **1.** A person who acts for another person (usually to vote in place of the other person in a meeting the other cannot attend).   **2.** A piece of paper giving the right mentioned in no. 1.   **3.** A *proxy marriage* has someone standing in for either the bride or groom (or both) at the wedding ceremony.   **4.** A *proxy statement* is the document sent or given to stockholders when their voting *proxies* are requested for a **corporate** decision. The **S.E.C.** has rules for when the statements must be given out and what must be in them.

Prudent person rule   A **trustee** (see that word) may invest **trust** funds only in traditionally safe investments or risk being personally responsible for losses. These safe investments may be restricted to a state-selected group of **securities** called *legal investments* or the *legal list.*

Prurient interest   A shameful or obsessive interest in immoral or sexual things. "Appealing to prurient interest" is one of many criteria for deciding whether a book is **obscene.**

Public   **1.** Having to do with a state, nation, or the community as a whole. For example, a tax or a government function that will benefit the community as a whole and not merely individual members has a *public purpose.*   **2.** Open to all persons.

Public defender   A free lawyer, employed by the government to represent poor persons accused of a crime.

Public domain   **1.** Land owned by the government.   **2.** Free for anyone to use; no longer protected by **patent** or **copyright.**

Public figure   Anyone who is famous (or infamous) for what he or she has done or who has come forward to take part in a public controversy. This may be important in **libel** or **privacy** law.

Public interest   **1.** A broad term for anything that can affect the general public's finances, health, rights, etc. For example, a business that is on public property and that the public must deal with is called "affected with" or "clothed by" a *public interest*. **2.** *Public interest law* is a nonprofit legal practice for a public cause, such as protection of the environment.

Public lands **1.** Land owned by the government. **2.** Land owned by the government and not set aside for a particular purpose, so subject to possible sale.

Public law   **1.** The study of law that has to do with either the operation of government or the relationship between the government and persons. Examples are **constitutional law, administrative law, criminal law,** etc.).   **2.** The name for the original form that United States and some state laws come out in; for example, "Public Law No. 223."

Public office   A vague term for a government job with independent duties. A mayor is a *public official*; a police chief might be, and a police officer is probably not.

Public policy   A vague word that can be as broad as "what is good for (or will not harm) the general public" or "the law."

Public service commission (or public utilities commission)   A state agency that **regulates** private businesses that have a public **charter**, perform a necessary public function, and need special government help, such as the power of **eminent domain.** These private businesses (such as railroads or power companies) are called *public utilities*, are often **monopolies**, and must provide service to all persons without **discrimination.**

Public utility   **1.** See **public service commission.** **2.** The *Public Utility Holding Company Act* is a federal law that broke up large power and other companies and forced them under state or local control.

Public works   Government construction projects.

Publicly-held corporation   A **corporation** with **stock** sold to a large number of persons.

Publication   Making public. For example, in **copyright** law, *publication* is offering a book, a movie, etc., to the public by sale or distribution; in the law of **defamation**, *publication* usually

Publici juris

means communicating the information to another person; in the law of **wills**, *publication* is telling a **witness** that you intend a document to be your will; and in the law of court procedure, *publication* of a legal notice is publishing it in a newspaper.

Publici juris   (Latin) "Of public rights." Common, public property, such as the right to breathe the air.

Publish   1. See **publication**.   2. To try to collect on a forged document (check, dollar bill, etc.).

Puffing   1. Salesmanship by a seller that is mere general bragging about what is sold, rather than definite promises about it or intentionally misleading information.   2. Secret bidding for the seller at an auction to raise the price.

Puis (or puisne)   Lower ranking or **junior.**

Punitive damages   Money awarded by a court to a person who has been harmed in a particularly **malicious** or **willful** way by another person. This money is not related to the actual cost of the injury or harm suffered. Its purpose is to keep that sort of act from happening again by serving as a warning. It is also called "exemplary damages."

Pur autre vie   See **autre** vie.

Purchase   1. Buy.   2. According to the **Uniform Commercial Code,** *purchase* includes "any voluntary transaction creating an interest in property, including a gift."

Purchase money mortgage   A buyer financing part of a purchase by giving a **mortgage** on the property to the seller as **security** for the loan.

Purchase money resulting trust   When one person puts up money to buy something to be held in another person's name, **title** to that property is held by a *purchase money resulting trust* in favor of the person putting up the money.

Purchase order   A document that authorizes a person or a company to deliver goods or perform services. It promises to pay for them.

Pure plea   1. An **affirmative defense.**   2. A legal **pleading** that requires no further paperwork to be acted upon by a judge.

Pure race statute (or act)   See **recording acts**.

Purge   1. Cleanse, clear, or exonerate from a charge, from guilt, or from a **contract.**   2. In the law of wills, "purge" means to omit the gift to a person named in a will (because that person is prohibited from getting anything) without destroying the rest of the will.

Purport **1.** To imply, profess outwardly, or give the impression (sometimes, a false impression). **2.** The meaning, intent, or purpose of something.

Purpresture Taking something public for private use; for example, fencing in part of a public park as part of your private land.

Pursuant In accordance with; in carrying out. For example, "pursuant to my authority as governor" means "I have the authority to do what I am about to do because I am governor, and that thing is . . . . "

Pursuit of happiness Constitutional rights not specifically mentioned, such as personal freedom, freedom of contract and occupation, domestic rights, etc.

Purview The purpose, scope, and design of a **statute** or other enacted law.

Put An **option** (see that word) to sell a particular **stock** or **commodity** at a certain price for a certain time. The person who buys a *put option* expects prices to fall. If they don't, he or she loses the purchase price of the *put,* but does not have to **exercise** (use) it.

Putative **Alleged,** supposed, or commonly known as. For example, a *putative father* is the alleged father of an "**illegitimate** child."

Pyramid sales scheme A type of sales pitch that promises that once you buy an item, you get paid for each additional buyer you find for the company. It is also known as a "referral sales plan," a "chain referral plan," and a "multilevel distributorship." It is illegal in many forms.

Pyramiding The use of a small amount of money or of "paper profits" to finance buying large amounts of **stock,** to control companies, etc. This is **leverage** plus the additional idea of adding on as you go along.

Q **1.** Quarterly. **2.** Question.

Q.B. Queen's Bench (see **King's Bench**).

Q.V. (Latin) Quod vide; "which see" or "look at." This is a direction to the reader to look in another place in the book (or in another book) for more information. This dictionary uses the phrase "*see that word*" where most lawbooks would say "*Q. V.*"

Qua (Latin) As; considered as; in and of itself. For example, "the *trustee qua trustee* is not **liable**" means that the **trustee** is not liable as a trustee (but might be liable as an individual).

Quae (Latin) Things; those things; things already mentioned; etc.

Quae est eadem (Latin) "Which is the same." Two apparently different things are the same thing.

Quaere A **question**, query, or doubt. When used before a phrase *quaere* means that what follows is an open question. [pronounce: <u>quee</u>-ree]

Qualification **1.** Possessing the personal qualities, property, or other necessary things to be eligible to fill a public office or take on a particular duty. **2. Limitation** or restriction.

Qualified acceptance A *qualified acceptance* is not an **acceptance** at all, but a **counteroffer** (see that word) because an acceptance of a deal must be unqualified and unrestricted.

Qualified endorsement Signing a **negotiable instrument** "without recourse" and limiting your **liability** for payment.

Qualified privilege **1.** The right to say or publish something derogatory about a person if done with no **malice**. See **privilege**. **2.** The right, under certain limited circumstances, to withhold information from the other side in a lawsuit. "Attorney work product" is a *qualified privilege*.

Qualify (or qualified) **1.** See **qualification**. **2.** For *qualified pension*, see **pension plan**.

Quality of estate *When* a person gets property rights, and the *type* of rights (**joint, common,** etc.).

Quando (Latin) When.

Quantum <u>mer</u>uit (Latin) "As much as he deserved." An old form of **pleading** a lawsuit for compensation for work done. The *theory* of fair payment for work done is still used in modern contract law. See also **quasi contract**. [pronounce: <u>quan</u>-tum <u>mer</u>-u-it]

Quantum va<u>le</u>bat (Latin) "As much as they were worth." An old form of **pleading** a lawsuit for payment for goods sold and delivered.

Quarantine The legal right of a government to hold and isolate a ship, isolate a person, forbid the transportation of goods, etc., in order to prevent the spread of a disease, of a pest, etc.

Quare (Latin) "Wherefore." For example, *"quare clausum fregit"* (wherefore he broke the close) is an old form of **pleading** a lawsuit for **damages** against someone who **trespasses** on your land. [pronounce: <u>kwa</u>-re]

Quarters of coverage The number of quarters of the year (January–March, April–June, July–Sept., Nov.–Dec.) that a person has made payments into the social security fund. **Benefits** depend on this.

Quash Overthrow; **annul;** completely do away with. (*Quash* usually refers to a court stopping a **subpoena,** an **order,** or an **indictment.**)

Quasi (Latin) "Sort of"; analogous to "as if." [pronounce: kwai-si]

Quasi (or constructive) contract An obligation "sort of like" a **contract** that is created, not by an agreement, but by law. The principle of *quasi contract* is used to bring about a fair result when a person's actions or the relationship between persons makes it clear that one should owe an obligation to the other that is similar to a contract. For example, if a homeowner stands and watches while another person mows the homeowner's lawn, the homeowner may have to pay for the mowing.

Quasi corporation A **joint stock company** (see that word).

Quasi in rem See **in rem.**

Quasi-judicial The case-deciding function of an **administrative agency;** when an agency acts like a court.

Quasi-legislative The rule-making function of an **administrative agency;** when an agency acts like a **legislature.**

Queen's Bench See **King's Bench.**

Query Question (see **quaere**).

Question 1. A subject or matter to be investigated, looked into, debated, etc. 2. A point in dispute in a lawsuit; an issue for decision by judge or jury. 3. For **leading** questions, **hypothetical** questions, questions of **fact** and **law,** etc., see those words.

Questman (or questmonger) In old England a person who started lawsuits or prosecutions, checked weights and measures, and generally investigated public **fraud** and **abuse.**

Qui (Latin) He (or she); he (or she) who. For example, *qui non negat fatetur* ("he who does not deny something admits it").

Qui tam (Latin) "Who as well as." A lawsuit based on an informer's tip. If the government collects a fine or penalty from the lawsuit, the informer gets a share.

Quia timet

Quia timet (Latin) "Because of fears." A request to a court, similar to a request for an **injunction** (see that word).

Quick assets A company's cash, plus its **assets** that are easily turned into cash for immediate use or to meet emergencies. *Quick assets* are **current** assets *minus* **inventory** (see those words.) "Net quick assets" are quick assets *minus* **current** liabilities (what the company owes that comes due soon). The *"quick asset ratio"* (or *"quick ratio"* or *"acid test"*) is quick assets *divided by* current liabilities. These are measures of whether a company can meet unexpected obligations, can take advantage of unexpected opportunities, and has good short-term prospects and even survivability.

Quid pro quo Something for something. The giving of one valuable thing for another. **Consideration** (see that word) that makes a **contract valid.**

Quiet Free from interference or disturbance. For example, an *action to quiet title* is a way of establishing clear ownership of land, and a *covenant for quiet enjoyment* is, among other things, that part of a **deed** that promises that the seller will protect the buyer against claims or lawsuits based on ownership rights.

Quietus A final **discharge** from a debt or obligation.

Quit **1.** Leave and give up possession of a place. **2.** Free or clear of a debt, of a criminal charge, etc.

Quitclaim deed A **deed** that passes on to the buyer all those rights or as much of a **title** as a seller actually has. A *quitclaim deed* does not **warrant** (promise) that the seller actually has full title to the land to pass on.

Quo animo (Latin) "With what intention or motive" (see **animo** for examples).

Quo warranto (Latin) "With what authority." A proceeding in which a court questions the right of a person (usually a public official) to take a certain action or to hold a certain office. This is a **writ.**

Quod (Latin) **1.** That which; that. **2.** For *quod vide,* see **Q.V.**

Quorum The number of persons who must be present to make the votes and other actions of a group (such as a **board**) valid. This number is often a majority (over half) of the whole group, but is sometimes much less or much more.

Quota **1.** An assigned goal, such as a certain minimum amount of sales a salesperson must make. **2.** A limit, such as the maximum number of cars that may be imported from a particular country. **3.** A proportional share of a **liability.**

Quotation (or quote) The selling or asking price of a **stock**, other **security**, or **commodity. Brokers** exchange *quotes.*

Quotient verdict A **jury's** deciding the amount of **damages** to **award** by each **juror's** writing down a dollar amount, then adding them all up, and dividing by the number of jurors. This is permitted to help discussion, but not as a way of computing an amount for a final decision.

R **Registered**, as in registered **trademark®**.

R.A.R. Revenue agent's report. An **I.R.S.** document explaining changes in tax owed resulting from an **audit.**

R.E.A. Rural Electrification Administration.

R.E.I.T. **Real estate investment trust** (see that word).

R.E.S.P.A. Real Estate Settlement Procedures Act. A federal law concerning **disclosure** of **settlement** (**closing**) costs in real estate sales financed by federally insured lenders.

R.F.P. Request for proposals. A government notice soliciting applicants to perform a contract or receive a grant.

R.I.F. Reduction in force. A **layoff** done by eliminating the job itself. See also **bumping.**

R.I.L. **Res ipsa loquitur** (see that word).

R.O.I. Return on investment.

R.O.R. Release on own **recognizance** (see that word).

R.S. Revised **statutes.**

Race statute (or race-notice statute or race recording act, etc.) See **recording acts.**

Racketeering **Extortion** by organized crime (usually threats of violence against a person or business to stop competition or to extract "protection money" or illegal interest on loans) or the large-scale, organized conduct of illegal gambling, narcotics traffic, prostitution, etc.

Rack-rent Exorbitantly high rent.

Raid

Raid One company's attempt to take over another company by buying its **stock** to gain control of its **board** of directors. This is often accomplished by a **tender** offer. The takeover is more often called a *raid* when the raiders want something the company *has* (such as **retained earnings** or a salable **asset**) rather than wanting the company's ongoing business.

Railroad Force a **bill** quickly through a **legislature** over the objections of some of its members.

Railway Labor Act A federal law that set up a procedure for handling labor disputes between railroad companies and their employees.

Raise **1.** To *raise funds* is to solicit or collect money. **2.** To *raise an issue* is to make it a subject of discussion or for decision in a lawsuit. **3.** To *raise a* **presumption** is to say or do something that creates an **inference** that something happened or something is true. **4.** To *raise a check* is to alter it fraudulently so that the amount paid on it is higher.

Raising portions An old word from the time when the oldest son inherited all land. It meant that the oldest son gave money to the other children.

Rake-off An illegal bribe, payoff, or skimming of the profits of a business.

Range **1.** A six-mile-wide row of **townships** running North-South within a state on government maps. See also **tier**. **2.** A large, open grazing area, whether public or private.

Ransom **1.** Money or property paid to free a kidnapped person or to free persons or property captured during war. **2.** In old English law, money paid to obtain a **pardon** for a major crime.

Rap sheet A police document listing a person's **arrest** and **conviction** record. Other law enforcement agencies also use *rap sheets*.

Rape The crime of a man imposing sexual intercourse by force or otherwise without legally valid consent. Also, *statutory rape* is the crime of a man having sexual intercourse with a girl under a certain state-set age. The definition of what precise acts constitute rape (and whether or not a man can be raped or a woman can rape) differs from state to state.

Rapine An old word for taking a person's property by force.

Rasure **1.** Scraping a paper to remove letters or words. **2.** Any obliteration of a document, including erasure, lining over, etc.

348

Ratable **1.** Proportional; adjusted by some formula or percentage. **2.** A proportional, but unequal division. **3.** Capable of being evaluated. **4.** Taxable.

Rate **1.** An amount fixed by mathematical formulas or adjusted according to some standard; for example, an **interest** rate. **2.** A charge that is the same to all persons for the same service; for example, a shipping rate. **3.** A classification by quality; for example, a "first-rate" **insurance risk**. **4.** For **discount** rate, **prime** rate, etc., see those words.

Rate base The property value (or investment amount) upon which a **public utility's** profit is calculated.

Rate fixing The power of some **administrative agencies** (such as state power commissions) to set the charges a company may get for its services. This is *not* the same as **price fixing,** which is done by sellers of goods or services and may be illegal.

Rate of return Profit as a percentage of money or property value invested.

Ratification Confirmation of a previous act done by you or by another person. For example, when the president signs a **treaty,** the Senate must *ratify* it (make it valid from the moment it was signed). Also, if a child makes a **contract,** it is probably not enforceable, but if the child *ratifies* it after becoming an adult, it becomes a binding contract.

Ratio decidendi (Latin) The central core of a judge's **decision.** The basic point that a judge uses to decide a case. [pronounce: ra-shi-o des-i-den-di]

Ratio legis (Latin) **1.** The reason or purpose for passing a law; the problem or situation that makes a law necessary. **2.** The basic reasoning or principle behind a law; the legal *theory* on which it is based.

Rational basis (or purpose) test A court should not second-guess a **legislature** (or an **administrative agency**) about the wisdom of a law (or of an administrative decision) if the law (or decision) has some *rational basis.*

Ravishment **1.** **Rape** (see that word). **2.** An old word for unlawfully taking away a person who is in the care of another.

Re (Latin) "Concerning"; see "**in re.**"

Reacquired stock **Treasury stock** (see that word).

Readjustment A **reorganization** of a company in financial trouble that is done voluntarily by the owners without court or other intervention.

Reaffirmation

Reaffirmation   Agreeing to pay a prior, possibly now uncollectable debt. Under **bankruptcy** and **contract** law, if you *reaffirm* a debt (with court approval in the case of bankruptcy), you are again **liable** for it.

Real   **1.** Having to do with land and things permanently attached to the land, such as buildings.   **2.** Having to do with a thing, rather than with a person. For example, a *real defense* is a defense based on the validity of a document, rather than on the circumstances surrounding it. Real defenses include **forgery,** the fact that the person signing was a **minor, alteration** of the document, etc.

Real estate   Land, buildings, and things permanently attached to land and buildings. Also called realty and *real property.*

Real estate investment trust   An arrangement in which investors buy shares in a **trust** that invests in **real estate.** To qualify for special **income tax** benefits, a *R.E.I.T.* must meet certain requirements, such as being unincorporated, having fewer than a certain number of investors, and gaining most of its income from real estate and related financial ventures.

Real Estate Settlement Procedures Act   See **R.E.S.P.A.**

Real evidence   Objects seen by the jury; for example, wounds, fingerprints, weapons used in a crime, etc. It is a type of **demonstrative evidence.**

Real party in interest   **1.** Someone who has a legal right to bring a lawsuit, whether or not the person is the one who will ultimately benefit from winning.   **2.** The person who will ultimately benefit from winning a lawsuit, whether or not that person brought it initially.

Realized   Actual; cashed in. For example, a *realized profit* is a cash-in-hand gain as opposed to a *paper profit,* which is the increase in value of property (such as a **stock**) that might be lost again if the value goes down; and a *realized gain or loss* is the difference between the **net** sale price of something and its net cost (or, in tax terms, its **adjusted basis**). Income or loss is *realized* when a "taxable event" takes place, typically a sale or exchange of property. *"Realization"* means "now is the time to see whether income or loss will have tax consequences." **Recognition** (see that word) means "the income or loss *does* have tax consequences now." In most cases, *realization* and *recognition* are the same.

Realtor A *real estate agent* (see **real estate** and **agent**) who belongs to the National Association of Realtors.

Realty **Real estate** (see that word).

Reapportionment Changing the boundaries of **legislative districts** to reflect changes in population and ensure that each person's vote for **representatives** carries equal weight. See also **gerrymander.**

Reasonable A broad, flexible word used to make sure that a decision is based on the *facts* of a particular situation, rather than on abstract legal principles. It has no exact definition, but can mean "fair," "appropriate," "moderate," "rational," etc. When reading the following examples, remember that the definitions tend to be circular and depend on the actual situation, not on the precise words used. For example, *reasonable care* has been defined as "that degree of care a person of ordinary prudence (the so-called *reasonable person*) would exercise in similar circumstances"; and *reasonable doubt* "is not mere conjecture, but doubt that would cause prudent persons to hesitate before acting in matters important to themselves."

Reasonable inference rule A **jury** may draw all reasonable inferences from **evidence,** even if the conclusions drawn are not necessary.

Reasonable person (or man) doctrine See **reasonable** (*reasonable care*) and see **foreseeability.**

Reassessment The government's reestimating of the value of property and changing the official value it gives to that property for tax purposes.

Rebate A discount, deduction, or refund.

Rebellion Organized, armed resistance to the government. If it succeeds, it may become a **revolution.**

Rebus sic stantibus (Latin) "At this state of affairs." A doctrine in **international law** that if conditions change greatly after making a **treaty** or other agreement, the treaty will have no more effect.

Rebut Dispute, defeat, or take away the effect of facts or arguments. *Rebuttal* is contradicting statements made by an adversary.

Rebuttable Disputable. For example, a *rebuttable presumption* is a conclusion that will be drawn unless **evidence** is presented that counters it.

Rebutter

Re<u>but</u>ter   A *common-law* **pleading**, the third by the **defendant**.

Re<u>call</u>   **1.** Remove an elected official from office by a vote of the people.   **2.** Take away a diplomat's job and bring him or her back from a foreign country.   **3.** Notify car (or other product) owners of a safety defect and offer to fix it.   **4. Revoke,** cancel or **vacate** a **judgment** because facts originally relied upon to grant it are found to be wrong.

Recaption   Taking something back that has been taken away.

Recapitalization   Readjusting the types, amount, values and priorities of a **corporation's stocks** and **bonds.**

Recapture   **1.** The **I.R.S.** requirement that a person pay taxes on profits created by some prior **deductions** or **credits,** such as the *investment tax credit.* For example, when *accelerated* **depreciation** is taken on some types of property that is later sold at no loss, the I.R.S. *recaptures* this depreciation by then treating it as **taxable income.**   **2.** A **contract** provision that limits profits or provides for the recovery of goods in special situations.   **3.** A **lease** provision giving the landlord a percentage of profits and allowing the landlord to end the lease if profits are not high enough.

Receipt   **1.** Written acknowledgment that something has been received or put into your hands.   **2.** The act of getting or receiving.

Receipts   Money that comes into a business (usually through sales).

Receivables   See **accounts receivable.**

Receive evidence   See **admission** of evidence.

Receiver   **1.** An outside person appointed by the court to manage money and property during a lawsuit.   **2.** A person who gets stolen goods.

Receivership   A court putting money or property into the management of a **receiver** (see that word) in order to preserve it for the persons ultimately entitled to it. This is often done when the **creditors** of a business suspect **fraud** or **gross** mismanagement and ask the court to step in and watch over the business to protect them.

Receiving stolen goods   The criminal offense of possessing any property known to be stolen.

Recent theft rule   If a person is found with recently stolen property, there is a **presumption** that he or she is the thief.

Recess   **1.** A brief break taken by a court, usually lasting an hour or two at most.   **2.** A break in a **legislative** session, sometimes lasting many weeks.

Recidivist   **1.** A repeat **criminal** offender.   **2.** A **habitual** criminal.

Reciprocal   Mutual; bilateral (two-sided or two-way). For example, *reciprocal wills* are **wills** made by two persons, and enforceable against each other because each person put something in his or her will that the other asked for; *reciprocal sales* involve buying from customers on terms better than others get (or favoring customers by buying goods from the customer), in possible violation of **antitrust** laws; and *reciprocal trade agreements* are agreements between countries to lower **import** taxes on goods traded between the countries.

Reciprocal Enforcement of Support Act   A law, adopted in most states, that allows a spouse (or parent of a child) in one state to enforce **support** obligations on the other spouse (or parent) in another state.

Reciprocity   **1.** Two states (or countries) giving identical privileges to the citizens of the other state.   **2.** See **reciprocal.**

Recision   See **rescission.**

Recital   **1.** A formal statement in a document that explains the reasons for the document or for the transaction involving the document.   **2.** Any formal listing of specific facts.

Reckless   "*Reckless*" can mean anything from "careless and inattentive" or "indifferent to consequences" to a "willful disregard for danger to the life or safety of others."

Reclamation Act   A federal law setting up a system of water storage and diversion projects in Western states, primarily for making dry lands productive.

Recognition   **1.** In most cases, when a taxpayer has received some financial gain, it is *recognized*. This means that it must be reported on tax forms, and tax must be paid on it. Some gains, however, are *nonrecognized*. This means that paying taxes on them may be put off to a later year. One example of possible "nonrecognition" of a gain comes when you sell a house at a profit, but within two years buy another equally or more expensive one in which to live. See also **realized** for a more complete understanding of *recognition*.   **2.** Acknowledgment that something done by another person in your name was authorized by you.   **3.** *Recognition picketing* is **picketing** to force an employer to **bargain** with a particular **union**. This is usually not permitted.

Recognizance   A formal obligation to do a certain act that is recorded in court. For example, a person accused of a crime may be allowed to go free before trial without putting up a **bail bond.** The person gives the court a formal written statement that failure to show up will mean payment to the court of a certain amount of money. This is called getting out on your *own recognizance.*

Recollection   The act of remembering. This may be done by a **witness** who *refreshes the memory* by using an object or a document. This is called *"present memory refreshed"* or *"present recollection revived."* For example, the witness might look at a document to remember what it was about, then put it down and **testify** about events mentioned in the document. If the witness still cannot remember clearly, the document might then be **introduced** into **evidence** and the witness might then read from it and testify as to its authenticity and accuracy. This is called *"past recollection recorded"* or *"recorded past recollection."* It is an exception to the **hearsay** rule.

Reconciliation   **1.** The renewal of a broken relationship with forgiveness on both sides. See also **condonation.**   **2.** Bringing two differing **accounts** into agreement; for example, adjusting the **balance** in a checking account to agree with the bank's monthly **statement.**

Reconstruction   The process of making changes in the governments of the Southern states in order to bring them back into the United States after the Civil War.

Recontinuance   An old word for a person's getting inherited rights that had been wrongfully taken away.

Reconveyance   The return of **title** to property; for example, the return of title papers to a house when the **mortgage** is paid off.

Record   **1.** A formal, written account of a case, containing the complete formal history of all actions taken, papers filed, **rulings** made, **opinions** written, etc. The *record* also can include all the actual **evidence (testimony**, physical objects, etc.) as well as the evidence that was *refused* **admission** by the judge. A *court of record* includes all courts except for the lowest level courts in which no permanent records of proceedings are kept.   **2.** A *public record* is a document filed with, or put out by, a government agency and open to the public for inspection. For example, a *title of record* to land is an ownership interest that has been properly filed in the public land records. The official who keeps these records is usually called the *recorder of deeds,* and the filing process is called *recordation.* **3.** A **corporation's re-** cords include its **charter, bylaws,** and **minutes** of meetings. The *record date* for payment of a company's **stock dividends** or for voting is the date on which stockholders must be **registered** on the company's books to vote or to receive dividends.

Recording acts State laws establishing rules for **priority** among persons who claim the same **interests** in **real estate** (and, some- times other property). These laws have many different forms and time limits in different states, but the three basic types are: **1.** *Race statutes.* In a state with a "race statute," a person who first **records** (files) a claim (such as a **deed**) has the legal right to that claim. For example, if Tom sells a house to Dick, then sells it again to Harry, then Harry files the deed, Harry's deed will probably be good against Dick because he won the "race." **2.** *Notice statutes.* In these states, the person with a *later* valid claim (whether or not recorded) has priority over an earlier unrecorded claim unless the later person *knew* about the earlier claim. For example, if Tom sells to Dick (who does not record the deed), then sells again to Harry, Harry's deed will probably be good against Dick *even if* Dick then records the deed and Harry doesn't, *unless* Harry knew about the prior sale. **3.** *Race-notice statutes.* In these states, the first person to record without knowledge of a prior unrecorded claim wins. For example, if Tom sells to Dick (who does not record), then sells to Harry, who then records without knowing about Dick's claim, Harry wins.

Recorded past recollection See **recollection.**

Recoupment **1.** Keeping or holding something back that you owe because there is a fair, just reason to do so. **2.** Taking or getting something back (especially money lost). **3.** A **counter- claim** (see that word).

Recourse **1.** The right of a person who holds a **negotiable instru- ment** (see that word) to get payment on it from anyone who en- dorsed (signed) it if the person who made it out in the first place fails to pay up (unless the signer signs it "no recourse" or "with- out recourse." **2.** The means of enforcing a **right.**

Recovery **1.** The thing received when a lawsuit is decided in your favor. **2.** The amount of money given by a **judgment** in a successful lawsuit.

Recross examination See **examination.**

Rectum (Latin) **1.** A right. **2.** A trial or accusation.

Recuperatio (Latin) Recovery by court action of something kept from you.

Recusation The process by which a judge is disqualified (or disqualifies himself or herself) from hearing a lawsuit because of **interest** or **prejudice.**

Red herring An advance copy of a **prospectus** that must be filed with the **S.E.C.** before a company sells **stocks** or **bonds.** It is "for information only" and marked in red for identification.

Reddendum A **clause** in a **deed** that keeps some right of **reversion.**

Reddition An old word for giving something back or being told by a court that something should be given back.

Redeem **1.** Buy back. Reclaim property that has been **mortgaged** or **pledged.** **2.** Turn in for cash.

Redeemable bond **1.** A **callable** bond (one that can be called in by the company and paid off at any time before **maturity**). **2.** Any bond that *has* a maturity date (as opposed to a **consol**).

Redemption Repurchase or turn in for cash (see **redeem**). A *redemption period* is the time during which a **mortgage** or similar debt that has gone into **default** can be paid off without losing the property. Some states have **mandatory** redemption periods for home mortgages.

Redhibition An old word for getting out of a deal because of a serious defect in the thing sold.

Redirect examination See **examination.**

Rediscount rate The rate at which a *federal reserve bank* can make loans to *member banks* on **commercial paper** (**bills, notes,** etc.) already discounted (resold) by those banks. See also **discount rate.**

Redlining A bank or **mortgage** company's refusal to make loans in a particular neighborhood solely because of deteriorating conditions. This practice violates federal laws and is often a "cover" for racial discrimination.

Redraft **1.** A second **note** or **bill** offered for payment after the first has been refused payment. It includes the costs of delayed payment and collection in addition to the original amount. **2.** A second writing (of a **legislative** bill, etc.).

Redress   1. Satisfaction or payment for harm done.   2. Access to the courts to get no. 1.

Reductio ad absurdum   (Latin) "Reduce to the absurd." Disproving an argument by showing that it leads to a ridiculous conclusion.

Reduction   Turning something abstract into something concrete. For example, *reduction to possession* is turning a right to something (such as a debt) into the thing itself (getting payment), and *reduction to practice* is turning an idea for a device or process into a useful device or process or filing a **patent** application on it. This often includes a demonstration of workability by a working model. See also **conception**.

Redundancy   Unnecessarily repetitive, superfluous, or irrelevant matter in a **pleading** (see that word).

Reenactment rule   If a **legislature** *reenacts* a law (to prevent it from expiring or to make minor changes), it automatically **adopts** any long-standing interpretation of the law made by the courts or the **executive** branch.

Reentry   Taking back possession of land by a right you kept when you left the land before.

Reexchange   The expenses caused by the refusal to pay a bill of **exchange** in a foreign country.

Refer   1. Point to; direct attention to.   2. A judge's action of turning a case or part of a case over to a person who has been appointed to sort things out by taking **testimony**, examining documents, and making decisions and recommendations. This person is often called a "referee" or "*special master.*"

Referee in bankruptcy   An old word for a federal judge who runs **bankruptcy** hearings.

Reference   1. An agreement in a **contract** to submit certain disputes to an **arbitrator** for decision. This may be an *arbitration clause*.   2. The act of sending a case to a referee for a decision (see **refer**).   3. A person who will provide information for you about your character, credit, etc.   4. Mention in a book or document of another place to find information on a subject or of the place from which the information used was taken. See also **citation**.   5. See **incorporation by reference**.

Referendum   Putting an important law to a direct vote of the people rather than passing it through the **legislature** (or in addition to passing it through the legislature).

Referral plan

Referral plan (or referral sales scheme) **Pyramid sales scheme** (see that word).

Refinance Pay off a debt with money from a new debt.

Reformation A procedure in which a court will rewrite, correct, or "reform" a written agreement to conform with the original intent of the persons making the deal. The court will do this only if there was **fraud** or mutual mistake in writing up the original document.

Reformatory A prison for **youthful offenders**.

Refunding Refinancing a debt.

Reg. **1.** **Regulation.** **2.** **Registered.**

Regalia (Latin) A king or queen's royal rights.

Regent **1.** A person who governs a kingdom while the king or queen is too young, disabled, or away for a long time. **2.** The name for the heads of some public institutions such as the *Board of Regents* of a state university system.

Register **1.** A book of public facts, such as births, deaths and marriages (also called a "registry"). **2.** The public official who keeps the book mentioned in no. 1. **3.** To place information into the book in no. 1. **4.** Other examples of public record books are the *register of patents* (a list of all patents granted) and the *register of ships* (kept by **customs**). **5.** Other examples of public record keeping officials are the *register of deeds* (land records) and the *register of wills* (**clerk** of **probate** court). They are often called "Recorder" or "Registrar." **6.** A chronological list; for example, of checks written.

Registered Listed on an official record. For example, a *registered stock* can only be cashed in by the person who is listed as the owner, and each time ownership changes that fact must be registered. A *registered bond* might have the **bond** or only the interest payments registered this way. A *registered check* is a check sold by a bank but not **certified**. And a *registered representative* is a person approved by the government to sell **securities**.

Registrar **1.** See **register** definition no. 5. **2.** A **transfer agent** (see that word).

Registration **1.** Recording (see **record**). **2.** Making up a list. **3.** Putting yourself on a list of eligible voters. **4.** A *registration statement* is a financial and ownership **statement**, including a **prospectus** and other documents, required by the **S.E.C.**

of most companies that want to sell **stock** or other **securities** and of all companies that want their securities traded in **markets** such as the New York Stock Exchange. Some stocks sold to small numbers of persons may meet the lesser requirements of the S.E.C.'s *"Regulation A."*

Registry   See **register** definition no. 1.

Regnal years   **Statutes** in England are usually dated by the name of the king or queen on the throne at the time and the year of their reign.

Regressive tax   Opposite of **progressive tax** (see that word).

Regs.   Abbreviation for **regulations**.

Regular   **1.** Steady; uniform; with no unusual variations. **2.** Lawful; legal; in conformity with usual practice. **3.** *Regular course of business* means books and records kept or sales made normally and in **good faith** (see that word).

Regulate   To control. For example, a government *regulates* businesses that have a big effect on the general public (such as power companies) by writing laws on the subject and setting up government organizations called "regulatory agencies" (or **administrative agencies**) to write rules and **regulations** that explain what (power) companies can and cannot do and how they may operate. The agencies also administer and enforce the rules by giving **orders**, holding **hearings**, etc.

Regulation   A "mini-law." A rule that is put out by a low-level branch of government, such as an **administrative agency**, to **regulate** (see that word) conduct. For example, **I.R.S.** *regulations* are rules about how the tax **code** applies to specific situations, and local governments put out parking *regulations*. Many *regulations* are known by name to insiders in the field. For example, *Regulation A* of the **S.E.C.** exempts some **stocks** from some **registration** requirements, and *Regulation Q* of the Federal Reserve Board limits the interest rate banks can pay on small deposits. See also **"Z."**

Regulatory agency   See **regulate**.

Regulatory offense   **1.** A **statutory** crime. **2.** A minor offense, defined by **regulation** rather than by **statute**.

Rehabilitation   **1.** The restoring of former rights, abilities, authority, credibility, etc. For example, *rehabilitating* a witness means asking questions to restore the witness's believability after the other side has destroyed it or put it in question, and *re-*

habilitating a prisoner means preparing him or her for an honest productive life once released. **2.** See **Chapter Thirteen.**

Reinstate   Place back in a condition that has ended or been lost. For example, to *reinstate* a case is to put it back into court after it has been dismissed (thrown out).

Reinsurance   A **contract** by which one **insurance** company insures itself with another insurance company to protect itself against all or part of the **risk** it took on by insuring a customer.

Rejoinder   A *common-law* **pleading.**

Relation   "Relating back" or having retroactive effect.

Relative fact   **1.** An **evidentiary fact** (see that word).   **2. Circumstantial evidence** (see that word).

Relator   A person in whose name a state brings a legal action (the person who "relates" the facts on which it is based). The name of the case might be *State ex rel* ("on the relation of") *Smith* v. *Jones.* [pronounce: re-<u>late</u>-or]

Relaxatio   (Latin) A **release** (see that word).

Release   **1.** The giving up or relinquishing of a claim or a right, by the person who has it to the person against whom it might have been enforced.   **2.** The piece of paper in no. 1. For example, most persons demand a *release* in exchange for paying money to settle an accident claim.

Release on own recognizance   See **recognizance.**

Relevancy   Applicability to an issue in a lawsuit (see **relevant**).

Relevant   Having an impact on a question or issue; having to do with a disputed issue in a lawsuit. **Evidence** is *relevant* if it tends to prove or disprove a theory or position (by one side in a lawsuit) that will influence the result of the lawsuit. Evidence must be relevant to be admitted (accepted) by the court.

Relevant market   The geographic area in which a particular type, price, and quality of product is sold.

Reliance   Belief in something, plus acting on that belief. See also **detrimental reliance.**

Relict   An old word for widow or widower.

Reliction   Slow **dereliction** (see that word).

Relief   **1.** The help given by a court to a person who brings a lawsuit. The "relief asked for" might be the return of property taken by another person, the enforcement of a contract, etc.   **2.** Public assistance to poor persons.

Religion   See **freedom of religion** and **establishment clause.**

Rem (Latin) "Thing;" see "**in rem.**"

Remainder **1.** An interest or **estate** in land or **trust** property that takes effect only when another interest in land or trust property ends. For example, if Mary's **will** says "I leave my house to Joe for ten years and then to Jane," Jane's interest is a *remainder.* See also **reversion** for a similar interest that also takes effect when another one ends. **2.** As used in a will, "remainder" may mean "leftovers"; for example, "My house and clothing to Joe and the remainder to Jane."

Remainderman A person who gets **trust** property after the trust is ended. Another name for this person is *"ultimate beneficiary."*

Remand To send back. For example, a higher court may *remand* a case to a lower court for the lower court to take some action ordered by the higher. Also, a prisoner is *remanded* if he or she is sent back to jail after a day in court.

Remargining See **margin call**.

Remedial statute **1.** A law that is passed to correct a defect in a prior law. **2.** A law passed to provide a **remedy** (for example, creating a new **lien**) where none previously existed.

Remedy **1.** The way a right is enforced or satisfaction for a harm done is received. The means by which a violation of rights is prevented, redressed, or compensated. For example, Ron's *remedy* against Don if Don refuses to give back Ron's book might be to take it back, to argue with Don until he gives it back, or to go to court to either get it back or make Don pay for it. **2.** Lawyers often mean "legal remedy" or "court remedy" when they say "remedy." In this sense, it might mean an **injunction**, **damages**, etc.

Remise **Release,** give up, or forgive.

Remission **1.** **Release** (ending or forgiving) of a debt. **2.** Forgiving an offense, injury, or harm done. See also **condonation**.

Remit **1.** Send; send in or send back. **2.** Give up or pay.

Remittance Money (or a check, etc.) sent by one person to another, often as payment for a debt owed.

Remitter Being "sent back" to an earlier, better right. For example, if a person who owns property and **leases** it to another is left the lease rights in the renter's **will**, the owner gets full original rights to the property.

Remittitur **1.** The power of a trial judge to decrease the amount of money awarded by a **jury** to a **plaintiff**. **2.** The power of an appeals court to deny a new trial to the **defendant** if the plaintiff agrees to take a certain amount of money less than that given in the trial. See also **additur**. **3.** *Remittitur of record* is the return of a case from appeals court to trial court for the trial court to carry out the higher court's decision.

Remonstrance   A formal protest against government policy or actions.

Removal   The movement of a person or thing from one place to another. For example, *"removal* from the state" means absence from the state long enough to be a change of residence, and "removal of a case" is the transfer of a case from one court to another (most commonly, from a state to a federal court).

Render   **1. Pronounce,** state, or declare. For example, a judge *renders judgment* by giving a decision in a case in court. **2.** Give up or return. For example, *rendition* is the duty of one state to return a **fugitive from justice** (see that word) to the state seeking the return.   **3.** Pay or perform.

Renegotiation board   A federal agency that **negotiates** with **contractors** on federal projects to lower payments when it decides that costs to the government have been unfairly high or excessive. It is not a permanent agency.

Renewal   Keeping an agreement alive by a fresh agreement.

Renounce   Reject, cast off, or give up openly and in public.

Rent strike   An organized **tenant** refusal to pay rent in order to force the **landlord** to do something.

Renunciation   **Abandonment** of a right; giving up a right without transferring it to anyone else or dedicating it to public use.

Renvoi   A legal rule by which a court uses a foreign country's rules to choose which laws should apply to a case, and the foreign rules say that the law where the *court is* should apply. *Renvoi* is also used in choosing which state's law to apply. See also **whole law**. [pronounce: ron-<u>vwa</u>]

Reorganization   **1.** See **Chapter Eleven** for a *reorganization* in **bankruptcy**.   **2.** Any restructuring of a large organization.

Rep.   **Reporter** or **reports**.

Repair   **1.** Fix a defect. *Repairs* and **improvements** are treated differently for tax purposes. A *business* repair can be taken as an immediate **deduction**, while a *home* repair has no tax benefits unless made soon before sale of the home, when it can be added to the tax **basis** of the house. Both business and home *improvements* can be added to the property's basis.   **2.** Repair and *reconstruction* (making something new) of *patented* objects are treated differently under **patent** laws. Reconstruction may be an **infringement**.

Reparable injury   A wrong that can be compensated by money.

Reparation   Payment for an injury; redress for a wrong done.

Repeal   The complete wiping out of an earlier **statute** by a later one.

Repetition   Trying to get back a payment made by mistake.

Replacement cost   The cost of buying something that does the job of something lost; for example, to build a house comparable to one that burns down. Compare this with **reproduction cost** (see that word).

Repleader   **Motion** for a new trial.

Replevin   A legal action to get back personal **property** in the hands of another person.

Replevy   To give back personal **property** to a person who has brought a lawsuit for **replevin** of the goods.

Replication   An old form of **pleading** similar to the modern **reply** (**plaintiff's** response to a **defendant's** first pleading).

Reply   In federal **pleading**, the *reply* is the **plaintiff's** response to the **defendant's answer** or **counterclaim**. The usual order is: complaint, answer, reply. The reply denies some or all of the facts in the answer. Sometimes, it adds new facts, but only to counter facts in the answer.

Repo.   **1.** A "repurchase agreement" in which a **dealer** agrees to buy back a **security** at a set time and price.   **2. Repossession**.

Report   An official or formal statement of facts or proceedings.

Reporter   **1.** Published volumes of decisions by a court or group of courts.   **2.** A person who compiles **reports**.   **3.** The *court reporter* is the person who records court proceedings in court and later makes good copies of some of them.   **4.** A **loose-leaf** book on current developments in an area of law, such as the Poverty Law Reporter.

Reports   Published volumes of case decisions by a particular court or group of courts.

Repossession   Taking back something sold because payments have not been made.

Represent   **1.** To say or to state certain facts.   **2.** To act for, do business for, or "stand in" for another person. See also **agent**.   **3.** To act as another person's lawyer.

Representation

Representation   **1.** See **represent**.   **2.** In the law of **contracts**, a *representation* is any statement (or any attempt to give an impression about a state of facts) that was done to convince the other person to make a contract.   **3.** In the law of **inheritance**, *taking by representation* is the same as taking **per stirpes** (see that word).

Representative   **1.** A person who **represents** (see that word) another.   **2.** A public official elected to the lower **house** of a **legislature**.

Representative action   **1.** A lawsuit brought by one stockholder in a **corporation** to claim rights or to fix wrongs done to many or all stockholders in the company. It is also called a **derivative action**.   **2.** Any **class action**.

Reprieve   Holding off on enforcing a criminal **sentence** for a period of time after the sentence has been handed down.

Reproduction cost   The cost of replacing a lost or destroyed item with an *exact* duplicate. See also **replacement cost**.

Republic   A country with a government by elected officials and, in theory, with ultimate power in the hands of the citizens.

Republication   Renewing the validity of a **will** that has been revoked.

Repudiation   Rejection or refusal. For example, *repudiation of a* **contract** is the refusal to go through with it, usually with a legal right to do so.

Repugnancy   **1.** Inconsistency. A condition which occurs if one part of a document is true (or correct), so that another part cannot be true (or correct).   **2.** The *repugnancy doctrine* is the principle that if two parts of a document contradict each other, the first clear one will be given effect.

Reputation   What people in a community think about a person.

Request for admission   One side in a lawsuit may give a list of facts to the other and request that they be admitted or denied. Those admitted need not be proved at the trial.

Request for instructions   Either side in a lawsuit may give the judge a written list of **instructions** about the law that it would like the judge to give to the jury.

Requirements contract   A **contract** for the supply of goods in which the exact amount of goods to be bought is not set, but will be what the buyer needs for the life of the contract (so long as the needs are real, reasonable, and the buyer's total needs for that type of goods).

Requisition   **1.** A demand or a request for something to which you have a right; for example, one state governor asking another to hand over a **fugitive from justice** (see that word, and see **extradition**), or the taking of private property by the government during an emergency.   **2.** A routine written request for supplies or services, made from one department of an organization to another.

Requisitory letters   **Rogatory letters** (see that word).

Res   (Latin)   **1.** A thing; an object; things; a status.   **2.** The subject matter or contents of a **will** or **trust**.

Res adjudicata   **Res judicata** (see that word).

Res controversa   (Latin) "A thing in controversy." The opposite of **res judicata**.

Res derelicta   (Latin) Abandoned property.

Res fungibiles   (Latin) **Fungible** goods.

Res gestae   (Latin) "Things done"; the entire event or transaction. Everything said and done as part of a single incident or deal. Statements that are part of an occurrence that has already been shown to have existed are *res gestae*. This means that they can usually be admitted in **evidence**, despite the fact that out-of-court statements cannot usually be used as evidence because they are **hearsay**.

Res immobiles   (Latin) Immovable things such as land and buildings.

Res integra   (Latin) "A whole thing." An undecided point of law. A legal question without **precedent**, and probably without any prior discussion.

Res ipsa loquitur   (Latin) "The thing speaks for itself." A **rebuttable presumption** (a conclusion that can be changed if contrary **evidence** is **introduced**) that a person is **negligent** if the thing causing an accident was in his or her control only, and if that type of accident does not usually happen without negligence. It is often abbreviated "res ipsa" or "R.I.L." [pronounce: rez ip-sa lock-we-tur]

Res judicata   (Latin) "A thing decided"; "a matter decided by **judgment**." If a court decides a case, the subject of that case is firmly and finally decided between the persons involved in the suit, so no new lawsuit on the same subject may be brought by the persons involved. See also **collateral estoppel** and **double jeopardy**.

Res publicae

Res publicae (Latin) "Public things"; things belonging to the public.

Resale price maintenance See **fair trade** laws.

Resale rights The right of a seller to resell (usually perishable) goods if the buyer does not pay or does not claim them in time.

Rescind To take back, "unmake," or **annul**. To cancel a **contract** and wipe it out "from the beginning" as if it had never been.

Rescission **1.** The "unmaking" of a **contract** (see **rescind**). **2.** The president's request to Congress that certain money already appropriated not be spent.

Rescript **1.** A judge's short note to a clerk explaining how to dispose of a case. **2.** An **appeals** court's short, usually unsigned, written **decision** in a case that is sent down to the trial court.

Rescue **1.** The *rescue doctrine* is that if one person negligently puts a second person in danger, and a third person is hurt while attempting a rescue, the third person can collect **damages** from the first person and cannot be charged with **contributory negligence** unless he or she acted recklessly. See also **emergency doctrine** and **Good Samaritan doctrine**. **2.** An older meaning of "rescue" is the forcible and unlawful freeing of a prisoner or taking back of goods that have been lawfully taken away.

Reservation **1.** See **reserve**. **2.** Land owned by an American Indian nation as a whole for the use of its people.

Reserve **1.** Hold back a thing or a right. For example, a **deed** to land can *reserve* the right to cross the land for the person selling it, and to *reserve* **title** is to keep an ownership right as **security** that the thing will be fully paid for. Also, a judge may *reserve* **decision** of a legal question in a case by putting it off until the end of the trial. **2.** *With reserve* in an auction means that the thing will not be sold if the highest **bid** is not high enough, and *without reserve* means that the thing will be sold at whatever is the highest price bid. **3.** A fund of money set aside to meet future needs, losses or claims (such as a **sinking fund** *reserve* to repay long-term debt or a **bad debt** *reserve* to cover losses). **4.** A *reserve bank* is a member of the *Federal Reserve System* and the *Reserve Board* is the Federal Reserve *Board of Governors*. **5.** A *reserve clause* in an athlete's **contract** puts restrictions on his or her right to change teams. **6.** The *primary reserve ratio* in banking is a comparison between the cash a bank has in its vault plus what it has with the *Federal Reserve Banks* and the amount of its **demand** deposits (money that could be withdrawn by depositors at any time). The *secondary ratio* is a comparison between government **securities** held by a bank and its demand deposits. **7.** *Reserved powers* are those that the Constitution leaves to the states, rather than to the federal government.

Resettlement   A judge's reopening of an **order** or **decree** to include something accidentally left out.

Residence   A place where a person lives all or part of the time. Sometimes this is the same as **domicile.** *Residency requirements* are state laws on how long a person must live in a state to get a **divorce, welfare, admission** to the bar, etc.

Resident agent   A person living in a state who is **authorized** by a **corporation** to accept **service** of **process** against that company.

Resident alien   A foreigner who lives in or moves to a country intending to become a **citizen.**

Residential cluster   A piece of land developed as a unit with open common land and grouped housing.

Residual   1. Residuary.   2. A payment to a writer, actor, etc., for re-use of a t.v. movie, etc.

Residuary   The part left over. For example, a *residuary clause* in a will disposes of all items not specifically given away (the "leftovers").

Residuum   (Latin) Leftovers.

Resisting an officer   The criminal act of attempting to stop or hinder a police officer from performing a duty such as making an **arrest,** serving a **writ,** or keeping the peace. This may be a crime whether or not force is used.

Resolution   A formal expression of the opinion of an organized group (such as a club, a professional organization, a **legislature,** a public assembly, etc.). In the case of a *congressional resolution*, a *concurrent resolution* is passed by one **house,** agreed to by the other, and expresses the "sense of Congress" on a subject though it does not become a law. A *joint resolution* is passed by both houses of Congress and, in general, is the same as a **bill** that has been passed by both houses.

Resolve   1. A **resolution** (see that word).   **2.** A mind that is made up; a decision to do something; a strong will to achieve a goal.

Resort   A *court of last resort* is a court whose decision cannot be appealed within the same court system.

Respondeat superior   (Latin) "Let the master answer." A legal rule that an employer is responsible for certain (often **negligent**) actions of an employee done in the course of employment. This is a type of **vicarious liability**.

Respondent 1. The person against whom an **appeal** is taken. (This person might have been either the **plaintiff** or the **defendant** in the lower court.) Also called the "**appellee**." 2. The person against whom a **motion** is filed.

Responsible bidder A company competing for public work must be financially sound, honest and competent to do the job bid on. The government may reject a low **bid** if the bidder is not "responsible."

Responsive Answering. A *responsive pleading* is a court paper that directly answers the points raised by the other side's **pleading**. Also, if a **witness** does not answer a question directly, the answer may be objected to as *not responsive*.

Rest To *rest a case* is to stop putting on **evidence** and let the other side do so (with, sometimes, the possibility of putting on more evidence later) or let the decision be made.

Restatement of Law Books put out by the **American Law Institute** that tell what the law in a general area is, how it is changing, and what direction the authors think this change should take; for example, the *Restatement of the Law of Contracts*.

Restitution 1. Giving something back; making good for something. 2. There are various rules for how much "giving back" is full *restitution*. For example, in **contract** law, restitution is usually the amount that puts the **plaintiff** back in the financial position he or she was in before the contract. 3. *Restitution programs* in some states make a convicted **criminal** pay back the crime victim in money or work.

Restrain 1. Prohibit from action; hold back. 2. Hinder or obstruct.

Restraining order A **temporary restraining order** (see that word).

Restraint of marriage A provision in a **will**, gift, or **trust** that prohibits the person getting the gift from marrying. These provisions are rarely enforced by courts.

Restraint of trade An illegal agreement or **combination** that eliminates competition, sets up a **monopoly**, or artificially raises prices. See **anti-trust acts**.

Restrictive covenant A **clause** in a group of **deeds** that forbids all the landowners (and all later owners) from doing certain things with their land; for example, a prohibition on erecting outhouses.

Restrictive indorsement   Signing a **negotiable instrument** (see that word) in a way that ends its negotiability; for example, "Pay to Robert Smith only."

Resulting trust   If Peter gives money to Paul to be held in **trust**, and the trust fails for some legal reason, Paul holds the money in a *resulting trust* for Peter. If Peter buys a house, but puts the **title** in Paul's name, it may be called a *purchase money resulting trust* in favor of Peter.

Retained earnings   A company's yearly **net profit** minus the **dividends** it paid out that year. *Accumulated retained earnings* is that year's retained earnings plus profits left over from prior years. It is a measure of what a company can use for future improvements and expansions as well as to ride out possible bad years. The *retained earnings statement* is a required part of most **corporate annual reports**. See **statement**. Most payments to shareholders made by a company with "*retained earnings and profits*" will be taxed as dividends, no matter what they are called.

Retainer   **1.** The act of a client employing a lawyer.   **2.** The specific agreement in no. 1.   **3.** The first payment in no. 1, either for one specific case or to be available for unspecified future cases.   **4.** Holding something back because you have a right to.

Retaliatory eviction   A landlord's attempt (prohibited in many places) to throw out a tenant for complaining to the health department, forming a tenants' union, etc.

Retaliatory law   A state law "evening up" taxes or restraints placed by other states on businesses from the first state. For example, if Maryland taxes Virginia insurance companies higher than Virginia does, Virginia might raise the tax on Maryland insurance companies.

Retirement   Making the final payment owed on a **bond**, **note**, or other **security** and ending its existence and all obligations under it.

Retorsion   Treating the citizens of a foreign country harshly because that country treats your citizens harshly.

Retraction   Taking something back; for example, taking back something you said and admitting that it was false.

Retraxit   A **plaintiff's** complete and voluntary **abandonment** of a lawsuit. In federal practice, this would be done by a *voluntary dismissal*.

Retreat to the wall See **flee to the wall doctrine**.

Retribution A theory justifying criminal punishment on the basis that society must "get even" with wrongdoers (rather than because wrongdoers must be rehabilitated).

Retro Back; backwards; behind; past. For example, a *retrospective* or *retroactive* law is one that changes the legal status of things already done or that applies to past actions. See also **ex post facto** laws.

Retrocession Giving a person back a **title** to property that the person once held, but no longer holds.

Return **1.** The act of a **sheriff** or other **peace officer** in delivering back to a court a brief account of whether or not (and how) he or she **served** (delivered) a court paper to a person. **2. Yield** or profit. **3.** See **tax return**.

Return day (or date) **1.** The date by which a **sheriff** or other **peace officer** must make a **return** (see that word). **2.** The day by which a **defendant** must **file** a **pleading** after receiving a **summons** to come to court.

Return on equity **1.** The profit a company makes compared to its value; especially the annual profit made compared to the total cost of its **common stock**. See also **statement** and **equity**. **2.** The profit an investor makes on shares of stock or other investments, such as rental housing.

Reus (Latin) **Party**.

Rev. **1.** Review. **2.** Revised.

Revaluation Raising the value of a country's money relative to other countries' money.

Revendication **1.** Demanding that someone return something you sold. **2. Replevin**.

Revenue **1.** Income. **2. Return** on an investment. **3.** Money raising or taxing by the government. For example, *revenue bills* raise tax money, and *revenue bonds* are sold by governments and backed by money-making public projects.

Revenue officer **1.** A tax collector. **2.** A tax investigator, such as a person who hunts for illegal whiskey stills.

Revenue procedures and rulings *Revenue procedures* (Rev. Proc.) are **I.R.S. opinions** on procedural tax matters and *revenue rulings* (Rev. Rul.) are I.R.S. interpretations of the tax law as it applies to specific cases. They are first published in an *Internal Revenue Bulletin* (IRB), then collected in *Cumulative Bulletins* (C.B.). They have slightly less legal "weight" than tax **regulations** and slightly more than *private* **letter rulings**.

Reverse **1.** Set aside. For example, when a higher court *reverses* a lower court on **appeal**, it sets aside the **judgment** of the lower court and either substitutes its own judgment for it or sends the case back to the lower court with instructions on what to do with it. **2.** For *reverse discrimination*, see **affirmative action**. **3.** A *reverse stock split* is a calling in of all **stock**, reducing the number of **shares**, and increasing the value of each share, without changing the total value of all the stock.

Reversion Any **future interest** (see that word) kept by a person who transfers away property. For example, John rents out his land for ten years. His ownership rights during those years, his right to take back the property after ten years, and his **heirs'** right to take back the property after ten years if he dies are *reversionary interests*.

Reverter See **reversion**.

Revised statutes **1.** A **code** (see that word). **2.** A book of **statutes** in the order they were originally passed, with temporary and repealed statutes removed. This is abbreviated Rev. Stat., Rev. St., or R.S.

Revive Bring back to life. Restore to original force or legal effect. For example, if a **contract** has expired, it can be *revived* by acknowledging it and making a new promise to perform it.

Revocation **1.** The taking back of some power or authority. For example, taking back an **offer** before it is accepted ends the other person's power to accept. **2.** The ending or making **void** of a thing. For example, *revocation of a* **will** takes place when, for example, a person tears it up intentionally or makes another will.

Revoke Wipe out the legal effect of something by taking it back, canceling, rescinding, etc. (see **revocation**). If something can be revoked, but has not yet been revoked, it is *revocable*.

Revolution The complete overthrow of a government. A successful **revolt**, **insurrection**, or **rebellion**.

Revolving charge Credit, often provided through credit cards or department stores, by which purchases may be charged and partially paid off month-by-month. New purchases may be made, charged, and paid off during the same period.

Rex   (Latin) The king.

Reynolds v. U.S.   An 1879 Supreme Court case that excluded the right to do illegal acts from the protection of **freedom of religion** (see that word).

Richard Roe   A common name used for a **fictitious party** or a name used along with "**John Doe**" to illustrate a legal situation.

Rider   An additional piece of paper attached to a larger document. For example, a *rider to a bill* is an addition made late in the **legislative** process and usually unrelated to the subject of the **bill**, but "tacked on" anyway.

Rigging the market   Artificially driving up the price of a **stock** by making a series of **bids** that make it look like demand for the stock has soared.

Right   1. Morally, ethically, or legally just.   2. One person's *legal* ability to control certain actions of another person or of all other persons. Every *right* has a corresponding **duty**. For example, if a person has a *right* to cross a street on a green light, most drivers have a *duty* to avoid hitting the person with their cars. (When lawyers speak of "a right," they mean a legal, not moral right.)   3. For **bill of rights**, **riparian** rights, **stock rights**, or the rights of **privacy**, **redemption**, **survivorship**, etc., see those words.

Right from wrong test   The **M'Naghten rule** (see that word).

Right of action   A claim that can be enforced in court.

Right of first refusal   The right to have the first chance to buy property when it goes on sale, or the right to meet any other offer.

Right of way   1. The right to cross another person's property, or the crossed-over strip of land itself.   2. The land on which a railroad is built.   3. The vehicle (or person) with the legal right to go first and be safe from harm by others. This might be the right to enter an intersection, use a waterway, etc.

Rights issue (or offer)   **Stock** (or other **securities**) that is sold only to current stockholders.

Right-to-work laws   State laws that forbid **labor agreements** requiring **union** membership, preferential hiring, or similar provisions. See also **union shop**.

Ringing up   **Brokers** exchanging sales **contracts** in order to cancel them out, with leftover differences paid.

Riot   Three or more persons who commit or threaten to commit an act of violence, commit a crime, prevent or coerce official action, or use a deadly weapon. Exact **statutory** definitions differ, but this is the central core of the crime.

Riparian Having to do with the bank of a river or stream. *Riparian rights* are a landowner's rights to use water and the land around and under it. See also **water rights**.

Ripe 1. A case is *ripe* for selection and decision by the U.S. Supreme Court if the legal issues involved are clear enough and well enough evolved and presented so that a clear decision can come out of the case. Any court or agency that has the power to turn down cases may use *ripeness* as a way of deciding whether to take the case. *Ripeness* also includes the idea that the case involves a real **controversy**, not merely potential harm. 2. A case is *ripe for decision* by a **trial** court if everything is completed and in order, and nothing remains but the **decision** itself.

Rising of court 1. The final **adjournment** of a court **term**. 2. Any break in the court's work (for the day, for a **recess**, etc.). 3. The start or stop of court business when a court official calls out "all rise" and the judge enters or exits.

Risk 1. A **hazard** (fire), the danger of hazard or loss (one chance in ten thousand per year), the specific possible hazard or loss mentioned in an **insurance** policy (John's house burning down), or the item insured itself (the house). 2. Money or property invested in a business (usually as **stock** or a share of the business) as opposed to loans or bonds (even "risky" bonds are not *risk capital*).

Robbery The illegal taking of property from the person of another by using force or fear of force.

Roberts rules *Roberts Rules of Order* are a set of rules by which many **legislatures** and other meetings are conducted. They are *official* **parliamentary laws** only where they have been specifically adopted.

Robinson-Patman Act A federal law that prohibits **price discrimination** and other anticompetitive practices in business.

Rogatory letters A request from one judge to another asking that the second judge supervise the examination of a **witness** (usually in another state and usually by written **interrogatories**).

Roe v. Wade A 1973 Supreme Court case that used the *right of privacy* to protect a woman's right to an abortion in the earlier stages of a pregnancy.

Roll

Roll 1. A record of official proceedings. 2. A list of taxable persons or property.

Rolling over 1. Extending a short-term loan for another short period. *Rollover paper* is a short-term **note** that can be extended. 2. Refinancing a debt.

Roman law The collection of laws from Roman times that provides the basis for the **civil law** in several European countries and for many legal words and ideas in the United States, especially in Louisiana.

Roomer A lodger. A person who rents rooms in a house, as opposed to a **tenant** (see that word). Roomers have fewer legal rights than tenants, especially in terms of **evictions** and the right to deny others access to the room.

Root of title The land transaction (usually the most recent one at least forty years old) relied on as the original basis for a claim to land ownership.

Rota (Latin) The order of rotation or **succession** for a job or temporary office.

Round lot A normal unit of trading in **stocks** or **bonds**. Fewer shares are an **odd lot**.

Royalty A payment made to an author, an inventor, an owner of oil or other mineral lands, etc., for the use of the property.

Rubric 1. General purpose. 2. Title. 3. Category. 4. Rule.

Rule 1. To settle a legal issue or decide a **motion, objection,** etc., raised by one side in a legal dispute. The *ruling* is made by the person in charge (judge, hearing officer, chairperson, etc.). 2. An established standard, principle, or guide. 3. A **regulation.** A "mini-law" made by a group or by an **administrative agency**, often to govern its internal workings.

Rule against accumulations A state law that prevents a **trust** from storing up money for too long. It is similar to the *rule against perpetuities*.

Rule against perpetuities See **perpetuity.**

Rule of four If four **Supreme Court** (see that word) **justices** want the Court to take a case that reaches the Court by **certiorari**, the Court will.

Rule of law 1. There are many different definitions of this phrase. According to Kelso's *Programmed Introduction To The Study Of Law*, a "rule of law" is "a general statement that is intended to guide conduct, applied by government officials, and supported by an authoritative source." 2. A governmental

374

system in which the highest authority is the law, not one person or a group of persons.

Rule of lenity If it is not clear whether a law should be read as harsher or more lenient, choose the more lenient interpretation.

Rule of 78 A method of computing **interest** on early loan repayments. The sum of the months in a year (1–12) is 78. If repayment is made in the first month of a one-year loan, 12/78ths of the total interest must be paid; in the second month, another 11/78ths, etc. This is more than paying 1/12th for each month the money was used.

Rule 999 (or other nonexistent rule or law) Slang for necessity, especially military necessity, that requires "making up the rules" as you go along. See also **Catch-22.**

Rules committee A **committee** of a **house** of a **legislature** that acts as a preliminary sifting place to decide which **bills** from the various committees will be voted on by the house, and in which order.

Rules (federal) Congress has given the Supreme Court **rule**-making power for the lower federal courts. The main *rules* are now the *Federal Rules of Civil, Criminal, and Appellate Procedure and the Federal Rules of Evidence.* (These rules also serve as models for many state rules.) Specialized rules also cover **bankruptcy, admiralty,** and other specialized proceedings, as well as proceedings before U.S. **magistrates.**

Rules of Decision Act The federal law making state **substantive laws** applicable to lawsuits in federal court.

Ruling A judge's decision on a legal question raised during a trial.

Run **1.** To have legal validity. For example, the law *runs* throughout the state. **2.** To apply during a time period. For example, a **statute of limitations** *runs* when the time to bring a lawsuit of a certain type has ended or run out. **3.** To be attached to another thing. For example, a **covenant** (see that word) may *run* with the land.

Runaway shop A business that closes and moves away to avoid unionization or the effects of union wages, etc.

Running account An open, as yet unsettled account; a charge account.

Rylands v. Fletcher The old English case that established the principle of **strict liability** for dangerous things and abnormally dangerous activities.

Ss

S 1. Section. **2. Statute.** **3. Senate.**

S.A. Abbreviation for **corporation** in French and Spanish.

S.B. **Senate bill**.

S.B.A. Small Business Administration. A U.S. agency that provides loans and advice for small businesses.

S.B.I.C. Small Business Investment Company.

Sc. **Scilicet.**

S.C. 1. **Supreme Court.** 2. Same **case.**

S.D. Southern **district.**

S.E. South Eastern Reporter (see **National Reporter System**).

S.E.C. **Securities and Exchange Commission.** A U.S. agency that **regulates** the sale and trading of **stocks, bonds,** etc.

S.E.P. Simplified Employee Pension. An employer's contribution to an employee's **I.R.A.** (Individual Retirement Account) that meets certain federal regulations.

S.E.S. The federal senior executive service or top management.

S.I.P.C. Securities Investor Protection Corporation. A government agency that protects, up to a certain amount, investor accounts in brokerage firms.

SM **Service** mark (see that word).

S.P. 1. **Sine prole.** 2. Same principle or point.

SS A vague and unnecessary symbol found on many **affidavits;** its meaning is not known for sure, but may be **scilicet.**

S.S.A. Social Security Administration. The U.S. agency that runs the federal program of retirement and disability insurance.

S.S.I. Supplemental security income.

S.S.S. Selective service system.

S.U.B. Supplemental unemployment benefits. A private plan that adds to or takes over after state benefits.

S.W.   South Western Reporter (see **National Reporter System**).

Sabotage   **1.** The intentional destruction of or interference with national defense production, material, or premises.   **2.** The intentional destruction of or interference with an employer's property or operations during a **labor dispute** (see that word).

Safe harbor   **1.** An approved way of complying with a **statute** when the statute is phrased in general terms. For example, **S.E.C. regulations** (see those words) list ways that are sure to keep you out of trouble when making certain types of **stock offerings** (even though other ways might be legal also).   **2.** "Safe harbor leasing" is a way for companies to sell tax breaks to each other.

Safe investment rule   **1. Prudent person rule** (see that word).   **2.** One way to calculate **future earnings,** by estimating what sum of money, safely invested, would equal the earnings.

Said   An unnecessary word, used in legal writing to mean "the one mentioned before"; for example, *"said table."* Usually "the" or "this" will do.

Sailor's will   An oral **will,** made by a sailor at sea, that can be used to give away personal, but not real **property.**

Salary   A rate of pay (usually based on a yearly amount) that does not depend primarily on hours worked. It is usually earned by managers and professionals who get paid as long as they do their jobs. See also **wages.**

Sale   **1.** A **contract** in which property is exchanged for money.   **2.** The actual exchange of property for money.   **3.** For **approval, bootstrap, bulk, consignment, foreclosure, judicial, sheriff's, short,** and other types of *sales,* see those words.   **4.** A *sale and return* is a sale in which the buyer may return any unused items; a *sale-note* is a summary of a sale, given by a **broker** to the seller and buyer; and a *sale against the box* is a **short sale** in which the seller actually owns that **stock.** "*Sales*" is a field of law, now covered primarily by the **Uniform Commercial Code,** that deals with the sale of **goods** and that partly replaces general **contract** law for those sales.

Sales finance company   **1.** A company that buys **accounts receivable** (money owed by customers to a merchant) at a discount and then tries to collect the debts.   **2.** A finance company that specializes in **consumer** sales.

Sales tax   A state (or local) tax on sales, paid by the buyer to the merchant, then sent on to the state. Some states tax items (such as cars) at different rates, and some states do not tax some items (such as food) at all.

Salvage   **1.** Property recovered after an accident or other damage or destruction.   **2.** Business property that has only scrap value, or, sometimes, business property that is disposed of simply because it has been replaced or is of no further use to the company, whether or not it is still valuable.   **3.** Money paid to someone who rescues property from destruction at sea.   **4.** *Equitable salvage* is a **lien** in favor of the *last* person to make a payment that prevents the loss of property through **lapse, foreclosure,** etc.   **5.** In tax law, a value given to property for **depreciation** calculations.

Same evidence test   If the same evidence would **convict** a person in two separate prosecutions, the second prosecution is prohibited because of **double jeopardy.**

Sample   A *sale by sample* usually means that the items bought must "conform to" the sample. In commercial law, this may mean "substantially identical," and it may mean "similar and accepted in the trade as of equal quality."

Sanction   **1.** To agree to or confirm another person's actions.   **2.** A penalty or punishment attached to a law to make sure it is obeyed.

Sandwich lease   A lease in which the person who leases property then sublets it for more money; for example, leasing a shopping center and renting out the stores in it.

Sanitary code   Local laws regulating the cleanliness of places dealing with food (and sometimes with medical services).

Sanity   **1.** Of sound mind; the opposite of **insanity.**   **2.** A *sanity hearing* is a court proceeding to determine whether a person is mentally fit to stand trial, is committable to a mental hospital, or other related matters. Also called a **competency hearing,** a *sanity trial* (where it is a separate proceeding), and other names. See also **insanity.**

Satisfaction   **1.** Taking care of a debt or **obligation** by paying it. See also **accord** and satisfaction.   **2.** A *satisfaction contract* is one in which one person promises to do work or supply goods that will satisfy another. "Satisfactory" in this sense does not mean "to every personal whim" but "to any reasonable need" or "according to the judgment of an impartial expert."   **3.** A *satisfaction* of **judgment, lien,** or **mortgage** is a written document signed by the person paid, stating that an obligation has been paid. A *satisfaction piece* is a written document, made to be recorded, similar to the one above or stating that two sides in a lawsuit have agreed that payments have been made, and the lawsuit should be ended.

Satisfactory A general word for "enough," or "good enough," used when it is hard to pin down how much is enough.

Save Hold until later; reserve; preserve.

Save harmless **Hold harmless** (see that word).

Saving clause **1.** A provision in a law or **contract** that makes its parts **severable** (see that word). **2.** A provision in a repealing law that *saves* some of the rights or penalties of the repealed law (until a new law can take its place).

Saving property rule The little-used rule that a person is liable not only for damage done to another person's property, but also for that person's injuries caused by an attempt to save the property.

Saving to suitors clause A federal rule that allows persons to bring **admiralty** (maritime) lawsuits in either a state or federal court. The laws followed in either place must be those of the federal admiralty court. (Other types of cases that can be brought in either state or federal court must use *state* laws in either place.)

Savings and loan associations One of several different types of institutions that primarily make loans to home buyers. Some are **cooperatives;** some banks; some state chartered; some federally chartered under the *Federal Home Loan Bank Board.* The difference between most of these associations and ordinary banks is not as great as it used to be.

Savings bank trust A **Totten trust** (see that word).

Scab Slang for a person who works for lower than union wages, works under nonunion conditions, takes the place of a striking worker, passes through a picket line, etc.

Scale order See **order.**

Scale-down A composition.

Scalper **1.** A small-scale speculator in **stocks, bonds,** theater tickets, etc. See **speculate. 2.** An investment advisor who buys **securities** such as stocks, and then recommends them without disclosing the fact that a price rise will be to his or her benefit.

Scandal **Slander** (see that word).

Schedule

Schedule **1.** Any list. **2.** A list attached to a document that explains in detail things mentioned generally in the document. For example, *scheduled property* is items on a list attached to an **insurance** policy, with the value of each piece and what the company will pay if it is lost or hurt. The supporting pages of calculations attached to the main sheet of a **tax return** are called *schedules*, as are the charts for computing the tax rates of high-income persons.

Scheme **1.** Any general plan or system, especially one to produce a business profit. **2.** A plan to trick or **defraud** someone. **3.** See **common scheme**.

Schempp v. Abington School District A 1963 Supreme Court case that forbade Bible reading and prayer in the public schools.

Scienter (Latin) Knowingly; with guilty knowledge; with intent to deceive. [pronounce: si-<u>en</u>-ter]

Scilicet (Latin) "That is to say." An unnecessary word, often used after a general statement to introduce a list of specific examples.

Scintilla A very little bit. The word is often used in the phrase "a mere scintilla of evidence" ("*is* enough to let the jury decide the case"; "is *not* enough to let the jury decide the case").

Scire facias (Latin) **1.** A judge's command to a public official to come to court and explain why a record in that person's possession should not be wiped out. **2.** Other **writs** called *scire facias* were used for various purposes, but all had to do with some public record or the record of a case. Most states no longer use these writs.

Scope of employment An action of the general sort a person was employed to do, even if not exactly what the employer wants.

Scott *Scott on Trusts*; a **treatise**.

Scrip A piece of paper that is a temporary indication of a right to something valuable. *Scrip* includes paper money issued for temporary use; partial **shares** of **stock** after a stock split; **certificates** of a deferred stock **dividend** that can be cashed in later, etc.

Script A manuscript, especially the original copy.

Scriviner "Writer." An old word for a person who drew up **contracts, deeds,** and other legal papers; also for a person who managed **securities** and investments for a percentage of the interest.

Seal   An identification mark pressed in wax. Originally, for a document to be valid, it had to have a wax seal on it to show that it was done seriously, correctly, and formally. Later, the use of the letters "**L.S.**" took the place of wax. Now, there is no need for the seal at all, except for making sure that the right person actually signed (like in front of a **notary public,** who has a seal), or to formalize certain **corporate** documents with a corporate seal. See also **sealed** and **contract under seal.**

Sealed   **1.** *Sealed bidding* is a way of taking offers to do work or supply materials. Each **bid** is submitted in a sealed envelope, all are opened at the same time, and the best bid is chosen. **2.** *Sealed records* are a way of keeping some criminal, juvenile, divorce, adoption, etc., records secret by sealing them to all but a court **order.**   **3.** A *sealed verdict* is a way of allowing a jury to go home after they have made a decision when the court is out of session. They seal it in an envelope and have it read when the court is in session again.   **4.** "Sealed and delivered" are old, now unnecessary, words following the signatures on a **deed.** **5.** A *sealed instrument* is a document that is signed and bears a **seal** (see that word).   **6.** See **contract under seal.**

Search   **1.** An examination of a person's clothing, car, house, etc., by a law officer to discover **evidence** of a crime. If done without either **probable cause** or a **search warrant** (or without its being a very limited, necessary search at the time of legal arrest or on suspicion of a concealed weapon), the search may be forbidden by the **Constitution** and any evidence obtained excluded from use in a **criminal** trial.   **2.** A warship may have the right to *search* a merchant ship during time of war.   **3.** A *title search* is an examination of all proper land records to see who legally owns property and whether there are any **mortgages, liens,** etc., on it.

Search warrant   Written permission from a judge or **magistrate** for a police officer (or **sheriff,** etc.) to search a particular place for **evidence,** stolen property, etc. The police must give a good reason for needing these items, a likely reason why they might be in the place they want to search, and some indication that the information on which they are basing their search request is reliable.

Seasonable   In a reasonable amount of time.

Seasoned   A **stock** is *seasoned* if it has already sold in a stock market, and a company or business venture is *seasoned* when it has been in existence for a while and has made some money.

Seat

Seat Capital, or place where the main government offices are located.

Seated land Land that is used in any way (farmed, occupied, etc.).

Seaworthy A ship that is properly constructed, maintained, supplied, crewed, and instructed.

Sec. Section.

Secede Withdraw from membership in a group. This is called *secession*.

Second Lower ranking; coming later or farther away. For example, a *second degree crime* is less serious than a *first degree crime* ("second degree **murder**" is without **premeditation**); a *second mortgage* ranks below a *first mortgage* in its right to be paid; and *secondhand evidence* is **hearsay evidence** (that has passed through other persons or media to the witness).

Second Amendment The U.S. constitutional amendment that grants to the people the right to keep and bear arms. This right has been defined restrictively by state and federal laws.

Second look statute A **wait and see statute** (see that word).

Secondary Lower ranking; coming later or farther away. For example, a *secondary distribution or offering* is the sale of a large block of **stock** that is not a new **issue,** but one that has been held by the company or an investment firm; *secondary evidence* is not as good as **best evidence** (such as a photocopy of a document); and *secondary liability* is a duty that does not come due unless someone else fails to perform his or her duty. Other "secondary" words follow.

Secondary authority 1. **Persuasive authority** (see that word). 2. A comment about the law, such as an **annotation** or an article in a legal periodical or encyclopedia.

Secondary boycott A **boycott** (see that word) aimed at a business that does business with the one a union is actually having a dispute with. It is indirect pressure. This also applies to secondary **picketing** and **strikes.**

Secondary easement The right to do what it takes to fully use or maintain an **easement.**

Secondary market A **stock exchange** or other organized, regular method for buying already **issued securities.**

Secret service The federal organization that investigates offenses against the currency, **securities,** or banks of the United

States and protects the president, vice-president, ex-presidents, presidential candidates, certain family members, high foreign visitors, etc.

Secret trust   A **trust** in which the **trustee** gives only a verbal promise to hold the property in trust.

Secretary   **1.** An organization's official record keeper, such as a **corporate secretary** (see those words).   **2.** The head of a government department, such as the *secretary of defense*.   **3.** *Secretary general* is the name given to the head of the United Nations and of some other public organizations.

Secretary of state   **1.** In the U.S. government, this is a **cabinet** member who heads the State Department and is in charge of foreign relations.   **2.** In most state governments, this is the official who takes care of many types of formal state business, such as the licensing of **corporations**.

Secrete   Hide something away, especially to keep it from **creditors** by putting **title** in someone else's name.

Secta   (Latin) **Lawsuit.**

Section   **1.** A subdivision of a chapter in a book or document.   **2.** A subdivision of a township that is one mile on a side, containing 640 acres.   **3.** A subdivision in some **bureaucracies**.

Secundum   (Latin)   **1.** "According to," as in the phrase *secundum regulam* ("according to the rule").   **2. Second.**

Secure   To give **security** (see that word). To guarantee the payment of a debt or the keeping of a promise by giving the person a **mortgage, lien, pledge,** etc. (see those words).

Secured   Protected by a **mortgage, lien, pledge,** or other **security** interest. The person whose money is protected is called a "*secured* **creditor**" or "*secured* **party**" and the money protected is a *secured loan.*

Securities   **1.** See **security.**   **2. Stocks, bonds, notes,** or other documents that show a share in a company or a debt owed by a company.

Securities acts   Federal and state laws regulating the sale of **securities (stocks, bonds,** etc.). These include the *Securities Act of 1933* (which requires the **registration** of securities to be sold to the public and the disclosure of complete information to potential buyers); the *Securities and Exchange Act of 1934* (which regulates stock **exchanges** and **over-the-counter** stock sales); the *Uniform Securities Act* (a model for the states that includes

Securities and Exchange Commission

Blue sky laws and *broker-dealer* requirements); and several others involving investments (the *Public Utility Holding Company Act,* the *Investment Adviser's Act,* etc.). Federal securities acts are administered by the **Securities and Exchange Commission.**

Securities and Exchange Commission A federal agency that administers the federal **securities acts** (see that word).

Securities Investor Protection Corporation A private agency set up by the U.S. government to help stockbrokers and others in financial trouble.

Security **1.** Property that has been pledged, mortgaged, etc., as financial backing for a loan or other obligation. A *security interest* is any right in property that is held to make sure money is paid or that something is done. Most property **secured** this way may be sold by the **creditor** if the debt it backs is not paid. **2.** A share of **stock,** a **bond,** a **note,** or one of many different kinds of documents showing a share in a company or a debt owed by a company or a government. There are different technical definitions of *security* in the various **securities acts,** the **Uniform Commercial Code,** the *Uniform Probate Code,* the *Federal Bankruptcy Act,* the *federal tax code,* etc. Some of these definitions overlap, and some conflict. **3.** For **assessable, equity, hybrid, listed,** etc., *security,* see those words.

Security Council The **executive** body of the United Nations. It has eleven members from eleven countries and handles major problems of world peace.

Security deposit Money put up in advance by a **tenant** to pay for possible damage to property or for leaving before the end of the **lease.**

Security for costs Giving a court money, property, or a **bond** to hold to pay **costs** in case you lose. This is done, for example, when the **plaintiff** is from another state.

Sed vide (Latin) "But see." A reference to something that conflicts with the statement just made.

Sedition Stirring up persons to armed resistance against the government.

Segregation **1.** The separation of property into groups. *Segregation of assets* involves identifying and setting aside the property belonging to one person from a common fund or pot. **2.** The **unconstitutional** practice of separating persons in housing, schooling, etc., based on color, nationality, etc.

Seisin Full and complete present ownership and possession of land. [pronounce: <u>size</u>-in]

Seize 1. See **seisin.** 2. See **seizure.**

Seizure 1. The act of a public official (usually the police or a **sheriff** or **marshall**) taking property because of a violation of the law, because of a **writ** or **judgment** in a lawsuit, or because the property will be needed as **evidence** in a criminal case. 2. The act of a **peace officer** taking a person into **custody** and detaining the person in a way that interferes with liberty of movement.

Select committee A **legislative committee** set up for a limited time and purpose.

Select council The upper branch of some city councils.

Selective tax A sales or use tax on particular items, such as tobacco products.

Selectman A member of some local **legislatures** or town councils. When a town is too small to have a mayor, the role of mayor is taken by the "first selectman."

Self-authentication Some official documents and some other signed writings need not be otherwise **authenticated** to be used as **evidence**.

Self-dealing A **trustee** acting to help himself or herself, rather than the person for whom he or she is supposed to be working.

Self-defense The right to use physical force against a person who is committing a felony, threatening the use of physical force, or using physical force. This is a right if the person's own family, property, or body is in danger, but only if the danger was not provoked or involves deadly force. See also **true person doctrine** and **flee to the wall doctrine**.

Self-employment tax The social security tax on the earnings of self-employed persons.

Self-executing Laws or court decisions that require no further official action to be carried out.

Self-help Taking an action without obtaining official authorization when that action may need authorization. For example, a *self-help eviction* may be a **landlord's** removing the **tenant's** property from an apartment and locking the door against the tenant. In some situations this is legal, in others, not.

Self-incrimination Anything said or done by a person that implicates the person in a crime. It is **unconstitutional** to force or require a person to do this or to be a **witness** *against self*, except in

Self-insurance

limited circumstances such as when a **criminal defendant** voluntarily **takes the stand** to **testify.**

Self-insurance   Setting aside a fund of money to pay for future losses rather than purchasing an insurance policy to cover possible losses *or* merely not providing for such losses at all (whether or not this is proper).

Self-liquidation   Paying off a loan by the short-term sale of the items bought with the loan money. For example, a loan to a car dealer might *self-liquidate* through the sale of the cars bought with borrowed money.

Self-serving declaration   **Hearsay** (see that word) that involves statements a person made out of court that, if admitted as **evidence,** would help his or her case.

Selling short   A **short sale** (see that word).

Semble   (French) "It seems that." An introduction to an uncertain point of law.

Senate   The upper **house** of a state or the U.S. **legislature.** The members are senators.

Senatorial courtesy   The informal right of home-state senators to have the **Senate** reject presidential nominations for judges and other important federal jobs.

Senior interest   An **interest** or right that takes effect or that collects ahead of others; for example, a *senior mortgage* has preference or priority over all others.

Seniority   Preference or priority; often, but not always, because the person or thing came first in time.

Sentence   **1.** The punishment, such as time in jail, given to a person convicted of a crime. The process is called *sentencing* and is usually done by the trial judge, but sometimes by a jury or a *sentencing council* of judges.   **2.** A *determinate, fixed, straight,* or *flat sentence* is an exact penalty set by law. A *mandatory sentence* is a determinate sentence that cannot be suspended and that does not allow the judge to order **probation.** An *indeterminate sentence* is one having a minimum and maximum, with the decision of how long the criminal will serve depending on the criminal's behavior in prison and other things.   **3.** For **concurrent** and **cumulative** *sentences,* see those words.

Separability clause   A **saving clause** (see that word).

Separable controversy rule   Even if only one claim (out of several in some lawsuits in state courts) is the type that can be removed to a federal court, the whole case can be removed. The federal judge can then decide whether to keep the whole case or only that one claim.

Separate but equal doctrine   The rule, established in the Supreme Court case *Plessy* v. *Ferguson* and then declared **unconstitutional** in the case *Brown* v. *Board of Education,* that when races are given substantially equal facilities, they may be segregated.

Separate estate (or property)   The property owned by a person as an individual, rather than jointly as a partner in a business or marriage.

Separate maintenance   Money paid by one married person to the other for support if they are no longer living as husband and wife. In some states, this term refers to only *temporary* **alimony** or **support.**

Separation   **1.** A husband and wife living apart by agreement, either *before* a **divorce** or *instead of* a full divorce. It is sometimes called a *mensa et thoro* or "from bed and board." There is often a *separation agreement,* a document about child **custody, support, alimony,** property division, etc. If it is by **order** of a court, it is a *judicial* or *legal separation.*   **2.** *Separation of powers* is the division of the federal government (and state governments) into **legislative** (lawmaking), **judicial** (law interpreting), and **executive** (law carrying-out) branches. Each acts to prevent the others from becoming too powerful.   **3.** *Separation of witnesses* is a court **order** in some cases that **witnesses** stay out of the courtroom until each is called to **testify.** This is also called *"the rule on witnesses."*

Sequester   To isolate or hold aside. For example, to *sequester a* **jury** is to keep it from having any contacts with the outside world during a trial, and to *sequester property* is to have it put aside and held by an independent person during a lawsuit. This process is called *sequestration* and may also apply to such things as the **judicial impounding** of a bank account and the taking of private property by the government of another country during war.

Sergeant at arms   A person appointed to keep order in a **legislature,** court, or large meeting.

Serial bonds   Groups of **bonds** put out at the same time, but with different cash-in times for each group. *Not* **series** bonds.

Serial note   A **promissory note** that is paid back in **installments.**

Serial right

Serial right   The right to publish a book by installments in, for example, a magazine.

Seriatim   (Latin) One at a time.

Series   A set of lawbooks in numerical order. A new (second, third, etc.) *series* follows, not replaces, an older one.

Series bonds   Groups of **bonds** put out at different times with different cash-in times, but all part of the same deal. *Not* **serial bonds**.

Servant   A person employed by another person and subject to that person's control as to *what* work is done and *how* it is done. An employee is called a *servant* and an employer is called a **master**.

Service   **1.** The delivery (or its legal equivalent, such as publication in a newspaper in some cases) of a legal paper, such as a **writ**, by an officially authorized person in a way that meets all the formal requirements. It is the way to notify a person of a **lawsuit**.   **2.** Regular payments on a debt. This is called *servicing* the debt or *debt service*.   **3.** *Service charges* for **consumer credit** include every cost that has anything to do with the credit, no matter what they are for or what they are called. These include **time-price** differentials, credit investigations, "**carrying charges**," creditor insurance, etc.   **4.** *Service establishments* include any place that sells services to the public (barbershops, laundries, auto repair shops, etc.).   **5.** The *service life* of property is how long it should be useful. This is not necessarily the same as its depreciable life.   **6.** *Service marks* are marks used in the sale or advertising of services (including such things as the character names on television programs), usually to identify a company by a distinctive design, title, character, etc.; for example, Lazy Transport's "*Slotruk Service*^{SM}." See also **trademark**.

Servient   Land subject to a **servitude** (see that word), **charge**, or burden is *servient*. (For an example of how "servient" is used, see **easement**.)

Servitude   **1.** A **charge** or burden on land in favor of another. For example, the owner of a piece of land may be required by the **deed** to allow the owner of adjoining land to walk across a part of the land. This type of *servitude* is called an **easement**. The land so restricted is the *servient estate* and the land benefiting from the restriction is the **dominant** estate.   **2.** The condition of being a slave or servant.

Session Either a day or a period of days in which a court, a **legislature**, etc., carries on its business.

Session laws **Statutes** printed in the order that they were passed in each session of a **legislature**. See also **Statutes at Large**.

Set aside **1.** Cancel, **annul**, or **revoke** a court's **judgment**. **2.** A program of keeping potential cropland out of production to conserve soil and stabilize crop prices. **3.** Any program of saving **assets** for future use.

Set down Put a case on the list (or court **docket**) for a **hearing**.

Set of exchange An original and copies of a foreign **bill** of exchange.

Setback A distance from a street, property line, building, etc., within which building is prohibited by **zoning** laws, **building codes**, etc.

Set-off A **defendant's counterclaim** that has nothing to do with the **plaintiff's** lawsuit against the defendant.

Settle **1.** To come to an agreement about a debt, payment of a debt, or disposition of a lawsuit. **2.** Finish up; take care of completely. **3.** Transfer property in a way that ties it up for a succession of owners. **4.** Set up a **trust**.

Settlement **1.** See **settle**. **2.** The meeting in which the ownership of real **property** actually transfers from seller to buyer. All payments and debts are usually adjusted and taken care of at this time. These financial matters are written on a *settlement sheet*, which is also known as a **closing** statement.

Settlor A person who sets up a **trust** by providing the money or property for it.

Seventeenth Amendment The U.S. constitutional amendment that changed the election of senators from a vote by state **legislature** to a popular vote.

Seventh Amendment The U.S. constitutional amendment that guarantees a **jury** trial in most federal **civil** cases.

Sever Cut off. For example, to *sever* the trial of a person from others is to **try** that person's case separately and at another time. It is often called "severance."

Severable Capable of carrying on an independent existence. For example, a *severable statute* is one that can still be valid even if one part of it is struck down as **invalid** by a court. A *severable contract* is one that can be divided up without harm to the part

Several

remaining. Most **statutes** and some **contracts** have a *severability* or "saving" clause.

Several 1. More than one. 2. Separate, individual, independent. See also **joint and several**.

Severally Distinctly; separately; each on its own.

Severalty ownership Sole ownership; ownership by one person.

Severance Separation. For example, separating **joint** rights in property into individual rights to pieces of it, harvesting crops or taking minerals from land, ending a person's employment, etc.

Severance tax A tax on the volume or value of a **natural resource** (oil, coal, etc.) taken from the land.

Sewer service Telling the court that you have properly served (officially delivered) a court paper when it has actually been thrown away.

Sexual harassment Using a position of power over a person's job, salary, etc., to gain sexual favors or punish the refusal of such favors. It may be as "small" a thing as unwarranted sexual innuendos.

Shall Almost always *must*, but sometimes merely *may* if the **context** definitely reads that way.

Sham False or fake. For example, a *sham pleading* is a court paper that is formally correct, but that is so clearly false as to facts that it will be rejected, and a *sham transaction* is one that will be disregarded by the **I.R.S.**

Share 1. A portion. 2. One piece of **stock** in a **corporation**. 3. A *share* **certificate** (or **warrant**) is a document certifying that a person is entitled to own (or buy) a certain number of shares of stock.

Shared equity A **real estate** purchase arrangement in which an investor puts up part of the purchase price and pays part of the **mortgage** in exchange for tax benefits and a share of the eventual profits of a sale.

Sharp A **mortgage** or other **security** document is *sharp* if it allows the **creditor** to take quick **summary** action to collect if the debtor fails to pay.

Shave A slang expression for buying **notes** or other **securities** at a discount; for cutting prices secretly to a few persons; for illegally holding down the score in a sporting event to help bettors; or for using **extortion** to get something.

390

Shelley's case The *Rule in Shelley's Case* is that when a **life estate** is given to a person, followed by a **remainder** given to **heirs**, the heirs take nothing, but the holder of the life estate gets an interest in **fee** (see these words). (Under the rule, if John gives land to Sue to use for life and, in the same document, gives it to someone else after that and then to Sue's children, Sue gets it all to do with as she pleases.) This rule is *no longer followed*; life estates and remainders *are* permitted.

Shelter 1. The principle that a buyer has as good a **title** to property as the seller had. For example, under the **U.C.C.** *shelter doctrine*, the *holder* of a **negotiable instrument** has **holder in due course** rights if the person who sold the instrument was a holder in due course. 2. A way of investing money to minimize your total tax burden.

Shepardizing Using a Shepard's **citator** (see that word) to trace the history of a case *after* it is decided to see if it is **followed**, **overruled**, **distinguished**, etc.

Sheriff The chief law officer of a county, who, with the help of deputies, is in charge of serving **process**, calling **jurors**, keeping the peace, executing **judgments**, operating a county jail, etc.

Sheriff's deed A document giving ownership rights in property at a *sheriff's sale* (a sale held by a **sheriff** to pay a court **judgment** against the owner of the property).

Sheriff's jury An old form of a **coroner's** inquest.

Sherman Act The first **antitrust** or anti**monopoly** law, passed by the federal government to break up "combinations in restraint of trade."

Shield law 1. A law that protects a writer's sources of information. This type of law is based on, but not required in all cases by, the **First Amendment**. 2. A law that protects any informer's sources or protects anonymity.

Shifting Changing; varying; passing from one person to another. For example, *shifting income* is moving it from the person who owns it to someone who will pay lower taxes on it.

Shipping 1. Transporting goods for a charge. *Shipping documents* include **bills of lading**, **letters of credit**, etc. 2. Having to do with ships or moving goods by sea. *Shipping articles* are a written agreement between a sailor and the ship's master concerning the voyage, the pay, etc.

Shop right rule When an employee gets a **patent** on an invention worked on during work hours and using employer's materials, the employer has a right to use the invention free, but not to take the patent away from the inventor.

Shop steward A **union** official elected to represent workers and collect dues in one department of a business.

Shop-book rule An older, more limited version of the **business records exception** (see that word) in **evidence** law.

Short cause (or short calendar) A lawsuit, or part of a lawsuit, that must be heard by a judge, but is usually scheduled early because it can be disposed of quickly.

Short sale A **contract** for the sale of something, such as a stock, that the seller does not own. It is a method of profiting from the expected fall in price of a stock, but risky because if the stock goes up, the person will have to buy at whatever price it reaches to *cover* the short sale. A person is called *short* or in a *short position* if he or she owns less of a **stock**, **commodity**, or **futures** contract than may be needed to meet future obligations. The number of shares *short* is called the *short interest*.

Short summons A **summons** that may bring a **debtor** to court quickly if the court agrees that the debtor may run away or fraudulently dispose of property.

Short swing profits Profits made by a company **insider** on the **short term** sale of company **stock**.

Short-term *Short-term* is defined for various tax and other financial purposes as less than a week, a month, six months, nine months, and a year.

Short-term trust A **Clifford trust** (see that word).

Shotgun charge An **Allen charge** (see that word).

Show cause A court **order** to a person to show up in court and explain why the court should not take a proposed action. If the person fails to show up or to give sufficient reasons why the court should take no action, the court will take the action.

Shower A person who takes a **jury** to a crime scene, an accident scene, or other place and points things out.

Show-up A pretrial identification procedure in which only one suspect and a **witness** are brought together. See also **lineup**.

Shut-in royalty Money paid to keep a mineral **lease** active when nothing is being produced.

Shyster A dishonest lawyer.

Si (Latin) If.

Sic (Latin) Thus; so; in such a way.

Sight   *At sight* means **payable** when shown and requested. A **bill** or **draft** payable when shown is a *sight bill* or *sight draft*. *Sight drafts* can be sent by a seller to a new, faraway buyer's bank. When the buyer tells the bank to pay the draft, the ownership documents for the goods are given to the buyer.

Signature   **1.** A hand-signed name.   **2.** In some commercial situations, any mark that normally serves as a hand-signed name.   **3.** A crime's *"signature"* is the recurring method of operating of the criminal.

Silent partner   See **partner**.

Silver platter   Federal officials using **evidence** that was gathered illegally by state officials. This is no longer permitted.

Simple   **1.** Pure, unmixed, or uncomplicated.   **2.** Not aggravated. (See **aggravated assault**.)   **3.** A *simple contract* was one not under **seal** (see that word and see **contract under seal**). A *simple trust* is a **trust** that is for individuals and does not accumulate income or reduce the original trust property by giving it out. It is where property is held by one person for another's benefit.

Simulate   Take on the appearance; imitate; fake. For example, a *simulated sale* is a fake sale to make it look to **creditors** as if the property is out of their reach. This is also called a *fraudulent conveyance*.

Simultaneous death act   A law, adopted in most states, that if there is no **evidence** as to who died first in an accident, each dead person's property will pass as if that person survived longer. Some states have a **presumption** that the younger, healthier, etc., person lived longer.

Sine   (Latin) Without. For example, *sine die* means "without day," or a final ending or **adjournment** of a **session** of a court or a **legislature**. [pronounce: si-ne de-ay]

Sine prole   (Latin) "Without children"; abbreviated s.p.

Sine qua non   (Latin) A thing or condition that is indispensable.

Single juror charge   A judge's **instruction** to a jury that if even one **juror** does not agree that the **plaintiff** should get something, the plaintiff gets nothing.

Single proprietorship   A business owned by one person. It is also called a *sole proprietorship*.

Single publication rule   When a person sues for **libel**, the number of copies of a book or magazine may influence the *amount* of **damages**, but multiple copies may not be the basis for multiple lawsuits.

Single-name paper   **A negotiable instrument** (see that word) that has only one **maker** (original signer) or, if more than one original signer, persons signing for exactly the same purpose (for example, as **partners**). This is opposed to **accommodation paper** (where one person signs as a favor to another) or a **surety**ship (where, usually for a fee, one person cosigns to back up another person's debt).

Sinking fund   Money or other **assets** put aside for a special purpose, such as to pay off **bonds** and other long-term debts as they come due or to replace worn-out or outdated machinery or buildings.

Sister corporation   Two companies with the same or mostly the same owners.

Sit   1. To hold court as a judge.   2. To hold any session (a court, **legislature**, etc); to be formally organized and carrying on official business.

Sit-down strike (or stay-in strike)   A work stoppage plus a refusal to leave.

Sitting   1. **Session** (see that word).   2. The place or way a court does its business; for example, *sitting* **en banc** (see that word).

Situs   (Latin) Site or fixed location; place. Usually the place where a thing has legal ties.

Sixteenth Amendment   The U.S. constitutional amendment that made **constitutional** a federal income tax.

Sixth Amendment   The U.S. constitutional amendment containing various criminal trial rights, such as the right to a prompt public trial by **impartial jury**, to know the accusation right away, to confront **witnesses**, to a lawyer's help, etc.

Sixty-day notice   The federal requirement that both employers and unions must give a notice sixty days before reopening or ending a labor contract. During this time **strikes** and **lockouts** are prohibited.

Skeleton bill   A **bill** of exchange written or signed **in blank** (see that word).

Skiptracing   A detective service that finds missing **debtors**, **heirs**, **witnesses**, etc.

Slander   Oral **defamation** (see that word). The speaking of false and **malicious** words that injure another person's reputation, business, or property rights.

Slating   **Booking** (see that word).

Slip decision (or slip sheet or slip opinion)   A printed copy of a U.S. Supreme Court **decision** (or certain other court decisions) that is distributed immediately.

Slip law   A printed copy of a **bill** passed by Congress that is distributed immediately once signed by the president.

Small business   A company may be a *small business* if it has few employees, a low sales volume, few **stock**holders, etc. The definition differs, depending on who (Small Business Administration, Workers' Compensation, the I.R.S., state law, etc.) defines it.

Small claims   The name for a court that will handle cases under a certain money limit (often about one thousand dollars). These courts have a more streamlined procedure, faster action, and fewer formalities than regular courts have. They were originally set up to help the "little person" get a day in court, but are mostly used by stores and collection companies to collect overdue bills. Not all states, and not all places within each state, have *small claims courts.*

Small loan acts   State laws setting maximum interest rates on **consumer** loans or on all small short-term loans.

Smart money   1. Punitive damages (see that word).   **2.** Profitable investing generally, but more often profitable investing because of inside information. See **insider.**

Smorgasbord plan   A **cafeteria plan** (see that word).

Smuggling   The crime of secretly bringing into or taking out of a country things that are either prohibited or taxable.

So.   Southern Reporter (see **National Reporter System**).

Social contract   The theory that the only basis for the existence of a government is the consent of those governed.

Social Security Administration   A federal agency, set up by the *Social Security Act* and the *Federal Insurance Contribution Act (FICA),* that administers a national old age, survivors, and disability insurance program and other **insurance** and **welfare** programs.

Socialism   A government system in which many of the means of production and trade are owned or run by the government and in which many human welfare needs are provided directly by the government. *Socialism* may be democratic, or it may be a form of **absolutism.**

Societé   (French)   **1.** See **society.   2.** A **partnership.   3.** A *societé anonyme* is a **corporation.**

Society **1.** Any group of persons organized for a common purpose. Often an unincorporated business. **2.** The love, care, companionship, help, and earning power of a family member. See also **consortium**.

Sodomy A general word for sexual intercourse involving a man's genitals and almost anything other than a woman's genitals. It is a crime in most states. Some states limit it to situations involving penetration of the anus, and some states broaden it to include all "unnatural" sex acts by men or women.

Soil bank A federal program in which farmers are paid to keep cropland idle or in noncrop use. This helps preserve the soil and makes crop surpluses less likely.

Soldiers' and Sailors' Civil Relief Act A federal law that suspends or modifies a military person's **civil** liabilities, or requires persons who want to enforce their **claims** against persons in the service to follow certain procedures.

Soldier's will The same as **sailor's will** (see that word).

Sole Single, individual, or separate. For example, a *sole proprietorship* is a business owned by one person.

Sole actor doctrine The rule that a **principal** (such as an employer) will be held legally responsible for knowing what his or her **agent** (such as an employee) knows and for what that agent does.

Solemn Formally correct and seriously done.

Solicitation **1.** Asking for; enticing; strongly requesting. This may be a crime if the thing being urged is a crime. **2.** A lawyer's drumming up business in too aggressive a way. This is prohibited by the lawyer's **Code of Professional Responsibility**.

Solicitor **1.** An English lawyer who handles all legal matters but trial work, which is done by a **barrister**. **2.** The name for the head lawyer for many towns and other government bodies.

Solicitor general The second-ranking U.S. government lawyer; in charge of all **civil** suits involving the U.S.

Solidarity A contract with **joint and several** (see that word) liability on one or both sides.

Solvency **1.** The ability to pay debts as they come due. **2.** Having more **assets** than **liabilities**.

Solvent See **solvency**.

Sophisticated investor A person who has the background and knowledge to understand what he or she is getting into by buying shares in a business venture. Some **stock** sales can avoid

S.E.C. registration requirements by selling to only *sophisticated investors* who can afford the investment.

Sound **1.** Whole; in good condition; healthy. **2.** "Of the type." For example, a lawsuit *sounding in tort* is one where more than one **remedy** might be appropriate, but "**tort**" was chosen. Or, *sounding in tort* means that *tort* was chosen, but a *different* legal theory, such as **contract**, better supports the facts.

Sovereign immunity The government's freedom from being sued for **damages** (money) in all but those situations where it consents to suit by passing **statutes** allowing it (for example, the Federal Tort Claims Act). See also **government instrumentality doctrine**.

Speaker The chairperson or head of many **legislative** bodies, such as the speaker of the U.S. **House of Representatives**.

Speaking Bringing up matters that are not found within the legal papers of the case. This was not previously allowed (such things as *speaking demurrers* and *speaking motions* were prohibited), but bringing up new things is now permitted by the Federal Rules of Civil Procedure.

Special **1.** Limited. For example, a *special indorsement* is the signing over of something to one particular person; and a court of *special jurisdiction* can handle only limited matters, such as **probate** cases. **2.** Unusual. For example, a *special session* is an extra meeting of a court or **legislature**. **3.** For *special* **master, partner, verdict**, etc., see those words. Some other "special" words follow.

Special act (or law) **Private law** (see that word).

Special appearance Showing up in court for a limited purpose only; for example, to argue that the court has no **jurisdiction** (see that word) over you.

Special assessment A **real estate tax** that singles out certain landowners to pay for improvements (such as a sidewalk) that will, at least in theory, benefit all those owners, but not the rest of the taxpayers.

Special facts rule The rule that **corporate insiders** must reveal certain types of financial and ownership information to **stockholders**, especially when fairness should prevent holding back on the information.

Special interests Groups that have common interests such as consumers, banks, milk producers, etc. Each *special interest*

Special interrogatories

tries to lobby the government to influence the passage of laws and their enforcement.

Special interrogatories   Written questions asked by a judge to a **jury**. If the jury's answers to these questions conflict with the jury's **verdict**, the judge has several options as to what, if anything, to accept as correct.

Special trust   Either a **ministerial** trust or a **discretionary trust** (see that word).

Special use permit (or permit of exception)   Government permission to use property in a way that is allowed by **zoning** rules, but only with a permit. (This is *not* a **variance**.)

Special use valuation   The option of a person handling a dead person's land to have it valued for tax purposes at the value of its current use, not what it would be worth if used most profitably. Users of this option must conform to several provisions of the tax code.

Special warranty deed   **1.** A transfer of land that includes the formal, written promise to protect the buyer against all claims of ownership of the property that are based on relationships with or transfers from the seller. See also **general warranty deed**. **2.** The same as a **quitclaim deed** (see that word) in some states.

Specialist   A stockbroker who handles other brokers' orders in a specialized type of stock.

Specialty   **1.** Formerly, a **contract under seal** (see that word). **2.** A building that can be used only for limited purposes without expensive conversion.

Specie   **1.** Coins, especially gold and silver coins. **2.** *In specie performance* of a **contract** means according to the exact terms; and return of an item *in specie* means return of the same, not "an identical" item.

Specific   Exact. For example, *specific intent* is an intent to commit the exact crime charged, not merely a general intent to commit *some* crime or merely a generally guilty mind; and a *specific bequest* is a gift in a **will** of a precisely identifiable object such as "the family Bible."

Specific performance   See **performance**.

Specification   A detailed listing of all particulars, such as the things a soldier is accused of in a military trial or the "how to build it" part of a **patent** application.

Spectrograph   A machine used for identifying persons from their "voice prints," the visual plotting of the pitch, intensity and timing of a person's speech.

Speculate   **1.** Hope to profit from rapid changes in a **stock's** (or other item's) price, or to profit from a huge price increase in a very risky (*speculative*) investment. A person who does this is a *speculator*. **2.** Conjecture; wonder. *Speculation* is usually accepted in a trial only from **expert witnesses** and only in limited ways.

Speech   Speaking, writing, gesturing, and any other way of communicating ideas. See also **symbolic speech**.

Speech or debate clause   The U.S. **constitutional** protection (from lawsuits for **libel** and **slander** and from criminal prosecutions) of nearly everything a member of the House or Senate says in the line of duty.

Speedy trial   A trial free from unreasonable delay. A trial conducted according to regular rules as to timing; not necessarily a fast trial or a trial as soon as you want one. The federal government has a *Speedy Trial Act* to implement this **constitutional** requirement. Several states have similar laws.

Spendthrift   A person who spends money wildly and whose property the state may allow a **trustee** to look after. This protection of a person's property against himself, herself, or **creditors** is called a *spendthrift trust*. These trusts are also set up privately through **wills** and **trusts** to enable one person to give money or property to another without fear for its loss.

Spin-off   A **corporation** sets up and funds a new corporation and gives the **shares** of this new corporation to the old corporation's stockholders. This new corporation is a *spin-off* and the process is a *spin-off*. See also **split-off** and **split-up**.

Split action   A lawsuit to recover only part of a single claim. When this is done, the rest of the claim usually may not be raised in a second lawsuit.

Split income   Allowing a married couple to pay taxes as if each earned his or her income separately or as if each earned half the total income separately.

Split order   See **order**.

Split sentence   A **criminal sentence** in which one part is enforced and another part is not.

Split-dollar insurance   One person helping another to pay **insurance** premiums. This may have tax advantages.

Split-off

Split-off A **corporation** sets up and funds a new corporation and gives the **shares** of this new corporation to the old corporation's stockholders in exchange for some of their shares in the old company. This new company is a *split-off* and the process is a *split-off*. See also **spin-off** and **split-up**.

Split-up A **corporation** divides into two or more separate new corporations, gives its shareholders the shares of these new corporations, and goes out of business. This process is a *split-up*. See also **spin-off** and **split-off**.

Spoliation 1. Destruction by an outsider; for example, alteration of a check by someone who has nothing to do with it. 2. The failure by one side in a trial to come forward with **evidence** in its possession (and the inferences that the other side may draw from this failure). 3. Destruction of evidence.

Spontaneous statement (or declaration or exclamation) rule The rule that makes most statements about an event or condition **admissible** as **evidence** (even though they are **hearsay**) if they were spoken during or immediately after the event or condition. The older rule was that the statement had to be an **excited utterance** (made while still under stress), but most courts now allow **present sense impressions** (no need for excitement).

Spot Immediate. For example, a *spot* exchange rate is the conversion rate for money exchanged at the time the rate is quoted.

Spot trading Selling something for immediate delivery with immediate payment. The *spot price* is the price of things sold this way.

Spot zoning Changing the **zoning** of a piece of land without regard for the zoning plan for the area.

Spread The difference between two prices, amounts, or numbers; for example, between **bid and asked** (see that word) prices in **commodity** trading.

Sprinkling trust A **trust** that gives income to many persons at different times.

Spurious Not genuine. For example, a *spurious class action* is a joining together of several persons' claims in one lawsuit for the sake of the court's efficiency, even though the claims are different and couldn't normally be part of a **class action**; and a *spurious* $5 bill is one that has some things right about it (such as the fact that it was made on proper plates), but some things wrong (such as the signature). It is not genuine, but only partly **counterfeit**.

Squatter's rights   The "right" to ownership of land merely because you have occupied it for a long time. This is different
from **adverse possession** (see that word) and is not recognized
as a right in most places.

Squeeze out   A **merger** or other change in a **corporation's** structure that is done by majority owners to get rid of (or further reduce the power or claims of) **minority stockholders** (see that
word). See also **freeze-out**.

Stakeholder   A person chosen by others to hold something that is
in dispute between them while the dispute is worked out in
court or some other way; also, a person who holds a bet for
others.

Stale check   A **check** that has been made uncashable because it
has been held too long. This time period is often set by state law.

Stamp tax   A tax on certain legal documents, such as **deeds**, that
requires that revenue stamps be bought and put on the documents in order to make them **valid**.

Stand   1. The place where a witness sits or stands to **testify**.
2. Remain; refuse to change.

Stand mute   A refusal by a criminal **defendant** to **plead** "guilty"
or "not guilty." The judge will usually enter a "not guilty" **plea**
for the defendant in this situation.

Standard   1. Conforming to accepted practice. 2. A model;
something accepted as correct. 3. A legal rule. For example,
the *standard of care* in **negligence** cases is the level of care a reasonable person would use in similar circumstances, and the
standard of need for receiving **welfare** is the total need of that
size and type of family as determined by the state. 4. For *standard of proof*, see **burden of proof**.

Standard deduction   A term no longer used for a fixed amount of
money subtracted from **taxable income** by persons who did not
want to **itemize** (list) all their possible individual deductions
when they did their **income tax returns**. This has been replaced
by the **zero bracket amount** (see that word).

Standing   1. A person's right to bring or join a lawsuit because
he or she is directly affected by the issues raised. This is called
"standing to sue." 2. Reputation. 3. A *standing committee*
of a **house** of a **legislature** is a regular **committee**, with full power to act within a subject area.

Star chamber   A court in old England that had the power to arbitrarily punish persons who disobeyed the king. It was abol-

ished for this reason, but the phrase "star chamber law" is still used to mean the lack of procedural fairness or the handing out of overly harsh punishments by a judge.

Stare decisis (Latin) "Let the decision stand." A legal rule that when a court has decided a case by applying a legal principle to a set of facts, that court should stick by that principle and apply it to all later cases with clearly similar facts, unless there is a good, strong reason not to, and courts **below** *must* apply the principle in similar cases. This rule helps promote fairness and reliability in judicial decision making. See also **precedent**. [pronounce: star-e de-sI-sis]

State **1.** Say; set down; or declare. **2.** The major political subdivision of the U.S. (*State action* is action by a state, such as New York.) **3.** A nation. (An *act of state* is by a country, such as France.) **4.** Condition; situation. **5.** Department of State, the U.S. **cabinet** department that handles relations with foreign countries.

State of mind exception An **exception** to the **hearsay** rule: An out-of-court statement by a person of the reason why that person did something, spoken when the thing was done, may be used as **evidence** even if the person is available to **testify**.

State of the case Whether a case is not ready for trial, ready, in trial, or awaiting **appeal**.

State secret Facts that the United States need not reveal to a court (or to anyone else) because they might hurt national security or another equally important national interest.

Stated **1.** Regular. For example, a *stated meeting* of a **board** of directors is one held at regular intervals according to law or **charter**. **2.** Settled or agreed upon. For example, a *stated account* is an agreed amount owing.

Statement **1.** Any assertion, whether oral, written, or by conduct, intended to be an assertion of fact, of intent, etc. **2.** A document laying out facts. For example, a *statement of account* or *bank statement* lists all the transactions made by a customer for that month; and a *statement of affairs* is the summary financial form filled out when filing for **bankruptcy**. **3.** There are several technical **accounting** *statements* that supplement a **corporation's** basic **balance sheet** in its reports. These include statements of **income** (profits and losses; **earnings per share**; money in and out for such things as wages, supplies, interest, taxes, etc., all compared with prior years); *changes in financial* *position* or *sources and application of funds* (cash **balances**, **working capital**, etc.); *changes in accounting* (the way **inventory** is valued, the way **assets** are depreciated, etc.); *owners' equity* (basically, **assets** minus **liabilities**, but for a corporation, it is measured by **paid-in** capital plus **retained earnings**); and *retained earnings* (basically, profit kept by a corporation after paying out profits as **dividends**, etc.).

State's attorney   See **district attorney**.

State's evidence   A general word for **testimony** for the **prosecution**, given by a person who is involved in a crime against others involved in the crime. This is called *"turning state's evidence."*

Station house   Police station.

Status   **1.** A basic condition. The basic legal relationship of a person to the rest of the community. A *status crime* is one that depends solely on a person's status (what the person *is*) rather than on something he or she has done. Most status crime laws are no longer **constitutional**, but states have gotten around the problem by defining a prohibited *status* (for example, being an alcoholic) as a prohibited *act* ("found intoxicated in a public place"), or by restricting behavior without calling it a crime (for example, putting a child in an institution for being "beyond parental control").   **2.** The state of things. For example, *status quo* is the existing state of things or the way things are at a particular time.

Statute   A law passed by a **legislature**. [pronounce: <u>stah</u>-chute]

Statute of frauds   Various state laws, modeled after an old English law, that require many types of **contracts** (especially large or long-term ones) to be signed and in writing to be enforceable in court.

Statute of limitations   See **limitation**.

Statute of wills   Various state laws, modeled after an old English law, that require a **will** to be in writing, signed, and properly witnessed to be valid. See also **holographic** wills.

Statutes at large   A collection of all **statutes** passed by a particular legislature (such as the U.S. Congress), printed in full and in the order of their passage. The U.S. *Statutes at Large* also contains joint **resolutions**, **constitutional amendments**, presidential **proclamations**, etc.

Statutory   Having to do with a **statute**; created, defined, or required by a statute. For example, *statutory rape* is the act of a man having sexual intercourse with a female under an age defined by state statute. A *statutory crime* is an act that is a crime only because a law or **regulation** was passed against it, not because it is basically evil. See also **malum prohibitum** and **strict liability**.

Stay **1.** To stop or hold off. For example, when a judge *stays a judgment*, the judge stops or delays its enforcement. **2.** A stopping or suspension. For example, the act mentioned in no. 1 is called a "stay of judgment." **3.** *Stay laws* are **statutes** that hold off legal actions, usually to protect **debtors** in times of national financial crisis.

Stenographic recording The taking down of **testimony** by a court reporter who uses a paper-punching device, a tape recorder, a shorthand notebook, or other device to take down testimony and court proceedings, and then types an exact copy later. *Nonstenographic* recording involves the use of a tape recorder, videotape, etc., without the court reporter to run or transcribe it.

Step up (or down) basis An increase (reduction) in the **basis** of a property for income tax purposes. This usually occurs when **heirs** take a dead person's property and their basis becomes the **market value**.

Steward A **shop steward** (see that word).

Stifling a prosecution Taking money for agreeing not to **prosecute** a person for a **criminal offense**. This may be a crime.

Stipulation **1.** An agreement between lawyers on opposite sides of a lawsuit. It is often in writing and usually concerns either court procedure (for example, an agreement to extend the time in which a **pleading** is due) or agreed-upon facts that require no proof. **2.** A demand. **3.** One point in a written agreement.

Stirpes See **per stirpes**. [pronounce: stir-pees]

Stock **1.** The **goods** held for sale by a merchant. **2.** Shares of ownership in a **corporation**. Stock is usually divided into **preferred** (getting a fixed rate of income before any other stock) and **common** (the bulk of the stock). **3.** There are various types of **corporate** stock. Some of these are: *assessable* (the owner may have to pay more than the stock's cost to meet the company's needs); *blue-chip* (excellent investment ratings); *callable* or *redeemable* (can be bought back by the company at a prestated price); *control* (that amount of stock, often less than a **majority**, that can control the company); *cumulative* (unpaid **divi-**

dends must be paid before any **common stock** gets paid); *donated* (given back to the company for resale); *floating* (on the open market for sale); *growth* (bought for an increase in value, not dividends); *guaranteed* (dividends guaranteed by another company); *letter* (a letter is required stating that the buyer will not resell before a certain time); *listed* (traded on an **exchange**); *participation* (gets a share of profits); *penny* (cheap and speculative); and *registered* (**registered** with the **Securities and Exchange Commission**). **4.** For **capital, common, convertible, issued, preferred**, etc., stock, see those words. **5.** For *stock*: **broker, dividend, exchange, jobber, market, option, warrant**, etc., see those words. **6.** Other "stock" words follow here.

Stock association   A **joint-stock company** (see that word).

Stock control   Maintaining records of **inventory** (goods held or for sale).

Stock dividend   Profits of **stock** ownership paid out by a corporation in more stock rather than in money. This additional stock reflects the increased worth of the company.

Stock law district   An area where cows, sheep, etc., are prohibited from running free.

Stock rights   Documents (usually **warrants**) that give existing stockholders (or those to whom the documents are later sold) rights to buy new **stock** later. See also *pre-emptive rights* under **pre-emption**.

Stockholder's derivative suit   A lawsuit in which a shareholder of a corporation sues in the name of the corporation because a wrong has been done to the company and the company itself will not sue.

Stockholder's equity   A **corporation's** net worth (**assets** minus **liabilities**) expressed, not in terms of the assets themselves (buildings, **inventory**, etc.), but in terms of the way the assets are owned by the stockholders. It consists of **capital** stock, **capital** surplus, and **retained earnings** (see those words).

Stop and frisk   A police officer temporarily detaining and "patting down" a person whom the officer suspects of being armed. This is called a "*Terry*-type stop and frisk" for the case establishing less stringent rules for less than a full search.

Stop order   **1.** A customer's notice to his or her bank to tell the bank to refuse payment on a check the customer has written to another person.   **2.** Instructions from a customer to a stockbroker to buy a particular stock at a price above the current market price or sell it at a price below the current price. A *stop-limit order* gives a price above which it can't be bought and below which it can't be sold, and a *stop-loss order* is to buy or sell at a particular price. **3.** An **order** from a judge, from an **administrative agency**, etc., to stop doing something, such as building a house without a **permit**. See also **injunction** and **cease and desist order.**

Stoppage in transit   The right of a seller to stop the delivery of goods even after they have been given to a **carrier** (railroad, etc.) if, for example, the seller finds out that the buyer is **insolvent** and will not be able to pay for the goods.

Straddle   A combination of **put** and **call options** in which a person buys the right to buy or sell a **stock** at a certain price within a certain time.

Straight-line depreciation   Dividing the cost of a thing used in a business by the number of years in its **useful** *life* and deducting that fraction of the cost each year from **taxable income**. See also *accelerated depreciation* under **depreciation.**

Stranger   A person who takes no part in a deal in any way; a **third party.**

Straw man   **1.** A "front"; a person who is put up in name only to take part in a deal. See also **street name.**   **2.** A man who stood around outside a court in old England and was hired by lawyers to give false **testimony.**   **3.** A legal argument set up purely to be knocked down. This is sometimes done to divert attention from the real point because your opponent will win that one.

Stream of commerce   Goods held within a state for a short while, but which come from another state and will go to another state, are in the *stream of commerce* and cannot be taxed by the state.

Street certificate   A **share** of **stock** signed in **blank**, so anyone can transfer it.

Street name   **1. Stock** or other **securities** held in the stockbroker's own name instead of the customer's (for convenience, to hide the owner's name, because the stock was bought on **margin**, etc.) are held in a *street name.*   **2.** The made-up name used by investment companies, banks, etc., to hide the real owners of stock, of a business, etc. Also called *"straw," "front name,"* and *"nominee."*

Strict   Exact; precise; governed by exact rules. For example, *strict construction* of a law means taking it literally or "what it says, it means."

Strict foreclosure A **creditor's** right, in some circumstances, to take back property and cancel the debt. In these situations, the property acts as an exact cancellation of the debt, and neither the creditor nor the **debtor** can sue the other for any additional money.

Strict liability **1.** The legal responsibility for damage or injury, even if you are not at fault or **negligent**. For example, a manufacturer may be **liable** for injuries caused by a defective product even if the person hurt cannot prove how the manufacturer was careless. **2.** Guilt of a **criminal** offense even if you had no criminal intention (**mens rea**). Only minor offenses (such as speeding) and special **regulatory offenses** (such as polluting) can be *strict liability* offenses. See also **statutory crime**.

Strike **1.** Take out. For example, to *strike* a word is to remove it from a document. **2.** Employees stopping, slowing down, or disrupting work to win demands from an employer. **3.** An *economic strike* is to make changes (in wages, hours, conditions, etc.) as opposed to one caused by an employer's **unfair labor practices**; a *general strike* is throughout an industry or country; a *jurisdictional strike* protests assignment of work to members of another union; a *secondary strike* is by one union against an employer who does business with another employer whose employees are on strike; a *sit-down strike* includes a refusal to leave the workplace; a *sympathy strike* is where one union helps another against the same employer; and a *wildcat strike* is unauthorized by union officials. **4.** See also **blue flu**, **job action**, **recognition**, and **work-to-rule**. **5.** In some states, a *motion to strike* (the **evidence**) is similar to a **motion** for a **judgment** of **acquittal**.

Strike suit A **stockholder's derivative suit** (see that word) brought purely for the gain of the stockholder or to win large lawyer's fees.

Striking a jury Choosing individuals from a jury **panel** to serve on one case.

Striking price The price at which a person can *exercise* an **option** (see that word) to buy or sell a **commodity**.

String citation A series of case names and **citations** that is printed after an assertion or legal conclusion in order to back it up.

Strong-arm provision A part of the federal **bankruptcy** law. It says that a bankruptcy **trustee** has all the powers of the most powerful **secured creditor**, whether or not one actually exists, so he or she has the *strong-arm power* to gather in all the bankrupt's property.

Struck jury   A group of persons chosen as supposedly "best qualified" to try a criminal case.

Style   Official name.

Sua sponte   (Latin) **1.** Of his or her own will; voluntarily. **2.** On a judge's own **motion**, without a request from one of the **parties**.

Sub   (Latin) Under. For example, *sub modo* means "under a restriction or condition."

Sub judice   (Latin) "Under judicial consideration." As yet undecided because a judge is considering it. [pronounce: sub joo-di-se]

Sub nom.   (Latin) Abbreviation for *sub nomine* or "under the name of." Under the title of.

Sub silentio   (Latin) "Under silence"; in silence; without taking any notice or giving an indication.

Subchapter S corporation   A legal status, sometimes chosen by small (defined by number of owners) business **corporations**, that allows them to be taxed primarily as **partnerships**, thus avoiding the **corporate** income tax and passing on *tax losses* to the owners.

Subcontractor   A person who contracts to do a piece of a job for another person who has a contract for a larger piece of the whole job.

Subdelegation   Same as **delegation** (see that word) of authority.

Subdivision   Land divided into many lots by a developer and sold to different persons under a common plan.

Subinfeudation   The process in the middle ages of kings owning all the land and granting only the use of it to nobles, who then gave use only of smaller parts to others, and so on down several layers. The **statute** of *quia emptores* ended this process in England, leaving the power of *infeudation* (granting *feuds*, the basis for feudal law) only to the king and making all lower land transfers more similar to modern sales and **grants**.

Subjacent support   See **support**.

Subject to   Subordinate to; governed by; affected by; limited by; etc.

Subletting   A **tenant** renting property to another person, either for the rest of the tenant's own lease or for a portion such as a "summer *sublet*."

Submit **1.** To put into another's hands for decision. **2.** Allow; yield to. **3.** Introduce **evidence**. **4.** Offer something for approval.

Subordination **1.** Signing a document that admits that your **claim** or **interest** (for example, a **lien**) is weaker than another one and can collect only after the other one collects. **2.** Any ranking of rights. **3.** *Not* **subornation**.

Subornation of perjury **1.** The crime of asking or forcing another person to lie under **oath**. **2.** *Not* **subordination**. [pronounce: sub-or-<u>nay</u>-shun]

Subpoena A court's **order** to a person that he or she appear in court to **testify** (give **evidence**) in a case. Some **administrative agencies** may now **issue** subpoenas. [pronounce: sub-<u>pee</u>-na]

Subpoena duces tecum A **subpoena** (see that word) by which a person is commanded to bring certain documents to court or to an **administrative agency**. [pronounce: sub-<u>pee</u>-na due-ces <u>tay</u>-kum]

Subrogation The substitution of one person for another in claiming a lawful right or debt. For example, when an **insurance** company pays its policy holder for damage to his or her car, the company becomes *subrogated to* (gets the right to sue on or collect) any claim for the same damage that the policy holder has against the person who hit the car.

Subscribe **1.** Sign at the end of a document (as the person who wrote it, as a **witness**, etc.). **2.** Agree to purchase some initial **stock** in a **corporation**. **3.** The person who does no. 1 or no. 2 is a *subscriber* and the act is *subscription*.

Subsidiary **1.** Under another's control; lesser. **2.** *Subsidiary* is often short for *subsidiary corporation*, or one that is controlled by another company which is called the **parent corporation**.

Substance **1.** Reality, as opposed to mere appearance. **2.** The "gist" or meaning of something.

Substantial **1.** Valuable; real; worthwhile. **2.** Complete enough. **3.** "A lot," when it is hard to pin down just how much "a lot" really is.

Substantiate Establish the existence of something or prove its truth; verify. See also **corroborate**.

Substantive evidence Evidence used to prove facts rather than to discredit or back up a **witness's** believability.

Substantive law The basic law of **rights** and **duties** (**contract** law, criminal law, accident law, law of **wills**, etc.) as opposed to **pro-**

cedural law (law of **pleading**, law of **evidence**, law of **jurisdiction**, etc.).

Substituted service   **Service** of **process** by any means other than personal delivery; for example, by mail, publication in a newspaper, or service on a member of the family at the person's usual residence.

Subtraction   The old offense of keeping from another person money, rights, or services that person is entitled to.

Subversive activities   Espionage, **treason**, **sedition**, **sabotage**, and other acts to undermine a government.

Succession   **1.** The transfer of a dead person's property. *Intestate succession* is the transfer of property by law to **heirs** if the person does not leave a **will**. A *succession law* is an **inheritance** law, and *successors* is another word for heirs.   **2.** Taking over a predecessor's official duties.   **3.** The continuation of a **corporation** even though its owners, **directors**, and managers change.

Sudden emergency doctrine   See **emergency doctrine**.

Sudden heat of passion   See **heat of passion**.

Sue   To start a **civil** lawsuit.

Sue out   Ask a court to **issue** a **writ**, a court **order**, or other court papers.

Suffer   Allow or permit something to happen. To *suffer* something usually means to willingly permit it, but in the case of *sufferance*, it may mean neglect to enforce a right.

Sufficient cause   **1.** *Legal cause* to remove a public official from office. It must be for something basic to the person's job qualifications as they affect an important public interest.   **2.** **Probable cause** (see that word).   **3.** Legal cause generally.

Suffrage   The right to vote.

Suggestion   A mere hint or insinuation that does not make a fact probable or even possible, but only introduces the idea that it *might* be possible; less than an **inference** or **presumption**.

Sui generis   (Latin) One of a kind. [pronounce: sue-ee jen-er-is]

Sui juris   (Latin) "Of his or her own right." Possessing full **civil** and **political rights** and able to manage his or her own affairs.

Suicide   **1.** Killing yourself. *Attempted suicide* may be a crime, as may be the accidental killing of another person during an attempt or persuading another person to attempt suicide.   **2.** A person who kills him or herself.

Suit   A lawsuit; a **civil action** in court.

Suit money   Lawyer's fees and costs that a judge orders one side in a lawsuit to pay to the other.

Suitor   A **party** or **litigant** in a lawsuit; usually the **plaintiff**.

Suits in Admiralty Act   Similar to the **Federal Tort Claims Act** for maritime (seagoing) suits against the U.S. government.

Sum certain   An exact amount of money, usually of money owed. The amount is exact even if it includes interest, costs, etc., so long as these added amounts are exactly computable. A *sum certain* is a legal requirement for such things as the *negotiability* of a **negotiable instrument**.

Summary   Short; concise; immediate; without a full trial. For example, *summary judgment* is a win for one side in a lawsuit before the start of a trial. It may be a **judgment** based on **pleadings**, **depositions**, **affidavits**, etc., which show that there is no need to resolve any factual questions at trial.

Summary process   An abbreviated type of court hearing available in some situations; for example, an **eviction** where the tenant's failure to pay rent automatically ended the **lease**.

Summing up (or summation)   Each lawyer's presentation of a review of the **evidence** at the close of a trial.

Summons   A **writ** (a notice delivered by a **sheriff** or other authorized person) informing a person of a lawsuit against him or her. It tells the person to show up in court at a certain time and place to present a case or risk losing the suit without being present.

Sumptuary laws   Laws controlling the sale or use of socially undesirable, wasteful, and harmful products.

Sunk costs   Past spending that no longer directly affects current decisions. For example, the original cost of a car is not as important as its current sale value, except for taxes.

Sunset law   A law authorizing an **administrative agency** that puts the agency automatically out-of-business unless the law is renewed after a careful reexamination of the agency by the **legislature**.

Sunshine law   A law requiring open meetings of government agencies or a law making public access to government records easier. See also **Freedom of Information Act**.

Suo nomine   (Latin) In his or her name.

Superior   1. Higher. However, a *superior court* may be a court of different levels in different states.   2. Having control. For ex-

Supersede

ample, a *superior estate* (which might be quite small) might have an **easement** against an *inferior estate* (which might be quite big). These are generally called **dominant** and **servient estates**.

Supersede 1. Set aside; wipe out; make unnecessary. 2. Replace one law or document by another, later one.

Supersedeas (Latin) A judge's order that temporarily holds up another court's proceedings or, more often, temporarily **stays** a lower court's **judgment**. For example, a *supersedeas bond* may be put up by a person who **appeals** to hold off the person's obligation to pay a judgment until the appeal is lost. [pronounce: sue-per-<u>see</u>-de-as]

Superseding cause **Intervening cause** (see that word).

Supervening New; newly effective; interposing. For *supervening cause*, see **intervening cause**, and for *supervening negligence*, see **last clear chance**.

Supervisor 1. An individual or a member of a **board** that runs a county or town in some states. 2. Anyone with authority over others, but in **labor law** this does not include low-level persons who do not need to use "independent judgment" in their supervision of others.

Supplemental pleading A **pleading** that brings up events that happened after the start of the lawsuit.

Supplementary proceedings A **judgment creditor's** (see that word) in-court examination of the **debtor** and others to find out if there is any money or property available to pay the debt.

Support 1. The obligation to provide for your immediate family. 2. The payments made to a wife, husband, child, etc. (with or without court supervision or formal agreement) to meet the obligation in no. 1. 3. *Lateral support* or *subjacent support* is the obligation landowners have to avoid the collapse of adjoining land (due to digging, etc.).

Suppress 1. To *suppress evidence* is to keep it from being used in a **criminal** trial by showing that it was gathered illegally. This can happen at trial or a pretrial *suppression hearing*. 2. Refuse to give evidence in a criminal trial. This may be a crime. 3. The prosecution's holding back requested evidence favorable to the defendant. This may be **unconstitutional**.

Sup-pro **Supplementary proceedings** (see that word).

Supra (Latin) Above; earlier (in the page, in the book, etc.).

412

Supremacy clause The U.S. **constitutional** provision that the U.S. Constitution, laws, and **treaties** take precedence over conflicting state constitutions or laws.

Supremacy of law A government in which the highest authority is in law, not in persons.

Supreme Court The highest U.S. court and the highest court of most, but not all, of the states.

Surcharge **1.** An extra charge on something already charged. **2.** A special payment, such as the personal payment a **trustee** must make to a **trust** if he or she has negligently handled the account and it has lost money. **3.** An overcharge. A charge beyond what is right or legal. See also **surtax**.

Surety A person or company that insures or guarantees that another person's debt will be paid by becoming **liable** (responsible) for the debt when it is made. See also **guaranty**.

Surface A vague word which, when used in land **deeds**, may mean anything from "the top few feet of land with no **mineral rights**" to "all the land and minerals except oil and gas."

Surplus Money left over. A **corporation's** surplus, or its "**capital** *surplus*," has been defined in several different, overlapping, and sometimes conflicting ways including "**assets** minus **liabilities**," "assets minus **stock** value," etc.

Surplusage **1.** Extra, unnecessary words, or matter not relevant to the case, in a legal document. **2. Surplus**.

Surprise The situation that occurs when one side in a trial, through absolutely no fault of its own, is faced with something totally unexpected that places an unfair burden on its case. When this happens, a **continuance** is often granted and, occasionally, a new trial may be granted.

Surrebutter (or surrejoinder) Two old forms of **pleading** no longer used. Modern court practice usually stops with two or three pleadings, not the five or more it would take to reach these.

Surrender Give back; give up; hand back or return.

Surrogate **1.** The name for the judge of a **probate** court in some states. **2.** A person who stands in for, takes the place of, or represents another.

Surtax **1.** An additional tax on what has already been taxed. **2.** A tax on a tax. For example, if you must pay a hundred dollar tax on a one thousand dollar income (10 percent), a 10 percent *surtax* would be an additional ten dollars, not an additional hundred dollars.

Survey

Survey **1.** Measuring or mapping land boundaries. **2.** An investigation, examination, or questioning, such as taking an opinion poll.

Survival statutes State laws that allow a lawsuit to be brought by a relative for a person who has died. One type is a **wrongful death** statute.

Survivorship The right to property which is held by more than one person when the others die.

Suspect classification Making choices (in employment, etc.) based on race or religion. These choices may be legitimate, but must be strongly justified if challenged.

Suspended sentence A **conviction** of a crime followed by a **sentence** that is given formally, but not actually served. See also **probation**.

Suspicion **1.** "Held on suspicion" is being temporarily held by the police without specific charges against you. **2.** More than a guess, but less than full knowledge.

Sustain **1.** Grant. When a judge *sustains an* **objection**, he or she agrees with it and gives it effect. **2.** Carry on; bear up under. **3.** Support or justify. If the evidence fully supports a **verdict**, it is said to *sustain* the verdict.

Swear Give or take an **oath**. For example, the *swearing in* of a **witness** or a person about to become a public official in an official oath-taking ceremony.

Sweat equity The increase in property value due to an owner's making improvements.

Sweating Harsh, threatening, or overly aggressive questioning of a **criminal** suspect.

Sweetheart contract A **labor contract** containing unusually favorable terms for one side or the other. Many *sweetheart contracts* are gained by actions unrelated to the employment relationship, such as bribery.

Swift witness A **witness** who seems overeager to give information or who shows a **bias** toward one side.

Syllabus A **headnote**, summary, or **abstract** of a case.

Symbolic delivery Giving something by giving a valid symbol of ownership. For example, giving a key to a safety deposit box may be the actual gift of what is in the box.

Symbolic speech Actions to express an opinion or to say what otherwise might have been expressed in words; for example, holding your nose. This may be protected by the **Constitution** if the actions are more speech than conduct and if the speech itself would be protected.

Sympathy strike   A **strike** by one **union** to help another union. These are now mostly prohibited.

Synallagmatic   **Bilateral**.

Syndicalism   The theory that trade unions should control the means of production and, ultimately, the government. *Criminal syndicalism* is advocating a crime, **sabotage**, etc., to take over an industry or affect the government.

Syndicate   **1.** A **joint adventure** (see that word).   **2.** Any business venture, whether permanent or temporary, **incorporated** or not.   **3.** Slang for organized crime.

Synopsis   A summary of a document, book, etc.

T   **1.** An old abbreviation for the Latin "testamentum" (**will**); also, a mark that used to be put on a criminal's clothing or body.   **2.** Term; territory; title; etc.   **3.** A form of keeping financial records, also called a *T-Account*, in which the title is above the top part of the "T," the **debits** are on the left side of the vertical bar, and the **credits** are on the right.

T.C.   Tax court. (A "T.C. Memo" is a **memorandum decision** [see that word] of the *U.S. Tax Court.*)

TM   **Trademark**.

T.R.O.   **Temporary restraining order** (see that word).

Table   **1.** Suspend consideration of a **legislative bill**; put something aside temporarily or permanently.   **2.** Lists of figures, such as the federal precomputed tax-rate charts for most taxpayers' incomes.   **3.** A *table of cases* is an alphabetical list of cases mentioned in a book with page numbers on which they are found.

Tacit   **1.** Understood without being openly said; done in silence; implied.   **2.** Customary.

Tacking

Tacking   Attaching something later, smaller, or weaker to something earlier, larger, or stronger. For example, if the owner of a third **mortgage** buys the first mortgage on a property and joins them together to get **priority** over the owner of the second mortgage, this is called *tacking*. The term is also used for joining rights together to make **adverse possession** (see that word) claims, to beat statutes of **limitations,** to extend trucking routes, etc.

Taft-Hartley Act   A federal law, passed in 1947, that added several employers' rights to the union rights in the **Wagner Act.** It established several union "unfair labor practices" (such as attempting to force an employee to join a union).

Tail   Limited; limited to only children, grandchildren, etc. See **fee tail**.

Taint   **1. Attainder** or **attaint** (see those words).   **2.** The shame or untrustworthiness that results from **conviction** of a serious crime.   **3.** *Tainted* **evidence,** money, or property is that gained by illegal means.

Take   *Take* has a wide variety of meanings in the law, but most are close to the ordinary language meaning. For example, in the criminal law, to *take* something is to take it without the owner's consent and with the intent to cheat or steal; the government *takes* a person's property even if it is only lowered in value by a public use; when you **inherit** property, you *take* by **descent;** *take-home pay* is pay after deductions for such things as taxes, insurance, savings plans, etc.; a *take-over* is the gaining of control, but not necessarily **majority** ownership of a company (see **tender** offer); and to *take up* a **note** or other **negotiable instrument** is to pay or **discharge** it.

Take the stand   **Testify** as a **witness** in court.

Take-down   **1.** The time when a deal is actually performed, such as when goods have been both delivered and paid for.   **2.** The time when prearranged credit is actually used.

Take-out loan   A permanent **mortgage** that pays off a construction loan.

Talesman   A person taken from off the street or inside the courthouse to serve as a **juror.**

Tamper   Make changes by meddling; interfering. For example, *jury tampering* is attempting to bribe, threaten, or otherwise illegally influence a **juror.**

Tangible   Capable of being touched; real.

Tare   Box or container weight substracted from the total weight of goods.

Target   The thing aimed at. For example, a *target company* is the subject of a takeover by a **tender** offer; a *target offense* is the contemplated crime in a **conspiracy;** and a *target witness* is a person called before a grand **jury** because the government wants to indict that person.

Tariff   **1.** An import tax or a list of articles and the import tax that must be paid on that list. A *protective tariff* is to protect local businesses from foreign competition; a *retaliatory tariff* is in exchange for a foreign country's tax on goods from your country; and an *antidumping tariff* is to prevent foreign countries from selling cheaper here than there.   **2.** A public list of services offered, rates, charges, and rules of a public utility, such as an electric company.

Tax   **1.** A required payment of money to support the government. Some of the hundreds of different types of taxes are listed in no. 2.   **2.** Types of taxes defined in this dictionary include: **ad valorem; capital** gains; **capital** stock; **capitation; collateral inheritance; direct; estate; excess profits; floor; gift; head; holding company; income; indirect** (see **direct**); **inheritance; intangibles; investment credit; luxury; payroll; poll; progressive; property; regressive** (see **progressive**); **sales; selective; severance; sinking fund; stamp;** stock **transfer; succession; surtax; tonnage; transfer; undistributed profits; unified transfer; use; withholding;** etc. (see those words).   **3.** For *tax* **certificate, foreclosure, lease, lien, sale,** and **title,** see those words or see **tax deed.**   **4.** For *tax* **assessment, audit, credit, deduction, exclusion, exemption, fraud, roll, schedule, shelter, table,** etc., see those words.   **5.** All other *tax* words follow alphabetically.

Tax avoidance   Planning finances carefully to take advantage of all legal tax breaks, such as **deductions** and **exemptions.**

Tax benefit rule   If a loss or expense deducted from taxes in one year is recovered in another year, the recovery will be taxed as income in that later year to the extent of the deduction.

Tax court   A U.S. court that takes **appeals** from taxpayers when the **I.R.S.** has charged them with deficiencies (underpayments) in their payments of **income, estate,** and **gift** taxes. (The *U.S. District Courts* also handle tax cases.) There are also specialized *tax courts* in some states.

Tax deed   A proof of ownership of land given to the purchaser by the government after the land has been taken from another person by the government and sold for failure to pay taxes. Also, a *tax certificate* is a temporary proof of ownership that can be turned into a **deed** if the original owner does not **redeem** the property by paying the taxes due by a certain date; and a *tax lease* is a proof of ownership for a number of years when state law prohibits **absolute** sales for tax reasons. (All of these are *tax* **titles** given at a *tax* **sale** after a *tax* **warrant** has been issued for a *tax* **foreclosure** on a *tax* **lien;** see those words.)

Tax evasion   Illegally paying less in taxes than the law allows. Committing **fraud** in filing or paying taxes.

Tax exempt(s)   **1.** Property (such as that belonging to schools, churches, etc.) that is not subject to property taxation.   **2.** Investments (such as **municipal bonds**) that give income that is not subject to income taxation.   **3.** Income that is free from taxation, such as income *received* by a **charitable** organization.   **4.** Certain charitable organizations.

Tax ferret   A person who searches out property that has not been taxed (for a state fee) or who turns in tax cheaters (for a percentage of the tax recovered).

Tax fraud   The deliberate nonpayment or underpayment of taxes that are legally due; **tax evasion.** *Tax fraud* can be **civil** or **criminal,** with criminal fraud having higher fines and the possibility of a prison sentence upon the showing of "willfulness." The line between the two types of fraud is fuzzy.

Tax home   That base of business operations from which, if you travel on business, travel expenses may be deducted from taxes as business expenses.

Tax rate   The percentage of **taxable income** (or of inherited money, things purchased subject to sales tax, etc.) paid in taxes. The federal income tax has a *graduated* tax rate. This means, for example, that the first ten thousand dollars of a person's taxable income might be taxed two thousand dollars and the next one thousand to two thousand dollars at 25 percent. This percentage is called the "tax bracket" or "marginal rate."

Tax return   The form used to report income, **deductions,** etc., and to accompany tax payments and requests for refunds.

Tax (taxable) year   See **fiscal** year.

Taxable estate (or gift)   The property of a dead person (or a gift) that will be taxed after subtracting for allowable expenses, **deductions,** and **exclusions.**

Taxable income Under federal tax law, this is either the "**gross income**" of businesses or the "**adjusted gross income**" of individuals (see these words) minus **deductions** and **exemptions** (see these words). It is the income against which **tax rates** are applied to compute tax paid before any **credits** are subtracted.

Taxing costs Making one side in a lawsuit pay the other side's costs of the suit when legally required.

Taxpayer suit A lawsuit brought by an individual to challenge the spending of public money for a particular purpose.

Technical **1.** Having to do with an art or a profession. Technical terms are often called "**words of art.**" **2.** Minor; merely procedural. For example, *technical errors* are mistakes in trial procedure that cause no real harm to either side.

Technical analysis Deciding whether to buy or sell a particular **stock** or other **security** based on its price and its sales patterns. (See also **fundamental analysis**.)

Teller A person who counts, such as a *bank teller* who takes in and pays out money or a *vote teller* in a **legislature**.

Temporary restraining order A judge's **order** to a person to keep from taking certain action before a full **hearing** can be held on the question. Abbreviated **T.R.O.**

Tenancy The condition of being a **tenant**; the **interest** a tenant has; the **term** (amount of time) a tenant has. See **tenant**.

Tenant **1.** A person who holds land or a building by renting. Tenants include persons who have a **lease**; tenants at **will** (started out with a lease and still living there with permission); tenants at **sufferance** (started with a lease, but holding onto property against the wishes of the owner); etc. **2.** A person who holds land or a building by any legal right including ownership. For example, tenants in **common** each hold a share of land that can be passed on to **heirs** or otherwise disposed of; **joint** tenants are like tenants in common except that they must also have *equal* interests in the property and, if one dies, that person's ownership interest passes to the other owner(s); and tenants by the **entireties** are like joint tenants except that they must also be husband and wife and that neither has a share of the land, but both hold the *entire* land as one individual owner. Different states vary these definitions slightly.

Tender **1.** An **offer**, combined with a readiness to do what is offered. **2.** An offer of money. **3.** Cash on the line. Actually putting money forward, as opposed to merely offering it. In this

Tenement

sense, U.S. cash is *legal tender* in the U.S.   **4.** A *tender offer* is an offer (usually public) to buy a certain amount of a company's **stock** at a set price. This is often done to get control of the company.

Tenement   **1.** Any house, apartment, or place where people live. **2.** Particular kinds of living places, such as apartment houses. The word may be defined differently by different **statutes** or **regulations.**   **3.** In its original sense, anything that could be held, including offices, rights, etc.

Ten-K (10-K)   The annual report required by the **S.E.C.** of publicly held **corporations** that sell **stock.**

Tenor   A vague word that can mean anything from "the exact words" to "the general meaning" or "train of thought."

Tentative trust   A **Totten trust** (see that word).

Tenth Amendment   The U.S. constitutional amendment that says all powers not specifically given to the federal government are kept by the states and the people.

Tenure   **1.** Term of office. The length of time ("four years," "life and good behavior," etc.) a person may hold a job.   **2.** A right to lifetime employment, subject to specific restrictions.   **3.** The **feudal law** right to hold property as a subject of a higher lord.

Term   **1.** A word or phrase (especially one that has a fixed technical meaning).   **2.** A fixed period; the length of time set for something to happen. For example: a *term of court* is the time period in which the court may hear cases (hold **sessions**); a *term loan* is a bank loan for over a year; and a **lease** or **jail** *term* is how long each lasts.   **3.** A part of an agreement that deals with a particular subject; for example, a *price term*.   **4.** For *term* **bonds** and *term* **insurance,** see those words.

Termination   Any ending; an ending before the anticipated end; an ending as specifically defined under some law. For example, under the **Uniform Commercial Code,** *termination* marks the end of a **contract** without its being broken by either side.

Terra   (Latin) Land.

Territorial   **1.** Having to do with a particular country. For example, *territorial waters* are the oceans surrounding a country. These waters "belong" to the country out to a certain distance. **2.** Having to do with a particular area. For example, *territorial jurisdiction* is the power of a court to take cases from within its particular geographical area.

Territorial courts   U.S. courts in each **territory**, such as the Virgin Islands. They serve as both federal and state courts.

Territory   Land that is administered by a country, but not a permanent part of that country or completely integrated into its governmental workings.

Test case   **1.** A **lawsuit** brought to establish an important legal principle or right; or breaking a law to challenge it in court. **2.** One case selected from many similar ones to be tried first, with all persons involved in the other cases agreeing to be bound by the **decision.**

Test oath   A **loyalty oath** (see that word).

Testacy (or testate)   Leaving a valid **will.** *Testate succession* is the giving and receiving of property by a will.

Testament   A **will** (see that word).

Testamentary   **1.** Having to do with a **will.** For example, *testamentary capacity* is the mental ability needed to make a valid will; and a *testamentary class* is the group of persons who will eventually **inherit** from a will.

Testator   A person who makes a **will.**

Testify   Give **evidence** under **oath.**

Testimonium clause   The part of a **deed** or other document that contains who signed and when and where it was signed.

Testimony   **Evidence** given by a **witness** under **oath.** This evidence is called *testimonial* and is different from **demonstrative** evidence.

Testis   (Latin) **Witness.**

Theft   Stealing of any kind. In many states, various **common law** crimes such as **larceny** and **embezzlement** have been combined as *theft*.

Theocracy   Government by the dominant religious group in which church law is the highest law.

Theory of pleading doctrine   The **common-law** principle that a person must prove a case *exactly* as pleaded and will lose even if the facts could have won if used to prove a different **pleading.** This theory is *no longer valid* in most courts because pleadings may usually be amended to match the proof.

Theory of the case   **1.** An interpretation of facts and law that fits the facts of a case. It may be one of several theories based on the **evidence** or it may be *the* legal theory that properly explains the evidence. **2.** The facts on which a case is based; the **cause of action** (see that word).

Thereabout

Thereabout (and other "there" words) A vague, overly formal word meaning "approximately there." Like all other "there" words *(thereafter, thereat, thereby, therein, thereof, thereto, theretofore, thereunder, thereupon, therewith, etc.),* it is best left out of a sentence or replaced by the exact thing referred to.

Thin corporation A **corporation** that owes its **stockholders** so much money that the **I.R.S.** will call some of the debt **equity** and call some of the debt payments **dividends**, thus raising the owners' taxes.

Third degree Illegal methods of interrogation to force a person to confess to a crime.

Third market The sale, outside the usual **exchange**, of **stocks** and other **securities**. This is also called "off-board," and is sometimes done by institutional traders of large blocks of stock.

Third party (or person) A person unconnected with a deal, lawsuit, or occurrence, but who may be affected by it. For example, a *third party beneficiary* is a person who is not part of a **contract,** but for whose direct benefit the contract was made. A *third party complaint* is a **complaint** brought by a **defendant** in a lawsuit against someone not in the lawsuit. It brings that person into the lawsuit because that person may be **liable** for all or part of what the **plaintiff** is trying to get from the defendant.

Thirteenth Amendment The U.S. constitutional amendment that abolished slavery.

Thirty-day letter An **I.R.S.** letter to a taxpayer stating a tax **deficiency** (or refusing a refund request) and explaining **appeal** rights.

Threat A communicated **intent** to harm another person by an illegal act. *Threats* against the president, threats of terrorism, threats using the mails, and certain other threats are federal crimes.

Three-judge court A special federal trial court for certain limited types of cases specified by federal **statute. Review** of these cases goes directly to the **Supreme Court.**

Three-mile limit One distance used as a measure of a country's rights to claim control of offshore **territorial** waters.

Through bill A **bill of lading** for goods that will be carried by more than one shipper in sequence.

Throwback rule If the **beneficiary** of a **trust** receives income from the trust in excess of the trust's income that year, and the trust has not in previous years paid out all its income, the excess will be taxed to the beneficiary that year minus a **credit** for tax previously paid by the trust.

Ticket **1.** A list of candidates for political office from one political **party**. **2.** A traffic law violation notice. **3.** A certificate showing a **right** (theater tickets, train tickets, lottery tickets, etc.).

Tie-in See **tying in**.

Tier A six-mile-wide row of **townships** running East-West within a state on government maps. See also **range**.

Time draft (or time bill or time loan) A **draft** (or **bill** or loan) payable at a certain time.

Time immemorial **1.** Since before the memory of anyone now alive. **2.** Since before any oral or written records on the subject.

Time is of the essence When this phrase is in a **contract**, it means that a failure to do what is required by the time specified is a **breach** (breaking) of the contract.

Time-price doctrine Courts may allow a higher price charged for things bought on **credit** than for the same things paid for in cash. This is a way for a seller to get around state *usury* (see that word) laws.

Timely Done in time. For example, a *timely* **suit** is one that is brought to court soon enough to be valid (not barred by a statute of **limitations**, by **laches**, etc.).

Tippee A person given information about a company by an **insider** whose duty to the company and the general public forbids giving out such information.

Title **1.** The name for a part of a **statute**. For example, "Title VII" of the 1964 Civil Rights Act is known to specialists in the field as simply "Title Seven." **2.** The formal right of ownership of property. **3.** A document that shows no. 2. **4.** For **abstract** of; **chain of; clear; color of; defective** (see **defect**); **document of; lucrative; marketable; onerous; paper; perfect; record; root of; torrens**; etc., *title*, see those words. **5.** A *title search* is a search of the land records to see if title is good or restricted; a *title guaranty company* makes this search, then guarantees the title for the buyer; *title standards* are criteria set up by state organizations of banks, real estate lawyers, etc., to evaluate whether or not a title is good; and a *title state* or *title theory jurisdiction* is a state in which the title to mortgaged property is held by the lender until the debt is paid. See also **lien theory state.**

To have and to hold   An unnecessary phrase used in many deeds. At one time this phrase had to be used to make the transfer of land valid, but it is now just excess words.

To wit   An unnecessary phrase meaning "that is to say" or "namely." It can usually be replaced by a colon (:).

Toll   **1.** A fee to use a road, bridge, etc.   **2.** To *toll* a statute of **limitations** (see that word) is to do something to put it off, in effect, "stopping the clock from running."

Tombstone ad   A **stock** (or other **securities**) or land sales notice that clearly states that it is informational only and not itself an offer to buy or sell. It has a black border.

Tonnage tax   A tax on ships based on either their weight or carrying capacity.

Tontine   A reverse type of life **insurance,** now illegal, in which many persons pay into a fund and only those living by a certain date split it up.

Torrens title system   A system of land ownership **registration,** used in some states, in which the actual **title** is recorded and formally approved (usually by a judge) as a "Certificate of Title," rather than the more usual procedure of recording only **evidence** of title, such as a **deed.** *Torrens* registration is supplemental to the regular title system and is voluntary for each purchaser.

Tort   A legal **wrong** done to another person. A **civil** (as opposed to **criminal**) wrong that is not based on an obligation under a **contract.** For an act to be a *tort*, there must be: a legal **duty** owed by one person to another, a **breach** (breaking) of that duty, and harm done as a direct result of the action. Examples of torts are **negligence, battery,** and **libel** (see those words).

Tortfeasor   A person who commits a **tort** (see that word).

Tortious   Having to do with a **tort.**

Total   Complete for legal purposes. For example, a *total disability* may not be "total" in the common language sense, but merely be that which stops a person from doing his or her normal work; and *total loss* by fire need not be a burning to the ground, but merely be a complete commercial loss.

Totalitarianism   **Absolutism** (see that word) in which the government controls most of the small details of each person's life.

This is done through propaganda, an intrusive military and police, etc.

Totten trust Putting your money into a bank account in your name as **trustee** for another person. You can take it out when you want, but if you do not take it out before you die, it becomes the property of that other person.

Touch and stay A ship's right, under its **insurance** policy, to stop and stay at certain ports, but not to carry on any trade there.

Town A type of local government or local area. It means different things in different states. It is important in some states, trivial in others, large in some, small in others.

Township **1.** A division of state land having six miles on each side and varying in importance as a unit of government from state to state. **2.** A division of a **county,** having different meanings and powers in different states.

Tract index A public record containing all recorded **deeds, mortgages, liens,** etc., piece of land by piece according to numbered lots with map references, so if you know exactly where the land is you can easily find out about transfers of ownership and other recorded matters. Compare this with a **grantor-grantee index.**

Trade **1.** Buying and selling; commerce. **2.** A job or profession. **3.** Barter; swapping. **4.** A *trade agreement* is an agreement among countries to allow the sale of certain items (and at certain import tax rates); a *trade association* is a group of similar businesses organized for idea exchange, maintaining standards, and **lobbying;** *trade credit* is **credit** sales made by one business to another (commercial **accounts receivable**); *trade debt* is credit purchases by one business from another (commercial **accounts payable**); a *trade discount* is a price reduction to certain types of business customers (from a lumber dealer to building **contractors**); a *trade dispute* is any **labor dispute** (excluding such things as the refusal to cross **picket** lines); a *trade secret* is a process, tool, chemical compound, etc., that is not generally known to the public and is not patented; and *trade usage* is common, regular practice or custom within a type of business or trade.

Trade name The name of a business. It will usually be legally protected in the area where the company operates and for the types of products in which it deals.

Trademark A distinctive mark, motto, or symbol that a company can reserve by law for its own exclusive use in identifying its products; for example, a picture of a dancing rabbit on the pocket of a particular brand of shirt or the name Hareshirt®. (The ® stands for **registered**, a requirement to protect a *trademark*.)

Traditionary evidence   What a dead person said long ago.

Traffic   Regular commerce, trade, or transportation.

Transaction   **1.** A business deal.   **2.** An occurrence; something that takes place. A group of facts so interconnected that they can be referred to by one legal name, such as a "crime," a "contract," a "wrong," etc.

Transactional immunity   See **immunity**.

Transcript   A copy; especially the official typed copy of the **record** of a court proceeding.

Transfer   To change or move from person to person (sell, give, or sign something over, etc.) or from place to place (court to court, etc.).

Transfer agent   A person (or an institution such as a bank) who keeps track of who owns a company's stocks and bonds. Also called a **registrar**. The transfer agent sometimes also handles **dividend** and **interest** payments.

Transfer payments   Government payments (such as **welfare** or social security) for which the government gets nothing directly in return.

Transfer tax   The name for different types of taxes in different places; for example, an **estate** tax, a gift tax, a tax on the sale of **stocks**, etc. See also **unified transfer tax**.

Transferred intent rule   If a person tries to hit another, but hits a third person instead, the rule says that he or she legally *intended* to hit the third person. This legal **fiction** allows the third person to sue the hitter for an *intentional* **tort** and allows the government to charge the hitter with an intentional **crime**.

Transgressive trust   A **trust** that violates the rule against perpetuities. (See **perpetuity**.)

Transitory action   A **lawsuit** that may be brought in any one of many places.

Trauma   **1.** An injury to the body caused by an external blow.   **2.** Sudden psychological damage.   **3.** Severe psychological damage caused by a specific past event.

Travel Act   The law that makes it a federal crime to travel interstate or to use any interstate or foreign means of transportation, communication, or commerce to commit a crime.

Traveler's check   A **cashier's check** (see that word) bought from a bank to safeguard travel money. It can be cashed only when signed a second time with a matching signature by the purchaser of the traveler's check.

Traverse   An old form of **pleading** in which facts in the other side's pleading were denied.

Treason   The act of a U.S. citizen's helping a foreign government to overthrow, make war against, or seriously injure the U.S.

Treasurer   The person in charge of an organization's money (taking in, paying out, etc.), but not necessarily its financial decisions.

Treasure-trove   Hidden money or other valuables with no known owner. Depending on state law, it may belong to the finder, to the land owner, to the state, or part to each.

Treasury   Department of the Treasury. The U.S. **cabinet** department that handles most national financial, monetary, and tax matters. It runs the Internal Revenue Service (taxes), the Mint (coins), the **Secret Service** (see that word), etc.

Treasury bill, bond, certificate and note   Documents showing that the U.S. Treasury has borrowed money. A *treasury bill* comes due in three, six, nine, or twelve months. It pays no interest, but is sold at a **discount**; a *treasury certificate* comes due in one year and pays interest by **coupon**; a *treasury note* is like a *certificate*, but comes due in one to five years; and a *treasury bond* is issued for long-term borrowing.

Treasury stock (or treasury shares)   Shares of **stock** that have been rebought by the **corporation** that issued them.

Treatise   A large, comprehensive book on a legal subject.

Treaty   A formal agreement between countries on a major political subject. The *treaty clause* of the U.S. **Constitution** requires the approval of two-thirds of the **Senate** for any treaty made by the president.

Treble damages   Triple the amount of actual **damages** will be given in some lawsuits to strongly discourage certain kinds of wrongful actions. A **statute** must authorize treble damages.

Trespass   **1.** A wrongful entry onto another person's property. **2.** An old term for many types of civil wrongs or **torts**. For example, the *trespass* in no. 1 was called *trespass quare clausum fregit* (see **quare**); modern **contract** lawsuits grew out of *tres-*

pass on the case and *trespass vi et armis* (force and arms) became modern lawsuits for both **negligence** and **battery** (see those words).

Trial The process of deciding a case (giving **evidence**, making **arguments**, deciding by a judge and **jury**, etc.). It occurs if the dispute is not resolved by **pleadings**, pre-trial **motions**, or **settlement**. A trial usually takes place in open court, and may be followed by a **judgment**, an **appeal**, etc.

Trial balance A separate totaling of all **credit** entries and all **debit** entries in an **account** (or of all accounts with a *credit balance* and all accounts with a *debit balance*) to compare the two. If they are not equal, there is a **bookkeeping** error.

Trial list (or calendar) See **calendar**.

Tribal lands Lands held by an Indian nation as a whole; a **reservation**.

Tribe **1.** American Indian nation. **2.** *American Constitutional Law* by Tribe; a **treatise**.

Tribunal Court.

Trier of fact **1.** The **jury** or the judge if there is no jury. **2.** An **arbitrator**, an **administrative law judge**, etc.

Trover An old type of lawsuit, now rarely used, in which a piece of property was claimed to be lost by you and then found by the person from whom you want it back. This got around the problem of proving the thing was wrongfully taken because all you had to prove was that it was yours and that the other person had it.

True bill An **indictment** approved and made by a grand **jury**.

True lease A lease that qualifies under **I.R.S.** rules for the **lessor** to claim ownership benefits (such as investment tax **credits** and **deductions** for **depreciation**) and for the **lessee** to deduct payments from income. *True leases* are different from **installment** sales.

True person doctrine The "rule" that a totally blameless person need not try to escape before killing a person who suddenly attacks with deadly force. Contrast this with the **flee-to-the-wall** doctrine.

True value rule If **corporate stock** is not fully paid for in "real money" or its equivalent, stockholders may be **liable** to **creditors** of the company for the difference.

Trust **1.** A group of companies that has a **monopoly** (see that word). **2.** Any transfer or holding of money or property to one person for the benefit of another. For example, a mother signs over **stocks** to a bank to manage for her daughter with instructions to give the daughter the income each year until she turns thirty and then to give it all to her. In this example, the mother is the **settlor** or **grantor** of the **trust**, the bank is the **trustee**, and the daughter is the **beneficiary**. However, a trust need not be set up explicitly by name; for example, if a father gives a son some money saying "half of this is for your brother," this may be a *trust* too. Also, a trust can be set up in a **will**; created by formally stating that you *yourself* hold money in trust for another person; and created several other ways, both intentional and unintentional. **3.** There are hundreds of types of trusts. Some of those defined in this dictionary are: **accumulation; active; alimony; annuity; bond; business; charitable; charitable remainder; Clafin; Clifford; common law; community; complete voluntary; complex; constructive; contingent; direct; directory; discretionary; dry; equipment; estate; executed; executory; express; fixed; foreign; foreign situs; generation-skipping; governmental; grantor; honorary; imperfect; implied; indestructible; instrumental; insurance; inter vivos; investment; involuntary; irrevocable; limited;** life **insurance; life estate (or interest);** living; marital deduction; **Massachusetts; ministerial; mixed; naked; nominal; nominee; passive; perpetual; personal; pourover; power of appointment; precatory; private; public; real estate investment; reciprocal; resulting; revocable; savings bank; secret; shifting; short-term; simple; special; spendthrift; sprinkling; tentative; testamentary; Totten; transgressive; unitrust; vertical; voluntary;** and **voting.** (See those words.) **4.** Other *trust* words follow here.

Trust account   See **trust deposit.**

Trust allotment   Land given to Indians that is held in **trust** for them by the government for a certain time.

Trust certificate   A document showing that property is held in **trust** as **security** for a debt based on money used to buy the property. See also **deed of trust.**

Trust company   A bank or other organization that manages **trusts,** acts as **executor** of **wills,** and performs other financial functions.

Trust deed   A **deed of trust** (see that word).

Trust deposit   Money or property put in a bank to be kept separate (often for ethical or legal reasons) or used for a special purpose.

Trust estate   The legal right of the **trustee**, the legal right of the **beneficiary**, or the property itself.

Trust ex delicto (or ex maleficio or ivitum)   (Latin) "From crime or wrongdoing." A **constructive trust** (see that word).

Trust fund   **1.** Money or property set aside in a **trust** or set aside for a special purpose.   **2.** Money or property that *should* be treated as a trust. For example, the *trust fund theory* (or doctrine) says that certain funds (such as those improperly used by a corporation's **directors** or others) will be considered as held in trust for **creditors** or others.

Trust indenture   **1.** A document that spells out the details of a **trust**.   **2.** The *Trust Indenture Act* is a federal law requiring certain investor-protection provisions in documents used to **issue** some kinds of **bonds**.

Trust instrument   A **deed of trust** (see that word) or a formal **declaration** *of trust*.

Trust officer   A person in a **trust company** who manages **trusts**.

Trust receipt   A document by which one person lends money to buy something and the borrower promises to hold the thing in **trust** for the lender until the debt is paid off. These deals are now usually handled by **security** agreements.

Trust state (or trust theory jurisdiction)   A state in which **title** to mortgaged property is transferred to a **trustee** to hold until the debt is paid. See also **title** state and **lien theory state**.

Trust territory   An area put under one country's administration by the United Nations.

Trustee   **1.** A person who holds money or property for the benefit of another person (see **trust**).   **2.** A person who has a **fiduciary** relationship towards another person; for example, a lawyer, an **agent**, etc.   **3.** A *trustee in bankruptcy* is a person appointed by a court to manage a **bankrupt** person's property and to decide who gets it; and a *trustee de son tort* (French) is a person who is held responsible for his or her acts because of some wrongful or **negligent** conduct while improperly claiming the right to take on and taking on the duties of a trustee.   **4.** A prisoner whose good behavior has earned a position of trust.

Truth-in-Lending Act   The **Consumer Credit Protection Act** (see that word).

Try   To *try* a case is to argue it in court as a lawyer, decide it as a judge, or participate in it in one of several ways.

Turncoat witness A **witness** who is expected to give helpful **testimony**, but who **testifies** for the other side.

Turning state's evidence See **state's evidence**.

Turnkey contract **1.** A **contract** in which a builder agrees to complete a building to a specific point, usually "ready to move in," and in which the builder assumes all construction risks. **2.** A drilling contract in which the driller does all the work up to the point when a well can begin production and in which, for a set fee, the driller assumes all construction risks except the risk of a dry hole.

Turnover (or turnover rate) The rate at which **inventory** or financial **assets** are replaced during a time period.

Turnover order A court order that something be given to someone else (property from a **defendant** to a **plaintiff** who has won the case, property that is in dispute to the court for safekeeping, a **bankrupt's** property to the **trustee**, etc.). This is a general word for many different **orders**, **writs**, etc.

Turntable doctrine **Attractive nuisance** (see that word).

Turpitude Unjust, dishonest, or immoral activity.

Twelfth Amendment The U.S. constitutional amendment that requires separate voting by **electors** for president and vice-president.

Twentieth Amendment The U.S. constitutional amendment that moved up the presidential inauguration and the congressional session from March to January, eliminating a "**lame duck**" **legislative** session.

Twenty-fifth Amendment The U.S. constitutional amendment that set up procedures for appointing a president and vice-president in case of death, removal, or resignation.

Twenty-first Amendment The U.S. constitutional amendment ending national **prohibition** (the banning of alcoholic beverages).

Twenty-fourth Amendment The U.S. constitutional amendment forbidding a **poll tax**.

Twenty-second Amendment The U.S. constitutional amendment prohibiting three-**term** presidents, limiting one person to no more than ten consecutive years as president.

Twenty-sixth Amendment The U.S. constitutional amendment that made the voting age eighteen.

Twenty-third Amendment The U.S. constitutional amendment that gave Washington, D.C. residents the right to vote in presidential elections.

Twisting

Twisting Misrepresenting policies to convince a person to switch insurance companies.

Two issue rule If a judge makes an **error** in a jury **charge** on one **issue**, but there is more than one issue in the trial, and it cannot be proved that the jury based its **verdict** on that issue, the verdict is good. This rule is not followed in all states.

Two witness rule Under this rule a person cannot be convicted of **perjury** (or, in some states, of **first degree murder** or other crime with a possible death penalty) unless two witnesses **testify** that the person's statement was false (or that the person committed the crime).

Two-tier method Double taxation of **corporate** income (when the company gets it and when the owners get it).

Tying in A seller's refusal to sell a product unless another product is bought with it. If a seller has a **monopoly** on a product, *tying in* the sale of another product may be a violation of the **antitrust** laws, especially if the *right* to sell a **patented** product is tied into selling a non-patented product.

Uu

U.C.C. **Uniform Commercial Code** (see that word).

U.C.C.C. Uniform Consumer Credit Code. (Also called the *U.C.3.* or *U3C.*) A **uniform act** adopted by some states to **regulate** the way merchants and lending institutions give **credit** to **consumers.**

U.C.M.J. Uniform Code of Military Justice. Rules of conduct and criminal behavior for members of the armed forces. See **Code of Military Justice.**

U.L.A. Uniform Laws Annotated.

U.L.P.A. Uniform Limited Partnership Act.

U.N. United Nations.

U.P.A. Uniform Partnership Act.

U.S.C. *United States Code.* The official lawbooks where all federal laws are collected by subject matter. They are recompiled every six years, and supplements are published when needed.

U.S.C.A. **1.** *United States Code Annotated.* The lawbooks where all federal laws are collected by subject and partially explained. Cases from state and federal courts referring to each federal law are listed. **2. United States court of appeals** (see that word).

U.S.C.C.A.N. United States Code Congressional and Administrative News. A series of books with the texts of and cross-references to all federal laws and some Congressional committee reports and federal **administrative regulations**.

U.S.C.S. A set of lawbooks similar to **U.S.C.A.**

U.S.D.A. United States Department of Agriculture. The **cabinet** department that **regulates** farm activities, sets agricultural policy, carries on agricultural research and education programs, etc.

U.S.D.C. United States District Court.

U.T.I. Undistributed taxable income.

Ubi (Latin) Where.

Ukase A wide-sweeping decree by a king or other person in full control of a country.

Ullage The amount of liquid missing from a closed container.

Ultimate facts Facts essential to a **plaintiff's** or a **defendant's** case. Basic or "core" facts.

Ultimate purchaser A consumer or business purchaser who intends a product for use, not resale.

Ultra (Latin) Beyond; outside of; in excess of. For example, *ultra vires* actions are things a **corporation** does that are outside the scope of powers or activities permitted by its **charter** or **articles of incorporation.**

Umpire A person chosen to decide a **labor dispute** when the original **arbitrators** disagree.

Unauthorized practice Nonlawyers doing things that only lawyers are permitted to do. Who and what fits into this definition is constantly changing and the subject of dispute. If, however, a clear case comes up (for example, a nonlawyer pretending to be a lawyer and setting up a law office), the practice may be prohibited and the person punished under the state's criminal laws.

Unavailability A **witness** is unavailable if dead or insane or in the federal courts and some state courts, if the witness is beyond the reach of the court's **summons,** or beyond the ability of the person who wants to use that witness's **testimony** to bring the witness to court. Once the witness's *unavailability* is shown, past testimony, **dying declarations**, and certain other types of **hearsay** by that witness may be used in court if it is properly verified.

Unavoidable accident (or casualty, cause, danger, etc.) An accident in which everyone was careful, yet it happened. In some states this could result in a lawsuit with no **damages** awarded, in the reopening of a lawsuit because the **defendant** was prevented by an accident from answering the court papers or showing up in court, etc.

Unclean hands See **clean hands**.

Unconscionability Sales practices that are so greatly unfair that a court will not permit them. For example, the use of small print and technical language in contracts with poorly-educated persons, combined with prices that were three times higher than normal, was called *unconscionable* by one court. The **Uniform Commercial Code** permits **rescission** ("unmaking") of unconscionable contracts.

Unconstitutional Laws or actions that conflict with the U.S. **Constitution.**

Under protest See **protest.**

Undersigned The person (or persons) whose name is signed at the end of a document.

Understanding A vague word meaning anything from silent, informal agreement to a valid, written **contract.**

Undertaking 1. A promise. 2. A promise made in the course of a lawsuit to the judge or to the other side. 3. **Bonds** or other financial **securities;** the process of putting out these bonds. 4. A venture of any kind.

Underwrite 1. To insure. An *underwriter* is an insurer. 2. To guarantee to purchase any **stock** or **bonds** that remain unsold after a public sale, or to sell an **issue** of stock or bonds *for* a company or purchased *from* a company. The person (or organization) who does this is an *underwriter.*

Undistributed (or undivided) profits tax A tax on a company's profits that are kept (rather than paid to stockholders) in excess of reasonable needs (paying bills, expansion, contingencies, etc.). The federal tax is called an **accumulated earnings tax.**

Undivided right (or title) Property held by two or more persons under the same right. These persons may have different financial stakes in the property, but they all have full rights of possession.

Undue More than necessary; improper; illegal. For example, *undue influence* is pressure that takes away a person's free will to make decisions. Undue influence involves misusing a position of confidence or taking advantage of a person's weakness or distress improperly to change that person's actions or decisions.

Unearned income **1.** Money that has been received, but not yet "earned"; for example, a landlord's getting a January rent payment in December. **2.** Income from investments, rather than from salary or wages. This was formerly taxed at a higher rate than the rate on **earned income**.

Unemployment benefits (or compensation or insurance) State payments to persons who have worked a certain minimum length of time, given when they are laid off or have lost their jobs. Plans have varying payment rates and different qualifications rules, such as the person being "available for work."

Unethical conduct Actions that violate professional standards such as the lawyers' **Code of Professional Responsibility.**

Unfair competition **1.** Too closely imitating the name, product, or advertising of another company in order to take away its business. This is called "passing off." **2.** Some states recognize various other dishonest trade practices, such as using someone else's work unfairly, as *unfair competition.* **3.** *Unfair methods of competition* is a slightly broader phrase, used by the *Federal Trade Commission,* to bring in more types of unfair conduct than the courts had previously recognized.

Unfair labor practice An action by a **union** or by an employer that is prohibited by law; for example, an employer's attempt to force an employee to give up union organizing activities.

Unified transfer tax A federal tax on transfers by **gift** or death. It replaced the separate federal gift and **estate** taxes. The *unified transfer credit* is a **credit** against the unified transfer tax. It replaced the lifetime gift and estate tax **exemptions.**

Uniform Regular; even. Applying generally, equally, and evenhandedly.

Uniform acts (or uniform laws) Laws in various subject areas, proposed by the commissioners on Uniform State Laws, that are often adopted, in whole or in part, by many states. Some of

Uniform Code of Military Justice

these are the Uniform Anatomical Gifts Act, the **Reciprocal Enforcement of Support Act**, and the **Uniform Commercial Code**.

Uniform Code of Military Justice   See **Code of Military Justice**.

Uniform Commercial Code   A comprehensive set of laws on every major type of business law. It has been adopted by almost every state, in whole or in major part. It replaced many older uniform laws, such as the Uniform Negotiable Instruments Law and the Uniform Sales Act.

Unilateral   One-sided. (For *unilateral contract,* see **contract**.) A *unilateral mistake* about a contract's *terms* usually will not get a person out of the contract unless the other side knew about the mistaken idea all along.

Union   1. Any joining together of persons, organizations, or things for a particular purpose.   2. An organization of workers, formed to **negotiate** with employers on wages, working conditions, etc. **Labor unions** include: *closed* (highly restricted in members by small numbers, long apprenticeships, high fees, etc.; see also **closed shop**); *company* (sponsored by employer; now usually forbidden by labor laws); *craft* or *horizontal* (persons in the same craft, no matter where they work); *independent* (persons working for one employer who form a union with no affiliations); *industrial* or *vertical* (working in one industry, regardless of job type); *local* (workers in one company or place who affiliate their union with a larger one); *open* (easy to get into; (see also **open shop**); and *trade* (refers to either a labor union generally or a craft union).

Union certification   See **certification proceeding**.

Union security clause   The provision in a **contract** between a **union** and an employer that sets out the union's status and explains which types of employees must belong to the union.

Union shop   A business in which all workers must join a particular union once employed.

Unit of production   One barrel of oil (or an equivalent measure of a different **natural resource**) out of the estimated number that will be produced from a particular well, **lease,** or property. The "unit" is each barrel's fractional part of the whole estimated production. The total costs and profits of each venture are divided among each barrel for tax purposes.

Unit ownership acts   State laws on **condominiums**.

Unit pricing   Pricing by item and not by a flat **contract** price on a total deal involving many items. *Unit pricing* may also mean pricing by each unit of weight (per ounce of peanut butter rather than per jar), by length (by board-foot, rather than by board), etc.

Unit rule **1.** A way of valuing **stocks** and other **securities** by taking the sale price of one **share** of stock sold on a stock **exchange**, ignoring all other facts and assumptions about value. **2.** A rule binding all members of a group to vote the way the majority of the group votes.

United States attorney A lawyer appointed by the president to handle U.S. **civil** and **criminal** legal matters in a U.S. **judicial district** (all or part of a state). Also called **district attorney** (see that word).

United States commissioner (or magistrate) See **magistrate.**

United States court of appeals These are federal courts (one to each "**circuit**," an area of several states) that hear **appeals** from the U.S. district courts. They used to be called the "U.S. circuit courts."

United States courts The U.S. **Supreme Court, courts of appeals, district courts, court of claims,** Customs Court, Customs and Patent Appeals, etc. These are *U.S. courts* as opposed to *state* courts.

United States Government Organization Manual An annual U.S. publication that summarizes most information on the branches, agencies, and persons running the U.S. government.

United States Reports The volumes in which decisions of the U.S. **Supreme Court** are collected.

United States Statutes at Large See **Statutes at large.**

Unitrust A **trust** (see that word) in which a fixed percentage of the trust property is paid out each year to the **beneficiaries.** To qualify for special tax benefits, a unitrust must comply with several **I.R.S.** requirements.

Unity **1.** An identical interest in property held jointly. There are the *unities* of *time* (the property was received at the same time), *title* (received in the same **deed** or event), *interest* (each person getting the same ownership rights), and *possession* (each has the same right to possess the whole property). In addition, *unity of person* refers to the way property is held "as one person" by **tenants** *by the entireties.* **2.** *Unity of possession* also refers to the **merger** (see that word) of rights in land.

Universal Everything or everyone.

Unjust enrichment The legal principle that when a person obtains money or property unfairly, it should be returned. (This does not include merely driving a hard bargain or being lucky in a deal.)

Unlawful Contrary to law; unauthorized by law. Not necessarily a crime, but at least either a **tort** or disapproved of by the law.

Unlawful detainer Holding on to land or buildings beyond the time you have a right to them.

Unliquidated See **liquidated.**

Unmarketable title See **marketable** title.

Unnatural act **1.** Sodomy (see that word). **2.** A **will** that gives away most of a person's property, without apparent reason, to other than immediate relatives.

Unprofessional conduct **1.** Conduct that violates a profession's ethical code, such as the lawyer's **Code of Professional Responsibility** (see that word). **2.** Conduct that is generally considered immoral, unethical, or dishonorable. (This conduct must generally relate to the performance of the person's duties for it to be included in no. 1.)

Unreasonable See **reasonable.**

Unrelated offenses Crimes or other wrongdoings not related to the subject of a prosecution. These *unrelated offenses* may not be used to show a person's general character.

Unwritten law **1.** Things people do because they are considered right, just, or usual. **2.** Any one of several commonly held assumptions about the law that are *not* laws and will not be enforced by a court; for example, the "law" that a husband will not be punished if he kills his wife's lover. **3.** **Common law** or judge-made law as opposed to **statutes, regulations,** etc.

Upset price A **reserve** (see that word) price.

Urban easement The right of most streetside property to get light, air, and free entrance from the street side. See also **ancient lights.**

Usage A general, uniform, well-known course of conduct followed in a particular area or business. *Usage* is important in interpreting ambiguous **contracts.**

Use An old method of transferring and holding land, similar to a **trust,** in which one person got legal ownership, but another person got the use of the land. For such exotic "uses" as *shifting use* or *springing use,* see a book on the history of land law.

Use immunity   See **immunity**.

Use tax   Tax on some products brought into a state without paying the state's **sales tax**.

Useful   **1.** In **patent** law, something is *useful* if it actually *does* something (as opposed to merely existing for its own sake or conveying information) that can be "applied to some practical use beneficial to society." This is a prerequisite for **patent**ability.   **2.** In **tax** law, *useful life* is one measure of the time period for the **depreciation** of business property. It need not be the actual length of time something will be used.

Usufruct   An old word for the right to use something as long as it is not changed or used up.

Usurious   Involving **usury** (see that word).

Usury   Charging an illegally high rate of **interest**.

Utility   A requirement for a device or process to be **patented**. See **useful**.

Utter   **1.** Put into circulation. **Issue** or put out a **check**.   **2.** Say.   **3.** Enough so that it will be considered complete, total, or **absolute**.

Uxor   (Latin) Wife. Abbreviated *ux*.

V.   **1.** An abbreviation for *versus* or "against" in the name of a case. For example, *Smith v. Jones* means that *Smith* is suing *Jones*.   **2.** Volume.

V.A.   Veterans Administration. The U.S. agency that administers benefits and programs for armed services veterans. These programs include hospitals, college tuition assistance, etc.

V.A.T.   **Value added tax** (see that word).

V.R.M.   **Variable rate mortgage** (see that word).

Vacate   **1. Annul;** set aside; take back. For example, when a judge *vacates a judgment*, it is wiped out completely.   **2.** Move out or empty.

Vadium   (Latin) A **pledge**.

Vagrancy

Vagrancy   A vague, general word for "hanging around" in public with no purpose and no honest means of support.

Vague   **1.** Indefinite; uncertain; imprecise. **2.** The *vagueness doctrine* is the rule that a **criminal** law may be **unconstitutional** if it does not clearly say what is required or prohibited. A law that violates the **due process clause** in this way is void *for vagueness*. See also **overbreadth**.

Valid   **1.** Binding; legal; complying with all needed formalities. **2.** Worthwhile; sufficient.

Valuable consideration   Same as **consideration** (see that word).

Value   **1.** Worth. This may be what something *cost*, what it would cost to *replace*, what it would bring on the open market, etc. *Actual value, cash value, fair value, market value*, etc., may all mean the same. See **market value**. **2.** *For value* or *value received* means "for **consideration**." These phrases often go in a **contract** or **note** to show that it is meant to be valid even if no *consideration* is mentioned in the document itself.

Value added tax   A tax on each step of a manufacturing process based on the value of what is produced minus the value of the materials bought.

Value rule   One measure of **damages.** It is the difference between what was received and what was promised.

Valued policy   An **insurance** policy in which the items insured are given an exact value. This is in contrast to an *open policy* in which a value need not be placed on items until they are lost, damaged, etc.

Vandalism   The intentional destruction of another person's property.

Variable annuity (or insurance)   An **annuity** (or **insurance** policy) with payments that depend on the income generated by particular investments. It is also called "**asset**-linked."

Variable rate mortgage   A **mortgage** with payments that change (every year, two years, five years, etc.) based on a standard index such as the **prime** rate.

Variance   **1.** A difference between what is alleged (said will be proved) in **pleading** and what is actually proved in a **trial**. **2.** Official permission to use land or buildings in a way that would otherwise violate the **zoning** regulations for the neighborhood.

Vel non   (Latin) Or not.

Vendee   Buyer.

Vendor   Seller.

Vendor's lien   A catchall phrase for various types of **liens** held by the seller of property, including the *purchase price lien* (not usually recognized by law) of a person who sells land with no **security** and the lien of a seller who holds goods until the price is paid.

Venire facias   (Latin) A command to the **sheriff** to assemble a **jury.**

Venireman   Juror.

Venue   The local area where a case may be tried. A court system may have **jurisdiction** (power) to take a case in a wide geographic area, but the proper *venue* for the case may be one place within that area for the convenience of the parties, etc. Jurisdiction is the subject of fixed rules, but venue is often left up to the **discretion** (good judgment) of the judge.

Verba   (Latin) Words; as in *verba artis,* "words of art" or technical terms.

Verbal   Spoken; partly spoken and partly written; written but unsigned; or lacking some other formality.

Verdict   The **jury's** decision.   **1.** The usual verdict in a **civil** case, one where the jury decides which side wins (and how much, sometimes), is called a *general verdict.* When the jury is asked to answer specific questions of **fact,** it is called a *special verdict.* For **compromise, directed, sealed,** etc., *verdicts,* see those words.   **2.** The jury's verdict in a **criminal** case is usually "guilty" or "not guilty" of each **charge.** A jury might also make *sentencing* decisions.

Verify   **1. Swear** in writing to the truth or accuracy of a document.   **2.** Confirm; prove the truth of; back up; check up on.

Versus   Against.

Vertical   In a chain, such as from manufacturer to wholesaler to retailer (as opposed to among various manufacturers, among various retailers, etc.). In **antitrust** law, a *vertical trust* is the combining of several of these levels under one ownership or control.

Vertical union   An **industrial union** (see that word).

Vest   **1.** Give an immediate, fixed, and full right.   **2.** Take immediate effect (see **vested**).

Vested   **1. Absolute, accrued,** complete, not subject to any **conditions** that could take it away; not **contingent** on anything. For example, if a person sells you a house and gives you a **deed,** you have a *vested interest* in the property even if the sale **contract** allows the seller to stay in the house for ten years; and a pension is *vested* if you get it at retirement age even if you leave the company before that.   **2.** There are several types of **pension plan** *vesting.* For example, *"cliff"* *vesting* (until you work a certain number of years, you get nothing; after that, you get all your accrued **benefits**); *"graded"* *vesting* (additional percentages of your accrued benefits are added the longer you work); and *"rule of 45" vesting* (after your age plus the number of years you have worked for the company equals 45, part of your accrued benefits become vested, with the rest vested in the next few years). There are variations on all of these methods.

Veterans Administration   See **V.A.**

Veterans preference   Federal and state laws giving honorably discharged war veterans various hiring preferences, with the strongest usually going to disabled veterans.

Veto   A refusal by the president or a governor to sign into law a **bill** that has been passed by a **legislature.** In the case of a presidential veto, the bill can still become a law if two-thirds of each **house** of Congress votes to *override* the veto. An *item veto* is the veto by a state governor of only part of an **appropriations** bill, and a *pocket veto* is the holding by the president of a bill at the end of a **legislative session.** This acts as a *veto.* Also, any member of the *United Nations* **Security Council** can *veto* a **resolution** of the Council.

Vexatious litigation   Lawsuits brought without any just cause or good reason. Also see **malicious** *prosecution.*

Vi et armis   (Latin) "Force and arms" (see **trespass**).

Via   (Latin) A right of way or road.

Viable child   A child developed enough to live outside the womb.

Vicarious liability   Legal responsibility for the acts of another person because of some relationship with that person; for example, the **liability** of an employer for the acts of an employee.

Vice   **1.** Illegal (and considered immoral) activities such as gambling and prostitution.   **2.** An imperfection or defect.   **3.** Second in command, or substitute.

Vide   (Latin) See. For example, *vide ante* means "look at the words or sections that come before this one."

Videlicet   (Latin) "That is to say." An unnecessary phrase used to separate a general statement and specific things that explain it.

View   1. The right in some cases to have your windows free from new obstructions. See also **ancient lights**.   2. An inspection by a jury or by persons appointed by a court (called "viewers") of an accident scene, a crime scene, a route for a proposed road, etc.

Vigilance   Watchfulness. Reasonable promptness in pursuing or guarding a **right,** enforcing a **claim,** etc.

Vinculo matrimonii   (Latin) See **a vinculo matrimonii**.

Violent presumption   Full, if indirect proof. For example, the fact that the sun was shining is a *violent presumption* that an event did not take place at midnight in New York.

Vir   (Latin) A man; a husband.

Virtual adoption   See **equitable** adoption.

Virtue   1. By *virtue* of means "by the power of" or "because." 2. Something worthwhile or good (in a practical, rather than a moral sense).

Vis   (Latin) Force or violence. For example, *vis major* is an irresistible force or a natural disaster. See also **act of God** and **force majeure**.

Visa   Permission to travel in a country, given by officials of that country who usually mark it into a person's *passport*. A *visa* is also sometimes required as permission from your *own* country to travel to an otherwise "off-limits" country.

Visitation   1. The right to see children after a **divorce** or **separation**. 2. Outside inspection or supervision.

Vital statistics   Births, deaths, diseases, marriages, divorces, etc.

Vitiate   Cause to fail. Destroy (either totally or partially) the legal effect or binding force of something. For example, **fraud** *vitiates* a **contract**.

Viva voce   1. (Latin) "Living voice"; orally, as opposed to in writing. 2. A *viva voce vote* is usually taken on minor questions. The person leading the session decides who wins based on which side sounds louder.

Viz.   An awkward term, meaning "that is to say" or "these are." Usually a colon (:) alone will do.

Void   Without legal effect; of no binding force; wiped out. For example, a *void contract* is an agreement by which no one is (or ever was) bound because something legally necessary is missing from it. See also **voidable**.

Voidable

Voidable Something that can be legally avoided or declared **void** (see that word), but is not automatically void. For example, a *voidable contract* is a **contract** that one or both sides can legally get out of, but is effective and binding if no one chooses to get out of it.

Voir dire (French) "Look-speak." The examination of a possible **juror** by the lawyers and the judge to decide whether he or she is acceptable to decide a case. *Voir dire* is also the preliminary examination of a **witness** to decide whether that person should **testify**. [pronounce: vwah deer]

Volentia non fit injuria (Latin) "A willing person cannot be injured legally." See **assumption of risk**.

Volstead Act A now dead federal law prohibiting liquor. The law was passed under the now repealed **Eighteenth Amendment** to the U.S. **Constitution.**

Voluntary **1.** With complete free will; intentional. In this sense, a *voluntary trust* is one set up intentionally, rather than imposed by law. **2.** Free; without **consideration.** In this sense, a *voluntary trust* is set up as a gift, rather than as a way of protecting, for example, a **mortgage** holder.

Voter A person who has the legal qualifications to vote; a person who has **registered** to vote; a person who has actually voted.

Voting Rights Act A federal law that prohibited literacy and character tests, provided for federal voter **registration,** and prohibited states from certain other practices.

Voting stock Usually **common stock** (see that word). However, other types of stock can sometimes vote within their type (or *class*).

Voting trust A deal in which stockholders in a company pool their **shares of stock** for the purpose of voting in stockholders' meetings.

Vouch Give personal assurance of the truthfulness, validity, or existence of something.

Voucher **1.** A document that authorizes the giving out of something, usually cash. **2.** A **receipt** or **release;** the **account** book that shows these receipts.

Vs. Versus. See **V.**

W   West or western.

W.D.   Western **district**.

Wage and hour laws   Federal and state laws setting minimum wages and maximum hours of work, especially the *Fair Labor Standards Act.*

Wage assignment   An arrangement in which a person allows his or her wages to be paid directly to a **creditor.** It is illegal in most situations in many states. See also **garnishment.**

Wage earner's plan   See **Chapter Thirteen.**

Wager of law   A practice in old England by which a person accused of something, such as owing money, could swear that the money was not owed and could bring eleven neighbors (called *compurgators*) to swear to the person's general truthfulness.

Wager policy   A **gambling policy** (see that word).

Wages   **1. Salary. 2.** Salary *plus* **commissions,** bonuses, company housing, tips, etc. **3.** Regular payments based on hours worked or work produced, as *opposed to* salary.

Wagner Act   A federal law, passed in 1935, that established most basic union rights. It prohibited several employer actions (such as attempting to force employees to stay out of a union) and labeled these actions "unfair labor practices." It also set up the National Labor Relations Board to help enforce the new labor laws.

Wait and see statute   A state law that avoids some of the problems with the rule against perpetuities (see **perpetuity**) by allowing time to pass to find out if a **will** or **trust** violates the rule.

Waive   Give up, renounce, or disclaim a privilege, right, or benefit with full knowledge of what you are doing.

Waiver   The voluntary giving up of a right (see **waive**). For example, *waiver of immunity* is the act of a **witness** who gives up the **constitutional** right to refuse to give evidence against himself or herself and who proceeds to **testify. A criminal defendant waives immunity** merely by **taking the stand.**

Waiving time   Allowing a court to take a longer time than usual to **try** you on a criminal charge.

Walsh-Healey Act   A federal law that set up minimum wage, hour, and work condition standards for employees working for **contractors** on federal jobs.

Want   **1.** Desire.   **2.** Lack.

Wanton   **1. Reckless**, heedless, or **malicious**.   **2.** Weighing about two thousand pounds.   **3.** Floating in broth.   **4.** In need.

War crimes   Crimes committed by countries and individuals that violate **international laws** of the conduct of war.

War powers clauses   The U.S. **constitutional** clauses that give Congress the power to declare war and raise armies and give the president the power to carry on the war.

Ward   **1.** A division of a city for elections and other purposes.   **2.** A person, especially a child, placed by the court under the care of a **guardian**.

Warehouse receipt   A piece of paper proving that you own something stored in a warehouse. It may be a **negotiable instrument**.

Warehouser (warehouseman)   A person in the business of storing goods. A *warehouser's lien* is the right of a person storing goods to keep them until charges have been paid.

Warrant   **1.** To promise, especially in a **contract** or in a **deed** (see **warranty**).   **2.** Permission given by a judge (or **magistrate**, etc.) to a police officer (or **sheriff**, etc.) to **arrest** a person, conduct a search, seize an item, etc.   **3.** An **option** to buy **stock**.   **4.** To promise that certain facts are true.   **5.** The name for certain written authorizations to pay or collect money.   **6.** For **bench warrant, distress** warrant, etc., see those words.

Warranty   **1.** Any promise (or a presumed promise, called an *implied warranty*) that certain facts are true.   **2.** In land law, a *warranty* is a promise in a **deed** that the **title** of land being sold is good and is complete ("**marketable**"). (See **general** and **special warranty deeds**. See also **quit claim deed**).   **3.** In the law of buildings, a *construction* or **home owner's warranty** is the promise that it was built right, and a *warranty of habitability* is the implied promise to buyers or renters that a house is fit to live in.   **4.** In commercial law, a *warranty* is either no. 3 or no. 2.   **5.** In **consumer** law, a *warranty* is the same as in the previous definitions, plus any obligations imposed by law on a seller for a buyer; for example, the *warranty* that goods are **merchantable** and the warranty that goods sold as fit for a particular purpose are fit for that purpose. Also, under recent federal law, if a written consumer warranty is not "full" (as to labor and material for repairs) it must be labeled *limited warranty* in the sales contract.

Wash sale   1. Selling something and buying something else that is basically the same thing. The word often is used to describe the nearly simultaneous buying and selling of **shares** of the same **stock.   2. Rescission** (see that word) is sometimes called a "wash" because all original rights, **liabilities,** and property are returned.   **3.** Breaking even financially on a sale.

Waste   Abuse or destruction of property in your rightful possession, but belonging to someone else, or in which someone else has certain rights.

Waste-book   A merchant's log of rough notes of transactions as they occur. Also called a "blotter."

Wasting   Can be used up. For example, a *wasting asset* (or property) can be an oil **lease** or **patent** right that has a limited useful life and can be given a **depletion allowance** (see that word) for tax purposes; and a *wasting trust* is one that uses up the **principal** to make payments.

Water rights   The right to use water from a river, stream, ditch, pipe, etc. (sometimes for a specific purpose or amount). See also **riparian rights.**

Watered stock   A **stock issue** that is put out as if fully paid for, but that is not because some or all of the shares were sold (or given out) for less than full price.

Waybill   A document made out by a **carrier** that includes the "who, what, where, how, and when" of goods shipped. See also **bill of lading.**

Weight of evidence   The more *convincing* **evidence** in a legal dispute, not necessarily the larger quantity.

Welfare   1. Public financial assistance to certain categories of poor persons.   **2.** Health, happiness, and general well-being.   **3.** The *welfare clause* of the U.S. **Constitution** gives the federal government the power to pass laws for the "general welfare" of the people.

WEST LAW   A computerized legal research source.

Wharton rule   Concert of action rule (see that word).

Whereas   A vague word, often used to mean "because" when placed at the beginning of a legislative **bill** (in the explanation for why the bill should be passed and made law).

Whereby

Whereby (and all other "where" words) A vague word meaning "by means of," "how?" or several other things. This word, like all the other vague, formal "where" words (*whereas, wherefore, whereof, whereon, whereunder, whereupon,* etc.), is best left out of a sentence or replaced by a specific thing, place, idea, etc.

Wherefore A vague word, often found in a **complaint** (see that word) to begin the section where the **plaintiff** spells out exactly what he or she wants from the **defendant** or wants the court to do.

Whipsaw strike **1.** A **strike** that is particularly harsh to convince other companies to give in to **union** demands. **2.** A strike against a company in which the union uses the added pressure of allowing the company's competitors to continue working by not striking them.

White acre See **Black acre.**

White slave The original word for a woman involved in a **Mann Act** (see that word) violation.

White-collar crimes **1.** Commercial crimes like **embezzlement, price-fixing,** etc. **2.** Nonviolent crimes.

Whole law A state or country's **internal law** plus its **conflict of laws** rules. See also **renvoi.**

Whole life See **insurance.**

Wholesale Selling (usually in quantity) to intermediaries or to retailers rather than to consumers of the product.

Widow's (or widower's) allowance That part of a dead spouse's money and property that a person may take free of all claims under some state laws.

Widow's (or widower's) election That part of a dead spouse's money and property that a person may choose to take under state law, rather than accepting what was given in the spouse's **will.** This is usually equal to what the person would get if there is no will and is sometimes called "waiving the will."

Wigmore *Wigmore on Evidence;* a **treatise.**

Wildcat strike A strike without the consent of the union.

Wild's case An old English case that said if a person gives property in a **will** "to John and his children," unless the will clearly means something else, if John has children at the time the will is made, they take the land jointly with John; but if John has no children when the will is made, John gets the land, but it goes to any children after he dies.

Will **1.** Desire; choice. For example, a *tenant at will* is a person who is permitted to use land or a building only as long as the owner desires the tenant to stay. **2.** A document in which a person tells how his or her property should be handed out after death. If all the necessary formalities have been taken care of, the law will help carry out the wishes of the person making the will. For the various types of wills (**holographic, joint, mutual, nuncupative,** etc.), see those words.

Will substitutes Life **insurance, joint** ownership of property, **trusts**, and other devices to partially eliminate the need for a **will.**

Willful **1.** Intentional; deliberate; on purpose. **2.** Obstinate; headstrong; without excuse. **3.** With evil purpose.

Williston *Williston on Contracts*; a **treatise.**

Wind up Finish current business, settle accounts, and turn property into cash in order to end a **corporation** or a **partnership** and split up the **assets.** See also **dissolution.**

Windfall Profits that come unexpectedly or through no effort or financial cost.

Wish Anything from "mildly desire" to "strongly command."

With all faults **As is** (see that word).

Withholding of evidence Hiding, destroying, or removing objects, records, etc., because they may be needed by a court. This may be a crime.

Withholding tax **1.** The money an employer takes out of an employee's pay and turns over to the government as prepayment of the employee's **income tax.** **2.** A tax on **dividends**, interest, and other income paid to people in other countries.

Within the statute **1.** Defined by the **statute.** **2.** Prohibited by the statute. **3.** Allowed by the statute.

Without day See **sine die.**

Without recourse Words used by an endorser (signer other than original "**maker**") of a **negotiable instrument** (check, etc.) to mean that if payment is refused, he or she will not be responsible.

Witness **1.** A person who is present at an occurrence (such as an accident), an event, or the signing of a document. **2.** A person who makes a statement under **oath** that can be used as evidence (in a court, **legislature, hearing,** etc.). **3.** For **material witness** and **expert witness**, see those words; and for "*witness against self,*" see **self-incrimination.**

Words and phrases

Words and phrases A large set of lawbooks that defines legal (and many nonlegal) words by giving actual quotes from cases.

Words of art Technical terms that are used in a special way by a profession. They are also called *"terms of art."*

Words of limitation The words in a **deed** or **will** that tell what type of **estate** or rights the person being given land receives.

Words of purchase The words in a **deed** or **will** that tell who is to get the land.

Work release program Daytime release of prisoners to work, with return to the prison for nights and weekends.

Work-to-rule A work slowdown in which formal work rules are so closely followed that production slows down.

Workers' compensation laws Laws passed in most states to pay money to workers injured on the job, regardless of **negligence**. Businesses pay into a fund to support those payments. These laws are also called *"workman's compensation laws."*

Working capital A company's **current** *assets* minus **current** *liabilities*. It is one measure of the company's ability to meet its obligations and to take advantage of new opportunities. See also **current** *ratio* and **quick assets.**

Working papers Proof-of-age certificates to satisfy minimum age laws.

Work-product rule The principle that a lawyer need not show the other side in a case any facts or things gathered for the case unless the other side can convince the judge that it would be unjust for the things to remain hidden and that there is a special need for them. This is also called the "qualified *attorney work-product* **privilege**."

World Court The **International Court of Justice** (see that word).

Worthier title doctrine **1.** Historically, the rule that if persons who inherit something in a **will** would get exactly the same thing by being **intestate heirs** (see those words), their "worthier title" is to get it as heirs instead. **2.** Today, in different forms in those states that use it, the rule creates a **rebuttable presumption** that a person did not mean to limit a **remainder** interest to his or her heirs. Applying this rule is extremely difficult.

Wraparound **1.** A **second** mortgage on a property that includes payments on a low-interest-rate first **mortgage**. This is done by buyers who don't want to lose the first mortgage and sellers who can't finance the sale without being willing to keep their names on the first mortgage. It is also done by lenders who finance work on older buildings. **2.** A new mortgage that makes payments on old mortgages on several properties at once.

Wrap-up clause A **zipper** clause (see that word).

Wright and Miller *Federal Practice and Procedure*; a **treatise**.

Writ A judge's **order** requiring that something be done outside the courtroom or authorizing it to be done. The most common *writ* is a notice to a **defendant** that a lawsuit has been started and that if nobody comes to court to defend against it, the **plaintiff** may win automatically. If the writ cannot be served (delivered properly), a second one (called an *"alias writ"*) may be used. Other types of writs include **prerogative** (unusual) writs such as **habeas corpus, mandamus, certiorari** and **quo warranto** (see those words), writs of **attachment, error, execution** (see those words) and many others. These include papers that are no longer strictly "writs" but have become part of the court's ordinary processes as **judgments** and **orders.**

Writeoff **1.** An uncollectible debt. **2.** A business or investment loss that can usually be claimed as a tax loss.

Writer A person who sells **options.**

Write-up Update financial records to show the increased value of property.

Writings Anything expressed in words, symbols, and numbers, whether written, printed, photocopied, etc.

Written law **Statute** (see that word) law.

Wrong A violation of a person's legal rights, especially a **tort.**

Wrongful death action A lawsuit brought by the **dependents** of a dead person against the person who caused the death. Money **damages** will be given to the dependents if the killing was **negligent** or **willful.**

Wrongful life action Lawsuits against doctors for malpracticed sterilizations and similar operations and advice. These suits are new and have an unsettled legal status, whether brought by the child "wrongfully born" or by the parents.

Yy

Year-and-a-day rule   The principle that a death cannot be attributed to another person's wrongful conduct unless it occurred within a year and a day of the conduct. This principle has been abandoned in some states.

Year books   Reports of old English cases.

Yeas and nays   Oral voting in a **legislature**, usually one-by-one, calling each name in turn.

Yellow dog contract   An employment contract in which an employer requires an employee to promise that he or she will not join a **union**. These are now illegal.

Yield   Profits as measured by a percentage of the money invested. For example, a ten dollar profit on a hundred dollar investment is a 10 percent *yield*.

York-Antwerp rules   Agreed international rules for **contract** provisions dealing with **bills of lading**, for settlement of disputes about maritime losses, etc.

Youthful offenders   Persons treated as juvenile **delinquents**, rather than adult **criminals**.

Zz

Z   **1.** *Regulation Z* is the set of rules put out by the **Federal Reserve** Board under the Truth-in-Lending law. It describes exactly what a lender must tell a borrower and how it must be told.   **2.** "**Z**" is the mark used to fill in unused blank spaces on a legal document to keep them from being filled in later.

Z.B.B.   **Zero-base budgeting** (see that word).

Zealous witness   A **swift witness** (see that word).

Zenger   The 1735 colonial case in which a man imprisoned for defaming New York's governor was freed, establishing the principle that truth is a valid **defense** to **libel**.

Zero bracket amount A flat **deduction** from income on personal income taxes. It is built into the **tax tables** and **tax schedules**, so some taxpayers must subtract it from their **itemized deductions**. It replaced the *standard* **deduction**.

Zero-base budgeting Looking closely at an entire program's funding when planning its next budget, rather than looking only at that program's need for additional money.

Zero-rate mortgage A **mortgage** in which a large down payment is made, and the rest of the purchase price is paid off in equal **installments** with no **interest**.

Zipper (or wrap-up) clause A statement that an agreement is **integrated** (see that word).

Zone of employment The physical area (usually the place of employment and surrounding areas controlled by the employer) within which an employee is eligible for **worker's compensation** benefits when injured, whether or not on the job at the time.

Zone pricing Charging everyone within a geographical area the same price for the same delivered goods.

Zoning 1. The division of a city or county into mapped areas, with restrictions on land use, architectural design, building use, etc., in each area. 2. *Cluster zoning* allows housing closer together than minimum lot size if open space is maintained; *Euclidean zoning* excludes businesses, apartment houses, etc., from single family residential areas; *floating zoning* is the setting aside of a certain amount of land in each district for otherwise nonpermitted buildings, with the exact place for them not yet settled; and *spot zoning* is changing the zoning for a piece of land without regard for the zoning plan.

APPENDIX A
Where to Go for
More Information

If you cannot find the word you want in this dictionary, if the definition given here does not fit the context in which you found the word, or if you need a more elaborate definition, there are several places to look. They are listed here with the most convenient first and the most comprehensive last.

1. Standard English Dictionaries

Try a regular dictionary. Often, legal documents will use an ordinary English word in its ordinary way, but because of some special emphasis or because of its use in an unfamiliar place, the word looks "legal." A regular dictionary may reassure you that the word's ordinary meaning fits perfectly. *American Heritage*, *Merriam-Webster*, and *Random House* are helpful dictionaries. For older words or for more complete definitions try the *Oxford English Dictionary*.

2. Large Law Dictionaries

These books are especially helpful for long Latin phrases, historical words, and situations in which you need several examples of how to use the word properly. Their definitions are sometimes confusing or out of date, but they have more words and more extensive definitions than this dictionary. The two best known are *Black's* (5th ed., West Publishing) and *Ballentine's* (3d ed., Lawyers' Cooperative Publishing).

3. Hornbooks

If you know the legal subject your word comes from, the best starting place is a students' summary of the law in that field. This is called a "hornbook." For example, if the word belongs in the field of torts, try the index in the back of *Prosser on Torts*, West Publishing.

4. Legislation and Cases

If the word comes from a statute, ordinance or regulation, the law itself may have a "definition section" or several definition sections scattered through it. This is always true of the "Uniform

Laws" and usually true of major Federal and State legislation. For example, the most important definitions for many commercial terms are found in the definition section of the Uniform Commercial Code. (If all you have is the popular name of a statute or a case, you can find it by using *Shepard's Acts and Cases by Popular Name*, found in most law libraries.)

5. Words and Phrases

If you want to be buried by every conceivable use of a term or if the word you want has not turned up in any of the preceding sources, go to a law library and use *Words and Phrases,* a multivolume set of books by West Publishing. It has excerpts from every judge's decision that ever explained a word. It is the best place in a law library to get a start with complicated legal language. But be careful; the excerpts are frequently from cases that have been long overruled or discarded, from cases that were decided in the opposite way from what the quote would lead you to believe, from "dicta" (words that have nothing to do with the basis for the decision) or from inaccurately quoted cases. Also, do not forget to look in the supplement inside the back cover of each book for more recent uses of the word.

6. Descriptive Word Index

If the word you want is not a legal word, but you need to know if the word ever became entangled with the law, try the *Descriptive Word Index* to West Publishing Company's *American Digest System.* For example, if you want to know whether there was ever a case about a pet skunk spraying a meter reader (because your skunk gets edgy when the reader comes into the basement), you might try looking up "skunk," "pets," or "meter readers." If you find nothing, try more general topics, such as "animals," "household liability," etc.

7. Legal Encyclopedias

If you want to get into the general legal subject that your word came from and if "hornbooks" are no help, try a legal encyclopedia. The two major ones are *Corpus Juris Secundum* by West Publishing Company and *American Jurisprudence* by the Lawyers' Cooperative Publishing Company.

APPENDIX B
Lawyer Talk

This section is written primarily for lawyers, paralegals, law students and others who use legal words professionally. Its message is simple: legal words are valuable technical tools, but they can be used to excess. This smothers clear thinking, clear writing, and clear speaking.

The section is also written for the "person on the street" who uses the dictionary to help with legal questions that come up in everyday life or to learn something about the law. The ability to sort out useful legal language from "Legalese" is a big advantage.

There are many reasons why legal language is overused and misused. Lawyers, paralegals, and legal writers get carried away by legal jargon because of their training. Traditional law schools teach by the "case method." Students spend most of their time studying how appeals judges (who have never seen the actual trial or any of the persons involved in the case) decide cases. This involves applying abstract legal concepts to abstract summaries of facts. After three years of dealing with legal words and abstract ideas, law students have problems talking about the real world in clear English.

Even after working for real clients who have real problems, many lawyers and paralegals still use legal jargon either from habit or to cover up fuzzy thinking. There are several different ways that legal words are overused or misused. Some of these ways are:

1. Using TECHNICAL legal words when dealing with non-lawyers.
2. Using VAGUE legal words when clear English would be more precise.
3. Using TOO MANY legal words.
4. Using certain WORTHLESS legal words.

1. Technical Words

Even when used accurately, legal words may be out of place when speaking to or writing for nonlawyers. For example:

Lawyer talk	English
An "annulment" voids the marriage ab initio.	An "annulment" wipes the marriage off the books as if it never happened.
Plaintiff alleges Jones is the vendee.	Smith claims he sold it to Jones.
If you don't bequeath it in a codicil, it will go by intestate succession.	If you don't change your will to put it in, some cousin may get it.
I'll move for a continuance, but it may be denied as dilatory.	I'll try to put it off, but the judge will think we are stalling.
You hold the estate in fee, but if you alienate it, you activate the acceleration clause in the security interest.	You own the house, but if you sell it or give it away, the whole mortgage comes due.
You hold legal title on the face of the instrument, but extrinsic evidence shows that Smith has equitable title.	The papers are in your name, but a court would give it to Smith.

2. Vague Words

Some legal words have a "built in" vagueness. They are used when the writer or speaker does not want to be pinned down. For example, when a law talks about *reasonable* speed" or "*due* care," it is deliberately imprecise about the meaning of the words because it wants the amount of speed allowed or care required to be decided situation-by-situation, rather than by an exact formula. Vague words, however, just as often accompany vague thoughts. A small list of vague words, drawn from many possibilities, is given below:

Sounds precise	But is it?
Above cited	Earlier on the page? In the chapter? The book?
Accident	Intentional? Negligent? Pure chance?
Adequate	For what? Buy what standard? Who decides?
Civil death	For all legal purposes? Just some? Permanent?

Sounds precise	But is it?
Community	The "block"? That section of town? The state?
Face	The whole document? The first page?
Facsimile	Exact copy? Close copy? How close?
Fair hearing	Fair in what way?
Final decision	Final before appeal? Final with no appeal?
Fixture	May be removed? May not be removed?
Foreign	Different country? Different State? City?
Heirs	Children? All who may inherit? One only?
Infant	Baby? Young child? Under legal age?
Reasonable person	By what standards? With hindsight?
Stranger	Not part of the deal? Knew nothing about it?
Substantial	A lot? More than a little? Above a cutoff?
Undue	A lot? Too much? By force? Illegal?

Some legal words have been in dispute in thousands of cases. Judges have decided that many of them "clearly" mean a dozen different, conflicting things. These words can rarely be avoided but should be replaced by specific objects, facts, or concepts whenever possible even if this requires using extra words. For example, lawyers almost never agree about the following words:

Consideration
Conspiracy
Holding
Insanity
Jurisdiction

Law
Obscenity
Preponderance of evidence
Proximate cause
Willful

3. Too Many Words
Doubling legal words that mean the same thing can be confusing. The best examples of legal word-doubling (and tripling) are found in pages 346 to 366 of *The Language of the Law* by Mellinkoff (1963, Little, Brown, Co.) Some of these are:

Fit and proper
Force and effect
Give, devise and bequeath

Have and hold
Known and distinguished as
Last will and testament

459

Mind and memory	Over and above
Name and style	Rest, residue and remainder
Null and void	Written instrument

There are a few useful doublings such as "aid and comfort" (describing treason) or "cease and desist order" (an administrative equivalent of an injunction by a court). Most doublings, however, are just clutter.

4. Worthless Words

Many legal words are worthless. Some are useless because they are almost meaningless. Others mean exactly the same thing as a clear English word. Here are some of both types:

Aforesaid	Hitherto	Here (or There) about
Ambulatory	Issue (for	after
And/or	"children")	by
Firstly	Party of the	for
Forthwith	first part	from
Four corners	Re (for	in
	"about")	inafter
	Said (as in	to
	"said table")	tofore
	To wit	upon
	Viz	with
	Whereas	unto

What can a legal professional do about jargon? Before using a legal word, stop and think. Even if it is precise and useful, is it too technical for the situation? Is a vague word being used to smooth over vague thinking? Would fewer words do the job? Is the word on the "worthless list"?

What can a nonlawyer do about legal jargon? First, learn to recognize it. Legal language is less imposing once the garbage is stripped away. Next, ask for a translation when something you hear is confusing. And finally, don't use it.

APPENDIX C
Legal Research

Only practice can teach you to do legal research, but some basic legal knowledge plus a reference guide will get you started.

This appendix is divided into three sections. *Concepts* introduces the important legal ideas (such as "**authority**," "**holding**," and "**jurisdiction**") that you must keep in mind while doing research. *Techniques* explains the basic skills of analyzing your problem, finding the law, and using the law you find to solve your problem. And *Sources* describes the places (such as statute books, case reporters, and digests) where you will find the law.

Here are some hints for using the material:

If you have never seen a law library, read the *law libraries* section before going to one.

If this appendix seems too basic, but you still need more help, read the *books on doing legal research* section.

Use the dictionary with this appendix and while doing research. Dictionary-defined words in this appendix are usually in **boldface**.

Use the table of contents that follows as a checklist of things to consider while doing your research.

Keep at it. Frustration is the first step on the path to True Legal Enlightenment.

CONCEPTS IN THE LAW

These are the basic ideas you should have "under your belt" before starting any serious legal research. You do not need to know their every jump through a scholar's hoop (and none of those jumps are presented here). You do not need to keep them in mind all at once. But you *do* need to know what they mean when you come across them.

The ideas are presented as a series of short questions in the heading of each section. The use of separate questions breaks apart interrelated concepts, but it presents them in a way that will allow you to run through the questions as a list when deciding how to approach a legal problem, how to look for the right books, or how to read the legal material you have found.

LEGISLATIVE, JUDICIAL, OR EXECUTIVE?

First, a quick "civics" review of the U.S. government: The **legislative** branch writes **statutes** (see that word), the **judicial** branch decides **cases** ("interpreting" those statutes and deciding a good deal more besides), and the **executive** branch runs the country, primarily by carrying out those statutes. Figure 1, reprinted from the 1981 *U.S. Government Manual* shows these branches.

Notice "The Constitution" in the top box. The Constitution is not a statute, but the document establishing the basic principles for the entire government and setting up the basic structure and procedures for running it. Nothing done by the government may conflict with what the Constitution says.

Now notice the large Executive Branch box in the center. (The chart *was* prepared by the executive branch.) This is the source for several types of written laws (such as **executive orders** and **treaties**) that are also not statutes.

And finally, look at all the small boxes near the bottom and the one large box at the bottom. These are the **cabinet departments** and independent **agencies** that actually run the government, primarily by issuing **regulations** and administering them (see **regulation** and **regulate**). These departments and agencies also hold trial-like **hearings**. The process is called **administrative law**. Since some things done by administrative agencies *look* "judicial" or "legislative," you must keep your government branches straight.

For more on statutes and cases, see the next question.

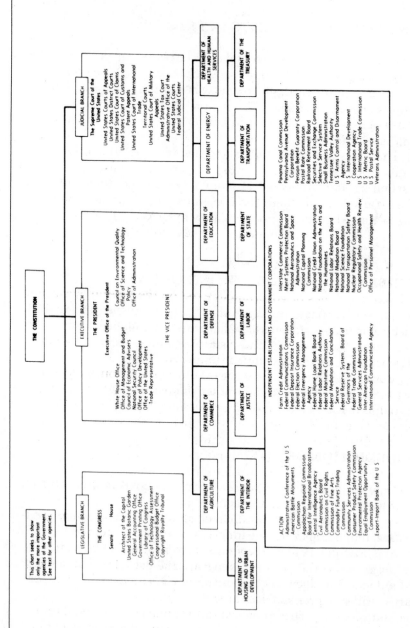

Figure 1 Organization of federal government.

Source: *The United States Government Manual* (Washington, D.C.: Government Printing Office, 1981), p. 815.

STATUTE OR CASE?

Most of "the law" you research will be clearly recognizable as **statutes** or **cases**. "**Statutory** law" is a **legislature's** official statement about conduct it wants to encourage, permit, or forbid. It is collected in statute books.

"**Caselaw**" is a statement by a court that is based on legal principles developed from past case decisions. It is a judge's decision, plus the facts and reasoning behind that decision. It is collected in books of case *reports*.

See **statute**, **statutory**, **case**, and **caselaw** for more information. And see the next question for the levels of government that produce statutes and cases.

FEDERAL, STATE, OR LOCAL?

All three branches of government exist on the federal, state, and local levels. Each has a chart similar to the U.S. chart in Figure 1. The words used at each level are generally the same, except at the *local* level. Local constitutions are usually called **charters** and local statutes are usually called **ordinances**.

You must always know whether the constitution, statute, regulation, or case decision you are dealing with is federal, state, or local. For one major reason why, see the next question.

JURISDICTION OR NOT?

The United States is a *"jurisdiction."* So are Virginia, Fairfax County, and Falls Church City.

A *statute* rarely has legal effect outside its geographic jurisdiction. (For exceptions, see **long-arm statute** and **comity**.) Public officials, such as police officers, usually have jurisdiction to take official action within only one geographical area. Further, a judge usually has jurisdiction to decide cases about people or places only within one geographical area.

The federal (U.S. as opposed to Virginia) court system, for example, has a Supreme Court (with "geographical jurisdiction" over the whole country), several Courts of Appeals (most with a numbered "circuit" of several states), and many District Courts (each for a "district" that is a state or part of a state). See Figure 2 for a view of the jurisdictions of the various Federal courts.

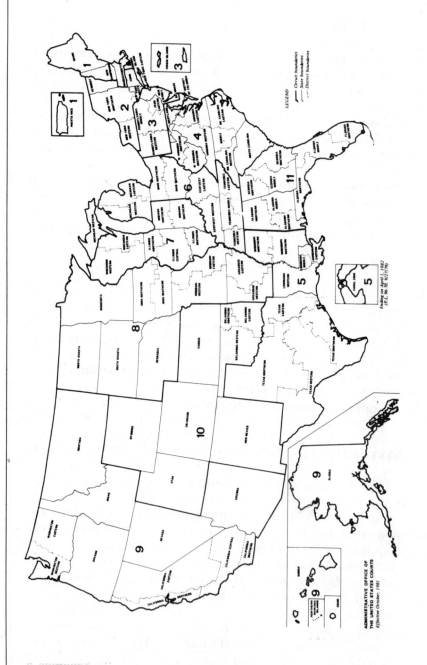

Figure 2 U.S. Courts of Appeals and U.S. District Courts

You should always make sure you know which geographic jurisdiction your statute or case comes from because that will tell you where it has legal effect. This is important, but easy to check.

There is, however, another meaning of jurisdiction that can get more complicated. This is the right and power of a court (or a public official) to take actions involving only certain types of people, property, or subject areas. In the simplest case (where a statute defines the jurisdiction), a "small claims court" might have jurisdiction over only "money claims under eight hundred dollars," and a court with **appellate** jurisdiction would be able to handle only **appeals**.

The situation becomes even more complicated when there is no clear statute, and courts must decide whether a judge, police officer, administrative agency, etc., had jurisdiction to take an action. The next question is about another jurisdictional difference.

CIVIL OR CRIMINAL?

Criminal statutes describe conduct that will be punished by the government. Courts with criminal **jurisdiction** decide whether or not a person is guilty of this conduct and decide the punishment. These courts must follow special **constitutional** safeguards beyond those required of civil courts.

Civil statutes establish the rules for legal relationships between persons, for noncriminal matters involving persons and the government, and for the workings of the government itself. Courts with civil jurisdiction handle primarily lawsuits brought to enforce a right or to gain payment for a wrong.

There is a "grey area" within the matters handled by civil courts that may look somewhat "criminal," either because punishment can be handed out (for example, revoking a sales license) or because what may *feel* like punishment is not *called* punishment (for example, **civil commitment** to a mental hospital).

In any event, it is important to know under *which* sets of statutes and court procedures your legal problem is likely to fall.

The next question must also be asked about statutes.

CLEAR OR NOT?

First, another brief "civics" review: A **bill** generally becomes a **statute** by being voted on and passed by a **legislature** (with each

house, if there are two, holding **committee hearings**, sometimes **floor** debate, etc.), signed by (or sometimes passed over the **veto** of) the president (or a governor, etc.) and printed as a law. This process, and the documents it produces along the way, provide a **legislative history**.

If a statute or other written law is not clear on paper, there is not much chance that its application to the real world will be clear. You need to know "What does it really say?" Judges sometimes use the **legislative history** when deciding what a statute means, and sometimes use various "rules" for statutory **interpretation** and **construction** (see those words).

The next question is about the two settings in which judges work.

TRIAL OR APPEAL?

Most courtroom activities take place in **trial** courts. This is where witnesses give **testimony**, lawyers argue before **juries**, and facts are sorted out to resolve disputes. Trials usually take place long after the blood is spilled.

Appellate court hearings usually take place long after even the echoed sound and fury of the trial court fades away. "Issues of fact" (what really happened on the street years ago) have been decided by the trial court. Courts of appeal decide primarily "issues of law" (disputes about how the law applies to the facts).

The facts have by now become "the **record**" (an information package consisting of a summary of facts prepared by the trial judge plus **transcripts** of testimony, other evidence, etc.). The appeals court then writes a short summary of legally relevant facts and proceeds to "apply the law."

The law that is applied is a combination of the relevant **statutes** and the decisions of past judges in legally similar cases. These legally similar past decisions are called **precedents** (see that word).

If you do not look at the process closely, it seems as if the appeals court has absolutely nothing to do but take the facts in one hand, the law in the other, and put them together mechanically. (See **stare decisis** for more about this.) After all, if the trial court judge and jury decide "the facts" and hand them on as a record, and past judges have handed down "the law" in the form of precedents, what thinking needs to be done?

In fact, the appeals court has great freedom to decide which past cases are legally relevant, and the freedom to decide what those cases really say. The appeals court makes the whole decision. It is these appellate decisions that are preserved in published collections of case **reports**.

If, later, a "legally similar" case *is* appealed, the prior decision of the appeals court becomes one more precedent to be accepted, rejected, or changed by the court.

The next question explains more about precedents.

HOLDING OR DICTA?

Precedents (see the last question, *Trial or appeal?*) are those past cases with morsels of wisdom that should be used to decide today's **appellate** cases, to guide **trial** court judges, and to provide standards of behavior for mere mortals. But what qualifies a case with a morsel of wisdom as a precedent?

First of all, the morsel must be part of the decision of the case. This eliminates morsels from the dissenting or concurring (see **dissent** and **concur**) judges whose opinions, no matter how favorable to your position, didn't decide the case. It also rules out, unfortunately, everything the main deciding judge *did* say that *was not a logically necessary part of the decision*. These interesting, sometimes forcefully argued words are called **dicta** (see that word). (One example of dicta would be a judge's statements that Joe was definitely right in a dispute when the judge actually decided the case in favor of Moe.)

What is left as **precedent**, after the dicta is removed, is the **holding** (see that word), the central core of the judge's decision. If you find a "holding" in a case with facts that are legally similar to your situation, and the case has not been **overruled** or **distinguished** (see these words) by a later court, you have found a precedent.

Precedents, however, are not all alike. The next question explains how precedents can be strong or weak, and where they fit into all other kinds of **authority**.

BINDING OR PERSUASIVE?

Precedents (see *Trial or appeal?* and *Holding or dicta?* for their definition and use) are only one type of **authority**. An authority is a reference to a statute, case decision, legal encyclopedia, treatise, etc., used in support of a legal argument.

Statutes and cases are called **binding** (or *mandatory*) **authority** if they *must* be taken into account by a judge in deciding a case.

A case decision by an appeals court is "binding authority" for a legally identical case in a court **below** the appeals court. A statute is "binding authority" if it is in effect in the geographic **jurisdiction** where it is claimed as an authority (see *Jurisdiction or not?*). The detailed rules for whether case decisions and statutes are binding are complicated. As you pursue your research, you will need to know more of these rules. Most authority is not binding, but persuasive only. *Persuasive authority* can be such things as case decisions from other jurisdictions, **dicta** (see *Holding or dicta?*), legal encyclopedias, articles, or anything that *might* legitimately persuade a judge to decide a case a certain way. It is anything that carries legal "weight" and, just as persuasive authority comes in all types, it comes in all weights.

Authority is either binding or persuasive. There is no such thing as "sort of binding" authority. But persuasive authority can be more or less persuasive. While "how persuasive" depends on how persuasive the judge *decides* the authority is, there are some general rules of persuasiveness. For example, in Virginia, a decision of the Maryland Supreme Court is more persuasive than is a decision of a low-level Arizona court. This is so both because Maryland is closer and because the supreme court is higher.

"Authority" is what you will be looking for in your research. The next section supplies some basic search techniques.

TECHNIQUES OF RESEARCH

ANALYZING THE FACTS

"An ounce of thinking is worth ten pounds of research."

Know Your Facts
Much of research is listmaking. Your first, most important list will be of everything you know about the facts of your problem: The *things, happenings, persons,* and *places* involved. Note beside each fact what you know, how you know about it, and how sure you are about each of the subfacts. Add no legal observations or conclusions to these facts.

Know Your Objectives

Analyze what you want to accomplish. What results do you (your client, etc.) want? Are they realistic? Make a list and look at it often throughout the research process.

FINDING THE LAW

Create a Word List

Most research tasks involve either too few potentially useful reference sources or too many. In neither case should you flounder in near-random flip-flops through more and more books. The solution is to *cartwheel*.

Cartwheel is a method of creating and expanding word lists to use your sources best and to lead you to new sources. (Cartwheel was developed by William Statsky, and can be seen in greater detail in either of his two books mentioned in the "Books on doing legal research" section.)

Cartwheel lets you turn your lists of facts (things, persons, happenings, places) and your list of objectives (see *Analyzing the Facts*) into words to "plug into" the indexes, tables of contents, references, and word lists of your sources. It helps you phrase each word or idea *in as many different ways as possible* to find more leads to useful information. You should take each word or phrase on your list and put it into the cartwheel, as seen in Figure 3.

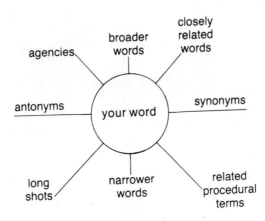

Figure 3   Cartwheel

Suppose that one important word from your fact lists was "bloody nose." Under *broader words*, you might list "injury" and "trauma"; under *procedural terms*, "battery" or "tort"; under *long-shot*, "fight" or "insult." It doesn't matter where you put the words or how words overlap. The purpose is to plug as many new words as possible back into as many indexes, tables of contents, and other finding aids as possible.

Cartwheel is a good "word-plugging system," but it doesn't matter whether you use Cartwheel, a system devised by another author or publisher, or your own system. (Some researchers prefer a system that includes a memory device such as TARP (Things, **Actions**, **Remedies**, and **Parties**). Generating new words (especially when you run out of ideas) is the master-key to unlocking closed sources.

Do Your Search

It is time to begin the "library research." You will need a general knowledge of the *Sources* listed in the third section of this appendix and a detailed knowledge of how to use those you have selected. Here are some guidelines to help you along:

If in doubt about the workings of the law library itself, see the section on *Law libraries*.

Keep the information on *Sources* handy as you work.

Start with *primary sources* (statutes, cases, regulations, etc.) if you have possible leads into them.

Make a "strange critters" list. If you do not know what a word is, look it up in this dictionary. If you come across a strange critter (such as a "**pocket part**" or a "**slip law**" "live" on a library shelf, pick it up and identify it.

Finally, *be flexible*. Let the words on your lists, new Cartwheeled words, and the references suggested by your sources tell you where to go next. Take some chances. Follow some side paths. As the Sage of the Cartwheel says, "You may not know what you are looking for until you find it."

ANALYZING THE LAW

Reading Cases

Most law school training is based on the "case method." Students read, "brief" (take notes on and analyze), and discuss the reported decisions of **appellate** courts.

You will need to brief cases for many research problems. What follows is only a basic outline—enough to get your job done. Assume that you have found a case decision that is central to your research problem. What should be in the brief?

1. Read all the material printed in front of decision itself. There is a sample page of these preliminary **headnotes** in the *Sources* section. This will give you an orientation to the case.
2. Write down all the **citation** information that identifies the court and the reporter volume by official name.
3. Write down *who wrote the decision*. If it lacks a name, but says "**per curiam**," it is an anonymous decision for all the judges.
4. Write down the *procedural history* of the case. From where did it come on appeal? Anything unusual?
5. Write down the *result*, the judge's **holding** (see that word). This is the most important part of your job, and by far the hardest. (Refresh your memory now on the questions from "*Jurisdiction or not?*" to the end of the *Concepts* section.)
6. Write down the *reasoning justifying the holding* point-by-point. The judge may summarize for you, but be careful. Both here and elsewhere in the opinion, the words the judge used may be **dicta** (see that word). Number 7 will help you decide what is dicta.
7. Write down the *action* taken in the case. This might be to **affirm**, **reverse**, **remand**, etc. Many of the judge's words will reveal themselves as *dicta* at this point if the judge took an action that did not depend on the words. You may even find at this point that the action taken was the opposite of what was argued in prior words.
8. Write down any important points made by judges who **concur** or **dissent**.
9. Write down the case's *later history*, if any, that you find when you **Shepardize** (see that word) it.

Reading Statutes and Regulations

Reading statutes and regulations is as hard as reading cases. You must read them word by word because they are often very precise in places and very vague in others. Each comma may matter.

"*Briefing*" statutes is not as hard as briefing cases. The form of the brief doesn't matter as long as it contains the statute's **citation** and information on who is *included in* and *excluded from* the statutes reach, on *when* and *how* it operates, on whether it *commands* or only *permits* something, and on any details directly bearing on your problem. Quote directly when the exact words are important.

If anything important about the statute is unclear after a careful reading, you must use the cases and historical data given in the statute's **annotations** to find the **legislative history**. You should always at least look at the annotations to see if you are interpreting something incorrectly.

Briefing **regulations** is generally similar to briefing statutes. You must also include information on the statutes that authorize the regulations.

USING THE RESEARCH

Validate with Shepard's
You have found what you want. Now what? First, make sure you have what you think you have. Are your cases, statutes, or regulations still good **authority**? The only way to find out is to trace them down through later cases, commentators, or other sources to see if they have been criticized, **overruled**, changed, etc. Read the section in *Sources* on **Shepard's Citations**.

"Cite It Rite"
A case or other authority is worthless if you (and those to whom you offer it as authority) cannot find it again. This means that you must always get its correct citation.

For example, *Ex parte Grossman* 267 U.S. 87 (1925) gives the case name, volume, **reporter**, page and date in order. If you find the case in one reporter, but another reporter is its *official* place of publication, you must always use at least the official citation.

There are many rules for proper citation form, but most important, "cite it rite." Copy down the citation *before* you take notes and check it against the original. (If you are not sure of the proper form, consult *Uniform System of Citation* (see "Other helpers" under *Sources*.)

Analyze Both Sides' Positions
Once all your research is "in the bag," reanalyze your arguments for loose ends. Then analyze its strength and the strength of the other side's arguments. Upon what will *they* likely rely? Does that mean more research for you?

Write It Up
Order and label all your papers; make an informal index; and write a summary of what you *have*, what you *did*, and what you *concluded*. Keep it short, clear, and simple. Check your work against a book such as *Legal Writing: Sense and Nonsense* (see "Other helpers' under *Sources*).

LAW LIBRARIES

If you use a law library as a warm, cozy place to curl up with a few thousand good books, you do not need this section. Nor do you need this section if you use a law library as a "knowledge store" where you regularly "spend" time and "buy," if not exactly what you came looking for, at least what you need. If, however, you imagine a law library as a huge, dark cave, filled with dangerous ambiguities lurking to embarrass you, read on.

How do you find a law library? Small libraries exist in most law firms. They have enough books to handle many problems of state law and simple problems of a broader nature. Large law libraries exist in large law offices, bar associations, courthouses, and administrative agencies. They can handle almost any research problem, but not always in the most convenient way. Complete law libraries exist in law schools, some large agencies and courthouses, and some major city research centers and general libraries. They can handle any legal problem.

How do you get in? First, call around. Some are open to the public, especially some courthouse and law school libraries. Some lawyers will let you use their libraries or get you into one. Some law librarians will bend loose policies, even ignore "no public entrance" signs, if you begin by asking a research question.

Before you go. Do the preliminary fact analysis and problem definition before you go. Not in detail, but enough to know why you need the library. Read the *Concepts* and *Sources* sections of this appendix, but do not bother reading the "*How to use it*" parts of the *Sources* section before you have the books in hand. Take copier change.

You're in. Now what? Take the books and run! No, calm down. Ask the librarian for a brief orientation. Show your ignorance. Be effusive with thanks. Look around. Take your time. Get acquainted with where each type of book sits, using *Sources* to sort things out.

Then, before you start using the lawbooks, briefly review *why* you are there and what you hope to accomplish. Perhaps put this information on a 3×5 card and look at it once in a while as you work.

Finally, think about some of the "rules for library use" from the HALT pamphlet (see *Books on doing research*): 1) Write down complete source information before you take notes, including date, volume, section, and page. 2) Read all prefaces and content descriptions. 3) Put a bookmark in abbreviation tables. 4) When you see a reference you *might* want, write it down with a note why. 5) Take breaks before you get tired. 6) Do not rush or take short-cuts. 7) Do not hoard books. Take only what you need; find out library policy on reshelving and follow it. This is not merely an "ecological ethic." You will come to hate hoarders when the book you need is at the bottom of a napper's headrest pile. 8) Go to it and keep at it!

SOURCES OF THE LAW

The rest of this appendix contains answers to the following legal research questions:

What *are the materials used in legal research?*

Where *are they?*

When *do you use each of them?*

How *do you use them?*

Because of the small size of this appendix compared to its large topic, many of the answers will be in outline form.

If you want an overview of the various materials, read on. If, however, you want to use these materials to solve a legal problem, do not continue until you have a basic understanding of the materials in the "Concepts" and "Techniques" part of the appendix, especially the techniques of defining your problem. Otherwise, you will soon be adrift in a sea of interesting, but probably useless, facts. Remember also that the words you come across in **boldface** are defined in this dictionary. That should throw light on some of the murkier passages.

Sources of the law are divided into two types: primary and secondary. *Primary sources* are original legal documents such as statute books, case decision **reporters**, and collections of **regulations**. *Secondary sources* are books and other materials *about* the primary sources and include **digests,** encyclopedias, and **citators.** This appendix adds a third category of source, *computer-assisted legal research.*

Figure 4 is a chart of various types of primary and secondary sources. I have reprinted it with thanks from William Statsky's *Legal Research, Writing, and Analysis* (West Publishing, 1982) because it has a larger scope than that of this appendix. Read the chart, however, with two things in mind:

Much legal research concentrates on the top four rows of the chart.

The appendix is not organized according to the chart.

PRIMARY SOURCES

Federal Statutes and Regulations

Where Do You Find Them? The official source for the text of federal statutes while they are still **bills** going through Congress is the *Congressional Record.* It is also one of the earliest sources because it comes out daily while Congress is in session. Information in the *Congressional Record* helps provide a **legislative history** for statutes. The best unofficial source for *Congressional Record* information (legislative history, including some **committee** reports) is printed in the *U.S.C.C.A.N.* (see below).

The official source for federal statutes in the order they become law is the U.S. *Statutes at Large.* The main unofficial source is West Publishing's *United States Code Congressional and Administrative News* (*U.S.C.C.A.N.*).

The official source for statutes once they have been sorted by subject into a permanent order is the *United States Code* (*U.S.C.*). (Those statutes that have not been enacted as part of an organized **code** can still be found here, but they must be officially **cited** by their *Statutes at Large* text.) The two unofficial sources are West's *United States Code Annotated* (*U.S.C.A.*) and Lawyers Co-operative's *United States Code Service* (*U.S.C.S.*). The two unofficial sources are the main places to go for federal statutory research because they contain the law in the most useful form, come out sooner than the official *U.S.C.*, and have **annotations** to **caselaw,** legislative history, regulations, etc.

KIND OF LAW	SETS OF BOOKS THAT CONTAIN THE FULL TEXT OF THIS KIND OF LAW	SETS OF BOOKS THAT CAN BE USED TO LOCATE THIS KIND OF LAW	SETS OF BOOKS THAT CAN BE USED TO HELP EXPLAIN THIS KIND OF LAW	SETS OF BOOKS THAT CAN BE USED TO HELP DETERMINE THE CURRENT VALIDITY OF THIS KIND OF LAW
(a) Opinions	Reports Reporters ALR, ALR2d, ALR3d, ALR4th, ALR Fed Legal newspapers Loose leaf services Slip opinion Advance sheets	Digests Annotations in ALR, ALR2d, ALR3d, ALR4th, ALR Fed Shepard's Legal periodicals Encyclopedias Treatises Loose leaf services Words and Phrases	Legal periodicals Encyclopedias Treatises Annotations in ALR, ALR2d, ALR3d, ALR4th, ALR Fed Loose leaf services	Shepard's
(b) Statutes	Statutory Code Statutes Statutes at Large Session Laws Laws Compilations Consolidated Laws Slip Law Acts, Acts & Resolves	Index volumes of statutory code Loose leaf services	Legal periodicals Encyclopedias Treatises Annotations in ALR, ALR2d, ALR3d, ALR4th, ALR Fed Loose leaf services	Shepard's
(c) Constitutions	Statutory code Separate volumes containing the con- stitution	Index volumes of statutory code Loose leaf services	Legal periodicals Encyclopedias Treatises Annotations in ALR, ALR2d, ALR3d, ALR4th, ALR Fed Loose leaf services	Shepard's
(d) Administrative Regulations	Administrative Codes Separate volumes or pamphlets contain- ing the regulations of certain agencies Loose leaf services	Index volumes of the administrative code Loose leaf services	Legal periodicals Treatises Annotations in ALR, ALR2d, ALR3d, ALR4th, ALR Fed Loose leaf services	Shepard's (for some agen- cies only)
(e) Administrative Decisions	Separate volumes of decisions of certain agencies Loose leaf services	Loose leaf services Index or digest vol- umes to the deci- sions	Legal periodicals Treatises Annotations in ALR, ALR2d, ALR3d, ALR4th, ALR Fed Loose leaf services	Shepard's (for some agen- cies only)
(f) Ordinances	Municipal code Official journal Legal newspaper	Index volumes of municipal code	Legal periodicals Treatises Annotations in ALR, ALR2d, ALR3d, ALR4th, ALR Fed	Shepard's
(g) Charters	Separate volumes containing the charter Municipal Code State session laws Official journal Legal newspaper	Index volumes to the charter or munici- pal code	Legal periodicals Treatises Annotations in ALR, ALR2d, ALR3d, ALR Fed	Shepard's
(h) Rules of Court	Separate rules vol- umes Statutory code Practice manuals	Index to separate rules volumes Index to statutory code Index to practice manuals	Practice manuals Treatises Annotations in ALR, ALR2d, ALR3d ALR4th, ALR Fed Encyclopedias Loose leaf services	Shepard's
(i) Executive Orders	Federal Register Code of Federal Reg- ulations U.S. Code Congres- sional and Admin- istrative News USC, USCA, USCS (for some orders only)	Index volumes to the sets of books listed in the second col- umn	Legal periodicals Treatises Annotations in ALR, ALR2d, ALR3d, ALR4th, ALR Fed	Shepard's Code of Federal Regula- tion Citations
(j) Treaties	Statutes at Large (up to 1950) United States Trea- ties and Other In- ternational Agree-	Index within the vol- umes listed in sec- ond column	Legal periodicals Treatises Annotations in ALR, ALR2d, ALR3d, ALR 4th, ALR Fed	Shepard's (for some treaties only)

Figure 4 Sources of the Law

The official source for the text of federal **administrative** rules and regulations, both while they are still proposed and in the order of their final approval, is the *Federal Register*. Published daily, it is the administrative law equivalent of both the *Congressional Record* and the *Statutes at Large*. (See below for unofficial sources.)

The official source for most administrative regulations once they have been sorted by subject into a permanent order is the *Code of Federal Regulations* (*CFR*), although individual agency collections also exist. It is the administrative law equivalent of the *United States Code*. There is no complete unofficial source for administrative regulations, but *U.S.C.S.* prints bits and pieces, as do various **looseleaf services** discussed under the section on secondary sources).

How Do You Use Them? The *Congressional Record, Statutes at Large,* and *Federal Register* are easy to use. The *United States Code* is rarely used when either annotated version is available. None of these is explained here.

The *United States Code Annotated* (*U.S.C.A.*) republishes the fifty **titles** of the *U.S.C.* in over one hundred volumes. Each title is printed whole, then repeated section-by-section with annotations.

There are three ways to find the section (subdivision of a title) you need. If you know the statute's popular name, go to the Popular Name Tables in the end volumes, then consult the subject index of the volumes they lead you to. If you know the general area of law you need, read through the index of the fifty titles. Once you choose a title, use that title's individual subject index. And, if you know only certain specific facts or legal catchwords, go to the general subject index in the end volumes first. (If nothing turns up, you may have to go through a word-list expansion exercise such as "Cartwheel" or "TARP" mentioned earlier in this appendix.)

Once you have the section you need, there is a wealth of information on **legislative, executive,** and **judicial** handling of the subject, all in one place with references, and mostly organized by the West **Key Number System** (see those words).

To update the *U.S.C.A.* volumes, you must use **pocket parts,** "Supplementary Pamphlets," and "Special Pamphlets." Also, make sure you are using the latest hardback volume because volumes are revised on separate schedules.

To update the *U.S.C.A.* and its pamphlets with the most recent news, you need the *United States Code Congressional and Admin-*

istrative News and its supplementary pamphlets. These both contain easy-to-use tables that tell you whether or not your section was affected by later legislation, and both include recent regulatory developments.

The *United States Code Service* works generally the same way as *U.S.C.A.* Its main annotations are to Lawyers Co-operative materials rather than West's. Check its "how to" pamphlet for special features.

The *Code of Federal Regulations*, currently published entirely in pamphlet form due to frequent revision, is the only complete source for administrative law materials. Its fifty titles correspond only generally to the *U.S. Code* titles, and its individual sections do not correspond at all. (The titles do group generally by the federal agency that administers them.) In the **citation** "2 CFR § 7.1" the "title" is 2, the "part" or major subdivision is 7, and the "section" (everything after the "section symbol") is 7.1.

If you have a *U.S. Code* citation (for statutes in your area of law), the best way to find the right *CFR* section (for administrative regulations put out under the authority of these statutes) is to convert the Code citation directly through tables in the *CFR* pamphlet containing finding aids. Lacking that, you should use the general index in *CFR*. Don't forget to check for index supplements. (If you find nothing and suspect that you are dealing with an entirely new area of law, check the various *Federal Register* indexes.)

To update your *CFR* research, first make sure that you have the latest volume. (The titles are revised once each year in quarterly batches.) Then find the latest *CFR* monthly update pamphlet called "Cumulative List of CFR Sections Affected." It tells which *CFR* sections have been recently affected by new regulations, new proposed regulations, etc. Read the text of these changes in the *Federal Register* (the page number is given). Finally, for last-minute updates, check the "Cumulative List of Parts Affected" in the latest issue of the *Federal Register* and read the changes in the daily issue you are referred to. **Shepards** also has a *CFR* **citator** for the same purpose.

State Statutes

Many researchers use state statutes more often than they use federal statutes, but not too much is said about them here because there are fifty different states. There are, however, some similarities that should be mentioned.

Most states have both official and privately printed, **annotated** versions of their statutes. Many of the annotated versions are based on the model of West's *U.S. Code Annotated* (see the prior section). Even when the state version is not based on *U.S.C.A.*, many of its features, such as references to encyclopedias and other secondary sources, will be similar.

To find state statutory law, you can start by looking up your subject in *Martindale-Hubbell*. Its use is explained later in this appendix. This may give you a quick, if not conclusive, answer to your question and a reference to the state statute with the answer. Otherwise, go directly to the statutes and take a few minutes to read the explanatory material at the front of the first volume. This will alert you to anything unusual about the set's organization. For example, some states organize their statutes in chronological order. Other states organize their statutes into integrated **codes.** This can be confusing. (While you are using the first volume, also check the table of contents, if any, for a shortcut to what you need.)

Next, check to see if there is a general index in the last volumes of the set. These vary in size and quality, so you may have to do some word-expansion exercises such as "Cartwheel" or "TARP" to expand your search possibilities. Once you find the right volume, check to see if *it* has an index, and use that also. (Some code titles fill more than one volume, so check for an index in other volumes of that section too.)

Finally, update your research with any **pocket parts**, supplements, or binders of **slip laws** available, and don't forget to **Shepardize** the statute. (*Reminder*: If you do not know what the words in the last sentence mean, look them up.)

State Administrative Regulations and Local Ordinances

These lower-level sources of law are not always collected in one place. Their organization, style, and quality vary widely. They are often highly detailed, and at the same time vague, and they sometimes conflict with the state laws that authorized them. Footwork, persistence, and care are needed to track them down and to understand them.

There are three general approaches to finding this material. First, you can check to see if your library collects it in one place. Second, you can write, call, or visit the agency, department, or city government in question. And third, you can search the secondary sources (**Shepard's** state and ordinance law volumes, **A.L.R.**, digests, articles, etc.). Do not assume that finding nothing means that nothing is there. And do not assume that what you found is complete or accurate.

Caselaw: The National Reporter System

What Is In It?   Only about one percent of the cases decided by courts in the U.S. have ever been collected and printed, yet there are well over a million cases now on library shelves. Most of these are in the *National Reporter System* (*NRS*), published by West Publishing. A "reporter" publishes cases in chronological order from one geographical area or court system. Some states have their own "official" reporters that are separate from the *NRS* and some use West to publish their official reporters. Most state and federal **appellate** court decisions are collected in the *NRS*. Figure 5 summarizes the *NRS*.

How Do You Use It?   The *NRS* is simple to use, which is fortunate because you cannot avoid using it. Each *volume* has a Table of Cases Reported (contents by court); Table of Statutes Construed (a listing of all statutes used in the reported cases); a Table of Words and Phrases (words and phrases defined in the cases); and a small **Key Number** Digest that is especially useful for new cases.

Each case in the *National Reporter System* has the same type of cross-referencing information plus summaries related to only that one case. Figure 6 is a typical first page from a case in a reporter.

Each reporter series in the *NRS* also has **advance sheets.** These are sometimes the quickest way to find out about newly decided cases from state courts. The advance sheets have all the research aids of the bound volumes.

Finally, the two ways of going back and forth between corresponding pages of official and *NRS* volumes, are by using the *National Reporter Blue Book* (which has matching columns of volumes and pages from each) or by using the **Shepard's Citator** for either set.

Caselaw: Other Sources

Non-*NRS* Federal Reporters   The official **reporter** for decisions of the U.S. Supreme Court is called *United States Reports*. A frequently-used annotated version is *United States Supreme Court Reports*, Lawyer's Edition, put out by Lawyer's Co-operative. It is known simply as "Lawyer's Edition" (L.Ed.). Some volumes contain the **briefs** in the case as well as extensive cross-referencing to

REGIONAL REPORTERS	COVERAGE BEGINNING	COVERAGE
Atlantic Reporter	1885	Connecticut, Delaware, Maine, Maryland, New Hampshire, New Jersey, Pennsylvania, Rhode Island, Vermont, and District of Columbia Municipal Court of Appeals
North Eastern Reporter	1885	Illinois, Indiana, Massachusetts, New York and Ohio
North Western Reporter	1879	Iowa, Michigan, Minnesota, Nebraska, North Dakota, South Dakota and Wisconsin
Pacific Reporter	1887	Alaska, Arizona, California, Colorado, Hawaii, Idaho, Kansas, Montana, Nevada, New Mexico, Oklahoma, Oregon, Utah, Washington and Wyoming
South Eastern Reporter	1886	Georgia, North Carolina, South Carolina, Virginia and West Virginia
South Western Reporter	1887	Arkansas, Kentucky, Missouri, Tennessee and Texas
Southern Reporter		Alabama, Florida, Louisiana and Mississippi

FEDERAL REPORTERS

Federal Reporter	1880	United States Circuit Court from 1880 to 1912; Commerce Court of the United States from 1911 to 1913; District Courts of the United States from 1880 to 1932; U.S. Court of Claims from 1929 to 1932 and since 1960; the U.S. Court of Appeals from its organization in 1891; the U.S. Court of Customs and Patent Appeals from 1929; and the U.S. Emergency Court of Appeals from 1943
Federal Supplement	1932	United States Court of Claims from 1932 to 1960; United States District Courts since 1932; United States Customs Court since 1956
Federal Rules Decisions	1939	United States District Courts involving the Federal Rules of Civil Procedure since 1939 and the Federal Rules of Criminal Procedure since 1946
Supreme Court Reporter	1882	U.S. Supreme Court beginning with the October term of 1882
Bankruptcy Reporter	1980	Bankruptcy decisions of U.S. Bankruptcy Courts, U.S. District Courts, U.S. Courts of Appeals and the U.S. Supreme Court
Military Justice Reporter	1978	United States Court of Military Appeals and Courts of Military Review for the Army, Navy, Air Force and Coast Guard

Figure 5 National Reporter System

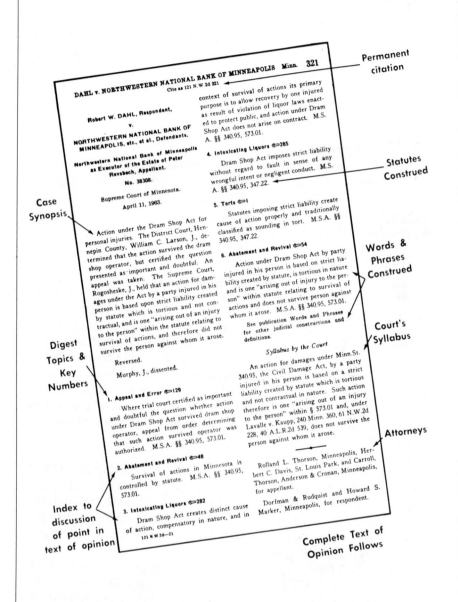

Permanent citation

Statutes Construed

Words & Phrases Construed

Court's Syllabus

Attorneys

Case Synopsis

Digest Topics & Key Numbers

Index to discussion of point in text of opinion

Complete Text of Opinion Follows

Figure 6   Example of a Case in the National Reporter System

digests such as *ALR*. (As we saw earlier, the *National Reporter System* version is *Supreme Court Reporter*.)

Two **loose-leaf services** print weekly copies of Supreme Court decisions. These are *Commerce Clearing House Supreme Court Bulletin* and Bureau of National Affairs' *United States Law Week*. *Law Week* is more frequently used because of its news coverage of other legal matters. All other collected reports of federal court cases are in the *National Reporter System*.

Other State Reporters

As mentioned before, some states have official reporters that are not part of the *NRS*. Special problems with their use are minor.

SECONDARY SOURCES

Martindale-Hubbell

What Is In It? The first several volumes of the *Martindale-Hubbell Law Directory* contain a state-by-state listing of practicing lawyers and law firms. Unless you need this information, go right to the last volume: It contains summaries of the law of each state by legal topic. It also contains copies of more than fifty **Uniform Acts**, short summaries of the law of over fifty foreign countries, and reviews of a few areas of federal law. In short, while *Martindale-Hubbell* is not an authoritative source, it is very useful for quick, preliminary answers to questions about state statutory law.

How Do You Use It? *Martindale-Hubbell* is not hard to use. It has a topical index with good cross-referencing to find the right subject areas. These subjects are the same for each state and include all the areas of everyday law. And *Martindale-Hubbell* has fifty individual state digests, each with a preface that explains what the citations and abbreviations mean.

There are, however, a few things to keep in mind. First, even though *Martindale-Hubbell* comes out every year, there is still the chance that state law has changed. Second, it is *very* condensed, so you may be missing some of the fine points of the original statute. And third, it uses technical legal language, so its apparent simplicity may be deceptive. But it is easier to use for simple questions than most alternatives. Merely remember: do not rely on it and do not cite it.

Key Number Digests

What Is in Them?   West Publishing Company's *Key Number Digests* have been called one of the three pillars of legal research. (The other two are the Lawyer's Co-operative *ALR Annotations* and *Shepard's Citators,* plus there is now a "fourth pillar," computer-assisted research). *Key Number Digests* are the most comprehensive (but not quick to use) method of categorizing, indexing, and finding the legal subjects discussed in American courtrooms.

A Key Number is a permanent number given by West Publishing to a specific legal subject as categorized by West. It is usually preceded by the Key symbol   ⚷   . West first subdivided all possible legal subjects into seven main headings, then broke these headings into thirty-two subdivisions and over four hundred "Key Topics" the same way. Figure 7 is a part of that breakdown. Finally, each of these Key Topics is broken down into many Key Numbers *all its own,* so to use the system you must know both the Topic and the Number. New Numbers are added to Topics regularly, and old ones are further and further subdivided, but they never change.

A West editor who reads a case decision that comes into the *National Reporter System* picks out *each legal point* and writes a brief summary of that point in a single paragraph. These paragraphs are given a Key Topic and Number, printed in front of their decisions in case Reporters (see the sample page under *National Reporter System*), and collected into *Key Number Digests* by Topic and Number.

There are *Key Number Digests* for most individual state reporters, for most regional reporters, most *United States Court Reporters,* and most individual volumes of these sets. (The digests for the U.S. courts are: *Federal, Modern Federal Practice, Modern Federal Practice 2d,* and *Court of Claims*). The material in all these digests is then collected into the *American Digest,* a massive master index of caselaw summaries covering the whole country and most of its appeals courts since colonial days. The *American Digests* is divided into a *Century Digest* (1658–1896), a series of *Decennial Digests* (1897–1905, 1906–1915, etc.), *General Digests* (yearly between the last and the next Decennial), and updating pamphlets.

How Do You Use Them?   All the *Key Number Digests* (except the *Century Digest,* which predates the Key System) work exactly the

1. PERSONS
2. PROPERTY
3. CONTRACTS
4. TORTS
5. CRIMES
6. REMEDIES
7. GOVERNMENT

---

1. PERSONS

RELATING TO NATURAL PERSONS IN GENERAL

Civil Rights
Dead Bodies
Death
Domicile
Drugs and Narcotics
Food
Health and Environment
Holidays
Intoxicating Liquors
Names
Poisons
Seals
Signatures
Sunday
Time
Weapons

PARTICULAR CLASSES OF NATURAL PERSONS

Absentees
Aliens
Chemical Dependents
Citizens
Convicts
Illegitimate Children
Indians
Infants
Mental Health
Paupers
Slaves
Spendthrifts

PERSONAL RELATIONS

Adoption
Attorney and Client
Employers' Liability
Executors and Administrators
Guardian and Ward
Husband and Wife
Labor Relations
Marriage
Master and Servant
Parent and Child
Principal and Agent
Workers' Compensation

ASSOCIATED AND ARTIFICIAL PERSONS

Associations
Beneficial Associations
Building and Loan Associations
Clubs
Colleges and Universities
Corporations
Exchanges
Joint-Stock Companies and Business Trusts
Partnership
Religious Societies

PARTICULAR OCCUPATIONS

Accountants
Agriculture
Auctions and Auctioneers
Aviation
Banks and Banking
Bridges
Brokers
Canals
Carriers
Commerce
Consumer Credit
Consumer Protection
Credit Reporting Agencies
Detectives
Electricity
Explosives
Factors
Ferries
Gas
Hawkers and Peddlers
Innkeepers
Insurance
Licenses
Manufactures
Monopolies
Physicians and Surgeons
Pilots
Railroads
Seamen
Shipping
Steam
Telecommunications
Theaters and Shows
Towage
Turnpikes and Toll Roads
Urban Railroads
Warehousemen
Wharves

2. PROPERTY

NATURE, SUBJECTS, AND INCIDENTS OF OWNERSHIP IN GENERAL

Abandoned and Lost Property
Accession
Adjoining Landowners

Figure 7   Example of Legal Subjects Subdivided

same way. If you want to know about "Theaters and Shows ⌦ 6(18) athletic events" in Florida only, use the Florida Key Digest; for "Theaters and Shows ⌦ 6(18) athletic events" in the whole Southern region, use the *Southern Key Digest;* do the same for federal courts and the Supreme Court. For the whole country, use the American Digest.

The most direct way into the Key Numbers is to start with a case that discusses the question that you want to answer. Few researchers are so lucky, but if you *do* have a printed case on point, you can go straight from the case's Key Number summary paragraphs to a digest. If all you have is a case *name,* you can look it up in the Table of Cases for the digest you want to use. This will give you, in addition to more information about the case, the Key Numbers that summarize its legal points.

A Descriptive Word Index is the best way into the digests. You start by categorizing your problem and generating an expanded list of *related* words using the "Cartwheel" or "TARP" method (explained earlier), or your own method of adding to the concepts of your search with the help of this dictionary. You then look up these new words alphabetically in each digest's Descriptive Word Index. Those that exist in the index will lead you to Key Topics and Numbers. Once you find the Key Numbers you need, look them up in the Digest.

It may take a long time to wade through the summary paragraphs. If you are working with the *American Digest* (rather than with one of the regional, state, or U.S. court digests), every digest in the system, plus the updates, must often be consulted. (Be sure to see the Cumulative Table of Key Numbers to avoid having to look through every *General Digest.*) Only use the *American Digest* approach if you have no quicker or less all-inclusive alternatives.

Finally, *do not rely completely* on the *Key Number Digest* paragraphs because they are overly condensed and sometimes wrong. Read the reporter case referred to in each paragraph to see what the judge really said. And never cite the summary as authority for a legal point. It isn't.

American Law Report (A.L.R.)

What Is In It? A.L.R. is probably the most complex-to-use law finder, but it is well worth mastering because, if you find what you need, it comes in highly concentrated form.

A.L.R. has hundreds of volumes, each containing several selected cases, each case followed by long **annotations** (see that word). Each annotation references hundreds of other cases based on the same area of the law from various **jurisdictions**. The lead case is a way of pulling together the "core" of a legal subject area, such as "product liability: heating equipment." The references both go into greater detail and take the subject into related fields. In this respect, *A.L.R.* (with its various indexes) is a combination of case reporter, digest, and encyclopedia. Its most frequent outside cross-referencing is to the *American Jurisprudence* (*Am. Jur.*) encyclopedia and to the rest of the Lawyers Co-operative Publishing (LCP) system.

In recent volumes, each main case is followed by three outlines: an organization of the article by major issues, by descriptive words, and by jurisdictions with cases mentioned. The annotation itself then follows. While earlier volumes lack some features, it now begins with a table of contents called "Scope," references to other annotations called "Related Matters," a "Summary," and a section on "Practice Pointers." The bulk of the annotation is a detailed discussion of the caselaw with complete statutory and other references.

How Do You Use It? With practice and great care. *American Law Reports* is divided into five series of books: *A.L.R. 1st* (State and Federal cases from 1919–1948), *A.L.R. 2d* (State and Federal 1948–1965), *A.L.R. 3d* (State and Federal 1965–1969, State only 1969–1980), *A.L.R. 4th* (State only, 1980 on) and *A.L.R. Federal* (1969 on). Volumes are updated on different schedules. Also, the indexes and updates are somewhat limited and complex. How, then, to find the law?

Of course, lightning might strike. You will occasionally be referred directly from a **citator, treatise,** or encyclopedia to the one *A.L.R.* article that gives you almost everything you need. For more usual situations, start by using the Quick Indexes. You must go through a Quick Index for each *A.L.R.*, and, in particular, a pocket part (inserted supplement) for each. These contain Annotated History Tables that show how each article has been updated. (For *A.L.R. 1st,* you must use the separate *A.L.R. Blue Book* for updates). This involves looking carefully through several books, but it is not a tedious process, and it usually does the job.

If the Quick Index system fails, the other approaches are less promising. There is a descriptive work index and a digest system for some of the sets, but neither is easy to use or as comprehensive as the competing West Publishing volumes.

Finally, once you have material you need, make sure to update it by checking separate volumes called Later Case Service for *A.L.R. 2d*, and by checking the pocket parts in each main article volume of *A.L.R. 3d, 4th*, and *Federal*. This can be crucial. Also, *A.L.R.* is still growing, with new indexes and services coming out all the time.

Shepard's Citators

What Is In Them? A *citator* is a method of finding out what has happened to a case, a statute, or some other legal authority (such as a regulation, a law review article, etc.) by listing the places it has been cited (mentioned). Since Shepard's puts out all the most important legal citators, "Shepardizing" has come to mean "using a citator to trace and document a legal authority's subsequent history."

Shepardizing is a good way to find cases, statutes, etc. It is the only good way to validate your research by proving that the statutes you quote are unchanged and legally valid, and that the cases you rely on are still good **precedent** (have not been **overruled, reversed,** or **distinguished**) and are the best available to prove your points (still mentioned and followed in recent cases, annotations, articles, etc.). *You should never formally use a case, statute, or other authority without Shepardizing it.* On a complex,time-consuming project, you probably shouldn't even bother to take notes on a long case or article without Shepardizing it first.

A typical listing under a case will give parallel citations (other places the same case has been printed), the history of the case (appeals, overrulings, etc.), and the cases, annotations, and articles that have mentioned it since.

Figure 8 shows a piece of a Shepard's case citation page.

How Do You Use Them? While the *process* of Shepardizing is simple to learn and easily remembered, there are three pitfalls:

1. Because the process is repetitive, it is easy to skip accidently a crucial book, flip past a crucial page, or skim by a crucial cite. Be methodical.

2. *Shepard's Citators* use dozens of symbols of their own (for example, A³ is *A.L.R. 3d*). Since crucial information may be missed or misinterpreted by working without full knowledge of the symbols, take the time to refresh your knowledge by checking symbol explanations at the front of each different type of Shepard's.

Vol. 179   NORTHWESTERN REPORTER, 2d SERIES

f454F2d^{6}1203	– 336 –	Calif	– 377 –	– 398 –	215NW342
553F2d^{8}129	182NW^{2}118	95CaR28	(384Mch55)	(384Mch42)	227NW^{12}1
f409FS^{2}691	182NW419	484P2d1372	218NW^{1}383	s166NW552	235NW^{1}30
409FS^{1}692	188NW^{3}363	Fla	Calif	j190NW^{7}104	251NW^{1}53
435FS^{8}187	188NW^{5}367	262So2d434	107CaR919	219NW43	NM
Iowa	189NW^{4}580	Ind	114CaR103	223NW^{6}639	505P2d124
225NW^{2}113	193NW^{5}88	285NE271	522P2d663	448FS915	15AE170s
DC	196NW^{2}529	La	77AE241n		56AE13s
365A2d386	j196NW^{2}531	259So2d563		– 405 –	32AE1227s
Ga	196NW^{2}548	Md	– 379 –	(23McA688)	55AE593n
226SE147	197NW568	361A2d118	(384Mch38)	205NW^{1}867	59AE216n
Md	199NW^{2}330	Ore	s167NW834	208NW^{1}51	
349A2d251	200NW824	493P2d747	f188NW^{1}239		– 471 –
Mont	203NW^{2}307	28LE1065n	f189NW^{1}868	– 409 –	182NW^{4}11
564P2d166	203NW587	35LE754n	f193NW^{1}393	cc179NW413	182NW^{2}16
NJ	204NW^{5}608	97AE549s	f194NW^{1}93		183NW^{4}20
319A2d784	f204NW^{4}612	33AE335s	194NW^{1}695	– 413 –	188NW^{4}30
385A2d917	219NW^{5}499		204NW^{1}334	cc179NW409	196NW^{2}52

Figure 8   Example of a Shepard's Case Citation Page

3. The "how-to" information that follows here is very brief. To learn the process best, work through the practice problem given at the front of each new type of Shepard's you use (*Regional Reporter Cases, Federal Statutes,* etc.). Now on to the barebones of how to do it.

Each major set of case reporters or statutes is usually followed on the library shelf by its corresponding set of *Shepard's Citators.* Sometimes, however, the Citator's supplements are for more than one set of hardbound volumes, so you may have to look around a bit.

First, make sure that you have found a *complete* set of Citator main volumes and supplements. You do this by getting the latest pamphlet (no more than one month old) and reading the box on the cover, which lists all volumes and supplements currently in use. If your set is incomplete, your research is suspect and, perhaps, worthless.

Second, use all the volumes, and check each carefully for citations. If a supplement has no citations to your case, statute, etc., there may be no citations, but you may be on the wrong page or even in the wrong book.

And third, "milk" the citations for everything you can. For example, if one of the citations in the list is "j224NW^{11}231," you know that the case was mentioned on page 231 of volume 224 of the *Northwest Reporter, Second Series.* You also know from the "j" that the case was mentioned in a **dissenting opinion** (because you checked what "j" meant in the front of the book). And you know from the raised "11" that the judge in the later case discussed the specific legal point mentioned in the eleventh summarizing introductory **headnote** to the earlier case.

Finally, assume there is a citator to the books you are using unless you *know* there is none. Assume you lack some volumes until you *know* you have them all. Assume you're skimming too fast unless you're constantly double-checking for completeness. Assume some worthwhile symbols have slipped through your fingers unless you have refreshed your memory in the tables at the front of each book. And assume that you must continue tracking down each chain of citations until you know that you have come to the end. It's easier than it sounds.

Legal Encyclopedias

What Is In Them? Legal encyclopedias, like general encyclopedias, are multivolume information sets arranged alphabetically by topic. They usually have extensive cross-referencing, so they are a good way to get a reasonably quick general handle on a legal topic, especially if you need background material or initial leads to major cases and statutes. They are not, however, good books to quote as authoritative sources of law.

The two large national legal encyclopedias are *Corpus Juris Secundum* (CJS) and *American Jurisprudence, Second* (*Am. Jur. 2d*). CJS is published by West, and is tied into West's *Key Number Digest* and *National Reporter Systems. Am. Jur. 2d* is published by Lawyers Co-operative and works with its lead case digest, *American Law Reports.* Many states also have state legal encyclopedias, most of which are published by Lawyers Co-operative.

How Do You Use Them? CJS and *Am. Jur. 2d* have huge general index volumes at the end of the series. Use these indexes fully. Be creative. Then, even if the general indexes lead you straight to a topic, section, or page number within a subject volume, do not bypass the subject and analysis outlines at the front of these volumes. They may lead you to more necessary material. (Once you reach the right topic sections, do not forget to check the **pocket part** for updates.)

Finally, *CJS* cross-references with comprehensive West materials and is keyed into the WESTLAW computer service. *Am. Jur.*

2d, however, is often more readable. Plus, it has some specific features lacking in *CJS*, such as a Table of Statutes and Rules Cited and a New Topics Service.

Other Important Secondary Sources

Words and Phrases   *Words and Phrases* is a West Publishing set of hardbound books plus supplements that list alphabetically thousands of legal, technical, and everyday words. Each word or phrase is followed by short summaries of how it was defined by judges in various cases. *Words and Phrases* is large, but easy to use (see Appendix A for more information).

Looseleaf Services   A looseleaf service is a three-ring binder with information on one specialized area of the law (such as tax law, family law, or even medical devices law), on one court, or on more general legal topics. Looseleaf services often send out supplements every week, which either add to or replace older sections. They often combine relevant **statutory** law, **regulatory** law, **case-law** and practical advice with news about major activities and prominent persons in the field. The four largest looseleaf publishers are Commerce Clearing House (CCH), Bureau of National Affairs (BNA), Prentice-Hall (PH), and Matthew Bender (MB).

Treatises and Law Review Articles   Treatises are individual books or small sets written for lawyers and law students. (Treatises for students are sometimes called hornbooks.) They cover specialized areas of the law, such as contracts or federal practice. You can find treatises through your law library's card catalogue.

Law Review and *Law Journal* articles analyze legal issues. They are written by top law students or by professors. The footnotes can lead to recent important cases. You can find these articles through the *Index to Legal Periodicals*, the *Legal Resources Index*, or the *Current Law Index*.

Form, Practice, and Procedure Books   Form books are collections of sample forms that have been used in legal practice (rental agreements, wills, **pleadings**, jury **instructions**, etc.). They often have blanks to be filled in.

The larger form books (by West, Lawyer's Co-operative, and others) annotate the forms with extensive information on the statutes they are based on, case decisions interpreting them, and practical advice. These forms, however, must always be tailored to the individual legal situation.

Practice and procedure books (sometimes also called form books) contain the detailed technical rules by which each system of courts, and each individual court, operates. Many are annotated with case decisions and practical examples. Attempting to practice before a court without a knowledge of these rules is embarrassing at best.

Books by Advocacy Groups Organizations such as HALT (see "books on doing legal research"), the **ACLU**, and others publish paperbacks and pamphlets on areas of the law private individuals face. These include such things as probate law, mental patients' rights, etc. Publications from trade associations, consumer groups, and other advocacy organizations are often found in bookstores and general libraries. They should be relied on for general information only.

Other "Helpers" The following is a small list of helpful secondary sources that need only brief mention.

The *Uniform System of Citation* is a tiny paperback put out by a consortium of law reviews. It is the "bible" for proper citation form and also a good quick skim-review of possible legal sources.

The law library's *Kardex* or other system for recording new arrivals and its general *card catalogue* are valuable resources. Take time to learn them early, before you need them in a crunch.

Legal Writing: Sense and Nonsense by David Mellinkoff (West Publishing, 1982), can teach you to strip legalese from your writing.

The *U.S. Government Manual*, a large, inexpensive paperback from the Government Print Office, has many of the details you will need about the federal government's organizations and agencies.

The best way to learn about doing *nonlegal* research is *Finding Facts Fast*, a small, cheap paperback by Alden Todd (Ten Speed Press, Box 7123, Berkeley, CA, 94707). Its chapters on finding and using each different type of reference material will help you zero in on what you need.

Another good, small book to keep on hand is *Reference Books: A Brief Guide* by Bell and Swidan (Enoch Pratt Free Library, Baltimore, MD), which contains lists of useful general sources.

Books on Doing Legal Research

You may already know the basics of legal research, or you may want to start off with more detailed information. Here is a list of books and materials.

Small "Freebies"

> West's Law Finder
> West Publishing Co.
> Box 3526
> St. Paul, MN 55165

A free catalogue from the company that produces the most extensive collection of legal research materials. It explains the *National Reporter System, Key Number Digests, Corpus Juris Secundum, United States Code Annotated, Words and Phrases,* etc.

> The Living Law
> Lawyers Co-operative Publishing Co.
> Rochester, NY 14694

A free catalogue of the second most extensive collection. It explains *American Jurisprudence, A.L.R., U.S.C.S., the U.S. Supreme Court Reports and Digest Lawyers Edition,* etc.

> How to Use Shepard's Citations
> Shepard/McGraw-Hill
> Box 1235
> Colorado Springs, CO 80901

A free catalogue of the Shepard's Citation books and services, explaining how to *Shepardize* cases, statutes, regulations, etc. These books, plus West's and Lawyers Co-op's, make up a large proportion of all commonly used legal reference materials.

> CCH   and   BNA
> 4025 W. Peterson   1232 25th N.W.
> Chicago, IL 60646   Washington, D.C. 20037

You can also get free catalogues from these two largest *loose-leafs services.* CCH and BNA provide specialized, current information through the *Bankruptcy Law Reporter, Environmental Reporter, Labor Relations Reporter, Tax Court Reporter,* and many more.

Using a Law Library
HALT, Inc. 201 Massachusettes N.E.
Washington, D.C. 20002

This is the cheapest and most concise research guide. It comes free with paid membership in HALT, an organization devoted to fighting legalese and to lessening the public's need for lawyers. The guide contains a good flow chart of the HALT research method and a list of guides to state law research, but not much nuts and bolts information.

Paperbacks

Legal Research, Writing, and Analysis, 2d
William P. Statsky
West Publishing Company
Box 3526
St. Paul, MN 55165

This is the most innovative and easiest to use research paperback. It integrates the "what," "where," "why," and "how" of research extremely well and provides many excellent step-by-step charts plus detailed instructions on how to read cases and statutes.

Legal Research in a Nutshell
Morris Cohen
West Publishing Company

Small in physical size, easy to handle, and broad in coverage, but better as a survey or review than as a "how-to" learning tool.

Hardback "Combos"

Introduction to Paralegalism 2d William P. Statsky West Publishing Company	*N.A.L.A. Manual for Legal Assistants* Roger Park West Publishing Company

The Career Legal Secretary
N.A.L.S.
West Publishing Company

Each of these books combines chapters on legal research with chapters on other skills, such as interviewing, as well as other areas, such as the court system. Statsky's is strongest on research, and the emphasis in other chapters varies from book to book. (The N.A.L.A. also produces a set of cassettes and materials on research.)

Big Hardbacks for Courses and Reference

Fundamentals of Legal Research 2d
Jacobstein and Mersky
Foundation Press

How to Find the Law
Morris Cohen
West Publishing Company

Effective Legal Research 4th
Price, Bitner and Bysiewicz
Little, Brown

Legal Problem Solving 3d
Marjorie Rombauer
West Publishing Company

These books all give a full overview and applications, except for *Legal Problem Solving*, which concentrates on techniques, not sources.

COMPUTER-ASSISTED LEGAL RESEARCH

What Is In It? Legal research can often be done most quickly, easily, accurately, and completely by computer. A researcher using a computer typically uses a video display terminal, computer keyboard, and printer to connect by telephone to a computer that holds a complete legal research system such as WESTLAW or LEXIS.

WESTLAW, for example, contains the full text of most recent federal and state court decisions, categorized summaries of these decisions, most federal statutes and regulations, and a wide range of other legal materials. These other materials include the resources of other companies' data banks, such as indexes of law-related newspaper articles.

Once you learn how to use the system, a process that takes very little time for a person who already knows some traditional legal research methods, computerized research can be incredibly fast. The computer can search through millions of words in seconds to find the cases you need. You can ask it to search broadly or narrowly, by legal or nonlegal subject, by a list of specially coordinated West Key Number topics or any set of words you choose (such as product names or persons), etc.

The computer will then give you a list of cases or other materials that have what you want. It can show them to you by summary, by whole text, or by only those parts that contain the words or ideas that interest you. You can then either take notes, go to the right books, or automatically print out the part you need.

What are some of the other advantages of computer-assisted research? First of all, computer data banks contain many things unavailable in most law libraries. WESTLAW, for example, has many legal decisions before they get into print. It also has many federal agency rulings that never get bound and generally distributed.

Computer research services also allow greatly simplified **Shepardizing** (tracing a case or other authority's "afterlife" as mentioned in later authorities). Old research from past projects can be quickly updated this same general way.

Computer-assisted research is sometimes the *only* way to work because some types of library research take huge amounts of time. Time problems can limit you to a quick library scan for what you need or, worse yet, force you to forget the point entirely (and hope that everyone else does too)!

For example, suppose you need to know whether a Federal District Court in the First Circuit is likely to overturn a particular federal agency's decision that has been appealed. Courts will usually do this only when the agency's decision is not based on substantial evidence. But what is "substantial evidence"? A general definition does no good; you need to know how courts in the First Circuit, particularly the Court of Appeals, used the words in cases as similar to yours as possible. How do you find these cases?

Library research would require so many boring days of case reading that you might be tempted to rely on general definitions plus quotes from cases "sort of" like yours. With access to WESTLAW or LEXIS, however, you could, with a few numbers and phrases typed on a terminal, ask the computer for all those cases in the First Circuit that used the words *substantial evidence*. An easy series of further requests would get you right to the paragraphs using the words, with those words highlighted on the screen.

Computer-assisted research is sometimes the only way to work even if you have all the time in the world. Only by using a computer can you turn many nonlegal ideas that support your case into solid legal precedents.

For example, a Washington, D.C. lawyer recently handled a case in which a wily businessman saw changes in federal rules coming down the pike. The businessman tried to rush through some soon-to-be-prohibited purchases and sales before the agency got around to changing the rules. When the sales took longer than expected, he was stuck with a huge pile of goods, so he went to court to get an exemption when the agency refused to help him. The lawyer represented people who wanted to *prevent* the businessman from selling the goods.

The lawbooks are full of cases in which persons who used trickery were prevented from winning in court, but this businessman had not clearly done anything sneaky. How was the lawyer to make a case against what was either hard luck or mere stupidity?

Easy, he thought. There might not be any obvious legal phrases to lead him to the cases he needed, but there were some good nonlegal ideas floating around that judges might have used in the past. So he asked his computer to give him all the cases in which the word *chestnuts* appeared near *fire*, and all the cases containing the word *catspaw*. He included various spellings like *chestnut* and *cats-paw*, just to be sure.

To be sure of *what*, you ask? To be sure that every time a judge used phrases from the old story about the monkey who convinced a cat to pull hot chestnuts out of a fire, the lawyer would find the judge's opinion. This may seem like an unnecessarily cute way to do serious research, but the WESTLAW system came up with several totally unrelated cases in which a judge essentially said, "The Federal Courts are not in the business of being used as a cats-paw to pull a private businessman's chestnuts out of the fire." Instant **precedent**.

Not a person to rely on one type of precedent, the lawyer then plugged *orphan, mercy, murder,* and *court* into the computer, asking for sentences with all four words. Before you read on, try to guess why, for it is this type of reasoning that makes computer research most worthwhile.

Got it? The computer quickly scanned millions of words and churned out several cases in which a judge disgustedly told a businessman, "This reminds me of a man who murders his parents and throws himself on the mercy of the court as an orphan." One of the cases was quite similar to the lawyer's. To find that case in a law library, he might as well have thrown darts at a wall of books.

How Do You Use It? The first steps in most computer research systems are to connect with the computer by telephone, identify yourself by a user number and password, and tell the computer which information source or data base you want. To see a list of

499

data bases in WESTLAW, for example, you could type in "**db.**" You could then choose a particular data base—for example, choosing the cases decided by the U.S. Supreme Court by typing in "**sct.**" Now you are ready to ask your questions.

Suppose you want to know what the Supreme Court has said about attorney fees. One way would be to ask for all Supreme Court cases with the words *attorney* and *fees* in the same sentence. This is done by typing in "**attorney /s fees**," where the "/s" means "in the same sentence." If this doesn't give you enough information, there are several things you could do to broaden the search. For example, you could ask for cases with the two words in the same paragraph ("**attorney /p fees**"); you could ask for cases containing all varieties of *attorney*, such as *attorney's*, in the same sentence with all varieties of **fee**, such as *fees* ("**attorney* /s fee***"); or you could ask for cases with words similar to *attorney*, such as *lawyer* or *counsel* ("**attorney, counsel lawyer /s fees**").

If, on the other hand, you come up with too many cases even to skim, you could narrow the search to only those types of cases that interest you, such as negligence cases, by asking for all three words in the same paragraph ("**attorney /p fees /p negligence**"). Or you could rule out a type of case that you know doesn't help by asking the computer to skip this type ("**attorney /p fees % negligence**").

Remember also that this is an example of only *one* type of research. You could also look for specific phrases by putting them in quotes ("**negligence per se**"). You could search only one field, such as case topics, from a preselected and organized list of major subjects ("**#45 Attorney and Client**"). You could even search for particular types of cases decided by a particular judge. And these choices barely scratch the surface of possible computer research techniques.

About the Author

Mr. Oran is a graduate of Hamilton College and Yale Law School. He has practiced law in Connecticut and the District of Columbia. In addition, he has been Assistant Director of the National Paralegal Institute, Professor of Law at Antioch Law School, and staff counsel to a congressman and the House Appropriations Committee. He has written an internationally reprinted novel and text as well as professional and popular articles on paralegal education, psychiatry and law, poverty law, and individual rights.

†